Latin American and Caribbean Foreign Policy

Latin American and Caribbean Foreign Policy

Edited by
Frank O. Mora
and Jeanne A. K. Hey

ROWMAN & LITTLEFIELD PUBLISHERS, INC.
Lanham • Boulder • New York • Toronto • Oxford

ROWMAN & LITTLEFIELD PUBLISHERS, INC.

Published in the United States of America
by Rowman & Littlefield Publishers, Inc.
A wholly owned subsidiary of The Rowman & Littlefield Publishing Group, Inc.
4501 Forbes Boulevard, Suite 200, Lanham, MD 20706
www.rowmanlittlefield.com

P.O. Box 317, Oxford OX2 9RU, UK

British Library Cataloguing in Publication Information Available

Library of Congress Cataloging-in-Publication Data

Latin American and Caribbean foreign policy / edited by Frank O. Mora and Jeanne A.K. Hey.
p. cm.
Includes bibliographical references and index.
ISBN 0-7425-1600-8 (Cloth : alk. paper)—ISBN 0-7425-1601-6 (Paper : alk. paper)
1. Latin America—Foreign relations—1980- 2. Caribbean Area—Foreign relations—1945- I. Mora, Frank O. II. Hey, Jeanne A. K.
F1415.L375 2003
327'.098—dc21 2003009712

Printed in the United States of America

∞ ™ The paper used in this publication meets the minimum requirements of American National Standard for Information Sciences—Permanence of Paper for Printed Library Materials, ANSI/NISO Z39.48-1992.

To Mirka, Ivette, and Daniella

For the inspiration and love
provided by three generations of women

To E. Berry Hey Jr. and Jeanne C. Hey

For the best foundations a child
could ask for

Contents

Part II. Andean Region

Part III. Brazil and the Southern Cone

Preface and Acknowledgments

Why a volume about Latin American and Caribbean (LAC) foreign policy? The theoretical, empirical, and policy contributions of such a volume are numerous. The twenty-first century presents a series of enormous global challenges and opportunities for the region. From a policy perspective, an effective foreign policy allows Latin America and the Caribbean to adjust its strategies in ways that limit the costs while enhancing the benefits. From a methodological standpoint, the literature on foreign policy analysis retains an outdated emphasis on the so-called great powers and on the "trouble spots" in the world. As a result, in the post–Cold War era, LAC foreign policy has suffered from much neglect. This volume attempts to address this problem. This volume also fills an important void by linking the dominant questions in foreign policy analysis with empirical study in the region. In the final analysis, this volume is important and possible because a growing number of scholars within and without the region have foreign policy expertise and field experience in Latin America and the Caribbean, and because the editors of this volume have a passion about the subject and were able to bring together a diverse and exceptional group of authors to write about it.

This volume was the brainchild of Frank Mora, who approached Jeanne Hey, a scholar with an established record in the field of foreign policy analyses, in the spring of 2000 with a new idea: a comprehensive and current collection of foreign policy analyses that would become the largest volume of its kind. Whereas numerous books collected chapters on Latin American foreign policy, none had the scope Mora envisioned. Furthermore, he imagined authors from "both sides of the border" working together in a way that could meld scholarly traditions and practices in Latin America, the Caribbean, and North America. Hey could hardly turn down such an offer, and with the patronage of Rowman and Littlefield, the project was born.

After more than three years of data collection, analysis, and editing, we are delighted to present *Latin American and Caribbean Foreign Policy*. Throughout the process, we have accumulated numerous debts to friends and colleagues. Space does not permit recognizing the many people who played an invaluable role in this project, but the contribution of some need to be acknowledged.

First, we thank our chapter contributors. Each author not only worked generously within our framework but also managed editorial changes and demands for more information. Their professionalism and patience were greatly appreciated. We especially thank Gerhard Drekonja-Kornat, whose chapter finally did not appear in the volume but who has put significant effort and commitment toward the volume. Special thanks also go to Susan McEachern, our editor at Rowman & Littlefield. She has worked with us from the point of the initial proposal through the final editing. Jessica Gribble, assistant editor, took great care of the project and manuscripts in its final stages.

The support and vibrant intellectual environment provided by the Department of International Studies at Rhodes College gave birth to the idea. Brenda Somes, the department's administrative assistant and indispensable friend to all of us, helped coordinate the labor in the early stages of the project. The meticulous and committed work of the department's work-study students, especially Jill Reifsteck and Gelsey Bennett, was greatly appreciated. Several deans were also instrumental. Deans Mark McMahon, John Planchon and Robert Llewellyn provided the financial support by way of the J. S. Seidman Research Fellowship and the Senior Latin American Studies Fellowship that made this project possible. At the University of Miami, Jaime Suchlicki, director of the Institute for Cuban and Cuban-American Studies, and Andy Gomez, special assistant to the provost, provided a home and resources during Mora's sabbatical that helped us complete the bibliography and final edits of the manuscript. Norma Laird's editing was nothing short of spectacular. If it were not for Norma, this book would not have come out on time. Tania Mastrapa was also instrumental in the final editing phase of the manuscript. Finally, we both thank our families for their love and support, and for their willingness to give us the time to complete the book.

Introduction

The Theoretical Challenge to Latin American and Caribbean Foreign Policy Studies

Jeanne A. K. Hey and Frank O. Mora

Latin America and the Caribbean (LAC) have had an impact on international relations since the early nineteenth century. Not long after independence, LAC embarked on an effort to build regional institutions and a body of rules and norms, some of which are now part of international law and the Charter of the United Nations. For example, the principle of nonintervention was first established in the Western Hemisphere long before the League of Nations established it as a principle of international law. During the Cold War, many LAC countries played leadership roles in such organizations as the United Nations Conference on Trade and Development (UNCTAD), the Non-Aligned Movement, and the Organization of Petroleum Exporting Countries (OPEC), to name just a few. Some countries, like Brazil, Cuba, and Mexico, had a truly global foreign policy, maintaining an active and at times vital presence in countries and regions outside the Western Hemisphere.

Today, LAC are crucial players in modern global economics and politics. The region is central to any debate about globalization, as it is fully integrated into the world economy yet remains "underdeveloped." Regional leaders are known around the world for their daring political initiatives and challenges to Western powers, specifically related to economic policy. For example, many LAC presidents have expressed deep concern about the impact of globalization on their societies. As a result, they are helping to focus the international community's attention on resolving the deleterious social effects of global integration and free trade. For these reasons, understanding LAC foreign policy behavior is crucial to discerning not only LAC regional politics and economics but global trends as well.

Research in Latin American and Caribbean foreign policy (LACFP) is abundant and rich in detail. Two common, interrelated critiques of foreign policy research (especially as practiced in the United States) charge that it (1) overlooks the "third world" and (2) relies on theoretical models that ignore the realities of politics in underdeveloped regions. The latter argument is often valid, as models designed to explain U.S. decision making often do not apply to Latin American and Caribbean states, many of which have small bureaucracies, limited financial and military resources, and very different foreign policy problems from the United States. Yet the first critique rings hollow when applied to Latin America since it has received more scholarly attention than other so-called third world regions. Perhaps most importantly, research from the region itself is integrated into the broader scholarly literature. Thus, LACFP has avoided some, though certainly not all, of the intellectual imperialism that damages and undermines mainstream writing on Africa, Asia, the Middle East, and even the former Soviet Union.

Unfortunately, the abundance of studies has not generated an integrated theory of LACFP (Hey 1997). As a body, this research is grounded in so many different theoretical traditions that it is a cohesive paradigm. Examples of the wide range of theoretical traditions include diplomatic history, "great leaders," dependent foreign policy, and regional and subregional relations. Because of these widely diverse approaches, few scholars have incorporated empirical findings and theoretical reflections into a unified whole. Certainly, some themes emerge throughout the literature (as we discuss in the next section), but the lack of theoretical coherence is remarkable.Beginning with an overview of the crucial questions facing LACFP, this chapter then introduces the "level of analysis" framework all the country chapters follow. We hope this common structure will answer the call (Van Klaveren 1996: 55) for comparative research into LACFP that not only is descriptively rich but also moves us toward an integrated explanation of LACFP.

CRUCIAL QUESTIONS FACING LACFP: SYSTEM, INDIVIDUAL, AND DEVELOPMENT

LACFP has been studied long and hard.[1] Much of the post–World War II research consisted of largely atheoretical descriptions of diplomatic activity as well as examinations of individual Latin American and Caribbean leaders' international behavior. More theory-driven explanations entered the picture in the 1970s and 1980s as more theory injected into LACFP as political realism and dependency theory entered foreign policy analysis, especially as it applied to the third world. Scholars asked to what extent the region's dependence (primarily on the United States) was reflected in its foreign policy behavior. Dependency theorists focused on U.S. economic hegemony and its political-strategic implications. Realists, while also paying attention to the asymmetries in the relationship between the United States and Latin America, focused on the overall power capabilities, particularly in terms of military strength and global influence, that the United States possessed vis-à-vis Latin America and the Caribbean. Early research (e.g., Wittkopf 1973; Richardson 1978) began a two-decade-long focus on the model of compliance, whereby dependent states fulfill the demands of core countries because failure would provoke painful economic punishment. Moon (1983, 1985) was an early contributor to this research, demonstrating that pro–core country foreign policies were not necessarily "compliant"—in other words, forced on the dependent state. Moon argued that "consensus" was a better depiction of the U.S.–Latin American relationship because in many cases Latin American foreign policymakers agreed with and even shared economic interests with elites in the United States. Perhaps most interesting are the very weak results from quantitative studies of foreign policy alignment between core and dependent countries. Mostly relying on UN voting data, many studies revealed that dependent countries failed to follow their "benefactors," even when the latter pressured them (Richardson and Kegley 1980; Armstrong 1981; Menkhaus and Kegley 1988; Kegley and Hook 1991).

Beginning in the 1980s, LACFP largely left behind the quantitative studies of behavior based on UN votes and looking for compliance. Case study–based research became more popular, as did the notion that Latin American and Caribbean states often do not follow the lead of the United States (Menkhaus and Kegley 1988; Biddle and Stephens 1989; Hey 1995). Researchers also returned to an examination of myriad inputs to the policy process, from leader ideology and domestic politics, to the influence of the United States. The single focus on systemic influences that had dominated the compliance and consensus literatures abated (Ferris and Lincoln 1984; Muñoz and Tulchin 1984, 1996). During this time, the international relations–trained scholars focusing on foreign policy analysis joined with those in comparative politics who had traditionally engaged in case study analyses.

In the 1990s, a number of works appeared that together generate an understanding of the "state of the discipline" (Muñoz 1996; Van Klaveren 1996; Hey 1997, 1998). From those articles and chapters emerges a series of questions this volume addresses. These questions aim at *explaining* LACFP, which is at the heart of this book's objectives.

The two dominant explanatory themes emanating from the LACFP literature reside at the system and individual levels. In other words, much of LACFP has been about the region's role within the Western Hemispheric and global system and the influence that (usually subordinate) role has had on foreign policy options and choices. Van Klaveren (1996: 37) argues that although the distinction between the internal and the external is largely false, conceptually it remains useful. Much of LACFP's concern with the interplay between these two themes has focused on *dependence*. LACFP has been concerned especially with the Unites States and the degree to which its activities and policies constrain Latin America's foreign policy aspirations and behavior. In Muñoz's (1996) language, a core theme of LACFP is "autonomy," the inverse of dependence. This emphasis reveals the influence of two, often thought contradictory, models of politics: realism and dependency. While the first is designed to explain international relations and the second to explain underdevelopment in Latin America, both find their roots in the asymmetrical power relations that pervade the Western Hemisphere.

On the other hand, this same body of research pays much attention to the role of presidents in determining foreign policy. Latin America's political culture, specifically its tradition of personalism and authoritarian rule, has accentuated the role of the executive. Latin American foreign policy, more so than domestic policy, has traditionally been the preserve of the executive and a narrow elite. Many LAFCP studies are indeed organized according to a presidential chronology, telling the story through the lens of presidential administrations.

In the post–Cold War era, for example, is LACFP still about dependence? One could argue that the Unites States was vigilant about Latin American compliance with U.S. goals during the Cold War because Washington was so afraid of losing allies to the Soviet sphere. Certainly, U.S. policy in the wake of Cuba's "defection" to the communist bloc indicates that Washington was fully committed to keeping the rest of the region in line. Thus, the disappearance of the Soviet enemy might give Latin America and the Caribbean more foreign policy latitude. Conversely, the rise of the United States as the sole superpower might give it even more power to coerce or cajole its Latin American neighbors into compliance, because now the latter have no other patron to which to turn. Possible indicators of this idea include the hemisphere-wide move toward economic neoliberalism (i.e., the deregulation and privatization of the economy emphasizing the market over the state as the main engine of growth and development), the free trade of the Americas movement, and the friendly sentiments expressed during the Summit of the Americas in Quebec City in 2001. This leaves us to ask, What is the role of system-level variables on LACFP in the post–Cold War era?

In terms of individual factors, research on LACFP has traditionally emphasized the role of political culture, personality or leadership styles, and excessive concentration of power in the hands of the executive as important explanatory variables. However, with democratization, legislatures and societal groups have had the opportunity to organize and become important participants in foreign policy. Other than Fidel Castro, there are no nondemocratic caudillos, as such, but presidential personalities, particularly populist leaders such as Hugo Chavez in Venezuela and Alberto Fujimori in Peru, dominated foreign policy decision making with little regard to legislatures and public opinion. An enduring question, then, concerns the degree to which democratization has diminished presidential power and heightened that of societal groups.

The fact that much of the region remains desperately poor, especially after the so-called lost decade of the 1980s, means that development has remained a crucial issue for LACFP (Muñoz 1996; Hey 1997). Over twenty years ago, Coleman and Quiros-Varela (1981) wrote an influential chapter that used a state's development strategy to explain its foreign policy behavior (see also Snarr 1995). While perhaps too little research has continued explicitly on this path, many research efforts have been directed toward understanding Latin America's development strategies, especially the extent to which they are externally derived (Canak 1989; Williamson 1990; Green 1995). Development is generally considered a state-level matter. It is probably the most important state-level determinant that needs to be better integrated into LACFP. Some research (see Hey 1997) suggests that international pressure on LACFP is strongest on economic issues such as development policy. An important question then, concerns how autonomously regional leaders are able to make and implement their own development programs. Even after the "lost decade," research suggests that they are heavily dependent on, or in agreement with, core actors.

THE LEVELS OF ANALYSIS: THE MISSION OF THE BOOK

We need empirical scholarship that addresses these questions in a systematic way in order to identify foreign policy trends and to establish the grounding for a theory of LACFP. This volume offers an ideal place to address these questions in an integrated way, providing empirical research in the hope of offering some theoretical precepts. The editors of this book, Jeanne Hey and Frank Mora, are political scientists who have devoted much of their careers to studying Latin America. They are trained in the two "international" subfields of the discipline: Hey in international relations (IR) and foreign policy, and Mora in comparative politics, especially in Latin America and the Caribbean. The complexity of the questions surrounding LACFP, as well as that of the globalized world in which it is created, require an integrated analysis of LACFP that brings together these two subfields of political science. The chapter contributors are also political scientists and country specialists (many of them Latin American) with extensive experience conducting research on site. Since much of LACFP analysis stems from IR (realism and dependency) and comparative politics (single-country case studies), the editors hope to provide a framework that allows the contributors from both subfields to present their analysis.

The levels of analysis employed in IR research serves the conceptual purpose at hand. The objective of this book is not to establish a theory per se but to collect a series of foreign policy case studies all examined through a single conceptual lens. Of the numerous categorizations of levels of analysis (e.g., Singer 1961; Rosenau 1966; Jervis 1976), we chose a three-tiered one that includes the individual, the state, and the system. In general, the *individual* level of analysis focuses on the importance or weight of idiosyncratic or the personality of individual leaders—namely, presidents or prime ministers—in foreign policy. In addition to political culture, psychology is a variable that is often used in foreign policy analysis. In terms of the *state*, the role of domestic political institutions, such as legislatures, political parties, and civil society organizations, are examined to discern the impact of state or societal institutions in the formulation of foreign policy. Finally, the *systemic* level of analysis studies macro or international variables such as the structure of the global system, interstate conflict, role of international governmental and nongovernmental actors, and dominant values or norms of the international system (i.e., democracy and economic neoliberalism) to distinguish the key determining factors shaping foreign policy.

The seventeen contributors were asked to evaluate their empirical evidence of foreign policy behavior within a levels-of-analysis framework. Taken together, the chapters present a rich body of research on LACFP that can be compared in a way that allows us to answer the questions presented earlier. The editors contend that each level of analysis remains vital to understanding LACFP, but, as the chapters demonstrate, the relative weight of each level varies by country and circumstance.

Together these chapters provide two contributions that enhance our understanding of LACFP. First, they present a wealth of descriptive information about the content of recent LACFP behavior. This is of special interest because it documents the trends in the region's international behavior since the end of the Cold War. The most recent efforts to bring together numerous works on LACFP were published in 1996 and thus did not benefit from many years' experience beyond the collapse of the Soviet bloc (Mace and Therien 1996; Muñoz and Tulchin 1996).[2] Second, the chapters organize their analytical findings according to individual-, state-, and system-level categories. This book is unique in imposing a common conceptual framework that enables us to examine whether the system and individual levels remain as important as they were prior to the end of the Cold War and whether democratization has allowed for a rise in the importance of state-level actors on foreign policy. Organized as it is, the volume also permits us to examine the interaction among the three levels, as well as their relative weights under different circumstances.

CONCLUSION

In this section, we provide some "introductory concluding" remarks about the composite findings of the contributors' chapters in this volume. It is difficult to generalize about the foreign policies of countries as different as Cuba and Brazil. Also, the chapter authors examine different issue areas and different time periods. Space constraints did not permit including all thirty-four countries of the hemisphere. However, the volume offers analyses of seventeen different countries (a chapter on CARICOM countries as a whole is included) carefully selected not only because of their influence in hemispheric and global affairs but because of their comparative value in analyzing countries not included in the volume. Comparing them offers some conclusions about foreign policymaking and behavior in Latin America and the Caribbean as a region.

The reader will find that nearly every contributor to the volume finds that the best explanation resides in the nexus among all levels of analysis. This is no surprise, as any thorough and detailed analysis requires appreciation of the inputs from the system, state, and individual levels. From policy initiative to full implementation, factors at each level contribute. Yet conclusions about the relative weight of the factors are discernible. The first conclusion is that the international system, in most cases the influence of the United States, is a ubiquitous presence in LAC foreign policymaking environments. Whether it be Soviet support enabling a proactive and global Cuban foreign policy, Paraguay forced to accept the terms of the Southern Cone Common Market (Mercosur) without considering its consequences, or Argentina buckling to core pressure to adopt a neoliberal economic model, LAC states can almost never remove themselves from global and regional systemic pressures. In the smaller and weaker countries such as those of the English-speaking Caribbean, Panama, Paraguay, and Uruguay, the systemic influences are most keenly felt, to the detriment of the relative weight of other inputs to foreign policy. Yet even Chile and Mexico have had their foreign policy profiles profoundly shaped by behaviors and events beyond their borders. This finding is consistent with both political realist and dependency approaches, as both hold that the global distribution of power will be one of the heaviest determinants of foreign policy outcomes.

Individual LAC leaders have certainly made a name for themselves in the foreign policy realm. Global awareness of names such as Arias, Castro, Manley, Salinas, and Fujimori indicate the degree to which some individuals can overcome their country's poverty and low world status to develop a foreign policy that attracts attention. Yet numerous authors in this volume have demonstrated how that influence is moderated by other factors. A weak state in Peru, economic crisis in Cuba, and a favorable global environment in Panama are all examples of nonidiosyncratic variables that intervened to detract from or enhance the leader's ability to develop and enact policy. In places like Colombia and Ecuador, where foreign policy behavior vacillates according to the presidential ideology, it is specifically those presidents' attitudes *toward the United States* that are the defining feature of each regime's foreign policy profile. In other words, the role of the leadership is fully tied up in those countries' subordinate relationship vis-à-vis the regional hegemon. LAC leaders can distinguish themselves, but they cannot separate themselves from their hemispheric and global systems.

The types of state-level variables important in explaining LACFP vary. Chapter authors include public opinion, the strength of the state apparatus, fragility of democratic institutions, and legislative pressures among the many domestic inputs into foreign policy. Despite nearly fifteen years of democracy, the quality and strength of democratic practices and institutions in LAC remain weak affecting the cohesiveness, decision making and implementation of foreign policy. This is particularly the case in Central America, Ecuador, Peru, and Paraguay. One state-level institution, the government bureaucracy, receives little attention here. Except in Brazil, a large country with a large bureaucracy playing an unusually important role in international affairs, most LACFP reflects the regime's, rather than the bureaucrats', proclivities. There is one common domestic concern that influences foreign policy in all the LAC countries under study, be they large or small: the state of the domestic economy. Because the region is "underdeveloped," and especially because of the chronic economic crisis it has suffered since the 1980s, LACFP orients itself toward economic survival. In Mexico, this meant a reorientation away from a protectionist, anti-U.S. stance. In Peru, foreign policy changed dramatically when free marketer Alberto Fujimori replaced a leftist leader with a devastating economic legacy. In Ecuador, foreign policy has been pared down to the bare essentials, as economic crisis means that little can be done beyond dealing with border conflicts and other immediate concerns. Even in Cuba, the economic crisis brought on by the collapse of the Soviet Union saw Havana make adjustments that few would have expected.

It would be dangerous to rank the levels of analysis, as the chapters do not collectively make a statement that one level is always the most important in explaining LACFP. Rather, it is appropriate to conclude that the system level nearly always plays a role, sometimes the most important, in determining LACFP behavior. This contradicts expectations that the end of the Cold War would create a more flexible environment for LAC countries. According to that logic, the less developed states in the Western Hemisphere, and indeed in the world, would gain greater foreign policy freedom because the collapse of the East–West conflict would remove the U.S. incentive to keep its allies in line. Certainly anticommunism no longer infuses U.S.-LAC relations as it once did. But economic matters appear to have replaced political ones as the fulcrum upon which core influence is pressed on LAC. In addition, now that antiterrorism is a primary U.S. foreign policy goal, we can expect it to replace anticommunism as the primary global political force weighing on makers of LACFP.

A preliminary conclusion about LACFP is that we need all the same tools to explain it as we do to explain foreign policy in the developed world or in any other region. These chapters demonstrate that individual leaders and their advisers, legislative bodies, popular input and international forces all have an effect on LACFP, just as they do in the United States, New Zealand, or Malaysia. Yet, LACFP also has its own flavor, and that is one strongly peppered by the role of core actors and domestic economic crisis. While these play a role in every country, local idiosyncrasies, circumstances, and events determine the relative weight and the direction of the influence that these two factors have in any given policy. This dual focus in LACFP suggests that future research should examine the intersection between system- and individual-level politics.

NOTES

1. Hey (1997, 1998) reviews this scholarship in greater detail.
2. One important exception to the dearth of research since 1996 is Tulchin and Espach (2001).

I

MIDDLE AMERICA AND THE CARIBBEAN BASIN

1

Mexico

The Challenges of a Latin American Power in the U.S. Backyard

Ana Covarrubias

Mexican foreign policy since the end of World War II has oscillated between periods of moderate global activity and visible regional and world participation and leadership ambitions. Several variables explain these changes in Mexican foreign policy. This chapter will resort to three main categories: the international level, the state level, and the individual level. The international level includes first and foremost the United States, which is closely linked to the structure of the international system (bipolar/multipolar; Cold War/post–Cold War). It also includes opportunities in international politics that Mexican governments have engaged in and events that Mexican governments have had to react to. The state level will consider the economic development model (import substitution/export promotion), power capabilities (economic vulnerability/strength), and the nature of the Mexican political regime characterized mostly as authoritarian. The fact that the Institutional Revolutionary Party (Partido Revolucionario Institucional [PRI]) was in power until December 2000 is very important since its self-proclaimed revolutionary origin provided foreign policy with a discourse that underlined its revolutionary/progressive nature. Such discourse proved to be very useful on certain occasions. The PRI also claimed to be the heir and performer of a traditional diplomacy centered on international law principles such as nonintervention and self-determination. Finally, the individual level becomes relevant in terms of changes in leadership and ideas.

This chapter will make a very brief reference to Mexico's foreign policy prior to 1970, to analyze in more detail the presidential periods (*sexenios*) of Luis Echeverría (1970–1976), José López Portillo (1976–1982), Miguel de la Madrid (1982–1988), Carlos Salinas de Gortari (1988–1994), Ernesto Zedillo (1994–2000), and Vicente Fox (2000–2006). The chapter is divided into three sections: the first and the second describe general tendencies of Mexican foreign policy during and after the Cold War, and the third attempts to assess the influence of different variables in foreign policy.

Mexican-U.S. relations will have priority because of their dual importance as a point of reference of Mexican foreign policy in general and because of its own logic. Given the complexity of the bilateral relationship, the chapter will identify only the most difficult issues such as illegal immigration, trade, debt, and drug trafficking.

MEXICO IN THE COLD WAR: THE DIFFICULT TASK OF PARTICIPATING IN INTERNATIONAL POLITICS

The Early Postwar Years

Generally speaking, prior to 1970, Mexican governments were concerned mainly with economic development and political stability in the country. An active role in the international system was not a priority. Mexican foreign policy, however, cautiously responded to specific interests, unilaterally and according to international law. The inter-American system provided Mexico the occasion to implement a distinct foreign policy: differing from the position of the Organization of American States (OAS) members, the Mexican government condemned the invasions of Guatemala (1954) and the Dominican Republic (1965), rejected the imposition of sanctions on the Cuban government and refused to break diplomatic relations with it. Another issue, in which Mexico had an important role, was that of disarmament both at the United Nations and regionally, by sponsoring the Treaty for the Proscription of Nuclear Weapons in Latin America and the Caribbean, signed in 1967.

Despite disagreements at the OAS, relations with the United States were stable after a period of cordiality during World War II. From the 1970s on, however, the bilateral relationship became increasingly problematic. In 1971, the U.S. government imposed a 10 percent surcharge on all its imports and refused to exempt Mexican and Canadian products despite their claim of an existing "special relationship" with it. It was clear that Mexico could not expect privileged treatment from the United States.

Looking for Global Leadership

The end of the "special relationship" with the United States, as well as domestic circumstances characterized by political and economic deterioration, prompted president Luis Echeverría (1970–1976) to implement an active foreign policy to diversify Mexico's international relations (Shapira 1978; Rico 2000). Echeverría traveled worldwide, increasing the number of countries with which Mexico had diplomatic and economic relations, supported the third world movement, and strengthened relations with some Latin American countries, especially Salvador Allende's Chile and Cuba. Echeverría's specific initiatives included the promotion of political pluralism at the OAS and various efforts to encourage Latin American economic unity, such as the Latin American Economic System (SELA) and, most importantly, the Charter of States' Economic Rights and Duties. The charter pretended to be the counterpart of the Universal Declaration of Human Rights and proposed a new international economic order (NIEO) that, based on equity, sovereign equality, interdependence, and cooperation, would reduce inequality in the international system.

A Short-Lived Middle Power

Despite a temporary retreat from the international scene as a result of economic crisis at the end of Echeverría's presidential term, president López Portillo (1976–1982) continued a policy to redress international inequality. He proposed the World Energy Program at the UN to improve the position of oil-producing countries. Mexico hosted the North/South Dialogue in Cancún, to discuss economic relations between rich and poor countries. López Portillo's discourse, however, significantly differed from Echeverría's (Green 1977a).

López Portillo's main undertaking was to encourage political change in Nicaragua and El Salvador as guerrilla fighting spread in Central America at the end of the 1970s. The Mexican government decisively supported the Sandinista revolution in Nicaragua and, to a lesser extent, the guerrilla movement in El Salvador. Mexico's discourse favored political change in these countries as the only way in which peace, stability, and progress would be achieved in the area. During the first months of the Sandinista government, Mexican assistance was just behind that of the United States and Cuba. By 1983, Mexico's aid to Nicaragua exceeded U.S.$500 million (Rosenzweig 1983; Herrera and Ojeda 1983; Pellicer 1983). In the case of El Salvador, the Mexican government, along with the French government, issued a declaration that considered the opposition (Frente Farabundo Martí para la Liberación Nacional [FMLN]), and (Frente Democrático Revolucionario [FDR]), as "representative political forces," while maintaining diplomatic relations with the Salvadoran government (Herrera and Ojeda 1983; Rico 2000). According to Lorenzo Meyer, Mexico's policy toward Central America since the late 1970s intended to advance regional pluralism so that Mexican nationalism could survive in the face of the United States (Vázquez and Meyer 1982).

López Portillo's most comprehensive proposal was the 1982 peace plan that contemplated the creation of mechanisms to encourage the parties involved, including the United States and Cuba, to engage in discussion concerning differences between the two. The plan was not enthusiastically received by either country. As the Central American conflict took on regional dimensions, the Mexican government was faced with the need to stop the flow of refugees, especially Guatemalan, from entering Mexican territory. President Miguel de la Madrid (1982–1988) decided to act jointly with Panama, Colombia, and Venezuela in the Contadora Group. The group's central purpose was to find a peaceful solution to conflicts within and between Central American countries (Heller 1984; Herrera and Chavarría 1984). In Contadora's perspective, this was going to be easier if the United States abstained from military intervention on a large scale.

By joining the Contadora Group, the Mexican government maintained a moderate presence in the region. As part of a multilateral diplomatic effort, the Mexican government had to adjust previous positions: it gradually distanced itself from the Sandinistas, recognized democratic progress in El Salvador, and improved relations with Guatemala, once a civilian government assumed power (Herrera and Chavarría 1984; Purcell 1985).

Mexican-U.S. Relations: A Troubled Agenda

Depending on the economic situation in the two countries, and on nationalist and xenophobic sentiments in the United States, illegal immigration has become a serious source of conflict in the bilateral relationship. For many years, the United States handled the problem from a criminal and police perspective, while Mexico insisted on the need to protect immigrants' human rights and wanted to deal with it as a bilateral issue. Although consultations and talks between the two governments have been frequent, the U.S. government has taken unilateral measures against illegal immigration. A good example is the Immigration Reform and Control Act (IRCA) of 1986, which prohibited employers from hiring illegal immigrants. IRCA provoked a strong reaction from the Mexican government and public opinion, and it contributed in turn, to deteriorating the state of the bilateral relationship. As will be seen later, cooperation would not reenter the bilateral relationship until the 1990s (García y Griego and Verea Campos 1998).

Trade and investment have also been a source of disagreement, ideologically and in practice. For many years, the U.S. support for a market economy and free trade confronted a predominantly state-ruled and highly protectionist Mexican economy. Advocacy for free trade by the United States, however, was not absolute: the United States demanded access to foreign markets but tended to protect its own (Toro 1983; Meyer 1985). A good example is that of the tuna embargo imposed on Mexico as a result of U.S.

ecological groups complaints that Mexican methods to catch tuna resulted in dolphins' deaths. The embargo was seen as a means to force Mexican authorities to adopt a new technique. In the last analysis, however, the embargo also served as a means to protect tuna production in the United States (De la Mora 1995).

Mexico and U.S. perspectives on economic matters began to converge in the 1980s when, forced by a major debt crisis, president Miguel de la Madrid initiated a process of economic liberalization. After the Mexican government announced in 1982 that it could not meet its debt commitments, mostly with U.S. banks and the government, the United States and the International Monetary Fund (IMF) reluctantly supported De la Madrid's government on condition that it initiated a recovery program that required economic liberalization, reduction of imports, and cuts in public expenses (González 1986; Green 1986). To settle the debt issue, Mexican governments complied with the Baker (1985) and Brady (1990) Plans that also required the debtor country to adopt neoliberal policies. At the beginning of the 1990s, Mexico was considered a "model debtor" and was also praised for its economic opening that had included joining the General Agreement on Tariffs and Trade (GATT) in 1986 (Meyer 1992). The North American Free Trade Agreement (NAFTA) would consolidate changes in Mexico's economic orientation, although it has not ended trade problems with the United States. On the other hand, though debt continues to be a heavy burden for the Mexican economy, it is not currently a matter of dispute between the two countries.

Like illegal immigration, drug trafficking between the United States and Mexico has existed for many years but became a highly sensitive issue in the 1980s (Toro 1995). The U.S. and Mexican views on the drug issue diverged as to what caused the problem: The former blamed it on drug supply, while the latter blamed it on demand. As Mexico became not only a producer but also a transit country, drug trafficking posed a problem of sovereignty and authority to the state since the government had to deal both with traffickers and U.S. officials working illegally in the country (Toro 1998). Tension between the two countries arose when an agent of the U.S. Drug Enforcement Agency (DEA), Enrique Camarena, was murdered in Guadalajara in 1985 by alleged drug dealers. In response, the United States launched Operation Intercept to check on every single person wishing to cross the border. In practice, it meant the closing of the border. Moreover, in 1986 the U.S. Congress approved a law to certify other countries' cooperation with the United States in the fight against drug trafficking. The Mexican government condemned the process of certification as a unilateral policy infringing on the sovereignty of the countries under review (certification of Mexico was suspended in 2001). The United States, however, disregarding Mexico's protest over unilateral measures, arrested a Mexican citizen, Humberto Álvarez

Machain, in Mexico to be judged in the United States in connection with Camarena's murder.

The assassination of Camarena and the ensuing dispute over drug trafficking and the activities of U.S. police in Mexican territory seriously damaged bilateral relations. Diverse political and social sectors in the United States, including the media, used drug trafficking as evidence of the deterioration of the Mexican political system in general. According to this view, inefficiency and corruption pervaded Mexico's administration up to the highest levels, and the government could no longer maintain political stability as the opposition gained strength (Chabat 1992; Gil Villegas 1992). Senator Jesse Helms organized a series of hearings that summed up the view of important groups in the United States: Mexico was close to chaos as a result of general corruption, state intervention in the economy, and electoral fraud (Gutiérrez 1987).

The 1980s, in brief, were characterized by a troubled bilateral relationship. As debt, immigration, drug trafficking, and a policy supportive of political change in Central America became a source of dispute, some U.S. officials, senators, and the media expressed a rather unusual concern for Mexico's lack of democracy and openly supported political change (Bagley 1989; Chabat 1992). In the end, however, democracy in Mexico—or the lack of it—ceased to be a matter of discussion in the United States when the 1988 elections demonstrated that it was the leftist Frente Democrático Nacional (FDN)—and not the Partido Acción Nacional (PAN), -which coincided more with U.S. positions—that had obtained more electoral support (Meyer 1991). The PRI still won the presidential election amid allegations of fraud.

THE END OF THE COLD WAR: "INTERMESTIC" POLICY?

NAFTA and Afterward: Bilateral Conflicts in a Cordial Framework

There is consensus among scholars that Salinas' government contemplated the possibility of negotiating a free trade agreement with the United States once it realized there were no other options for economic recovery (Del Castillo and Vega 1995; Smith 2000; González 2001; Domínguez and Fernández de Castro, 2001). Before turning to the United States, however, Salinas tried, unsuccessfully, to engage Europe in such a recovery. But Europe was more concerned about Eastern Europe. At the International Conference at Davos in 1990, Salinas could not attract the participants' attention to the economic reforms that his government was implementing.

The free trade agreement with the United States and Canada would boost economic growth by stimulating industrialization, promoting exports, and attracting foreign investment. It would guarantee access to Mexican products in the U.S. market and would also formalize rules and procedures to solve disputes. Finally, the treaty would consolidate Mexico's market-oriented reforms, thus giving them more credibility (Del Castillo and Vega 1995; Domínguez and Fernández de Castro 2001). The Bush administration, in turn, considered NAFTA a good start for a wider multilateral process of trade liberalization given the poor results of the GATT's Uruguay Round negotiations. Thus, the Mexican proposal would not only redefine troubled relations between the United States and Mexico but also defend U.S. general trade interests. As a matter of fact, the proposal would be useful in Bush's attempts at shaping a new world order. It would also be a good example of how relations between rich and poor countries could be conducted (Domínguez and Fernández de Castro 2001).

Some sectors were especially difficult to negotiate in NAFTA. Textile and apparel, agriculture, and automotive goods proved difficult due to consequences that their liberalization would bring to any of the two countries. Moreover, the Mexican government excluded transport, telecommunications, and energy for nationalistic reasons. Meanwhile, labor and environmental groups in the United States opposed the conclusion of the free trade agreement. To appease these nongovernmental organizations (NGOs), and by refusing to include labor issues in the main text of the treaty, the NAFTA partners signed two side agreements: the North American Agreement on Environmental Cooperation (NAAEC) and the North American Agreement on Labor Cooperation (NAALC). Both treaties provide for the imposition of sanctions when national laws concerning labor and environmental issues are violated (Del Castillo and Vega 1995; Domínguez and Fernández de Castro 2001).

The opening up of the Mexican economy in the 1980s and NAFTA incorporated new actors, issues, and procedures to deal with conflict and cooperation concerning the bilateral relationship. Government officials from the federal, state, and local levels, business executives, NGOs, and media organizations have all become influential actors in the bilateral relationship (Domínguez and Fernández de Castro 2001). In the case of Mexico, the Bank of Mexico and the Ministries of Finance and Industrial Promotion and Foreign Trade became important voices in designing foreign policy, occasionally opposing the Ministry of Foreign Relations.

NAFTA has contributed to shaping a more cordial attitude by the two governments when they face disagreement. During the 1990s, Mexican and U.S. authorities discussed more openly and more frequently the matter of illegal immigration, although with few specific results. In 1995, for example, the Mexican government admitted that it should encourage investment in the country as a way to stop Mexicans from leaving the country, and it accepted deportation of immigrants as a fact (García y Griego and Verea Campos 1998). The United States, in turn, continued to take measures to stop illegal immigration. Proposition 187, sponsored by California's governor Pete Wilson in 1994, provoked a strong reaction from the Mexican government and public opinion. The proposition excluded illegal immigrants from certain public services such as education. Additionally, partly as a result of Republican pressures, President Clinton signed the Personal Responsibility and Work Opportunity Act, the Antiterrorism and Effective Death Penalty Act, and the Illegal Immigration Reform and Responsibility Act in 1996. In general terms, these acts denied illegal immigrants certain social welfare benefits, increased vigilance at the border, and higher penalties for U.S. employers who hire illegal immigrants and forge documents (García y Griego and Verea Campos 1998; Smith 2000).

President Fox intends to shape a "strategic" relationship with the United States. As far as Mexican immigration is concerned, the Mexican government proposed to the United States a five-point program that included granting amnesty for those illegal immigrants already living in the United States, an increase in the number of annual visas for Mexicans, the establishment of a visiting workers' program, heightened border security, and the promotion of economic development in the Mexican regions that provide for illegal immigration. The United States did not react very enthusiastically to Mexico's proposal, and the terrorist attacks of September 11, 2001, reduced its possibilities of success, as security became the priority of the U.S. national and international agenda.

The fight against drug trafficking remains an important issue with regards to the bilateral agenda. Although the U.S. government has recognized that the root of the problem is not drug supply alone, it continues to employ unilateral measures since widespread corruption in police forces and the incompetence of the judicial system hinder effective actions from Mexican authorities. The Casablanca Operation, completed in 1998, was a case in point. The U.S. Customs Service implemented an undercover operation to identify money-laundering mechanisms in Mexico, without the knowledge of the White House, the State Department, and Mexican authorities. The operation resulted in the arrest of some Mexican banks' employees in the United States. According to the Mexican government, these arrests as well as the U.S. agents' activities in Mexico had been illegal (Smith 2000; Domínguez and Fernández de Castro 2001). Once again, Mexican authorities rejected the extraterritorial application of U.S. laws.

Mexico and the New International Agenda

Salinas's concern about Mexico's image abroad contributed to making Mexico's political and social conditions the subject of external criticism. The

Zapatista uprising in January 1994, and the assassinations of the PRI presidential candidate, Luis Donaldo Colosio in March and of the PRI secretary general, José Francisco Ruiz Massieu in September of the same year, were major causes for the deterioration of Mexico's image. But it was president Ernesto Zedillo's government (1994–2000) that faced more severe foreign censure concerning democracy and human rights. The government's response was to become gradually more willing to discuss domestic matters with foreign actors: governments, the OAS, and the UN especially (Covarrubias 1999).

As far as the OAS was concerned, the Mexican government in 1996 invited members of the Human Rights Inter-American Commission (HRIC) to assess the state of human rights in Mexico, as an indication that it realized the convenience of "ventilating" human rights–related problems as long as its authority was not challenged. Two years later, the Mexican government announced its decision to accept the jurisdiction of the Human Rights Inter-American Court, also as a means to reinforce its standing vis-à-vis foreign judgment and to have a legitimate and recognized forum to defend itself.

Representatives of diverse UN commissions as well as the secretary-general also visited the country. Some of them included the special rapporteurs on torture, Nigel Rodley (1997) and on extrajudicial, summary or arbitrary executions, Asma Jahangir (1999), and the High Commissioner for Human Rights Mary Robinson (1999). These visits demonstrated the same pattern in Mexico's behavior: the willingness to welcome and collaborate with the organization's representatives while clearly stating the limits of their participation in Mexican affairs. Secretary-General Kofi Annan and Mexican authorities, for example, declared that the UN would not act as a mediator in the Chiapas conflict. The Mexican government's new attitude assumed that international organizations were no longer "questioning" the country's performance, but, on the contrary, they could collaborate in creating a culture for the protection of human rights.

The promotion of democracy and the protection of human rights are so important for the new government installed by President Fox that they have become foreign policy objectives. In this sense, the government actively supported the Quebec Declaration and the Inter-American Democratic Charter (2001). Both documents take democracy as a condition to participate in the Free Trade Agreement of the Americas, in the first case, and at the OAS, in the second case. The idea that democracy and human rights are not strictly domestic issues but may be discussed and promoted internationally is certainly one of the most important changes in Mexican foreign policy.

NAFTA is the most obvious example of Mexico's endorsement of free trade, but it is not the only one. An agreement with the European Union as well as numerous agreements with Latin American countries is worth mentioning. The peculiarity of the agreement with the EU is the inclusion of a democratic clause. Initially, the Mexican government was uncomfortable with the clause because it underlined the centrality of democratic principles and human rights with the *domestic* and international policies of Mexico and the EU, thus implying intervention (*El Financiero*, June 20, 1997; *La Crónica*, April 8, 1997). The treaty, however, became Zedillo's principal foreign policy goal, and his government finally acquiesced.

As a result of Mexico's economic liberalization initiated in the 1980s, the Mexican government turned to Latin America as a potential market for Mexican products and investment, however limited. Mexican governments signed free trade agreements with the following countries in the region: Chile (1992), Costa Rica (1995), Venezuela and Colombia (1995), Bolivia (1995), Nicaragua (1996), and Guatemala, El Salvador, and Honduras (2000). The agreements impact, however, have been minor on both the Mexican and the Latin American economies.

EXPLAINING FOREIGN POLICY

With the United States as one of the key variables explaining Mexican foreign policy, it is necessary to explain the recurrent statement of Mexico's dependence on the United States. Traditionally, Mexico has sold about 60 to 70 percent of its exports to the United States, more toward the end of the twentieth century. For many years, tourism from the United States and border transactions were significant income sources for the Mexican government, which helped to compensate for Mexico's trade deficit. U.S. investment in Mexico before NAFTA reached about 80 to 85 percent. Additionally, the United States has been Mexico's major creditor: 70 percent of the $85 million that comprised Mexico's debt in 1985 was contracted with official and private U.S. sources, as well as with international financial organizations with which the United States has had great influence (Ojeda 1986; Meyer 1972, 1985; Toro 1983). As the century came to an end, this kind of relationship transformed into "partnership," although it was not an easy process. Moreover, even though the economies of the two countries have become closely linked, asymmetry in development and power between the two countries has not disappeared.

It is also worth mentioning a few traditional propositions that have aided in understanding the peculiarities of Mexico–U.S. relations. The first is the so-called dilemma of Mexican foreign policy—namely, the need to "maintain its anti-interventionist position and not to oppose the United States too much" (Ojeda 1976: 80). Mexico disagrees with the United States on fundamental issues concerning Mexico that are not necessarily important to the United States, but Mexico cooperates with regard to fundamental issues important to the United States that have little benefit for Mexico (Ojeda

1976: 93). Support for nonintervention, in turn, has served two purposes: to protect Mexico from excessive and direct U.S. intervention and to underline Mexico's independent foreign policy. An "agreement to disagree" is essential to understand divergent positions that have not led to serious confrontation in the bilateral relationship (Ojeda 1976). Another crucial consideration that explains the agreement to disagree is the U.S. interest for stability in Mexico, which has prevented the U.S. government from extreme reactions against Mexico, for example, where a lack of democracy is concerned (Meyer 1991; Mazza 2001).

As already mentioned, Mexican governments did not have an interest or capacity to participate actively in international politics during the early Cold War years. This does not mean, however, that Mexico was isolated in the international system or that it lacked a foreign policy. A bipolar international system was important in shaping Mexican foreign policy in two somewhat contradictory ways. First, given Mexico's economic dependence on the United States, engaging in international politics at a time of highly ideological definitions was extremely risky, such that Mexican governments reacted to international events more so when it was convenient to their interests. At the same time, and for the same reasons, Mexican governments needed to find a means to reaffirm Mexico's independence from the United States. Foreign policy appeared to be a good alternative, and the OAS provided the opportunity to consolidate an "autonomous foreign policy" (Ojeda 1976; Pellicer 1965–1966). Therefore, based on a diplomatic tradition, which privileged the use of international law principles, especially nonintervention and self-determination, Mexico differed from U.S. policies in dealing with the cases of Guatemala, Cuba, and the Dominican Republic. International law principles therefore allowed Mexican governments to diverge from U.S. positions, mostly as a unilateral reactive and defensive policy, and not by implementing bold initiatives beyond diplomatic declarations.

In brief, Mexico's predominantly legalistic and defensive policy before the 1970s may be explained by (1) a domestic situation characterized by a closed economy, which avoided much contact with foreign actors; a centralized regime in which only a few actors designed and implemented foreign policy: the president and the Ministry of Foreign Affairs mainly, and a party in power that had to underline its revolutionary origins and progressive stands expressed paradoxically in nonintervention and self-determination; (2)) an international system in which Mexico was a relatively less powerful country that depended on but had to underline its independence from the United States, and where Mexico was, in the security sphere of the United States, in a contested bipolar system; and (3) regional events that offered opportunities to serve Mexico's interests in proclaiming a foreign policy of its own.

The more active foreign policy implemented by Echeverría and López Portillo responded originally to domestic circumstances but found a favorable international system, and it was also influenced by the personalities of the two presidents. In time, foreign policy acquired a life of its own but was finally frustrated by both internal and external restraints. President Echeverría inherited a very deteriorated political system after the 1968 confrontation between protesters and the army in Tlatelolco Square in Mexico City. The student movement initially began as a reaction to police violence after a clash between students from two higher education institutions. The movement soon widened and acquired a political agenda. On October 2 at Tlatelolco Square, students and other social groups demanded a more open political system. The police in turn, opened fire on the group. Echeverría, who was the interior secretary at the time, was responsible in the public eye for ordering the military to subdue the demonstration. Once he became president, Echeverría had to restore the democratic and progressive image of the Mexican government by improving relations with the left, which had been the most affected sector besides the students. An active foreign policy gradually became a convenient counterpart to a democratic opening, especially as this domestic objective became more difficult to accomplish. In this sense, foreign policy also distracted attention from domestic problems (Shapira 1978; Pellicer 1972a; Green 1977b). Close relations with Cuba and Allende's Chile would contribute to underlining the progressive stand of the government (Arriola 1974; Shapira 1978; Pellicer 1972a). Furthermore, given Castro's prestige in the third world, an improvement in relations with Cuba also reinforced Echeverría's standing among third world leaders when promoting the Charter of States' Economic Rights and Duties. Additionally, as the "special relationship" with the United States came to an end in 1971, economic difficulties increased. The import substitution model had reached a stalemate and needed fresh money to continue with the following stage of producing capital goods. As a result, the Mexican government had to look for alternative markets abroad and opt for strategies of export promotion while at the same time increasing the government's participation in the economy through state enterprises and restricting foreign investment (Shapira 1978; Anguiano 1977). A foreign policy that intended to shape the international economic system corresponded with greater regulation of the Mexican economy.

Echeverría could not have implemented this foreign policy without an international system characterized by détente and the emergence of Japan and Europe as economic powers, on the one hand, and the third world, on the other. More important, the United States was more preoccupied with ending the war in Vietnam than with events in Latin America (Pellicer 1972a). Finally, as Echeverría's foreign policy gained momentum, his aspirations to become the UN secretary-general and to obtain the Nobel Peace Prize also influenced his foreign policy: The support of the third world would be decisive in his election (Green 1977b). Mexican foreign policy became inseparable from Echeverría's name.

Echeverría's domestic and foreign policies were unsuccessful, and his presidency ended in severe economic crisis characterized by a significant increase in external public debt (approximately U.S.$20 million), the devaluation of the peso, capital flight, and deterioration in the balance of payments. Export had not increased at the same rate as imports. Border transactions decreased, as did foreign investment because of Echeverría's turn to the "left" (Green 1977a; Rico 2000). On the other hand, the most industrialized countries rejected the charter of the UN, dashing hopes for a new economic international order.

López Portillo had to adhere to an economic austerity program imposed by the IMF, and he ended Mexico's active foreign policy for about two years (Green 1977a). However, toward the end of the 1980s, oil reserves, and to a lesser extent Mexico's accumulated economic growth, gave the country a new standing in the international system (Ojeda 1984). At the same time, guerrilla fighting in Nicaragua and other Central American countries was intensifying, without an initial strong visible reaction from the Carter administration. Carter's regional policy was characterized by support for nonintervention, cooperation, and the protection of human rights, and the hostage crisis in Iran allowed for a more visible Mexican presence in the isthmus (Pastor 1992). Speaking in realist terms, Mexico was more powerful, and the international system provided the opportunity to act more assertively. Conditions were ripe for the Mexican government to develop a committed policy toward its southern neighbors, to act as a middle or regional power (González 1983; Bagley 1981). In this sense, Mexico's policy responded to its perceived national interest, which was to avoid general war on its southern border, by having a leading role. A second interpretation suggests that the Mexican government was looking for a "sphere of influence" based on the oil card (Castañeda 1987).

Mexico's position as a middle power, however, did not last very long. The fall in oil prices in 1981 and the ascension of Ronald Reagan to the U.S. presidency limited Mexico's actions in Central America. Reagan's ascension to power in the United States led to an upsurge of the Cold War, and his policy of rolling back communism was a determinant in closing spaces for Mexican actions in two ways: by exacerbating differences within and between Central American countries, thus reducing the prospects for peace, and eventually by exercising pressures on the Mexican government. The fall of the international price of oil deprived the Mexican government of the resources that had previously sustained its foreign policy (Bagley 1983; Ojeda 1983). The peace plan is the best example of Mexico's diminished influence in the region.

The comparison between Echeverría and López Portillo's policies is interesting in terms of the nature and scope of Mexican foreign policy. In both cases, the personality and ambitions of the two presidents were fundamental. There are significant differences: Echeverría acted at a global level, mostly diplomatically in the field of ideas. López Portillo, in turn, acted regionally with a concrete objective for his policies: the Sandinistas and the Salvadoran guerrilla. Moreover, López Portillo had the resources to back his foreign policy initiatives not only by directly aiding the Sandinista government and by diplomatically recognizing the Salvadoran opposition, but also by undertaking joint initiatives such as the San José Agreement (1980), which supplied oil on favorable terms to Central American and Caribbean countries. In both cases, restraints escaped the government's control. Domestic weakness marked the end of both presidencies, and their diplomatic initiatives did not prosper. In the case of Echeverría, the charter was rejected; López Portillo, in turn, confronted direct interests of the United States in the region, opposite to Mexico's. Mexico and the United States seemed to be competing in the context of an intensified Cold War. Moreover, Mexico needed to sort out a new crisis with U.S. assistance; the weight of the United States was more easily felt by Mexico, directly or not (Green 1977a). If this argument is true, however, why did Miguel de la Madrid continue with a foreign policy toward Central America that so irritated the United States (Purcell 1981–1982)?

Perhaps the most immediate answer pertains to the Mexican government's perception that the conflict had become a national security problem in terms of its southern border and flows of refugees, and that a regional war in which the United States was directly involved would worsen such a situation. Bagley (1983) argues that it was also difficult to abruptly end Mexico's foreign policy toward Central America due to the Mexican left, which supported it. Moreover, as De la Madrid's government became more vulnerable vis-à-vis the United States, as a result of the debt problem and drug trafficking issues, the Mexican government may have understood the need for independent action. There are different theories concerning U.S. pressures on Mexico. According to Bagley, the U.S. government was ready to press the Mexican government to change its policy toward Central America. According to Chabat, Mexico and the United States agreed to disagree once more (Bagley 1989: 47; Chabat 1992: 93). In the last analysis, Mexico's participation in the Contadora Group reflects this dual purpose: to bring peace and stability in the region as a means to avoid flows of refugees into the country and the spread of the war, and the need to act independently of the United States. Mexico's internal weaknesses in facing U.S. policy against revolution explains the Mexican government's choice of collective action. Contadora's failure may be understood primarily as a result of the influence of U.S. actions against communism in the Central American countries—that is, radicalizing the Sandinista government while creating alliances against it. "National" solutions in Central America were difficult to reach (Rico 1986; Bagley and Tokatlián 1987; Purcell 1985).

Two different kinds of interaction between the domestic and international spheres during the 1980s account for changes in Mexican foreign policy in the medium term. The first one refers to the change in the economic model toward liberalization as a major condition imposed by international actors such as the IMF, the World Bank, and the U.S. government to help Mexico solve the debt crisis. Agencies other than the Ministry of Foreign Affairs intervened more actively in the design and implementation of a gradually more economic and pragmatic foreign policy (González 2001). A concrete result was Mexico's entrance to the GATT. Second, as the political process in Mexico became more complex, PAN complained to the Human Rights Inter-American Commission about electoral fraud. It was unusual for a Mexican political actor to resort to external agencies in order to judge the validity of internal procedures. International actors therefore had something to say about Mexican politics when requested by Mexican actors or on their own initiative. Salinas's decision to accept international monitoring of the elections of August 1994, for example, was a last-minute reaction to increasing external disapproval of the Mexican political process. In the long term, foreign policy had to adjust to this reality.

The end of the Cold War influenced Mexico's domestic and foreign policies powerfully and in a variety of ways. The crisis that marked the beginning of Salinas's and Zedillo's presidencies seemed to be more of a constant: The way in which it was resolved depended very much on the international system. In the first case it was a lack of options for economic recovery, except for U.S. aid; in the second, it was resolved by economic partnership with the United States. But a key variable without which these results would not have taken place was a new generation that came to power during Salinas's sexenio. Such new leaders had been educated in the United States and were ideologically closer to U.S. positions, especially concerning economics. An ideological convergence between Mexican and U.S. leaders facilitated contacts between the two countries, and the former thought it was no longer necessary to disagree with the United States. Additionally, the regional and world context did not offer major opportunities for divergence, and the Mexican government was able to acknowledge the existence of shared interests with the United States. Nationalism and sovereignty in Mexico were understood differently (Domínguez 1998; Pastor 1992; Domínguez and Fernández de Castro 2001). The revolutionary and progressive categories lost relevance and utility for foreign policy. Moreover, the "traditional" PRI gave way to the new leadership.

The most visible change in terms of U.S.–Mexico relations from the Salinas presidency onward concerns a disposition toward bilateral cooperation. Domínguez and Fernández de Castro identify four factors that account for this new attitude: (1) the international system—specifically, the removal of barriers to cooperation, such as the ending of the Central American conflict, and the weakening of Cuba after the collapse of the Soviet Union; (2) domestic crises in Mexico since the 1980s that compelled Mexican leaders to change the economic strategy dramatically; (3) the simultaneous ascension of president Salinas and president Bush that enabled them to refashion relations—Mexican leaders were from a younger generation, their U.S. counterparts were Texan politicians who were closer to Mexican realities, and the end of the Cold War allowed both governments to use the ideas of international institutions that were available since the 1980s; and (4) the idea of institutionalized cooperation that became fashionable in the post–Cold War world reached several important issues in the bilateral relationship (Domínguez and Fernández de Castro 2001: 34).

President Zedillo's foreign policy also changed in areas other than the bilateral relationship with the United States. An increase in social participation that strengthened political opposition and demanded a transformation of the political system offered President Zedillo the opportunity to present himself as the leader who consolidated Mexico's democratization process. On the other hand, the legacy of the Chiapas uprising, the assassinations of Luis Donaldo Colosio and Francisco Ruiz Massieu, together with cases of human rights violations during his sexenio (mostly the killing of peasants and indigenous people in the states of Guerrero and Chiapas), urged Zedillo to find a means to control external criticism. Foreign policy in consequence had to incorporate democracy and human rights issues. The Mexican government therefore invited members of the Inter-American Human Rights Commission, accepted the jurisdiction of the Inter-American Human Rights Court and the International Penal Court, and signed a commercial treaty with the EU, which contained a democratic clause. It is important to say that the United States did not officially criticize human rights violations in Mexico but, on the contrary, supported Zedillo's policies to strengthen democracy. On the basis of its democratic legitimacy, as it has been said, Fox's government has included the promotion of democracy and the protection of human rights as foreign policy objectives.

CONCLUSION

It is difficult to determine the most important level for explaining Mexican foreign policy since it is a combination of different variables that account for specific results. However, since the international system has been both a constraint and a provider of opportunities to act, a good starting point to assess the influence of key variables is the suggestion to take the international system as a framework, within which particular foreign policy outputs are shaped by domestic considerations.

Before the 1970s, in the context of the Cold War, Mexican governments could have actively participated in international politics in two ways: by joining the United States or, on the contrary, by opposing it. The international system offered opportunities in both directions. However, Mexican governments focused mainly on domestic development without many links with foreign economic actors, and they reacted to specific regional events on the basis of a diplomatic tradition that privileged international law and the defense of Mexican nationalism. The PRI claimed to be the legitimate performer of such tradition. President Echeverría faced a more flexible international system but strictly speaking did not have to implement an active foreign policy. That is, the Mexican government may have well concentrated on domestic problems that were especially delicate. Instead, Echeverría opted for an active participation in world politics precisely because of these domestic circumstances. The Mexican president seems to have seized ideas available in the international system, which were easily made compatible with the PRI ideological standing. López Portillo's foreign policy is a very interesting case since the international system significantly changed during his sexenio. Before Reagan came to power, Mexico had the possibility of reacting to revolution in Central America without major interference from the U.S. The question, however, is the same: Why did López Portillo choose to act in Central America if the region had been unstable many times in the past, without threatening Mexico? The "power of oil," nationalism, and the ambitions of the president may be the answer. After Reagan became president, the international system clearly reduced the spaces for successful Mexican action. Moreover, the "power of oil" ended as international prices fell in 1981. Nevertheless, López Portillo maintained an active presence in the region perhaps as a matter of nationalism, personal ambition, and inertia.

Another relevant explanation may be the direct consequences that the Central American conflict was having on Mexico's southern states. Miguel de la Madrid also faced an adverse international system and domestic weaknesses, but he decided to continue promoting peace and stability in the region. The option of multilateral diplomacy, however, was consistent with the country's circumstances. It was foreign policy that acknowledged serious constraints but did not surrender to these constraints, as the containment of war was a national security priority. In a post–Cold War world, Salinas admitted that the only real alternative to economic external support was, as it had always been, the United States. Once more, taking advantage of ideas available in the international system, the Mexican government acted according to them, but only as economics was concerned. As a matter of fact, Salinas resisted international trends in favor of democracy and human rights surely as a strategy in the domestic struggle for power. On the contrary, Ernesto Zedillo joined, or was forced to join, international political trends, in a context of more domestic political diversity, which he had to acknowledge. His task was then to lead Mexico to democracy.

The July 2000 elections were a turning point in Mexico's contemporary history. However, foreign policy change began at least in the 1980s as a result of the change in the economic model and the emergence of political and social opposition. Therefore, within a PRI-dominated regime, foreign policy changed according to specific international and domestic circumstances. Toward the end of the century, the PRI governments gradually accepted different issues of the newly emerging international agenda. In this sense, as the regime formally changed in 2000, foreign policy had already adjusted to a different world and to a lesser extent, a different Mexico. President Vicente Fox's government has of course accepted a new foreign policy agenda, and it has underlined its intention of participating actively in international politics, by joining the UN Security Council, promoting the Inter-American Democratic Charter and the Free Trade Agreement of the Americas, for example. Why is such activity necessary if there is no guarantee as to Mexico's democratic and economic viability? Once again, domestic considerations may help us to gain understanding: Foreign policy seems to be another instrument to underline change in Mexico. Restraints on Mexican foreign policy, however, will never disappear, although it is difficult to say which form they will take in the future. It is true that a successful foreign policy should be flexible, but it is also true that in the cases of countries like Mexico, it has to adjust to each country's primary interests and capabilities.

DISCUSSION QUESTIONS

1. Why has it been so difficult for Mexico and the United States to reach successful agreements in the fields of immigration and drug trafficking?
2. What have periods of active foreign policy demonstrated about the nature of Mexican foreign policy?
3. How influential have the principles of international law been in shaping Mexican foreign policy?

2

Costa Rica
Neither Client nor Defiant

John Peeler

As small and weak as Costa Rica is, and as close to the United States, one might assume that its foreign policy would be nothing more than a reflection of the will of the hegemon. This chapter will show that such a view would be extremely simplistic. Both domestic forces and idiosyncratic factors have at times shaped Costa Rican policy in unexpected ways (for the best overview, see Rojas Aravena 1990a; see also Araya Incera 1990). The normal foreign policy of Costa Rica since World War II has had three characteristics: (1) support for the United States on issues of strategic importance to the latter; (2) partial disengagement from Central American affairs, especially as regards political integration; and (3) moderate idealism with regard to international law and organization, if that idealism did not conflict with the first two characteristics.

As a small Central American country, Costa Rica could not possibly, early in the twentieth century, ignore the influence of the United States at a time when the latter country had come explicitly to assert its right to control international affairs in Central America and the Caribbean. For the most part, Costa Rican governments contrived to avoid giving offense and thus to preserve for themselves some limited autonomy. After World War II, most Costa Rican presidents provided reliable support for the chief foreign policy priorities of the United States. In turn, the United States has almost always treated Costa Rica gently, using persuasion and positive incentives more than coercion or pressure, to influence Costa Rican behavior. As exceptions in the first half of the twentieth century, two Costa Rican governments

(Tinoco's in 1919 and Picado's in 1948) were brought down at least in part because of U.S. policy.

A key component of Costa Rican strategy has been an isolationist stance toward Central American affairs (Gutiérrez 1956: 14–15; Salisbury 1974: 454). When it has become involved, there has usually been trouble. Costa Rica played a critical role in the successful Central American battle against the North American soldier of fortune, William Walker, in Nicaragua in the 1850s (Sáenz Carbonell 1996: 191–228). Its relations with Nicaragua have always been prickly, with the border along the Río San Juan a chronic friction point. Its southeastern neighbor, Panama (part of Colombia until 1903), has also posed occasional border problems and tensions (see Sáenz Biolley 1990; Carreras 1990). It did, however, join the Central American Common Market and the Central American Development Bank in the 1960s, and in recent years it has generally favored economic integration.

Costa Rica has long been a supporter of international law and organization, providing early support for Latin American doctrines of nonintervention, joining the League of Nations, becoming a charter member of the United Nations, and taking an active role in the Organization of American States (OAS), relying on the OAS for its own security in countering two Nicaraguan invasions in the 1950s. But it has also hung back from such involvement when its other interests appeared threatened. For example, in the 1980s, Costa Rica refused to join the Central American Parliament,[1] even as it was taking the lead in forging a regional peace settlement.

Costa Rican policymakers have generally shown an acute sense of how to manage domestic political forces while pursuing perceived national interests within boundaries set by systemic forces. Since the country is a highly institutionalized, presidential democracy, its foreign policymaking processes involve highly complex interactions of several interacting spheres (Vega 1990; Wilson 1994; Clark 1997). The executive branch, of course, contains many officials and agencies competing for the ear of the president. The legislature has important investigatory and budgetary powers, and it is the principal arena of action for the opposition. Research institutes and university faculties are integral parts of the system of circulation of elites and frequently sponsor symposia and reports intended to influence policy. Private corporations, trade associations, labor unions, and other civil society organizations will frequently seek input on foreign policy. Finally, other states will influence policy: The U.S. ambassador and other embassy staff in particular are likely to be closely consulted and usually heeded. In the final analysis, it is the president who makes policy, but it is important to understand the domestic and international forces bearing on the decision. The relative dominance of the president in the foreign policymaking process has increased in the last twenty years, particularly in response to the crises of the 1980s (Booth 2000: 94).

FOREIGN POLICY FROM WORLD WAR II: A SUMMARY

The government of Rafael Angel Calderón Guardia (1940–1944) had to deal with the effects of World War II. Although Costa Rica did not become militarily involved in the war, Calderón sought to support the United States, by declaring war on the Axis powers immediately after Pearl Harbor, by providing the United States with raw materials, and by facilitating intelligence gathering. This policy was continued by Calderón's ally and successor, Teodoro Picado (1944–1948). However, Picado confronted a shift in U.S. priorities after the end of the war and especially as the Cold War emerged in 1947. The Vanguardia Popular (the Costa Rican Communist Party) had formed an essential part of the governing coalition under both Calderón and Picado, both of whom faced strong opposition. While communists in the government were acceptable to the United States during World War II when the Soviet Union was an ally, under Cold War conditions this view changed. Picado, however, could not sack the communists without leaving his government vulnerable to the internal opposition. Thus, he was unable to satisfy the United States on a matter of great importance to that country. When opposition elements led by José Figueres Ferrer mounted a civil war in 1948, the United States did not spring to support Picado, even though it was also ambivalent about Figueres. This failure of Picado's foreign policy led to his defeat in the civil war and the emergence of a Junta of National Liberation led by Figueres (Bell 1971; Cerdas Cruz 1992; Facio 1979; Longley 1997; Schifter 1982, 1986; Yashar 1997).

Figueres was closely allied to the revolutionary government of Juan José Arévalo in Guatemala, which helped him to create the army that brought him to power. At the same time, Calderón was closely allied to the Nicaraguan dictator, Anastasio Somoza García, who gave Calderón asylum and facilitated the attempts of the latter to attack Costa Rica. Since Somoza was a close ally of the United States (which had deep misgivings about the Guatemalan regime), Figueres distanced himself from the Guatemalan regime after he came to power in order to come to an accommodation with the United States. By associating his government with anticommunism and a commitment to establish democracy, Figueres succeeded in reestablishing warm relations between Costa Rica and the United States.

Costa Rican foreign policy after 1948 reverted to the normal pattern of nonconfrontation with the United States, even though politics continued to be polarized around José Figueres and the party he founded, the Partido de Liberación Nacional (PLN). The presidency tended to alternate between the PLN and the noncommunist opposition (including both his former conservative allies and the calderonistas).[2] Neither the PLN nor its opponents adopted foreign policies that challenged or confronted the United States.

Regardless of the party in power, Costa Rica's foreign policy from 1948 to 1978 was strongly supportive of the United States, especially on issues related to the Cold War, such as the embargo against Cuba after 1960. Costa Rica did capitalize on its pacific image derived from the 1949 abolition of the army, by pushing for the strengthening of international institutions and the peaceful settlement of disputes, and specifically by relying on the OAS to counter two Nicaraguan invasions in the 1950s. But it consistently avoided crossing the United States. In the 1960s, Costa Rica was cautiously supportive of the Central American Common Market and the Central American Development Bank, and it benefited substantially from the Alliance for Progress foreign aid program of the United States (Facio 1979).

The presidency of Rodrigo Carazo (1978–1982) marks the beginning of a decade of twin systemic crises, economic and political (Carazo 1989; Rovira Mas 1988; Abarca Vásquez 1995). Economically, soaring world petroleum prices posed intractable problems for countries that, like Costa Rica, imported their oil. Gambling that prices would not stay high, Costa Rica under Carazo went deeply into debt to maintain supplies while avoiding cutbacks in social programs such as social security and medical care, which had provided Costa Ricans with an unusually high quality of life as compared with the rest of Central America.[3] Then the monetary policy of the Carter administration in the United States sent global interest rates up sharply. Costa Rica, along with such major Latin American countries as Mexico and Brazil, could not service its loans. Carazo spent the better part of his term trying unsuccessfully to cope with this externally imposed economic crisis (Rivera Urrutia 1982).

He did so, moreover, in a context of political crisis in Nicaragua, where the long-standing Somoza family dictatorship (widely unpopular in Costa Rica) came to an end in 1979. The Sandinista revolutionary movement (finally gaining traction by 1978, after nearly two decades of insurgency) was extremely popular among Costa Ricans, at least in the final stages of the insurrection and the early revolutionary regime. Carazo thus responded to domestic forces in openly supporting the Sandinistas, both verbally and materially, in a manner quite out of keeping with the country's isolationist tradition, though consistent with its commitment to democracy. Carazo's policy was somewhat at odds with that of the Carter administration, deeply ambivalent about the Sandinistas but welcoming the prospect of getting rid of Somoza if it could lead to a moderate, democratically elected government. Ronald Reagan's 1980 victory over Carter was partly impelled by the accusation that Carter was soft on communism and had failed to stand behind reliable allies such as Somoza. After he took office in early 1981, Reagan's policy toward Sandinista Nicaragua was implacably hostile, and Carazo was not in tune with the Reagan policy (Edelman 1983; Furlong 1987).

Carazo was succeeded by Luis Alberto Monge (1982–1986), a stalwart of the PLN with strong roots in the labor movement. Monge returned to a much more characteristically Tico (i.e., Costa Rican) foreign policy, in which he went as far as he had to in supporting U.S. policy in Nicaragua (including tacit but substantial support for U.S.-funded Contra forces and CIA covert operations out of Costa Rica), and received in return substantial aid on terms less exacting than those of the International Monetary Fund (IMF). The U.S. aid would permit Monge's government to begin to turn the economy around. At the same time, Monge reaffirmed Costa Rica's traditional unarmed neutrality, resisting U.S. pressure to make the lightly armed Civil Guard a more credible military force. Furthermore, he encouraged the Contadora peace initiative of Colombia, Mexico, Panama, and Venezuela and was ready to sign their peace plan in 1985 until pressure from Washington forced Costa Rica, along with El Salvador, Guatemala, and Honduras, to back off (Sojo 1991; Furlong 1987; Rovira Mas 1988; Rojas Bolaños 1992).

Monge was succeeded by Oscar Arias, also of the PLN, in 1986 (Rojas Aravena 1990b). While Arias basically embraced the neoliberal economic program that the United States and the IMF had been pushing (Vega 1990), he pursued a remarkably independent policy with regard to settling the political-military crisis in Central America (Rojas Aravena and Solís 1988; Child 1992; Moreno 1994). The Contadora initiative had failed (essentially blocked by the United States) between June 1986 and April 1987. The U.S. policy of support for the Contras had broken down in the course of 1985 and 1986, as Congress first blocked military aid for the counterrevolutionaries, then exposed the Iran-Contra scandal in 1986. The Central American presidents indicated as early as May 1986 during the first summit meeting in Esquipulas, Guatemala, that they were disposed to taking control of the peace process. With support in Washington from congressional Democrats but over the opposition of the Reagan administration, Arias gave the Central American presidents the means to do so in a summit excluding Nicaragua in February 1987 in Costa Rica. At this meeting, Arias first laid out a peace plan based on the Contadora proposal, but he went beyond it by proposing to commit each Central American country to a process of internal reconciliation and democratization. That is, each government would negotiate a cease-fire and the incorporation of insurgents into an open, competitive democratic political process. Arias managed to get the somewhat grudging agreement of the other three presidents to the principles of his plan, contingent on the agreement of Nicaraguan president Daniel Ortega. A second Esquipulas summit was called for August 1987, for all five presidents.

The Reagan administration, on the defensive and internally divided about strategy, negotiated an alternative peace plan with Democratic House Speaker Jim Wright, which was floated shortly before the Esquipulas summit but was promptly undercut by hard-liners in the Administration. As a result, Wright encouraged the Central Americans to proceed with their own plan

(Moreno 1994: 88–89). Thus, the Arias Peace Plan was adopted by the five Central American presidents at the Esquipulas II Summit on August 7, 1987.

The plan entailed these points: (1) national reconciliation—amnesty for insurgents and political dissidents, and implementation in each country of a National Reconciliation Commission to monitor implementation of the plan; (2) cessation of hostilities; (3) democratization—freedom of press and speech, pluralism of political parties, rule of law, and termination of states of siege or emergency; (4) free elections—creation and election of a Central American Parliament, as well as national elections in each country, with international observers; (5) cessation of aid to irregular forces and insurgent movements; (6) nonuse of territory to attack other states; (7) arms control negotiations (and disarmament of irregular forces willing to accept amnesty); (8) ways to deal with refugees and displaced persons; (9) consolidation of democracy and the creation of an economy of well-being and economic and social democracy; (10) international verification and follow-up by the OAS and UN secretaries-general, Central American foreign ministers, the Contadora, and support group foreign ministers; and (11) a timetable for implementation (Child 1992: 178–84).

The signing of the peace plan was a major triumph for Arias (and won him the Nobel Peace Prize), but its success was dependent on further diplomacy over the next three years (indeed, the Guatemalan peace settlement was not finally signed until 1996). Although the Reagan administration was unable to block the signing of the plan, it continued to drag its feet about disarming the Contras. At the same time, mutual mistrust among the Central American governments, and between governments and insurgents, posed repeated obstacles to implementation. Arias thus devoted continual attention to the diplomacy of the peace plan for the rest of his term. In mid-1988, a combination of U.S. intransigence and Nicaragua's inability to come to an internal settlement brought the process close to failure. A summit meeting scheduled for mid-1988 was canceled lest it end in open failure (Moreno 1994: 105).

With a new administration in Washington, the Central American presidents were able to get the peace process back on track. At a summit in Tesoro Beach, El Salvador, in February 1989, Nicaragua offered major concessions on issues of internal reconciliation and democratization, including committing to democratic elections by February 1990. Weak compliance continued to be a problem on all sides through 1989, but the process was not derailed, and the Nicaraguan elections were indeed held on February 25, 1990. The unexpected defeat of Daniel Ortega by Violeta Chamorro transformed the political environment of the region and made it easier for the other countries to carry through with their own peace settlements. As Arias himself left office in 1990, the most difficult challenge to the peace plan had been met in a quite unanticipated manner.

As the Cold War evaporated and the several Central American conflicts inched painfully toward settlement, Central America (including Costa Rica) had to adjust both politically and economically. Politically, the successful implementation of the peace plan in Nicaragua, El Salvador, and (eventually) Guatemala meant an end to outright war and the advent of a precarious and still oft-times violent peace. It meant that Costa Rica could revert to its traditional arm's-length posture toward Central American affairs, including resistance to joining the Central American Parliament (Vega 1990) and to anything else resembling political integration. The main focus of Costa Rica's foreign as well as domestic policy would be the management and structural adjustment of the economy. Because it was seen as good economic management and was congruent with advice received from the IMF and World Bank, Costa Rican governments in the 1990s generally favored steps to revitalize the Central American Common Market and worked closely with other governments of the region to present a common front in international negotiations.

The three presidents of the 1990s (Calderón Fournier, Partido Unidad Socialcristiana [PUSC], 1990–1994; Figueres Olsen, PLN, 1994–1998; Rodríguez, PUSC, 1998–2002) would basically continue the policy of neoliberal structural adjustment started by Monge and continued in earnest by Arias. Overall, by the end of the 1990s, Costa Rica's economy and society were in better shape than they had been in the 1980s and better than those of its neighbors. Having lost ground economically and stagnated in human development in the early 1980s, Costa Rica adapted to neoliberalism in the 1990s.

The Calderón Fournier administration focused its foreign policy heavily on securing more favorable financing for its foreign debt, continuing the trend of cutting social services and controlling budget deficits, in order to reach the third structural adjustment plan (SAP) with the IMF in 1994 (earlier SAPs had been concluded in 1985 and 1989). It also continued to promote exports, especially nontraditional ones, and to push for what it saw as equitable treatment in world markets. The administration's free market and export orientation was reflected in its deliberate devaluation of the *colón* in 1992 (Booth 2000: 100; Gudmundson 1996: 88–89; Clark 1997; Goss and Pacheco 1999).

Figueres Olsen (1994–1998), in spite of coming from the PLN, with its traditional commitment to social services and industrial promotion, pursued economic policies very similar to those of Calderón (and indeed to those of Arias), while dealing with a variety of political issues involving both Central America and the United States. A free trade pact between Costa Rica and Mexico was signed in 1995, leading to a 365 percent increase in Costa Rican exports to Mexico by 1997 (*Ecocentral*, March 19, 1998). Nontraditional exports were promoted and continued to increase as a proportion of total exports (*Ecocentral*, September 19, 1996). In 1996, Costa Rica won a case in the World Trade Organization (WTO) against the United States on the issue of U.S. quotas on Costa Rican undergarments (*Ecocentral*, November 21, 1996). In 1997, the Central American presidents (including Panama) signed a treaty to integrate the region's network of electricity generation and distribution (*Ecocentral*, January 16, 1997). Also in 1997, Figueres Olsen participated in a summit in Santo Domingo where a framework agreement was signed to facilitate bringing the Dominican Republic into a free trade treaty with Central America (*Ecocentral*, November 13, 1997). The final agreement with the Dominican Republic was signed on April 16, 1998. Shortly thereafter, a preliminary trade agreement with Chile was signed (*Ecocentral*, May 7, 1998).

Following on the Central American peace process begun under Arias, in December 1995 the Central American presidents signed a Treaty of Democratic Security in Central America, committing them (with support from the United Nations Development Program and the Spanish government) to work to reinforce the security of democratic institutions in the region (*Ecocentral*, December 19, 1996). On the other hand, Costa Rica continued to abstain from joining the Central American Parliament (*Ecocentral*, July 17, 1997).

Responding to continuing United States interest in controlling the movement of illegal drugs, the Figueres Olsen administration in 1997 agreed to establish joint antinarcotics operations in Costa Rican waters (*Ecocentral*, October 9, 1997). A source of irritation in U.S.–Costa Rican relations was the unsolved murder of a U.S. citizen involved in a land dispute in the southwestern part of the country, in November 1997. In March 1998, the U.S. ambassador was quoted as threatening sanctions against Costa Rica if the case were not solved (*Ecocentral*, March 5, 1998).

The third president of the 1990s, Miguel Angel Rodríguez (PUSC, 1998–2002) again represents more continuity than change, particularly on economic policy. Like his predecessors, Rodríguez was more interested in economic than political integration. In July 1998, the Central American group (including Belize and Panama) signed a series of pacts with Mexico on economic integration, but Costa Rica was cited as being notably reluctant to commit to political integration (*Ecocentral*, July 30, 1998). Much the same report about Costa Rica emerged after the next summit with Mexico in August 2000 (*Ecocentral*, August 31, 2000). Also in August 2000, in response to reports that President Portillo of Guatemala favored abolishing the Central American Parliament, President Rodríguez (whose country remains outside the parliament) criticized it as being too costly for a poor region (*NotiCen*, August 10, 2000). On the occasion of a 1999 summit between European Union (EU) governments and those of Latin America and the Caribbean, Rodríguez's foreign minister stated his government's priority is "to maintain the present opening [the isthmus] has with Europe" (*NotiCen*,

July 1, 1999). On April 23, 2001, Costa Rica signed a free trade agreement with Canada, its first with a member of the G7 group of industrialized countries (*NotiCen*, May 3, 2001).

Costa Rica staked out a position contrary to that of the United States in a dispute regarding EU banana quotas. On April 6, 1999, the WTO ruled in favor of the United States in a dispute with the European Union involving quotas on banana sales in the EU. Designed to protect high-cost producers in the eastern Caribbean who were former European colonies, the quotas were opposed by large U.S. corporations such as Dole and Chiquita and by Ecuador, Guatemala, Honduras, Mexico, and Panama. Costa Rica, the second largest world producer of bananas, was not a party to the complaint, having accepted the quota system and received a share (*NotiCen*, April 15, 1999).

Rodríguez supported the arrangement negotiated by Figueres with the United States for joint antinarcotics patrols in Costa Rican waters, and the National Assembly approved the arrangement in a bipartisan vote in August 1999 (*NotiCen*, September 2, 1999, and March 2, 2000).

Relations with Nicaragua returned to the agenda under Rodríguez in a series of border-related disputes. In July 1998, the two countries resolved tensions resulting from the request by fourteen Nicaraguan communities in the southwestern department of Rivas that they wished to secede from Nicaragua and join Costa Rica, because of neglect by the Nicaraguan government (*Ecocentral*, July 23, 1998). Also in July, Nicaragua sought to restrict access by armed Costa Rican Civil Guards on the San Juan River. The river forms the border on the Atlantic side and is Nicaraguan territory, but Costa Rica has free navigation rights under a treaty of 1858. Underlying the tension was a chronic problem of illegal Nicaraguan migration into Costa Rica (*Ecocentral*, August 13, 1998; *NotiCen*, July 15, 1999; March 9, 2000; and July 13, 2000).

Taking up Costa Rica's traditional role as an advocate of democracy, Rodríguez refused to attend the IX Ibero-American Summit held in Havana in November 1999, on grounds that the regime would not assure that dissidents who spoke with visiting delegations would not be punished (*NotiCen*, December 9, 1999).

FOREIGN POLICY FROM WORLD WAR II: AN ANALYSIS

In normal times (i.e., 1949–1978 and 1990–present), Costa Rica's foreign policy behavior is best explained by a combination of conformity to the policy of the United States[4] and response to domestic pressures. These two pressures have normally been congruent and therefore mutually reinforcing. For example, anticommunism and liberal democracy were basic tenets of United

States foreign policy during the Cold War and were also values widely and consistently held by elites and public opinion in the domestic Costa Rican environment (Booth 2000: 104). Thus, it was relatively easy for Costa Rican governments between 1949 and 1978 to pursue the first and most important component of what this chapter has characterized as the normal Costa Rican foreign policy: (1) support for the United States on issues of strategic importance to the latter; (2) partial disengagement from Central American affairs, especially as regards political integration; and (3) moderate idealism with regard to international law and organization, if that idealism did not conflict with the first two characteristics. The second and third components of normal Costa Rican foreign policy are largely attributable to domestic pressures. The second point reflects a widespread sense, again among both elites and masses, that the rest of Central America is distinct from, and perhaps inferior to, Costa Rica (Biesanz et al. 1979: 30). Thus, while it may be to the economic advantage of Costa Rica to have a common market, few Costa Ricans would see any advantage in political integration with the rest of Central America. The third point reflects a consciousness of long standing among political elites that Costa Rica is a small, weak country whose best defense will be found in support of international law and international organization.

After 1990, with the end of the Cold War and the gradual termination of the Central American conflicts, Costa Rica could return to its normal foreign policy under the leadership of Calderón Fournier, Figueres Olsen, and Rodríguez. The primary preoccupation of the United States in the 1990s was no longer the Cold War but rather the promotion of neoliberal economic reform. Again the balance of domestic forces in Costa Rica proved generally congruent with this U.S. priority, though not without significant and persistent opposition, particularly from the left and from some sectors of the PLN. Costa Rica also continued with its traditional ambivalence about Central American integration, here reflecting both widespread domestic skepticism and considerable systemic support for economic integration, from both the United States itself and from international financial institutions. Finally, Costa Rica in the 1990s also recapitulated its traditional devotion to international law and organization, particularly by its successful use of WTO proceedings even against the United States.

We have noted two main periods when the normal Costa Rican foreign policy did not prevail: the 1940s and the 1980s. From 1940 to 1945, Costa Rican foreign policy was a normal response to the highly abnormal situation of world war. Costa Rica under Calderón Guardia in fact responded faithfully to the strategic priorities of the United States. However, it should be noted that this pro-Allied foreign policy was pursued in spite of domestic pressures. Elements of the right-wing opposition showed some sympathy for the Germans as well as being anticommunist, while elements of the Social Democratic opposition were strongly anticommunist. With the end of the war and the advent of the Cold War, the U.S. attitude toward the communists shifted radically, but the Picado government was prevented by domestic pressures from following suit: Had Picado divested himself of communist support, he would not have had the means to stay in power at all. Thus, the anomalous Costa Rican foreign policy at the outset of the Cold War is directly explicable at the domestic level of analysis (Aguilar Bulgarelli 1980; Longley 1997; Yashar 1997; Facio 1979; Bell 1971; Schifter 1982, 1986). Picado paid the price for not responding to the anticommunist policy of the United States when the latter failed to back him in the civil war, notwithstanding his strong support (and that of his mentor Calderón) for the United States in World War II.[5]

The second period of anomaly, the 1980s, takes in the twin crises of debt and revolution. There were actually two distinct anomalous periods, that of Carazo (1978–1982) and that of Arias (1986–1990), separated by the relative normality of Monge (1982–1986). The Carazo anomaly was in some ways reflective of domestic forces: widespread hatred for Somoza and sympathy for the insurgent Sandinistas, and widespread support for maintaining the welfare state in the face of the debt crisis. Yet in this case the domestic explanation does not suffice because Carazo's successor, Monge, confronted the twin crises in even more acute form and responded, as noted earlier, in a much more "normal" manner: by accommodating the top priorities of the United States to the degree necessary to elicit the economic aid he needed.

That Carazo did not respond in this way may be attributed to idiosyncratic factors. Carazo was, as it were, quixotically tilting at two windmills with interacting blades: He could not pay the country's bills, and he would not make the cuts in social programs demanded by the IMF as conditions for a bailout. With the influence of the United States over the IMF, he might have gotten easier terms, but his pro-Sandinista stance meant that the Reagan administration, rather than helping him, would pressure him. His domestic political standing steadily declined with the national economy, and the initial popularity of the Sandinistas had evaporated by 1980 and 1981, in response to political discord in Nicaragua and the flow of refugees into Costa Rica. In short, Carazo's well-intended attempt to confront the twin crises was nothing short of disastrous.

In contrast, Monge's policy was quintessentially Tico: knowing how much one must bend in order to avoid being broken. Like Calderón Guardia's policy in World War II, it was a "normal" Costa Rican foreign policy in abnormal times. Monge left office still quite popular, as if people understood just how difficult his position had been.

The other period of anomalous foreign policy was that of Oscar Arias (1986–1990). While Carazo had defied the systemic forces confronting him and been beaten for it, and while Monge to a great extent bowed to those forces in order to save what he could, Arias found himself in a more favorable position to take the initiative. It is to his ever-lasting credit that he was able to lead the way to a comprehensive peace settlement for Central America (Hey and Kuzma 1993; Rojas Aravena 1990b; Rojas Aravena and Solís 1988; Child 1992; Moreno 1996; Sojo 1991; Rojas Bolaños 1992).

Arias was in a more favorable position because of several changes on both domestic and systemic levels. Domestically, the economy was still in recession, but it had turned the corner as a result of Monge's policies and the substantial aid he had received. The country was thus less vulnerable to U.S. pressure than it had been four years earlier. Also, while Costa Rican public opinion remained critical of the Sandinistas, few loved the Contras, and most wanted to see Costa Rica escape involvement in the U.S. attempt to subvert the neighboring regime. Thus, Arias could count on solid domestic support for his peace initiative (Hurwitz, Peffley, and Seligson 1993).

Internationally, the success of the United States in scuttling the Contadora initiative in 1985 proved a Pyrrhic victory: Both Latin American and European governments were, with few exceptions, opposed to the U.S. policy and receptive to Arias's initiative. The Reagan policy had never been strongly supported within the United States, and congressional Democrats had succeeded as early as 1984 in cutting off funds for the Contras. That in turn had led to the illegal attempts to fund the Contras, led by Colonel Oliver North, which blew up into the Iran-Contra scandal and crippled the administration's Central American policy, precisely as Arias was mobilizing (Honey 1994; Child 1992: 40; Moreno 1994: 87–88).

Calculating that Costa Rica's security was gravely endangered by a continuation of this multifarious crisis bleeding across national boundaries, Arias believed that a solution would have to come through a comprehensive negotiation among all the Central American governments. Beginning as soon as he took office, by August 1987, Arias had gotten the other Central American presidents to agree to a plan that required each country to pursue parallel plans that focused on negotiation with insurgent forces pursuant to national reconciliation, cease-fires and the disarmament of insurgents, absorption of insurgents into political life, and free elections. Each government committed itself to stop giving aid to rebel movements in its neighbors and not to use its territory for aggression against other states (Rojas Aravena 1990b: 61–62). The plan thus imposed symmetrical obligations on Nicaragua and on the states allied with the United States. Its implementation would make it impossible for the United States to continue to use Central American countries to attack the Sandinista regime.

As noted earlier, Arias still had substantial diplomatic work to do to overcome mistrust among Central Americans and muted hostility from the Reagan administration. The Bush administration (1989–1993), its attention increasingly focused on the turmoil in Eastern Europe and the deepening crisis in the Soviet Union, was less obsessed with Central America than its predecessor but loath to withdraw until the Sandinistas had been removed. The Sandinistas ran a second honest election (after that of 1984), and they lost this time, much to the surprise of the Bush people. The defeat of the Sandinistas in 1990 is unlikely to have occurred without the Arias Peace Plan, which brought a cease-fire, a political opening in Nicaragua, and a coalescence of opposition forces with strong U.S. backing for the campaign.

The Arias policy requires all three levels of analysis for explanation. Arias was responding to and trying to manage a systemic crisis of major proportions, one in which the United States was deeply involved in a manner he thought ill considered. He had significant domestic support for his peace initiative. Finally, what distinguished this episode was the idiosyncratic factor of his understanding of the complex interplay of forces in the Central American arena and how, even from a position of weakness, it was possible, under those unique circumstances, to move toward a comprehensive settlement even against the will of the U.S. government. The point is not that Arias could have done what he did under any circumstances but that he understood what could be done in the circumstances that faced him and had the capacity to make it happen.

CONCLUSION

"Normal" Costa Rican foreign policy, as we have seen, is cooperative toward the United States, isolationist toward Central America, and moderately favorable toward international cooperation. This chapter has focused on instances where this normal posture has not prevailed. These are especially instructive in illustrating how idiosyncratic factors of personality and historical circumstance may impinge on and alter the normal interplay of domestic and systemic forces. This chapter has reviewed two such anomalous periods: (1) the crisis of the 1940s and (2) the crises of the 1980s.

The complex crisis of the 1940s involved domestic forces temporarily trumping the normal Costa Rican tendency to follow the lead of the United States. Calderón's alliance with the communist VP was a master stroke during the war, helping to secure Picado's election. But as the Cold War dawned, Picado and Calderón could not do the expedient thing and jettison the communists without giving up power entirely. Conversely, Figueres astutely used U.S. anticommunism to gain U.S. support for his reformist regime. In this case, the lack of congruence between domestic and systemic forces undermined Calderón's position and opened the way for the highly idiosyncratic and brilliantly innovative intervention of Figueres.

The crises of the 1980s provide illustrations of both disastrous idiosyncrasy and astute management of a unique historical conjuncture. Carazo's idiosyncrasies locked him into a set of policies that seemed to make sense at first but would ultimately lead to disaster. His commitment to social justice and suspicion of Somoza led to his enthusiasm for the Sandinista rebellion, an enthusiasm largely reflected, at first, in Costa Rican public opinion. But as the United States became more hostile and the revolution radicalized, Carazo was slow to change. Similarly, Carazo's commitment to the Costa Rican welfare state led him to resist adjustments in economic and fiscal policy that might have mitigated the economic crisis of the 1980s. A more typically "Tico" president—such as Monge—would have been more flexible in adjusting to systemic realities.

Oscar Arias was able to take advantage of the peculiar conjuncture of circumstances in 1986–1987 to bring about a comprehensive Central American peace settlement over the objections of the Reagan administration and to keep the peace process on track until the Sandinistas lost the 1990 election and the Bush administration lost interest in obstructing peace in Central America. Arias could not have accomplished what he did in a different set of circumstances. For example, had he been elected in 1982, the United States would have been able to frustrate his plan just as it did the Contadora plan. Had the Iran-Contra scandal not erupted when it did, the Reagan administration would have been able to stop Arias in 1986. But we must also allow for the genuine originality, genius, and audacity of Arias, a most fortunate idiosyncrasy in Central American affairs.

The diplomacy of the Arias Peace Plan is an excellent illustration of how, in the right circumstances, even a small and weak power operating in opposition to a hegemonic power can have a transformative impact on an international crisis.

DISCUSSION QUESTIONS

1. Given that the United States has intervened forcefully in Central America on numerous occasions, why did it not do so in Costa Rica in 1948?
2. Explain how, when both President Carazo and President Monge faced with the twin crises of revolution in neighboring Nicaragua and economic crisis at home, Monge's administration was generally more successful at managing the crises than was Carazo's.
3. What conditions permitted Oscar Arias, confronting the twin crises, to succeed in getting his peace plan adopted and implemented?

NOTES

1. The Central American Parliament (PARLACEN) was negotiated in the later 1980s as part of a renewed drive for regional integration, but Costa Rica, after exten-

sive debate, chose not to become a member. See *Ecocentral*, July 17, 1997 (http://ladb.unm.edu).

2. Presidents after 1948: Otilio Ulate (Unión Nacional, 1949–1953), José Figueres Ferrer (PLN, 1953–1958), Mario Echandi (UN, 1958–1962), Francisco Orlich (PLN, 1962–1966), José Joaquín Trejos (UN, 1966–1970), José Figueres Ferrer (PLN, 1970–1974), Daniel Oduber (PLN, 1974–1978), Rodrigo Carazo (Unidad, 1978–1982), Luis Alberto Monge (PLN, 1982–1986), Oscar Arias (PLN, 1986–1990), Rafael Angel Calderón Fournier (PUSC, 1990–1994), José María Figueres Olsen (PLN, 1994–1998), and Miguel Angel Rodríguez (PUSC, 1998–2002).

3. Morgan (1990) shows how the Costa Rican government commitment to community participation in health care in the Carazo and Monge administrations was to a great extent a function of international pressure and shifting international priorities.

4. From the point of view of Costa Rican policymakers, the policy preferences of the United States are effectively part of the international system within which they function. Costa Rican leaders may be able to affect the policy of the United States toward Costa Rica itself but will not normally be able to effect any change in the grand structure of U.S. foreign policy. Thus U.S. policy is, *for Costa Rica,* part of the systemic level of analysis.

5. Costa Rica might have suffered covert U.S. subversion such as that later perpetrated on Guatemala in 1954, but the United States confronted many cross-pressures in dealing with Costa Rica in 1948. Calderón had been a strong ally during the war, but his alliance with the Vanguardia Popular (VP) was now suspicious. Calderón was also a close friend of dictator Anastasio Somoza in neighboring Nicaragua. This should have been a good thing from the U.S. point of view, since Somoza had been virtually installed by the United States in the 1930s and had been an unswerving ally. But the United States and Somoza were at that moment having some difficulty over whether Somoza should perpetuate himself in power. The U.S. preference was that he not do so, but his compliance was not yet assured. On the other side, Figueres was strongly anticommunist and an avowed democrat, but he was a close ally of the Guatemalan revolutionaries who had overthrown Ubico, and whose ranks included communists. Inasmuch as the United States was already quite nervous about the Guatemalan situation, it was reluctant to see Figueres come to power in Costa Rica. Finally, however, it was the U.S. ambassador, along with the papal Nuncio, who presided over the negotiations that saved San José from a direct assault by Figueres' troops. Picado, Calderón and the VP leadership fled into exile, and Figueres came to power at the head of a Junta of National Liberation.

3

Nicaragua

Foreign Policy in the Revolutionary and Postrevolutionary Era

JoAnn Fagot Aviel

After presenting a brief history of Nicaraguan foreign relations, this chapter will focus on the foreign policy of three different administrations: those of the Sandinistas from 1979 to 1990, Violetta Chamorro from 1990 to 1996, and Miguel Alemán from 1996 to 2002. Using James Rosenau's three levels of foreign policy analysis, similarities and differences in the idiosyncratic, domestic, and systemic characteristics of each administration will be examined in an effort to understand the extent of change and continuity in Nicaraguan foreign policy.

HISTORY

Throughout its history, the primary goal of Nicaraguan foreign policy has been to obtain the resources the governing elite needed to remain in power. Nicaraguan political elites have used external groups or states to obtain power or sustain themselves in power and in turn have been used by external forces for their own ends. Due to its geographic location, relations with its Central American neighbors and the United States have been the two most important foci of its foreign policy. Nicaragua shared a common history with its Central American neighbors from the time of the Spanish conquest until 1838. After gaining independence from Spain, they were first part of Mexico and then formed the United Provinces of Central America, which disbanded in 1838. Since then Nicaraguan history has been marked by internal conflict and foreign intervention. Its geographic location as a possible route for a canal helped to motivate foreign interest and intervention. The U.S. soldier of fortune, William Walker, who had been invited by the Liberals to help them defeat the Conservatives, later declared himself president but soon after was defeated with the help of forces from other Central American countries. Later when the Liberal dictator Jose Santo Zelaya began negotiations for a canal with European and Japanese interests, the United States encouraged a Conservative rebellion and then directly intervened in 1912. Augusto Cesar Sandino led a rebellion that helped to force the withdrawal of U.S. Marines in 1932. However, the United States backed the new regime of Anastasio Somoza García, the first Nicaraguan commander of the National Guard, who assassinated Sandino in 1934.

Anastasio (Tacho) Somoza García was succeeded by his sons. The administrations of both father and sons owed their power to their control of the National Guard and their ability to cultivate close relations with the United States. Nicaragua's votes in the United Nations consistently followed those of the United States. The Somozas frequently portrayed the country as being the target of international communism and offered it as a base for U.S. covert operations against Guatemala in 1954 and Cuba in 1961 (Gambone 1997: 219–20). Nicaragua was also used as a base for operations against Costa Rica. Tacho Somoza supported his friend and business partner, Costa Rican president Teodoro Picado, when he annulled elections and attempted to prevent the victory of Pepe Figueres in Costa Rica in 1948 and later sent forces into Costa Rica in efforts to overthrow him (Crawley 1979: 109–13).

Elections were manipulated to ensure either their own victory or that of their chosen successors. Anastasio Somoza Debayle, the third and last Somoza to hold the presidency, was first elected in 1967 with 70 percent of the vote (Crawley 1979: 135). It was often said that "Somoza runs this place as if it were his own *finca*." Foreign relations were conducted primarily by Somoza himself, whether between other heads of state in Central America or on personal trips to Washington, D.C. With a phone in each hand, he cajoled the presidents of El Salvador and Honduras into stopping the "football war" of 1969. After being told that Panamanian general Torrijos had stated that if Somoza kept up this "direct diplomacy" business much longer, his foreign ministers would become obsolete, he was asked whether he agreed. Somoza responded, "Yes. But after the Heads of State reach an agreement, someone has to do the carpentry. That is what you need the Foreign Ministers for" (Crawley 1979: 2–4). Under Somoza, only seventy people worked in the ministry, and many never even came to work (author interview with Miguel d'Escoto, Managua, July 1992). A U.S. official remarked that "Somoza was a cunning fellow. Not only was he friends with (Nixon's crony) Bebe Robozo . . . he cultivated lots of people in the U.S. government and in the Congress over the years. And because of that, he was a difficult man to go up against and change policy on. Somoza knew people in government, banking, investments, and different political parties" (Morley 1994: 66). As a graduate of the U.S. Military Academy at West Point, he had special ties to the U.S. military.

The idiosyncratic level was thus most important in explaining Somozan foreign policy, but its importance was made possible by domestic and systemic characteristics in which there was no counterbalance to the power of the Somozas and the United States. When challenges to their influence occurred, the Somozas and the United States mutually reinforced the cooperation between themselves. However, after Somoza pocketed much of the aid sent for the victims of the 1971 earthquake in which twenty thousand had died and had opposition newspaper editor Pedro Joaquin Chamorro assassinated in 1978, popular discontent exploded, and the U.S. Carter administration withdrew support. The Sandinista Front for National Liberation (FSLN) won broad national and international support. Somoza went heavily into debt to obtain arms abroad in an unsuccessful effort to quell the ensuing uprising. The United States failed in its efforts to negotiate an interim government and to send an Organization of American States (OAS) peacekeeping force (Cockcroft 1996: 211). After years of armed struggle, the Sandinista front succeeded in overthrowing Somoza and sending him into exile in July 1979. However, the conflict had resulted in the deaths of about 2 percent of the population (Walker and Armony 2000: xxii–xxiii; Walker 1997: 7).

SANDINISTA ADMINISTRATION (1979–1990)

From 1979 to 1985, the Sandinista regime governed through first a five-member executive junta and then a three-member junta that had emergency powers and consulted closely with the directorate of the FSLN. Elections were held in 1984, which Daniel Ortega, one of the members of the junta, won. His foreign policy view was influenced by his experience as a military leader who had been victorious over Somoza and the Sandinista socialist ideology. The foreign minister was a Catholic priest, Father Miguel d'Escoto, but one of the administration's major critics was Cardinal Miguel Obando y Bravo. Divisions among supporters of the revolution on what the nature of the new regime should be and opposition to the regime by supporters of the previous Somoza administration caused difficulties in decision making. The Carter administration's more accommodationist policy shifted to that of the Reagan administration's confrontationist Cold War policy and at the end to the first Bush administration's policy of transition to a post–Cold War system.

Whereas the Somoza regime had relied on its close relationship with the United States, the Sandinista regime sought to break Nicaragua's dependency on the United States and to extend its relations worldwide. On a trip to Washington soon after the victory over Somoza, Foreign Minister d'Escoto talked with members of the U.S. Congress who he said told him that if his nation didn't vote with them in the United Nations, it would not get $75 million in aid. He angrily responded that they could keep their aid (d'Escoto 1992). Although some aid continued under the Carter administration, when President Reagan took office in January 1981, the U.S. government attempted to ensure the overthrow of the Sandinista government. It suspended all U.S. aid on January 23, successfully worked to cut off aid from the World Bank and Inter-American Bank, and in 1985 imposed an economic embargo. It authorized support for a counterrevolutionary exile army (Contras) based in Honduras. After the Iran-Contra scandal, the U.S. Congress in 1987 cut off all military support to the Contras, resulting in a military stalemate and improving the possibilities of a negotiated peace (Merrill 1994: 42–43, 47).

The Sandinista government made much use of the United Nations to mobilize support (Aviel 1988). Becoming a member of the Non-Aligned Movement was one of the first foreign policy decisions made by the new revolutionary government, and its voting record in the United Nations was similar to that of other members. In October 1982, Nicaragua won a seat on the UN Security Council as a nonpermanent member (Vanderlaan 1986: 323). In the first year after Somoza's fall, Nicaragua more than doubled the number of countries with which it had diplomatic relations. New relations were established with practically all the socialist countries in Eastern Europe and with many African countries (Bendana 1982: 322). Whereas the Somoza regime had relations with only forty-one states, the Sandinistas had diplomatic ties with 117 by 1989 (Vanden 1991: 305). After the revolution, the number of people in the Foreign Ministry rose from seventy to over seven hundred, and a new Ministry of Foreign Cooperation was established to coordinate foreign aid. In an effort to avoid international economic isolation, the new government immediately announced its willingness to service the huge foreign debt incurred under the Somozas (Walker and Armony 2000: 73). It also incurred huge debts of its own. From 1979 to 1989, foreign debt grew by an average of 17.2 percent annually. By the end of 1989, Nicaragua depended on foreign aid to finance 81.5 percent of its needs. Although in 1981 65.1 percent of this aid had come from market economies, by 1985 90.3 percent of total resources came from countries with planned economies (Instituto de Investigación, Capacitación, y Asesoría Económica [INICAE] 1991: 61–63).

The Sandinistas' greatest foreign supporter was Cuba. In 1979, Cuba had been one of the first countries to initiate a line of credit and later gave $950 million in donations. Cuban advisers could be found throughout the government, including the intelligence and military services. Cuban teachers aided in the literacy campaign and Cuban doctors served throughout Nicaragua (INICAE 1991: 137). Nicaragua participated in the Council of Mutual Economic Assistance (COMECON) as an observer until its demise. However, due to economic and political problems in the socialist countries and political accords between the United States and the Soviet Union, aid from Eastern Europe decreased (author interview with Erwin Kruger, Managua, July 1992). By mid-1988, the Soviets had begun to press the Sandinistas to seek greater economic and financial support elsewhere (Vanden 1991: 313). Although Western Europe had provided 33 percent of all loans to Nicaragua from 1979 to 1982, aid had decreased due to diplomatic pressure by the Reagan administration and European dissatisfaction with Nicaraguan actions. Spanish financial, technical, and economic cooperation in its relations with Nicaragua during 1979–1989 were the most ample and stable of any European Community members (INICAE 1991: 103). Although even after the U.S. embargo in 1985 the European Community continued to give aid, by the beginning of 1988 West Germany had ended all aid, and France and the Netherlands had cut back. Only Sweden had promised to increase its support. With the decrease in aid from the Soviet bloc, President Ortega initiated a major diplomatic effort to obtain more aid from Western Europe, which was forthcoming only after significant concessions were made to hold supervised elections and permit more political freedom (Vanden 1991: 307–9). From 1979 to 1989 Latin American countries provided 11.1 percent of external resources. However, there was a cooling of initially good relations with most Latin American nations and a decline in trade that the Sandinista administration later worked to restore (INICAE 1991: 106). Its relations with Colombia were marred by Nicaragua's 1980 declaration that the 1928 treaty in which Nicaragua acknowledged that the San Andrés and Providencia islands belonged to Colombia was invalid because of U.S. pressure for it to sign (*Honduras News This Week*, October 5, 2000).

Nicaragua sought not only economic resources especially needed after the imposition of the U.S. economic embargo and civil war but also political solidarity. The government hosted international conferences and sent delegates to conferences worldwide. Links not only with governments but also with nongovernmental organizations (NGOs) became especially important. Foreign NGOs contributed money and advisers and pressured their own governments in an effort to counteract the U.S. embargo. In 1984 and 1985, the government took its case against U.S. support for the Contras and the Central Intelligence Agency's mining of its harbors to the World Court. Although the United States attempted to prevent the court from hearing the case, the court found the United States guilty in 1986 of eleven violations of international law and ordered the payment of reparations (Vanderlaan 1986: 352–53). Although the government supported rebels in El Salvador while fighting Contra rebels at home, it backed the failed peace efforts of the Contadora nations (Mexico, Panama, Colombia, and Venezuela). It participated in the Central American negotiations that resulted in the signing of the Esquipulas peace accord in 1987. The war had killed 30,865 Nicaraguans. Nicaragua became the first independent country to request that the United Nations supervise its electoral process in 1990 (Merrill 1994: 47–49; Walker 1997: 12).

During the 1990 election campaign, the worldviews of the two candidates appeared quite different, as did their sources of external support and likely foreign policy. The very religious, pro-U.S. views of the National Opposition Union (UNO)'s candidate, Violetta Chamorro, contrasted sharply with the socialist, prorevolutionary stance of the FSLN's candidate, President Daniel Ortega. A vote for Chamorro was seen to be a vote to end the war and U.S. embargo and obtain U.S. aid to rebuild the economy. A vote for Ortega seemed to mean a continuation of the war and U.S. embargo with even less external support due to the breakup of the Soviet bloc. U.S. aid to the Contras and later to the electoral process helped to bring about the Sandinista defeat.

The idiosyncratic level appears least important in explaining Sandinista foreign policy. Not only was there initially a plural executive, but the Sandinistas consciously eschewed a cult of personality. Most important were the domestic and international systems and the interaction between them. The Sandinista-led revolution owed much of its success to its ability to unite diverse groups in opposition to the U.S.-supported Somoza and his allies and to its ability to gain wide international backing by sending spokespersons around the world (Walker and Armony 2000: 72). The Sandinista attempt to maintain this diverse domestic and international support was initially aided by coming to power during the Carter administration, which had a moderate Cold War policy. The coming to power of the Reagan administration with its more extreme anti-Soviet and anti-Sandinista policy affected both domestic and foreign policy as the Sandinista administration had to focus on defeating the U.S.-armed Contra rebels. Although the Cold War helped it to obtain Soviet and Cuban assistance, the decline of the Soviet Union and end of the Cold War meant a decline in assistance and the need to accept a negotiated peace settlement and supervised elections.

CHAMORRO ADMINISTRATION (1990–1996)

At the idiosyncratic level, the principal decision maker had changed from an ardent revolutionary to the widow of a slain newspaper editor and mother of children who included both Sandinista and Contra supporters. At the domestic level, the revolutionary Sandinistas had been defeated electorally but still remained the largest single party, and the coalition that had united behind Chamorro's candidacy was very much divided. At the systemic level, the transition to the post–Cold War era and a capitalist global economy was well underway. The Republican Bush administration was followed by the Democratic Clinton administration that, however, had to govern with a Republican-dominated Congress after its first two years.

Perhaps the greatest change was Nicaragua's loss of presence in foreign affairs due to internal changes as well as the end of the bipolar era. Its huge debt and international lenders forced the administration to reduce the size of government and cut the size of the Foreign Ministry by over 100 employees (author interview with Edmundo Castillo, Managua, July 1992) and the Ministry of Foreign Cooperation by 120 (author interview with Kruger, July 1992). The Foreign Ministry attempted to comply with a law professionalizing the civil service so that the majority of the personnel remained from the previous regime (author interview with Castillo, July 1992).

The primary goal of Nicaragua's foreign policy continued to be obtaining foreign support. From 1990 to 1995, aid represented $1,000 per capita, of which one-third was for debt repayments (Oxfam International 1998). However, the source of much of the aid changed. In response to a question on what was the greatest change in Nicaraguan foreign policy since the Sandinista defeat, Chamorro's vice minister of the presidency stated, "The greatest change is that the United States is now a friend" (author interview with Alejandro Bolanos, Managua, July 1992). After President Chamorro took power, the United States ended its trade embargo and increased its aid from almost nonexistent to 27.2 percent of external resources in 1992. The Agency for International Development (AID) program in Nicaragua became its largest per capita and the fourth largest in the world in 1992 (author interview with Janet Ballantyne, Managua, July 1992). Under the Bush administration's threat of suspending bilateral aid and blocking multilateral credits, the government withdrew Nicaragua's suit with the World Court to obtain the $12 billion in indemnization owed it by the court's 1986 ruling (Walker 1997: 38).

Political leaders in Nicaragua perceived having ties with those in positions of power in the United States as necessary to obtain support for desired policies or for them to remain in power or to attain power. As the UNO coalition broke up, Chamorro's minister of the presidency denounced Alfredo Cesar, then president of the National Assembly, for being an "employee of Washington" (*Envio* 1992: 14). Cesar's close ties to Senator Jesse Helms helped to bring about a freeze in U.S. aid in June 1992 as a means to pressure the Chamorro government to hasten the return of land to former owners and to remove Humberto Ortega, the Sandinista commander-in chief of the army, and other top officials in the police and military. This occurred despite Ortega's own attempts to ensure good relations with the United States by awarding the highest military honor to the U.S. military attaché and by accepting a U.S. military team to advise on arms security measures (Latinamerica Press 1995: 3). Sandinista leaders attempted to obtain U.S. support. After a trip to Washington in 1992, Sandinista leader Henry Ruiz stated, "[T]he macro times are changing in the international scene, and therefore, we can't clutch onto traditional dogmatic and rigid criteria. It is within this search for new elements that we are trying to build a new relationship with the U.S. administration" (*Barricada Internacional*, February 24, 1992: 24).

Fearing that the aid suspension could become permanent, in September 1992, President Chamorro announced that thousands of people whose property had been confiscated in the 1980s were entitled either to get their properties back or to receive compensation (*San Francisco Chronicle*, September 10, 1992). She later reached agreement with the Sandinistas enabling the National Assembly to pass a law in 1995 that granted current occupants provisional title (Walker and Armony 2000: 80).

Relations also changed with the Soviet Union and Cuba. Following the announcement of Chamorro's electoral victory, the Soviet government sent an official message congratulating her and turned down a Sandinista proposal to install a parallel diplomatic office in Moscow (Federal Broadcasting Information Service [FBIS], June 8, 1990: 17). Although some aid continued to be sent in 1990 and $6.6 million in loans were made in 1991, no aid was sent in 1992 (Ministerio de Cooperación Externa 1992: 14, 20). After a meeting between U.S. and Soviet officials in Madrid over alleged shipments by the Sandinista army to leftist groups, the Soviets announced that they would send no more arms or spare parts to Central America and "asked other countries, including the United States, to abstain from shipping arms" (FBIS, April 8, 1991). After a Russian parliamentary visit in 1996, Russia forgave 90 percent of the $3.5 billion Nicaragua owed (Agence France Presse, November 27, 1998). Although change in Soviet relations had begun under the previous administration, changes in relations with Cuba were major. After the 1990 elections, Castro removed military advisers, construction workers and doctors and suspended the yearly supply of petroleum and rations of food for people on the Caribbean coast (FBIS, April 5, 1990: 1–2, 37). When asked about Cuban aid, the secretary-general of the Foreign Ministry said that Nicaragua would receive aid from anywhere so long as it was not conditioned or politicized but that they did not want to have Cuban advisers in the different state institutions, as had existed under the previous government. Nicaragua also wanted to reassure the United States that it would not help to break the embargo imposed on Cuba (author interview with Castillo, July 1992).

To limit its dependency on the United States, the government has sought aid from other sources and indeed was encouraged to do so by the United States. The Republic of China (Taiwan) and Japan began their aid programs only after the victory of President Chamorro. While both administrations would have preferred to maintain relations with both Chinas, when forced to choose they chose differently. Whereas the Sandinistas opened diplomatic relations with the People's Republic of China (PRC) in 1985, the Chamorro government established relations with Taiwan in 1990, thus resulting in the PRC suspending diplomatic relations. Its decision was influenced by the hope of obtaining development aid and investment (FBIS, November 8, 1990) and resulted in a $60 million loan in 1991 and $30 million, or 5.7 percent of bilateral external resources, in 1992 (Ministerio de Cooperación Externa 1992: 14, 20). In March 1992, President Chamorro visited Taiwan, where she signed a series of cooperation agreements (Reuters, February 29, 1992). Although the United States initially opposed it, Taiwan gave nonmilitary aid to the army. When the United States froze U.S. aid to Nicaragua, the Taiwanese chancellor sent a letter to Senator Helms stating that he had confidence in Chamorro and that the U.S. aid should be resumed (author interview with Kruger, July 1992).

Although the Sandinista government had diplomatic relations with Japan, there was little exchange and no aid until 1988 when some natural disaster relief was given. The first secretary of the Japanese Embassy in Nicaragua in 1992 stated that with the change in regimes, it was natural that more cooperation began because of the restoration of democracy and that technical-economic assistance was coordinated with the United States (author interview with Naohito Watanabe, Managua, July 1992). President Chamorro traveled to Japan in February 1991 in an attempt to obtain more aid. Japan agreed to participate in the granting of two soft long-term credits of approximately $50 million each to pay bills owed to the World Bank and the Inter-American Development Bank and to strengthen the economic stabilization program. In 1991, Japan sent volunteers to Nicaragua and increased the number of scholarships. In 1992, it contributed $43.1 million, or 8.2 percent of all bilateral financing, and aid increased in succeeding years (FBIS, February 20, 1992: 115; Ministerio de Cooperación Externa 1992: 20; Ministerio de Relaciones Exteriores de Nicaragua 2001).

The Chamorro government continued the policy of courting European support, but with more success. European Community members contributed only 8.6 percent of bilateral external resources from 1979 to 1989, but 24.1 percent in 1992. Germany increased its aid from zero in 1988 to 10.4 percent of Nicaragua's bilateral external resources in 1992. From 1990 to 2000, its aid totaled more than $200 million. Relations with Scandinavian countries continued to be good. From 1979 to 1989, they had contributed $360.5 million, amounting to 5.2 percent of bilateral external resources. In 1992, this percentage had increased to 16.0 percent (INICAE 1991: 146; Ministerio de Cooperación Externa 1992: 20; Ministerio de Relaciones Exteriores de Nicaragua 2001). Spain continued its aid but also advised on ensuring a peaceful transition of power from Ortega to Chamorro (Aviel 1992:

295–312). Spain gave aid to professionalize the police, intelligence, and military services as well as interceded with President Bush in an attempt to unfreeze U.S. aid (*La Prensa*, June 23 and 29, 1992). Since the Central American Peace Accords, Europe has minimized bilateral relations with individual nations and focused on multilateral meetings and aid to Central America as a whole. Nicaraguan relations with Europe have thus increasingly been conducted in coordination with its Central American neighbors.

A unified Central America was a primary theme in President Chamorro's first address to the United Nations in September 1990, as it has been in subsequent expositions on Nicaraguan foreign policy (FBIS, September 28, 1990; author interview with Castillo, July 1992). The Chamorro government worked to help bring about a negotiated solution to the conflict in El Salvador by meeting with both government and FMLN leaders and promoted the demilitarization of Central America. However, Nicaragua was reluctant to join the Central American Parliament. In an attempt to exert pressure on Nicaragua and Costa Rica to join, the Central American Integration Bank granted aid only to coffee producers in Honduras, El Salvador, and Guatemala (*La Prensa*, June 26, 1992: 3). Since then, Nicaragua has elected deputies to the Parliament (Fundación Arias 1997: 190). Central American presidents supported the government when it was faced with internal unrest as well as when confronting the freeze in U.S. aid funds (FBIS, July 11, 1990, and May 14, 1991). Chamorro's foreign minister, Enrique Dreyfus, stated that "each of the Central American countries are now convinced that their future depends on the regionalization concept within the framework of a common market" (FBIS, July 11, 1990: 12–20). In 1991, Nicaragua supported reforming the treaty of Central American integration of 1960 and the charter of the Organization of Central American States of 1962, which resulted in the new Central American Integration System (SICA) (Fundación Arias 1997: 189). At the 1992 summit meeting in Managua, agreements were signed on establishing maximum limits for arms and military personnel and on regional cooperation, economic development, and the environment (*Notimex*, June 5,1992).

Relations with Mexico and South America improved under the Chamorro administration. In 1991, Colombia, Mexico, and Venezuela helped provide "bridge" loans and Venezuela provided concessionary loans to pay Nicaragua's debt to the World Bank and the Inter-American Development Bank (Ministerio de Cooperación Externa 1992: 11–12). Venezuela and Mexico each agreed to restructure Nicaragua's debt at very favorable rates (FBIS, July 3, 1990: 24; and April 25, 1991: 11). President Chamorro met with the presidents of Brazil and Argentina on a March 1992 tour to seek renegotiations of their debt and to encourage investment in Nicaragua. She also sought Brazilian support for a new international coffee export quota agreement (Reuters, March 20, 1992). Later the government signed a Free Market Trade Agreement with Mexico (*Barricada Internacional*, September 1992: 6).

The Middle East as an area with rich developing nations was of special interest to both the Sandinista and Chamorro administrations, but President Chamorro placed more emphasis on conservative Arab nations (Aviel 1990: 13–41). Good relations continued with Iran, which agreed to provide additional oil and to renegotiate Nicaragua's debt (FBIS, January 22, 1991, and June 10, 1991). The Chamorro administration supported UN Security Council resolutions against Iraq (FBIS, September 14, 1999: 15). Acting in accord with UN Security Council resolutions, it expelled a Libyan diplomat in April 1992 (InterPress Service, April 2, 1992, and May 5, 1992). In 1992, relations with Israel were restored (*Jerusalem Post*, October 6, 1992).

In September 1992, President Chamorro attended the summit conference of the Non-Aligned Movement in Indonesia and continued the previous government's policy of voting with the Non-Aligned Movement and thus the majority in the United Nations (United Nations 1991). In 1993, Nicaragua's votes coincided only 35.2 percent of the time with those of the United States on recorded votes. However, the following year the coincidence of votes increased to 47.8 percent. The United Nations continued to be an important part of Nicaragua's foreign policy. While cutting a large number of foreign embassies particularly in the developing world, the Foreign Ministry attempted to maintain contact with these nations through its United Nations mission (author interview with Castillo, July 1992). The United Nations' importance as a source of aid for Nicaragua increased. With the United States no longer voting against aid to Nicaragua in multilateral organizations and with the UN's desire to support the peace process, multilateral aid increased from 12.5 percent of external resources in 1989 to 29.6 percent in 1992 (Ministerio de Cooperación Externa 1992: 3, 20). The UN General Assembly endorsed Nicaragua's request for preferential treatment from the international community and international lending agencies. As the poorest country in Central America, Nicaragua received "special support" from the World Bank's regional office, which was set up in Nicaragua (*NICCA Bulletin* April–June 1992: 6). The number of both national and foreign nongovernmental organizations (NGOs) increased. The Ministry of Economic Cooperation provided foreign nongovernmental organizations with a list where the ministry wanted them to work (author interview with Kruger, July 1992).

While both the principal decision maker and many foreign policies changed from the administration of Daniel Ortega to that of Violetta Chamorro, idiosyncratic factors were not the most important influence on foreign policy. Due not only to her own experience and beliefs but also to the domestic power situation in which the Sandinistas were the largest single party and as her own coalition had splintered, Chamorro had to follow a policy of reconciliation. This policy earned her the enmity of hard-liners both in Nicaragua and the United States and resulted in the freezing of U.S. aid funds. Chamorro continued the Sandinista policy of searching for more diverse sources of aid, but with more success due both to the change in regimes as well as changes in the international system. While Ortega was more interested and involved in expanding Nicaragua's foreign relations than was Chamorro, the cutback in Nicaragua's foreign presence was largely due to its economic difficulties as well as to the new post–Cold War international system. Again the interaction between domestic and systemic levels is most important in explaining Chamorro's foreign policy.

ALEMÁN ADMINISTRATION (1997–2002)

Arnoldo Alemán defeated Daniel Ortega in the 1996 elections. A lawyer and farmer and member of the same Liberal Party as Somoza, he became mayor of Managua during the Chamorro administration. As a neopopulist mayor, he had used USAID funds to build popular support and had strong ties to U.S. Republican congressional leaders. Due not only to systemic changes but also to ideology, he took the most pro-U.S. stance of any administration since that of the Somozas, but he also had to negotiate with the Sandinistas. Agreement was reached on a pact to share power and provide immunity from prosecution for Ortega, who had been threatened with civil and criminal charges (González 2000). The post–Cold War era diminished international support and interest in Nicaragua. Aid increased only after Hurricane Mitch struck Nicaragua in October 1998, resulting in the deaths of over twenty-four hundred people and rendering homeless nearly a fifth of the population (Walker and Armony 2000: 81–85).

The Alemán government further reduced the size of the Foreign Ministry. In 1997, it announced the closure of many embassies of which some were later to remain open after public debate. The consulates in the United States were placed under the control of the Finance Ministry, which collected funds for visas and other services to maintain them (*La Prensa*, May 9, 1997). In 2000, Nicaragua had embassies in thirty countries. In August 2000, the National Assembly passed the first Foreign Service law in the history of Nicaragua with the objective of establishing a professional nonpolitical service (Ministerio de Relaciones Exteriores de Nicaragua 2001).

Although Alemán stressed in his presidential campaign that the resolution of the property issue reached in 1995 was unacceptable, his attempt to change it resulted in months of strikes and challenges, which forced him to reach an agreement with the Sandinistas on a new property law in 1997 (Close 1999: 168, 216–17). Nicaragua continued to be required to apply annually for a waiver to unfreeze the aid that had been granted in recognition of progress made in dealing with the property disputes. In spite of his pro-U.S. stance in 1997, the year Alemán took office Nicaragua received U.S.$450.2 million, which was 21.2 percent less than the annual average from 1990 to 1996. After the devastation caused by Hurricane Mitch, the United States increased its aid to U.S.$554.7 million in 1999. However, in 2000, only $467.1 million had been promised; by the end of November, only $357.7 million had been received (Ministerio de Relaciones Exteriores de Nicaragua 2001; *La Prensa* January 29, 2001). Alemán had discussed with President Clinton in 1999 increasing bilateral aid, encouraging support for Nicaragua's inclusion in the Highly Indebted Poor Countries (HIPC) initiative of the World Bank and IMF, and raising its quota for products exported to the United States (*La Nación*, February 28, 1999). The United States forgave 90 percent of the bilateral debt and in September 1999 announced that it would forgive the remaining 10 percent as part of the HIPC initiative (Alemán 2000: 33).

As had occurred during previous administrations, Nicaraguan parliamentary delegations traveled to Washington to lobby members of the U.S. Congress (*La Prensa*, June 28, 2000). In July 2000, the United States announced it would grant a waiver permitting Nicaragua to receive $65 million in bilateral aid and U.S. support in international financial organizations for it to receive $300 million (*La Prensa*, June 30, 2000). In March 2000, after Sandinista members abstained, the administration won assembly approval of controversial plans for the deployment of five hundred U.S. soldiers to help reconstruction efforts (BBC World Service, March 22, 2000). In June 2001, it signed a treaty of cooperation to combat illicit drugs (Ministerio de Relaciones Exteriores de Nicaragua 2001).

Under the Alemán administration, Nicaragua's coincidence of voting with the United States in the United Nations ranged from 42.4 percent to 44.9 percent (U.S. State Department 1999: 24, 36). Nicaragua supported U.S. initiatives for the United Nations to investigate alleged human rights abuses in Cuba (FBIS, March 2, 1991). President Alemán refused to attend the Ninth Inter-American Summit in Havana, Cuba, in November 1999 to protest Cuba's lack of implementing commitments for democratization and human rights made in earlier summits (Alemán 2000: 36). In February 1997, the new Alemán administration announced plans to open Nicaragua's first-ever embassy in Israel (*Jerusalem Post*, February 2, 1997). However, three years later Nicaragua had an embassy in only one country in the Middle East: Qatar (Ministerio de Relaciones Exteriores de Nicaragua 2001). Nicaragua's support for Israel and for the United States in the United Nations was demonstrated by its abstaining with two other nations on a resolution in 1998 calling for Palestinian self-determination in which only two nations voted against, the United States and Israel (Agence France Presse, December 2, 1998).

Relations with Taiwan and South Korea increased. Taiwan funded the construction of a new building for the Foreign Ministry and a presidential palace as well as other projects (Alemán 2000: 37; Walker and Armony 2000: 155). During a visit by the president of Taiwan in August 2000, a joint communiqué called for efforts to increase Taiwanese investment and appreciation for technical assistance given in agriculture. President Alemán stated that he would continue to support Taiwan's membership in the United Nations and other international organizations (Ministerio de Relaciones Exteriores de Nicaragua 2001). Nicaragua joined with twenty-eight other nations in petitioning the UN secretary-general to support Taiwan's entry into the United Nations (Kyodo News Service, August 4, 2000). After a meeting of the Nicaraguan and South Korean presidents in May 2000, their foreign ministers signed treaties on investment guarantees and economic partnership (BBC World Service, May 15, 2000).

The destructive effects of Hurricane Mitch in 1998 helped to bring Central American leaders together in efforts to obtain aid for reconstruction. At the October 1999 Twentieth Summit, the presidents of Central America, the Dominican Republic, and Belize agreed to the Declaration of Antigua defining a regional strategy to reduce the region's social and ecological vulnerability (Alemán 2000: 33). President Alemán joined with the presidents of El Salvador and Guatemala in agreeing to push ahead with plans to integrate their infrastructure and coordinate security, foreign, and economic policies. They invited Belize, Costa Rica, Honduras, and Panama to join the process (BBC World Service, May 2, 2000). In September 2000, Guatemala, El Salvador, Honduras, and Nicaragua agreed to measures to strengthen the customs union between them and to create a mechanism for resolving commercial disputes (*La Prensa*, September 30, 2000).

In what some saw as an effort to defuse attention from corruption scandals, the Alemán administration engaged in several territorial disputes with its neighbors. In 1998, it prohibited Costa Rican police boats from navigating on the San Juan River and later refused Costa Rica's request for mediation of the dispute. However, in June 2000 at a meeting with Mexican and Central American leaders, Nicaragua stated that Costa Rican patrols could resume (BBC World Service, June 30, 2000). After Honduras recognized Colombian sovereignty over an area in the Caribbean claimed by Nicaragua, Nicaragua mobilized its forces and broke off trade relations. Several incidents of Nicaraguan and Honduran patrol boats exchanging fire occurred. In March 2000, after talks with a mediator from the Organization of American States, both countries agreed to freeze the deployment of ground forces along their border and carry out joint naval patrols until the World Court could settle the dispute. Nicaragua also brought the dispute to the Central American Court of Justice (BBC World Service, December 9, 1999; January 4, 2000; February 25, 2000; and March 8, 2000). However, Nicaragua is the only Central American country not to approve a system for the settlement of disputes proposed by the secretary-general of the Central American Secretariat for Economic Integration (SIECA) (*La Prensa*, June 10, 2000).

Much of Nicaraguan diplomacy with nations outside the region continued to be carried out in conjunction with its neighbors. For example, in 1999, meetings between Central American nations and the European Union, China, Japan, and the United States were held that approved aid projects to the region and, in the case of the European Union, granted a special tariff regime (Alemán 2000: 35–36). In 2000, Nicaragua and the other Central American nations joined the Rio Group that now composes nineteen nations whose leaders meet annually to coordinate foreign policy (Agence France Presse, June 15, 2000).

Both national and foreign NGOs became increasingly important participants in policymaking. At the EURODAD annual conference in Vienna in November 1997, NGOs from Europe, the United States, and Central America agreed to take common action on Nicaragua to push for civil society participation in the new national economic reform program and for speeding up the process of debt relief under the HIPC Initiative (Eurodad 2000). Disaffection with government handling of aid and reconstruction resulted in a coordinated plan by NGOs in Central America to deal with the disaster and the channeling of much of foreign aid through NGOs. President Alemán attempted to deflect the flow of international assistance away from NGOs and toward local governments where Liberals were in power or to Liberal Party organizations where they were not (Walker and Armony 2000: 84). However, the Nicaraguan delegation to the Stockholm meeting in May 1999 of the Consultative Group for the Reconstruction and Transformation of Central America was composed of representatives from all branches of government, political parties, the private sector, workers, and NGOs (Alemán 2000: 30–31).

The idiosyncratic level of analysis helps to explain President Alemán's nationalistic policy regarding territorial disputes with Nicaragua's neighbors. However, the interaction of domestic and systemic levels was most important for other foreign policy issues. In spite of his previous close association with the United States and fervent opposition to the Sandinistas, he found that he had to reach an accommodation with them to prevent domestic strife and in doing so he also incurred U.S. opposition. The search for more foreign aid met failure until the destruction of Hurricane Mitch. In the new post–Cold War global era Nicaragua's presence in world affairs was even further diminished.

CONCLUSION

According to Rosenau's classification of countries, Nicaragua can be classified as small and underdeveloped with an open and penetrated polity. This study agrees with Rosenau's ranking of the systemic level as most important in such countries. However, his ranking of the idiosyncratic level ahead of societal factors was valid for Nicaragua during the Somoza period, but not after the Sandinista revolution (Rosenau 1990a: 175). Reasons for this difference need to be further examined, but a partial explanation lies in the success of the Sandinista revolution in changing some fundamental aspects of government and society and the continuing strength of the Sandinista forces. Since 1979, the idiosyncratic level has been the least important in explaining Nicaraguan foreign policy. Certainly the very different values and personal backgrounds of Presidents Ortega, Chamorro, and Alemán influenced their decisions, but the domestic and systemic levels of analysis and the interaction between them were more important. Although Rosenau (1990a) describes the fusion of domestic and international systems that characterizes a penetrated system as new (169), Nicaragua has had a penetrated system throughout its history.

As a small country in the sphere of influence of a great power, that penetration has been greatest by the United States, which in the past has physically occupied the country. The nature of relations with the United States is the main determinant of both domestic and foreign policy. The revolutionary Sandinista government, which attempted to lessen dependency on the United States, welcomed penetration by Cuban advisers and many international supporters while combating the penetration of counterrevolutionary forces supported by the United States. As chair of the U.S. Senate Foreign Relations Committee, Jesse Helms and other U.S. leaders and AID officials influenced both domestic and foreign policy during the Chamorro and Alemán administrations. Links with foreign leaders, organizations, and governments have been important to the survival of national leaders, organizations and regimes.

Changes in the international system helped to bring about changes in government as well as changes in Nicaraguan foreign policy. While the change in policy toward China was due to the change in decision makers, many changes were under way even before the 1990 elections and would have occurred no matter who was in government. Even the Socialist Sandinista administration found it necessary to begin to implement domestic structural reform policies in 1988 as required by the global economic system. However, the most important change, improvement in relations with the United States, was possible only because of the change in regimes due to the refusal of the United States to accept the Sandinistas in power. As the second poorest country in the Western Hemisphere (U.S. State Department 2000), Nicaragua has a need for aid that continues to dominate foreign policy, but until Hurricane Mitch, aid had been decreasing. Changes in domestic and foreign policy have so far not brought great increases in foreign or national investment, thus capital requirements continue to be a problem. Future administrations are likely to face similar domestic and systemic constraints on their foreign policymaking.

DISCUSSION QUESTIONS

1. Discuss the relationship between internal elites and external group states in Nicaraguan history. To what extent is the Nicaraguan situation similar or different from that of other Latin American countries?
2. Do you agree that the idiosyncratic level is least important in explaining foreign policy after the defeat of Somoza? Why or why not?
3. Do you agree that relations with the United States are the most important determinant for domestic and foreign policy in the past and currently? Do you expect the same for the future?

4

Panama
The Limits of Sovereignty

Peter M. Sanchez

THE SALIENCY OF POWER, WEALTH, AND GEOGRAPHY

Two geographic factors—size and location—have limited significantly Panama's foreign policy potential. Nation-states that influence the world community—such as the United States, the former Soviet Union, Germany, and Japan—typically are large and wealthy. Panama is practically bereft of any significant instruments of power necessary for affecting world affairs, primarily because its population, size, and economy are small. Second, as Panama is a natural equatorial passage between the Atlantic and Pacific Oceans, great powers have always attempted to control the isthmus. Location worked against Panama in the last two centuries since the isthmus' proximity to the United States meant that Washington fixed its sights on the small region.

Like all other states, Panama's foreign policy is also affected by factors that are less static than size and location. In the study of international relations, these variables are often grouped by level of analysis. Following this popular framework, this chapter looks at the importance of key individuals, the attributes of the Panamanian nation-state, and the characteristics of the international system to better understand Panama's foreign policy.

This chapter will analyze Panama's foreign policy in the latter half of the twentieth century, emphasizing key individuals, events, and sociopolitical changes that have affected such policy.[1] Perhaps the most important change in the international system during this period was the end of the Cold War.

The termination of this highly competitive, bipolar international context prompted most U.S. policymakers to stop seeing Panama simply as a chess piece in U.S. strategic policy. Despite this watershed systemic change, however, Panama's foreign policy continues to be highly conditioned by its small size and relative power disparity vis-à-vis the United States. Domestically, Panama's politics were marked by fundamental changes that included a transition from oligarchic and military rule to democratic politics and the development of a state with some relative autonomy. Also during this period, influential national leaders emerged in Panama, who helped to forge a truly national foreign policy and who left their personal imprint on Panama's foreign relations.

THE COLD WAR ERA: THE CLASH BETWEEN U.S. GEOPOLITICS AND PANAMANIAN NATIONALISM

Panama's foreign policy after World War II cannot be understood fully without an awareness of some important aspects of the nation's previous history. First and foremost, since the mid-1800s, the United States held a position of dominance on the isthmus. U.S. interest started in earnest with the construction of the transisthmian railroad during 1851–1855, and it increased dramatically with the creation of the U.S.-controlled Canal Zone in 1903 and the construction of the canal during 1904–1914. The Panamanian isthmus and the canal became U.S. "prized possessions," vital for U.S. military and economic expansion in the nineteenth and twentieth centuries (Major 1993). Panama's rapid and bloodless independence from Colombia in 1903, in fact, resulted from a Washington ploy to gain the rights to build a maritime passage across the isthmus after Colombia's congress refused to ratify a treaty with the U.S. government that would allow Washington to build a canal through the isthmus. The ploy entailed a conspiracy that included U.S. and French investors who stood to gain handsomely from the sale of the French concession, granted by Colombia, to build a canal there (Diaz Espino 2001). The leaders of the fledgling nation of Panama, indebted to Washington and fellow conspirators for their success, felt compelled to ratify an accord, the 1903 Hay–Bunau–Varilla Treaty. The treaty gave Washington complete control, in perpetuity, over a ten-mile-wide zone that cut the nation in two, the right to build the canal, and the right to intervene at will in the domestic affairs of the isthmus. From the time of independence, then, Panama's foreign policy was dominated by its relations with the United States yet imbued with a desire to acquire the sovereignty it never fully achieved in 1903. In the early 1900s, it was impossible for Panamanians to acquire true independence or to influence their nation's foreign policy since politics on the isthmus were controlled by a small, urban, and commercial oligarchy and by the United States, both focusing their energies on the safe and efficient operation of the canal.

By the 1930s, however, Panama had begun to experience an increasing sense of nationalism and a desire for self-determination. As a result of the 1903 treaty, Panama was essentially a U.S. neocolony, or "protectorate." The ruling oligarchy's wealth derived from a trickle of business opportunities from the canal's presence, such as housing and the sale of goods, and maintained its power partly with the help of the U.S. military and diplomatic presence on the isthmus.

However, in 1931, Acción Comunal, a political organization, representing nationalist, middle-class forces, led by Harmodio and Arnulfo Arias, took the presidential palace and paved the way for the election of Harmodio Arias as president in 1932. The election of a president who was not from the traditional oligarchy marked the initial rise of the middle and lower classes into national politics. This important change allowed Panama to push for changes to the hated 1903 treaty, culminating in the 1936 Hull–Alfaro Treaty that ended Panama's protectorate status and gave some economic benefits to the isthmus, including a greater share of the canal's proceeds.

These emerging middle-class and popular sectors shared two important perspectives. One was their adherence to nationalism that translated often into anti-U.S. sentiments, owing principally to Washington's overwhelming power and influence on the isthmus. Their other shared sentiment was a scorn for the ruling oligarchy. Many Panamanians saw the traditional oligarchy as economically selfish and as lackeys of the United States. The oligarchy and the United States responded to these popular and democratic pressures by cooperating in the establishment of a more powerful constabulary force called the National Guard. This new Panamanian paramilitary force, supplied and trained by Washington, very quickly became one of the most important political institutions on the isthmus (Guevara Mann 1994).

In the 1930s, therefore, Panama experienced important domestic, state-level changes that ultimately changed the nation's foreign policy goals. The rise of nationalism, the clamor for greater participation in the political system, and the institutionalization of a small but increasingly powerful military all were domestic transformations that conspired to check the traditional oligarchy's power. These emerging forces would at times also challenge the dominant U.S. position on the isthmus. Decades would pass, however, before these new national sentiments would translate themselves into a more coherent, national foreign policy, since Panama's international relations were still the purview of a relatively small, inner circle of national elites and key U.S. officials.

The Cold War affected significantly how the United States perceived its role in world affairs and how it sought to protect its strategic interests.

Because U.S. decision makers became preoccupied with this East–West conflict, employing a policy of "containment," Washington increasingly viewed Panama predominantly as a chess piece in a bipolar international conflict. Within this competitive international system, a small country like Panama could hardly be expected to formulate an effective and independent foreign policy. Thus, during the Cold War period, the United States became less tolerant of Panamanian nationalism and desires for sovereignty, stressing political order and pro-U.S. policies.

An important case in point was the U.S. effort in 1946 to keep over one hundred military installations that it had acquired in Panama during World War II. The Panamanian president quickly rejected the U.S. request since Washington had agreed to turn these facilities over to Panama one year after the end of hostilities. Eventually Panama agreed to allow the U.S. military to retain just over ten defense facilities, but even this more limited concession led to popular disenchantment that forced the National Legislature to vote unanimously against the agreement. Despite the pressure to force the United States completely out of these facilities, culminating in anti-U.S. riots in 1947, Washington was able to engineer an accord that allowed it to keep a dozen facilities. The rejection in 1947 of the initial bases agreement, though, showed not only that nationalism and mass politics were becoming powerful forces but also that Panama's oligarchy had some limits when it came to allowing the United States carte blanche on the isthmus. Washington kept some bases, but with the unintended effect of raising isthmian national consciousness.

The Panamanian oligarchy, and even the middle class, had over the years simply wanted Washington to amend the U.S.–Panama relationship, so that the isthmus could enjoy greater economic benefits and achieve some symbolic respect. The 1936 treaty had made some positive changes to the 1903 treaty. But, in 1954, Panama again asked Washington to amend the hated 1903 treaty. Interestingly enough, Panama's president at the time, Jose Remón, was the former head of the country's armed forces that Washington had helped to forge. Although Remón was a staunch anticommunist, he carried out many needed social reforms, was nationalistic, and also wanted Washington to make some important changes to the U.S.–Panama partnership. The resulting 1955 Remón–Eisenhower Treaty gave Panama some economic concessions, but Washington still resisted any fundamental changes to the 1903 Treaty. For example, one of Panama's principal concerns about the economics of the Canal Zone that did not change as a result of the treaty was the unequal wage scale giving U.S. citizens larger salaries than Panamanians for the same work. Nevertheless, the new accord yielded Panama a larger annuity from canal proceeds. Typical of U.S.–Panama agreements, Washington believed it was forfeiting too much, while Panama thought that U.S. concessions were miserly.

In 1959, Panamanian nationalism expressed itself again in the form of anti-U.S. violence. The rising tide of nationalism was increasingly concerned with sovereignty issues. The fact that the isthmus was divided by a ten-mile zone controlled by a foreign country was injury enough. Panamanians felt additional insult by the pervasive presence of U.S. flags on their titular territory. Thus, on Panama's Day of Independence, scores of students, led by two prominent leaders, attempted to plant small Panamanian flags in the U.S.-controlled Canal Zone. The ensuing violence, between Panamanians and U.S. Zonians, prompted Washington to deploy U.S. troops. The conflict left sixty-four Panamanians and more than forty-five U.S. citizens wounded. Nine young Panamanians were injured by birdshot when U.S. troops fired at students who attempted to enter the Canal Zone, generating greater resentment toward U.S. neocolonialism on the isthmus. The U.S. Congress affirmed its stance that Panama's flag not be flown in the Canal Zone. President Eisenhower, however, resorting to executive privilege, ordered that both nations' flags be flown together in specified locations in the zone.

The 1960s were such tumultuous years in Latin America that Panama and Washington were sure to clash once more. The Cold War was at its peak, and the 1959 Cuban revolution brought the bipolar struggle directly into the Western Hemisphere. In 1964, conflict emerged once again over the issue of flags. Panamanian students who attempted to raise their nation's flag at Balboa High School in the Canal Zone encountered resistance by U.S. students. This seemingly minor incident mushroomed into mass demonstrations in Panama City and Colon directed against the Canal Zone and the U.S. government, eventually leaving twenty-one Panamanians dead. The zone police and U.S. military forces initially suppressed the demonstrations, but the crisis did not end until Major Omar Torrijos and Lieutenant Manuel Noriega flew in from the province of Chiriquí and enforced order (Janson Pérez 1997: 63). President Chiarí broke diplomatic ties with Washington, a first in U.S.–Panama relations. This crisis galvanized the nation. After 1964, elites and masses alike called for the abrogation, rather than the amendment, of the hated 1903 treaty. A foreign policy consensus, which would challenge U.S. interests on the isthmus, finally emerged in Panama.

U.S. policymakers became increasingly concerned about Panama. The 1959 Cuban revolution had brought a pro-Moscow, socialist state to the Western Hemisphere, and Washington was convinced that the 1964 riots in Panama were instigated and directed by communists. Panama's emergence as a second Cuba would be unacceptable to Washington. To avert this possibility, President Johnson quickly announced that the United States would begin negotiations designed to alter fundamentally the "special relationship." Panama reestablished relations and talks ensued, but the negotiations diminished neither Panama's surging nationalism nor Washington's proprietary sentiments about the canal and the zone. By 1967, an agreement had been reached, but neither the United States nor Panama was prepared to sign any new treaty, as both nations were embroiled in domestic politics that called for a hard line to triumph.

THE REGIME OF GENERAL OMAR TORRIJOS: DECLINING U.S. INFLUENCE?

In 1968, ardent nationalist Arnulfo Arias won the presidency in Panama; however, within eleven days the armed forces overthrew him. Washington quickly gave the new military junta its blessing and material support, despite the regime's flimsy base of support.

Panama's foreign policy during the initial period of the military regime was principally anticommunist and pro–United States. In fact, some analysts have argued that General Omar Torrijos' progressive domestic policies were designed principally to thwart any sort of social unrest, policies that could have come right out of John F. Kennedy's Alliance for Progress blueprint, fashioned to prevent socialist revolutions. But like Remón before him, Torrijos desired to be a beloved, nationalist leader, so he carried out land reform, strengthened the Panamanian state (and military), and brought into his government people from the middle classes as no other government had done before. Eventually Torrijos would demand that Washington reward him for his ability to prevent a repeat of the Cuban revolution in Panama, by asking for the abrogation of the 1903 treaty.

In 1970, when his foreign ministry announced that the proposed treaty of 1967 could not serve even as a foundation for a new U.S.–Panama relationship, General Torrijos began to appeal to the world community in a concerted effort to force the United States to abrogate the 1903 treaty. Torrijos scored a major victory when he was able to convince the United Nations Security Council to hold a special session in Panama in March 1973. The Security Council meeting represented an important propaganda victory for Panama, since Washington eventually vetoed a resolution that vaguely called for a renewed relationship between the United States and Panama, while all other countries supported the document and England abstained. Torrijos also highlighted Panama's cause within the Non-Aligned Movement and began to make friends with nations that he knew would rally behind Panama's grievances against Washington, including Cuba and Libya. Although U.S. officials suggested that the Maximum Leader had gone too far, in fact, only two months after the Security Council's special session, President Nixon informed the U.S. Congress that it was "time for both parties . . . to develop a new relationship" (quoted in Jorden 1984: 199). The Nixon administration deplored Torrijos's tactics and actions. However, the general's actions also worried Washington at a time when the United States seemed to be losing its hegemony in Latin America. Washington, in fact, had begun a dialogue with the Soviet Union and China, in an attempt to ameliorate Cold War tensions and improve global U.S. stature. A serious crisis in Panama, especially if it led to the inauguration of an anti-U.S. regime, was something that U.S. policymakers felt they could not afford.

Torrijos' multilateral strategy forced Washington to fashion a new relationship with Panama. The now-famous 1977 Panama Canal Treaties, which abrogated the 1903 treaty, included two accords: the Panama Canal Treaty, and the Treaty Concerning the Permanent Neutrality and Operation of the Panama Canal. The treaties gave Panama sovereignty over most of the Canal Zone in 1979, the United States retaining control only of the Canal Operating Area and existing U.S. military bases. Panama would finally take possession of the canal and all U.S. military facilities at noon on December 31, 1999. During the life of the Canal Treaty, 1979–1999, Panama would also receive a much larger remuneration from canal proceeds.

It would seem that General Torrijos had won the isthmus's greatest victory. However, the Neutrality Treaty was a large price to pay for the new relationship. First, this treaty gave the U.S. government the right to intervene in Panama in perpetuity for the sake of the canal's operation and safety. Additionally, the new accords legitimized the myriad of U.S. military facilities and operations that had grown up in Panama since 1903, thus giving Washington the right to carry out strategic operations throughout Latin America from the isthmus at least until the end of 1999. While U.S. critics saw the accords as "giving away" the canal, Panamanian critics viewed the treaties as more of the same. Nevertheless, Panama did finally achieve a new relationship with Washington, whereby it would acquire full sovereignty over its territory and take control of the canal. These achievements, impossible earlier in U.S.–Panama relations, came only after a long, difficult struggle and with a great deal of controversy.

Panama's ability to achieve sovereignty over its entire territory after decades of frustration can be attributed to several factors that we can group according to level of analysis. At the international level, the relaxation of the Cold War, during the period called *détente* in the mid- to late 1970s, allowed Panama to assert itself diplomatically without Washington fearing a Soviet or Cuban victory in the region. In fact, the Carter administration had opened an Interest Section in Havana, providing for the first direct diplomatic ties between the United States and Cuba since 1961. This more relaxed bipolar environment allowed the developing nations to assert themselves more in international forums such as the Non-Aligned Movement. A huge power asymmetry still existed between the United States and Panama, but with Washington's strategic imperative diminished, Panama could assert its nationalist aspirations. Also, by the mid-1970s, the canal had declined in its military and economic importance to the United States, and defense analysts had concluded that the waterway was virtually indefensible.

Significant domestic changes in Panama also prompted this more positive response from Washington. While geopolitics remained at the center of U.S. international strategy, Washington virtually ignored Panama's sentiments of nationalism and self-determination, dismissing them as misguided or communist inspired. As Panama's middle and lower classes became increasingly involved in politics, however, ignoring these national sentiments became more dangerous, as highlighted by the 1959 and 1964 anti-U.S. riots. Ironically, it was the U.S.-supported military regime that was able to forge these sentiments into a strong and more effective foreign policy. Although, General Torrijos was not elected to power, he turned the desires of nationalists into a national foreign policy and coaxed Washington to alter the U.S.–Panama relationship. Panama's military regime was somewhat immune from U.S. pressure since it dominated the political arena on the isthmus and had received a great deal of backing from international financial institutions, thanks to support from the United States (Ropp 1992). In essence, the U.S. government had created a Frankenstein it eventually could not control. U.S. senators voted for the canal treaties that would finally abrogate the infamous 1903 treaty principally because U.S. policymakers and experts convinced them that Panama could explode in anti-U.S. social violence if Washington did not treat the isthmus fairly. The domestic, state-level changes that occurred in Panama during the 1930s to 1970s, along with the changed international system, paved the way for a restructured U.S.–Panama relationship. Simply stated, Torrijos's repressive yet populist military regime pieced together a stronger, more autonomous state that could forge a more independent Panamanian foreign policy.

Although important changes at the international and state levels were vital elements in allowing Panama greater success in its relations with the United States, individuals also played a strong role in creating the new U.S.–Panama relationship. Four national leaders stand out in pressing for a more nationalistic and independent Panamanian foreign policy: Arnulfo and Harmodio Arias, Jose Remón, and Omar Torrijos. These were men who rose from outside the oligarchy to assume political power in a country where politics had been dominated by a small, urban oligarchy in collusion with the U.S. government. Ironically, Remón and Torrijos were military men who owed much of their rise to prominence to the U.S. government, in its quest to promote an anticommunist military on the isthmus. Many Panamanian military officers and members of the middle class cooperated with the oligarchy and with U.S. interests. These and other less prominent men, however, chose to challenge Washington at certain times in their political careers, sometimes risking their power, as happened to Arnulfo Arias on several occasions. We are left with a sort of tautology: Individuals make foreign policy; therefore, individuals are important agents in foreign policy formulation. These individuals, however, cannot be separated from the domestic socioeconomic changes taking place in Panama that brought the middle classes into the political arena. The generals and politicians who emerged after the 1930s may have left their personal legacies but they were also representatives of new, important social sectors that were having greater influence on Panama's political landscape.

More important changes to come—namely, the Cold War's end and the inauguration of democracy in Panama—would further influence Panama's foreign policy. But before such changes could transpire, Panama had to rid itself, with U.S. assistance, of the powerful military regime that controlled the isthmus.

THE NORIEGA CRISIS AND THE U.S. INVASION

General Torrijos would never see the fruits of his labor. In July 1981, he died in an airplane crash that some observers still consider suspicious. Nevertheless, Torrijos had left an important legacy. Panama had started down a path of democratization that the Carter administration demanded as a quid pro quo for the U.S. concessions in the canal treaties. Torrijos had allowed political parties to organize once more and had scheduled national elections for 1984. Implementation of the canal treaties was also moving forward.

By 1983, however, important domestic and systemic changes, that would dramatically alter the U.S.–Panama relationship, had occurred. Within Panama, General Manuel Noriega, Torrijos's chief of intelligence, took control of the military, renaming it the Panamanian Defense Forces (PDF). The new PDF commander had an unusually close and long-standing working relationship with the Central Intelligence Agency and had become PDF commander by double-crossing other top officers who had signed a secret plan with him to control the PDF and the nation's presidency. Second, the Cold War had flared up anew, owing to the Nicaraguan revolution and the Soviet invasion of Afghanistan, both occurring in 1979. Washington, forgetting détente, was once again looking at Panama as a strategic chess piece, rather than as a sovereign nation state. The renewed tension prompted Washington to support General Noriega, simply because he was cooperating with U.S. military and intelligence operations in Latin America, designed to undermine the Nicaraguan regime and to shore up pro-U.S. regimes in Central America. The fact that Noriega was involved in the illicit narcotics and weapons trade and was undermining the democratic process in Panama was less important to U.S. decision makers than his cooperation with U.S. strategic policies in the region.

Like his mentor Torrijos, Noriega was a complex man. At the same time he was obliging Washington in matters of U.S. national security, he was pursuing independent, "nationalist" policies. In 1983, Noriega spearheaded the foundation of the Contadora Group, formed by Panama, Venezuela, Mexico, and Colombia. These countries agreed to promote a peaceful solution to the internal conflicts raging in the Central American nations of Nicaragua, El Salvador, and Guatemala. Washington viewed this diplomatic approach with skepticism, preferring a unilateral strategy of providing military and economic assistance to the pro-U.S. Salvadoran and Guatemalan regimes, and to the counterrevolutionaries, known as Contras, that were fighting to bring down the anti-U.S. Nicaraguan government. In 1984, the facilities and land that comprised Fort Gulick, one of the many U.S. military facilities on the isthmus, was to revert to Panama, as stipulated by the canal treaties. Washington had a strong interest in keeping the School of the Americas, housed at Fort Gulick, open and in Panama, since the school trained Latin American military personnel who went on to support U.S. strategic goals in the region. After some rocky negotiations, Noriega decided to take over Fort Gulick and force the United States to relocate the school, much to the displeasure of the Reagan administration. General Noriega was also involved in numerous illegal activities that should have concerned Washington greatly from the start. He became involved in the drug trade at least by the early 1970s, but his involvement was now growing dramatically. He provided intelligence and Western goods to the Castro regime. He supplied the Salvadoran leftist rebels with weapons. And, he cleverly infiltrated U.S. electronic intelligence operations in Panama. Ironically, at the same time, Washington conferred on the general glowing commendations for his assistance with U.S. antidrug operations.

Eventually, executive-legislative branch dynamics changed in Washington, leading to Noriega's falling out of favor with U.S. policymakers. By 1986, the U.S. Congress discovered that the Reagan administration had been violating U.S. law by providing lethal aid to the Contras. As a result of the subsequent Iran–Contra affair, several key members of the Reagan team lost their jobs or resigned, and consequently Noriega lost his principal backers. Once the Reagan administration became disenchanted with the general, the U.S. Congress and media began to receive information on Noriega's activities, leading quickly to a national outrage that centered on the evils of the general and the lack of democracy in Panama. The leaked information did not oust Noriega, so the Reagan, then the Bush, administration began to take a series of steps to force the general from power. Washington employed many tactics, including bribing the general, inciting popular rebellion, funding armed insurgents, carrying out shows of force, promoting *golpes* from within the PDF, applying economic sanctions, indicting Noriega on drug charges, and funding opposition candidates. Finally, after all of these steps failed, President Bush adopted the most extreme option and authorized the invasion of Panama on December 20, 1989 (see Scranton 1991).

Although the Bush administration gave a variety of official reasons for the invasion, the U.S. government invaded Panama because General Noriega was no longer valuable and was in fact hindering important U.S. goals in the region. The Canal Treaty specified that on January 1, 1990, a Panamanian would become administrator of the Panama Canal Commission. U.S. policymakers felt they could not allow that person to be a Noriega appointee, which helps to explain the specific timing of the invasion. Additionally, Washington wanted to come to some sort of agreement on the status of U.S. military bases after 1999, but, since 1983, General Noriega had been putting off any serious negotiation on that vital issue. Finally, Washington would not allow a de facto military leader, who was knee-deep in the illegal narcotics traffic, to lead Panama through the final disposition of the canal treaties, particularly to allow him to take possession of the canal on December 31, 1999. The 1989 U.S. invasion of Panama, therefore, demonstrates quite clearly that despite the autonomy achieved by the military governments of Torrijos and Noriega, Panama was still vital to U.S. interests in Latin America and was sovereign only to a limited extent.

THE POST–COLD WAR ERA: THE REALIZATION OF "SOVEREIGNTY" AND THE PROMISE OF DEMOCRACY

The postinvasion period is important to an analysis of Panama's foreign policy for two reasons. First, it represents the nation's transition to a potentially stable democracy. In the 1990s, Panama finally inaugurated a democratic regime that, despite its potential frailties (Pérez 2000), could be considered more representative than previous oligarchic and military regimes. Additionally, the U.S. invasion led to the elimination of the PDF, reducing the prospects of future military involvement in politics. Consequently, Panama's foreign policy would now be potentially formulated by a larger number of sectors than ever before, perhaps being more truly the reflection of national interests rather than the narrow interests of a few individuals or institutions. Second, by the 1990s, the international system was finally devoid of the Cold War tensions that had characterized the system since soon after the end of World War II. U.S. strategists quit viewing Panama simply as a pawn in a Cold War chessboard. By 1991, the Soviet Union had dissolved, the leftist regime in Nicaragua had been voted out of power, leftist rebels in El Salvador had negotiated a peace settlement with the government, and Cuba had lost Soviet economic support. As a result, Panama could now assert a more independent foreign policy without raising Washington's concerns about Soviet or Cuban influence in the region.

Soon after the U.S. invasion, a new government was sworn in on a U.S. military base in Panama. Guillermo Endara, the presidential candidate who had received the most votes in the May 1989 elections, attained political power thanks to U.S. troops. He had won the vote count in the May 1989 election but had not assumed the presidency because Noriega, insisting there had been "foreign" intervention, annulled the contest.

The Endara government did not chart out a clear foreign policy for Panama during his administration, being concerned principally with his government's legitimacy and with economic recovery. Other nations in the region remained aloof toward the isthmus, owing to the manner in which Endara attained power. Practically every government in the region had condemned the U.S. invasion and viewed Endara as an accomplice in the invasion. While some effort was made to integrate Panama into the Central American community, such integration was limited and not economic in scope. Although the U.S. government urged Endara to begin negotiations over a continued U.S. military presence on the isthmus past the year 1999, the new president resisted, owing to his scant popularity and his political party's resistance to a continued U.S. military presence. Although he resisted on the issue of bases, the Endara administration was beholden to the United States for assuming power and for Panama's economic recovery. Economic sanctions in the late 1980s, the devastating effects of the invasion, and postinvasion rioting had devastated the country's economy. Consequently, with the exception of the issue of U.S. military bases, the Endara government cooperated fully with Washington in economic and other matters. Financial aid became a foreign policy imperative, thus minimizing the government's ability to make any attempts to chart out an independent foreign policy. For example, U.S. economic assistance was tied to Panama's adopting new legislation that would reduce bank secrecy, something that Washington demanded for its "war" on drugs.

The Endara administration, nevertheless, took a number of steps that helped to restore some of Panama's position in the international arena. One accomplishment was the reincorporation of Panama into the Rio Group, which had grown out of the Contadora Group and included other influential nations in the region. The Contadora nations had expelled Panama from the group late in the Noriega crisis. Panama also took the bold step, although at Washington's urging, to eliminate its armed forces, thus making it difficult for security matters to be prominent in the nation's foreign policy. One hitch in this demilitarization plan was that the elimination of the PDF, which was approved by the national assembly, was nevertheless rejected in a national referendum. Finally, the Endara government established the Inter-Oceanic Regional Authority, or ARI by its Spanish acronym. ARI was designed to oversee the disposition of the lands and facilities that Panama would receive pursuant to the 1977 canal treaties. The vast majority of these properties were still held by the United States, since Washington wanted to keep its military bases as long as possible, and the Noriega crisis had significantly slowed down the reversion process.

Perhaps Endara's greatest achievement was his ability to stay in office for a full term. In 1994, Panama had its first truly free and fair election. Ironically, Ernesto Pérez Balladares, the candidate of the Democratic Revolutionary Party (PRD), won this contest. Founded by Omar Torrijos in 1978, the PRD supported the Noriega regime throughout the 1980s. With the inauguration of the Pérez government, Panama initiated a slightly more independent foreign policy. The new president was able to distance himself from Washington principally because Panama had recovered quite well from its economic crisis, the Cold War was clearly over, Panama was more democratic, and his political party called for a more independent foreign policy.

During the Pérez administration, Panama applied a two-pronged strategy in its relations with the United States. First, the country fully cooperated with the neoliberal economic policies promoted by Washington throughout Latin America. Pérez accelerated the privatization program the Endara government started, even though the PRD had promoted statist, protectionist policies in the past. Cable and Wireless, a British telecommunications firm, purchased the state-owned INTEL, the nation's telephone company. Also up for sale were Panama's social security, sewage, and utilities systems. Panama privatized its ports and began selling to investors the former Canal Zone properties it was slowly acquiring from the U.S. government. Consistent with neoliberal reforms, the Pérez administration slashed tariffs, allowing the country to join the World Trade Organization in 1997. These policies pleased Washington greatly.

Along with privatization, however, Pérez began to diversify Panama's economic and political ties. The Hong Kong–based firm Hutchinson-Wampoa led a consortium that won concessions to develop Panama's two principal ports, Balboa on the Pacific side and Cristóbal on the Atlantic. From the U.S. perspective, a "foreign" company for the first time ever would be operating a major economic operation adjacent to the canal. Most troubling to some key players in Washington was that this particular company was now home based in the People's Republic of China, since Britain had turned Hong Kong over to China in July 1997. Panama's new strategy was to open Panama to investment from all over the world, in order to grow its economy but also to minimize Washington's economic influence. In this effort, President Pérez increased the isthmus's ties to Central America, joined the Andean group, and started bilateral trade negotiations with Chile and Mexico.

Panama's most important resources—its geographic location and the canal—provided the greatest potential for allowing the nation to become more independent and economically vibrant. Since Panama was but years away from assuming control of the canal, the Panamanian government did what it could to convince the global community that Panama would be able to efficiently operate and defend the vital waterway, holding a Universal Congress on the Panama Canal, designed to let the world know of Panama's upcoming control of the canal, in September 1997. To assure the international community and Washington that Panama was prepared to operate the canal, the Pérez administration established the Panama Canal Authority, the government agency that would assume control of the waterway from the U.S.-led Panama Canal Commission at noon on December 31, 1999. The legislation creating the Canal Authority stipulated that the organization would be an autonomous, national agency, in an effort to depoliticize the canal. When President Pérez appointed the authority's governing board, however, criticism rapidly ensued, since several appointees were relatives or political cronies.

In the political realm, Panama also attempted to distance itself as much as possible from the United States. Perhaps the most important step taken was Panama's resistance to a continued U.S. military presence on the isthmus past 1999. Early in the Pérez administration, the U.S. government negotiated with Panama to keep U.S. military bases on the isthmus. However, since Washington refused to pay a lease for the bases, Panama declined to continue negotiating the permanence of bases. President Pérez then suggested that the negotiations center on a Multilateral Anti-drug Center (Centro Multilateral Antidrogas [CMA]). Washington liked the CMA idea, since it would be a less offensive way to keep U.S. troops in Panama and would highlight the U.S. antidrug effort. Negotiations on a CMA began in earnest in mid-July 1997. However, the talks eventually failed one year later when Pérez decided that a continued U.S. military presence was not in his or the nation's best interest. By September 1998, the two countries were at an impasse, disagreeing over the duration of the agreement, the legal status of U.S. troops, and the functions of the CMA (Sanchez 2003).

The most problematic aspect of efficient canal operation was the issue of the waterway's security. Washington argued that Panama, devoid of a military, would be ill equipped to defend the canal effectively. Panama, on the other hand, agreeing with a long line of domestic scholars and leaders, insisted that neutrality assured the best canal defense. The issue became particularly salient when several incursions into Panama's Darien region by paramilitary forces and guerrillas took place during the negotiations over a continued U.S. military presence. In April 1998, the Defense Intelligence Agency leaked a report concluding that 40 percent of Colombia's territory was controlled by armed rebels (*Latin American Weekly Report*, April 21, 1998: 175). The border incidents, along with leaked information, convinced many Panamanians and even some outside observers that Washington was directing a covert campaign to make the situation in Panama seem at near-crisis level, necessitating a continued U.S. military presence. Nevertheless, Pérez and his key advisers remained confident that neutrality would better protect the canal than U.S. forces stationed in Panama. As a precautionary measure, however, the president initiated "Operation Peace and Sovereignty," sending over one thousand police to the Darien frontier.

Panama's democratic development continued with the election of the nation's first woman president in 1999. Mireya Moscoso de Gruber, a presidential candidate from the Arnulfista Party and the widow of Arnulfo Arias, assumed power in September 1999 and continued the two-pronged strategy of the previous administration. Although the Arnulfistas were vocal and longtime critics of the PRD, both parties were forged in populist doctrine that pointed to Panama's exploitation by the "gringos." Consequently, even though Washington tried to renew its efforts to keep U.S. military personnel in Panama, or at minimum reach a Status of Forces Agreement, President Moscoso stood firm and refused to entertain the idea of a continued U.S. military presence on the isthmus. Her administration also continued the policy of diversifying Panama's economic and political relations.

Within four months of taking office, President Mireya Moscoso enjoyed the privilege of presiding over the transfer of the famous canal from the United States to the Republic of Panama. While PRD supporters thought it fitting that Martin Torrijos, son of the late General Torrijos and losing presidential candidate, should have had the honor of receiving the canal, Mireya Moscoso, as the widow of Arnulfo Arias and presidential candidate of the Arnulfista Party, also merited the honor. Arias and Torrijos above all others had personified Panamanian nationalism and populism, if not democratic ideals. This great moment in Panamanian, and indeed world, history was bittersweet, however. The Clinton administration decided to minimize the importance of the event and slighted the Panamanians by sending former president Jimmy Carter, as the principal but unofficial U.S. representative. Many Panamanians, while not necessarily surprised, were certainly deeply disappointed.

Despite Moscoso's populist rhetoric, Panama continued its move toward privatization, free trade, and promotion of foreign investment—policies normally viewed as detrimental to the masses by populist leaders. Although these steps were consistent with Washington's neoliberal mantra, they also promoted a move toward diminishing Panama's historical, economic dependence on the United States. ARI continued its plan to allow many nations and investors to partake in the reverted Canal Zone property bonanza. In addition to the modernization of two ports by the Hong Kong–based Hutchinson-Wampoa, the Taiwanese firm Evergreen acquired rights to operate a container facility at the Atlantic side of the canal, near the city of Colon. Several Taiwanese companies also established manufacturing plants in a recently created industrial park, located in the former Fort Davis military base. Other projects include a cruise ship port and shopping facility on the Pacific entrance of the canal, an ecotourism facility in the town of Gamboa, a "City of Knowledge" at the former site of Albrook Air Force Station, and a multimodal transportation hub at what used to be Howard Air Force Base.

In the political arena, the Moscoso administration continued to diversify and strengthen Panama's diplomatic ties. In November 2000, Panama hosted the Tenth Ibero-American Conference, bringing together the leaders of Spain, Portugal, the Spanish-speaking countries of Latin America, and Brazil. The United States was notably excluded from this annual event. Additionally, Panama continued to be active in the Central American parliament and other international bodies. In fact, Panama has offered former Canal Zone facilities to many international and regional groups at substantial savings. Panama diversified its political universe most effectively, however, by insisting on the departure of the U.S. military from Panama, an action that helped to minimize U.S. power and influence on the isthmus.

Like her predecessor, President Moscoso stood firm on not allowing Washington to keep troops and bases on the isthmus. Before taking office, Moscoso was quoted as saying, "As long as I'm president, there will be no foreign military bases in Panama" (quoted in *Latin America Weekly Report*, July 13, 1999: 321). In November 1999, newspapers reported that Moscoso was working on a "secret deal" with Washington that would allow U.S. troops to remain on isthmian soil. Although the Moscoso administration attempted to dispel those rumors, negotiations were certainly taking place on some sort of maritime intelligence agreement and on the status of U.S. troops that might be operating in Panama in the future. The U.S. government was certainly not giving up on firming up some sort of security agreement with Panama prior to the transfer of the canal. But, finally, when Washington attempted to sign a "status of forces" agreement with Panama, the Moscoso administration flatly rejected the accord.

Panama, however, still needed to convince critics that the canal would be secure, despite the problems along the Colombian border and the departure of U.S. troops. Consequently, the Moscoso administration embarked on a project to develop a Strategic Plan for National Security. While not receiving complete national support, the strategic plan elucidates long held Panamanian beliefs about the isthmus' role in the world. The plan was developed principally through the initiative of the Arnulfista Party, but with the assistance of the Christian Democratic Party and even the PRD. An underlying principle of the plan is the notion of neutrality as the underpinning for canal defense and Panamanian national security. Consequently, the plan prohibits the stationing of any foreign troops or the establishment of any foreign military facilities on Panamanian territory, of course alluding to the United States. Additionally, the plan promotes the principle of multilateral, rather than unilateral, security, which once more indirectly maligns the U.S. "right" under the Neutrality Treaty of 1977 to unilaterally assure the defense of the canal in perpetuity. In fact, the plan states that Panama's greatest threat to its national security lies in a unilateral (U.S.) determination that the safety of the canal is in danger.

To assure that such an eventuality would not arise, Moscoso continued to deal with the Colombian so-called spillover problem.[2] The Moscoso government took several actions: doubling the number of police in the Darien region, calling for the United Nations to be involved, meeting with Colombian president Andrés Pastrana, and promoting an agreement that arranged for the security chiefs of Colombia's five bordering neighbors to meet regularly to discuss border and security concerns. These multilateral efforts were designed to deal with the serious Colombian conflict but also to ensure that the United States would not act unilaterally or completely monopolize the situation.

In the 1990s, Panama was able to begin to formulate a nascent but truly national and more representative foreign policy, not dominated completely by a small oligarchy, U.S. interests, or the armed forces. First, the Cold War had ended and thus Washington had begun to relinquish the strategic imperative that had guided its policy since as early as 1947. Second, Panama transitioned to democratic rule for the first time since its independence from Colombia, holding two clean and fair national elections. Panama was thus finally able to focus on the type of foreign policy that through the years had been advocated by many of its scholars, politicians, and opinion leaders—a foreign policy with an emphasis on sovereignty, economic and political multilateralism, and neutrality.

CONCLUSION: POWERFUL SYSTEMS, CHANGING STATES, AND ASSERTIVE DIPLOMATS

The post–World War II history of Panama's foreign relations has been fascinating, frustrating and, at limited times, somewhat successful. Despite its vulnerability, owing to its small size and weak economy, at the end of 1999, Panama achieved sovereignty over its entire territory and gained control of the Panama Canal. This is a most impressive accomplishment given the fact that, for most of the twentieth century, Panama could be said to be devoid of a national foreign policy, owing to the nation's control by a small oligarchy and by U.S. interests. Panamanians did not achieve a national consensus over one vital aspect of Panama's foreign policy—the abrogation of the 1903 Hay-Bunau-Varilla Treaty—until the 1960s. Before then, Panama had no national consensus on foreign policy, was devoid of a diplomatic corps, and lacked any real input into foreign policy formulation from sectors other than the oligarchy and Washington. Clearly, nationalist sentiments, expressed by middle-class and popular sectors, were making themselves heard, especially beginning in the 1930s. However, no real institutionalized process of foreign policymaking that included other than a small inner circle was present as late as the 1960s.

Beginning in 1969, with the military regime of Omar Torrijos, the Panamanian state began to assert itself and nonoligarchic sentiments were injected into Panama's foreign policy, even if in an autocratic manner. Subsequently, in the late 1970s, General Torrijos coerced Washington into overhauling the U.S.–Panama relationship, leading to the 1977 Panama Canal Treaties. In the late 1980s, General Noriega challenged the United States on many issues but was eventually forced out of office by a U.S. invasion in 1989, demonstrating that Panama was still subject to U.S. power and interests. In the 1990s, democratic presidents were able to effectively resist Washington's efforts at retaining U.S. bases in Panama past the year 1999. Additionally, these presidents were able to achieve increased diversity in Panama's economic relations. For some observers, these triumphs represent the ability of a small nation to challenge the United States.

A more critical view of these events, however, suggests that Panama has been able to achieve its policy goals only after a great deal of struggle, at significant cost, and later than most other "developing" countries. In 1999, almost all of the nations of the world had achieved self-determination, even many that had been under communist, imperial tutelage. While General Torrijos was able to force Washington to the bargaining table in 1977, these negotiations came more than ten years after President Johnson had stated that the U.S.–Panama relationship would be revamped. Even then, the canal treaties of 1977 passed the U.S. Senate by the narrowest of margins, one vote, and came only after Washington was convinced that the canal had lost much of its importance and only because Washington feared another Cuba might emerge in Panama. Additionally, Washington insisted on retaining its right to intervene in Panama for as long as the canal was in operation. Noriega directly challenged the U.S. government, but he was eventually "arrested" and brought to the United States for trial by way of a military invasion. Presidents Pérez and Moscoso were able to prevent the U.S. government from retaining a U.S. military presence in Panama, but both leaders closely followed Washington's blueprint for economic restructuring. Consequently, historical evidence suggests that Panama's victories have been limited and have come at great cost and sacrifice, principally because of its weakness as a nation-state. The power of a nation-state is a highly important factor when trying to explain foreign policy success. Using a levels of analysis approach, state-level factors stand out as very persuasive in understanding Panama's difficulty in achieving its foreign policy goals, since size, wealth, and location, as key characteristics of the Panamanian state, seem to be most salient in explaining Panama's limitations in foreign relations.

Nevertheless, the United States has not always gotten exactly what it has wanted from its relationship with Panama, as some Panamanian critics have argued. The actions of individuals, the characteristics of domestic politics, and the features of the international system help us to explain Panama's foreign policy behavior and efficacy. First, powerful leaders who have developed popular backing and have attained some autonomy of action, like Omar Torrijos and Manuel Noriega, can be successful in foreign policy, albeit at some level of risk. What is problematic with this conclusion is that such leaders tend to be dictatorial and thus are subject to exposure or vilification by a powerful nation that disagrees with them, as happened with Noriega. However, Torrijos and Noriega, although militaristic and repressive in their rule, helped to strengthen the Panamanian state, which later helped democratic leaders to formulate a more representative Panamanian foreign policy. Second, under a democratic system, nations can achieve some degree of foreign policy success, as Panama did by preventing a U.S. military presence past the year 1999. When it negotiated with Pérez for a continued U.S. military presence, Washington accepted Panama's rejection of the CMA-proposed accord and eventually withdrew all of its troops from the isthmus. Pérez was able to accomplish this goal because it was clear to Washington that he was a legitimate leader and had the backing of his party and other important political groups in Panama. Likewise, when President Moscoso rejected Washington's Status of Forces Agreement, there was little that the U.S. government could do. Forcing a U.S. military presence on a democratic Panama would be much more difficult to justify than the 1989 invasion, which was severely criticized by almost all of the countries in Latin America.

The characteristics of the international system are very important in understanding Panama's foreign policy successes and failures. Panama was able to achieve foreign policy goals only when international conditions encouraged the United States to accept Panamanian demands. Torrijos was able to get Washington to consent to a new relationship with Panama when U.S. decision makers became convinced that conceding to Panamanian demands would not create an advantage for the Soviet Union. When Washington needed Noriega for its strategic goals in Central America, Panama was able to undertake the Contadora Process and close down the School of the Americas. Presidents Pérez and Moscoso could press for the end of U.S. military bases on the isthmus because the bases there were no longer necessary for U.S. strategic interests. Thus, although Panama's asymmetrical power relationship with the United States severely restricted the small nation's foreign policy efficacy for most of its history, the actions of key leaders, combined with the end of the Cold War, a stronger Panamanian state, and the inauguration of democratic politics, have allowed the isthmus some greater leeway and limited success in its foreign policy. The U.S. government, however, because of its power and interests in the isthmus, will still retain the ability to influence Panamanian affairs, even if less powerfully than in the past.

In addition to these limited victories, Panama has been able to formulate a foreign policy that is more attuned with the wishes or interests of the nation. Panama's ability to develop a national foreign policy can be attributed directly to domestic, state-level developments occurring this past century. As early as the 1930s, the Panamanian oligarchy and the United Sates began to lose their monopoly on isthmian international affairs. In that decade, the middle-class sectors began to have a greater, if indirect, say in the nation's international dealings. It was those nonoligarchic sectors that convinced the Panamanian legislature in 1947 to reject a military bases agreement with Washington. Eventually students became increasingly involved in foreign policy and made daring attempts to restore Panama's national pride in 1959 and 1964. Now that Panama has had two free and fair postinvasion national elections, democracy seems to have returned to the isthmus. With the inauguration of a democratic regime, Panama will have the potential for generating a truly national foreign policy. The isthmus will always be small and thus vulnerable to powerful nation-states, but Panama can now begin to take better advantage of its geographic location. With proper leadership, the isthmus can perhaps become, as some Panamanians hope, the Singapore of the Western Hemisphere.

DISCUSSION QUESTIONS

1. Could a small country like Panama ever achieve its foreign policy goals in the current international system? Why or why not?
2. What changes took place at the international and state levels in the last half of the twentieth century that allowed Panama to assert itself more in the international arena and develop a foreign policy?
3. Did the inauguration of democracy after the 1989 U.S. invasion alter Panama's foreign policy goals and efficacy?

NOTES

1. The author acquired much of the information used in the development of this chapter from a variety of sources while in Panama on a lecturing/research Senior Scholar Fulbright grant, from July 1997 to July 1998, and on additional research trips in June 1999 and December 1999. The newspapers *El Panamá América* and *La Prensa* provide much of the chronology and Panamanian perspective. Over one hundred for-

mal and informal interviews yielded a great deal of inside information from both the U.S. and Panamanian perspectives.

2. Analysts are concerned that the high levels of violence in Colombia, resulting from the guerrilla warfare, the illegal narcotics trade, and paramilitary forces, will spill over into Panama and threaten the canal and the isthmus's political system.

5

Cuba
Talking Big, Acting Bigger

Damián Fernández

The Cuban revolution of 1959 inaugurated an unprecedented phase in the island's international relations. Not only did the revolutionary government represent a break with the foreign policy actions of the republican governments (1902–1959), but it broke the mold of how small, relatively poor states are supposed to behave in world politics. The most dramatic aspect of the new Cuban foreign policy since 1959 was its support for revolutionary groups worldwide, culminating in the deployment of tens of thousands of Cuban troops in Angola (post-1975) and Ethiopia (post-1976). Other dimensions of Cuba's role on the global stage, if not as sensational, were nonetheless as atypical. The island provided extensive development assistance to neighbors and friends and assumed leadership roles in a host of multilateral forums advocating radical global transformation. Cuba since 1959 exhibited a will to act big, even if it never amassed the wherewithal to be considered a world power. From this perspective, 1959 ushered in a radical departure from the past (Domínguez 1978a; Erisman 1985; Fernández 1987). But did it?

This chapter will answer that question. It does so by examining Cuban foreign policy after 1959 through the lens of an analytical model closely resembling that of Rosenau's. Four main factors in tandem explain the island's behavior in world affairs: (1) leadership and ideology, (2) the domestic political system, (3) the connection to an exogenous source of power (i.e., the USSR until 1990), and (4) the international environment. But such an approach has its limits (not only the unresolved issue of differential weighing of variables), but most notably the neglect of an important dimension of social life that is all too often absent in foreign policy analysis: political culture. Traditional explanations of foreign policy tend to focus on decision making, power capabilities, and international structures—all important dimensions—but neglect cultural factors of what can be considered a national style of diplomacy. Even when it is included, political culture is usually portrayed in an amorphous fashion; specificity is lacking. Moreover, until recently, international relations theory did not take into account the connection between words and deeds. This chapter is an attempt to deal with these omissions. It does so by examining points of encounter in pre- and postrevolutionary practice and discourse and by connecting a national foreign policy style forged during the republic with that of post-1959 Cuba.

While the argument that the socialist government's actions on the global stage signaled a radical departure from the past is essentially correct, it fails to locate, acknowledge, and understand the roots of Cuban internationalism in the history and culture of republican Cuba. By including the cultural aspect, a nuanced understanding of Cuban foreign policy in specific and politics in general through time (i.e., from 1902 to the present) emerges. The cultural factor expressed in the norms and attitudes of foreign policy discourse and practice helps to frame the worldview of Cuban elites and how they conceptualized Cuban identity, interests, and aspirations in the world. It also provides a more connected perspective of politics before and after the revolution.

Rather than exclusively underscoring the watershed the revolution marked on the island's foreign affairs, the inclusion of culture uncovers a level of continuity that is usually unrecognized. Pre-1959 diplomacy provided a foundation for post-1959 foreign policy by establishing a will to grandeur in Cuba's internationalism. Before Cuba acted big, Cuba talked big about international affairs. The propensity to grandeur was clearly evident in the actions and rhetoric of Cuban officials of the republic and later was manifest in Fidel Castro's discourse and practice. Foundational codes of the national style of grandeur were established in the republic, especially between the 1920s and 1940s, but can be traced back to José Martí, the founding father of the nation. Tracing such lineage shows that revolutionary internationalism had a basis in Cuban political culture, even if the revolution took it to unexpected turns.

First, this chapter revisits Cuba's republican past, from 1902 to 1958, to uncover a series of developments and patterns of ideology and action that were decisive in creating a culture of international politics that foreshadowed features of post-1959 diplomacy. Second, I offer a sketch of the different stages of Cuban foreign relations from 1959 to the present in an attempt to trace a profile of the principal characteristics of the island's foreign policy under socialism. The purpose is to establish a foundation to understand the nature and scope of the Cuban government's international actions. Third, and based on the historical experience, I present a four-dimensional model that explains how Cuba was able to break the mold assigned to weaker states in traditional conceptions of international relations. The chapter ends arguing that the traditional four-factor model should be completed with a cultural dimension. In the Cuban case, revolutionary foreign policy cannot be fully understood if the republican past is not considered. Talking big in the republic ushered in acting big post-1959.

THE WILL TO GRANDEUR: CUBA'S LIBERAL INTERNATIONALISM IN THE REPUBLIC

Did the Cuban revolution inaugurate a watershed in the island's international behavior? The answer to this question is yes and no. As the historical account and analysis of foreign policy post-1959 will show, the revolution of 1959 gave way to a dramatically active era of diplomacy in which the island behaved as if it were a mini–world power. Several structural and coincidental factors intertwined to explain this. However, fundamental commonalities are found in the pre and post-1959 period once one takes a close look at Cuban diplomacy in the republic.

The Cuban republic was established in 1902 after three years of a U.S. protectorate that resulted from Spain's (and Cuban independence fighters') defeat in the Spanish-American War of 1898. The republic was born with limited sovereignty as the U.S. Congress imposed the Platt Amendment on the Cuban constitution as a condition for "independence." The amendment (finally abrogated in 1934) restricted many of the conditions that are usually associated with statehood, including nonintervention by foreign powers. The Platt Amendment gave Washington the right to intervene in domestic national matters. It also circumscribed Cuba's autonomous actions in world affairs. Compromised sovereignty notwithstanding, Havana surprisingly played a relatively important role in regional and international forums, adopting at times positions contrary to those of the United States. Even before the abrogation of the Platt Amendment, but especially post-1934, Havana challenged Washington and manifested a will to grandeur in international issues.

Cuba's will to grandeur was expressed in issues of international law and governance. It was the result of material and ideational factors that jointly forged a national style of diplomacy in the first half of the twentieth century. Among the socioeconomic factors that help to explain the rise of a distinct culture of foreign policy is that by the mid-1920s, the island had achieved a modicum of development (if uneven, for sure) and had a political and professional elite highly educated and "modern." These individuals traveled to the

United States and Europe and were in tune with the latest developments of their times. In addition to the material infrastucture that facilitated the emergence of a community of diplomats and international legal experts on the island, political and cultural factors intervened. For Cuba, a diplomatic corps was a necessity, for the state had to conduct frequent negotiations with the United States. Domestic politics were intimately tied to foreign politics Cuba, like many Caribbean and third world states, was born internationalized. In the case of Cuba, though, the proximity to the United States geographically, culturally, and economically exacerbated the international aspects of domestic politics. Domestic and international politics in this context were intimately intertwined, one never knowing where the first ended and the other started (especially under the provisions of the Platt Amendment).

The legacy of José Martí, the father of Cuban independence, provided the cultural grounds for an internationalist perspective. A progressive, liberal, and highly moralistic internationalist discourse originated in Martí. Martí, both an admirer and a critic of the United States and a proponent of Latin American solidarity, had an egalitarian spirit imbued with lofty ideals for peace and cooperation between nations. Martí provided the ideational ground on which republican diplomats sowed the seeds of Cuba's foreign policy. Cuba's chief delegate to the UN Third General Assembly in 1948, Guy Pérez Cisneros y Bonel, who along with another Cuban Ernesto Dihigo, a prominent professor of law, were two of the most influential third world delegates in drafting the Universal Declaration of Human Rights, linked the spirit of Martí with Cuba's position in support of the Declaration. In his address to the assembly minutes before the approval of the Declaration, Cisneros y Bonel said:

> The members of the Cuban delegation are deeply moved when—as they review the articles of the important Declaration that we will adopt in a few minutes—they recognize that all its provisions could have been adopted by that generous spirit who was the apostle of our independence: Jose Marti, the hero who—as he turned his homeland into a nation—gave us forever this generous rule: "With everyone, and for the good of everyone." (*Miami Herald*, December 10, 1998)

The profile of the political culture of Cuban foreign policy during the republic had two principal features: (1) international assertiveness (despite limits on sovereignty), particularly in multilateral organizations; and (2) a moral impetus that was strikingly progressive. During the republic, Cuba acted bigger and spoke louder than what its size would seem to indicate, even when its sovereignty was compromised by its close economic and political relations with the United States. Havana's international assertiveness can be seen in the discourse, practice, and institutions of republican policy and was made possible by the existence of a community of competent diplomats and skilled international lawyers. One of the early architects of Cuban foreign relations, Cosme de la Torriente (1951), claimed that "from the foundation of the Republic we put our efforts so that our nation would have relations with all the countries of the world. And I can say that from the first decades of our independence we have a very competent diplomatic corps" (352).

Cuban lawyers successfully represented the government in negotiations and international forums. They participated in the Treaty of Versailles independent from the United States as the island had entered the war autonomously. In the mid-1920s, a group of prominent lawyers established the Sociedad de Juristas Internacionales (Society of International Lawyers) in Havana. One of its members served on the International Court of Justice in the Hague; another one (Cosme de la Torriente) became president of the Assembly of the League of Nations.

In negotiations with the United States over the crucial and sensitive issues such as the sugar quota, Cuba sought and gained at particularly difficult moments what Domínguez (1978b: 61) labels "strategic advantage." Cuban officials negotiated the withdrawal of the United States from the Isle of Pines and the abrogation of the Platt Amendment. Despite the asymmetry of power and the ties of dependence between Havana and Washington, Cuba had a tendency to violate the reciprocity agreement with the United States, which prompted a State Department official to claim that the islanders "have a tendency to flaunt their 'independence' in small ways" (quoted in Domínguez 1978b: 61). Cubans lobbied the U.S. Congress successfully to guarantee a profitable sugar arrangement (Perez-Stable 1993).

The Cuban government assumed other policy positions that were in conflict with those of the United States. For instance, it did so when it entered the League of Nations (when the United States did not) and supported Puerto Rican nationalists who were advocating the withdrawal of the United States from their country and took their cause to the UN. The nationalist liberal underpinning of such actions are clear; if not as radical as post-1959, they do manifest a decisively independent, activist, and progressive streak in the island's foreign relations.

The second aspect of the island's foreign policy political culture that foreshadows post-1959 development is the missionary zeal. Cuban foreign policy from 1902 to 1958 manifested a moral imperative that drove it to activism in multilateral organizations, regional forums, and international crises. Although the island's diplomatic ventures helped to secure pragmatic and economic interests, one of the features of Cuban foreign policy was its tendency to crusade. This propensity is evidenced not only in deeds but in words. Cuban delegates were known for their moralistic penchant, reflected in rhetorical inflation in international debates. The will to grandeur is literally expressed in talking big. In turn, talking big reflected Cuba's own sense of importance, agency, and efficacy.

In the late 1940s and early 1950s, Cuba was at the vanguard of the regional movement in defense of democracy. Under President Carlos Prío (1948–1952), the government supported the creation of the Inter-American Association for Democracy in 1950. With headquarters in Havana, the association institutionalized Prío's interest in coordinating "moral efforts in defense of democratic unity in the hemisphere" (Ameringer 2000: 90). The purpose was to support the people of the region against the power of tyrants. In this issue, Cuba assumed a highly moral position that advocated the establishment of multilateral mechanisms that would act to dislodge dictators. Prío put into practice Raul Haya de la Torre's and Romulo Betancourt's ideas for the protection of human rights and democratic governance in the hemisphere (Ameringer 2000). Initiatives such as these led the State Department to describe the Auténticos (the Party of Prío) as exhibiting a "crusading 'democratic' zeal." Such moral imperative is a precursor of the passion of Cuban foreign policy after 1959. But unlike the foreign policy after 1959, the missionary imperative of republican foreign policy was reformist rather than radical, liberal rather than Marxist—much more in line with Woodrow Wilson's internationalism than Lenin's.

The progressive essence of Cuba's international posture should not be neglected or underestimated. Pérez Cisneros and other Cuban diplomats of the times were firm supporters of social rights that were quite advanced for their times (i.e., fair labor practices, women's rights, and intellectual rights, many of which had been recognized in the Cuban constitution of 1940). They also defended the "right to protect one's honor, a high moral concept rooted in the soul of every Hispanic person" (*Miami Herald*, December 10, 1998). The position of Cuban diplomats was not divorced from domestic party politics, nor of national politics. The program of the Partido del Pueblo (Ortodoxo), not only of the Auténticos, resonated with the actions and discourse of the island's representatives abroad. The Ortodoxos called for the strengthening of international cooperation and the common defense of human rights and endorsed far more polemical positions such as the negation of the right of veto for the superpowers in the UN Security Council. Surprisingly, the Ortodoxos also endorsed the notion of limited sovereignty in favor of universal protection of human rights, a position that places them at the vanguard of the human rights struggle. Fidel Castro was a member of the Ortodoxo Party before he launched an armed insurrection against the dictatorship of Batista (1952–1958). Eduardo Chíbas, the leader of the Ortodoxos, was one of Castro's mentors and role models. Chíbas, with his moral crusade to sweep away the corruption endemic in Cuban politics, saw himself as an ideological descendant of Martí. Fidel Castro would make the same ideological connection with the founding father and would espouse progressive, even radical, positions in world affairs after 1959.

THE WILL AND THE WAY TO GRANDEUR: CUBAN FOREIGN POLICY FROM 1959 TO 2000

The experience of 1902–1958 laid the foundation for Cuban activism in the world after 1959. From 1959 to the present, Cuba's foreign policy can be divided into five stages: (1) the initial period (1959–1967); (2) the period of increasing internationalism (1968–1974); (3) the period of active internationalism (1975–1980); (4) the period of limited or restrained internationalism (1980–1990); and (5) contemporary times, in which Cuba has readjusted its international relations as a response to the breakdown of the Soviet Union and its impact on the island (1990 to the present). Throughout these one can distinguish the tenets of republican diplomatic culture, if radicalized. The radicalization was a result of the trajectory of the revolution itself with its polarization, the ideology and personality of Fidel Castro, U.S hostility to Cuban communism, and the bipolarity of world politics in the early 1960s.

The Initial Period: 1959–1967

During the first or initial stage, the main priority of the Cuban government was to stabilize, and consolidate, its revolution. However, at the same time the seeds of its future internationalism were being sown, partly based on a republican trajectory of actions and words. From 1959 to 1967, "Cuba's foreign policy can be viewed as exhibiting a restrained activism, restrained in the sense that many Cuban policy initiatives were responses and reactions to international conditions and were made necessary by the policies of other actors" (McShane 1979: 1). During this period, Cuba had neither the power nor the means to carry out extensive foreign activities, although the revolutionary elite had already begun to manifest its commitment to a globalist policy, especially in its support of revolutionary groups in Latin America and progressive causes worldwide.

While the antagonism of the United States served to circumscribe Cuba's foreign activities to some extent, Cuba did not respond passively—or in merely reactive fashion—to this posture. Since early in 1959, Castro consistently made decisions that served to foreclose U.S. economic assistance to, and trade with, the island (Carrillo 1985: 165–76). Moreover, Castro's anti-Americanism, a cornerstone of his ideology, antedated 1959. The U.S. embargo, the termination of diplomatic relations, and the expulsion of Cuba from the Organization of American States (OAS) isolated Cuba within the Western Hemisphere. Castro's *guerrillismo* alienated Cuba in official circles throughout Latin America as Havana preached revolutionary overthrow in other countries as well, and Ernesto ("Che") Guevara, one of Castro's revolutionary leaders, called for "many Vietnams." In practice, Cuba supported guerrilla movements at work in Argentina, Bolivia, Brazil, Chile, Colombia, Guatemala, Mexico, Nicaragua, Peru, Uruguay, and Venezuela. For this reason, this period has also been labeled the "period of the export of revolution" (Furtak 1983: 472).

As Havana's relations with Washington rapidly deteriorated onto a confrontation course, Castro sought out the economic and moral support of Moscow. From the Castro perspective, only the Soviet Union had the power to ensure the survival of his revolution from reprisal by the United States. Thereafter, the Soviet Union became the focus of Cuba's international relations despite the fact that Soviet-Cuban relations were often to suffer from their ups and downs. Cole Blasier (1978: 2) claims that, although Castro's collision with the United States has received the most public scrutiny, actually Cuba's biggest battles were with its Soviet patrons throughout the 1960s. Diverging interpretations of revolutionary strategy were not the only impediments to the Soviet-Cuban alliance.

The Soviets had their doubts about Castro's reliability as an ally: Not only was Cuba involved in the Non-Aligned Movement (NAM), but it had also courted the friendship of the Chinese in the early to mid-1960s. The Cubans had their doubts as well, particularly regarding the degree of Soviet commitment to defend the revolution. This was dramatized by the Kennedy–Khruschev negotiations at the time of the 1962 missile crisis, from which Castro was excluded, a situation that caused Castro to question the reliability of Soviet friendship. Tensions between Havana and Moscow continued to escalate up until 1968, when Castro resolved the conflict by agreeing (1) to endorse the Czechoslovakian invasion and (2) to abandon guerrillismo in Latin America.

Cuban involvement in Africa dates back to this initial period. In 1966, Havana hosted the First Conference of Solidarity with the Peoples of Africa, Asia, and Latin America, with the purpose of coordinating a common strategy to fight imperialism. Even before this date, Cuba had sent limited military aid to certain countries (such as Algeria and the Congo) in support of anticolonial groups. Also in the 1960s, Che Guevara had toured Africa to establish contacts and to offer assistance.[1]

During this stage, major foreign policy successes of the regime were the survival of the revolution and defeat of the U.S.-sponsored invasion at the Bay of Pigs. The combination of fending off U.S. hostility and securing Soviet assistance provided Cuba with an international coup. Jorge Domínguez (1980) analyzed "the management of success" in Cuban foreign policy to conclude:

> Above all, the Cuban revolutionary government wanted to survive after January 1959. For many regimes of the world, that might not necessarily be such an obvious foreign policy need, but it was by no means a foregone conclusion that the Cuban revolutionary regime would survive at any time between 1959 and 1962. The need for success was most pressing in the early years. (1)

Increasing Internationalism: 1968–1974

Cuba's revolutionary foreign policy entered its second stage in 1968, when the Soviets were able to pressure Cuba, successfully, to support the Moscow line regarding the appropriate road to revolution in Latin America, and when Castro agreed, albeit reluctantly, to endorse the Soviet invasion of Czechoslovakia. After 1968, idealism became tempered by pragmatism. The pressures on Castro were not only external. Within the country the economy had been steadily deteriorating, and the failure to reach Fidel's much-publicized projected ten-million-ton sugar harvest (in 1970) only underscored Cuba's need for Soviet economic assistance. In return for the latter, an "understanding" was reached with the Soviets regarding international policies, and Cuba's identification with the Soviets increased. As a result, Cuba accommodated to Soviet demands concerning its internal politics. By the early 1970s, Cuba had become integrated into the COMECON and had strengthened the Cuban Communist Party.

With military and economic aid guaranteed, the regime received the protection it needed to initiate global activism. In 1972, Castro traveled throughout Africa and Eastern Europe; in 1973, he gave a landmark speech in Algiers at the Non-Aligned Meeting. In this address, Castro condemned the notion of two imperialisms (that of the United States and the USSR), and he defended the thesis that the Soviet Union, as a socialist and, therefore, an anti-imperialist state, was a natural ally of the third world in the struggle for freedom and development.

It was during this period that Cuba increased its military missions to Africa and the Middle East, as well as the number of foreign socioeconomic assistance projects. By 1973, Cuban personnel were operating in Algeria, Angola, Equatorial Guinea, Iraq, Mozambique, Sierra Leone, Somalia, South Yemen, and Syria (Durch 1978: 34–74). In Latin America, Castro opted for conventional state-to-state relations, having abandoned, at least temporarily, the incitement to revolution. The island found diplomatic doors opening as several Latin American countries (Peru, Panama, Colombia, Venezuela, and Chile under Allende) reestablished relations with Havana.

At the same time, Cuba and the USSR decided that cooperation in the international arena could be mutually beneficial. Havana was assured of much-needed Soviet economic and military assistance as relations intensified between the two regimes. Furthermore, Fidel's personal dream of becoming a revolutionary figure of world stature was given added substance as Cuba was able to diversify its contacts around the globe. This development was also encouraging to a domestic nationalism that would have liked to reduce dependency on the Soviets.

In turn, the Soviets were compensated for assuming the financial burden of supporting, and the risks incumbent in having, an unpredictable ally, by the benefits produced through a lowered international visibility that reduced their risk of confrontation with other powers as well as the cost of potential failures. As the Angolan, Ethiopian, and Grenadian situations were to demonstrate, years later, Cuba could serve as a broker for Soviet influence and a proxy for the Soviet presence.[2]

Active Internationalism: 1975–1980

As the Soviet-Cuban connection grew stronger, the conditions Cuba needed to assume a more active international role were being met and the way paved to the third stage. In this sense, the 1968–1974 period served as a prelude for orchestration of the partners' diplomatic and military moves in several areas of the third world. In 1975, three events took place that marked a new era in Cuban foreign relations: (1) the First Congress of the Communist Party of Cuba was held, (2) OAS sanctions against Cuba came to an end, and (3) Cuban involvement in Angola escalated. As John McShane (1979) has pointed out, "the First Party Congress represented not the depersonalization of governance under Fidel, but rather a heightened concentration of power and responsibility on the *líder máximo* with respect to foreign policy" (3). Centralization of decision making is illustrated by the fact that Fidel holds the first position in the party, the Council of State, the Council of Ministers, and the Ministry of the Revolutionary Armed Forces (MINFAR).

With firm internal control, strong Soviet support, and the beginning of acceptance in the hemisphere, Castro embarked on a period of unprecedented foreign activism. The reinvigorated international role found expression in traditional state-to-state diplomacy, a leadership role in the third world movement, and in troop commitments abroad, specifically in Angola and Ethiopia. Cuba not only found new and old friends in the Caribbean (Panama, Mexico, Jamaica, Guyana, Trinidad-Tobago, and later Grenada) but also cultivated allies in the Middle East, Africa, and Europe. In 1977, Fidel made a successful tour of those continents. Two years later, in 1979, Cuba, as leader of the Non-Aligned Movement, acted as host for the Sixth Conference of Non-Aligned Nations, held in Havana.

The overthrow of Salvador Allende in Chile (1973), who had been the first socialist in Latin America to be elected head of state, had a profound impact on the Cuban-Soviet alliance. Both Havana and Moscow interpreted Allende's fall in the same way: by claiming that it was impossible for a progressive group to reach power by means of the ballot. Castro's line of the 1960s, that violence was the correct strategy to follow in the "liberation" of the third world, appeared to be vindicated by the Chilean case. As a result, Soviet and Cuban views on revolution began to converge, eventually to be justified by the successful revolution in Nicaragua (1979). This ideological concert between Cuba and the Soviet Union made possible their future collaboration on military campaigns and brought the two countries closer together.

The best known of these collaborative efforts are Cuba's missions to Angola and Ethiopia, both of which have been extensively documented.[3] Since 1975, Havana has sent Cuban soldiers (up to thirty-six thousand, according to Castro) to back the Marxist Popular Movement for the Liberation of Angola (MPLA) in its fight against opposition groups. In Angola, Cuba provided the manpower while the Soviets furnished the weapons and logistical infrastructure. It was a massive operation that decided the outcome in favor of the MPLA's Agostinho Neto. In spite of the apparent triumph, Cuba incurred considerable costs, not only financial but human as well, and few, if any, long-term benefits.

In the Ethiopian-Somalian conflict, Cuba found itself in the embarrassing position of supporting first one, then the other, side in this struggle. In 1974, Cuba had established a military mission in Somalia, at which time it had supported that country's territorial claim against Ethiopia. When, in 1975, there came to power in Ethiopia a radical, pro-Soviet faction, led by Lieutenant Colonel Mengistu Haile Mariam, Cuba established relations with the new government. This sufficiently offended the Somalis that they retaliated by seeking support from the West. During a visit to the area in 1977, Castro attempted to mediate the conflict between Ethiopia and Somalia personally, but the effort failed and Somalia invaded the disputed region (the Ogaden) in July 1977. The following year, when the Ethiopian forces were on the verge of defeat in 1978, Cuban forces staged a counteroffensive. By April 1978, fifteen thousand Cuban soldiers were fighting in Ethiopia, using Soviet-provided weaponry and under Soviet command. Confronted by counterattack, the Somalis were forced to pull back and the war was subsequently decided in favor of Ethiopia.[4]

Despite their cost, the African campaigns had a positive symbolic impact on Cuba's international relations. Cuba was perceived, and perceived itself, as a global player of import, although that self-perception was a bit misguided due to the physical and material limitations of Cuba's power. Initially, the third world and the African nations responded favorably to Cuban involvement. Increasingly, however, African governments began to equate Cuban objectives with those of the Soviets, a realization that served to undermine Havana's professions of nonalignment (especially after Cuban approval of the invasion of Afghanistan). Nevertheless, the African wars raised the prestige and power of revolutionary Cuba (Domínguez 1978b: 97). At the same time, the African wars increased Cuba's leverage vis-à-vis Moscow.

As Cuba's value to the Kremlin became more apparent, Soviet military and economic aid to the island climbed to unprecedented levels. A five-year economic agreement, signed in 1976, provided for a 250 percent increase in trade between the two countries as compared with the previous five-year period. The accord also provided for the building of a nuclear power plant and a steel mill, as well as for the indexing of the price of Soviet crude oil to the price of Cuban sugar (Gonzalez 1977: 12). The Angolan and Ethiopian actions also carried internal political ramifications. First, changes in the state and party organs enhanced the power of hard-line Fidelistas at the expense of the pragmatists (the technocratic and managerial elite) (Gonzalez 1977: 6–10).[5] Second, and related to the prior point, the Revolutionary Armed Forces (Fuerzas Armadas Revolucionarias [FAR]) gained prominence and clout. Pleased with the FAR's accomplishments, Moscow rewarded it with modern weaponry. For U.S.-Cuban relations, however, Havana's expanded activism proved detrimental. The thaw, which had begun under Ford and continued under Carter, ended abruptly when Washington asked Havana to withdraw its troops from Africa and Cuba refused.

Restrained Internationalism: 1980–1990

The fourth stage of Cuban foreign policy, that of restrained activism (or "partial paralysis"),[6] began in 1980. In 1979, when Cuba officially sanctioned the Soviet invasion of Afghanistan, it damaged its nonaligned credentials with the third world. Cuba also followed the Soviet position on Kampuchea (Cambodia) during the debate in the 1979 General Assembly, another position incompatible with nonalignment. As a result, the nonaligned nations failed to support Cuba's bid to become the nonpermanent Latin American representative on the United Nations Security Council.

During this period, a few Latin American neighbors distanced themselves from Cuba when the Castro regime refused, on several occasions, to recognize the right of asylum.[7] The regime's isolation was made obvious when Mexico, responding to U.S. pressure, failed to invite Castro to the North–South Conference held in Cancun (in October 1981) to discuss the economic situation of the third world and its relations to the industrialized countries. Cuba's absence underlined the extent to which its influence with the third world had deteriorated.

Cuba's problems worsened with the inauguration of a Republican president in the White House. A staunch anticommunist, Ronald Reagan came to office determined to halt radical leftist regimes from proliferating in the U.S. backyard. Viewing national revolutions as part of the East–West conflict, the administration blamed Soviet-Cuban subversion for fomenting instability in Central America. To deal with this situation, the president adopted a hard-line policy toward Cuba, including flexing military muscle in the Caribbean Basin by funding the contras in Nicaragua, supplying aid to fight the Salvadoran guerrillas, and eventually invading Grenada, a close ally of Havana.

Although Cuba scored a major foreign policy success when the Sandinistas overthrew Anastasio Somoza and took power in Nicaragua (in 1979), for the most part it had been losing friends in the region. A wave of neoconservatism in the Caribbean washed away left-of-center governments in Jamaica, St. Vincent, St. Kitts-Nevis, Antigua, and St. Lucia. Cuban support for Argentina during the Falklands/Malvinas war improved relations between both countries, and, although Cuba had partially mended its fences with Venezuela, overall Havana's relations with its neighbors in the Americas were at a low point in the early 1980s. Relations with Colombia suffered due to Cuba's support for the M-19 guerrilla movement, and relations with Costa Rica suffered due to Cuba's treatment of political prisoners. Ties with Panama, Peru, and Ecuador weakened as democratic centrist regimes took office.

By the mid-1980s, Cuban foreign policy no longer reflected the activism of the preceding decade. Havana retreated to a wait-and-see posture and pursued conventional diplomacy. Certainly, the reversal in Grenada made the Cuban leadership aware of its limitations and affected Cuban international behavior. Following Grenada, Castro warned Nicaragua that Cuba would not be able to rescue the Sandinistas in the event of a U.S. military invasion.[8]

Grenada provoked internal repercussions as well, specifically within the FAR. The invasion chilled Cuban-Soviet ties for approximately a year and a half due to what Havana considered Moscow's detachment from the Grenadian crisis. It seems that Castro, under attack from leftist groups in the region for "abandoning" his allies to U.S. imperialism, criticized Soviet lack of support for revolutions. Implicitly, he may have been drawing parallels between the Grenadian situation and his own under like circumstances, questioning Soviet resolve to come to the aid of its friends (*Latin American Weekly Report*, June 29, 1984, 6).

After a series of foreign policy setbacks in the 1980s and an extended stay in Africa, Cuba began to reemphasize traditional means of furthering its international aims. These included a renewed effort at establishing, or repairing, state-to-state relations and organizing regional conferences on topics of widespread interest (i.e., the debt crisis). Retreating from the activism suggested by military ventures, Havana returned to the political arena by courting domestic Latin American political actors, such as organized labor and religious groups. In a pragmatic vein, Cuba attempted to develop connections with capitalist and oil-exporting countries that may one day prove to be sources for much-needed capital and markets. Vis-à-vis Washington, Castro continued to oscillate between overt antagonism and overtures for normalization, a seesaw pattern that continues.

Redefining Cuba's Role in the World (1990 to Present)

Superseding this restrained internationalism, there has been a "new internationalism" characterized by diplomatic initiatives on a variety of fronts (i.e., the debt crisis; antiglobalization, among other causes) and by an ideological flexibility that allows for the cultivation of newfound friends (i.e., liberation theology). The new internationalism was dictated by international factors, principally the breakdown of the USSR and the end of its preferential trade and aid regime toward Cuba. As a result, the Cuban economy declined about 40 to 45 percent in the early 1990s; with this Cuban internationalism had to be reduced. The improved relationship between the superpowers and Gorbachev's "new thinking" made possible the end of key regional conflicts and codetermined Cuba's post-1990 strategy. The new internationalism of what on the island became known as the Special Period in Times of Peace is a four-dimensional one: (1) it casts Fidel Castro in the role of elder statesman; (2) it attempts to place Cuba in the position of power broker, in a new initiative to recapture worldwide influence; (3) it promotes Cuban economic selective integration in the world economy (through foreign investment, trade arrangements, and tourism, mainly) and in regional associations (the Caribbean Common Market [CARICOM], particularly); and (4) it resorts to international forums and to social movements, not only to state-to-state diplomacy as the locus of action in favor of "progressive" causes and the arena for influence. The new internationalism does not repudiate Havana's commitment to revolutionary change, but it does seek to extend diplomatic influence abroad without incurring high risks or costs for the island.

Therefore, statesmanship, moderation, and expansion of socioeconomic ties have become salient features of the island's international behavior. This is not to say that such an approach was absent from Cuban foreign policy in the past. Not at all. In fact, pragmatism has always been present to some degree. The only change has been one of emphasis, dictated by the material reality of economic decline and the structural change in the international environment.

THE MODEL OF CUBAN FOREIGN POLICY[9]

Clearly, the most dramatic aspects of Cuba's foreign policy, the military initiatives carried out in Angola (1975) and Ethiopia (1977), as well as the island's extensive program of development aid to dozens of third world countries, opened a chapter in the island's diplomatic history. That is why one can argue that in 1975, Cuba broke the mold in which small, underdeveloped states had been cast in international affairs. By increasing its contacts with the rest of the world and becoming a socioeconomic and a military powerhouse, Cuba created and epitomized a would-be new model for the weaker and the poorer countries: that of a miniature world power (an apparent oxymoron). What factors explain Cuba's "new role" in world politics? What are the elements of the Cuban prototype after 1959 (particularly between 1975 and 1990)? And, finally, how different is this model from the one pursued in the republic?

The coexistence and interaction of four factors have determined Cuba's foreign policy since 1959: charismatic leadership and ideology, the state and the domestic political system, connection to a major external source of power, and the regional and international context. First, we will discuss each of these four factors, how they interrelate, and how they have come together to bring about Cuba's international behavior. Second, we will assess the benefits, costs, and constraints that revolutionary internationalism places on Cuba. In concluding, we will evaluate the suitability of the model for other third world states.

Charismatic Leadership and Ideology

Fidel Castro has been the driving force behind the Cuban revolution. His leadership style and his ideology have defined the nature of the regime and its foreign policy. Among his other titles, Castro is the first secretary of the Cuban Communist Party (CCP) and the *comandante en jefe* (commander in chief) of the Revolutionary Armed Forces. Above all, he is the *líder máximo*. In spite of the process of revolutionary institutionalization of the 1970s, state and party organs continue to be subordinated to him. In Cuba, ultimate power rests with Castro, for not only is he in control of the state, but he enjoys the admiration of the mass of the Cuban people. His style is that of a charismatic leader. Through foreign policy, Castro has internationalized his charisma.

Cuba's foreign policy reflects Castro's ideology (and that ideology, as explained later, resonates with characteristic features of Cuban political culture). Although the regime's official ideology is Marxist-Leninism, Castroism is a distinct set of beliefs extrapolated from observable behavior rather than from government pronouncements. Castroism is characterized by centralization of state power in the líder máximo, social change through revolution, militarization of society, controlled social participation through mass organizations, anti-Americanism, and nationalism. Marxist-Leninism and Castroism share points in common, such as centralization of authority, but differ on other points, such as personalism.

Castroism is the key to unlocking the relationship between the domestic political system and foreign policy in post-1959 Cuba. Castro's ideology had to be put into practice internally before he could undertake major external campaigns. The domestic system, transformed according to Castroism, laid the foundation for revolutionary internationalism. The cardinal points of the líder máximo's worldview—anti-Americanism and revolutionary change through armed struggle—guide Cuba's actions in the world. Ideological zeal, however, has not always driven Havana. The regime calculates cost/benefit factors before implementing policies. Therefore, ideology by itself does not explain Cuba's foreign policy. Pragmatic conditions were in place before Cuba assumed the role of a mini world power. In brief, Cuba's international strategy is ideological, but when necessary, its tactics are pragmatic.

The State and the Domestic Political System

Since the triumph of the revolution, foreign policy has been intimately tied to domestic matters. U.S. support for the dictatorship of Fulgencio Batista coupled with Washington's animosity toward reformist populism in Latin America was the first obstacle the *guerrilleros* had to surmount to reach and to stay in power. Armed domestic insurgency and U.S. hostility aggravated the situation during the first years of revolutionary rule. Winning, assuming, and consolidating power were all internal and external successes for the regime.

Castro's ideal foreign policy required two domestic developments: the consolidation of power under his command, and a strong, well-equipped, and loyal military apparatus that would include paramilitary organizations and a large pool of ready reservists. The two prerequisites went hand in hand.

The First Congress of the CCP (1975) secured Castro's position as head of the state, the party, and the armed forces. At the same time, the congress continued the institutionalization of the revolution by strengthening fledgling state- and party-directed mass institutions through which popular participation was to be channeled. Loyal *Fidelistas* remained perched at the top of the power structure. By 1975, the year of the first major deployment of troops in Africa, the regime faced no overt internal threats (the opposition either sought exile or was eliminated in some way), the ideological training of the population and of the armed forces was well under way, and mechanisms of state supervision, such as the neighborhood Committees for the Defense of the Revolution (Comités de Defensa de la Revolución [CDRs]), reached all levels of society. Popular organizations, working as regime sustainers, would serve as recruiting grounds for internationalist duty, as transmission belts for the government's foreign policy programs, and as rallying points of support for foreign initiatives. By 1975, external threats had died down as well. The Bay of Pigs invasion (1961) had failed, and the Kennedy–Khrushchev Agreements, which ended the October 1962 missile crisis, safeguarded the island from U.S.-backed invasions.

By 1975, the Revolutionary Armed Forces had become the most modern and best-supplied army in Latin America. One of the first steps Castro took to consolidate his power and to reorganize the state was to forge a national military establishment out of the rebel army. Armed forces were needed to defend the revolution from its internal and external enemies, without rocking the regime. The loyalty of the military was of paramount importance. It was secured by placing Fidelistas in positions of command (i.e., Raul Castro was appointed minister of the armed forces); by creating an intelligence network capable of detecting unrest, dissent, and/or factionalism; and by providing ideological training to the rank and file.

The Soviet Union played a vital role in the development and professionalization of the Revolutionary Armed Forces. Moscow not only offered a model of military organization and ideological education but eventually supplied the weaponry that gave Cuba an offensive capacity. Soviet commitment to the Revolutionary Armed Forces was apparent since the early 1960s. After Havana endorsed the Soviet invasion of Czechoslovakia in 1968 and abandoned its policy of support of armed revolution in Latin America, the way was paved for a Cuba–USSR rapprochement after a period of tension. As a result, the USSR strengthened the Cuban armed forces by providing advanced military equipment. During the early 1970s, Castro, with Soviet input, tailored the Revolutionary Armed Forces for international campaigns.

At another level, domestic transformations facilitated the pursuit of internationalism. Socioeconomic changes, such as expansion of education and technical training for the population, made possible foreign developmental assistance, especially in terms of the export of personnel. Cuba sent thousands of workers to dozens of less developed countries each year, in fields ranging from construction to health. This is a significant dimension of Cuba's relations with other nations, not only quantitatively but qualitatively as well. Havana gained political goodwill and leverage in other areas of the world as a result of its paid and nonpaid foreign assistance programs.

Connection to an International Source of Power

Since the first days of the Cuban revolution, the political will to act as a great power in international relations was present in the form of Castroism. However, political reality and physical resources constrained Cuba. In rhetoric, as well as in aspirations, revolutionary foreign policy was maximalist. (One of the leaders of the revolution, Ernesto "Che" Guevara, promised many more Vietnams.) In practice, it was minimalist; it aimed for the survival of the regime and offered token assistance to national liberation groups.

(Guevara himself was killed in the jungles of Bolivia while trying to incite the *campesinos* to revolt.) Cuba, like most third world countries, was bound by its geographic and material limitations. This was the situation until 1975. By then, Castro had matched political will to political muscle. What made this development possible?

The connection to a source of economic and military strength made possible Cuba's great power aspirations. The island's military internationalism in Africa was a product of partnership with the USSR. The Soviets not only provided weaponry and logistical support; they also gave their approval to the campaigns. In Angola, Moscow stood behind Havana. In Ethiopia, deployment of Cuban troops was coordinated with the Soviets. In fact, Cuban troops served under Soviet command. Cuba could not have acted without the USSR's blessing or against the USSR's wishes. The costs and the risks of doing so would have been very high, for Havana would have had to face possible retaliation from both superpowers.

Cuba's actions, however, were not exclusively those of a proxy. Cuban-Soviet interaction in the international arena is best described as one of a convergence of interests and a relative mutuality of influence. Military internationalism brought Cuba tangible rewards from the Soviet Union. After 1975, Soviet aid to the island quadrupled. Moreover, it is likely that Havana's leverage in Moscow increased as a result of Cuba's role in Africa. For the Soviets, Cuba became a valuable power broker and an ally in the third world.

The Regional and International Context

Conditions in other countries and the regional and international context act either as a pull toward or as a push away from foreign involvement. These two opposing forces help to determine the type and the depth of Cuba's policy toward other nations. While the pull force sets the stage for success by guaranteeing a favorable reaction to Cuba's overtures, the push force increases risks and anticipates a negative or conflicting response from the target country and/or global powers.

The impact of the regional and international context on Cuban foreign policy was evident during the 1975–1979 period, the zenith of Cuba's internationalism, and during the following period, 1980 to the present, when external events restrained the island's activities abroad. One of the factors that pulled Cuba into Angola and Ethiopia, in addition to the ones mentioned previously, was the political climate in the United States. Suffering from the post-Watergate and post-Vietnam syndrome, the United States was not likely to respond forcefully to Cuba's military internationalism. Cuba realized this and took advantage of it.

Revolutionary ferment in other areas of the world, including the Caribbean and Central America, contributed to Havana's activism. Furthermore,

Moscow's willingness to push détente to its limits gave Havana a green light in the world.

Contrary to the favorable circumstances of the mid-1970s, events since the 1980s increased the risks of and the capability to pursue a revolutionary foreign policy. Several factors constrained activism and pushed back Cuba's expanding internationalism, but the principal one was Gorbachev's new foreign policy (which supported the end of regional crisis and the reduction of Cold War tension) and later the eventual demise of the Soviet Union and the communist bloc. With the break up of the USSR, Cuba lost its source of economic and military support that facilitated its activities abroad.

CONCLUSION

How exceptional is Cuban foreign policy? While it responds to the same factors that determine the foreign actions of other countries and therefore is not exceptional at all, the island's foreign policy has been rather unique. But its exceptionality is not only due to the fact that Cuba carried international military campaigns thousands of miles away from its shores. Cuban exceptionalism is also due to political cultural factors, which are reflected in the language and practice of foreign policy from 1902 onward, not exclusively post-1959. The national style, the will to grandeur, is a tradition in the island's foreign policy political culture that bridges the divide between pre- and post-1959. The will to grandeur with its tendency "to talk big" in pre-1959 Cuba later found a way to "act big" in 1975 due to a combination of factors, not least of which was the material assistance of the Soviet Union and the ideology of Castroism and the official norm of proletarian internationalism. Talking big was part and parcel of acting big. Talking big introduced the themes of nationalism, activism, international liberal reformism, and moralism into the island's foreign policy practice quite early in the republic. Talking big later served as one impetus for revolutionary activities abroad. The will to grandeur carried cultural codes of long genealogy (from Martí's latinoamericanism to the international democratic internationalism of the Autenticos and the Ortodoxos). These norms resonate as the cornerstone of much of the revolution's foreign policy behavior, if in a radical reinterpretation: From reformist to radical globalism was not an insurmountable stretch once the revolution took hold. The combination of nationalism, socially progressive agendas, and moralism with a hyperrhetorical flair were distinctive characteristics of pre- and post-1959 foreign policy practice. Even under U.S. hegemony during the republic, Cuban governments found ways of standing up to the United States and assuming positions not favored by Washington. (Similarly, the Cuban government collided with the Soviets.) An ample margin of autonomy, more ample than usually recognized, existed pre-1959. Confrontation with the United States and conflict of interest and values predated the advent of the revolution. So did anti–status quo postures and assertiveness in world organizations. The Cuban revolution merely radicalized an already-existing social global conscience among sectors of the elite and the society. Without that republican legacy, it is hard to imagine that the Cuban government would have had the norms and the practical experience to behave the way it has on the global stage. From this vantage point, political culture was as decisive as other factors in tandem (individual and structural, domestic and international, material and ideational) to codetermine Cuba's talking and acting big.

DISCUSSION QUESTIONS

1. According to the author, what additional factor should be included in the levels of analysis framework?
2. Identify and explain several factors of change in Cuba's foreign policy over time.
3. Identify and discuss at least one factor of continuity in Cuba's foreign policy from 1902 to the present.

NOTES

1. For a general account of this period, see Domínguez (1978b).
2. Jorge Domínguez holds this view.
3. For an overall assessment, see Mesa-Lago and Belkin (1982).
4. For more information, see Durch (1978) and Mesa-Lago and Belkin (1982).
5. See also Suchlicki (1984).
6. Also a rubric coined by Furtak (1983: 465).
7. Denial of asylum rights to Cubans who sought, in the late 1970s and early 1980s, entrance to the embassies of Costa Rica, Peru, and Venezuela damaged, at least temporarily, the relations of these countries with Havana.
8. This position is changing due to Cuba's increased military assistance to Nicaragua.
9. Based on Fernández (1987).

6

The Dominican Republic

From Nationalism to Globalism

Anthony P. Spanakos and Howard J. Wiarda

The foreign policy of any country is determined largely by representations of national interest and by the possibilities and constraints that form policy to further said interest. Rosenau's (1966) pioneering article on foreign policy located such possibilities and constraints as existing at the individual, governmental, societal, and systemic levels. Building on Rosenau's work, this chapter will focus on how much of the change and continuity in Dominican foreign policy can be traced to systemic and individual variables.

This chapter examines the change and continuity in Dominican foreign policy in the wake of the Cold War, and as the Dominican Republic experienced change in leadership from traditional nationalist politics to a more internationalist and globalist foreign policy. This has allowed for increased policy consensus between the Dominican Republic and the United States, improved relations with other countries, and increased Dominican activity in multilateral organizations. The one area of Dominican foreign policy that has seen the least change has been that of Dominican-Haitian relations, where deep-seated societal prejudices still predominate. Changes in leadership and in the international system are what best explain contemporary Dominican foreign policy, although societal perceptions, particularly regarding policy toward Haitians and sovereignty, explains resistance to change.

SYSTEMIC AND INDIVIDUAL CHANGE: FROM BALAGUER TO FERNÁNDEZ

The transition from a relatively closed authoritarian political system and a highly nationalized economy to a more open political system and a more liberal economy was not unique to the Dominican Republic. The loosening of international relations as the Cold War began to thaw, the emphasis of the Carter and subsequent administrations on democracy and human rights, the shift in the international left to a position that was supportive of democracy, and the increased hegemony of liberal economics over Keyneseanism (and import substitution industrialization) encouraged such liberalization. Such events opened possibilities that were ignored, defied, or exploited by leaders in "dependent" countries. The next five sections will analyze especially how Presidents Balaguer and Fernández reacted to such possibilities and to what extent the perceptions of Dominican national security changed.

From Isolationism to Internationalism

The Cold War between the United States and its allies and the Soviet Union and its allies was effective in providing a rigid ordering to the postwar international system. Although many countries were nonaligned, geopolitics had an air of inevitability, particularly for developing countries. Being in the U.S. "backyard" meant that significant incentives and disincentives were used by the United States to support governments in Latin America that shared U.S. conceptions of national security. Joaquín Balaguer flourished in this international environment since he was able to play to both domestic and international groups, satisfying the former by nationalist policies and economics and the latter by his staunch anticommunist position and by repressing the left. The end of the Cold War did not immediately affect much of official Dominican foreign policy since the isolationist, nationalist Balaguer remained in power until 1996, although changes occurred in the area of economics (see the later section on economics). Leonel Fernández, however, seized the opportunities presented by the new international environment to improve Dominican participation in multilateral organizations and in economic integration and free trade initiatives.

During the Cold War, not only could the Dominican political and economic systems be described as closed, but so could the international system. International organizations, such as the United Nations, were largely seen by developing countries as forums for debates and showdowns between the chief protagonists of the Cold War or their immediate allies. Legitimacy was even more lacking in regional organizations such as the Organization of American States (OAS) where there were disparities in power between one superpower and the rest of the countries. Since U.S. foreign policy was preoccupied with East–West conflict, which had little relevance to many Latin American countries, the OAS focused on themes that were more relevant to the United States than to the other states. The Dominican Republic especially considered the OAS an institutional façade for U.S. unilateralism largely because it was officially an OAS force that invaded the Dominican

Republic in 1965 to end the civil war and allow Balaguer to become president (Espinal 2000: 361).

The perception of regional and international organizations as groups who would intervene and erode Dominican sovereignty dominated Balaguer's conception of foreign policy, which was largely isolationist and passive. Domestic political and economic crises as well as the scarcity of international alternatives (see the section on economics) led to the Balaguer government's adoption of a stabilization program in 1990. The program, its inevitability and its design, reflected considerable changes in the international system, particularly the increased importance of nongovernmental actors in international affairs and the global consensus surrounding the neoclassical economic model. Balaguer resented the international influence; however, the economic turnaround was immediate, and Balaguer's administration passed more reform from 1991 to 1993. International concerns about human rights violations in Haiti and the Dominican government's role in supporting the Haitian military government, however, was seen largely as interference by Balaguer. Sovereignty remained a call word for Balaguer to defend human rights violations. The sanction/prevention of smuggling through the Dominican-Haitian border to circumvent the international embargo against the Haitian government was cleverly used by Balaguer to allow international observers to limit their pressure on the Dominican president after an especially dubious electoral victory in 1994.

The foreign policy of the U.S.-educated Leonel Fernández, who succeeded Balaguer in 1996, represented a significant change. As opposed to the isolationism and the defensive calls to sovereignty echoed by Balaguer, Fernández understood the end of the Cold War as opening considerable opportunities to the Dominican Republic. Such opportunities, however, required a more open political and economic system as well as an internationalist foreign policy. Former Dominican ambassador to the OAS Flavio Darío Espinal (2000) writes, "President Leonel Fernández defined as one of his fundamental priorities to articulate and put into practice a new foreign policy with the goal of converting the country into a dynamic and relevant actor in the changing and complex world of today" (359).

The end of the Cold War led to two major changes in the global arena: a new conception of security and the empowerment of multilateral institutions, largely to address this new conception of security. Security challenges were conceived less in national terms, such as geopolitics, military threat, and nuclear stockpiling, and more in terms of transnational issues, such as immigration, poverty, drug trafficking, corruption, democracy, and the environment. As Espinal (2000: 365) argues because such problems "cannot be seen as isolated by each of the countries," they require concerted effort, which tends to highlight the importance of multilateral institutions. Former foreign minister Eduardo Latorre explains, "'only the combined action of the countries of the Hemisphere could assure the realization of realistic, verifiable . . . goals in the strict respect of international norms of law' " (in Espinal, 2000: 376).

The opportunities opened by the end of the Cold War were not lost on Leonel Fernández, who pursued a vigorous foreign policy. Dominican membership in multilateral organizations and in free trade initiatives increased considerably. The Dominican Republic also hosted summits of the Central American presidents, the heads of state, and governments of the Association of Caribbean States and the Group of Africa, Caribbean, and the Pacific. Participation and leadership in such organizations show both Dominican commitment to international engagement and the effort to build south–south ties, to limit dependence on the United States. Such activities were certainly more possible due to U.S. security following the "victory" in the Cold War. This is particularly true of U.S. tolerance of an official visit of Fidel Castro in 1998 and the reestablishment of diplomatic relations between the Dominican Republic and Cuba in 1999.

The United States could hardly use fear of socialism as a motive for constraining Dominican relations with Cuba, since President Fernández actively pursued free trade. His involvement and membership in the Caribbean Basin Initiative (CBI) and the Central American Common Market (CACM) established his position as an economic liberal, and, in recognition of that, in May 2000, the Dominican Republic received textile parity with the North American Free Trade Agreement (NAFTA) countries. Similarly, on his many international trips, to the United States and elsewhere, Fernández emphasized how the Dominican Republic was an excellent location for investment, and he guaranteed the full repatriation of profits for foreigners.

Points of Conflict with the United States: Drugs and Immigration

Relations with the United States have improved in recent years for a variety of reasons. The collapse of the Cold War and a change in leadership in both countries have engendered more of a sense of partnership between the two countries, which has eroded the more traditional presentation of the Other as threat. Additionally, and perhaps more important, the presence of Dominicans living in the United States and the political and economic opening of the Dominican Republic has made the United States, U.S. foreign policy goals, and national security goals more familiar. With one-eighth of Dominicans living in the United States, the traditional view of the United States as an interventionist Other has been replaced by an increasingly hybrid picture. The presence of Dominicans in the United States has led to new conflicts between the United States and the Dominican Republic, primarily over immigration and drug trafficking. The nature of these conflicts, as opposed to issues in previous eras, is based on the very familiarity and proximity that has developed in the last twenty years.

Immigration from the Dominican Republic to the United States prior to the assassination of Trujillo was very limited due to strict control by the Dominican government and U.S. immigration law that issued quotas for immigration that limited the number of visas available for small countries like the Dominican Republic. Between 1961 and 1963, with the political turbulence and violence that followed the assassination of Trujillo, the number of visas offered to Dominicans quadrupled (Wucker 1999: 216). An additional boost to immigration came with the passing of the Hart–Celler Immigration Reform Act, which loosened country quotas and made it easier for immigrants in the United States to bring family members to the United States. Even still, between 1965 and 1969, an average of 8,156 Dominicans entered the United States as legally documented immigrants (Graham and Hartlyn 1996: 135). With political conflict in the Dominican Republic, the United States and the Dominican government saw immigration as an escape valve to prevent further instability.

By the 1980s, with the considerable worsening of economic conditions in the Dominican Republic and a generation of Dominicans living in the United States, the average number of immigrants was more than fifteen thousand, and 4 percent of all immigrants to the United States were Dominican (Vega 1996: 36). Most of these Dominicans settled in cities where there was already a Dominican population, such as the Washington Heights section of New York and Lawrence, Massachusetts. Dominican immigration was especially considerable at the local level as some 17 percent of immigrants to New York were from the Dominican Republic, the largest percentage for any country.

By 1992, there were one million Dominicans living in the United States, and an average of forty thousand Dominicans were entering the country legally. By 1996, the Dominican community in the United States sent approximately U.S.$1 billion in remittances to family and friends in the Dominican Republic. Dominicans in the United States became increasingly involved in Dominican politics, particularly with Fernández's appointment of Bernardo Vega as Dominican ambassador to the United States. Vega (1996: 21), an economist who was educated in the United States, had urged Dominicans to be more than "absent citizens" in his newspaper column in 1992. With a keen understanding of the importance of U.S. domestic politics in determining U.S. policies and the role that Dominicans in the United States could play in Dominican politics, Vega encouraged Dominicans living in the United States to become active in U.S. politics. Simultaneously, he encouraged the growth of the local affiliates of Dominican parties that had sprung up in the Dominican diaspora.

In 1990, only 18 percent of Dominicans living in the United States had become citizens. There was a good deal of reluctance among Dominicans to become naturalized since they did not want to lose their Dominican citizenship, primarily because most Dominicans maintained the intention of some day returning to the Dominican Republic. Those numbers have since improved following the 1994 constitutional change that allowed dual citizenship and with Vega's organizational efforts (Wucker 1999: 225). Since then, Dominicans in the United States have become increasingly important in New York City politics, although there are still few elected Dominican officials, and in Dominican politics, where the Dominican diaspora is a major source of finance for political parties, especially the Liberal Democratic Party (PLD) and the Dominican Revolutionary Party (PRD).

This is not to say that the subject of Dominican immigration is entirely pacific. As would be expected, increased immigration has led to an increase in undocumented immigration, which in turn has led to conflict between the two countries. The U.S. government has always been defensive about its borders, particularly when concerning non-European immigrants. Although Dominican immigrants do not have the stigma that has been placed on Haitian immigrants (articles in New York papers sensationalized the presence of HIV in Haiti), undocumented Dominican immigrants are perceived as "illegal" and threatening. In 1991, more than 3,500 Dominicans were intercepted and returned to the Dominican Republic. The number of undocumented Dominican immigrants is much higher than such a figure would suggest since so many Dominicans who come to the United States under tourist and student visas often overstay their visas.

Although only a minority of Dominicans living in the United States are involved in the drug trade, it is a very visible minority. Dominican participation in drug trafficking has increased along with Dominican immigration to the United States, leading to stereotyping in the Dominican diaspora and problematic relations with local and federal law enforcement agents. The town of San Francisco de Macorís, with a population of three hundred thousand, is the home of many of the Dominicans involved in the drug trade. In 1991 alone, the U.S. government sent 160 Dominicans killed in the drug war to San Francisco to be buried (Graham and Hartlyn 1996: 140).

President Fernández shared an interest in reducing drug trafficking, and, after considerable negotiation, he allowed for some extradition and invited New York City police officers to help train Dominican police, particularly the National Directorate for the Control of Drugs (DNCD). The Dominican Republic also hosted a meeting of drug enforcement agencies of twenty-six nations and territories that set out a comprehensive plan for drug enforcement in the Caribbean. The choice of Santo Domingo as the "Northern Command" for the operation highlights both the importance of the Dominican Republic in the drug trade as well as the Dominican government's willingness to combat it. Dominican participation in such an operation not only is necessary for success but also shows increased Dominican security about its sovereignty.

Democracy—Toward Free and Fair Elections

The shift in U.S. foreign policy that began with Jimmy Carter's highlighting of human rights and the later easing of Cold War tensions led to more political space for less traditional security concerns—such as democracy and immigration—and for less traditional actors, such as nongovernmental organizations (NGOs). There was also a marked shift in terms of the international left when it committed itself to elections and forsook socialist one party states. These conditions, in addition to the global repudiation of authoritarianism, contributed to making the global climate more hospitable to democracy. In the Dominican Republic, the shift from the *caudillo* Balaguer to the more liberal Fernández was also significant since Balaguer represented an authoritarian leader who was expected to ignore the very checks and balances that had been carefully written into the Dominican constitution. The shift to a president like Fernández, who was limited by the congress and who needed to seek partners in coalition, encouraged democratization, even if it made many reforms less possible.

U.S. support for democracy in the Dominican Republic has come largely as pressure applied by NGOs. This has led to some strains in U.S.-Dominican relations as Dominican governments have simultaneously supported the idea of NGOs, civil society, and electoral observation yet denounced such involvement as encroachment on its sovereignty when it was politically expedient. Dominican democracy suffers from many flaws, but perhaps the most obvious and the ones that have received the most attention, particularly in the international community, have been electoral irregularities and the treatment of Haitian laborers (discussed in the next section).

It would not be an exaggeration to report that every electoral contest between 1966 and 1996 has been denounced as fraudulent by the losing party, although not all have been. Not surprisingly, despite compulsory voting, abstention rates increased between 1978 and 1990, and only 1994 showed a decline in abstention (Hartlyn 1988: 231). The 1996 and 2000 presidential elections and the 1998 municipal elections were largely free of allegations of fraud and represented a significant improvement. This improvement was both a result of technical and financial assistance from international groups, as well as the observation by domestic and international groups.

Prior to the 1990 elections, PLD presidential candidate Juan Bosch invited former U.S. president Jimmy Carter to observe the elections. Carter accepted when he received a letter of invitation from the president of the Electoral Board (JCE), Froilán Tavárez (Espinal 1998: 98). Despite a remarkably close vote,[1] the Carter delegation found no evidence of fraud and made two reports to the Dominican people indicating such findings. Two months after the election, Balaguer was declared the victor, and Tavárez accused Carter of interfering with Dominican politics.

Following the numerous allegations and the lack of legitimacy accorded to the electoral results, there was a mandate for reform. The Electoral Board was expanded and made less partisan; however, allegations of politicization of JCE members surfaced prior to the 1994 elections. The Dominican elections of 1994 were especially important, not only because the last elections had been somewhat dubious but because an international embargo on Haiti's military government gave the Dominican elections a higher profile in the international community. Balaguer's reluctance to cut down on cross-border trade, which weakened the effects of the embargo, led to increased pressure from the United States. U.S. ambassador Robert Pastorino declared that the United States wanted to see free elections, and the U.S. Agency for International Development (USAID) and the International Foundation for Electoral Studies (IFES) invested considerable technical and financial assistance to improve the electoral process (U.S.$2.1 million) (Espinal 1998: 101; National Democratic Institute [NDI], August 15, 1994: 2).

Despite, or perhaps because of, the extra attention awarded the 1994 election, the JCE "delayed issuing an invitation to international delegations, insisting that it was not necessary to invite hundreds of international observers and that the Board itself should retain control of the electoral process" (Espinal 1998: 102). Delegations from the OAS, NDI, Center for Electoral Promotion and Assistance (CAPEL), IFES, and the Socialist International nevertheless observed the elections. The NDI delegation, led by former U.S. congressman Stephen Solarz, noted the presence of two different voting lists (NDI, August 15, 1994). Although the polls were allowed to stay open an extra three hours, the announcement that voting hours were to be extended was not made until after the polls officially closed.

The JCE created a Verification Commission whose final report estimated that forty-five thousand voters were disenfranchised in the election. The Verification Commission review approximated that 75 percent of those would have been for the PRD candidate, who officially lost by 22,281 votes (Ferguson 1994: 11; also Espinal 1994: 11). Despite the findings of the Verification Commission, the JCE ignored the results and declared Balaguer president. Domestic protests and international pressure led to a surprising "Pact for Democracy" negotiated between Dominican leaders and international representatives. The final agreement led to legislation preventing immediate reelection, the shortening of the actual presidential term of Balaguer from four to two years, and a congressional amendment allowing Dominicans overseas to vote.

The contestation of the electoral results led to more reform of the JCE, as it had four years earlier.[2] In addition, to reform of the JCE, increased exposure to foreign observers and experience observing elections abroad contributed to the formation of the Red Ciuduadania de Observadores Electoral (RED), a Dominican NGO that played a valuable role in electoral observation in the 1996 elections. Some controversy surrounded the RED since it was seen as having a bias in favor of the PRD.

The JCE invited a delegation of the NDI to observe the 1996 presidential elections. This delegation was led by Belisario Betancur and Ramón León Carpio, former presidents of Colombia and Guatemala, respectively. A survey by Rumbo-Gallup found that "fifty-four percent of Dominicans . . . thought that international and national observers should monitor the 1996 election; another 21 percent felt there should be only national observers" (Espinal 1998: 109). Support for international observers, despite the possible infringement on "sovereignty," was thus considerable. Clearly Dominicans considered the threat of another electoral crisis greater than the loss of sovereignty that international observation would engender. That the delegation was led by Latin Americans probably made such observation more palatable still.

It is not coincidental that the increased sense of security Dominicans felt regarding their sovereignty in 1996 corresponded with an election that did not feature Balaguer as a candidate. Both Fernández and Peña Gómez were much more comfortable with, and indeed welcomed, the presence of foreign observers. Additionally, Dominican national politics was less constrained since the U.S.-led blockade of Haiti had ended in 1994 with the return of Jean Bertrand Aristide to power.

The 1998 municipal elections and the presidential elections of 2000 were regarded as free. Some irregularities appeared, but they were minimal compared to previous elections. Concern emerged in 2000 since the PRD-dominated senate nominated members of the JCE who were largely thought to be biased toward the PRD (NDI, May 18, 2000). Nevertheless, Dominican elections are much more fair and free than they were six years ago. Even Balaguer's presence as a candidate in the 2000 election did not retard the progress that had occurred. International observers were invited for both elections, and the reports prepared by international observers and the activity of RED were accepted and did not receive the kind of challenge that they had in previous elections.

The improved administration of elections is illustrative of the more general improvements in Dominican democracy. They are the result of pressure from new actors in domestic and international politics—NGOs, whose role has been given increased importance due to changes in the international system, a new vision of U.S. security, and a diminished fear of intervention on the part of Dominican leaders. In this last area, the shift in leadership from Balaguer to Fernández and Peña Gómez has been essential. Despite the progress in Dominican democracy, there is still considerable room for further improvements. Institutions remain weak, the legal system is not applied equally to all citizens, and accountability remains low (Spanakos 2000). The accountability of the police is especially troubling, particularly in terms of its encounters with Haitian laborers living in the Dominican Republic.

Haiti—Human Rights Violations

One of the areas experiencing the least movement in terms of Dominican foreign and domestic policy has been the conditions of Haitian migrants. A shift from a racist president, Balaguer, who considers Haiti to represent a perpetual threat to Dominican national identity, to a more liberal president, Fernández, made some improvement in the relations between the two countries. However, human rights violations against Haitian migrants and laborers continue. Here, changes at the individual level and particularly the increasing openness of the political regime have not improved the situation, since it is rooted in the depiction of Haitian identity in Dominican political culture.

Despite the fact that Dominicans and Haitians generally coexist with little violence, there is a very clear hierarchical ordering to society that not only identifies Haitians at the lowest rung of the social pyramid but associates dark skin with all of the negative discourses implied by Haitian identity (Spanakos 2000). The fault lines that underlie Dominican-Haitian relations are more apparent in police activity and in periodic political posturing, which often leads to deportation of Haitian workers. The violation of Haitian human rights by police officers and the lack of transparency and lawful restraint used during deportation is legitimized by Dominican political culture. In a recent survey, 66.43 percent of the Dominicans believed that "Haitians bring problems to the country" (Brea et al. 1995: 227), and there is something of an inevitability in such a response because Haitians must bring problems—crime, disease, misery—into the country. After all, the representation of "Haiti/ans" correlates perfectly with any problems the Dominican Republic may suffer; even if such problems are domestic in origin, they become projected unto the outsider.

Balaguer (1985) writes, "Contact with the negro has contributed, without a doubt, to the relaxing of our public customs," and this has resulted in "the progressive ethnic decadence of the Dominican population" (45). He also explains that the difference between Dominicans and Haitians is not exclusively cultural but also biological, writing that "[t]he excess of population in Haiti constitutes . . . an increasing threat to the Dominican Republic. That is for a biological reason: the black abandoned to his instincts and without the reserve that a level of relatively elevated life imposes in all countries to reproduction, he multiplies almost in a similar way to a certain species of vegetables" (37).

Balaguer's use of the text of *Haitianidad* (Haitian identity) is not purely a literary one, since as president he used the equivocal status of Haitians to boost his role as a national protector and father figure. When the Dominican government decides to crack down on Haitians, those who are without papers are deported regardless of their place of birth. Police are reported to consistently tear up the official documents of legal Haitian residents, who are sometimes deported. In June 1991, Balaguer decreed that Haitian immigrants under the age of sixteen and over sixty be expelled from the country.[3]

There were no government investigations into the military's activity or any preventative measures installed to avoid future repetitions of such incidents. Pressure from nongovernmental and transnational organizations was rebuffed by Balaguer, who said that he had "the right to treat the Haitians the same way as the United States or Puerto Rico treat Dominicans" (in Ferguson 1992: 89). Human Rights Watch urged the U.S. Congress to review the conditions of Haitian laborers and to levy appropriate sanctions on the Dominican Republic because of its unwillingness to address these conditions (Vega 1996: 21).

Although some may find such blatant prejudicial politics out of place in a democracy, William Connolly (1991) argues that "[e]lectoral politics contains powerful pressures to become a closed circuit for the dogmatization of identity through the translation of difference into threat and threat into energy for the dogmatization of identity" (210). Since elections offer an opportunity to consider national identity, policies, and the future of the nation, important decisions need to be made as to who should be included and excluded. Balaguer cleverly identified former PRD presidential candidate José Francisco Peña Gómez as Haitian and Other, relying on classist, racist, and xenophobic texts to articulate Peña Gómez's inadequacy as a representative of the nation (Spanakos 2000: 265–67).

Fernández avoided the authoritarian ruling behavior of his predecessor and seemed to represent what political scientist Jacqueline Jiménez-Polanco (1999) considers a transition from a "charismatic leadership to contingent leadership." Contingency was not simply a matter of personality and ideology but also a result of a weak political base that was exacerbated by the inability to maintain a governing coalition in the congress. Contingency, deadlock, and perceived political weakness led to the need to use the "Haitian card" periodically to improve domestic popularity. In March 1997, Fernández sent the police in pursuit of undocumented Haitians, especially in Santiago, where there was rumored to be a "Haitian beggar network" (Wucker 1999: 247). Fernández justified this action by explaining that all sovereign states remove illegal immigrants and by citing the expulsion of Dominicans from Puerto Rico and the United States, and Mexicans from the United States as an example. Despite his internationalist appeal, in this area where Dominican national identity and his legitimacy as a leader were particularly weak and "threatened," he reverted to the same sovereignty-based defensiveness of his predecessor.

However, during the Fernández government, for the first time in thirty-one years, the Dominican government allowed the Interamerican Commission on Human Rights to visit the country (Espinal 2000: 378). Fernández also improved diplomacy with the government of Haiti. He visited Haiti, addressed the Haitian parliament, and engaged in warmer relations with the government of Haiti. At the same time, improved relations between Haitians and Dominicans may be made more possible by the increased importance of diasporic communities from both countries in the domestic politics of their home countries. The diaspora experience has led to considerable efforts at coalition building among Dominicans and Haitians and at challenging the racism that underlies traditional Dominican perceptions of Haitianidad.

Although the shift to a more liberal president, more committed to political and economic openness, should have led to an improvement of the situation of Haitian laborers, there has only been an improvement in interstate relations. The border remains a difficult area to police, and Haitian migrants, documented and otherwise, occupy a considerable portion of the labor force in the Dominican Republic. Additionally, the end of the Cold War led to a country that was more open to global voices, particularly those of NGOs. However, Dominican presidents remain defensive about sovereignty when concerns arise about Haitian migrants, which they see as a domestic issue. Improved diplomatic relations and relations between diaspora communities may help in the long run, but societal prejudices remain the crucial constraint in terms of Dominican policy toward Haiti.

Economics—from Nationalism to Liberalism

Unlike many of the other changes in Dominican foreign policy examined in this chapter, some of the most significant changes in policy, in terms of passed legislation, occurred while Joaquín Balaguer was president. Balaguer's implementation of a stabilization program, which was not only inconsistent with his longtime commitment to state-led development but also sought to undo the damage done by his previous administrations, particularly that from 1986 to 1990, was not a result of ideological commitment to liberalization. Balaguer viewed liberalization as a pragmatic measure, and he had no difficulty increasing the money supply in the electoral year of 1994. At the same time, he often blocked privatization and maintained a corporatist model of state-led growth, through which he maintained a considerable amount of control.

Leonel Fernández, on the other hand, was convinced of the necessity of further economic reform in order to make development sustainable and to increase investment in areas where there was considerable need, such as education, health, and other social spending. Balaguer's reluctant acceptance of the "rationality" and "inevitability" of a stabilization program, as well as Fernández's belief in reform, was largely due to a combination of pressure from international lending agencies as well as a global paradigmatic shift in economics in which liberal economics became dominant.

The international system responded to the Latin American debt crisis primarily through stabilization programs and contingent loans orchestrated by international and regional lending agencies, such as the International Monetary Fund (IMF), the World Bank, and the Inter-American Development Bank (IADB). Among the economists working for these organizations, and increasingly among policymakers in the West and in Latin America, there was a consensus that Keynesean demand side economics was no longer appropriate; that inflation, the most glaring problem faced by developing world debtors, was primarily a monetary problem; and that reform leading to more liberal, export-oriented, and open economies would return developing countries to growth.

Although Balaguer had the type of political mandate in previous administrations (1966–1970, 1970–1974, 1974–1978, and 1986–1990), bolstered by economic growth (for the first three periods) or by strong nationalist sentiment (in the last period), that allowed him to ignore international trends of liberalization and pressures from international financial institutions, in 1990 he benefited from neither. A sharp reduction in the gross domestic product (GDP) in 1990, high inflation, considerable exchange rate pressures, and an increased external debt to international financial institutions (IMF 1999: 11), compounded by a dubious electoral victory, left Balaguer in a weakened position, particularly in dealing with international financial institutions. Though an ardent nationalist who has always been wary of U.S. interest/intervention in domestic politics, Balaguer was convinced by international lending agencies that reform would improve the country's economic woes. The need for foreign capital, the seal of approval that countries receive when stabilization plans are negotiated with international financial institutions, as well as the demonstration effect of economic liberalization in Mexico, led to Balaguer's adoption of a stabilization program.

In 1990, President Balaguer announced the New Economic Program. Between 1990 and 1993, through presidential decree and later passed into legislation by the congress, a number of economic reforms were implemented. These reforms were also consistent with conventional wisdom among international economists and policymakers in the West, who saw the collapse of the Berlin Wall as positive proof of their triumph over interventionist economic models. Under the guidance of the United Nations Development Program (UNDP) and the World Bank, the Balaguer government implemented a stabilization program that was immediately successful. Public sector deficit in 1990 was replaced by a surplus of nearly 4 percent in 1991, tariffs were simplified, most import quotas and licensing requirements were abolished, fiscal discipline was generally maintained, tax collection improved, progress was made in terms of banking supervision, and the government removed ceilings on interest rates in 1991. The peg on the exchange rate was also made more flexible.

Since the New Economic Program, the Dominican Republic has enjoyed consistent growth, beginning at modest levels in the early 1990s and accelerating to an average of 7 percent, the highest in the world, during the Fernández government (1996–2000). Some of the more significant achievements are the reduction of public external debt from 72 percent of GDP in 1990 to 23.7 percent of GDP in 1998 and improved tax collection (IMF 1999). As a further sign of willingness to participate in reform, and as a foreshadowing of the internationalism that would occur during the Fernández government, the Dominican Republic joined the World Trade Organization (WTO) in 1995.

Balaguer's commitment to reform was not without its limits. Particularly telling was his reliance on a huge discretionary budget for the office of the presidency, which was used to expand patronage and thus to ensure political loyalty, and his deviation from fiscal discipline during the electoral year of 1994. The stalling of further reforms following the New Economic Program (1990–1993) and Balaguer's return to economic nationalist and populist language following his exit from power in 1996 suggest that the nonagenarian's turn toward liberalizing the economy was more the result of a pragmatist who had been pushed by domestic crisis and a consensus among international lenders.

Fernández, who assumed the presidency in 1996, was committed to further liberalizing the economy because he realized privatizing many of the state-owned enterprises would alleviate some state debt, improve services, and give the state added funds that could be transferred into education, health, and other social spending. Fernández's inability to maintain a workable alliance led to strained relations between the president and the congress, with the result being little further reform. Despite this, President Fernández attempted to push reform by appealing to international investors and by becoming more active in international organizations. His government showed its difference from the more nationalist Balaguer government by paying debts to the OAS, the UN, the WTO, the Association of Caribbean States (ACS), and the International Labor Organization (ILO), which were all overdue. He also negotiated free trade agreements with CACM and the Caribbean Community (CARICOM), although these are under review by the congress. He joined the Central American Free Trade Association (CAFTA) and CARICOM and was an active supporter of the Free Trade Area of the Americas. Fernández spent more time abroad than any president in Dominican history; he justified it by the need to adapt the Dominican

Republic to globalization, but he received intense criticism from the more inward-looking Dominicans.

In the same vein, Fernández opened the Dominican economy to foreign investment, joint ventures, and new economic initiatives as never before. Despite congressional obstruction, the free trade zones in the Dominican Republic have flourished and have proven themselves a reliable source of hard currency. The free trade zones, as well as the reforms undertaken since the New Economic Program, are largely responsible for the high levels of growth (7 percent) attained during the Fernández government. Reform has also made such growth sustainable without relying on external debt, which has actually been reduced sharply, while keeping inflation low.

Nevertheless, further reform, as international financial institutions suggest, is necessary. The Dominican Republic still maintains one of the highest simple average tariffs in the region (17.7 compared to Belize, 9.2; El Salvador, 10.2; Haiti, 10; Jamaica, 9.6), and its overall trade restrictiveness is significant (IMF 1999: 38–39). Additionally, growth has been largely dependent on the growth of remittances, which may have totaled as much as U.S.$2 billion in 1999 (Fernández 1996). Such an infusion of hard currency has clearly been beneficial, but it, along with the strong performance by the free trade zones and by the telecommunications sector, have delayed the urgency for further reform.

Domestic crisis coupled with a paradigmatic shift in the ideologies of international financial institutions pressured a politically weakened President Balaguer into abandoning the state-led growth model that he had used in previous administrations. The arrival of President Fernández, who was committed to economic reform and to being an active part of the international community and regional economic organizations, was met by resistance from Balaguer's Reformist Social Christian Party (PRSC) and from the left-of-center PRD. The lack of a majority or a tenable coalition as well as the lack of urgency of reform, since the economy had stabilized and was growing, led to little further reform being passed.

CONCLUSION

The contours of Dominican foreign policy and the changes that have occurred during recent administrations can largely be attributed to opportunities opened by the end of the Cold War and changes in individual leadership in the Dominican Republic. Continuities, particularly foot dragging in the area of human rights violations against Haitian workers, are best explained by the continuities in Dominican national identity. But even this has seen some movement, especially as diplomatic relations between the Dominican Republic and Haiti improve, the United States and NGOs pressure Dominican governments to be more responsible in their treatment of Haitian workers, and bonds of solidarity are forged in the Haitian and Dominican diasporas in the United States.

The quality of democracy must also be improved, but the heightened presence of domestic and international NGOs has made society more vigilant and aware of the excesses of government. Although it took quite a number of years, elections appear to be reasonably fair. This is in large part due to the work of international and domestic NGOs, whose presence is increasingly recognized as necessary. As the political system has become more pluralist and has opened space for nontraditional political actors, the Dominican economy has also opened. Considerable reform has taken place and has been very successful, but, again, more is necessary. With policy suggestions perceived as constructive rather than threats to national sovereignty, more reform may indeed be possible.

Finally, relations with the United States have improved markedly as the Dominican Republic has entered into partnership with the United States on many issues—fighting drugs, enjoying free trade, strengthening regional organizations—but the presence of Dominicans in the United States has made the positions of the two states more proximate. Problems still arise over the issues of drugs and immigration, but there is more of a spirit of partnership than ever before. This has been bolstered by U.S. and Dominican initiatives aimed at invigorating multilateral organizations.

DISCUSSION QUESTIONS

1. What level of analysis best explains the changes in Dominican policy?
2. How does the end of the Cold War affect Dominican foreign policy?
3. Has the Dominican Republic benefited from its shift toward a more internationalist foreign policy?

NOTES

1. In that election, 24,470 votes separated Balaguer and Bosch.

2. The most significant of these changes were that members must be approved by each of the major political parties, a reliable computer system must be used, parties must approve all parts of the electoral process, and new voter lists must be posted publicly before election (NDI, May 18, 1996, 2).

3. Those between sixteen and sixty were allowed to stay since they were considered workers.

7

CARICOM
The Pursuit of Economic Security

H. Michael Erisman

Compared to the rest of Latin America, the English-speaking Caribbean projects a somewhat peculiar international profile in the sense that countries in this area have always placed a very heavy premium on a multilateral approach to their foreign relations. The institutional vehicle that they have used to try to implement this strategy is the Caribbean Community and Common Market (CARICOM).

CARICOM is a regional cooperation/integration organization serving primarily, but not solely, the Anglophone islands of the West Indies. It was established in 1973 with twelve charter members, all of which were at the time or once had been part of the British Empire.[1] The Bahamas joined the fold in 1983, and in 1995, Suriname became the first country to be admitted that did not have an English heritage—it had been a Dutch colony. The group's most recent addition is Haiti, which was granted provisional membership in 1997 and then became a full participant in July 1999.[2]

Clearly, as James Rosenau's seminal conceptual work that is guiding this volume has shown, factors at various levels of analysis can influence the foreign policymaking process and subsequent external behavior. In CARICOM's case, for example, domestic (i.e., national) considerations have sometimes resulted in different and competing definitions of interest among its members. One manifestation of this phenomenon occurred in 1981 when seven smaller participants, complaining that their rewards from CARICOM's common market arrangements were insufficient, formed a parallel group known as the Organization of Eastern Caribbean States (OECS) in an attempt to service their distinctive needs.[3]

Nevertheless, despite occasional outbursts of such dissident sentiments driven by the exigencies of nationalistic or even more parochial interest group politics, CARICOM has remained the key instrument utilized by Caribbean governments to coordinate and pursue their international agendas. Consequently, the OECS, although a separate institutional entity, often finds itself functioning as a lobbying group within CARICOM for its members (all of which have maintained their affiliation with the larger association).

Those who were the driving force behind CARICOM's emergence conceptualized it in very ambitious terms. For instance, they envisioned it as a mechanism that hopefully would promote such diverse goals as joint educational programs, collaborative cultural projects, and greater ease of intraregional travel. In the final analysis, however, one central theme has always defined the very essence and core mission of the organization for its members—economic security. From this starting point, two basic, interrelated categories of CARICOM concern have evolved, which can be briefly summarized as follows:

1. *Promoting intraregional cooperation and momentum toward increased economic/political integration as a means to enhance the economic development of its participants.* This consideration always has and still today revolves around the proposition that small island nations such as those in the Anglophone Caribbean[4] must pursue integrationist strategies if they are to have a reasonable chance to enjoy any significant developmental successes.
2. *Coordinating its member's foreign policies.* At its most general conceptual level, the rationale for such collaboration is to enhance the international status and influence of all participants through a process of "power pooling." In practice, the primary goal has been to create conditions whereby the CARICOM countries can *collectively bargain* the terms of their trade and developmental relations with the major centers of world economic power (e.g., the United States and the European Union [EU]).

At the heart of the bureaucratic structure created to pursue these goals are two distinct institutional entities—the Caribbean Common Market and the Caribbean Community—that represent the basic division of labor within the larger umbrella organization. Common Market personnel concentrate primarily, of course, on such duties as administering programs related to maintaining uniform external tariffs and enhancing free trade among the participants. The community staff, on the other hand, is responsible for overseeing the political and functional facets of Caribbean integration (e.g., foreign policy coordination and the provision of infrastructural services).

The CARICOM policymaking hierarchy involves three main centers of authority and influence, which are the Heads of Government Conference (HGC), which takes place once a year with each meeting being hosted by a different member country; the Common Market Council of Ministers; and the Caribbean Community Secretariat. Officially, ultimate decision-making power is vested in the HGC, where each participating country has one vote and unanimity is required to pass recommendations (compliance here being voluntary) or binding resolutions. The conference also holds the mandate for concluding treaties on CARICOM's behalf and for overseeing its relations with individual states or other international associations. In practice, however, the HGC often merely ratifies proposals that have been worked out within the Council of Ministers, whose membership provisions and voting procedures are practically identical to those of the Conference. Although the council meets as needed throughout the year, it inevitably convenes just prior to the annual CARICOM summit to finalize the details of the agenda items that the prime ministers will consider (and usually accept without major modification). Naturally, one factor complicating the work of both the HGC and the council is that their members represent their governments and hence may be inclined to give priority to national rather than CARICOM interests. Thus, one must turn to the secretariat to find the true nerve center of integrationist sentiment since, like most other similar international bodies, its staff is prohibited from accepting instructions from any official at the national level, and they are obligated to assure that their actions serve the community rather than the parochial concerns of any of its members. According to Andrew Axline (1979), the secretariat

> has become the most dynamic element in the process of Caribbean integration. Drawing upon the expertise of the Secretariat, studies have been undertaken and policies designed which have provided the basis for inter-governmental negotiations and the adoption of integrative measures. The Secretariat, in fostering an ideology of integration, has provided a communications link among the various forces of the region, including intellectuals, the private sector and member governments. The Secretary General himself has played an important role in negotiating compromises among member governments, often through personal contact and face-to-face discussions with heads of government. The Secretariat has also participated in missions to various countries in order to develop support for compromises on the adoption of regional policies. The Secretariat represents the vanguard of the Caribbean integration movement by attempting to build a regional consensus around measures which will constitute an integration scheme likely to contribute to the development of the region. (78)

As has already been noted, numerous variables, both internal and external, can influence the formulation of an international agenda and the prioritization of items thereupon. But following CARICOM's lead, the material here will concentrate on the question of *economic security* for the region's peoples and CARICOM's efforts to promote it within the context of such issue areas as the following:

- Regional integration projects, with special emphasis on the questions of broadening/deepening CARICOM and CARICOM involvement in the Association of Caribbean States (ACS)
- Relations with the United States, looking particularly at the CARICOM response to the challenge presented by the North American Free Trade Agreement (NAFTA). Two other matters impacting U.S.–CARICOM affairs that will receive some attention are migration matters and the problem of drug trafficking.
- Relations with the EU, especially within the context of the Lomé/Cotonou process

  The analysis will conclude with some general observations about CARICOM's foreign policies and the relevance of its external behavior to Rosenau's level-of-analysis framework.

CARICOM Confronts the Cold War

The CARICOM nations were, in a sense, latecomers to the hothouse of Cold War politics, for, in comparison to the rest of the hemisphere and indeed the Third World in general, they lagged rather far behind in making the transition from colonies to independent states with the potential to chart their own courses in international affairs. But like many other small countries, they understood that breaking the colonial shackles would not necessarily guarantee that they were now masters of their own fates. Instead, they were painfully aware of the harsh reality that they remained highly susceptible to various kinds of control and exploitation by outside powers. William Demas (1986), president of the Caribbean Development Bank, has eloquently summarized the situation:

> Many people in the region . . . hold pessimistic and deterministic positions regarding our prospects for any degree of effective independence vis-à-vis the outside world. They believe that we are doomed to abject subordination because of our small and in some cases minuscule size, and because of our long colonial history as mere political, economic, military, and cultural appendages of the metropolitan countries. They consider that we can only be "specks of dust" [that are] impotent, unable to control our destiny, . . . and inevitably subject to the decisions, and indeed the whims, of outside countries. (12)

Demas's implication here is very important, especially for small island nations—the need within the policymaking process to distinguish clearly between *formal* and *effective* sovereignty. The former is in many respects symbolic, involving such things as admission to the United Nations and other similar badges of acceptance into the international community. Effective sovereignty, on the other hand, refers to circumstances where a country and its people *truly control* their own destinies; they are, in other words, exercising their right of national self-determination to the greatest extent possible.

Flowing from this concept of effective sovereignty is the concern about economic security that permeates the international agendas of the West Indian countries. Their long colonial experiences drove home in no uncertain terms the high level of vulnerability involved in their relations with external powers, and while classical colonialism has largely disappeared from the equation, the dangers inherent in such asymmetrical relationships (sometimes conceptualized in terms of neocolonialism or dependency) have not.

During the Cold War, CARICOM's interest in maximizing its members' effective sovereignty was to a great extent incompatible with Washington's strategy of global containment, which demanded that the United States maintain a tight rein over the political/economic dynamics of strategic regions such as the Caribbean. Thus, as the United States in effect "incorporated" the West Indies into its grand scheme of trying to prevent the expansion of Soviet influence in particular and the spread of Communist ideology in general, it often employed mechanisms of pressure or control that were at odds with CARICOM'S sovereignty-maximizing impulses. Some of the more blatant and controversial tactics that the United States employed were these:

- Waging economic warfare against "unacceptable" governments; using trade embargoes and other destabilization techniques to try to create so much chaos that the targeted regime would somehow be swept aside in the process. Among the most prominent CARICOM recipients of such attention were Michael Manley's first administration in Jamaica (1972–1980) and Maurice Bishop's New Jewel Revolution in Grenada (1979–1983).
- Launching covert operations, sometimes characterized as "dirty tricks" and usually carried out by the CIA (Central Intelligence Agency), to remove perceived challenges to containment. One example here, although not as well known as the infamous and ill-fated 1961 Bay of Pigs operation against Castro, was a successful joint U.S.-English campaign in 1964 to nullify the preindependence elections in British Guiana (later known as Guyana) won by Jeddi Jagan, an avowed Marxist.
- Finally, of course, the most drastic measure available—deploying regular U.S. armed forces to take control of a nation deemed to be threatened by or to have already fallen victim to communist subversion. This

option was employed only once against a CARICOM country—Grenada in 1983.

Despite such actions, which were obviously inconsistent with the core (sovereignty) values embedded in the West Indian perspective, the basic ideological conservatism of most CARICOM governments combined with heavy doses of pragmatism produced an operational scenario wherein they normally deferred to the Cold War concerns of the United States. In short, once all the policy chips had been laid on the table, Anglophone Caribbean countries usually opted for cooperation rather than confrontation with Washington, especially when there were potential benefits (or, conversely, avoidance of costs or risks) involved that could be seen as contributing to their economic security. The region's response to the Caribbean Basin Initiative (CBI) was illustrative of this phenomenon.

The CBI was conceived by the Reagan administration as a means to counter what was seen to be a growing leftist threat to the prevailing pro-Western ideological order and American influence in the Caribbean Basin. The first blow to Washington's complacent assumption that the area constituted a docile backyard came in March 1979 when a band of young radicals led by Maurice Bishop staged the West Indies' first successful armed coup in Grenada. Four months later (July 1979), the Sandinistas marched triumphantly into Managua, thus breaking the Somoza dynasty's long stranglehold over Nicaragua. Adding to Washington's regional anxieties were the escalating leftist insurgencies in both El Salvador and Guatemala as well as some indications that political instability might be brewing in Dominica, St. Lucia, and St. Vincent. The CBI represented the Reagan administration's attempt to bring American economic power to bear in order to help pacify the region.[5]

Three basic elements were incorporated into the CBI, which became fully functional in 1983 after having been formally proposed in February 1982. First, the flow of U.S. government developmental aid was increased. The initial package called for a $350 million emergency grant for 1982 followed by $750 million over the next three years (with administration officials clearly implying that more would be forthcoming if needed). Second, most Caribbean exports entering the American market were guaranteed duty-free status for twelve years. Finally, arrangements designed to promote private investment in the Basin were made that included various tax/financial incentives for U.S. companies as well as protection against nationalization and other forms of "unacceptable" government intervention in their affairs.

The CBI's promise to provide a special and highly advantageous relationship with the United States was generally greeted very enthusiastically in the English-speaking Caribbean. Overall, however, the CARICOM pessimists proved to be better prophets than the optimists, for the program's economic/developmental benefits did not live up to the initial expectations. For instance, the healthy trade surplus that the West Indies once ran with the United States shrank drastically (e.g., from $633 million in 1984 to $90 million in 1987), while Washington's aid disbursements plummeted by about 50 percent during the same period (González 1989: 69). Nevertheless, despite this somewhat lackluster performance, a revised and expanded version of the program—popularly termed CBI II—was instituted in 1990.

It would not, however, be accurate to portray the CARICOM countries as nothing more than abject client states that docilely marched to Washington's tune. Rather, their attitude toward the United States sometimes reflected the nationalistic cross-currents operative in the relationship, in which their desire to exercise effective sovereignty led them to take positions and pursue policies that diverged from Washington's Cold War agenda. Perhaps the most dramatic collective manifestation of this propensity occurred in December 1972 when Barbados, Guyana, Jamaica, and Trinidad/Tobago all reestablished diplomatic relations with Fidel Castro's Cuba, thereby abandoning the united front that the United States had been promoting in its efforts to isolate and hopefully destroy the government of its most hated Cold War protagonist in the Western Hemisphere. Jamaica in particular continued to display such defiance for the rest of the decade under Michael Manley's leadership (particularly following his 1976 reelection landslide), exhibiting a growing admiration for the Cuban socioeconomic model as well as interjecting an increasingly militant nonaligned coloration into its foreign policy.

But the brief forays into left-wing revolutionary politics by Manley and Grenada were the exceptions rather than the rule. For the most part, CARICOM governments were reluctant to mount any major Cold War challenges to the United States. Indeed, even in the Cuban case, their relations with Castro could be characterized as correct rather than cordial; in other words, they never developed any serious collaborative ties with Havana.

The major initiative that CARICOM states launched during this period in terms of pursuing increased economic security and attempting to assume a leadership role on the international scene that would enhance their effective sovereignty occurred outside the mainstream of Cold War politics. Specifically, the Anglophone Caribbean was at the center of the negotiations that produced the Lomé agreements between the European countries and a large group of their former colonies.

The roots of the Lomé process can be traced to England's decision in the late 1960s to join the European Community (EC), a move that very much alarmed developing countries who were members of the British Commonwealth (including the CARICOM nations) because they feared that it would cost them their privileged access to English markets. Consequently, when given the opportunity in 1972 to establish an institutionalized association with the *entire* European Community, they formed the ACP (Africa/Caribbean/Pacific) Group[6] to serve as their bargaining unit and proceeded to negotiate a comprehensive new relationship with the EC that became known as the Lomé I (1975) Convention. The key benefits for the ACP Group provided by Lomé I and its successors[7] were duty-free EC access for almost all their exports, a system that assured that trade would occur on the basis of stable and reasonable prices, and various developmental aid programs.

CARICOM states played a vanguard role in the Lomé process from the very beginning. They often, for example, served as the catalyst for a greater strategic consensus within the ACP and thereby enhanced its ability to present a more united front in its negotiations with the Europeans. In so doing, they contributed not only to the ACP's collective interests but also enhanced their own economic security by establishing the Lomé connection as an alternative to excessive dependency on the United States for trade and aid.

THE POST–COLD WAR PERIOD

The demise of the Cold War has been both a blessing and a curse to the CARICOM countries. Certainly most governments in the region were relieved that the United States no longer felt that it was necessary figuratively and sometimes almost literally to look over their shoulders to assure that they remained solidly within the boundaries of the political/ideological orthodoxy demanded by Washington's containment policies. On the other hand, the disappearance of whatever strategic significance the Cold War had conferred on the region had a very real downside, with the most serious negative implications emerging in the economic realm. One harsh new reality, for example, was the fact that the demise of the Soviet bloc as a superpower competitor removed the major incentive for such U.S. foreign aid initiatives as the CBI. Consequently, with Washington losing interest in such programs as vital tools for pursuing its foreign policy agenda, the CARICOM states could no longer draw upon the trade preferences and other benefits involved as a means to enhance their economic security.

Figures 7.1 and 7.2 shed some light on general long-term (i.e., Cold War and post–Cold War) patterns of economic development and trade in the West Indies. Using the per capita gross domestic product (GDP) data (which includes a few Caribbean countries outside CARICOM—e.g., the Dominican Republic) as a rough developmental/standard of living indicator reveals that the region basically made no significant progress in the twenty-year period; its per capita GDP was essentially the same in 1997 as it had been in 1979 and was down approximately 6.5 to 7 percent from its high point in the late 1970s/early 1980s. Elsewhere in the hemisphere, the mainland Latin American countries that had initially lagged behind the Caribbean had dramatically reversed that situation by the late 1990s.[8] CARICOM's problems

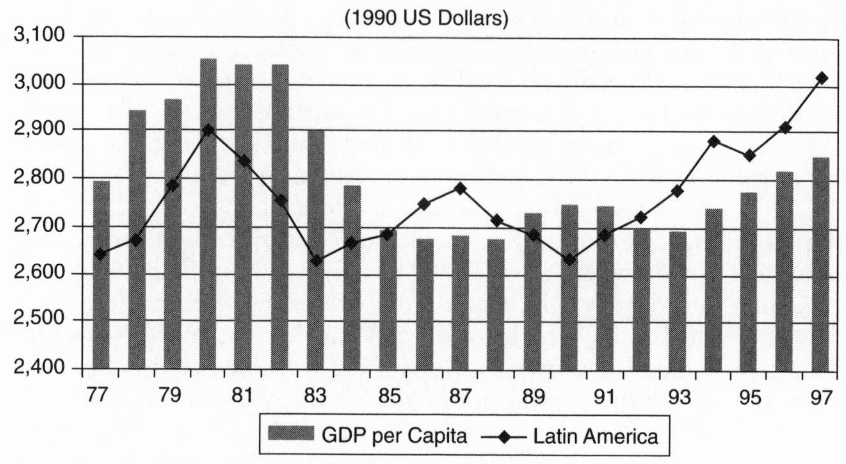

Figure 7.1. Caribbean GDP per Capita (1990 U.S. dollars)

Source: Inter-American Development Bank (IADB), Statistical and Quantitative Analysis Unit; www.iad.org.

are illustrated more dramatically when looking at the export/import situation (see figure 7.2), where the decent performance that is crucial to the well-being of small island economies has not been achieved in recent years.[9] Instead, increasingly severe West Indian trade deficits have characterized the post–Cold War era. Such patterns do not bode well with regard to CARICOM's economic security aspirations.

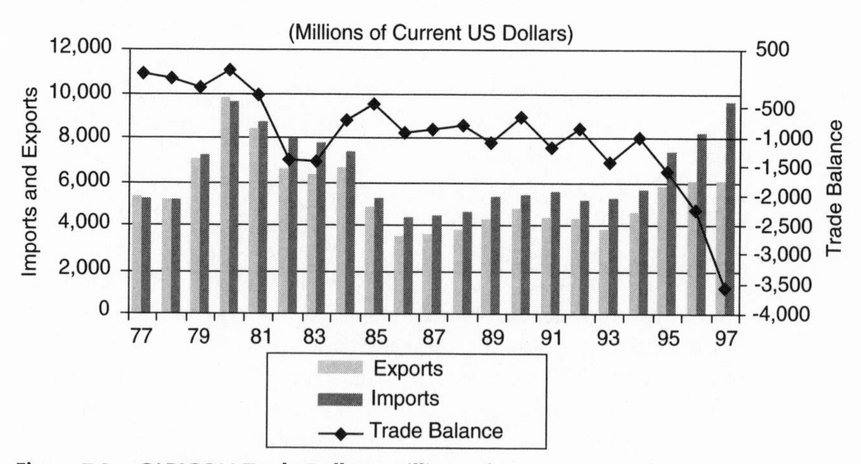

Figure 7.2. CARICOM Trade Dollars (millions of current U.S. dollars)

Source: Inter-American Development Bank (IADB), Statistical and Quantitative Analysis Unit; www.iad.org.

The basic configuration of the network of international trade relations within which the CARICOM countries have been trying to improve their developmental prospects is summarized in figures 7.3 and 7.4. The most obvious (and potentially dangerous) aspect of this profile is the dominant—indeed, some might say hegemonic—position that the United States has long occupied and that shows no signs of serious abatement. This disparity is especially apparent in terms of CARICOM imports, with its reliance on the United States growing steadily over the past two decades to the point it is now approximately three times greater than any other source. The export patterns are not quite so lopsided, although the EU and the (strengthening) Intra-CARICOM categories represent markets that are only one-half the size of their U.S. counterparts. The risks inherent in such a lack of trade diversification are considerable, especially for island economies that rely heavily on export revenue for developmental capital and to finance the importation of crucial goods that

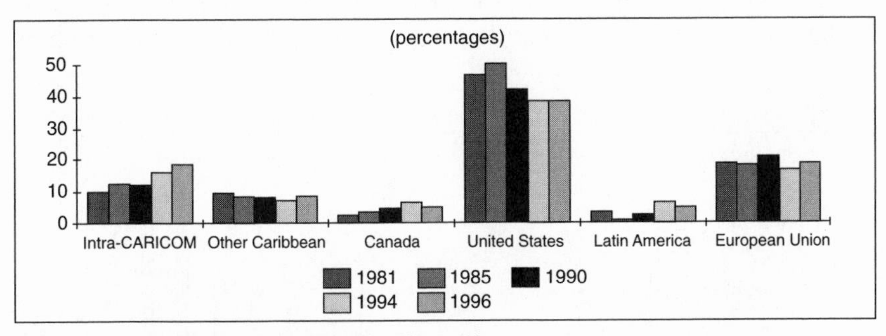

Figure 7.3. CARICOM Export Destinations (%)

Source: Constructed using data downloaded from CARICOM's website at www.caricom.org/statistics.

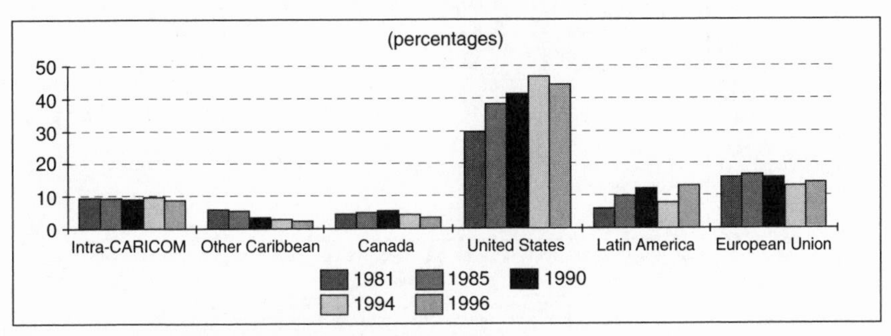

Figure 7.4. Sources of CARICOM Imports (%)

Source: Constructed using data downloaded from CARICOM's website at www.caricom.org/statistics.

cannot be produced domestically. Consider, for example, the crisis that engulfed Cuba when its special and highly lucrative ties to the Soviet bloc, with which Havana carried out over 70 percent of its trade transactions, simply disappeared as the international environment shifted to a post–Cold War mode.

In CARICOM's case, the problem, at least over the last ten to fifteen years, has revolved more around the dynamics of its U.S. relationship than any fears that it might somehow disappear. Quite simply, as illustrated by figure 7.5, the West Indian countries collectively have been doing very poorly in their business transactions with the United States, with trade deficits exploding as the 1990s progressed. If proportionate shortfalls were incurred with a minor trading partner such as Canada, the negative implications would not be all that great. But when dealing with the United States within the context of the trade profile detailed earlier, the shock waves generated can permeate a CARICOM country's entire economic structure.

Further complicating the U.S.–CARICOM relationship is the fact that in the post–Cold War period, Washington has lost interest in programs

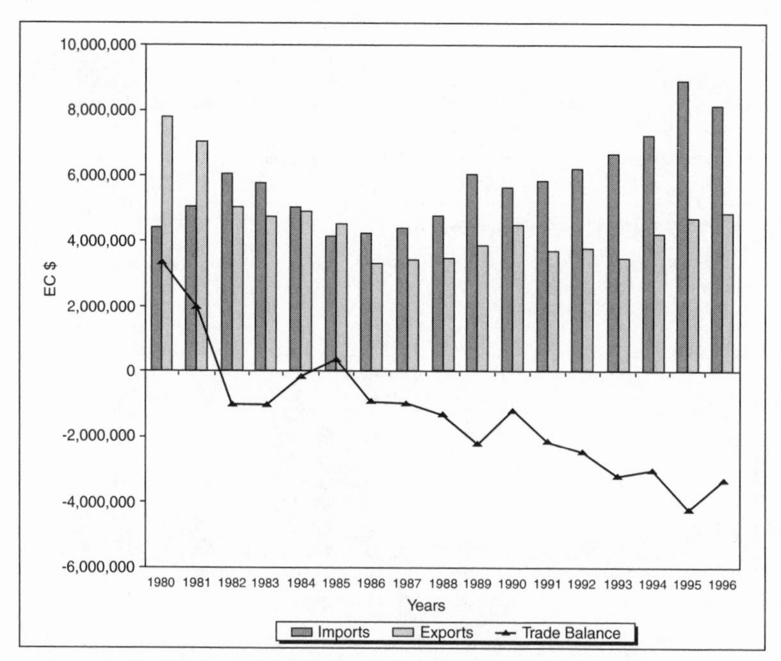

Figure 7.5. CARICOM's Trade Balance with the United States, 1980–1996

Source: Downloaded from CARICOM's website at www.caricom.org.

such as the CBI (where Cold War politics dictated that Caribbean countries receive some preferential treatment) and instead has emphasized structuring its economic relations within the Western Hemisphere along free trade lines. The centerpiece of this new approach is, of course, the North American Free Trade Agreement (NAFTA). By and large, the CARICOM countries have expressed serious doubts about their economic futures in a world dominated by a neoliberal ethos and free trade organizations such as NAFTA. An example of such sentiment was voiced in early 2000 by Sir Neville Nicholls, president of the Caribbean Development Bank (CDB):

> As the region gears itself for a world of trade liberalization, mega-trading blocs, and a dramatic increase in the trade in services, the CDB is ever mindful of the potential negative fallout and adverse social and human consequences of these seemingly inevitable, irresistible and irreversible changes in the global economy.
>
> There is a powerful school of thought which argues that the warm embrace of the market, trade liberalization and full integration into the global economy will yield increased opportunities for wealth creation and employment, and consequently, improved living standards for all our people.
>
> We in the Caribbean know only too well that this is not necessarily how it works. To us, the vulnerability of states such as ours to economic uncertainty . . . is beyond dispute. (International Press Service [IPS] 2000)

The key issue here is that CARICOM countries simply do not think that they can compete, particularly on an individual basis, with NAFTA members such as Mexico in terms of securing shares of the U.S. market for their exports or attracting private U.S. investment (e.g., to build original production facilities or to relocate factories from the United States). The World Bank echoed these concerns in the mid-1990s, estimating that more than one-third of the $12.5 billion of Caribbean goods exported annually to the United States might shift to Mexico due to its NAFTA membership. The Caribbean Textile and Apparel Institute reinforced such projections with hard data, reporting that during the 1995–1996 period more than 150 regional textile plants closed and 123,000 jobs were lost as a direct result of trade and investment diversion to Mexico (Rohter 1997).

Recognizing this problem, the CARICOM countries have lobbied hard for some kind of "CBI enhancement" or "NAFTA parity" ever since the free trade agreement went into effect in 1994. But over the following six years the U.S. Congress repeatedly voted down or tabled proposals to this effect. Finally, in May 2000, President Clinton signed the U.S.-Caribbean Basin Trade Partnership Act (CBTPA), which basically provided an opportunity for West Indian and Central American countries to enjoy greater duty-free access to the U.S. market for textiles and a few other product categories (White House 2000). Unlike NAFTA, this program does not require beneficiaries to lower their tariffs or other barriers to U.S. exports (although they must respect copyrights, patents, and other intellectual property rights as well as safeguarding foreign investors). Participation is not, however, automatic. Instead, prospects must satisfy various entrance requirements.[10] These along with other provisions have generated skepticism about the extent to which the West Indies will reap any significant benefits. By February 2001, five of the eleven regional countries thus far certified as acceptable were CARICOM members (Belize, Guyana, Haiti, Jamaica, and Trinidad/Tobago), but critics were charging that there are still so many regulations involved that exporting to the United States will not be easy in any case.

While these developments were unfolding on CARICOM's North American front, trends that likewise were potentially detrimental to West Indian economic security began to emerge with regard to the European Union. Beginning in the early 1990s, it gradually became evident that CARICOM's status on the EU's list of international priorities was eroding. Obviously various factors entered into this equation, although certainly one important consideration was the increasing attention being paid by the EU to the question of its evolving economic relations with former Soviet bloc states (e.g., which, if any, might be granted membership?). Probably the most significant impact of this downgrading could be seen in the EU's changing attitudes toward the Lomé Convention.

The first major indication of a reevaluation came in 1990. The EU insisted that the fourth version of Lomé being negotiated at that time run for ten years rather than the five-year duration that had always been the norm, thus indicating somewhat less willingness to make "adjustments" in the relationship than had previously been the case. In 2000, a much more radical shift occurred, with the Europeans now demanding a new treaty rather than just a revision of the existing accords. Consequently Lomé was allowed to expire and was replaced with a new arrangement called the Cotonou Agreement. Among its main provisions (compared with their Lomé counterparts) are the following (Cotonou 2000):

- Cotonou will be a twenty-year pact; some, but not all aspects, of the accord will be open to revision every five years. Usually Lomé as a whole was subject to renegotiation every five years (the ten-year 1990 version being the only exception).
- The system of trade preferences that the EU had granted ACP countries under Lomé will be gradually replaced by a series of new economic partnerships (which *are not* subject to the five-year review provision) based on *reciprocal* removal of trade barriers. In other words, Cotonou

is more akin to a conventional two-way free trade agreement than Lomé's one-way preferential system which gave the ACP countries privileged access to EU markets.

In general, the Cotonou system places heavy emphasis on EU aid and other types of programs concentrating on poverty reduction in the least developed countries. As such, the new system is less likely to contribute to the economic security of the CARICOM states (which are, comparatively, better off economically than many of their ACP counterparts) than was the case with the Lomé Accords.

In an effort to respond to these U.S.–EU developments that could undermine their economic security, the West Indian countries have attempted to *deepen* intra-CARICOM cooperation and to *broaden* the organization's international scope by seeking to forge new partnerships with other developing nations in the Western Hemisphere. Jacqueline Braveboy-Wagner (1995) has summarized this scenario as follows:

> Caribbean policymakers generally recognize the benefits of regionalism in a world of economic megablocs—the EC, NAFTA, and the informal Pacific bloc. Thus enhanced regionalism has become a cornerstone of the region's economic policy. . . . Two strategies for trade are predominant: the deepening of the movement for regional integration; and the preparation for [CARICOM] integration into Latin America and North America. (14)

The primary motivations in both cases have been to enhance CARICOM's developmental prospects and, especially in the "broadening" instance, to strengthen its potential collective bargaining position when dealing with the United States/NAFTA and the EU/Cotonou.

The effort to expand the flow of intraregional and Latin American trade can be seen in figures 7.3 and 7.4, which show a clear upward trend with regard to exports among CARICOM members as well as an overall improvement in the larger mainland Hispanic picture. This process of trade diversification (especially with regard to export destinations) is illustrated by table 7.1, which indicates that in 1985, the United States and the EU far overshadowed the other major centers of CARICOM export activity; their market share was almost five times greater than that of their less developed competitors. But by 1996, this differential had been cut almost in half. In other words, while still trading heavily with these traditional partners, the CARICOM group as a whole was succeeding in becoming *less* export dependent on them. This pattern can be seen as contributing to the CARICOM countries' quest for economic security, for they are moving away from (although certainly not completely escaping) a situation where their economic health can become so closely tied to their relationships with certain countries that

Table 7.1. Market Share of CARICOM Members' Exports

Percentage of Exports Going to	*1985*	*1996*
United States and the European Union	68.0%	56.9%
Other CARICOM members and Latin/ Central America	13.8%	23.8%

Source: Based on the data used to generate figure 7.3.

they may find themselves highly vulnerable to trade sanctions and other kinds of commercial blackmail.

Certainly, the most audacious and controversial move that CARICOM has made with regard to broadening its scope has been its overtures toward Castro's Cuba. This process began to gain momentum in late 1990 when the CARICOM heads of state decided at their Eleventh Summit Conference (Jamaica, August 1990) to launch serious discussions with Havana regarding the possibilities for increased economic cooperation. A series of meetings followed in which significant progress was made and trade between the two parties began to increase significantly. This budding relationship further expanded when CARICOM used its influence to promote Cuban involvement in economic negotiations with the European Union. In June 1998, Havana was admitted to the CariForum (which is the body used by CARICOM to formulate and represent its interests in negotiations with the European Union to update the Lomé/Cotonou accords) as an observer and in August 1998 its status was upgraded to full membership. In April 2000, however, CARICOM's efforts to broker an even stronger Cuban-ACP connection floundered when Havana, angered at growing criticism being leveled at its human rights record by some EU nations and especially their votes in support of an anti-Cuban resolution submitted by Washington to the UN Human Rights Commission, withdrew its application to join the Cotonou Agreement.

CARICOM's most ambitious attempt in recent years to establish an institutionalized economic link with its Hispanic mainland neighbors has involved the vanguard role that it played in the creation of the Association of Caribbean States (ACS), which officially appeared on the scene when the treaty establishing it was signed on July 24, 1994, in Cartagena, Colombia. The organization has twenty-five members who collectively (as of 2001) have a population of 948 million and a total annual trade volume of roughly $462 billion.

The basic objectives of the ACS, which not surprisingly are very similar to those of CARICOM due to the heavy influence of West Indian leaders in founding the association, can be summarized as follows:

1. To maximize regional trade and to promote the economies of scale needed to achieve insertion into the international economic system through trade liberalization;
2. To optimize bargaining power with third parties (given the area's post–Cold War decline in strategic importance) through the forging of tightly focused regional alliances based on identification of common (primarily geoeconomic) interests;
3. To move toward various forms of cooperation (and eventual integration) by forging consensus on matters of mutual interest and consolidating a regional identity, based on shared cultural and social traits, that will overcome existing divisions and heterogeneity and benefit the population of the entire region (Serbin 1994: 64).

But as the new millennium dawned, the ACS, unlike CARICOM, did not seem to be demonstrating any significant capacity to achieve its stated goals. Many observers were not particularly surprised by this turn of events, noting that the two main regional groups within the ACS—the West Indian islands and the mainland Hispanic states—have never displayed much capacity for sustained cooperation. Such institutional lethargy was put vividly on display in September 2000 at a major ACS meeting convened in Port-of-Spain, Trinidad, to assess its performance, to make any necessary revisions in its long-term strategic vision, and to set some concrete cooperative goals that could be met in the near future. Participation was lackluster; only fourteen (of the twenty-five) members attended with host Trinidad being the only CARICOM country present. Whether this development was just an anomaly or an indication that West Indian countries have essentially given up on the ACS remains to be seen.

The post–Cold War concerns of West Indian policymakers are not, of course, limited to economic issues. Certainly, the popular perception, especially in the United States, with respect to what should be the priority items on the international agendas of the CARICOM states tends to center on such matters as migration problems and, perhaps most important, drug trafficking. Migration has always been a prominent feature of Caribbean life. Indeed, in percentage terms, the region stands among the world's leaders with respect to its people relocating to other lands, the United States being the favorite destination. While emigration might benefit the individual participants, most of whom are motivated by such basic economic considerations as a desire for employment or a better-paying job, the "brain drain" involved can seriously undermine a country's developmental potential since those who leave are often the brightest and the most ambitious.

For the most part, such migration has not generated serious tensions between Washington and Caribbean governments, Cuba and Haiti being the main exceptions.[11] In fact, despite growing sentiment within the United States over the last two decades for more restrictive laws, legislation passed in 1990 actually increased the islands' total number of permissible immigrants (although reductions occurred in some subcategories).

Migration issues tend, for the most part, to capture the attention of policy professionals. Drug trafficking, on the other hand, resonates strongly with the general public in both the United States and the West Indies. The Caribbean is insignificant in terms of production when compared with such major supply centers as Colombia or Peru. But the region is a major hub in the industry's delivery network. It has, for example, been estimated that 40 percent of all cocaine produced in South America for the U.S. and European markets moves through the area. Initially, the Bahamas, Belize, and Jamaica were the main countries used as transshipment centers. More recently, however, such activity has expanded to include Barbados, the Dominican Republic, Guyana, Haiti, Trinidad/Tobago, and many of the smaller Eastern Caribbean islands. Also, drug cartels have often turned to the region to "launder" their huge profits, using friendly banks, paper corporations, and other ruses to hide their narcodollars in legitimate business activities.

The CARICOM countries have generally been willing to cooperate with Washington in its efforts to cut the flow of drugs. They have, for example, established mechanisms for sharing intelligence with such U.S crime-fighting organizations as the Drug Enforcement Agency (DEA) and have often participated in joint interdiction operations. The one major discordant note here has involved the "Shiprider Agreements," which permit U.S. antidrug agencies to conduct land, sea, and air patrols, maritime searches and seizures, and arrest/detention operations *within* the national boundaries of the Caribbean signatories. Critics have attacked these accords on a number of grounds, the most common complaints being: Washington has often used questionable tactics to pressure Caribbean governments to consent to such arrangements, the provisions in many respects infringe on West Indian sovereignty, and the United States has not reciprocated in any significant way (e.g., by providing increased developmental aid).

In the final analysis, however, it is the question of economic security that will have the greatest long-term impact on the viability of Caribbean societies as they confront the complexities of the post–Cold War world. Indeed, it will be the CARICOM community's performance in this issue area that will be most important in determining whether its people will be able to live fairly normal lives or whether they will turn to the drug trade or (illegal) immigration as possible panaceas for their problems.

CONCLUSION

Correlating the foregoing CARICOM material to the three basic tiers in James Rosenau's analytical framework suggests the following:

1. The idiosyncratic level sheds little light on CARICOM's external behavior, the main reason being that CARICOM basically functions as a multilateral institutional actor (i.e., an intergovernmental organization [IGO]) on the world stage wherein policy tends to reflect the consensus of all participating governments rather than the individual preferences of their leaders. It should, however, be noted that the "unanimity rule" required to pass resolutions opens the door for strong-willed prime ministers to essentially veto proposed courses of collective action.
2. The domestic level has some explanatory utility, this observation being consistent with the widely held view that international affairs are inherently intermestic in nature and hence can be affected by intrasocietal factors. In the West Indian arena, for example, nationalistic sentiments as well as the commercial self-interest of business groups in some countries have contributed to the willingness of both CARICOM as a whole and certain member states to develop (despite strong U.S. opposition) cordial relations with Castro's Cuba.
3. The systemic level is where, without any doubt whatsoever, CARICOM reality and Rosenau's conceptualization come together most clearly and most productively. Indeed CARICOM's experiences represent an excellent systemic case study to confirm that (to paraphrase Rosenau a bit) nonhuman aspects of an external environment and/or actions occurring abroad can condition or otherwise influence international behavior (Rosenau 1966: 43). This phenomenon has been demonstrated most vividly as CARICOM has pursued its top-priority concern of maximizing its participants' economic security.

Indeed, the utility of Rosenau's approach becomes increasingly apparent as one moves beyond this basic three-tiered configuration. At first, however, such does not seem to be the case, at least with respect to the CARICOM experience, for his preliminary classification scheme (Rosenau 1966: 48) suggests that individual/idiosyncratic rather than international/systemic variables will exert the greatest foreign policy influence on states whose traits are similar to those of CARICOM's members (i.e., countries with open political systems that are small and economically underdeveloped). But missing from this equation is the very important fact, recognized and heavily emphasized by Braveboy-Wagner (1989) in her outstanding work, that the economies of nations such as those in the CARICOM region are

> intimately linked to the global capitalist economy and that Caribbean economic dependence on Western countries has in large part determined the scope and direction of their security and diplomatic activities as well. Thus the role of international economic factors . . . must be incorporated into any model of Caribbean foreign policy. (20)

Ultimately, Rosenau does take such concerns into account by factoring the "penetration" concept into his calculations. A penetrated political system, he says, can be defined as "one in which nonmembers of a national society participate directly and authoritatively, through actions taken jointly with a society's members, in either the allocation of its values or the mobilization of support on behalf of its goals" (Rosenau 1966: 65). Clearly the international linkages and dependencies highlighted by Braveboy-Wagner would appear to justify characterizing CARICOM's members as penetrated states. When this attribute is added to those mentioned previously, the profile of CARICOM countries that emerges—small, economically underdeveloped, politically open, and externally penetrated—places them in a category where Rosenau contends that *all aspects* of their foreign policy agenda will be influenced primarily by international/systemic considerations (Rosenau 1966: 91). This hypothesis is supported by the survey presented here of CARICOM's quest for economic security, for it has been amply demonstrated that activity in this issue area has been and continues to be overwhelmingly dominated by the dynamics of CARICOM's relations with the larger global community (especially the United States and the EU).

Looking to the immediate future, it unfortunately appears unlikely that CARICOM will really be able to function as a catalyst for achieving a high level of economic security. It has lost its privileged Lomé connection with the EU, the new Cotonou Agreement representing at best a problematical replacement. Its situation with regard to NAFTA has not yet been fully clarified, with the present trends suggesting that Washington is not inclined to extend the CARICOM countries any kind of significant special treatment.

Under such conditions the nature of the CARICOM states' evolving relations with mainland Latin America would seem to be a key variable in the international equation that has always been central to their well-being. What is needed is for these ties to be solidified within the context of integration organizations that can serve as vehicles for significant developmental progress as well as effective collective bargaining agents with the world's major economic power centers. Unfortunately, experiences such as those with the ACS during its first seven years (i.e., through 2001) provide few assurances that this optimistic scenario will become a reality. In short, the CARICOM nations, like many other developing countries, face a very uncertain economic future in today's highly competitive neoliberal world.

DISCUSSION QUESTIONS

1. Is there a major contradiction for small states such as those found in the Caribbean between joining NAFTA and maximizing their effectiveness over sovereignty?
2. What are the most effective strategies for small states such as those found in the Caribbean to counter or manage Rosenau's penetration phenomenon?
3. Which of the following options is more likely to enhance the ability/effectiveness of Caribbean governments to bargain collectively with the United States: deepening the existing ties through CARICOM or broadening (beyond CARICOM) their networks of cooperation/integration?
4. Keeping in mind Rosenau's various issue area categories, would it appear to make more pragmatic sense for individual Caribbean governments to employ a bilateral or a multilateral (via CARICOM) approach to their relations with the United States and other non-Caribbean countries?

NOTES

This chapter draws on and at some points incorporates material written by the author for "Evolving Patterns of International Relations," in *Understanding the Contemporary Caribbean*, ed. Richard Hillman and Thomas D'Agostino (Boulder, Colo.: Rienner, 2003).

1. Four of the charter members were sovereign nations at the time CARICOM was established: Barbados, Guyana, Jamaica, and Trinidad/Tobago. The eight others, all of which except Montserrat would subsequently become independent, were Antigua, Belize (known at the time as British Honduras), Dominica, Grenada, St. Lucia, St. Vincent and the Grenadines, St. Kitts/Nevis, and Montserrat.

2. Like most similar groups, CARICOM also has associate members and official observer states. The three associates (as of early 2001) are Anguilla, the British Virgin Islands, and the Turks and Caicos Islands. The six observers are Colombia, the Dominican Republic, Mexico, the Netherlands Antilles, Puerto Rico, and Venezuela.

3. The seven members of the OECS are Antigua/Barbuda, Dominica, Grenada, Montserrat, St. Kitts/Nevis, St. Lucia, and St. Vincent and the Grenadines.

4. Of CARICOM'S full member states, five have populations of under 100,000 while another five fall into the 100,000–300,000 range. Only three break the one million mark: Trinidad and Tobago (approximately 1.2 million); Jamaica (approximately 2.6 million), and Haiti (approximately 6.8 million).

5. In Grenada's case, the Reagan administration went beyond economic measures to deal with its revolutionary government and resorted to its most extreme

option—an invasion by regular U.S. forces that was launched on October 25, 1983, and quickly took control of the island. Opinion within CARICOM regarding this matter was deeply divided: Antigua/Barbuda, Dominica, St. Lucia, St. Vincent, Jamaica, and Barbados all collaborated with Washington; Belize remained neutral; and Trinidad/Tobago, Guyana, and the Bahamas were strongly opposed.

6. ACP membership quickly expanded beyond British Commonwealth circles to include the former colonies of other European powers (especially France), with forty-six countries ultimately participating in the negotiations for the first agreement.

7. Normally, the Lomé accords were renegotiated every five years—Lomé II–1980, Lomé III–1985, and Lomé IV–1990. The 1990 version differed from its predecessors in that it was in force for ten years.

8. The most recent real per capita GDP data, which were not at this point available in graphic format from the InterAmerican Development Bank and hence do not appear in figure 7.1, indicate that the West Indies have been outperforming the mainland Hispanic countries. Specifically, CARICOM's real per capita GDP rose by 1.5 percent in 1998 and 3.2 percent in 1999. The corresponding figures for Latin America were 0.7 percent and −1.2 percent. Applying these percentages to the rough 1997 dollar amounts in figure 7.1 suggests that by 1999, the CARICOM had almost closed its per capita GDP gap with Latin America.

9. The trade data in figure 7.2 do not include tourism, which is a major industry in the Caribbean. In 1996, for example, the gross tourism revenues for the CARICOM region was $4.331 billion. Recognize, however, that foreign ownership of such enterprises as airlines and hotels means that a lot of tourist dollars do not stay in the host countries. Most estimates suggest that at least thirty-five to forty cents of every tourist dollar go to foreign companies, with some observers contending that the figures are actually as high as seventy-five to eighty cents. If we calculate for 1996 using the low and high estimates, the CARICOM states would lose anywhere from approximately $1.52 billion to $3.47 billion of the gross tourism revenues.

10. The criteria that the president must consider in determining whether a country is eligible to participate in the CBTPA fall into the following broad categories: (1) whether it has demonstrated a commitment to undertake its obligations under the World Trade Organization (WTO) and to participate in the Free Trade Area of the Americas (FTAA) or other free trade agreement negotiations; (2) the extent to which it provides protection for internationally recognized intellectual property rights; (3) the extent to which it respects internationally recognized rights of workers; (4) whether it has eliminated the worst forms of child labor; (5) the extent to which it meets U.S. counternarcotics certification criteria; (6) the extent to which it has implemented the Inter-American Convention against Corruption; and (7) the extent to which it has transparent, nondiscriminatory, and competitive procedures in government procurement programs. In addition, prospective participants must demonstrate that they have implemented or are making substantial progress toward implementing various customs procedures contained in the NAFTA agreement. For additional details, see the U.S. State Department's website at www.usinfo.state.gov/regional/ar/islands/trade03.htm.

11. Haitians illegally leaving the island who claim that they are fleeing oppression

have often been turned back by U.S. authorities, who contend that they are actually economic emigrants and hence not eligible for political asylum. This policy has often been denounced as racist by critics in both Haiti and the United States. Cubans, on the other hand, have usually been automatically classified as political refugees, welcomed with open arms, and put on a fast track to establish U.S. residency, a practice that Havana says creates unnecessary tensions and can lead to personal tragedies such as the Elian González case.

II

ANDEAN REGION

8

Venezuela

Petroleum, Democratization, and International Affairs

Elsa Cardozo Da Silva and Richard S. Hillman

Domestic as well as international events and processes have shaped Venezuelan foreign policy in the second half of the twentieth century and continue in the advent of the twenty-first. The leaders, institutions, and dynamics responsible for a nation's strategy toward the world beyond its borders are products of ideas, attitudes, and values that evolve over time. Even a cursory review of the origins of Venezuela's external relations reveals a complex political culture in which internal instability has filtered external influences. Contemporary Venezuela has had to establish its position in global affairs within the context of this historical legacy.[1]

The difficult process of independence from Spain, which included ten years of declared war, was accompanied by important diplomatic activity: from the declaration of independence on July 5, 1811, to victory at the Battle of Carabobo on June 24, 1821, and the attempt to unify Venezuela, Colombia, Ecuador, and Peru into Gran Colombia, which disintegrated in 1830. The political consolidation of the new Venezuelan state had to contend with wars and internal conflicts, the need for international recognition, boundary disputes with its neighbors, the pressure from the imperialist policies of the great powers, and the burden of foreign debts and claims of creditors. In light of these unstable and troubled initial relations with the rest of the world, the process of institutionalizing a systematic foreign policy was as slow and difficult as the consolidation of the state. During the first third of the twentieth century, Juan Vicente Gómez dealt with domestic instability by centralizing political, economic, and military power. Relatively isolated from the international system, the government's main concerns were debts and unresolved border demarcations. Otherwise, the world was considered "a potential buyer of coffee, until the arrival of oil" (Ferrigni, Guerón, and Josko de Guerón 1973: 199). Certainly, the acceleration of systemic change following World War I and the start of the production and export of oil had significant impacts on the country's self-perception and view of the world.

Venezuela's transformation into an oil-producing state contributed to redefining conceptions of stability and order that had governed domestic politics and foreign policy. Governments began to perceive the international political and economic context with growing realism. They recognized the realities of world power and slowly abandoned isolation, as evidenced by their participation in international organizations—such as the League of Nations and the Inter-American Conferences—as well as in the revision of outdated assumptions on trade policy. Venezuela entered into complex negotiations for a trade agreement with the United States—already the country's most important trading partner[2]—as well as modi vivendi with other countries. By the beginning of the Cold War, Venezuela's leaders were well aware of the growing importance of relations with the rest of the world.

The Cold War and post–Cold War drastically changed systemic conditions as well as the opportunities and threats affecting Venezuela. Domestic economic and political factors strongly influenced the country's responses to both the domestic and global transformations. The political, economic, and cultural benefits of the oil industry, along with a relatively long period of democratic stability, favored an increasingly active foreign policy. Despite visible discontinuities associated with regime change, Venezuela became active in the Americas and in democracy promotion and development.

To approach the evolution and influence of systemic and regime change—responding to James N. Rosenau's (1966) challenge for the development of middle-range theories and concrete knowledge on foreign policy, this chapter analyzes Venezuelan foreign policy in three subsections: (1) the influence of the Cold War, (2) transformations in the post–Cold War world, and (3) the relative impact of these changes on the process of foreign policymaking.

DICTATORSHIP AND DEMOCRATIC CONSOLIDATION DURING THE COLD WAR

In Venezuela, the Cold War era from 1947 to 1989 coincided with a short-lived democratic experience (1945–1948), a dictatorship (1948–1958), and a democratic period established by the Pacto de Punto Fijo (Pact of Punto Fijo, 1958–1998). Strongly impacted by regime change, foreign policy moved between adaptation and resistance to the challenges presented by the initiation, intensification, transformation, and termination of the Cold War.

At the beginning of the Cold War, profound domestic changes in Venezuela led to a brief democratic experiment. During the last years of World War II, governments in Venezuela and other Latin American countries reassessed their relations with the rest of the world. The visits of President Isaías Medina Angarita to Andean countries and the United States in 1943 and 1944 and a more complex foreign agenda, which ranged from treatment of the problems of postwar peace and security to issues of trade and political stability to relations with de facto governments, stimulated active participation in the Inter-American Conferences and in the creation of the United Nations (Consalvi 2000: 257–82).

The overthrow of the Medina administration by a civilian-military movement opened a trial period for democracy known as the Trienio (Triennium, 1945–1948). In these three years, an attempt was made to speed up the break with the legacies of the Caudillo. The "necessary gendarme" model of the Gómez dictatorship was already weakened by the enormous impact of an oil economy that engendered contradictions between authoritarianism and the policies of expanding public freedoms and developing institutional mechanisms of participation.

A civilian military junta headed by Rómulo Betancourt, the leader of Acción Democrática (AD), initiated a period of more rapid change after 1945. In 1947, a Constituent Assembly was called to draw up and approve a democratic constitution that recognized the need for an active foreign policy. Democratic political stability and economic development were understood to depend on effective participation in the definition of the rules regarding the domestic and international conditions of the postwar world. Elections were held after approving the new constitution. Nevertheless, the winner Rómulo Gallegos (AD), was ousted by a military coup in November 1948, only nine months after taking office.

A review of the Venezuelan foreign policy agenda and the priority given to its most important partners between 1945 and 1948—the United States, Latin America, and the Caribbean—demonstrates that changes in Venezuela had as much impact on foreign relations as the rapid polarization of the world between the United States and the Soviet Union after 1945.

Foreign policy during the Trienio assumed the so-called Política de las Buenas Compañías (Good Companions Policy), a commitment to promote democratic governments in the Americas. It was both an expression of ideological support for democratic ideas and practices as well as an attempt to create a secure democratic environment. Relations were terminated with nondemocratic countries such as the Dominican Republic, Spain, Argentina, and Nicaragua. During the ninth Inter-American Conference in Bogotá (1948)—which approved the charter of the Organization of American States

(OAS)—Venezuela championed principles that reflected the country's democratic perspective on international politics. In the words of Rómulo Betancourt (1969), the Venezuelan ambassador to that meeting, "[OAS] contributions in favor of the spread of democracy and the preservation of peace should be and can be of very great scope" (197).

Recognizing the asymmetry and interdependence of "the two Americas," Betancourt (1969: 207–10) advocated free access to markets and rejected economic aggression and coercive measures, insisted on legal limitations on free enterprise to prevent monopoly practices, promoted economic cooperation between Latin American countries while recognizing the advantages of sub regional agreements, proposed studies to eliminate double taxation, and advocated the holding of a continental economic conference to formulate a plan that would address the economic development needs of Latin America.

Participation in multilateral agreements was consistent with this new outlook. Venezuela signed the Bretton Woods agreements establishing the International Monetary Fund (IMF) and the World Bank in 1944; the San Francisco Charter, which led to membership of the United Nations in 1945; the Statute of the International Court of Justice in the same year; and, in 1948, the Universal Declaration of Human Rights. In 1947, Venezuela signed the Inter-American Treaty of Reciprocal Assistance and, in 1948, the Charter of the OAS and the American Declaration of the Rights and Duties of Man.

These three years of democratic experimentation left a deep imprint on the basic assumptions of foreign policy throughout the rest of the twentieth century. Venezuela's support of democracy nevertheless took place against a backdrop of conspiracies, growing political conflict, and the resurgence of military regimes in the region. The Venezuelan democratic trial was not an exception: it came to an end with the military coup of 1948 and the installation of a military junta headed by Lieutenant Colonel Carlos Delgado Chalbaud, a member of the revolutionary junta of 1945 and defense minister in the Gallegos administration. Thus, while the Cold War intensified, a ten-year period of military rule began in Venezuela. This military resurgence occurred in the context of a rise in Cold War tensions during which many Latin American governments aligned themselves with U.S. policies.

The Nuevo Ideal Nacional (New National Ideal) was the doctrinarian framework of the military regime. In domestic politics, this doctrine, which was embodied in the brief preamble to the 1953 Constitution, turned out to be "a mixture of repression, immigration and material progress" (Urbaneja 1992: 180). In foreign policy, the Ideal took an economic and political form. Economic policy was designed to stimulate the industrial development of both public and private sectors, with a strong impetus for foreign investment, particularly for U.S. capital in the oil sector.

The military regime's modernization project had a strong geopolitical component: the determination of policy by the strategic resources and advantages of Venezuela's geographic position and the priority given to the application of the principle of nonintervention in its active and passive forms. Geopolitics meant anticommunism and the building of a regional balance of power through alliances with the increasing number of regimes that shared authoritarian views and practices. Economic cooperation was used as a complementary and pragmatic resource for cultivating common points of view with those kinds of regimes.

The image of unconditional support for U.S. policies on the part of Venezuela during the military regime was due to several circumstances: the junta's initial preferential desire to win recognition from Washington; the opening to investment, especially the 1952 amendment to the Reciprocal Trade Treaty with the United States; and the decision to change the oil policies of the democratic regime (Mondolfi 2000: 345–48). Certainly, the close relationship was evident in the concentration of foreign trade with the United States, which took 38 percent of Venezuelan oil exports and 72 percent of total imports in 1952 (Vivas 1999: 127). Also, the junta agreed to increase production during the Korean War and later, during the Suez crisis in 1956, decided to resume oil concessions that had been suspended since the Trienio. The Pérez Jiménez dictatorship supported American positions and proposals in the OAS during the tenth Inter-American Conference in March 1954.

Complex coincidences and conflictive perspectives resulted in: rejection of the U.S. campaign for restrictions against Venezuelan oil imports since the early 1950s; the protection of basic industries; and in the proposed creation, at the meeting of American Heads of State in Panama in 1956, of an International Economic Aid Fund for Latin American countries with government contributions. The last of these met with strong opposition from the United States. In October 1953 the Venezuelan government adopted an anticolonialist stance in response to the violent confrontation in British Guiana between the leftist Popular Progressive Party and the colonial government (Gamus 1994; Vivas 1999: 149; Petrásh 1999: 647–49).

In relations with Latin America, the geopolitical concept designed to preserve territorial integrity and national security prevailed. This meant seeking alliances "between equals" from 1953 on. In this geopolitical game, Colombia was considered—at least until 1957—as a political and strategic antagonist. This explains, along with ideological and military affinities, the very close relations with Peru, which were intended to counterbalance Colombia's leverage in the region. In the Caribbean, this approach prompted the regime to develop its own "Good Companions" policy (Ferrigni, Guerón, and Guerón 1973: 340), characterized by solidarity with military regimes and the strengthening of Venezuela's economic presence in the Netherlands Antilles. This policy favored authoritarian regimes in Haiti, Ecuador, Bolivia, and Paraguay. The Venezuelan regime's views and fears produced a foreign policy that broke diplomatic ties with the democratic governments of Costa Rica and Uruguay, while confronting the International Labor Organization in 1955 as well as Argentina and Chile in 1957. After that year, the regime's domestic and international support plummeted and strong opposition organized around sectors that were critical for the reconstitution of the democratic system.

Finally, foreign policy as well as other governmental policies became isolated from domestic needs and expectations. On January 23, 1958, the military regime fell after a series of uprisings. A military junta took power and announced its intention to transform the country into a democratic state based on the rule of law. Following the municipal, legislative, and presidential elections of December 1958, a period of unprecedented democratic stability and institutional development began. The new regime was explicitly supported by a broad consensus among crucial actors, including political parties, unions, the church, armed forces and business. All were committed to a return to democracy based on a consociational agreement among elites (Rey 1989; Hillman 1994). The Pacto de Punto Fijo, signed in October of 1958 by the main political parties—AD Comité Pro Elecciones Independientes (COPEI), and Unión Republicana Democrática (URD)—initiated a complex democratic transition that was informed by the lessons of the failed Trienio (Jácome 1999).

The Venezuelan transition to democracy coincided with the intensification of the Cold War climate in the hemisphere. The triumph and radicalization of the Cuban Revolution and the emergence of guerrilla movements in Venezuela and elsewhere with Cuban ideological and material backing were important components of the new geopolitics. The Venezuelan political process was directly affected. Besides guerrilla attacks, the reaction of the military officers who had been displaced from power, and the attempts by the Trujillo regime in the Dominican Republic against the Venezuelan government and President Betancourt himself,[3] posed additional complications for the stabilization of democracy.

The Pacto de Punto Fijo provided a valuable formula for balancing treatment of the domestic and international dimensions of foreign policy and projecting its spirit into the international arena. A set of unwritten rules helped to promote responsibility, continuity, discretion, and prudence in foreign policy. The basic agreements were moderation in conflicts, interparty consultation and shared responsibility, discretion in the management of critical issues and rejection of their public debate, as well as affirmation of consensus (Josko de Guerón 1978: 329–441).

The 1961 constitution set out principles that were to give continuity to the foreign policy of administrations of different political tendencies over the next forty years. These principles included an explicit commitment to the defense and extension of democracy; promotion of development; cooperation based on respect for sovereignty; and repudiation of war, conquest, and economic predominance.

In the process of stabilizing the regime, foreign policy gained relevance as an important dimension of public policy designed to build abroad conditions that would favor domestic democracy and socioeconomic development. Concomitantly, the increasingly broad and complex agenda accelerated institutional development of the foreign policymaking process, creating a complicated system of negotiations within the traditional diplomatic system. Among the most important negotiations were issues concerning oil, trade and economic integration, debt and investments, democracy and human rights, economic cooperation, borders and frontiers, and the environment. These new dynamics overwhelmed the traditional decision-making process centered in the presidency, the Ministry of Foreign Relations, and the congress.

The evolution of foreign policy during the democratic period contains not only changes in the systemic opportunities and threats of the Cold War but also the significant influence of democratic regime transformations. The regime evolved from one searching for stability and the consolidation of democracy, reflected in the expansion and diversification of the foreign policy agenda, to a regime in a cycle of deconsolidation and crisis with a tendency to reduce the agenda and focus on specific priorities.

The search for democratic political stability dominated the administrations of Rómulo Betancourt (1959–1964) and Raúl Leoni (1964–1969) of AD, and the start of the first term of Rafael Caldera (1969–1974) of COPEI. During this time, foreign policy was expressed in a series of changing strategies.

The rigorous application of the precepts of the Betancourt Doctrine—a new version of the Good Companions Policy—promoted democracy and thus led to breaking diplomatic relations with regimes that came to power by force against democratically elected governments. It was activated toward Argentina and Peru in 1962 and Guatemala, Haiti, Ecuador, El Salvador, the Dominican Republic, and Honduras in 1963. Once the domestic situation was stabilized and the guerrilla movements pacified, a gradual shift to the thesis of Pluralismo Ideológico (Ideological Pluralism) replaced the doctrine. The request for OAS sanctions against the Dominican Republic (1959) and Cuba (1964) in reaction to their intervention in Venezuelan domestic affairs demonstrated the incompatibilities of domestic democracy with regional antidemocratic governments of the right or left. Venezuela became a "test case" for democratization vis-à-vis the insurgencies, guerrilla warfare, and assassination attempts supported by authoritarian regimes of the left (Cuba) and of the right (the Dominican Republic). Venezuela took its grievances to the OAS.

Complementing these policies, Venezuela's active participation in the creation of the Organization of Petroleum Exporting Countries (OPEC) in

1960 addressed the question of economic stability through the defense of oil prices. An outward-looking and strongly nationalist oil policy revived and projected the principles of the Trienio (Sánchez 1999). The restrictions on oil imports imposed by the United States in 1958 became one of the most important sources of irritation in the relations between the two countries (Tugwell 1977: 206; Tarre 1999: 668–89; Mondolfi 2000: 354–55). Apart from oil, the diversification and realignment of international economic relations was unquestionably part of the foreign agenda from the start of the democratic era, and became increasingly important as internal political stability was achieved. During the Leoni administration in 1964, Venezuela began to participate in the United Nations Conference on Trade and Development (UNCTAD). The country joined the Latin American Free Trade Association (LAFTA) in 1966, six years after its creation. In 1973, the Caldera administration signed the Andean Pact four years after its establishment. Participation in the Andean Pact required termination of the trade agreement with the United States because of its most favored nation clause. Engaging in these agreements and the new integration schemes were the most important examples of enhancing cooperative relations with Latin America and the Caribbean. These policies were accompanied by policies of cultural, technical, financial, and oil cooperation and have exhibited a high level of consistency since the 1970s.

Meanwhile, pending problems of border demarcation affected regional, political, and economic relations with neighboring countries. The claim to territory west of the Esequibo River in then British Guiana was reactivated in 1962. Also, negotiation of territorial waters with Caribbean islands under the new Law of the Sea intensified in the seventies. Most cases were resolved, including delimitation treaties with the Netherlands (1978), the United States (1978), the Dominican Republic (1979), and France (1980). Negotiations with Colombia on territorial waters and submarine areas to the north of the Gulf of Venezuela officially began in 1968. The demarcation of the Brazilian border was concluded in 1973.

The cycle of expansion and diversification of the foreign policy agenda reached its first peak during the administration of Carlos Andrés Pérez (1974–1979) when, in a period of high oil prices and OPEC protagonism, the administration advocated the "New International Economic Order," which ambitiously expressed third world aspirations of achieving favorable integration into the international economy based on fundamental transformations of the world order. The illusion of affluence and influence overextended Venezuela's international commitments (Bond 1977; Rey 1983; Romero 1986: 195–96). Paradoxically, an abundance of resources and foreign policy opportunities allowed for the overwhelming influence of systemic dynamics on foreign policy. Venezuela was able to escape neither the wave of indebtedness in the third world nor the new sources of tension and regional conflict.

Between the oil boom of the 1970s and the end of the 1980s, Venezuela received more income than in all its previous history. At the end of those twenty years, however, the country had only limited economic and sociopolitical gains and a huge foreign debt.[4] Since then, the debt became a strong determinant of foreign policy and domestic politics.

The revival of concern for regional democratic stability in the late 1970s revealed the emergent importance of international factors. Such concern, for example, led to Venezuela's deep involvement in the search for solutions to the conflict in Central America.

Relations with the United States suffered less than might have been expected from the third world and nationalist policies of the first Pérez administration. These policies included supporting Panama in the canal negotiations, nationalizing the Venezuelan oil and iron industries, and many other initiatives.[5]

Important changes on the world scene and growing domestic economic difficulties dramatically reduced the Venezuelan international agenda in the late 1970s. The North–South conference produced meager results, and détente between the United States and the USSR ended. The low priority of human rights in U.S. foreign policy, the escalation of the Central American crisis, the foreign debt crisis, and the Anglo-Argentine war meant a drastic change in regional priorities. Domestically, exhaustion of the sociopolitical pact and the pressing need for debt renegotiation decisively contributed to a reduction of the foreign policy agenda.

The administrations of Luis Herrera Campins (1979–1984) of COPEI and of Jaime Lusinchi (1984–1989) of AD diminished Venezuela's international presence by concentrating on critical issues for regime stability. Such issues as the growing pressure of the foreign debt, the aggravation of Central American conflicts, and regional crises such as Grenada (1983) and the Malvinas/Falkland Islands (1982) reduced attention to hemispheric security and alliances.

Despite the minimized agenda, the early 1980s were characterized by serious problems that revealed tensions in the country's relations with Latin America and the United States. Possibilities for regional coordination were hampered by the ideological (Social Christian) orientation of President Herrera's foreign policy toward the Central American crisis, specifically in Nicaragua and El Salvador. These difficulties were compounded by the reappearance of ideological and diplomatic tensions in relations with Cuba, domestic economic problems, and the bilateral animosity left by the rejection of a proposed demarcation of territorial waters with Colombia.

An important change in Venezuela's approach to regional issues emerged in the mid-1980s. A drastic fall in oil prices between 1985 and 1986 and renewed pressure to service the foreign debt fostered a new need for coordination with regional partners. Also, change was stimulated by the new wave of democratization in Latin America, which brought about a broad common regional agenda. Participating in a growing regional consensus on the Central American conflict, Venezuela contributed to enhancing regional cooperation by helping to transform the Contadora Group into the Group of Río (1986). Moreover, despite the idea of a regional security organization including Cuba and without the United States, not even the crisis in relations with Colombia in 1987 impeded regional coordination. The United States remained a source of investment and a market for Venezuelan oil, despite restrictive measures on a number of Venezuela's nontraditional exports.

This new impetus for regional cooperation revealed the gradual evolution of a democratic culture in Venezuela and was manifested in the country's foreign policy. The underlying cultural component was characterized by a commitment to democratic values, as reflected in an attitude of conciliation and consensus. Also, it implied the need to resolve differences between general political principles (regional cooperation and democratic solidarity vis-à-vis nonintervention) and sometimes conflicting special interests (trade, energy, environment, and financial). The recognition of interdependence, especially visible in the handling of the asymmetrical relationship with the United States, became an important part of Venezuela's democratic approach to foreign policy. It was explicitly stated by Rómulo Betancourt in his inaugural address (February 13, 1959): "With the United States . . . we will maintain cordial relations that, because they concern the most powerful country of the hemisphere, will have to be different from colonial submission or provoking rudeness" (cited by Mondolfi 2000: 355).

POLITICAL CRISIS AND DEMOCRATIC DECONSOLIDATION AFTER THE COLD WAR

Fundamental regime and systemic changes were both profound and rapid in 1989, producing instability despite the end of the Cold War. In that year, the Venezuelan "Caracazo" erupted. This popular revolt characterized by massive riots and looting in important cities left hundreds of victims and great material losses. In a society that many considered a model of democratic stability and prosperity, the revolt revealed exhaustion of the model and institutions of consociational democracy, its statist and rent-seeking economic supports, as well as perversion of its culture of conciliation and consensus. Venezuela was constrained once again by troubles common to the region.

The optimism created by the democratic wave in Latin America and the Caribbean as well as the expectation of prosperity following the adoption of economic reform programs changed to skepticism—if not pessimism—in response to poor political and economic results, accompanied by growing social conflict in the region. In this context, Venezuelan foreign policy rapidly lost its image of democratic exceptionality and oil affluence. The legacy of the Lusinchi administration included corruption scandals and "serious problems concerning the financing of State expenditures, the drying up of private investment, and capital flight. Inflation, devaluation, the depletion of foreign reserves, the loss of credibility of the political system and its elite, and the declining abilities of the political parties to articulate and satisfy social demands added to the crisis" (Guerón 1993: 5). Under the stress of acute domestic and international pressures, Venezuelan foreign policy underwent a radical shift beginning in the 1990s.

The second term of Carlos Andrés Pérez (1989–1993) brought with it an economic and political reform program called *El Gran Viraje* (The Great Turnaround). It was an attempt to expand and consolidate the market economy, reduce and rationalize state intervention, and stimulate political and administrative decentralization. The program and measures that inspired foreign policy focused on a geoeconomic strategy based on trade diplomacy and a revival of Latin American and Caribbean integration. Democratic solidarity also received renewed attention. Venezuela supported the creation of a Unit for the Promotion of Democracy in the OAS (1990), and the OAS Resolution on Representative Democracy (1991) aimed to respond immediately and collectively "to the sudden or irregular interruption of the democratic political institutional process or of the legitimate exercise of power by the democratically elected governments" with the convocation of a meeting of the Permanent Council. On the part of Venezuela, the commitment to democracy involved support for President Jean Bertrand Aristide of Haiti after his overthrow in 1991, condemnation of the extraconstitutional powers assumed by President Alberto Fujimori of Peru in 1992, as well as backing the peace process in Colombia and democratic stabilization in Central America.

Simultaneously with the policy of economic opening, which included the signing of an agreement with the IMF on renegotiation of the foreign debt, the Pérez administration worked to reactivate regional integration and cooperation in the Andean Group and the Group of Río. The Group of Three was formed with Colombia and Mexico for creating a free trade zone and coordinating foreign policies. Also, to stimulate trade with the Caribbean Basin, nonreciprocal free trade initiatives were proposed to the Caribbean Community (CARICOM) and the Central American Common Market (CACM). The dynamism of regional integration policies was promoted by the widespread adoption of economic liberation programs, expansion of democratic regimes, and renewed willingness to solve demarcation and other border problems. Establishing binational commissions to identify and address common problems and opportunities immediately gave renewed impetus to the relations with Colombia, an important partner in the new

Venezuelan strategy. Indeed, the careful attention to the common agenda—including the critical issue of sea delimitation—facilitated the coordination of the two governments in strengthening the Andean Community and their joint regional projection.

Despite Venezuela's new international image and improved credibility in foreign policy occasioned by improvements in the economy and international relations, domestic politics showed increasing stress. Social protest along with growing opposition to governmental policies on the part of political parties and the media culminated in two failed military uprisings in February and November 1992. These events contributed to the erosion of the legitimacy of the Pérez administration and its program. A trial for misappropriation of funds finally produced the impeachment of President Pérez in May 1993. The commitment to economic integration and liberalization, promotion of democracy, and cooperative approaches to border issues was compromised by this episode.

After the transition government of President Ramón J. Velázquez, the second Rafael Caldera administration (1994–1998) took office with a new party and an ad hoc coalition. Foreign policy, which during the inconclusive Pérez administration had been a high priority in public policy, was reduced in importance and modified in direction as well as in its thematic and geographic focus.

Economically, the domestic dimension was reflected in criticism of globalization and the IMF, although inevitably in 1996 an agreement had to be negotiated with it and a new version of the adjustment program implemented. Politically, the domestic dimension gained preeminence with a geopolitical and ethical emphasis on hemispheric relations, while the geopolitical shift generated a change in priorities (Cardozo 1997).

The new approach intended to reduce the priority of relations with Colombia in the midst of increasing guerrilla violence along the common borders and to redefine relations with the United States after enthusiasm declined for the proposed free trade Enterprise for the Americas and for an association to the North American Free Trade Agreement (NAFTA). Important complements to this strategy of changing priorities were efforts to overcome tensions and develop economic and political links with Brazil and the pursuit of opportunities for association with the Southern Cone Common Market (MERCOSUR).

The Summit of the Americas in 1994 provided another important opportunity for redefining the direction of foreign policy. There, as in the OAS and other international forums, Venezuela gave priority to the fight against corruption and poverty, which took precedence over free trade and the promotion and defense of democracy.

The continuity of economic relations with the United States was affected by changes of priorities in the common agenda. The United States' extraterritorial application of unilateral measures defined the tone of these relations. The Caldera administration, for example, resisted the installation of radar and flights over Venezuelan territory to fight against drug trafficking, although limited agreements were reached. Beyond this specific issue, Venezuela joined other Latin American countries in protests and condemnations against other unilateral measures, such as the approval of the Helms–Burton Act in 1996 and U.S. certification of the preservation of human rights and the fight against drug trafficking.

Overall, integration acquired a more geopolitical than economic focus. Since 1998, this trend intensified as the limitations of U.S. leadership and new geopolitical and economic complexities of the post–Cold War order became evident. Since the late 1990s, the unresolved conflicts of the post–Cold War period had produced growing sociopolitical instability. Economic volatility in Latin America became painfully apparent. In this context, the Venezuelan presidential elections of 1998 brought to power retired lieutenant colonel Hugo Chávez, one of the leaders of the failed military uprising of February 1992, whose program produced a dramatic change in the direction and style of foreign policy. The Chávez administration adopted a program that gave participatory democracy a prominent role, resulting in a strongly presidential and centralized regime with a weak system of checks and balances. It was accompanied by a system of popular consultation that—as it has worked in practice—could be defined as "democracy by referendum." The constitution, approved in 1999, renamed the country the "Bolivarian Republic of Venezuela." This attempt to shift the international image (and self-image) of the country was allegedly inspired by a new sense of independence, sovereignty, nationalism, Latin American unity, and antihegemonic orientation. These ideas were revealed both in the principles written in the new constitution and executed in the foreign policy of President Chávez's government, but they cannot be considered as a consistent doctrine.[6]

The new constitutional text replaced the specific commitment to supporting democratic institutions with vague ideas about promoting the democratization of the world order. As a complement, the defense of sovereignty and the principles of nonintervention and self-determination were accentuated. The new direction took the form of proposals in the OAS to change the concept of representative to participatory democracy. The proposals aimed at limiting the role of election observers and opposing the application of the Resolution on Representative Democracy in the Peruvian election crisis of 2000. Consistent with that idea, Chávez's government considered the ostensible threats to democratic institutions in Paraguay and Ecuador in 1999 and 2000 as questions of a strictly domestic nature. Also, there were ambiguities with respect to the Colombian peace process and the treatment of the Colombian guerrilla and other regional insurgent movements, as discussed later. Government-to-government relationships and the very principle of nonintervention were at issue.

The constitution expressly recognized the national interest in regional economic integration and the state's predominant role in economic policy. The prevailing concept of regional integration as geoeconomic with geopolitical trimmings was altered to give more weight to the idea of political and military integration. These were apparent in the president's insistence on proposals for a Latin American confederation and even a Latin American NATO. In the meantime, a long list of specific agreements signed by the governments in the Andean Community of Nations (CAN) and between it and MERCOSUR sought to stimulate economic and political integration. These, however, did not receive needed attention and commitment.

The president's international contacts, which were aimed at developing a more global foreign policy that was less dependent on traditional partners and relationships, had very specific effects on Venezuela's energy policy and on relations with Colombia, Brazil, Cuba, and the United States. Rising tensions with Colombia acquired an unprecedented complexity because, aside from the growing pressure of the Colombian conflict on the Venezuelan border, the Chávez administration's attitude toward the guerrilla movements damaged relations between the two neighbors and undermined the legitimacy of the country's traditional mediating role. The proposal to recognize the belligerency of the guerrilla movement, dealings with the insurgency to liberate guerrilla prisoners inside Colombia without the knowledge of the Colombian government, the mismanagement of complex situations such as the capture and liberation by Venezuelan security forces of a guerrilla accused of hijacking an airplane, and frequent presidential references against the Colombian oligarchy and media fostered tensions among the two governments. These tensions were exacerbated by increased agreement between the United States and Colombia regarding terrorism, trade, and the Plan Colombia, which was criticized in Venezuela, as well as Colombia's granting of political asylum to Pedro Carmona, who attempted to assume the Venezuelan presidency during the aborted coup of April 12, 2002.

The role of Cuban–Latin American relations intensified. Brazil and Cuba became close partners in 1999 and 2000 during the search for political affinities, regional and hemispheric balance, and new openings in economic relations. Brazil and Venezuela reached important economic agreements regarding the increasing sale of oil and energy. In October 2000, Fidel Castro's visit to Venezuela, the nature and content of the energy cooperation agreement, and President Chávez's open expression of ideological sympathy for the Cuban revolution, revealed a profound change in Venezuelan foreign policy toward Cuba. While previous rapprochement was designed to contribute to Cuban democratization, the new relationship tended to foster—with political and economic support—the Cuban socialist model. Since

October 2000, Cuba has benefited, more than any other Caribbean country, from a very generously financed supply of Venezuelan oil. Subsequent to the aborted coup in April 2002, however, Venezuela terminated this policy.

Relations with the United States, which at first refused candidate Chávez a visa to enter the country, also changed. Such change had manifested itself in a complex combination of pragmatic and ideological components. The Venezuelan government expressed disagreements and open opposition to American proposals and policies. For example, Venezuela voted in the UN (1999) against condemnations for human rights violations against Cuba, Iraq, and Libya; opposed OAS (2000) sanctions against Peru; and gave limited support to free trade and the democratic clause proposed in the Americas Summit in Quebec (2001). Venezuela also refused to accept antinarcotics overflights and strongly opposed the "Plan Colombia." This plan was severely criticized by the Venezuelan government because of the military component of the U.S. aid and the risks of regional conflict escalation. Also, between 1999 and 2000, charges by the assistant secretary of state of the new Western Hemisphere Affairs Bureau that the Venezuelan government had been supportive of insurgencies in the Andean region contributed to the intensification of the antiunipolar—and even anti-American—rhetoric of President Chávez, especially during his frequent travels abroad. After the terrorist attacks against the United States, the Venezuelan president condemned fighting terrorism with terrorism by showing photos of children as victims of U.S. bombings in Afghanistan. This brought bilateral diplomatic relations between the United States and Venezuela to its worst moment.

Both Venezuela and the United States, however, sought to manage their bilateral relationship due to the risks of further deterioration. Even after its thinly veiled statement of support for Pedro Carmona as an alternative to Hugo Chávez when he was temporarily ousted in April 2002, the United States denied complicity in the coup attempt and continued to seek improved relations with Venezuela. Indeed, since 1999, oil was clearly a dominant factor in the redefinition of Venezuelan foreign policy. This necessarily included relations with the United States, Venezuela's primary market.

OPEC and President Chávez's leadership in promoting effective responses to the decline in oil prices gained renewed importance. Both helped stimulate a recovery from the very low price levels of 1998. Higher oil prices, however, brought about a new governmental illusion of power. It is important to note that despite the president's defiant rhetoric challenging United States hegemony, especially on his visits to OPEC partners in 1999, including Saddam Hussein and Muammar Gadhafi, the practical execution of oil policy has been relatively realistic and prudent. In 2001, after a long Asian tour that included declarations in favor of communism in China and Russia, the Venezuelan leader made a stop in Texas to assure that his country continued to be a secure energy provider to the United States. Moreover, as the termination of oil subsidies to Cuba after the attempted coup in April 2002 demonstrated, the Venezuelan government adopted more conciliatory policies toward the United States.

Despite Chávez's efforts to diversify relations with the world, as expressed in his intensive contacts with leaders of Europe and Asia, the accelerated weakening of Venezuela's democratic institutions and the ambitious geopolitical focus of foreign policy produced a dualistic isolationism. On the one hand, the country lost influence in regional and hemispheric processes as its "revolutionary" commitment continues and as the economy increases its dependency on oil income. On the other hand, foreign policy did not contribute to the provision of adequate responses to the most urgent domestic economic and social needs.

REGIME AND SYSTEMIC CHANGES AND VENEZUELAN FOREIGN POLICYMAKING

This review of a half-century of Venezuelan foreign policy reveals the conditions in which domestic and international influences varied during and after the Cold War. As Rosenau (1966) suggests, "We are not talking [just] about levels of analysis but, in effect, about philosophies of analysis with respect to one particular level" (109). Accordingly, we have traced the evolution of Venezuelan foreign policy on the domestic level, describing how a relatively small and underdeveloped Latin American country perceived and reacted to the Cold War and post–Cold War circumstances. We have also described a more complex variety of policies and issues with respect to regime characteristics and the structure of the international system in the second half of the twentieth century and beginning of the twenty-first.

From the domestic perspective, three eras were fundamental in the process of regime change: (1) the democratic Triennium; (2) the dictatorship; and (3) the Punto Fijo democratic regime, including its deconsolidation. We have interpreted the impact of these regime changes on foreign policy through the variables of leadership, ideas and culture, institutionalization, and oil revenue.

It is impossible to exaggerate the importance of individual leadership in the evolution of Venezuelan foreign policy. Because of their recognition of the importance of foreign relations, certain presidents, foreign relations ministers, and diplomats have had a decisive impact in the making of Venezuelan foreign policy. This trait has not necessarily been more accentuated in the periods of dictatorship or institutional deconsolidation. During the democratic experiences, the influence of the executive, particularly the president, was decisive in foreign policy. This is illustrated by the impact of different personal styles and changing international interests on foreign policy. Good examples of strong presidential leadership are the assertiveness of Betancourt in 1945–1948 and during his presidency of 1959–1964, the activism of Pérez in both his terms, and the rebellious and controversial international presence of Chávez.

Venezuelan political culture evolved during these periods. The emergence of democratic ideas gave content and purpose to the institutional development that created the context for foreign policymaking. These ideas contributed to a growing recognition of the importance of foreign policy for society and the need to harmonize domestic needs with international possibilities. Thus, democratic culture slowly pervaded the orientations and strategies of Venezuelan foreign policy. Democratic culture has provided the sense of legitimacy required for cooperation, peaceful solution of controversies, interdependence and independence, as well as the search for democracy and consensus. These ideas, with a variety of emphases and levels of explicitness, are contained in the Venezuelan constitutional texts of 1947, 1961, and 1999.

The most general assumption is that institutional development, not merely in terms of constitutions and laws but also in the effective enforcement of institutionalized rules and procedures, produces legitimate and effective implementation of foreign policy. Hence, the domestic influence on Venezuelan foreign policy is profound. Without denying the achievements and merits of specific policies at different times in the slow process of building the internal order and its external projection, Venezuelan foreign policy was most stable and farsighted between 1958 and the late 1980s. The democratic and alternating character of government, to a certain extent controlled by institutional checks and balances, added a high degree of stability and continuity. Venezuela began to address (through foreign policy) new dimensions, or "Venezuelan identities," that included the image of a country that perceived itself as still in the process of development, dependent on oil income, democratic, and part of the American hemisphere with asymmetrical yet important relations with the United States (Josko de Guerón 1984, 1992). Around these dimensions, specific agencies, policies, and strategies were aimed at achieving democratic political stability with economic prosperity and development. Such institutional development notwithstanding, a changing mixture of individual leadership and decaying degrees of legitimacy and efficacy created the conditions for important shifts in foreign policy.

Major changes in Venezuelan foreign policy coincided with transformations in world affairs that impacted the Americas. Proactive or reactive Venezuelan policies depended not only on leaders and institutional support but also on citizens' perceptions of governmental legitimacy and efficacy. The Cold War produced cycles of heightened tension. The U.S. policy of containment of communism in the late 1940s and early 1950s ironically coincided with the demise of the Venezuelan democratic Triennium. During the intensification of the Cold War, the military government developed a foreign policy that was designed to assure regime stability by cooperating with other authoritarian governments as well as supporting the United States in its anticommunist policies. The Cuban revolution and its aftermath, including attempts to export the revolution, had a direct impact on Venezuelan domestic politics. The newly emergent democratic regime had to deal with guerrilla insurgencies in the 1960s as it was stabilizing itself through consociational pacts.

Venezuela played an important mediating role in the Central American crisis in the 1980s. Antidemocratic instability in the region, the need for a secure regional geopolitical and socioeconomic environment, and the relative affluence provided by oil revenues produced different measures of activism on the part of Venezuela's pacted regime. Hence, to a large extent the cycles of Venezuelan foreign policy can be understood in terms of the cushioning and stabilizing effects on the economy of oil revenues during "boom" periods. The very ideas that led to the emergence and consolidation of a culture of conciliation and consensus derived, at least in part, from a society transformed by cycles of prosperity and impoverishment. Both domestic and foreign policies have been influenced by these transformations.

Undoubtedly in the final analysis of the second half of the twentieth century, the most important influences on Venezuelan foreign policy were the democratic opening from 1945 to 1948 and the democratic experience since 1958. The constitutions, governmental programs, speeches, and international commitments aided in the construction of a democratic political culture and its institutionalization.

The ten-year military regime between 1948 and 1958 altered the process of institution building, particularly in the nature and purpose of hemispheric cooperation. Nevertheless, throughout the Cold War, the prevailing goal of Venezuelan foreign policy was to consolidate the country's identity based on oil, democracy, and "Western" economic, political, and cultural values; to maintain a close relationship with the United States; and to build relations of cooperation and integration with Latin America and the Caribbean in search of opportunities for independent action.

The speed of economic, technological, and cultural change as well as the transformation in the very nature of the international system after the end of the Cold War exposed Venezuela to the challenges of a very uncertain world. Thus, the country's domestic institutions became overwhelmed by an overextended agenda replete with contradictory demands. Venezuelan foreign policy reflected these contradictions thus weakening many of the geopolitical and economic commitments built up over half the twentieth century.

Given a situation in which democratic institutions in Venezuela have eroded despite their intended radical transformation, it is useful to compare and contrast the nation's authoritarian and democratic foreign policies. The dictatorial regime, notwithstanding its central preoccupation with stability and national development, was strongly exposed to the influence of the international environment and, therefore, generally more vulnerable, defensive, and adoptive of strategies to appease more powerful regional actors rather than concentrating on sustainable domestic development. The democratic regime, especially in its period of greatest stability at the end of the 1960s through the early 1980s, developed more autonomous and innovative foreign policies that were oriented around national development despite significant variability in their effectiveness.

In conclusion, stable, relatively efficient, representative domestic institutions generated Venezuelan foreign policy during the later Cold War era (1958–1989). Oil and democracy were well managed within the context of complex geopolitical and economic relations with "the two Americas." In the post–Cold War era, however, domestic institutions lost their effectiveness and legitimacy in an atmosphere of regional and world uncertainty, volatile oil income, and cultural conflicts. Understanding how regime change shapes Venezuelan policies toward the world, therefore, continues to be an important task for scholars, analysts, and practitioners.

DISCUSSION QUESTIONS

1. What contrasts between adaptation and resistance to pressures of the Cold War can be seen in Venezuelan foreign policy during the Trienio (1945–1948) and the dictatorship (1948–1958)?
2. What effects did the emergence of the Pacto Consociacional have on foreign policy between 1958 and 1989? What effects did its crisis and deconsolidation have after 1989?
3. How can the relationship between Venezuela and the United States be characterized during and after the Cold War in terms of convergence and divergence on two fundamental issues: democracy and petroleum?

NOTES

1. For the most explicit references, see Kelly and Romero (2002); Boersner (1978, 1987); Josko de Guerón (1984, 1992); Alfredo Toro Hardy (1986, 1992); Guerón (1991); Romero (1992, 1998); Cardozo (1992, 2000); Romero (2002).

2. Despite the early lead taken by the British in the development of the oil business between 1912 and 1932, by the end of World War II, over thirty U.S. companies were controlling the bulk of the country's oil exploration and production (Betancourt 1969: 43–61).

3. Betancourt narrowly escaped assassination by Trujillo's agents in 1960, when

both conservatives and communists attempted to foment insurrections against democratic regimes in Latin America.

4. In 1989, to honor the service of the foreign debt, the country was required to pay more than half of the total income in foreign exchange from exports (Guerón 1993: 2–5).

5. Franklin Tugwell (1977: 216) presents an extensive inventory of irritating Venezuelan initiatives, including the promotion of the Latin American Economic System (SELA) as an autonomous forum, support for Andean restrictions on private capital, the sponsorship of the move to reassimilate Cuba in the Inter-American System, the hostility to the Chilean military regime, and the special condemnation of the U.S. 1975 Trade Act.

6. "[T]he assumption that we are inheritors of Bolívar has been an important factor in Venezuela's foreign policy. But we must distinguish between Bolívar the dreamer of 1810 from the Bolívar who during the foundation of Bolivia then understood the forces of disintegration and anarchy" (Consalvi 1997: 143–45).

9

Colombia

U.S. Subordinate, Autonomous Actor, or Something in Between?

Arlene B. Tickner

The "crude pre-theory" of foreign policy developed by James N. Rosenau (1996) assesses the weight of systemic, state-level (governmental and non-governmental), and idiosyncratic (or individual-level) variables as a function of the size/strength of a given country, the relative development of its economy, and the open/closed nature of its political system. Rosenau (1996: 183) predicts that in small, underdeveloped countries with either open or closed political systems, idiosyncratic and systemic variables will have the greatest weight in explaining foreign policy behavior. In keeping with Rosenau's pre-theory, the major characteristics, trends, and underlying principles of Colombian foreign policy are analyzed in this chapter as a function of a specific systemic factor—namely, the country's relations with the United States, the idiosyncracies of individual presidential administrations, and state-level variables, including the domestic political regime and the armed conflict.

At first glance, the study of Colombia's foreign relations seems rather straightforward, given that these tend to reflect two conflicting views of the country's place in the international system: (1) that its peripheral, subordinate status allows marginal leeway in foreign policy and warrants strict alignment with the hegemonic power, the United States; and (2) that the diversification of foreign relations, in combination with greater protagonism, would increase Colombia's negotiating power and create relative margins of autonomy in its relations with the United States. Nevertheless, upon closer examination, it will become clear that Colombian foreign policy fails to fit perfectly into these neat categories. Rather, the search for general principles is largely defied by the conjunctural, incongruous, and changing nature of the country's foreign relations. This chapter provides a general explanation and analysis of this scenario.

GENERAL CHARACTERISTICS OF COLOMBIAN FOREIGN POLICY

Many of the central features of Colombia's foreign policy exhibit a strong correlation with two distinct dynamics: the particular nature of the Colombian political system and the country's relations with the United States. These features include (1) the presidentialist and bipartisan character of Colombian foreign relations; (2) their personalized nature; (3) significant degrees of fragmentation in the formulation of foreign policy; (4) the existence of "parallel" diplomacies; (5) the centrality of international law; (6) closeness to the United States, combined with a low international profile; and (7) lack of input/interest on the part of public opinion (Drekonja 1983; Pardo and Tokatlián 1989: 83–86; Cepeda and Pardo 1989: 9–11).

As in the case of most Latin American countries, the presidentialist character of Colombia's political regime, the absence of a true division of powers, and the marginal role played by the legislature in international matters has historically granted the executive a significant degree of autonomy in the formulation of foreign policy. In addition to the Ministry of Foreign Relations, formally charged with the planning and execution of the country's international relations, the Colombian president has an additional consultation mechanism, the Foreign Relations Advisory Committee (CARE), composed of all former elected presidents and several other members appointed by congress and the president. This committee is charged with advising the executive on diverse international issues of strategic importance. The original purpose behind the creation of the CARE was to forge an agreement between the Liberal and Conservative parties concerning Colombia's negotiations with the United States following the independence of Panama (Ardila 1991: 51). Since its creation in 1914, the CARE has thus constituted an important mechanism for nurturing bipartisan consensus concerning Colombian foreign policy that has remained intact throughout most of the country's history.

The extreme personalization of the Colombian political system, along with its presidentialist nature, has allowed for a marked distinction between the formal structure of the country's foreign policy apparatus and the actual execution of Colombia's external affairs, which has tended to revolve around an extremely personalized network of individuals directly associated with the president of the republic (Drekonja 1983: 206). In practice, this situation is reflected in the predominance of varying foreign policy orientations, depending on the idiosyncracies of specific administrations, resulting in the absence of consistent, long-term state policies.

Colombian foreign policy has also been characterized by high degrees of fragmentation, derived from the centrality that economic diplomacy acquired in the country's international relations beginning in the early 1900s, and the perceived inefficacy of the Ministry of Foreign Relations in conducting the country's commercial affairs. In 1925, coffee accounted for approximately 80 percent of the country's total exports and 25 percent of its gross national product (GNP) (Randall 1992: 140), which largely explains why coffee became the central axis of Colombian foreign policy. The National Federation of Coffee Growers, a business association combining private and state sector attributes, was created in 1927, and quickly became a "state within the state" (Drekonja 1983: 201), acquiring a central role in establishing Colombia's coffee policy, while marginalizing the Ministry of Foreign Relations completely from coffee negotiations on an international level. According to Fernando Cepeda and Rodrigo Pardo (1989: 10), Colombian coffee diplomacy, exercised primarily by the Coffee Federation, contrasted sharply with those political diplomatic efforts executed by the Ministry of Foreign Relations: While the first was characterized by its efficiency and professional nature, the second was inefficient and markedly politicized.

The relative weakness of the Ministry of Foreign Relations has facilitated the ascendence of distinct actors and institutions to fill this void over time. Traditionally, this ministry's activities have been concentrated in two areas: the resolution of territorial and border disputes, and the conduct of conventional diplomacy in international organizations. As will be discussed subsequently, the changing nature of Colombia's foreign relations has thus led to the creation of new public posts parallel to the Ministry of Foreign Relations and the ascendence of distinct state and nonstate actors in the formulation and execution of the country's foreign policy.

The existence of parallel diplomacies in the Colombian case is the result of all of the factors highlighted thus far. The inability of the Ministry of Foreign Relations to coordinate the country's foreign affairs has implied that distinct institutions and actors occupy roles of varying importance, depending on the issue area in question. As a result, foreign policy is often the result of diverse, uncoordinated, spontaneous actions taken by different players (Cardona 1997: 343).

The execution of coventional diplomacy by the Ministry of Foreign Relations has been characterized by the consistent application of the basic principles of international law, more than the satisfaction of specific political goals (Drekonja 1983: 65; Tokatlián and Cardona 1991: 9). The loss of Panama and the national humilliation caused by this event led Colombian policymakers to view international law as the principal means of guaranteeing the country's sovereignty, understood primarily in terms of its territorial integrity. Nevertheless, the strict application of juridical principles has at times led to political inconsistency. Following the onset of the Falklands/Malvinas war in 1982, for instance, Colombia abstained, along with the United States, from voting on the application of the Inter-American Reciprocal Assistance Treaty (TIAR) in support of Argentina. This decision, based entirely on legal considerations,[1] marginalized the country from its Latin American neighbors (Palacios 1983: 63).

Another central characteristic of Colombian foreign policy is the country's alignment with the United States, in both economic and political terms. Following the independence of Panama, Colombia began to seek the satisfaction of its foreign policy objectives through a close affiliation with the United States. In addition to becoming a passive recipient of U.S. policy, the country's insertion into the international system became strongly conditioned by its links with Washington (Pardo and Tokatlián 1989: 84).

Finally, the lack of input and interest on the part of the population has been notorious in the case of Colombia's international relations (Pardo and Tickner 1998: 18–19). During many years subsequent to the loss of Panama, Colombia adopted an inward-looking, isolated stance in relation to the rest of the world. For the vast majority of the population, the nearly continuous existence of civil conflict since the late 1940s has compounded this historical predisposition, given that the challenges inherent to the country's external affairs seem to pale in comparison with the domestic situation.

CONTENDING DOCTRINES: *RESPICE POLUM* AND *RESPICE SIMILIA*

Respice Polum

As mentioned previously, one of the most permanent characteristics of Colombia's international relations has been the impact of the United States on the country's foreign policy orientations. Gerhard Drekonja (1983) points to the independence of Panama in 1903, the deterioration of U.S.-Colombian relations, and Bogotá's subsequent efforts to normalize its ties with Washington, as the central backdrop through which Colombian foreign policy evolved. Before the loss of Panama, considered to be one of its richest provinces, the country had played an active international role, and was perceived as having significant potential on a global level given its strategic location and vast natural resources (Tokatlián 2000a: 33; Randall 1992: 98). Nevertheless, the "Panama syndrome" produced a national catharsis that led to a fundamental shift in Colombia's view of its own role in the world (López Michelsen 1989: 157)—namely, the incident highlighted the country's impotence alongside the United States. As a result, Colombian foreign policy became characterized by its introverted, low-profile nature.

Marco Fidel Suárez, in his capacity as a member of the CARE, minister of foreign relations, and then president of the republic (1918–1922), promoted the negotiation, signing and ratification of the Urrutia–Thompson Treaty, through which Colombia received a U.S.$25 million indemnization from the United States in recognition of the losses incurred by Panama's independence. In essence, Suárez's role in this process reflected the president's conviction that U.S. hegemony in the continent was inevitable and that the normalization of Colombia's relations with Washington constituted a sine qua non of development (Pardo and Tokatlián 1989: 97). Not surprisingly, during the 1920s, both the country's domestic and international objectives revolved around the promotion of economic development and modernization. Policies designed to attract U.S. firms interested in investing in Colombia were consequently promoted, while U.S. experts were invited to participate directly in national development efforts.[2]

The tendency to align Colombia's economic interests with those of Washington became widely known as the *respice polum* doctrine. This term, coined by President Suárez himself, implied that the country should direct its foreign policy toward the "polar star" of the North, the United States (Drekonja 1983: 70–71). In practice, this principle led the country to adopt a pragmatic position of subordination toward the United States, "in explicit recognition that Colombia was located in the North American sphere of influence" (Pardo and Tokatlián 1989: 81).

The onset of the Cold War led to a strong bipartisan consensus[3] concerning the need to maintain and strengthen Colombia's "special relationship" with the United States, mainly due to the fact that both Liberals and Conservatives were ideologically committed to fighting communism both at home and abroad.[4] As a result, the economic imperatives that had underwritten the respice polum doctrine during the first half of the twentieth century were complemented by ideological and political goals related to the communist threat. The unconditional alignment with the United States that came to characterize this second phase of respice polum was manifest in specific actions taken on an international level. Colombia was an eager participant in the construction of the postwar hemispheric order. Undoubtedly, Alberto Lleras Camargo, Colombian president between 1945–1946 and 1958–1962, best exemplified this role: Lleras was an active participant in the 1945 San Francisco Conference, was appointed as the first general secretary of the Organization of American States (OAS), collaborated directly in the crafting of the original text of the TIAR, and was invited by U.S. president John F. Kennedy to participate in the elaboration of the Alliance for Progress. All of these activities were indicative of Washington's high degree of confidence in the firmness of Bogotá's alliance with U.S. objectives (Drekonja 1983: 75).

The country also took part in many multilateral operations orchestrated by the United States. For example, Colombia was the only Latin American nation to send troops to Korea in 1951, and it also participated in a UN emergency force deployed to the Suez Canal in 1956. In addition, the country followed the lead of the United States in condemning the communist threat on a global level. At the 1961 meeting of Inter-American states in Punta del Este, a bipartisan Colombian delegation sustained that the existence of a Marxist-Leninist government in Cuba was incompatible with the security of the region, and favored the expulsion of that country from the OAS (Randall 1992: 270). Colombia supported U.S. military intervention in the Dominican Republic in 1965 on similar grounds.

In exchange for its loyalty, the country received substantial military and economic assistance from the United States. Colombia was one of the three largest recipients of U.S. military assistance in Latin America and the second largest recipient, after Brazil, of U.S. economic aid between 1949 and 1974 (Pardo and Tokatlián 1989: 86). Nevertheless, several authors maintain that the consistency with which Colombia applied the respice polum doctrine in its foreign relations, although allowing the country to avoid certain costs and risks, in particular in its relations with the United States, also provided an exaggerated degree of certainty in Washington concerning Bogotá's international conduct, with which it failed to derive as many benefits as it might have from its "special relationship" with the United States (Pardo and Tokatlián 1989: 85; Drekonja 1983: 77).

Respice Similia

Beginning with the presidency of Carlos Lleras Restrepo (1966–1970), however, Colombia began to reorient its foreign policy toward its Latin American neighbors and other nations with the goal of diversifying its international relations. On an economic level, the country adopted an increasingly independent stance regarding its monetary and commercial policy, while modernizing the institutional apparatus responsible for economic and commercial diplomacy. The Lleras Restrepo administration implemented an economic development policy that consisted of (1) gradual liberalization of imports, combined with efforts to increase the country's exports; (2) export diversification and the promotion of nontraditional exports; (3) the depoliticization of decision-making processes through the creation of semiautonomous government agencies; and (4) the regulation of multinational activity in the country (Juárez 1993: 25–26). In 1966, the Colombian government rejected IMF demands for a massive devaluation of the Colombian peso, and instead it adopted a novel and highly successful crawling peg system of gradual devaluations. The results of this policy in economic terms were considerable. By the end of the 1960s, the per capita growth of the Colombian economy reached a historical 3.8 percent, nontraditional exports grew in comparison to products such as coffee, and the country's exports and imports increased at similar levels, offsetting potential balance of payments problems (Fishlow 1998: 327–28).

On a political level, Colombia modified its stance regarding diplomatic relations with socialist countries and resumed commercial relations with the Soviet bloc countries. The argument used to justify this shift was that increased trade relations with such nations did not imply Colombia's acceptance of their ideology (Randall 1992: 277). The country also began to participate in the construction of the Andean Group, whose first meeting was held in 1967.

This shift in Colombia's foreign policy orientation has been associated with the *respice similia* doctrine, a term coined by Alfonso López Michelsen, foreign relations minister under the Lleras Restrepo administration and later president of the republic (1974–1978). Literally, the term implied that Colombian foreign policy should revolve around relations with similar countries, especially in Latin America. Following this principle, Colombia sought greater interaction with its Latin American counterparts, as well as increased leeway in the international system vis-à-vis the United States. Such changes resulted from a combination of two factors: the "permissive" systemic conditions created first by détente and afterward, by the apparent decline of U.S. hegemony in the mid-1970s; and the personal conviction of key individuals, in particular López Michelsen, in terms of the need to create relative distance between the country's foreign policy positions and Washington.

As in the case of the Lleras Restrepo government, the López administration assigned increasing importance to those economic aspects of Colombian foreign policy, while challenging the thesis, upheld by the respice polum doctrine, that a permanent harmony of interests existed between Colombia and the United States. Tellingly, President López rejected Colombia's traditional role as a "pawn" in the Cold War (Pardo and Tokatlián 1989: 105–6). Consequently, this administration sought to "universalize" Colombia's diplomatic relations even further through a series of measures designed to reduce the country's traditional dependence on the United States: (1) active participation in third world forums such as the G-77, the New International Economic Order (NIEO) discussions, and, to a lesser degree, the Non-Aligned Movement;[5] (2) explicit support of Panamanian sovereign interests in the negotiation of the Panama Canal (or Torrijos–Carter) Treaty (1977), in addition to support for Cuba's reentry into the OAS; and (3) pursuit of multilateral versus bilateral strategies (Drekonja 1983: 81–82).

The Hybrid Principle: *Ad Libitum Alternare Utrumque Principium*

The implementation of the respice similia doctrine between 1966 and 1978 led to a moderate diversification of Colombia's economic and political ties on an international level, as well as a relative degree of autonomy in the country's relations with the United States. Nevertheless, following the López administration, the use of this foreign policy doctrine, as well as that of its precursor, respice polum, became markedly transitory and interchangeable. In other words, Colombian foreign policy began to exhibit alternation between these two principles, depending on the administration, situation, issue area, and circumstances in question (Tokatlián 2000a: 37). Additionally, the impact of state-level factors on the country's foreign policy became stronger, in particular because of (1) the end of the National Front power-sharing arrangement, in place between 1958 and 1978,[6] and the progressive deterioration of the bipartisan system; (2) the intensification of the armed conflict between the late 1970s and early 1980s, as well as growing political and social unrest; and (3) the ascendence of the drug problem.

Undoubtedly, the Turbay (1978–1982) and Betancur (1982–1986) administrations provide the most poignant examples of this "hybrid approach," which I denominate *ad libitum alternare utrumque principium*—literally, "alternation between the two principles at will." The government of Julio César Turbay Ayala was characterized primarily by the staunch anticommunist stance of the Colombian president. As a result, the growth in the scope and nature of armed activity in the country, in combination with unprecedented social and political demonstrations, became interpreted increasingly through the lense of the bipolar conflict (Pardo and Tokatlián 1989: 139).

In terms of the country's foreign policy, the Turbay administration not only returned the country to its traditional status as a U.S. "pawn" in the Cold War but also converted Colombia into an active "soldier" in the struggle against communism. Notwithstanding this general trend, however, Colombian foreign policy became visibly ambiguous during this period. In the case of Nicaragua, for example, the country's original stance toward the 1979 revolution largely contradicted Turbay's later foreign policy tendencies. The country sided with the Sandinistas in the revolution, in addition to the other Andean Pact members, and Mexico and Costa Rica, while opposing any form of external (namely, U.S.) intervention in this situation. The Sandinistas were eventually recognized as a belligerant group by these countries in 1979. In 1980, Nicaragua initiated efforts to reclaim its sovereignty over the archipelago of San Andrés and Providencia, originally ceded to Colombia in 1928 through the Esguerra-Bárcenas treaty. This claim, interpreted in Bogotá as both unfounded in terms of international law principles and unjustifiably aggressive, given Colombia's earlier support of the Sandinistas during the revolution, led to increasingly strained relations between the two countries. The situation became complicated even further by Nicaragua's attempts to distance itself from the United States, and the implantation of the "socialist" model in that country.

On the other hand, Colombia's relations with Cuba during the Turbay administration were strained from the very beginning. In 1979, the country actively blocked Cuba's bid for a seat on the United Nations Security Council. In early 1980, the M-19 guerrilla movement seized the Embassy of the Dominican Republic in Bogotá, holding a number of ambassadors and other officials captive for a month. The crisis was resolved with the departure of the guerrilla members to Cuba, which tended to confirm the Colombian government's suspicions that Cuba was directly aiding armed actors in the country. In 1981, Colombia broke diplomatic relations with Cuba.[7]

The ascendence of Ronald Reagan to the presidency in 1981 provided a prime opportunity for Colombia to align its foreign policy with that of the United States even further given the ideological affinities characterizing both executives. As a result, the country adopted a high anticommunist profile on an international level, in consonance with U.S. foreign policy imperatives, that reached its maximum expression in Central America and the Caribbean (Pardo and Tokatlián 1989: 140). While gaining the favor of the United States, this posture tended to isolate the country diplomatically from its Latin American neighbors. Colombia's decision to abstain from voting on the application of the TIAR in the Falklands/Malvinas war (1982) provided a poignant statement of the distance created by the Turbay administration between Bogotá and other countries of the region.

The first years of the Betancur administration (1982–1986) constituted a staunch contrast with the Turbay period. During his inaugural address, President Betancur boldly expressed his determination to develop an "independent" foreign policy. In addition to announcing his decision to make the country a full member of the Non-Aligned Movement, the Colombian president called for a meeting of Latin America's leaders in order to discuss possible solutions to the debt crisis (Bagley and Tokatlián 1987: 178). For some authors (Cepeda and Pardo 1989: 79), the fact that the debt crisis failed to affect the Colombian economy as severely as other Latin American countries, in combination with Betancur's own personal disposition, facilitated a more assertive foreign policy, which allowed Colombia to break with a long tradition of unrestricted alliance with the United States.

During President Reagan's visit to Colombia in late 1982, Betancur urged him to abandon U.S. interventionism in Central America and proposed the renegotiation of Latin American debt (Bagley and Tokatlián 1987: 178). The Colombian president was also critical of U.S. drug policy and consequently refused to fumigate illicit crops, as well as to enforce the extradition treaty that the two countries had signed in 1979. Betancur worked to reestablish friendly relations with the countries of the region as well. In addition to recognizing Argentina's sovereignty in the Falklands/Malvinas Islands, Colombia sought to reverse the hostile posture that the Turbay administration had adopted toward Nicaragua and Cuba.

Two instruments, the Cartagena Consensus and the Contadora Group, illustrate the degree to which multilateral political strategies tended to dominate Colombian foreign policy during the first half of the Betancur administration. In mid-1984, the Colombian president sponsored a Latin American debtor's meeting in Cartagena, with the goal of creating a unified, regional position toward the debt problem and its possible solutions.[8] In turn, the country became a central figure in the Contadora Group, created by Colombia, Mexico, Venezuela, and Panama in January 1983 with the goal of counteracting U.S. interventionism in the Central American crisis through the constitution of an alternative regional conflict resolution mechanism. The active role that Colombia acquired in the Contadora Group reflected the perception that the country's domestic situation was in many ways interrelated with the Central American crisis and that the promotion of multilateral initiatives for resolving the latter could resonate in the assurance of regional and local support for Betancur's domestic peace initiatives, which included the declaration of a general amnesty (Cepeda 1985: 18).

By mid-1984, following the enthusiastic application of the principles of respice similia, both internal and external restrictions weighed on Colombian foreign policy, ultimately forcing the country to resort to a more subdued international stance. On the domestic level, international reserves diminished, and the country's commercial deficit and external debt both rose, creating a liquidity problem that was ultimately confronted through an economic monitoring agreement signed with the IMF (Bagley and Tokatlián 1987: 197). The assassination of Justice Minister Rodrigo Lara Bonilla in 1984, which highlighted the salience of the drug problem in the country, led the Betancur administration to begin extraditing Colombian nationals to the United States and to harden the government's antidrug strategy. Such shifts brought Bogotá, once again, much closer to Washington's posture toward this problem. Finally, the M-19 invasion and destruction of the Palace of Justice in November 1985, which led to the death of nearly one hundred persons, also created a marked shift in the government's peace policy that coincided with setbacks in the Contadora process itself.

COLOMBIAN FOREIGN POLICY IN THE POST–COLD WAR PERIOD: ECONOMIC RELATIONS AND DRUGS

Apertura, Modernization, and Economic Diplomacy

The foreign policy of the administration of Virgilio Barco (1986–1990) exhibited a relative degree of continuity with that of Betancur's government.

Barco continued to emphasize the nonideological nature of the country's international relations, intensified efforts to diversify them, asserted Colombia's independence in relation to the United States, and alternated frequently between the two central foreign policy principles described earlier. However, Colombian foreign policy during this period also differed noticeably from that of the previous administration on a number of issues.

Colombia's independence in relation to the United States was asserted primarily through explicit emphasis on foreign economic diplomacy and the expansion of commercial and diplomatic relations with other regions of the world, rather than those political measures characteristic of the Betancur period. The diversification of the country's external relations was viewed essentially as a means of increasing its international negotiating capacity. The Colombian president also took measures to modernize the country's foreign policy apparatus. A foreign service statute created in 1968 but never applied was finally passed into law, in an attempt to professionalize the Ministry of Foreign Relations. In addition, the Presidential Advisory was created with the goal of enhancing the coordination of strategic aspects of the country's domestic and foreign policy. The markedly pragmatic nature of Colombian foreign policy during the Barco government was derived primarily from the personal style of the president himself, characterized by the primacy of technical rather than political considerations in the design of public policy (Pardo and Tokatlián 1989: 199).

Colombian economic diplomacy between 1986 and 1990 revolved mainly around export diversification, the expansion of the country's economic relations, and the maintenance of positive relations with international financial institutions (Cardona 1990: 11–12). In the mid-1980s, coffee continued to represent a significant percentage of the country's export earnings, approximately 50 percent. By 1990, however, coffee's share in Colombian exports had dropped to around 20 percent and was replaced by nontraditional products, such as flowers, as well as petroleum and coal. In effect, by the decade's end, no one product represented more than 30 percent of the country's foreign trade (Juárez 1993: 3).

In February 1990, the Barco administration launched its Program of Modernization and Internationalization of the Colombian Economy, designed to promote economic growth, reduce inflation, and reform the country's commercial structure through a gradual process of *apertura* (openness) and internationalization of the Colombian economy. Two of the primary motors of this process included export-oriented growth and economic integration. In addition to attempts to rescusitate the Andean Group, President Barco, along with his Venezuelan counterpart, Carlos Andrés Pérez, initiated an ambitious program of integration in Feburary 1989, designed to expand the scope of bilateral relations beyond border disputes (the Gulf of Venezuela, in particular) that had traditionally been prioritized.[9] The Group of Three

(G-3) was also created in the same year, primarily with the goal of increasing political-diplomatic cooperation among Colombia, Venezuela, and Mexico.

In a number of ways, the election of César Gaviria (1990–1994) marked the continuation of those foreign policy strategies implemented during the Barco administration. Many former officials of the Barco government were reappointed by the new Colombian president, while Gaviria also gave priority to Colombia's foreign economic relations over the political realm as a means of asserting greater autonomy and gaining enhanced negotiating capacity in the international system. Like Barco, Gaviria saw the reform of the country's foreign policy establishment as imperative to achieving these goals. Not only did the Gaviria administration continue to implement the modernization and internationalization program launched during the previous government; this process was actually accelerated through the introduction of swifter tariff reductions and a more extensive liberalization of the Colombian economy. Economic integration was viewed as a central instrument of the internationalization process. In consequence, the Colombian government continued to participate actively in regional integration schemes such as the ALADI, G-3 and the Andean Group, while signing a number of new bilateral trade agreements with neighboring countries.

An integral part of the modernization of the state during this period included institutional reforms designed to create greater efficiency and effectiveness in the public sphere. One result of this process was the creation of the Ministry of Foreign Trade in 1991, charged with the centralization of Colombian foreign economic policy.[10] In comparison to the Ministry of Foreign Relations, this new ministry was conceived in markedly different terms: In addition to being smaller and based on a horizontal organizational structure, the hiring of personnel was largely linked to technical criteria, rather than those political considerations that traditionally dictated the distribution of diplomatic posts (Sanz de Santamaría 1993: 47). The Colombian president also divided the Presidential Advisory into specific issue areas, leading to the creation of the Presidential Advisory for International Affairs in 1990. Finally, international relations offices were gradually created in the great majority of the other ministeries. The end result of these changes was to presidentialize Colombia's international relations even further, to marginalize the Ministry of Foreign Relations from strategic areas of foreign policy decision making, such as foreign trade and relations with the United States, and to impede the effective coordination of Colombia's foreign affairs.

Notwithstanding efforts undertaken during both the Barco and Gaviria administrations to diversify Colombia's international economic relations, these remained concentrated in the United States and, to a lesser degree, Europe. For example, by the end of the Gaviria period Colombia continued to export 35 percent of its products to the United States, while 40 percent of its imports originated in that country as well. The approval of the Andean

Trade Preference Act (1991) in the United States and the Special Cooperation Program in Europe (1990), designed to assist drug-producing nations in the Andean region to diversify their commercial relations, reinforced this tendency (Tokatlián and Tickner 1996: 109). In macroeconomic terms, although economic growth remained stable, the acceleration of the apertura process during the Gaviria administration aggravated the country's balance of payments. Between 1992 and 1994, for instance, imports grew at 33.9, 48.7, and 22 percent, respectively, while exports increased at –3, 3.1, and 19.2 percent (Banco de la República 2001). Foreign investment levels were also static until 1996.

The Role of Drugs in Colombian-U.S. Relations

The salience of the drug issue in Colombian-U.S. relations beginning in the 1980s reinforced the dependent relations between these two countries. In the specific issue area of drugs, the Colombian political system became "penetrated," in Rosenau's terms (1996: 185), adding weight to the impact of U.S. pressures on Colombian domestic and foreign policy. As mentioned earlier, one important objective of Colombian foreign policy during the Barco period was to increase the country's autonomy on a global level, especially through economic strategies. On the drug front, the country inaugurated an unprecedented strategy of confrontation that brought Colombia much closer to U.S. counternarcotics recipes, for which it earned praise from Washington as a faithful ally in the "war on drugs." However, on an external level, the Barco government was firm in identifying the drug traffic as an international problem that needed to be met with concerted multilateral efforts.[11] Colombia also undertook an extensive advertising campaign in the United States designed to improve the country's image, illustrate the costs associated with the "drug war," and impress on the U.S. public that drug consumption was largely responsible for this problem (Cardona 1990: 15). This active stance was matched on a domestic level when U.S. intromission was perceived to be overly excessive. For example, when a report leaked in late 1990, with information that Washington was determined to deploy an aircraft carrier battle group off the coast of Colombia in order to interdict drug shipments, the Colombian president adamantly rejected this measure, and the plan was subsequently abandoned.

In the area of drug diplomacy, Gaviria's policy orientation differed dramatically from the hard-line approach advocated by the Barco administration. The reasons for this shift lie primarily in the social, political, and economic costs of the campaign of terror and violence inaugurated by the Colombian drug cartels in order to impede the extradition of drug traffickers to the United States.[12] The Gaviria administration's response was to establish a clear distinction between narcoterrorism and the drug traffic, two related but distinct manifestations of the drug problem. Hence, government efforts became largely concentrated on domestic problems, and foreign policy only became important to the extent that it satisfied specific domestic objectives (Tokatlián and Tickner 1996: 108). The Colombian government enacted a plea-bargaining system in 1990, in which those individuals accused of drug-related crimes would receive reduced jail sentences in exchange for their voluntary surrender and confession of their crimes. Nearly a year later, the 1991 Constitutional Assembly, under significant pressure from the country's drug trafficking organizations, voted to prohibit the extradition of Colombian nationals altogether.

The escape of Medellín cartel leader Pablo Escobar from prison in July 1992 led to increasing U.S. intolerance of the Colombian government's drug strategy. Although Escobar was ultimately killed in December 1993 by Colombian security forces, the permissive conditions surrounding the Medellín cartel leader's imprisonment, which were brought to light following his escape, led to growing apprehension in the United States concerning the effectiveness of the plea-bargaining system. Washington's uneasiness was intensified in May 1994, when the Colombian Constitutional Court decided to legalize the consumption of certain illegal drugs for personal use. This controversial decision came shortly after a series of public declarations by the country's general prosecutor, Gustavo de Greiff, that the war against drugs had failed miserably and that the consumption and traffic of illicit substances should be legalized (Tokatlián 2000b: 68).

The Samper Administration and the Breakdown of Bilateral Relations[13]

Although the Gaviria administration's propensity to stray from U.S.-inspired counternarcotics dogma led to a steady deterioration in U.S.-Colombian relations, Colombia continued to be considered a "showcase" for U.S. efforts in the region (Matthiesen 2000: 261–62). Nonetheless, with the inauguration of President Ernesto Samper in August 1994, the bilateral relationship experienced a severe breakdown following revelations that his presidential campaign had received financial contributions from the Cali cartel. A drawn-out series of accusations and denials concerning this allegation, labeled Proceso 8,000, polarized the country and irrevocably damaged the legitimacy and credibility of the Samper government on both the domestic and international fronts. Increasingly, the United States began to refer to Colombia as a "narcodemocracy" and a "narcostate," rather than a determined "ally."

At an initial meeting in New York, between officials from both countries in June 1994, Samper was given a U.S. document with a series of new and stricter criteria to be used to evaluate Colombia's antidrug performance in the 1995 certification process.[14] The implicit message set forth in the document was that the Gaviria administration's performance had not been completely satisfactory and that the standards for judging compliance toward the future would be applied more stringently. Colombia was subsequently certified for reasons of U.S. national interest in 1995. U.S. pressure led to a series of developments in Colombia's counterdrug policies: Rosso José Serrano was appointed head of the National Police in December 1994 and subsequently embarked on an aggressive campaign against corruption in this institution, an intensive antidrug effort was initiated, the main protagonists of the Cali cartel were successfully jailed, and crop eradication efforts were intensified dramatically.

The increasing importance of the drug issue in Colombian-U.S. relations, in combination with Samper's lack of legitimacy, also led to the ascendence of a series of new "players" in the foreign policy decision-making process, most important, the director of the National Police and the General Prosecutor's Office. Both actors established close relations with all three branches of the U.S. government, and often acted independently of the Colombian executive.[15] Given the growing complexity of the bilateral relationship, as well as the president's own weakness, Samper convoked a weekly meeting of presidential advisers, ministers of justice, defense, foreign relations, and foreign trade that sought to centralize all information regarding Colombia's relations with the United States, as well as to preserve a minimum degree of coherence in the formulation of foreign policy. Nevertheless, given the absence of formal policy coordination mechanisms, most notably in the Ministry of Foreign Relations, each Colombian institution achieved a great degree of leeway in establishing direct relations with U.S. counterparts.

As speculations in Colombia grew regarding Samper's level of awareness and involvement in the campaign scandal, U.S. policy toward the country became markedly aggressive and intransigent, reducing the country's margins for international action even further. Although arguably the U.S. government may not have identified Samper's removal from power as an explicit policy objective, the weakening of the Colombian president clearly became the policy of some, if not many, State Department officials (Franco 1998: 53). In June 1996, Samper's U.S. visa was revoked, with which direct relations with the Colombian president were precluded altogether. Notwithstanding the Samper government's vigorous compliance with the exigencies of U.S. antinarcotics policy, Colombia was decertified in 1996 and 1997, although economic sanctions were not applied.

Undoubtedly, the case of Samper provides a telling example of the extent to which external pressures can constrain the foreign (and domestic) policy of a peripheral country. Not only was the Colombian president himself ostracized by the United States, both domestically and internationally; increasingly, Colombia became identified as a pariah state within the global community. The political costs of this reduced status for the country's foreign policy were significant. During his entire period, the Colombian president received only two official state visits by neighboring heads of state in Venezuela and Ecuador. Ten of Samper's twelve international trips were taken in his capacity as president of the Non-Aligned Movement, not as president of Colombia, and were designed to counteract the U.S. nonrecognition (Ramírez 2000: 181–82). In addition to improving Colombia's international image, the presidency of the movement sought to increase the country's visibility, diversify its political and commercial relations, and increase its international negotiating power (Ramírez 2000: 161). On all of these counts, Colombia's efforts proved insufficient to overcome U.S. opposition.

The Pastrana Administration From Pariah to Friend

The election of Andrés Pastrana in 1998 was considered a prime opportunity for reestablishing a cooperative tone to the bilateral relationship. Pastrana established a clear distinction between Colombia's domestic priority, which revolved primarily around seeking a peaceful solution to the armed conflict, as well as U.S. interests in the country, based essentially on the drug problem. As in the case of Gaviria before him, the Colombian president prioritized those aspects of the country's foreign policy deemed crucial to resolving urgent domestic needs. In consequence, in June 1998 Pastrana presented a peace plan, in which he maintained that the cultivation of illicit substances constituted, above all, a social problem that needed to be addressed through a type of "Marshall Plan" for Colombia (Pardo and Tickner 1998: 24). In an interview in July, the president-elect also stated that narcotics, although an important aspect of Colombian-U.S. relations, had monopolized these for too long, and should be replaced by more important topics such as trade relations (Farrell 1998: 27).

Before his inauguration, Pastrana met with U.S. president Bill Clinton in Washington. One of his primary goals was to press for an "opening" of the bilateral agenda beyond the issue of drugs. During Pastrana's first official visit to the White House in late October 1998, Clinton made an explicit pledge to support the peace process with the FARC[16] and to work with other international institutions to mobilize resources to support this objective. In December 1998, Colombian defense minister Rodrigo Lloreda and his U.S. counterpart, William Cohen, also signed an agreement designed to strengthen military cooperation between the two countries.[17] This arrangement paved the way for the training of the first of several special counternarcotics battalions of the Colombian Army. Simultaneously, the United States stepped up its military assistance to Colombia, which reached U.S.$289 million for 1999.

By September 1999, the changing domestic climate in Colombia, as well as growing skepticism among key U.S. officials regarding the viability of the peace process, led to an important shift in the Colombian government's foreign policy strategy. Namely, with the presentation of Pastrana's "Plan Colombia" in the United States, the Colombian president no longer anchored his appeals for U.S. assistance to the peace process but, rather, to the drug issue and the country's inability to confront this problem alone (Office of the President of the Republic 1999). Thus, following initial attempts to gear Colombia's foreign policy toward domestic priorities (peace), rather than U.S. concerns (drugs), President Andrés Pastrana was forced to resort to a "drug war logic" in order to secure sorely needed U.S. support.[18] In practice, this shift signaled the return to the rationalized subordination characteristic of the respice polum doctrine in Colombian foreign policy. However, contrary to previous periods, in which Colombia's subservience was exchanged for relative economic and commercial benefits, the Pastrana administration's acquiescence in the "drug war" was conceived primarily as a means of increasing the country's domestic military strength.

In addition to Plan Colombia, the Pastrana administration placed strong emphasis on a "Diplomacy for Peace" initiative that sought to engage foreign support for the peace process with the FARC that was officially ended on February 20, 2002. However, these two pillars of foreign policy efforts have worked at cross-purposes. Increasing U.S. military involvement in Colombia has led to a deterioration in the country's relations with its Latin American neighbors, in particular the Andean countries, reducing the possibility that key regional actors might serve as facilitators in future attempts at peace. In addition, the members of the European Union have shied away from committing significant resources to Colombia as a direct result of what is perceived as an excessive U.S. military presence in the country and its potential for escalating conflict in the region. Finally, the Ministry of Foreign Relations, which lacks sufficient know-how in those topics highlighted by Plan Colombia and Diplomacy for Peace, such as the armed conflict, Colombian drug policy, and economic and social development, has been largely marginalized from crucial aspects of the country's international relations.

CONCLUSION

This brief overview of Colombian foreign policy lends itself to several concluding remarks. Caught between the enticements of reward for good behavior and the call for independent action, Colombian foreign policy has seemingly swayed between full acceptance of U.S. tutelage and the search for an autonomous place in the international system. However, these two patterns have not been applied consistently, nor are they mutually exclusive. As a result, what is commonly referred to as "Colombian foreign policy" is often the product of partial, uncoordinated actions that vary dramatically depending on the specific problems, governments, and historical moments in question.

The causes underlying this ambiguous foreign policy are varied but are largely related to (1) the centrality of individual-level variables, most notably the personalized nature of Colombian politics and variation among presidential preferences and those of the executive's closest advisers; (2) the incapacity of the Ministry of Foreign Relations to coordinate the country's foreign relations and the consequent absence of medium to long-term foreign policy strategies; (3) the historical role played by the United States in certain issue areas; and (4) the changing nature of the armed conflict.

The events of September 11 have highlighted two key factors that account for Colombia's international relations at present: the U.S.-led global "war against terrorism" and the domestic armed conflict. Washington's classification of all three of the country's armed actors (FARC, ELN, AUC) as terrorists who are also involved in drug-related activities, in combination with the intensification of the Colombian crisis, have led to a full alignment of Colombian foreign and domestic policy with U.S. goals, comparable perhaps only to the Cold War years. This tendency will most likely continue during the next several years, irrespective of the specific policy orientations of incoming president Alvaro Uribe Vélez[19]

DISCUSSION QUESTIONS

1. Given the marked power asymmetry between Colombia and the United States, as well as the salience of drugs and counterterrorism on the U.S. international agenda, to what extent does Colombian foreign policy simply mirror U.S. policy?
2. How can one explain the following "paradox" between Columbian and Mexican foreign policy: Historically, both countries lost significant portions of territory to the United States, while drugs figure prominently in each of their contemporary agendas with Washington. Yet, Colombia and Mexico chose markedly different paths, the first characterized by rationalized subordination and the second, only recently, that of independence and autonomy.
3. To what degree does the personalized nature of politics in Colombia hamper the achievement of more consistent, coordinated, long-term foreign policy strategies?

NOTES

1. However, Colombia was one of the only peripheral countries to vote against the veto power of the permanent members of the United Nations Security Council, on international law grounds, when this organization was created in 1945.

2. The Kemmerer Mission (1923) was the first of several groups of economic experts invited to Colombia for this purpose.

3. Although bipartisan consensus was a nearly permanent feature of Colombian foreign policy before the Cold War as well, on several occasions the Conservative party criticized the Liberal governments for their staunch pro-American stance, in particular during World War II.

4. The Bogotazo of April 9, 1948, which followed the assassination of Liberal political leader Jorge Eliécer Gaitan, sparked anticommunist fears in the country and led Colombia to break off its relations with the Soviet Union.

5. Colombia attended its first Non-Aligned meeting in 1970, during the administration of Misael Pastrana (1970–1974). In 1974, the country acquired observer status, and in 1983, it became a full member.

6. The first open presidential elections took place in 1974; parity between Conservative and Liberal Party posts in the presidential cabinet and the public sector was preserved until 1978. Article 120 of the 1886 Colombian constitution, however, mandated that the majority party offer adequate representation to the second-place party, with which power sharing continued until the Barco administration (1986–1990).

7. Diplomatic relations were resumed once again in 1991, during the administration of César Gaviria.

8. Notwithstanding Betancur's efforts, a debtor's cartel was never formed among the countries of the region.

9. See Diego Cardona et. al. (1992) for an extensive discussion of Colombo-Venezuelan integration during the Barco and Gaviria administrations.

10. The creation of the Ministry of the Environment one year later attested to the importance, at least in formal terms, of environmental issues in domestic and foreign policy as well.

11. In 1990, the presidents of Colombia, Perú, Bolivia, and the United States met at the Cartagena Drug Summit to discuss joint strategies for addressing this problem.

12. This situation reached its apex on August 18, 1989, when Liberal presidential candidate Luis Carlos Galán was assassinated by gunmen supposedly hired by the Medellín Cartel.

13. A more comprehensive discussion of Colombia's relations with the United States during the Samper and Pastrana governments appears in Tickner (2002).

14. Personal interview with Ernesto Samper Pizano, former president of Colombia, Bogotá, September 4, 2000.

15. Personal interview with Rodrigo Pardo García-Peña, the former Colombian minister of foreign relations and director of El Tiempo, Bogotá, August 24, 2001.

16. One aspect of the peace process that was received with a certain degree of alarm in Washington, however, was the creation of the demilitarized zone the size of Switzerland in five municipalities located in southern Colombia.

17. Beginning in the mid-1990s, military cooperation was dramatically reduced as a result of the Colombian Army's participation in human rights violations.

18. In June 2000, the U.S. Congress approved an aid package corresponding to the period 2000–2001, in which the Colombian Army received U.S.$512 million and the National Police, U.S.$123 million.

19. Uribe was elected in the first round of Colombian presidential elections on May 26, 2002.

10

Ecuador

Foreign Policy on the Brink

Jeanne A. K. Hey

> Ecuador's international reputation has hit rock bottom.
>
> —General Paco Moncayo (*Latin American Research Review* [*LARR*], May 19, 1998: 3)

General-turned-politician Moncayo uttered this statement during a dispute between then-president Fabian Alarcon and the Constituent Assembly. He could hardly have guessed how much lower the political circumstances, and Ecuador's international reputation, could go. With the new millennium came the ouster of Ecuador's second constitutionally elected president in four years, the abandonment of the national currency, and regional rumors about the viability of Ecuador's democracy.

Ecuador entered the 1990s under President Rodrigo Borja, a center-left politician who joined most of Latin America's leaders in moving toward neoliberal economic reforms (Hey and Klak 1999). The conservative Sixto Duran Ballen, elected in 1992, found he shared his predecessor's primary dilemma: how to placate and serve an increasingly impoverished population while also servicing the foreign debt and pleasing international creditor institutions. With the election of populist Abdala Bucaram in 1996, Ecuador added political instability to its list of crises. Known as "el loco," Bucaram incensed his domestic opponents, alienated his supporters, displayed corruption and nepotism, and engaged in bizarre behaviors. Citing "mental incapacity," the legislature ousted Bucaram in early 1997. Vice President Rosalia Arteaga presided just long enough for the congressional deputies to revise the constitution so that their own speaker, Alarcon, could assume the presidency. As if one such incident were not enough for this "fragile democracy" (Corkill and Cubitt 1988), Alarcon's successor, centrist Jamil Mahuad, was ousted from the presidency by an unlikely military-indigenous-judicial alliance. Convinced that a coup d'état would not be tolerated within the region, the military element abandoned the triumvirate and oversaw the seating of Vice President Gustavo Noboa in January 2000.

Throughout the 1990s, Ecuador faced perpetual economic and political upheaval. A review of the decade finds the country in constant negotiations with creditors and global financial institutions. It frequently suspended payments and even defaulted. All economic indicators fell below projections. In addition to a dismal economic situation, Ecuadoran presidents faced hostile political challenges both from the popular sector in the form of national strikes and street protests as well as from the legislature, which impeached government ministers at will. Ecuador during the decade was ravaged by natural disasters, including earthquakes, a cholera epidemic, and the El Niño devastation. Finally, Peru and Ecuador waged war along their disputed border in 1991 and 1995.

Compared with its neighbors, Ecuador has always been small and poor. But even facing these challenges, it has carved out a proud foreign policy history. Its diplomats were instrumental in founding the Organization of Petroleum Exporting Countries (OPEC) and the Organization of American States (OAS), and its presidents have launched important diplomatic and economic initiatives (Martz 1987; Hey 1995). In short, Ecuador in the past rarely allowed its shortcomings to keep it from global participation. But the 1990s trials made a significant dent in Ecuador's foreign policy profile. Its international behavior focused on putting out fires associated with immediate issues such as foreign debt and the border war, at the cost of long-range foreign policy planning. In that sense, Ecuador's was a foreign policy "on the brink" of crisis throughout the decade.

This chapter examines Ecuador's behavior in three key foreign policy areas in the 1990s: the border war, international economic policy, and subregional relations—namely, Andean integration and concerns about spillover from Colombia's drug and guerrilla wars. Following this empirical examination is an analysis of Ecuadoran foreign policy behavior through a levels-of-analysis lens.

THE BORDER WAR

Since the time of Simón Bolívar, Peru and Ecuador have argued over a significant portion of their national territories. In 1941, the spoils of war went to Peru in the form of a large swath of territory in the Amazon region. In early 1942, the Rio Protocol formalized the new and sovereign boundaries and was "guaranteed" by four nondisputants: Argentina, Brazil, Chile, and the United States. Ecuador renounced the treaty in 1960, arguing that it had been signed under unjust circumstances and was otherwise "inexecutable," because cartographers' errors made it impossible to demarcate a border on the ground. While Ecuador continued to claim a vast piece of Peru, including the city of Iquitos, the only real dispute concerns a small area in the Cordillera del Condor, where Peruvian and Ecuadoran forces sparred for decades (Palmer 1997).

Ecuador has long used the border dispute to foment nationalism. National maps claim Ecuador a "*pais amazonico*," a reference to the claim to territory controlled by Peru. Although Ecuador cooperated with Peru in trade and Andean regional issues, no Ecuadoran president dared visit Lima or speak of reconciliation. On this matter, Ecuadoran foreign policy assumed the role of the noble martyr, refusing to relinquish its claim but never going to war with much larger Peru. Former president Osvaldo Hurtado attempted to initiate reconciliation efforts, and he was pilloried by congressional deputies appealing to nationalist sentiment. Even Hurtado's Foreign Ministry balked at the very notion of developing a "national consensus" toward resolving the border conflict (Martz 1987: 326; Hey 1995: 51). The scholarly consensus is that the territory under dispute is of little real value to either party and that both sides have exploited the conflict for political gain.

President Borja inherited this legacy. Although he made some attempts at working toward a settlement, Ecuador's superior performance during the 1991 border skirmish actually bolstered his foreign policy image (although evidence suggests that the military acted on its own in sparking the conflict) (Hey 1996; Palmer 1997). The conflict peaked in 1995, when skirmishes led to a war over control of the Tiwinza military base, which both countries claimed lay within their territory. Local observers reported that the "base" was little more than an uninhabited thatched hut. The rhetorical and real warfare between Peru and Ecuador in this case was an example of "the surreal atmosphere surrounding the conflict in the Cordillera del Condor" (*LARR*, March 9, 1995: 3). This outbreak of hostilities nonetheless provided Ecuadoran President Duran Ballen an unexpected foreign policy opportunity. His foreign policy reputation had suffered in the wake of an unpopular decision to rescind Ecuador's OPEC membership and his waffling on a crucial vote for the OAS secretary-general. In the latter case, Ecuador supported two different candidates before casting the deciding vote in favor of Colombian president Cesar Gaviria, the first choice of the United States and a neoliberal champion. Duran Ballen's deft handling of the 1995 border war was in marked contrast to these poorly managed decisions. While seeking a diplomatic resolution abroad, Duran Ballen fomented a nationalist sentiment at home. He used the occasion to pass a tax increase in the congress and assembled thousands of school children in Quito's Plaza Grande to show support for Ecuador's claim. At the same time, he engaged in shuttle diplomacy, offering an immediate cease-fire and a resumption of peace talks. It helped Duran Ballen's image that Peruvian president Fujimori was largely uncooperative, especially during the first weeks of negotiations (Latinamerica Press [LP] 1995; Hey 1996). With the help of the Rio Protocol guarantors, Peru and Ecuador achieved a cease-fire and signed the Itamaraty Peace Declaration, a commitment to working out a final solution (Palmer 1997: 122–23; Fernandez de Cordoba 1998).

The rest of Duran Ballen's presidency was spent with Peru and Ecuador talking about how to talk about negotiations for peace. Nonetheless, Duran Ballen's peacemaking with Peru laid the foundation for future progress toward a lasting peace settlement, something that was unthinkable only years before. Abdala Bucaram, shortly before being removed from office, became the first Ecuadoran president to visit Lima. His visit reflected his trademark irreverence for political convention but also his commitment to resolving the conflict and his personal relationship with Fujimori. Such headline-making initiatives ended with Bucaram's ouster, but incoming president Alarcon made a crucial concession in a January 1998 agreement that created a timetable for completing negotiations (Schemo 1998). The impetus for a settlement derived mostly from Ecuador's decision to cease demands for sovereignty over the segment of the Amazon that Peru annexed officially in 1942. Ecuador under Alarcon chose to settle instead for "free and uninhibited access" for trade and commerce through the region (Faiola 1998). This allowed the guarantors to establish four separate and simultaneous negotiating sessions, each tackling a different aspect of the border conflict (*LARR*, January 27, 1998: 1). Although much of the progress that year was in the predictable areas of "confidence-building and cross-border cooperation" (and not on demarcating boundaries), these negotiations marked the high point of cooperation between the two nations since the Rio Protocol was signed (*LARR*, March 3, 1998: 8).

So it was with disappointment and surprise that, upon Jamil Mahuad's inauguration, Peru announced that it would cease all contact until Ecuador withdrew its troops from the disputed area. This was exactly the type of statement that had sparked the 1995 conflict (*LARR*, September 1, 1998: 1). In spite of this early setback, Mahuad and Fujimori made rapid progress, concluding a final peace agreement in October 1998 in which Ecuador relinquished its claim to the large Amazonian tract of land in exchange for access to Amazon ports and a war monument in the Cordillera del Condor (McConnell 2001: 74). Nearly all quarters responded with delight. Lending agencies immediately offered billions of dollars for development projects in the region, and a national poll found 80 percent of Ecuadorans supporting ratification of the accord (*LARR*, November 10, 1998: 6). The opposition congress passed a resolution that guaranteed its oversight of the treaty's implementation, but ratified it nonetheless (British Broadcasting Corporation [BBC], October 19, 1998). The only angry political player appears to have been the military, who helped to oust Mahuad from power halfway through his term. Mahuad argued after the coup that making peace with Peru and cutting the military budget had motivated the overthrow (McConnell 2001: 74).

As of this writing, Ecuador and Peru have not returned to hostilities in the disputed area. They began the decade without a glimmer of hope for a settlement and ended it with a final peace. In June 2001, the two countries signed a new agreement to cooperate on development projects along their common border, and in October of that year Peruvian president Alejandro Toledo traveled to Quito to cement the newfound pacific relationship between the two countries. The Andean region has rid itself of one of its most enduring and vexing conflicts.

FOREIGN DEBT AND ECONOMIC POLICY

Consider the *Financial Times*' recent assessment of Ecuador's economic situation: "In the mid–1990s, Ecuador's . . . final destination seemed to be economic meltdown. By the end of the 1990s there appeared no way back from the abyss. Only eternal optimists would have sought investment opportunities there" (Warner 2001). Debt had reached $14 billion, the highest per capita debt in Latin America (Warner 2001). Growth rates reached a staggering −7.3 percent in 1999 (Economist Intelligence Unit [EIU] 2001). Foreign income relied on oil and bananas, the former notoriously fluctuating and the latter reliably low. By decade's end, many educated and middle- to upper-class Ecuadorans had fled. An estimated 2.5 million Ecuadorans live abroad, with nearly 1 million leaving in 1999–2000 alone (*LARR*, May 15, 2001: 6–7). At least half of the urban population and two-thirds of the rural population live below the poverty line (*Economist* 1996). The 1990s ended with the *Economist* (2000) naming Ecuador "Latin America's most unstable country."

Ecuadoran leaders have managed this desperate situation with neoliberalism for the international sector and spending for targeted voters. Hey and Klak (1999) document the neoliberal path taken by socialist Borja and conservative Duran Ballen. Though the former rejects that he is "neoliberal," he implemented key starters of a neoliberal transformation, including reducing industrial protections, *sucre* devaluation, utility and gas price hikes, and industrial privatization. What a Borja supporter called a "gradual" approach to reform was replaced by his successor's "brutal capitalism" (Hey and Klak 1999: 78). Duran Ballen's buzzword was *modernization*, referring to vigorous privatization and making business more "transparent" to investors. By January 1993, foreign and domestic investors operated under equal rules.

Within months of his taking office, Ecuador withdrew from OPEC, pleasing foreign investors but infuriating the new president's domestic constituency (Hey 1996). Vice President Alberto Dahik, a Princeton-trained economist and strong proponent of economic restructuring, was impeached and fled the country in November 1995.

Although Duran Ballen promised to prioritize debt service, he found that, like Borja, he had to suspend commercial debt payments. A Zurich-based financial company froze Ecuador's assets for failure to pay in 1993 (*LARR*, June 24, 1993: 4). Such reprisals were the exception, as the International Monetary Fund (IMF), the Inter-American Development Bank (IADB), and bilateral creditors routinely worked with both administrations to discount Ecuador's debt and reschedule payments. Indeed, in early 1995, Ecuador completed a Brady Plan–type agreement, covering $7 billion in overdue principal and interest payments (Quest 1998). Duran Ballen made other strides toward economic "maturity." He produced a balanced budget in 1994 and negotiated entry into the General Agreement on Tariffs and Trade (GATT) and the World Trade Organization (WTO). In 1996, he reduced inflation from 60 to 25 percent and cut the bureaucracy by thirty thousand. Exports to Colombia and Venezuela, the country's chief trading partners, increased from almost nothing to $800 million a year during his term (Escobar 1996). The war with Peru and a politically disastrous midterm election forced Duran Ballen to lose much of the fiscal austerity he demonstrated at the beginning of his term.

Upon Bucaram's election, one observer noted, "Many of the country's bankers and businessmen, not to speak of foreign investors, shudder at Mr. Bucaram's victory" (World Politics and Current Affairs [WPCA] 1996). His campaign speeches avoided specifics on international economic policy, but promised to increase domestic spending. Such promises labeled him a "populist" and constituted a danger to Ecuador's reputation. Bucaram eschewed attempts at fiscal caution demonstrated by previous presidents. He attacked his predecessor's privatization of national industries and swore not to sell off state petroleum and telecommunications companies. He vowed to "make the rich vomit" (WPCA 1996). Such talk put off not only global creditors and investors but also Ecuador's congress, which ousted him just months into his term in office.

This drama and the bizarre nature of Bucaram's personal behavior undermined his economic team. It put forth a currency convertibility scheme aimed at buttressing the falling sucre. It approved tax increases, subsidy reduction and elimination, and partial privatization of the state telephone company. In other words, his ministers set out to undermine many of the president's campaign promises. Shortly before Bucaram lost his job and fled to Panama, *Latin Finance* (1997), a major investor publication, reported that

Ecuador "is on the brink of major economic reforms that could change its future economic prospects dramatically."

Alarcon understood that Bucaram's abandonment of populist promises contributed to his downfall. Upon entering office, Alarcon instituted a macroeconomic management program aimed at reducing the fiscal deficit, improving tax revenues and other goals attractive to the international sector. But he canceled plans to cut crucial subsidies and to broaden the value-added tax, a move that angered the IMF (*Latin Finance* 1998). Alarcon also modified growth forecasts downward in light of the El Niño devastation to coastal agricultural regions. Alarcon's term lasted less than two years, and investors, creditors, and development agencies appeared to give him and Ecuador the benefit of the doubt in light of the frightening extraconstitutional measures that had brought him to power (Quest 1998). The challenge of bringing Ecuador out of its "lost decade" fell to Jamil Mahuad, the first in three presidents to come to power by election.

Mahuad announced to the congress in January 1999 that Ecuador faced "its worst crisis in seventy years" and that under the best scenario it would require an additional $700 million to balance its budget (*LARR*, January 26, 1999: 4–5). Throughout the ensuing year, Mahuad struggled with an almost-unimaginable set of economic and political challenges: El Niño devastation, low oil prices, 40 percent of government income servicing foreign debt, capital flight, currency devaluation, inflation, and hostility from the congress and grassroots sectors. Mahuad attempted to put emergency economic measures into place to deal with the fiscal crisis, but the congress opposed it, leading Ecuador to become the first recipient of Brady bonds to default on them (McConnell 2001). Ecuador also lost an IMF agreement that would have supplied $400 million in emergency credits. Ecuador ended 1999 with a −7.3 percent growth rate. As a last-ditch effort, Mahuad announced in January 2000 his intention to "dollarize" the economy. His plan went beyond Argentina's policy of pegging local currency to the dollar. Instead, Ecuador would adopt the greenback as its currency, depriving the Central Bank of its ability to print money or implement monetary policy (McConnell 2001).

Dollarization's attraction lay in currency stability and low inflation. Trade unions, peasants, indigenous groups, and other popular organizations nonetheless called it "a death sentence for Ecuadorans and . . . virtually a declaration of war" (EFE News Service, March 24, 2000). To critics, dollarization was a foreign policy designed to marry Ecuador to the imperialist United States. Days after Mahuad announced the policy, a coalition of military, indigenous, and judicial leaders ousted him. It is at once ironic and expected that Mahuad's successor, Vice President Gustavo Noboa, not only went forward with the dollarization but was able to complete an IMF agreement that released $2 billion in credits within months of the coup (McConnell 2001: 77).

This review of the economic policy during the tumultuous times of the 1990s reveals that all Ecuadoran presidents worked under extreme conditions. All were caught between the rock of external debt and creditor pressure and the hard place of an increasingly impoverished and mobilized population to whom the legislature looked for political support. As such, Ecuadoran foreign economic policy was implemented in an atmosphere of emergency, in fits and starts, but always with an eye toward liberalization.

ANDEAN REGIONAL ISSUES

Outside of the border war with Peru, two issues dominated Ecuador's subregional policy in the 1990s: Andean integration and spillover effects from Colombia's drug and guerrilla wars. In both areas, Ecuador demonstrated a measured and consistent foreign policy across many presidencies and congressional coalitions.

Andean integration enjoys a proud history. Ecuador, Bolivia, Peru, Colombia, Venezuela, and Chile together committed to trade liberalization first in 1966. They officially launched the Andean Pact in 1969. Ecuador and Bolivia received special concessions owing to their status as the smallest and poorest members. The group's "Decision 24" restricted foreign investment and attracted criticism within and without the subregion. In 1976, Chile withdrew from the Andean Pact, citing Decision 24's hostility to foreign investors (Ferris 1979: 55). By the 1980s, the Andean Pact was in disarray, with some members, including Ecuador, threatening withdrawal. But with the 1990s came efforts to revive and renew Andean integration. Ecuador entered the decade in a heated national debate over the benefits of liberalizing subregional trade. Ecuadorans were particularly concerned that Colombian firms, which they saw as better financed and more competitive, would overwhelm Ecuadoran businesses in their own markets. In 1991, the Andean Pact abolished Decision 24, opening the subregion to unfettered foreign investment and creating an incentive for member countries to work together (*LARR*, May 23, 1991: 1).

Quito under Duran Ballen hosted an important meeting in November 1994, in which the Andean Pact announced the "last step toward a common market," an agreement to apply a common external tariff to 90 percent of subregional imports. Members insisted on many special exemptions, but all the members save Peru (which agreed to be a "non-active member") signed (*LARR*, December 22, 1994: 1). Less than a year later, Quito hosted another meeting in which Foreign Minister Galo Leoro argued that the Andean Pact should be restructured and reoriented with the aim of integrating it into a hemispheric free trade zone (United Press International [UPI] 1995). Concomitant with efforts toward a common foreign tariff and common market were those aimed at bolstering the Andean Pact as a negotiating bloc. The group in 1996 changed its name to the Andean Community (Spanish acronym, CAN) and moved immediately to negotiate with the Southern Cone Common Market (MERCOSUR) (*LARR*, April 11, 1996: 8). At this meeting in Trujillo, members announced that they would model their organization on the mother of economic integration, the European Union (EU).

Both the business and agricultural sectors in Ecuador opposed rapid integration. Despite their free market rhetoric, businessmen worried that CAN would protect the "basic" industries of the larger members while Ecuador's assembly plants would suffer. This is consistent with Ecuadoran business leaders' historical approach to government regulation. While they complain bitterly about bureaucratic hindrances, they lobby for government protection and financing (Conaghan 1988). The large Andean countries also lobbied for exemptions on agricultural products, where Ecuador had a comparative advantage (*LARR*, May 23, 1991: 1). Early in the process, Ecuador and Bolivia successfully argued for special treatment.

There is value in comparing Ecuador's participation in CAN with that of Peru. Fujimori created numerous obstacles for CAN and generally behaved in an obstreperous manner. His blatantly undemocratic *autogolpe* (self-coup) threw the organization into temporary disarray. In 1997, Fujimori announced Peru would negotiate with Brazil alone and not via CAN's offices. Months later he changed his mind (*LARR*, February 25, 1997: 1). In contrast, Ecuador remained a solid CAN citizen, working for national interests but always within the spirit of moving forward on integration. This is noteworthy given that the neoliberal model was so heavily challenged in Ecuador. Even the heavily conservative Jaime Nebot, presidential candidate in 1996, ran a populist "people first" campaign that promised an end to privatization and an increase in subsidies (Escobar 1996).

Throughout the second half of the decade, Ecuador intensified its Andean commitments. President Alarcon served as president of CAN and traveled in that capacity around the region. CAN began negotiating with MERCOSUR middecade. By 1999, the Andean group was calling for a "common foreign policy," another element modeled on the European Union (EFE 1999). CAN closed 2000 with U.S.$5 billion in intraregional trade, up more than 27 percent from the previous year. Sebastian Alegrett, Andean Community secretary-general, noted this progress was made amid severe political problems and predicted that export levels would reach $10 billion by 2005 (Dempsey 2001). At 2001's "Summit for the Americas" in Quebec City, Andean presidents met with President Bush and pressed him to renew the Andean Trade Preference Act (ATPA) and to prevent spillover from Plan Colombia's deleterious effects (White House Fact Sheet 2001).

Concern about that spillover from Colombia's drug and guerrilla wars undermined Andean cooperation. Because it is so small and poor, and because its border with Colombia is in a guerrilla and drug region, Ecuador had reason to worry the most. Ecuador expressed concern that drug cultivation, trafficking, and consumption would cross the border into Ecuador, which had historically remained mostly free of drug problems. Indeed, drug consumption increased in Ecuador in the 1990s. Colombian cartels also looked to Ecuadorans to carry the drugs and bear the risk of the legal consequences. As one report put it, "While Colombian drug traffickers earn millions of dollars in their lucrative business, many of the Ecuadorans they use to smuggle the drugs to the United States and Europe are rotting in jail" (Iturralde Andrade 1995). Furthermore, an unintended, though foreseeable, consequence of peace between Peru and Ecuador was that drug traffickers quickly filled the border area once occupied by sparring troops (Lama 1995). In addition, Colombian insurgent forces, especially the FARC, moved their activities into Ecuador, not only criminalizing Ecuador but inviting right-wing paramilitaries to cross the border as well. In 1999, dozens of foreign oil workers and tourists were kidnapped in Ecuador near the Colombian border (Semple 1999). The spillover effects from Colombia are terrifying to Ecuador, which has cherished its placid image and the tourist dollars it attracts.

At every CAN meeting in the decade, Ecuador and its neighbors took aim at the Colombian spillover issue. In December 1995, the eight foreign ministers of the countries that make up the Amazon Region Cooperation Treaty agreed to establish new policy guidelines for the sustainable development of the Amazon region. They included a reference to the contamination of the region by drug traffickers (BBC 1995). But it was within the context of the United States' "Plan Colombia" that Ecuador and its Andean neighbors collaborated most effectively on the spillover issue. Plan Colombia, of course, is the multimillion-dollar aid package, approved in 2000, aimed at curbing Colombian drug trafficking and guerrilla warfare. Largely lost in the U.S. debate on Plan Colombia were the effects that it would have on Colombia's neighbors. CAN members were keenly aware of Plan Colombia's threats and opportunities. Early on, Quito expressed concern about Plan Colombia and drew up a series of emergency measures including security for the northern border region, development plans to keep peasants from growing coca, and refugee camps for the expected influx of Colombians. In response, FARC guerrillas warned Quito that it should remain "strictly neutral" in the Colombian conflict, a warning that Ecuador rejected (BBC 2000).

Many observers have likened Plan Colombia to the beginnings of U.S. military involvement in Vietnam. Perhaps because the spillover from that conflict into Laos and Cambodia is indisputable, the United States has been open to Andean concerns. Colombia's Putumayo province is the site of 60 percent of Colombian coca cultivation and borders Ecuador. The United States acknowledged that anti–coca fumigation chemicals were crossing into Ecuador, damaging crops, livestock, and citizens. The Ecuadoran Army reported in 2000 that eight thousand soldiers guarded the Colombia–Ecuador border, more than participated in the 1995 border war with Peru. In 2000, Ecuadoran analysts estimated that up to five thousand Colombians crossed into Ecuador each month. The chairman of the Joint Chiefs of Staff described Ecuador's situation in reference to Colombian spillover as a "time bomb" (*LARR*, November 7, 2000: 9).

Ecuador and its Andean partners took these concerns to the United States throughout the development of Plan Colombia and especially during the Quebec Summit of the Americas. The United States responded favorably, arguing that the renewal and expansion of the ATPA was crucial to prevent spillover. The U.S. Senate's sponsor of the act, Ohio senator Mike DeWine, said that "For Plan Colombia to succeed, it is crucial that we help bolster the faltering economies of the Andean countries . . . so they don't turn to the drug trade for their economic livelihood" (Agence France Presse [AFP] 2001). In 2001, the Bush administration requested $882 million for funding democratic institutional development and counternarcotics programs in the Andes. The funding split evenly between "democracy promotion" on the one hand, and law enforcement and security measures on the other (WHFS 2001). Ecuador, as the most vulnerable country to Colombian spillover and also the least able to combat it, was crucial in securing the aid package.

Ecuadoran Andean policy reveals that Quito was a consistent and reliable member of the Andean team, despite political tumult and significant regional challenges. This adheres with Ecuador's history as a regional team player, owing at least in part to its small status and limited resources. But it should also be noted that Ecuadoran leaders could have taken the path of neighboring President Fujimori, who not only flaunted his antidemocratic tendencies but also abandoned regional alliances when it suited him.

ANALYSIS

What is most striking about this review of some elements of Ecuadoran foreign policy in the 1990s is its relative continuity across six presidents (although Arteaga ruled only a few days) and during a time of domestic and international political flux. This section reviews factors at the individual, state, and international levels and examines their role in the development of foreign policy during the 1990s.

Individual level

Ecuador could hardly have asked for a more diverse cast of political characters than those it enjoyed during the last decade of the twentieth century. Rodrigo Borja was a fairly colorless political animal, but one who spoke often and eloquently about the principles of social and economic justice embodied in the platform of his leftist party, Izquierda Democratica (Hey and Klak 1999). Despite implementing some crucial steps in Ecuador's neoliberal transition, Borja continued to hold that he does "not believe in neoliberalism," even after he left office and has been one of only a few Latin American ex-presidents to publicly question the neoliberal model in international forums (interview with Rodrigo Borja, Quito, June 1, 1994; Hey and Klak 1999). In typical social-democratic fashion, Borja's party also advocated "third worldist" principles in international diplomacy.

Sixto Duran Ballen offered a dramatic change from Borja, ideologically if not stylistically. He was Ecuador's oldest leader of the decade, a low-key insider without political flair. He was for decades an important figure in right-wing Ecuadoran politics but lost two presidential elections as the candidate for the Partido Social Cristiano party. He therefore launched his own new party, the Partido Union Republicana, and won the election in 1992 on a platform promising economic austerity, modernization and decentralization (Hey and Klak 1999). Although Duran Ballen had a long personal bureaucratic history, he appeared committed to dismantling Ecuador's bureaucracy in favor of privatized and more "modern" institutions.

Duran Ballen was the last president to serve out a full term in the decade. Abdala Bucaram called himself "el loco," a moniker with which most observers agreed. His ideology is difficult to pin down, though the label "populist" is omnipresent in media reports about him. His populism was aimed against government bureaucrats and toward the poor and indigenous populations whom he promised state subsidies and programs (*LARR*, September 5, 1996: 1). His campaign promises included increases in public housing, lower prices on basic goods, and free medicine and school breakfasts (Cisternas 1996). Once in office, however, Bucaram succeeded not only in blasting political opponents but in alienating admirers as well. He failed to consult with grassroots groups and engaged in blatant nepotism. His penchant for vulgarity embarrassed Ecuadorans. After he was inaugurated, Bucaram used public funds to charter a jet to Miami for obesity treatments. When asked why he used taxpayer money for a personal trip, Bucaram replied without hesitation that he would have been mad to use his own money (*LARR*, November 14, 1996: 3). Perhaps Bucaram regrets the "el loco" label, given that the congress ousted him for "mental incapacity."

Ecuador's next two presidents, Fabian Alarcon and Jamil Mahuad, have in common their homelands in the sierra region (as opposed to the coastal origins of the previous two presidents) and their profession as lawyers. Alarcon had changed parties several times before rising to the presidency of the congress with the Frente Radical Alfarista party. He entered the limelight of Ecuadoran politics with the political trial that he launched against former vice president Alberto Dahik in 1995. Bucaram's vice president, Rosalia

Arteaga accused Alarcon of an extraconstitutional power grab in the days following Bucaram's ouster. But soon the legislature, the military, the United States, and, reluctantly, Arteaga offered their support to Alarcon. All elements were no doubt eager to see political stability restored. Also, Alarcon's professional demeanor, respected negotiating skills and political experience warmed Ecuadorans who were aghast at Bucaram's style of "politics by insult." Although Alarcon served out his special term until 1998, he was unable to eliminate a perception that his was a controversial and caretaker interim presidency. "His mandate was not to do anything," commented the respected Ecuadoran economic analyst, Walter Spurrier, observing that Alarcon owed his presidency to a congress that is famous for obstructionism (Schemo 1997).

Jamil Mahuad, on the other hand, entered the presidency with great expectations. He was the mayor of Quito when he was legally elected to the presidency from the centrist Democracia Popular (DP) party. Self-described as left-wing on social issues and right-wing on economic issues, he was referred to elsewhere as a "moderate and competent politician, who contrives to keep on good terms with everyone" (*LARR*, April 7, 1998: 6). Observers should have recognized this as a recipe for disaster in Ecuadoran politics, where nobody remains on good terms with anybody for long. Despite Mahuad's reputation as a "calm and clear-headed" listener who "does not believe that he knows everything already," the congress ousted him when he suggested dollarization as an antidote to the economic crisis (*LARR*, June 23, 1998: 3). He was replaced by Gustavo Noboa, a member of the wealthy industrial and agricultural family from the coast.

Individual-level effects on Ecuador's foreign policy in the 1990s appear to be of little import. Especially in economic and regional issues, Ecuador's behavior stayed on track, although perhaps on a circuitous route, toward freer trade abroad and structural adjustment at home. All presidents contended with heavy pressures from the outside to service the debt and to restructure the local economy according to IMF guidelines. At the same time, domestic populations suffered increasingly brutal economic conditions and this vitalized their political activity. Indigenous, labor, women's, and other groups kept Ecuador in a steady state of political upheaval throughout the decade, sponsoring frequent national strikes and closing roads to the major cities. Business groups, too, argued for industrial protection. Bucaram's ouster showed that a president could not ignore these protests without facing a real threat of political suicide. Hence, Ecuador implemented a neoliberal program in fits and starts, with frequent back steps aimed at placating the domestic population. Thus we see that individual men with as different political stripes as Duran Ballen, on the one hand, and Borja and Mahuad, on the other, implemented similar policies. For example, both Borja and Duran Ballen, despite vastly different political rhetoric and ideology, suspended commercial debt payments and increased domestic spending in the second half of their terms (Hey and Klak 1999). Bucaram's populist rhetoric belied many of the policies he went on to enact, including promoting foreign oil deals and privatization. Perhaps the most illustrative example of the weakness of the individual level concerns Mahuad's ouster. Congressional and grassroots opponents painted Mahuad as a villain for even considering abandoning the national currency in favor of the imperialist greenback. Mahuad lost his job over the policy. But successor Noboa, more conservative and of an entirely different political background from Mahuad's, not only agreed with dollarization but went forward with its implementation.

The one area where the individual level appears to have some import is in the border war with Peru. While there is evidence that no individual, no matter how motivated, could work toward a real solution before 1990, the eruption of the 1995 border war created a political opening in which progress became possible. Duran Ballen and Mahuad both took advantage of that opportunity and used creative and cooperative diplomacy to arrive at a workable solution with Peru. Certainly the process was long, political, and difficult. But the agreement could easily have been lost if either president chose to win political points by appealing to Ecuadoran nationalism and refusing to cede one inch of Ecuador's territorial claim. That neither did indicates an individual choice to work for a solution.

State Level

Intense domestic pressures and concerns permeated policymaking in Ecuador throughout the 1990s. No president could expect public or congressional approval for any policy initiative. If he were lucky enough to receive such approval, it was often fleeting. Duran Ballen, for example, earned a 93 percent approval rating for his handling of the 1995 border war (Hey 1996). Yet, later the same year, Duran Ballen launched a plebiscite on eleven constitutional changes. These aimed at facilitating business transactions, changing the electoral process, allowing privatization of social security, depoliticizing judicial nominations, and achieving other goals. In what was widely seen as a referendum not on these specific issues but on the Duran Ballen presidency itself, all went down to resounding defeat (*LARR*, December 21, 1995: 2). As economic conditions worsened and Ecuador's international reputation suffered in the wake of political scandals, the population continued to express dissatisfaction. A 1998 poll found that 82 percent of the population felt the country was in a worse state than a year earlier during the Bucaram ouster. Perhaps most remarkable is that a separate poll found that half the population preferred an authoritarian to a democratic government (*LARR*, May 19, 1998: 3).

Much of this dissatisfaction was expressed in strikes and demonstrations by Ecuador's two most visible political groups: the United Workers Front (FUT) and the leading indigenous coalition, the Confederation of Indigenous Nationalities of Ecuador (CONAIE). By the time Duran Ballen entered office in 1992, CONAIE was talking openly of a civil war (*LARR*, October 8, 1992: 6–7). FUT and CONAIE called an "indefinite strike" against Duran Ballen's economic policies in mid-1994. This was typical. A review of the decade reveals nearly continual strikes and demonstrations, almost always in response to economic policy proposals from Quito. At times the demonstrations succeeded in closing roads to major cities and shutting down economic activity on a national scale. Famously, in 2000, CONAIE urged indigenous people from around the country to march on Quito and take over the national Congress. Antonio Vargas, the CONAIE leader, ousted President Mahuad with the help of a general and a supreme court justice.

If Ecuadoran leaders were hampered by popular protest, their difficulties in dealing with the congress were even worse. Political gridlock was often the order of the day. With over ten active political parties competing in each election, winners find it difficult to form lasting alliances. Individual congressional deputies' allegiances to their party and political futures are stronger than their interest in policy progress and cooperation. The problem has long been exacerbated by a strong regionalism, by which Ecuadorans sense of identity is based more in a "costa vs. sierra" sensibility than a national one. As McConnell (2001: 73) notes, "the result has been a formal democracy in which representatives go through the motions of elections and parliamentary procedure while the citizens' daily experience with government agencies is marked by corruption, inefficiency and alienation." *The Economist* (1999) put it more bluntly, stating that "the irresponsibility of Ecuador's feuding politicians knows few bounds." Executive-legislative relations were so bad as to make almost impossible the painful decisions Ecuador had to make in order to remain eligible for new loans and attractive to foreign investment. The fact that presidents have seldom been able to maintain supporting coalitions in the legislature for more than a few months has made it impossible to design and implement a four-year policy plan.

The congress's principal tactic in thwarting the executive branch's plans is an impeachment process known as "juicio politico." It involves bringing government ministers and advisers to the congress for a political drama aimed at undermining the administration's reputation with the public and its ability to execute policy. Charges of corruption are most common, but perceived policy missteps are fair game as well. President Borja saw six cabinet ministers ousted in less than two years in office (*LARR*, November 15, 1990: 3). In 1994, the congress sacked Foreign Minister Diego Paredes on charges of ineptitude, illegally importing a car, involvement in financial fraud, and vacillation on the OAS secretary-general vote (*LARR*, November 17, 1994: 4). Vice President Dahik was not only interpolated but arrested for misuse of public funds. In 1997, of course, the congress amplified the trend and impeached the president, only months after he came into office. That the president of the congress, Alarcon, assumed the office of executive made the impeachment look all the more like a blatant power grab by the legislative branch. A very fragile working coalition that Mahuad's DP party had with the Social Christians (PSC) fell apart, leaving Mahuad with no political cover when the economic crisis intensified. After the fall of Mahuad, the congress allowed President Noboa a honeymoon, even when he went forward with the controversial dollarization program that had been Mahuad's downfall. But by August 2000, a battle for control of the congress broke out that ended in the election of Susana Gonzalez as speaker. She led a center-left coalition that does not support the programs of the president (*LARR*, August 29, 2000: 3).

Another state-level factor in the later 1990s was constitutional crises and domestic political instability. This began with Bucaram's impeachment in early 1997 and surprised observers inside and outside of Ecuador. The small state had enjoyed a reputation for fierce political battles, but always within a firm democratic environment. Ecuador's military government in the 1970s was never as brutal or repressive as those of its Southern Cone neighbors. A new constitution, developed in the late 1970s, was lauded for its commitment to principles of democracy and human rights. From the end of military rule in 1979 through the early 1990s, Ecuador confronted serious economic crises and saw its share of colorful and eccentric presidents, most notably Leon Febres Cordero (1984–1988), who was kidnapped briefly by troops loyal to a rogue colonel. But never was there an extraconstitutional change in executive power, and Ecuador became known as the relatively peaceful place between its politically tumultuous neighbors, Peru and Colombia.

Even before Bucaram assumed power, concerns about Ecuador's political stability emerged. In the wake of Peruvian President Fujimori's auto-golpe, *The Economist* described Ecuador as a "high-risk" country and warned of the threat of military intervention. Rumors circulated that Duran Ballen was planning to stage a "Fujimorazo," prompting denials from the president and from the defense minister that either planned an unconstitutional power grab. At the same time, four former presidents warned publicly that democracy in Ecuador was in danger because of an absence of leadership (*LARR*, March 10, 1994: 1, 6). While there was no doubt political gain to be made by such statements, they also reflect a real and new concern about the viability of Ecuadoran democracy. When coups happened, in 1997 and again in 2000, news reports the world around questioned whether the 1979–1997 period in Ecuador had been but a democratic exception in an otherwise dictatorial culture.

A final "state-level" factor worthy of consideration here is Ecuador's status as a small state, at least in South American terms. Ecuador's population (which surpassed ten million in the 1990s) and territory are small when compared with all its Andean neighbors, especially with those in the Southern Cone region, save Uruguay. Ecuador is also among the poorest countries in the region. This means that Ecuador has a smaller voice, fewer resources and less prestige to bring to any regional or global bargaining forums. In prototypical "small state" fashion, Ecuador frequently seeks out regional or otherwise multilateral approaches to problem solving. Consider, for example, Duran Ballen's appeal to regional leaders and the Rio Protocol guarantors to solve the 1995 border conflict. Ecuador's embrace of Andean regionalism is a second example. Ecuador's support for CAN and Andean integration in general is an extension of its foreign policy approach since independence. A third is Ecuador's joining with its neighbors to make clear its concern about spillover from Colombia. Ecuador is dwarfed by Colombia and is therefore especially worried about the problem. Ecuador's multilateralism is not entirely consistent. Elsewhere I argue (Hey 2000) that because Ecuador is a small state with few resources to devote to diplomacy, it should use the OAS as a primary foreign policy instrument. The evidence suggests that Ecuador uses the organization sparingly and misses important opportunities to enhance its voice through the hemisphere's principal diplomatic organization. It should be noted that the OAS's bland foreign policy reputation no doubt contributes to its disuse, and Ecuador finds alternative multilateral venues to promote its interests. Hence, Ecuador demonstrates a greater commitment to Andean groups than to the OAS. Ecuador also occasionally goes it alone. Ecuador joined the WTO and used its offices to sue the European Union over EU preferences for banana growers in the Caribbean, Pacific, and Africa. The WTO ruled in favor of Ecuador. But when the United States and the EU reached a bilateral agreement that Ecuador felt was unacceptable to its interests as the world's largest banana exporter, Ecuador demanded corrections that were eventually adopted (*LARR*, May 15, 2001: 6–7).

The state level of analysis appears to be a strong determinant of Ecuadoran foreign policy in the 1990s. The country's constant state of crisis in large part explains the continuity in policy. The domestic components of that crisis took three forms: (1) an economy and fiscal deficits in such bad shape that structural reform (including budget cuts) appeared the only alternative; (2) demands by popular interests that the state maintain subsidies, increase wages and services, and put off international creditors; and (3) an obstructionist legislature that went so far as to oust the president. These competing demands never relented throughout the decade and account for Ecuador's slow movement toward open markets, regional integration, and neoliberalism, punctuated by promises and programs for the working classes. Whether right-wing or left-wing, populist or grounded in business interests, Ecuadoran presidents operated within a crisis atmosphere that left them very little maneuvering room.

The state level of analysis is less potent in explaining Ecuador's policy toward Peru. As has been addressed earlier, individual presidents were crucial in securing an end to the border conflict. But it is important to note that state-level factors, public opinion and congressional approval, were necessary preconditions to presidential initiatives. No president before Duran Ballen enjoyed a national atmosphere in which reconciliation with Peru was possible.

System Level

A contradictory dynamic permeated Ecuador's relations with the exterior throughout the 1990s. On the one hand, Ecuador was in such dire economic straits that it became especially vulnerable to foreign pressures. For example, in 1996, a London investment reporting firm gave Ecuador a D investment rating, not only because of the drastic economic situation but because of the political uncertainty Bucaram's election caused (*LARR*, November 14, 1996: 3). In June 1997, months after the first coup, the U.S. ambassador in Ecuador accused Ecuadoran judges of being "up to their necks in drug trafficking," and denied them visas to the United States. He also charged that foreign interests invested in Colombia and Peru because they were unable to rely on a consistent set of rules in Ecuador, since contracts changed with every change of government or cabinet ministers. Days later, the British ambassador said that legal and commercial insecurity were driving out foreign investors. At the same time, France's risk-rating agency placed Ecuador on a list of countries from which investors were warned to steer clear (*LARR*, July 22, 1997: 4–5). These and other economic punishments occurred throughout the decade. More noteworthy perhaps is the fact that Ecuador secretly allowed the U.S. military to conduct counternarcotic operations in the Ecuadoran Amazon region in 1993 (*LARR*, January 29, 1993: 8). Previously, in 1987, Ecuador and the United States entered into an ill-fated collaboration to build a road in the jungle. Code-named "Blazing Trails," the operation brought U.S. reserve troops to Ecuador and ended in utter practical and political failure. Almost no progress was made on the road as the troops got stuck in the mud, and the congress used the operation to vilify President Febres Cordero as a traitor (Hey 1995). At the end of that debacle, there was a national consensus that U.S. troops would not again work in Ecuador. Yet only six years later they did. And in 1999, Ecuador agreed to allow the U.S. military to use Manta air force base for drug surveillance flights (*LARR*, July 25, 2001: 1). These events point not only to

Ecuador's inability to resist U.S. demands but to its concerns about the proliferation of drug-related activities.

On the other hand, Ecuador's dismal political situation and fragile economy earned it attention. The constitutional crises prompted concerns about democracy in general in Latin America, where memories of brutal military dictatorships remain vivid. Even though Ecuador's generals were not guilty of the atrocities committed by their neighbors, political events in Ecuador still became a bellwether for the region. To that extent, the region and the world had an enormous interest in seeing Ecuadoran democracy restored and underplaying the significance of the events. Ecuador was not punished as such when it ousted democratically elected leaders. Instead, there seemed to be a global sigh of relief that the military had not taken over (and the United States made it clear there would be repercussions if it had) (*LARR*, January 25, 2000: 1). Furthermore, on the economy, Ecuador earned as many concessions and second chances as punitive measures. An economic history of the decade shows one debt rescheduling agreement after another, all followed by new credits from international institutions.

The international system's role on Ecuador seemed at once forceful and weak. While global actors used threats of credit and investment stoppages to force Ecuador to pay its loans and restructure its economy, they also knew that Ecuador was impoverished and in political gridlock, making it very hard for any democratic leader to implement the desired changes. International pressures moved Ecuador along the seemingly inevitable path of economic restructuring, but they were unable to prevent the legislature and popular groups from creating frequent obstacles along the way. Ecuador's participation in Andean integration reflects the global tendency toward common markets and Ecuador's sense of self-interest more than it does submission to any particular country's pressures. All the diplomatic skill and power of the four guarantor countries of the Rio Protocol could not force Ecuador and Peru to reconcile the border conflict until they were ready, and only then in the wake of a deadly war. Yet, it was a system-level event, the eruption of the 1995 border war, that created and set the stage for the eventual signing of the Itamaraty peace accord and later a resolution to the border conflict. In sum, Ecuador's options in the 1990s were limited because of its vulnerability to international forces. This meant that Ecuador did not take on many international initiatives or implement bold foreign policies. But the power of domestic political interests often delayed and modified what the international sector would have liked to dictate.

CONCLUSION

The predicaments faced by Ecuadoran leaders in the 1990s made creative foreign policy impossible and even reactive foreign policy difficult. Domestic and international pressures were so extreme as to make it nearly impossible to advance any notion of the "national interest." The word *crisis* appears so often in accounts of Ecuadoran political and economic events during the decade as to suggest that the crisis was chronic. *Crisis* is by definition a short-term condition, marked by severe, yet temporary, challenges and perils (Hermann 1990). Yet Ecuador worked under extreme conditions throughout the decade and could indeed be said to have experienced an unremitting state of crisis.

This state of affairs had two key elements, one domestic, the other international. The domestic component entailed a nearly constant gridlock between the legislative and executive branches. Although the Ecuadoran constitution provides the executive exclusively with the power of implementing foreign policy, the congress frequently used international activities as an issue on which to foil the president. Whether through impeachment or legislative obstructionism, the Constituent Assembly maneuvered to embarrass and impede the executive. This occurred in both economic and diplomatic policy. With the exceptions of some instances surrounding regional integration and the Peruvian border war, Ecuadoran presidents could not count on legislative approval of their policies. Indeed, going forward with a foreign policy meant grave political risk. The international component concerned Ecuador's extremely fragile economy. One might think that this is best considered a domestic issue, and indeed it is. Ecuador's depleted coffers meant it had few funds to address issues of poverty and services within the country. But the economy was in equal part a foreign policy problem, inasmuch as Ecuador owed billions of dollars to foreign creditors, who in turn took great interest in the country's national economic choices.

So it was in a tightly restricted atmosphere that foreign policymakers made choices. The policy output of such an environment entailed mostly moving toward economic restructuring, but in a haphazard and circuitous way. Beyond that, however, is the crisis's effect of limiting Ecuador's foreign policy initiatives. No president during this time, save perhaps Bucaram during his visit to Lima shortly before his impeachment, was able to make any bold foreign policy decisions or to launch any visionary policies. Gone were the days of Ecuador's hosting a hemisphere-wide conference on Latin American development, as President Hurtado had done in the 1980s. Gone also were the bold, if unwise, decisions to break diplomatic relations with the likes of revolutionary Nicaragua, because the president cared little about the international community's vision of Ecuador's diplomacy (Hey 1995). Ecuador was a solid regional citizen, hosting CAN meetings and managing the border conflict with Peru. But the country's foreign policy history in the 1990s reveals that it had neither the resources nor perhaps the energy to go much beyond management of its crises.

DISCUSSION QUESTIONS

1. How would Ecuador's foreign policy have differed in the 1990s if the country had not experienced political turmoil?
2. Do Ecuador's many coups in the 1990s suggest that democracy is threatened there?
3. Which is the stronger force on Ecuadoran foreign policy: foreign creditors and institutions or the domestic constituency?

11

Peru

Managing Foreign Policy Amid Political and Economic Crisis

Rubén Berríos

Peru is a middle-range power in South America without the economic or political clout to have a major role in international issues. It has faced economic and political challenges over four decades that in many ways mirrored general trends in Latin America: difficulties in its economic and diplomatic relations with the United States, the burden of foreign debt, territorial disputes with its neighbors, internal political instability that affected its fragile economy, insurgent groups, and narcotraffic. Peru's responses to the problems it has faced reflect the range of strategies employed by many of its neighbors in the foreign policy area to cope with political and economic difficulties.

Peru's course over the years has been a zigzag one, with policies that rocked between sharply different courses of action. Until the 1960s, Peru's leaders had maintained that it was in their interest to comply with the United States' policy dictates. But in the late 1960s, Peru took a stance as an active third world actor seeking more autonomous national development. In the early 1980s, the country shifted back to a much less defiant policy until 1985, when the García regime began to defy the United States and international banking institutions with increasing independence. During the Fujimori administration, however, the country reversed its efforts.

This chapter examines the foreign policy strategies employed by Peru since the early 1960s and seeks to explain how despite regime change, the country has maintained a degree of stability. It examines Peru's behavior in three areas over the past four decades: international economic relations, ties with the Soviet Union, and regional issues (economic integration, economic cooperation, and Peru's border conflict with its northern neighbor). The first part is an empirical section on Peru's foreign policy in these three areas. This is followed by an examination using a levels-of-analysis approach that considers the individual, the state, and systemic factors.

INTERNATIONAL ECONOMIC RELATIONS: OUTSIDE PRESSURES AND ECONOMIC FRAGILITY

An examination of Peru's foreign policy since the 1960s provides evidence of a cyclical pattern of foreign policy behavior. Electoral democracy (Belaunde: 1963–1968, 1980–1985; Fujimori: 1990–2000) has fostered a "convergent" attitude or an effort of "compliance." Under the neoliberal framework, foreign policy behavior exhibited cooperation in a pro–free market attitude. But during two other periods (Velasco: 1968–1975; García: 1985–1990), foreign policy had a strong nationalist orientation that was more defiant of the core.

Early 1960s and the First Belaunde Administration (1963–1968)

Latin America underwent considerable change when the Cuban revolution challenged hemispheric stability in 1959. The United States had to devise new policies to reassert its influence in the region. In 1961, the Kennedy administration announced the Alliance for Progress to help Latin America's political and economic development. In another initiative, the Peace Corps sent volunteers to promote the Good Neighbor policy. The United States was promoting its principled commitment to democratic political development, but it was also reacting to safeguard its national interests. This came to a test with Peru's military coup in 1962. The United States. suspended relations and canceled its aid program to Peru. The military had annulled the electoral victory by Alianza Popular Revolucionaria Americana (APRA), an old rival of the military. Since no party had a clear majority the decision was up to the Congress, and since APRA had control of 45 percent of the seats in the congress, it claimed to be the winner.

Although its rhetoric invoked idealistic principles of democracy that opposed military intervention, Washington only opposed certain types of coups. While the Kennedy administration denounced some coups as antidemocratic because of their mildly leftist or nationalist stands, it remained silent about others (e.g., in Argentina, Guatemala, Ecuador) that were more repressive. The Kennedy administration was displeased with the Peruvian military's increasingly nationalistic political direction (Van Cleeve 1976). There was also a contrasting difference with this coup. It was no longer the old-type *caudillo*; rather, for the first time the armed forces were acting as an institution.

Fernando Belaunde was elected president in the next year's national elections. He immediately entered into a legal and political debate with the U.S.-owned International Petroleum Company (IPC), a firm that claimed ownership of the subsoil of the oil fields. As a result of the controversy that ensued, the United States suspended aid for four of the five years Belaunde was in office (St. John 1992). Disputes over IPC became a major impediment as Belaunde faced pressure from the United States and the electorate to whom he had promised to settle the issue in ninety days (Pinelo 1973; Olson 1975). As the IPC controversy awakened nationalist sentiments, a resolution to the dispute became increasingly difficult (Ingram 1974). Belaunde was willing to come to a generous compromise because Peru's economy was in deep recession and its recovery depended in large measure on U.S. credits and assistance.

External pressure substantially weakened Belaunde, who faced growing foreign debt and economic problems that undercut his reform programs. He was ousted as president in 1968, according to Gorman and St. John (1982), "in part because of his administration's weak foreign policy, which did not satisfy nationalist expectations" (179). The coup was the product of the politicization of the Peruvian armed forces, many of whom had been graduates of the Centro de Altos Estudios Militares (CAEM) (Astiz and García 1972; Villanueva 1974). Different from the traditional mold that protected the status quo, they recognized Peru's need for structural change if it were to avert violent revolution.

Military Rule (1968–1975, 1975–1980)

In 1968, Peru's traditional passivity in foreign affairs ended as the nationalist government of General Velasco Alvarado (1968–1975) began to take a more assertive and autonomous position in the conduct of its foreign policy. Until then, a privileged landed oligarchy with strong links to the export sector and foreign interests had dominated Peru. The army adopted a reformist and nationalist attitude under Alvarado, whose first priority was to nationalize Peru's economic and foreign policy. In his first act, he forcefully seized IPC's oil fields and the refinery at Talara.

Compared to its predecessors, the nationalist military regime intended to raise Peru's diplomatic profile by becoming more active in international organizations and forums. Evidence of this is Peru's active involvement in the Non-Aligned Movement, its strained relations with the United States due to the nationalization of American firms, its call for an end to the embargo on Cuba, its unilateral recognition of all the socialist countries, its support for regional economic integration (the Andean Pact), and its staunch defense of its two-hundred-mile marine limit (Berríos 1986; Gorman and St. John 1982; Swansbrough 1975). Peru also demanded the overhaul of the OAS and the Inter-American Treaty of Reciprocal Assistance, and it called for the creation of a new body that would give Latin American nations a greater voice and the right to ideological pluralism.

Peru's new foreign policy orientation was part of a nationalist trend that swept several Andean countries in the late 1960s and early 1970s. Peruvian generals were determined to transform the domestic economic structure and to reorient Peru's foreign relations. In their efforts to achieve more independent and diversified foreign relations, the generals made common cause with Salvador Allende in Chile (1970–1973) and the short-lived reformist government of General Juan José Torres in Bolivia (1970–1971). Peru had also been outspoken in its solidarity with Panama's nationalist leader General Omar Torrijos's (1968–1981) call for Panamanian control of the Panama Canal. Peruvian diplomacy took major steps in the direction of greater geographical diversification, multilateral diplomacy, and ideological pluralism (García Bedoya 1981; Gorman and St. John 1982; Swansbrough 1975). On the economic front, it restructured ties with its traditional trade partners and sought expanded relations with the socialist countries of Eastern Europe, the former Soviet Union, China, Cuba, and a number of countries in Africa (Berríos 1986; Berríos and Blasier 1991).

This nationalist trend put the Peruvian military on a collision course with the United States, especially since the quest for state ownership of natural resources and basic industry would lead to the expropriation of a number of U.S. firms. Among others, subsidiaries of W. R. Grace, Standard Oil, Chase Manhattan, and Cerro de Pasco Corporation were nationalized (Goodsell 1975; Huerta 1977; Hunt 1975; Sigmund 1980). These large multinationals came to symbolize a foreign presence that undermined true Peruvian sovereignty and demonstrated continued dependence on the United States (Carey 1964; Clayton 1999; Goodsell 1974; Sharp 1972). However, the government argued that IPC was a special case and that foreign investment would be welcome but under different circumstances.

Peru also asserted its nationalist rights in other ways. It declared offshore fishing limits of two hundred nautical miles and began to seize large numbers of U.S. tuna clippers in Peruvian waters in the early 1970s. By championing the cause in multilateral forums, it gained strong backing from other nonaligned countries but aroused the wrath of the Nixon administration. In May 1969, the United States retaliated by suspending arms sales to Peru. Peru in turn evicted the local U.S. military mission. In continuing hostilities, Lima canceled a visit by then-governor Nelson Rockefeller of New York, who was on a fact-finding mission to Latin America, and went as far as asking the Peace Corps to leave the country in 1974.

In the late 1970s, many of the Peruvian reforms were undone under the "second phase of the Peruvian Revolutionary Government," headed by General Morales Bermudez (1975–1980). As the economic crisis continued to deepen, the military regime became increasingly unpopular and was forced to call for general elections. The Morales years brought an abandonment of progressive diplomacy, and Peru's nonaligned activism was deemphasized. Gorman and St. John (1982) label this period as "an illustration of Peru's new conservatism" resulting from its mismanaged economic crisis, failed development strategy, and external pressure. Peru faced tough conditionality from the International Monetary Fund (IMF) on its foreign debt, and a series of measures were taken to persuade foreign bankers of Peru's creditworthiness (Ferrero 1987; Kisic 1987). Peru's bargaining position in external affairs was no longer consistent with the policies outlined in the early years of the Velasco government. Faced with domestic pressure and increased labor unrest, Peru's foreign policy was trapped in its subordinate position in the international system.

Fernando Belaunde (1980–1985)

The sagging economy and growing civilian opposition to the military prompted a return to electoral politics. In 1980, Fernando Belaunde returned to the presidency, ending twelve years of military rule by the people who had overthrown him. One of the key reasons why the military had deposed the Belaunde government in 1968 was his favorable treatment toward multinational corporations, which the military interpreted as less than advantageous to Peru's national interests (Goodsell 1974; Lincoln 1984). Thus, it was not surprising that the first act of the military junta in 1968 was the expropriation of the IPC, a subsidiary of Standard Oil of New Jersey.

On the domestic front, Belaunde set out to dismantle many of the policies adopted by the military government, particularly turning over state enterprise to the private sector. Although there was some degree of continuity in his foreign policy, the main aim was to realign Peru with Washington in order to obtain preferential treatment (Madalengoitia 1987). The "privileged partnership" that Belaunde sought was broken only by a brief estrangement in 1982, when Peru attempted to mediate a peaceful settlement to the Malvinas/Falklands war after Washington had aligned itself with British prime minister Margaret Thatcher (Lincoln 1984). Another minor incident that year was Washington's imposition of countervailing duties on Peruvian textiles, which Peru labeled protectionist.

At the heart of the rapprochement between Washington and Lima was real ideological convergence. The Reagan administration hailed the two countries' "common interest," responded warmly to Peru's democratization, and applauded Belaunde's vehement anticommunism. Meanwhile, the ideals of regional integration collapsed in the phase of Peru's emphasis on liberalization and privatization, which ran counter to trends within the Andean Pact.

Belaunde's electoral victory paved the way to liberalize the economy and repay the foreign debt. Belaunde's trade policy laid squarely in the Western sphere of influence. The United States reinforced its position as Peru's main trading partner and its principal supplier of credits and technology (Lincoln 1984; St. John 1992). As a result, dealings with the socialist countries fell abruptly. Peru's exports to the CMEA countries declined from $169.5 million in 1979 to $77.7 million in 1982; imports from the socialist countries dropped from $32.8 million in 1980 to just $9.7 million two years later (IMF 1986: 320–21).

The pattern of military procurement also shifted. In 1984, Belaunde approved the purchase of twenty-six of France's advance Mirage 2000 aircraft. Eventually fourteen of these aircraft were delivered at the cost of $700 million in a deal that shocked Peru's foreign creditors. In any event, the deal was eloquent proof of the power of Peru's military in the country's decision-making power (Masterson 1991). Meanwhile, the arms buildup was reciprocated by Chile, which made tensions flare. In 1981, border clashes with Ecuador ensued over a disputed portion of territory seized by Ecuador.

Belaunde's foreign policy represented a return to the traditional association Peru had with the United States under his first administration (1963–1968). With his administration just under way, he confronted the emergence of the little-known Maoist-inspired guerrilla group Sendero Luminoso (Shining Path). In December 1992, Belaunde declared a state of emergency in the Ayacucho, Huancavelica, and Apurimac departments where Sendero was active. Belaunde allowed the military to launch a counterinsurgency campaign, and there were many indiscriminate killings from both sides. In his five years in office, the death toll surpassed seven thousand. The United States did not express much concern about the deteriorating human rights situation in Peru (Roberts and Peceny 1997). In fact, military aid to Peru under the Reagan administration had more than doubled during this period.

During Belaunde's term in office, he also had to confront declining terms of trade, adverse climatic conditions that affected agricultural output, and rising interest rates on the foreign debt. As the economy took a downturn, domestic savings and investment declined, capital flight increased, and foreign credits dried up. Unable to reduce its fiscal deficit and to find any relief on interest rates, Peru's economy became increasingly fragile.

Altogether, Belaunde's impact on Peru's world role was twofold. As the economy ran into trouble, Belaunde accelerated the process that Morales Bermudez had begun in the mid-1970s of mortgaging Peru's foreign policy to its huge commitments to Western banks and multilateral financial organizations such as the IMF. At the same time, Belaunde deactivated Peru as a force in the international arena and returned it to the diplomatic lethargy of its conservative past (St. John 1992). When Alan García took office in July 1985, he inherited a country experiencing enormous difficulties and promised to lead the country toward a more statist approach.

Alan García (1985–1990)

García's foreign policy agenda was centered on three principles: anti-imperialism, nonalignment, and support for Latin American unity. García painted a broad activist role for Peru in world affairs. He favored close relations with the nonaligned, sought closer ties to the third world, and emphasized active participation in international organizations. García asserted his independence from the United States and came out in defense of the Sandinistas' efforts to achieve greater Nicaraguan sovereignty as they battled against Washington-supported, anti-Sandinistas labeled as *Contras*. At the same time he restored relations with Cuba, which had been severed in 1980 after Cuban dissidents took refuge in the grounds of the Peruvian embassy in Havana—an event that led to the exodus of more than one hundred thousand refugees from the Cuban port of Mariel.

By invoking the principle of Latin American unity in his calls for a negotiated settlement to the Central American conflict, García was instrumental in creating the Lima Group—composed of Argentina, Brazil, Peru, and Uruguay—to support the Contadora peace effort. Even at the cost of antagonizing his own powerful military, he called for the reduction of military spending and an end to the regional arms race. He also urged the revival and strengthening of regional economic bodies such as the Latin American Economic System (SELA) and the Andean Pact.

García is best known for his anticore leadership position on the international debt issue. Upon assuming office, he was confronted with a growing foreign debt that had become a widespread problem for much of Latin America. The Belaunde administration had negotiated agreements with the IMF but found it difficult to live up to them and had to stop payments after 1984. In his inaugural speech in July 1985, García announced that the government was going to limit payment on the foreign debt to 10 percent of its export earnings. In addition, he announced that henceforth Peru was only going to negotiate with its creditors, not the IMF. Tensions with the United States and the international financial institutions increased when García began to advocate for collective action to third world debt. Peru was declared ineligible for new credits and was labeled a high-risk country (Ministerio de Relaciones Exteriores del Peru 1986). To make matters worse, hyperinflation soared to record levels, and the government found itself confronting the fierce guerrilla insurgency of Sendero Luminoso.

Peru's stand was not against financial institutions such as the World Bank, Inter-American Development Bank (IADB), and Corporación Andina de Fomento. Peru had been paying its debt fully and on time to all those institutions. The beef was with private foreign banks. But rather than rejecting the debt outright as Cuba's Fidel Castro had proposed, the Peruvian government was insisting that it would pay according to its means, without causing further hardship to its people. García's call for third world unity landed on deaf ears as some of the bigger countries (Brazil, Mexico, Argentina) were negotiating their debt burden unilaterally under IMF auspices.

García certainly had pragmatic reasons for pursuing the policies he did as well. On the one hand, it diverted attention from the harsh economic realities at home and was an intricate part of the charismatic populism with which García hoped to buy time for his domestic policies (Crabtree 1992). At the same time, broadening diplomatic contacts, projecting an image of regional leadership, and searching for potential supporters were among the few cards that García could play to ease Peru's economic predicament and escape from isolation.

Alberto Fujimori (1990–2000)

When Alberto Fujimori assumed the presidency in 1990, he inherited a country that had been ravaged by guerilla violence and had been experiencing hyperinflation, a major decline in real income, and high budget deficits. Although he campaigned on a platform of benign populism, he steered the country on a more orthodox course by initiating a drastic stabilization plan. The new program involved what is better known as "shock treatment." The immediate aim was to halt hyperinflation and to liberalize the economy. Although the policy worked in controlling inflation, the price paid was a further decline in the standard of living. Other aspects of these initial measures included lifting subsidies, freeing prices and wages, liberalizing trade and the financial sector, and setting the stage for the privatization of public enterprises (Gonzales de Olarte 1996).

On the political front, his most immediate commitment was to confront guerrilla violence and to combat political corruption. Reflective of how much conditions had deteriorated domestically was the 1990 cholera epidemic, the worst in Latin America in over a century. Externally, Fujimori's first priority was to seek Peru's "reinsertion" into the international financial system because the country had been ostracized for defaulting on its foreign debt. That move did succeed in facilitating the inflow of foreign capital from financial institutions to revive the economy.

With the emergence of a new international order, economic and international financial issues began to play a central role in the execution of foreign policy. After the Cold War, the United States stressed that democratization was a key objective of its Latin America policy. However, in the case of the Fujimori government in the latter part of the 1990s, basic democratic principles were often being undermined. The United States was more interested in supporting free markets and the war against narcotics (McClintock 2001). With the defeat of Sendero Luminoso and the Movimiento Revolucionario Tupac Amaru (MRTA) guerrillas, the traditional communist ideological threat had moved to second place, and the United States became more preoccupied with Peru's political stability.

Determined to muscle his way into a third consecutive term, Fujimori used autocratic methods to stifle the opposition. International observers, including the OAS, had insisted that there were no guarantees for free and fair elections, but the United States overlooked the issue and at no time did it suspend assistance to Peru. In fact, from 1993 to 1998, Peru received more aid from the U.S. Agency for International Development (USAID) than any other country in Latin America. McClintock (2001) also stresses that the U.S. government insisted that Peru without Fujimori would be immersed in chaos.

U.S. assistance to Peru has often had a strong military component. Concerned with the struggle against drug trafficking and internal insurgency, the U.S. government has tolerated human rights abuses under Belaunde, García, and Fujimori (Roberts and Peceny 1997). However, it was Fujimori who took the most significant steps to empower the armed forces. Since Peru has a relatively weak legislature and judicial system, there were no oversights or control of military activities. As an important donor in aspects of security, the United States often sent the wrong signals because it was not able to back up its rhetoric with a decisive policy to consolidate democracy and respect for human rights. The bitter truth at the end of the millennium was that the region was no longer of primary concern to the United States.

Although the Fujimori administration was slow to cooperate with the United States in the war on drugs, it did finally get on board to substantially reduce the area devoted to coca cultivation. In another area of cooperation, the United States served as an observer and guarantor to Peru's border dispute with Ecuador. The peace agreement signed with Ecuador in 1998 was an important achievement of the Fujimori government. The agreement formally ended a bitter conflict that had spanned four decades, resulted in an arms buildup, and erupted into war in 1995. The accord put a brake on military spending and a plan was drafted to foster economic development and trade in the Amazonian border region. The boundary demarcation, which had been a problem for Peru for about 180 years, was an issue that had finally been resolved.

The election of Fujimori in 1990 generated enthusiasm and support from Japan. Faced with serious political and economic troubles at home, Fujimori sought assistance from the land of his ancestors. Although the government of Japan was sympathetic to Fujimori, it was not fully committed to come to his aid. Instead, Japan was cautious with soft credits and technical assistance that often came in consultation with the United States. For much of the 1990s, Japanese foreign investment in Peru was conspicuously absent relative to European participation. Trade between the two countries did not reach the anticipated levels.

As Peru and the rest of Latin America emerged from the so-called lost decade of the eighties, the Asian countries enjoyed impressive economic growth and trade performance. Peru "rediscovered" the Asia–Pacific region in the late 1980s and early 1990s, and it showed its admiration for those countries by expanding its diplomatic representation in Asia to advance economic cooperation. Trade between Peru and the Asia–Pacific region did increase between 1990 and 1996 but suffered a setback due to the financial turmoil that devastated some Asian countries in 1996–1997. Asian countries did not prove to be significant partners, and Peru continued to face the void created by diminishing U.S. interest in Latin America and the loss of the socialist countries as supporters.

Since the late 1960s, Peru sought to diversify its relations in its efforts to seek a wider involvement in the international system. Although the United States had traditionally been Peru's main trading partner, the Andean nation looked first to the socialist countries and other third world nations. During the 1990s, Peru began focusing more attention on Japan and the Pacific Asian countries as important market outlets and possible sources of investment.

RELATIONS WITH THE SOVIET UNION

One of the most remarkable aspects of Peru's foreign relations was a close relationship with the former Soviet Union that developed in the 1970s. During a period of several years, the expansion of trade between the two countries made Peru the second largest Latin American importer of Soviet arms—second only to Cuba.

Until the late 1960s, the former Soviet Union lacked both the capability and the opportunity to conduct an active foreign policy in Latin America. Though a number of small Moscow-line communist parties have existed locally since the 1920s, geographic distance and the overwhelming weight of U.S. influence had blocked any wider Soviet presence in the region. However, the shift to the left in Peru, Chile, and Bolivia awakened Moscow's interest. Optimistic Soviet observers saw a wave of anti-imperialist and national liberation struggles that challenged U.S. interests and might shift the balance of power in favor of the Soviet Union. The "progressive" nature of the Peruvian military drew praise, and Soviet analysts even began to reassess the character and role of third world military elites that Moscow had previously dismissed as reactionary. On February 2, 1969, Peru and the former Soviet Union formally established diplomatic relations (Berríos and Blasier 1991).

Trade was initially modest but constituted a vital element in the strategy of the military government of the 1970s. The nationalist military government attempted to redirect the bulk of Peru's trade away from its traditional reliance on U.S. markets and toward new trading partners such as the Andean Pact countries, the rest of Latin America, and Eastern Europe. Even a limited volume of trade bolstered Peru's determination and ability to withstand U.S. economic pressure. Some observers believe that the Soviet decision to develop closer ties with Peru came as a response "to the deterioration in U.S.-Peruvian relations—even if Soviet analysts may have harbored private doubts about the true depth of the Peruvian military's radicalism" (Evanson 1985: 104).

With the connection to the Council of Mutual Economic Assistance (CMEA), the socialist countries became an important market for Peruvian exports such as minerals and fishmeal, though results on the import side were less impressive. Peru received a range of goods that reflected the specialties of these economies. There were also some projects in which Peru received technical assistance from some of these countries, mainly in fisheries, the construction of hydroelectric plants, and engineering services (Berríos 1986).

Much more striking than Soviet economic trade and aid, however, was Soviet military assistance. Until the late 1960s, Peru had been one of the continent's major recipients of U.S. military aid. But when Peru set out to modernize its defense capabilities, Washington was reluctant, and Peru had to look for alternative suppliers. The Soviet Union at the time offered generous terms and Peru could not resist. The Peruvian Army and Air Force took full advantage of Soviet credits to acquire a sophisticated array of military hardware, including hundreds of tanks, dozens of helicopters, and thirty-six supersonic SU-22 Sukhoi fighter-bombers (Berríos and Blasier 1991).

The various actions Peru took in the late 1960s and early 1970s to try to assert its independence carried a predictably heavy price. Washington reacted more sharply to the nationalization of U.S. companies than to the warming of relations with the Soviet Union.

The United States threatened to substantially cut its bilateral aid programs and its sugar quota. The level of new foreign investment declined sharply (Huerta 1977). The U.S. government and multinational corporations together brought enormous pressure to bear on Peru, demanding protection of U.S. capital and adequate compensation for its expropriated holdings (Milenski 1975). Peru found access to loans denied and foreign credits at favorable rates hard to come by. Between 1968 and 1972, the country received no loans from the World Bank. Under pressure, the military government quickened the pace of borrowing to finance the expansion of exports but on harsher terms from the international commercial banks (Sheetz 1986; Uriarte 1986; Kisic 1987).

The nationalist surge began to lose steam by 1974. U.S.-Peruvian relations improved as the military toned down its revolutionary rhetoric and in February 1974 reached settlements on U.S. assets that had been nationalized (Huerta 1977; Schwalb Lopez-Aldama 1979). In the aftermath of the agreement, Washington resumed bilateral aid and external financing. In 1975, the United States–owned Marcona Mining Company was expropriated but soon compensated to the satisfaction of both sides.

Under the García regime, though undoubtedly troubled by Peru's reliance on Soviet military aid, Washington found Peru's radical nationalist version of nonalignment manageable. Washington's response was to try to wean Lima away from its close military ties to Moscow by presenting itself as an attractive supplier. In the meantime, Peru had to renegotiate its debt with the former Soviet Union through the use of countertrade arrangements where Peru was obligated to pay in kind much of its debt (Berríos and Blasier 1991). These countertrade deals in the form of barter and other modalities also opened the door for renewed trade and fresh credits. But attempting to diversify Peru's international alliances in a bipolar context was difficult. Determined to minimize conditionality pressures from the West and its financial institutions, García became increasingly isolated and Peru's economy deteriorated to its worst levels ever.

With the collapse of the Soviet Union, Peru's already-waning ties were mostly severed. The new Fujimori regime had close ties to the United States, and the faltering economy of Russia was not in a position to work with its former partners in any case.

REGIONAL COOPERATION, INTEGRATION, AND BORDER DISPUTES

Dissatisfied with the lack of progress within the Latin American Free Trade Association (LAFTA) in the 1960s, Andean countries found a renewed enthusiasm to promote regional integration. Geographic proximity, cultural and historical similarities, as well as economic benefits that could be derived from increased intraregional trade and industrial programming, led to state-promoted formation of the Andean Group (AG), composed of Bolivia, Colombia, Chile, Ecuador, and Peru.

In a process that was to lead to increased trade opportunities and greater solidarity among members, Peru played a leading role in the late 1960s within the Andean regional integration effort. The signing of the subregional integration agreement is what came to be known as the Cartagena Agreement, which led to the formation of the Andean Pact in 1969 (Berríos 1980). The Andean Group became, without a doubt, the most serious attempt to advance regional integration. The objectives of the AG were consistent with the nationalist trend at the time: to create a free trade zone among its members, establish an internal market for industrial production, and regulate foreign investment.

As a regional grouping, the AG aspired to a free trade area by eliminating tariffs among members. It also paid special attention to the role of multinational firms (Decision 24). While acknowledging the role of foreign capital, the group decided to control it rather than exclude it. However, the push for regional cooperation did not produce the desired political or economic gains. Since its formation, the Andean Pact has encountered a series of difficulties due to political problems that hampered integration efforts. Targets and deadlines were not often met and the established rules were modified. The incorporation of Venezuela was a big boost in 1973, but a serious setback was Chile's unilateral withdrawal in 1976 over regulations on foreign investment, which led to substantial modifications of the rules (Mytelka 1979). After 1976, the agreement was substantially modified with a series of protocols and formal decisions. Decision 24 was altered, virtually abrogated, and in 1987 annulled. Industrial programming was delayed. The AG went through another crisis in 1980 and 1981, due to the coup in Bolivia and border fighting between Peru and Ecuador.

During the rest of the 1980s, the integration process faced a new set of challenges as countries had to deal individually with their foreign debt renegotiations, external disequilibrium, and finding a way out of recession. There were also further delays in the chronogram that had been set. During those years, progress was slow and the overall economic outcome mixed. At the end of the 1980s, the import substitution model was reevaluated and replaced by economic liberalization (Lozano and Zuluaga 2001).

In 1992, Peru autoexcluded itself from its obligations to the Andean Group, which impeded efforts to form a customs union. In the mid-1990s, Peru again engaged in a border war with Ecuador that left hundreds of casualties on both sides. The seriousness of the conflict put in doubt the hopes raised at the Summit of the Americas just weeks earlier. Soon after the AG tried to overcome its divisiveness, and in 1996, Peru rejoined and the group changed its name to the Andean Community (CAN). CAN moved to negotiate with the Southern Cone Common Market (MERCOSUR) and announced that its model of integration would be the European Union (EU). By the end of 2000, intraregional trade had surpassed $5 billion, 27 percent higher than the previous year.

Although significant progress was made toward creating a free trade area, it had also been undermined by external factors. These included the on-and-off border dispute with Ecuador, the institutional coup of Fujimori in April 1992, the suspension of diplomatic relations between Peru and Venezuela, and the spillover effect of Plan Colombia. These interruptions became impediments along the process. Moving forward on integration has proven to be challenging under the new international order given the neoliberal model all countries have adopted. Increased competition and the push for trade liberalization has not been altogether favorable for some sectors of the Peruvian economy because of its inability to withstand the avalanche of foreign imports.

A window of opportunity that became available in 1989 was the move by the Bush administration to bolster the faltering economies with the creation of the Andean Trade Preference Act (ATPA). This was a package extended to the Andean countries for their efforts to combat drug trafficking. The package included trade preferences as well as technical assistance. Since the ATPA has to be renewed annually, the U.S. Congress has to "certify" that these countries are in fact fighting drugs. But, on the other hand, it has made the Andean countries more dependent on the favorable terms of the legislation to promote their nontraditional exports, rather than going at it on their own.

In the arena of subregional cooperation, the restructured Andean Community continued with efforts to bring expanded trade links, increase regional cooperation, establish a relaxed treatment of foreign investment, and promote industrial development. Hampered by internal political disruptions, the pact's degree of commitment to a higher level of transaction was limited by various economic and political problems that the Andean nations had to face in the 1980s and 1990s. Peru withdrew after much criticism from members because President Fujimori had staged a self-administered coup (*autogolpe*) in April 1992 that suspended the constitution and dismissed the congress and the judiciary. Peru rejoined later, but the damage had been done. Furthermore, subregional integration efforts faced a rocky road ahead, the result of economic and trade liberalization under an increasingly globalized economy.

The signing of the peace agreement with Ecuador was an important achievement to reduce tensions in October 1998 (Einaudi 1999). The treaty also laid the groundwork for projects to develop the affected regions. Soon after, negotiations with Bolivia resulted in an agreement that provided for a corridor and duty-free port at the Peruvian port of Ilo. Other agreements have been signed to promote the economic development around Lake Titicaca. As a result of these achievements, discussions with Chile over its old disputed territorial claims have also taken place. These steps and Peru's commitment to regional integration will certainly lead to lower military expenditures and greater cooperation among the Andean neighbors.

LEVELS OF ANALYSIS

This section analyzes Peru's foreign policy through the level of analysis lens by considering individual, state, and systemic factors, thus focusing on what Hey (1997) lists as key variables: leader, relative power of the country, and global concentration of power.

To better understand Peru's foreign policy behavior in these three areas, we rely on the dimensions of a procore versus anticore framework. This approach uses the term *core* to refer to the Northern industrialized world and the institutions associated with its power, including the United States, the International Monetary Fund (IMF), and multinational corporations and private commercial banks based in the North (Hey 1997: 633). A *procore policy* refers to one that cultivates a close relationship with the core, tending to rely on it and comply with its dictates. An *anticore policy* is one that pursues greater autonomy from the core and tries to operate outside the dominant international system by increasing its relative power capabilities. Examples of procore policies are the Belaunde (1963–1968, 1980–1985), Morales (1975–1980), and Fujimori (1990–2000) administrations; anticore approaches were used by the Velasco (1968–1975) and García (1985–1990) administrations.

The Individual Level

Since the early 1960s, Peru has had a very diverse set of presidents. The political system has also shifted from authoritarian to democratic to authoritarian, to democratic, and back to democratic/authoritarian. The line between democratic government and authoritarian government is not entirely precise. For instance, Fujimori was democratically elected but then began to dismantle institutions and constitutional principles that undergird democracy, and in the end he attempted to remain in office indefinitely until he was forced out by a corruption scandal.

Fernando Belaunde was a neoconservative who during his first administration was unable to carry out his agrarian reform program and had difficulty solving the IPC issue. He relied on his reformist image, government spending, and his idealism, but his administration was characterized by low accomplishments. The opposition obstructed his reform proposals. The deepening political impasse left the military increasingly frustrated with politicians in general. Belaunde embraced liberal policies and took an accommodating stand toward foreign investment. He showed a pragmatic willingness to compromise but lacked decisiveness (Lincoln 1984).

Under Velasco, Peru sought to become a leader in third world causes, but after a few years, he was unable to build a consensus within his ranks and was deposed internally. Velasco did not have personal charisma. Yet he was determined to destroy the old power structure and therefore had to rely on the unity of the military. The revolution he tried to implement was populist and nationalist but also military elitist (Jaworski 1984; Rudolph 1992). He promoted a third alternative: "neither communist nor capitalist." Peru was not alone in seeking a way of negotiating a bipolar world, but Velasco went much further than any other leader, and he took Peru with him. He succeeded in generating a highly charged ideological atmosphere, but the military as an institution was still isolated from the rest of society.

Morales abandoned some of the progressive policies of the first phase, as he had to enforce harsh stabilization measures. Morales had little room to maneuver politically. While there was little change in foreign policy, it lacked the luster and pragmatism of earlier years. As the economic situation grew worse, Morales announced general elections and had to step down.

Under Belaunde, Peru reaffirmed its commitment to subregional integration and preoccupied itself with geopolitical issues such as the border dispute with Ecuador. Belaunde was a moderate and a conciliator. Although he was politically conservative, his economic policies were neoliberal. He relied on the goodwill of the United States and called for modifications in the foreign investment code to encourage foreign investment. Under his administration, Peru suffered from deteriorating fiscal conditions and had to submit to IMF adjustment programs. He made little impression on the country's economic problems, but he scored high marks when Peru threw its support behind Argentina in the Malvinas/Falklands conflict. Belaunde's stance went beyond verbal support as he offered military hardware and fighter aircraft (Rudolph 1992).

Driven by a clear convergence of core pressure and ideological bent, Belaunde had been a largely procore leader during his first term of office (1963–1968), and he reprised that role when he came back to power. But the underlying conditions had changed, so that there was no longer a drive to split with the United States. The attempt to seek greater independence left most of the country in worse shape, and no longer in a mood to try to stand alone against the United States. The interest of the United States during this period was high, and the pressure strong, chiefly because Peru had hit an economic and political trigger when it nationalized United States–owned enterprises. This was not an action the United States was likely to overlook.

García represented a swing of the pendulum. He was a charismatic, eloquent speaker and populist leader. When he assumed office, the foreign debt and economic conditions had gone from bad to worse. García was highly personalist and his government very centralized. He often employed strong language and a confrontational style, though his words usually went beyond the actions he was willing or able to take.

García's diplomatic campaign had strong local roots. His activism owes a debt—of style as well as substance—to the *tercermundismo*, or "third worldism," of the first phase of the military government (1968–1975). And the idea of continental solidarity as a way of increasing Latin America's bargaining power has a long history within his own party, the APRA, going back to the classic book by party founder Haya de la Torre, entitled *El Anti-imperialismo y el APRA*.

Because of his youth, García brought with him a renewed enthusiasm. One of his first defiant steps was to set a limit on debt service payments from export earnings. Restricting debt payment became official government policy. He was also highly critical of international financial institutions. García sought to mobilize fellow Latin American debtors but failed when each country was unilaterally dealing with the IMF on debt restructuring. His government tried to boost Peru's participation in the Andean Group, the Group of 77, and within the Non-Aligned Movement.

García's debt stance was a key ingredient in his government's efforts to renew Peru's position of leadership among the nonaligned nations. As Rudolph (1992) puts it, "He took those ambitions personally." The politics of multilateral solidarity coincided with APRA's ideology of promoting regional integration and anti-imperialism. García also took unilateral action in support of the Sandinistas, because he saw U.S. policy as a threat to the sovereignty of not just Nicaragua but of Latin America (Rudolph 1992).

Fujimori, a son of Japanese immigrants, was an outsider and a relatively unknown candidate. With no links to the established political order, he transmitted an image of a proper man with Asian efficiency and political independence. Fujimori was helped by the exhaustion of political parties, for they had been incapable of solving Peru's problems. He was a strong man politically but a liberal in economic matters (McClintock 2001; Youngers 2000), and his administration took a very pro-Western stand throughout his term in office.

Leader ideology is the critical variable during the two anticore periods. Though many other factors clearly contributed to the shift away from the core (including internal politics, economic problems, and failure of the procore policies to improve the lives of the majority of the population), those factors were present during procore periods and were also present in other countries that did not choose an anticore path.

It appears that the policies of Peru during the first phase of military rule were more staunchly anticore than those of other countries largely because it was headed by an administration that acted decisively and consistently in search of independence from the core—represented by the United States and international financial institutions. It took strong repercussions from the core, as well as a change in leadership, to reverse the trend set by Velasco.

The developing relationship with the Soviet Union during the 1970s can also be attributed to leader ideology, since so many pressures were exerted on Peru and other Latin American countries to shun the second superpower.

Peru was not alone in turning to the Soviet Union, but as in the other aspects of its foreign policy during this period, it went further than most of its neighbors. So while the relative power of the world hegemons and their interest in the area played a role in this relationship, those factors alone cannot explain Peru's policies, since they did not produce similar shifts in alliances in most other Latin American countries at that time.

Similarly, the policies of Peru under García went so directly against not only the desires of the core but political and economic trends in the region that they seem explicable only by the variable of a strong leader's influence.

While leader ideology certainly played a role in the return to a procore policy after each of Peru's detours, pressure from the core was the most important variable. One possible exception is Belaunde, who seemed to genuinely share Washington's ideological stance and sought to bring Peru back into the fold. Fujimori also was ideologically in tune with Washington, despite his populist campaign rhetoric.

State Level

During the entire study period, Peru was in a state of extreme economic and political fragility. The weakness of the state created a steady underlying set of constraints that hamstrung each successive administration and severely limited options. There were brief periods of increased stability, but they dissolved and tended to then undermine whatever initiatives had been undertaken. Each time the state tried to strengthen itself by expanding its reach, the resulting economic and political repercussions led to even greater weakness.

Under the first Belaunde administration, the state was structurally weak, the size of the public sector was small, and the country was ruled by a privileged oligarchy. Peru's foreign policy was mainly focused on its neighbors and not its international powers.

Under the military regime, as a result of nationalizations, the state began to acquire a more significant presence. Through the creation of agencies and government ministries, the government had a centralized control of the economy. A conscious effort was made to increase Peru's bargaining position with its major trading partners and diversify relations with other states. The government also set new rules for foreign investment and promoted new schemes, such as joint ventures, in which the state would have majority participation. Throughout this period, Peru became the most active state in Latin America, second to Cuba, promoting nonalignment, greater independence from the core countries, and more diversified relations with other states.

Conaghan and Malloy (1994) note that the fiscal limits of the Velasco period were evident by mid-1975. The state had overextended itself and its ambitious projects required more loans. As the economic crisis set in during the second phase of military rule, there was a retrenchment favoring fiscal conservatism and some of the original reforms were rolled back. The state, however, still had a vastly entrepreneurial role in all sectors of the economy. The ensuing economic crisis undermined and challenged the state-centric model of the first phase. In the second phase, Morales's position was severely weakened by increasing pressures from the IMF to impose austerity programs and drastic stabilization measures. Popular protests against his austerity programs rocked his government and it was not long before he had to step down. The conservative nature of the Morales administration paved the way for a more concerted neoliberal experiment of the subsequent government of Belaunde. The neoliberal project for much of the first half of the 1980s aimed at economic reform and trade liberalization, but it faltered, and the Belaunde administration was faced with a crisis-ridden economic management.

García's government advocated a multilateral foreign policy strategy, particularly when it championed the concerns of other countries of the periphery, criticized the OAS for its domination by the United States, and increased Peruvian activism within the Sistema Economico Latinoamericano (SELA). After 1987, there was an economic debacle. State enterprises were bloated, notoriously inefficient, and operating at heavy losses. This had become a major contribution to the government's fiscal deficit. Moreover, other policies such as the nationalization of banks brought about distrust from investors and the growing deficit sent the economy into a tailspin and into hyperinflation. By the end of the 1980s, Peru's governing institutions were also facing severe problems, and the country was considered an outcast in the international lending system.

As soon as Fujimori had been elected, he went to the United States and Japan to mend fences with the international financial system. He sought help in getting Peru back into the game. He agreed to institute stringent economic measures—which became known as "Fuji-shock"—to gain the acceptance of international investors and lending institutions. Again the extreme weakness of the state left its leaders little maneuvering room in setting policy.

Peru found itself internationally more isolated. The ties with the Soviet Union were weakened by the state's vulnerability to international financial institutions dominated by Western interests. To Peru, of course, the collapse of the Soviet Union itself was the loss of a friendly partner, but the inherent weakness of the Peruvian state had meant that leaders attempting to pull it away from the core's sphere of influence had few resources with which to work.

Peru's efforts toward playing a leading role in regional integration efforts were also hampered by its own state weaknesses. Efforts at solving the longstanding border conflict with Ecuador were undermined by popular and military resistance to settling the dispute that involved a humiliating defeat at the hands of the Ecuadoreans and nationalist pride in 1995.

The state level of analysis helps to explain Peru's behavior chiefly by revealing the constraints that the country faced as it sought to be an actor on the world stage and regional level.

System Level

Though a weak state set the stage for Peru, it was pressure from the exterior that consistently put things into action. The system level is the most powerful framework for examining Peru's foreign policy behavior. During the last four decades, a period in which a weak Peru made two sustained attempts to break free of the core, exterior pressure emerges as a shaping factor. The international political and economic situation guided much of the country's policy, and it was resistance to those forces that resulted in deviations from the core.

Turmoil over pressure from the United States over economic issues was one of the main factors that led to the overthrow of the first Belaunde administration. Though the result was a more anticore military regime, it too found itself under pressure to come into conformity with U.S. demands. By 1975, the second phase of the military regime under Morales began a gradual dismantling of the Velasco reforms. Peru's actions during this period were part of a nationalist trend throughout the Andean region in the 1970s and early 1980s, but they can also be understood as part of a broad reaction to the restrictions put on by the previous course.

Belaunde's resumption of the presidency was a return to civil rule. This was part of a continent-wide transition to democratic political structures. Belaunde's liberalism was well received by international financial institutions. His government initiated a reversal of state interventionist policies and became compliant with IMF mandates. It lifted restrictive rules on foreign investment, and trade liberalization became a centerpiece of Peru's neoliberal experiment (Conaghan and Malloy 1994). His government was accused of *entregismo*, of surrendering the national patrimony to foreign interests. Tensions flared up between Peru and Ecuador soon after he assumed office. His economic policies brought about further economic decline. Although a democrat, Belaunde was perceived as having been incapable of governing effectively.

In the late 1980s and 1990s, there was a shift back toward integration into regional and global markets in Latin America. Hey (1997, 1998) found a consensus in the literature that Latin America became economically weaker during the 1980s, driving many countries back toward the core. As discussed earlier, Peru did not go along with most of its neighbors during that time, charting a course that was strongly nationalist at a time when many others were abandoning such policies. However, it was the overwhelming pressure that came with this dissent, along with the economic fallout for the country and internal turmoil, particularly the increasing role of terrorism, economic hardship, and popular perception that García's policies had failed, that ended the attempt at independence from the core.

The warm relationship with the Soviet Union during this period indicates the role of a bipolar system under Cold War politics was capable of playing in Latin American nations' foreign policy. Peru was not alone in turning to the Soviet Union during this period, but as in the other aspects of its foreign policy during this period, it went further than most of its neighbors. So while the relative power of the world hegemons and their interest in the area played a role in this relationship, those factors alone cannot explain Peru's policies, since they didn't produce similar shifts in alliances in most other Latin American countries at that time. Relations with the Soviet Union were also affected by core pressure, though Peru was able to walk the line between the two superpowers for several years.

The Fujimori administration beckoned yet another swing back toward the core. In this instance, it can be argued that the economic, political, and security situation in Peru had deteriorated to such an extent that it had little freedom to pursue policies not backed by the United States—the new hegemon. Fujimori was the product of a northern education and was probably ideologically in accord with most of the policies he pursued—but the urgency of Peru's situation meant that most leaders probably would have found themselves forced to take similar actions. Thus, core pressure and the internal political-economic situation come to the fore as the key components in the shift back toward the core. Nationalism was no longer a potent force in the search for independence.

With the disintegration of the Soviet Union and the collapse of the Stalinist governments in Eastern Europe, the threat of a bipolar world had dissipated. Soviet capabilities in the Third World had substantially diminished. What was Peru's position under the new world order? Palmer (1992) argues that "Peru entered the 1990s far more vulnerable both internationally and domestically than the country was 25 years earlier" (20). Though Peru had very limited success in its attempts to use the Soviet Union and regional integration as a way of countering strong core pressure, the dominance of the United States that came with the end of the Soviet Union sharply curtailed the ability of any state to steer an independent, or even a middle-of-the-road, course.

CONCLUSION

The foreign policy of Peru over the last four decades has followed many broad patterns shaped by international economic forces and the political and economic situation of Latin America. Peru's course has also differed in several ways, however. In general, Peru shifted more dramatically between a pro- and anticore stance than most of its neighbors and returned to an anticore stance in the late 1980s, a time when few countries were doing so.

Leader ideology emerged as one of the important factors playing a predominant role during the anticore periods and a somewhat less important role during the procore periods. The variable that seemed to best explain the swings back toward the core was pressure from the core; regional and internal politics also played a role.

The Peruvian case shows that over the last four decades its foreign policy shifted between a passive, reactive role and a more active, defiant role. The former shows the cooperative relations with "core" actors. The latter was an effort to promote collective solidarity in search of greater independence. The two principal arenas in which Peru demonstrated its independence were in reaching out to the Soviet Union, attempting to chart a course between the superpowers, and seeking to be a leader in regional cooperation. Ultimately, the weakness of the state and external pressures undermined both efforts. The state level of analysis reveals the vulnerability of a weak state exacerbated by a worsening domestic environment due to mounting deficits, the burden of the foreign debt, ultraleftist insurgencies, natural disasters, and political bickering. Though ties with the Soviet Union helped Peru in its effort toward greater autonomy, they were not enough to withstand the pressure from the United States and international lending institutions.

After the collapse of the Soviet Union, Peru had no hope of sustaining a "third way" in its foreign policy. With the end of the Cold War, foreign policy adjustment began to respond to global trends for economic liberalization and free markets. Adapting to the neoliberal trend has moved Peru back toward the core. Peru's policy shift under Fujimori seemed to be, by most accounts, a function of the political and economic environment within which Peru actually found itself.

DISCUSSION QUESTIONS

1. How does Peru's foreign policy differ from its Andean neighbors during the 1970s and 1980s?
2. Over the past four decades, successive Peruvian governments have pushed for greater independence in the conduct of their foreign policy. What level of analysis is considered most significant in pushing Peru toward the core?

12

Bolivia

The Struggle for Autonomy

Waltraud Quesier Morales

STATE CAPACITY AND FOREIGN POLICY

In foreign as well as domestic policy, power matters greatly. In the absence of power, state sovereignty and national development may be compromised. This has been the case with Bolivia. Within the global power hierarchy, Bolivia is a weak state with a limited political and economic capability to effect its will and achieve core objectives. Historically, geopolitics and the international political system have imposed pervasive structural constraints that have conditioned Bolivian foreign policy and compromised its autonomy.

The country's turbulent domestic politics and chronic instability have often combined with the constraints of geography, powerlessness, and underdevelopment to inhibit a more proactive foreign policy. Internal factors, however, have been less decisive in the Andean nation's international role than have powerful external givens. Bolivia's limited geopolitical and economic assets have meant that Bolivian statesmen, more often than not, were compelled to play the role of policy "takers" in regional and international arenas rather than serve as foreign policy "makers" (Axline 1996: 214; Mace and Bélanger 1999). Indeed, Bolivia has often been the "victim" of foreign policymaking as a consequence of its own inadequacies as well as the aggressiveness of its neighbors and the limited support of the international community.

Bolivia is a third world developing nation, ranking near the lowest third of the international power hierarchy, and a secondary player on the periphery of the global stage. Traditionally, the country has struggled to contain powerful external forces and dominant hemispheric actors. Twentieth-century Bolivian governments—democracies and dictatorships alike—have been hampered equally by the persistent problems of instability, underdevelopment, landlocked status, and external interference in national affairs.

Working as both cause and effect, the interplay of these factors has caused Bolivian foreign policy to become, and primarily remain, highly dependent and externally penetrated. Although not a "small" country in terms of territory, Bolivian foreign policy typifies the limited state capacity and influence of smaller and weaker countries. Bolivia has been, and remains, not only a "prisoner" of geography but also one of poverty and underdevelopment (Hausmann 2001). As a consequence of its small-state dependency, Bolivian governments have lacked the vital resources and necessary state capacity for a more autonomous foreign policy.

SEMIAUTONOMOUS FOREIGN POLICY

From a theoretical perspective, Bolivian foreign policy typifies that of many "underdeveloped societies," which have been chronically subject to extensive external penetration of both their foreign and domestic policies (Rosenau 1966: 54–57). Underdevelopment limits state capacity and contributes to a country's relative powerlessness. In the case of Bolivia, the shortcomings imposed by underdevelopment have been central and constant determinants of foreign policy. Bolivian policymakers have had narrow and difficult choices in the ongoing struggle to retain autonomy and realize core foreign policy objectives amid the highly competitive global power game.

International and systemic factors have been paramount in explaining the successes and failures of Bolivian foreign policy. In effect, external penetration of foreign and domestic policies has virtually collapsed these two agendas. This phenomenon has been apparent especially in Bolivia's relations with the United States, the hemisphere's dominant political and economic actor. Bilateral relations with the United States have preoccupied and dominated Bolivian foreign policy since World War II, inherently bilateralizing the foreign policy agenda. In terms of Rosenau's (1966: 65) theory of foreign policy, such extensive external domination represents a "penetrated political system" wherein nonmembers of a national society participate directly and authoritatively in both internal and external policymaking.

Characteristic of a penetrated political system is "the fusion of national and international systems in certain kinds of *issue areas,*" contributing to the increasingly "intermestic" nature of foreign policymaking (Rosenau 1966: 53–54). As with Bolivian foreign policy, the boundaries between the national and international political systems are eroded by powerful external forces and hegemonic system level actors such as the United States. This steady internationalization or globalization of issues and agendas threatens the foundation of Bolivia's national sovereignty—the capacity of governments to determine with relative autonomy their own policies, whether domestic or foreign. U.S.-Bolivian drug war policy represents such a bilateralized and internationalized issue. At best, Bolivian policymakers have maintained but a limited semiautonomy in the conduct of the drug war.

Rosenau's (1966) theoretical typology further hypothesizes the "nonpenetrated" international political system, where "nonmembers indirectly and nonauthoritatively influence the allocation of a society's values and the mobilization of support for its goals through autonomous rather than through joint action" (65). In Bolivian foreign policy, the quest for a sovereign seacoast appears to represent a foreign policy goal, which is conditioned by systemic circumstances and actors but remains "nonpenetrated" and a relatively autonomous policymaking arena (Rosenau 1966: 54–55).

Therefore, Bolivia's limited state capacity has facilitated the internationalization of the domestic agenda, the penetration of its issue areas by external system-level actors, and the salience of system level explanations of its foreign policy. Nevertheless, despite extensive penetration of the political system's key issue areas, policymakers have been able to preserve "pockets of semiautonomy" (Rosenau 1966: 55). This chapter considers two issue areas that have been central to contemporary Bolivian foreign policy: *la salida al mar*, or the campaign to regain a sovereign seacoast on the Pacific Ocean; and the drug war campaign. Since 1982, the former has represented a nonpenetrated international system and the latter a highly penetrated one.

STRUGGLE FOR THE SEACOAST

Bolivia's determination to regain sovereign access to the Pacific Ocean has been a perennial and core foreign policy goal. Unfortunately, this territorial reclamation has been bedeviled by the competing and often incompatible interests of Chile and Peru ever since a defeated Bolivia lost its coastal province of Antofagasta in the War of the Pacific in 1879–1884 and became landlocked. In the Peace Settlement of 1904, Bolivia acceded to Chile's de facto occupation of Antofagasta in exchange for free transit rights in Arica, the seaport most accessible to its highland population centers.

During the twentieth century, repeated setbacks in Bolivia's seacoast diplomacy seemed to confirm that political and economic stability, so essential to state capacity, were important prerequisites for foreign policy success. Indeed, the failure of seacoast initiatives implied an inverse relationship between internal instability and foreign policy success. Decades of aggressive bilateral, trilateral, and multilateral campaigns had achieved wide moral and diplomatic support, but no concrete breakthroughs. How much did regime type matter, and were like-minded governments really better able to forge a diplomatic breakthrough? Or were external factors more significant than internal ones? Clearly, external and internal conditions were closely interrelated. However, in the final analysis, this study of seacoast diplomacy demonstrates that international systemic variables, over which statesmen had little influence and control, were more influential in determining the outcome of Bolivia's foreign policy.

Despite a general sympathy in the international and hemispheric community of nations, there were no powerful champions of the Bolivian cause. The United States avoided becoming actively engaged with the problem of Bolivia's landlocked status. Except for President Harry Truman, who briefly attempted to broker a solution, American presidents generally were sympathetic to the Bolivian seacoast question but basically believed that the issue was primarily a hemispheric and tripartite one, best resolved without direct U.S. intervention. At the Eighth General Assembly of the Organization of American States (OAS) in 1978, President Jimmy Carter skirted Washington's official position of nonintervention and pledged to "stand ready with the OAS, the UN and other countries to help find a solution to Bolivia's landlocked status" (Gumucio 1993; 1987: 212). Carter's personal stance represented a turning point. At the Ninth General Assembly in 1979, the U.S. delegation supported the resolution that "[i]t is of continuing hemispheric interest that an equitable solution be found whereby Bolivia will obtain appropriate sovereign access to the Pacific Ocean" (Gumucio 1993; 1987: 212; Orias Arredondo 2000a: 390). U.S. foreign policy has supported this hemispheric consensus consistently since 1979.

Generally, Bolivian statesmen believed that a convergence of like-minded regimes, whether authoritarian or democratic, could create a diplomatic opening and a more "conducive" regional environment for resolution. However, a series of Bolivian presidents of distinct personalities, political ideologies, and regime types failed to deliver positive results. For example, talks between the two socialist governments of Salvador Allende and Juan José Torres failed in 1971, as did the short-lived rapprochement between the conservative military governments of Hugo Banzer and Augusto Pinochet. Although the 1975 summit meeting between the two dictators and the resulting Act of Charaña briefly restored full diplomatic relations between Chile and Bolivia, the promised territorial breakthrough never materialized (Morales 1992a, 1988, 1984a, 1984b; Salazar Paredes et al. 2001; Shumavon 1981; St. John 1977; Yopo 1988, 1986a).

Banzer, like many Bolivian leaders, had manipulated irredentism over the seacoast to generate domestic political support. Thus, when his foreign policy strategy failed to deliver, the public frustration over thwarted expectations intensified demands for a speedy return to civilian rule and democracy. The diplomatic failure also provoked a strategic reassessment of foreign policy, so that in late 1970 Bolivia abandoned the bilateral approach for an extensive multilateral campaign. Diplomats vigorously advanced the problem of Bolivia's landlocked state in major hemispheric and international forums at the Andean Parliament, the OAS, the United Nations, and the Non-Aligned Movement. Armed with the 1979 OAS resolution, this multilateral diplomacy by subsequent administrations affirmed Bolivia's right to a sovereign, direct, and viable exit to the Pacific.

In the 1980s and 1990s, the transition to democracy in the Andes and Southern Cone brought closer bilateral contacts. Bolivian president Jaime Paz Zamora appealed to the democratizing sentiments in the region, hoping for an opening with the first democratically elected president of Chile since 1973. In the early 1990s, he met with his democratic counterparts, Alan García of Peru and Patricio Aylwin of Chile. Describing Bolivia's landlocked status as a constrictive geopolitical encirclement, he appealed for a twenty-first-century solution to the nineteenth-century maritime problem. In 1992, Bolivia and Peru signed the Ilo Convention of friendship, economic cooperation, and regional integration. The Chilean government also responded to Bolivian overtures with a "new mentality" regarding the seacoast dispute that promised mutual cooperation and reciprocal interdependence. However, a planned bilateral economic agreement and normalized diplomatic relations were never realized (Camacho 2000: 353; Morales 1992a: 180–81; Orias 2000a: 397–401; Seoane et al. 1997: 27–47; St. John 2001).

President Gonzalo Sánchez de Lozada continued to approach the maritime problem from a bilateral as well as a nontraditional perspective, framing it within the challenges of globalization, regional integration and economic development. And he met with the new Chilean president, Eduardo Frei Ruiz-Tagle, in 1994. The next Bolivian president, Hugo Banzer, pursued a similar mixed policy from 1997 to 2001. He met Chilean president Ricardo Lagos in 2000–2001 and reopened personal channels of communication. Both presidents were personally committed to resolving Bolivia's seacoast problem. Banzer, who had come so close to a breakthrough in 1975, made *la salida al mar* the heart of his foreign policy. His Chilean counterpart was equally intent on restoring diplomatic relations during his term in office, but once again, diplomacy failed to overcome important stumbling blocks (British Broadcasting Corporation [BBC] News 1999; Camacho 2000: 353–55; Orias 2000a: 401–3; St. John 2001).

Chile typically linked renewed talks to the "bilateralization" of the seacoast issue and the cessation of Bolivia's aggressive multilateral diplomacy. In turn, Bolivia conditioned the normalization of diplomatic relations with Chile to progress in negotiations. After 1962, Bolivia and Chile did not exchange formal diplomatic relations except for the brief hiatus of 1975–

1978. Bolivian governments persisted in this nonrecognition policy, maintaining only consular-level representation, in order to pressure Chile into dialogue on the seacoast issue. As long as Bolivian diplomacy primarily relied on bilateral or trilateral negotiations with Chile and Peru, its efforts produced only stalemate as each country played off the other against Bolivia. A chronic sticking point was the secret protocol to the 1929 treaty between Chile and Peru that precluded either country from ceding coastal territory to Bolivia without the prior agreement of the other (Gumucio 1987: 182–86; St. John 2001).

The geopolitical and strategic interests of the three countries were fundamentally at odds, and public opinion and intense political debate within the national polities derailed promising proposals and external mediation. Bolivia and Chile basically disagreed on territorial compensation with the Bolivians rejecting this condition, and the Chileans demanding it. The Chilean foreign office stubbornly insisted that it had no outstanding territorial issues with Bolivia. In 2000, the new bilateral and trilateral initiatives, such as the "Trinational Project," which proposed the economic development and integration of Bolivia, Peru, and Chile in the disputed region, complemented Bolivia's multilateral efforts. Bolivian administrations increasingly relied on the forces of economic globalization and aggressive regional development plans to further the ultimate resolution of the seacoast question in the future (Barrios 1997; Camacho 2000: 350–55; Gumucio 1993: 156–308; Orias 2000a: 390–410; St. John 2001).

From a theoretical perspective, Bolivia's struggle for a sovereign outlet to the Pacific was primarily conditioned by international systemic variables. Nevertheless, the territorial issue represented a nonpenetrated vertical system in which there was little direct or indirect interference by the United States or other external actors. Indeed since World War II, U.S. foreign policy was basically passive or formalistic in support of the Bolivian cause. Rosenau's typology suggests that systemic variables may vary inversely with the size or capacity of the country; thus, smaller and weaker countries are more dependent on the international system. Indeed, such international systemic dependence was central to Bolivia's seacoast diplomacy.

Moreover, according to Rosenau's theory, territorial disputes can be more difficult to resolve because such issues generally involve tangible ends but intangible means (1966: 86–87). On this point, the Bolivian seacoast issue confirms that, despite the tangible goal of a sovereign outlet on the Pacific, policy solutions remained elusive because the means, primarily diplomatic persuasion, were intangible. Nevertheless, Bolivia's success in consistently and ceaselessly raising the issue to one of hemispheric concern and international awareness was the direct result of aggressive bilateral diplomacy and combined multilateral initiatives in the OAS and the UN, as well as in other significant international forums.

DRUG WAR POLICY

Bolivia's assault against the traffic in illegal drugs dates to the 1960s. The United States, Bolivia, and Peru signed the Single Convention on Narcotic Drugs in 1961, and Bolivia finally ratified it in 1973. That same year U.S. policymakers grew serious about the coca/cocaine problem in Bolivia and conducted studies and informal bilateral exchanges. During a quick stopover in Bolivia in 1976, then–secretary of state Henry Kissinger discussed Bolivia's growing cocaine-trafficking problem with the Bolivian foreign minister. The two governments agreed to cooperate on socioeconomic development in the coca-producing zones of Bolivia to reduce the extent of coca leaf cultivation (Barrios Morón 1989: 37–40). In August 1977, a Washington summit between Bolivian president Banzer and U.S. president Carter focused on the drug issue. Secretary of Interamerican Affairs Terence Todman, who had accompanied a U.S. congressional delegation studying the illicit drug problem to La Paz, announced that "the new U.S. policy of cooperation with friendly governments would emphasize the suppression of the narcotics traffic" (Barrios Morón 1989: 44–45). Thereafter, Bolivia steadily began to receive the first of millions in U.S. narcotics control assistance (Dunkerley 1984: 318; Lehman 1999: 191; Painter 1994: 78).

Bolivian foreign policy suffered a major setback in 1980 after General Luis García Meza seized power in his infamous "cocaine coup." The United States, the Andean Pact members, and a majority of Latin American governments isolated the pariah regime for over a year, curtailing diplomatic relations and vital foreign assistance funds. After the "narcoregime" fell in 1981, democratic successor governments projected an aggressive antidrug stance at home and in the country's regional and international diplomacy in order to rehabilitate Bolivia's tarnished international reputation and restore desperately needed economic assistance and foreign investments. Bolivia's continued economic development depended on beneficial relations with the United States, its hemispheric partners, and the major international lending agencies, such as the International Monetary Fund (IMF).

Consequently, beginning with Ronald Reagan's drug war, the next two decades marked the steady "narcotization" of Bolivian foreign policy and the progressive intensification of the country's political-economic dependence on the United States. Bilateral counterdrug enforcement agreements and coca eradication programs escalated the external penetration of Bolivian society, and negatively impacted the country's political stability, governing capacity, and national sovereignty. Nevertheless, with the exception of the corrupt narcoregime of García Meza, bilateral relations with Bolivian governments remained largely cooperative (Barrios Morón 1989: 77–128; Dunkerley 1984: 320–38; Healy 1988; Lehman 1999: 180–216; Morales 1992a: 97–98, 127).

Over the next twenty-three years, counternarcotics enforcement remained the number one priority of all U.S. administrations in their relations with Bolivia. Although other important objectives, such as market privatization and democratization, were pursued as well, generally these were secondary and often conflicting concerns. Indeed, "neoliberal" economics exacerbated the drug problem and complicated the restoration and consolidation of democracy. Neoliberal reforms imposed stringent fiscal austerity, which heightened socioeconomic deprivation among workers and peasants. After the collapse of the tin market in 1984, thousands of redundant miners migrated to the lowlands and took up coca leaf cultivation. Within the decade, Bolivia became the second major source country for coca leaf and cocaine paste.

The U.S. drug war in Latin America sought to externalize the drug problem by reducing supply abroad rather than addiction and demand at home. As a consequence, U.S.-Bolivian antidrug policies emphasized prohibition and "criminalization" almost exclusively at the expense of economic development and other strategies proposed by Bolivia's citizens and governments (Gamarra 1997: 244; Hargreaves 1992: 98–99, 186–87). The history of the Bolivian-U.S. counterdrug relationship after the return to democracy reveals that both Bolivia's internal politics and foreign policy primarily responded to external and systemic constraints and pressure from one hegemonic actor—namely the United States (Léons and Sanabria 1997: 21–45; Gamarra 1997: 250–52). Repeatedly, U.S. ambassadors exerted direct personal influence on Bolivian domestic and foreign policies. Often the mere threat to cut off foreign aid achieved the reluctant compliance of Bolivian governments; sometimes it was necessary to turn the threat into reality (Hargreaves 1992: 163–68; Menzel 1996: 8–10).

Rosenau's theory of foreign policy posits that the pervasive external interference and infringement of a country's policymaking autonomy characterizes a vertically penetrated political system. The experience of Bolivian administrations since 1982 demonstrates that the United States, an external, system-level actor, determined Bolivia's drug policy over the fierce, and often armed, opposition of the country's citizens' groups organized on the national and subnational levels. As a rule, as long as Bolivian officials acceded to U.S. wishes and demonstrated serious drug enforcement efforts, overall bilateral relations with the United States continued on an even keel. Washington's hegemonic presumption worked to "bilateralize" and dictate Bolivia's antidrug policy and to "narcotize" its foreign policy (Aranîbar Quiroga 1987).

Between 1982 and 1985, Bolivia's first democratic president tried to chart an independent foreign policy, opening relations with Sandinistan Nicaragua and Castro's Cuba and supporting the Contadora peace process in Central America. However, Hernán Siles Zuazo was seriously out of step with the conservative Reagan administration and severely constrained by Bolivia's grave economic crisis and growing drug problem. The illegal drug economy brought in needed foreign exchange and revenues to the depressed economy, and politically, Siles was unable or reluctant to crackdown on this black market (Burke 1991; Morales 1992a: 161–62; Painter 1994: 7–16; Toranzo Roca 1997). At one point, Siles even considered opening negotiations with major drug figures in an attempt to contain the coca/cocaine problem. From Washington's perspective, Siles appeared "soft" on drugs, having failed to prosecute the drug war successfully. Bilateral relations cooled as the United States applied diplomatic and economic pressure, diverting hundreds of millions of dollars in economic aid to drug enforcement and market privatization programs (Lehman 1999: 192–96; Menzel 1996: 8–10; Morales 1992a: 185–86). As Siles's rule deteriorated, the United States openly welcomed his early retreat from office.

The next administration of Víctor Paz Estenssoro managed to improve U.S.-Bolivian relations, in great part, by acceding to Bolivia's aggressive "militarization" of the drug war. Paz Estenssoro sanctioned joint military maneuvers despite widespread internal opposition. His skillful political maneuvering and pressure from the American ambassador eventually forced a reluctant Bolivian congress to pass stringent antinarcotics legislation in 1988. The Coca and Controlled Substances Law (Law 1008), which the U.S. embassy had helped to draft, was a precondition for continued U.S. aid and amicable relations. The law criminalized traditional coca leaf cultivation and, in effect, made a quarter million of Bolivia's peasants and coca growers criminals in their own country. Major Bolivian interest groups from peasant and workers' unions, to the Catholic Church and human rights organizations, as well as Bolivian lawmakers denounced the law as unjust and repressive, and an infringement of sovereignty (Del Pilar Gumucio 1995: 153–54; Sanabria 1997: 21–23, 175–76). Militant opposition and anti-Americanism coalesced around the law, and difficulties with its enforcement hampered Bolivian presidents in their efforts to govern democratically.

The 1985 Foreign Assistance Act provided the United States with the extra leverage over Paz Estenssoro's government that made Bolivian concessions necessary. The act conditioned aid to major drug-producing countries on compliance with drug enforcement. Every March, the president released a list (which Congress could approve or reject) of countries that had been certified as compliant with U.S. law and counternarcotics policies. If a country failed to earn at least conditional certification, the United States imposed severe sanctions, such as the elimination of foreign aid, international loans from the IMF and World Bank, and preferential trading status. The law, therefore, exposed Bolivia's internal politics and foreign relations to Washington's vetting and the vagaries of congressional politics and the annual drug certification process.

Paz Estenssoro grappled with decertification as soon as he entered office because the Siles government had failed to meet the coca eradication targets mandated by the United States. Shortly after the suspension of over seven million dollars in aid in 1986, Paz Estenssoro signed off on Operation Blast Furnace, a joint U.S.-Bolivian military exercise against drug traffickers (Lehman 1999: 200). Thus, the militarized enforcement option of the United States became the basis of Bolivian narcotics control policy. On the other hand, as long as coca eradication targets were being met, Paz Estenssoro and succeeding presidents could rely on the drug war to provide continued U.S. economic and military aid (Healy 1997: 237, 239–40; Lehman 1999: 199). The danger, however, was that this "supposed partnership could easily devolve into hegemonic imposition" (Lehman 1999: 199).

Paz Estenssoro also risked the viability of his governing coalition and Bolivia's long-term democratic consolidation. Deadly confrontations between organized coca growers and security forces occurred almost daily after his government militarized the main coca-growing region and imposed "voluntary" crop substitution. Moreover, Paz Estenssoro skirted constitutionality when he unilaterally approved the active involvement of the U.S. military in drug enforcement within Bolivia (Menzel 1996: 17, 21). Nevertheless, the United States cut over $8 million in security assistance when Bolivia failed to meet its coca eradication quotas in 1986 and 1987 (Hudson and Hanratty 1991: 210–11; Menzel 1996: 26). However, Paz Estenssoro soon managed to mend relations and double U.S. aid, so that in 1989, the United States provided Bolivia close to $100 million to prosecute the drug war (Del Pilar Gumucio 1995: 166; Menzel 1996: 10–22; Morales 1992a: 187).

Internationally, Paz Estenssoro attempted to forge a limited autonomy on the coca problem through multilateral diplomacy. At the Vienna Convention in 1988, for example, the Bolivian representative aired the demand of the Latin American and Caribbean Group of nations for "an alternative approach to Washington's War on Drugs" (Del Pilar Gumucio 1995: 152, 164; Léons and Sanabria 1997: 22). Bolivian diplomats vigorously lobbied to redirect the drug war toward "alternative development" and "shared responsibility" and away from militarization. Bolivia consistently stressed this position in major hemispheric and international forums. Over the next decade, Bolivian presidents employed this strategy to appease conflicting domestic and foreign interests and chart a more independent antidrug policy. Given the complexity of the coca/cocaine problem, they had little success.

The drug diplomacy of President Jaime Paz Zamora (1989–1993) played itself out in a precarious balancing act. Paz simultaneously expanded the role of the armed forces in drug enforcement and touted alternative development strategies at home and abroad. His "Coca Diplomacy" planned to develop a legal export market that could capitalize on the healthful and medicinal properties of the coca leaf. However, Paz soon discovered that there was "little international support for opening markets for coca derivatives" (Healy 1997: 239). His ambitious coca diplomacy fundamentally clashed with Washington's drug war agenda.

In 1989, the administration of George H. W. Bush produced the National Drug Control Strategy Report and the Andean Initiative, which provided $2 billion in counternarcotics assistance to the region over five years (Morales 1992a: 188). At the 1990 Andean Summit in Cartagena, Colombia, Bush pushed law enforcement and drug interdiction measures instead of the alternative development and demand-side solutions that Paz and other Andean presidents had favored. As a result, the final declaration formalized militarization of the Andean region. Despite his public and international stand, Paz quietly signed the U.S.-Bolivian Anti-Narcotics Agreement in May and thereby officially escalated the militarization of Bolivia's coca/cocaine war. Caught between the public outcry against the treaty and the economic pressure of the United States, the Bolivian congress refused to approve the agreement until a year later (Morales 1992b: 353; Menzel 1996: 49, 51). News of the treaty and stepped-up drug enforcement provoked anti-American demonstrations and record levels of civil violence. The Bolivian media trounced the Paz government, portraying it as the willing dupe of U.S. imperialism and a neocolony of the U.S. narcotics control agencies, the Pentagon, and the Central Intelligence Agency (CIA) (Morales 1992a: 189; 1992b: 363).

Problems in the foreign policy process compounded the tense relations with the United States. The foreign ministry had assigned insufficient personnel to work with the many U.S. agencies operating in Bolivia, and there was inadequate coordination among Bolivian agencies, the foreign ministry, and the presidency (Gamarra 1997: 250–51). Another problem was the endemic conflict between the executive and legislative branches of government in the making of foreign policy. Bolivian presidents did not always inform or consult with the congress on foreign policy matters as required by the constitution. For example, the Anti-Narcotics Treaty was negotiated in secret to circumvent congressional opposition. In a similar case, the Bolivian congress refused to ratify the new extradition treaty with the United States in 1991, even after Bush held up aid and threatened decertification (Menzel 1996: 65–66; Morales 1992a: 189–90).

The presidencies of Gonzalo Sánchez de Lozada (1993–1997) and Hugo Banzer Suárez (1997–2002) conducted the war on coca/cocaine even more aggressively. The drug problem was increasingly seen as a threat to national security and economic growth and as a major international embarrassment for Bolivia. The governing class perceived the country's "economic woes, political instability and social misery as direct consequences of the transnational drug industry" (Del Pilar Gumucio 1995: 149). Consequently, national leaders became more intolerant of grassroots opposition to the coca war and more supportive of stringent counternarcotics measures.

At first, President Sánchez de Lozada seemed prepared to break with past policy. He considered alternative development a failure and debated decriminalizing coca production. Reflecting these views, the Bolivian foreign office rejected the United Nations' efforts to declare all coca production illegal and echoed the president's position that "Coca is not cocaine." Sánchez de Lozada also criticized the United States for insisting on higher eradication targets while severely cutting anti-narcotics funding. By 1994, however, he had largely returned to the enforcement strategy of his predecessors and initiated "the largest antidrug offensive in years" (Lehman 1999: 211). His "Option Zero" plan sought to eradicate coca from the Chapare region and break the economic dependency on this crop by agricultural development and light industrialization (Lehman 1999: 210–11).

The program, however, anticipated billions in international aid to fuel structural changes and compensate growers for eradicating coca plants. With the response at home and abroad negative, the pressure on the Sánchez government intensified. Coca farmers violently challenged the government's authority and U.S. aid shrank when eradication targets fell short. Finally in 1995, the Bolivian congress approved the bilateral extradition treaty, which legalized the extradition and prosecution of Bolivian drug criminals in the United States. Also that year, Bolivia met its eradication targets for the first time in five years (Del Pilar Gumucio 1995: 188, 213; Lehman 1999: 211–13; Menzel 1996: 95; U.S. Department of State 2001b).

Immediately after assuming office, Hugo Banzer turned full-scale militarization and coercive drug enforcement up another notch. To secure a $180 million loan from the World Bank, he promised to reform Bolivia's legal system and rid the country of all illegal coca production by 2002. In 1997, Banzer's "Dignity Plan" declared all-out war on coca, phasing out economic compensation to peasant producers and imposing forcible eradication. Over the next three years, thousands of armed troops uprooted some ninety-four thousand acres, or 90 percent, of illegal coca crops. As a result, Bolivia, once the world's second-largest source of coca leaf, dropped from the list of major drug-producing countries for the first time in decades (Faiola 2001).

The Zero Coca policy was only a partial success, however, and the social costs were very high. Economic and alternative development efforts failed to revive the economy and stem the growing impoverishment in the coca-growing regions. Renewed waves of civil violence and governmental repression beset the country, and the alarming increase in human rights violations tarnished Bolivia's democracy and image abroad (Amnesty International 2001; Faiola 2001; Farthing and Potter 2001; Kohl and Farthing 2001; Krauss 2000). Nevertheless, the ailing Banzer assured U.S. secretary of state Colin Powell only months before leaving office that all significant amounts of coca would be eradicated by 2002 (Associated Press 2001; BBC News 2001).

Over several decades, the coca/cocaine war had forged a tenuous collaboration and mutual dependency between the United States and Bolivia. In the area of drug policy, the United States had exerted a hegemonic and highly intrusive role that compromised the domestic and foreign policymaking autonomy of Bolivian presidents. As a rule, Bolivian governments, irrespective of whether the regime was democratic or authoritarian or functioned as an open or closed polity, had been severely constrained by the conflicting demands of civil society and a dominant external actor—the United States. And despite what one might have expected, U.S. intervention seemed to increase after the country's return to democracy, at the same time that Bolivia's newly mobilized civil society intensified its resistance against such external interference.

In summary, this review of Bolivia's foreign policy with the United States indicates that the issue of the drug war dominated bilateral relations for over two decades. In that period, Bolivian policymakers were more responsive to U.S. foreign policy goals and the authoritative decision making of bureaucrats in Washington than to the internal demands of their own national, regional, or local constituencies. Although it was necessary to appease the political opposition and public opinion at home, still, the critical audience of Bolivia's drug diplomacy was in Washington and the halls of the U.S. Congress. The constant threat of decertification and reduction in foreign aid dogged, and ultimately cowed, every civilian president and democratic government from 1982 to 2003. Such was the reality of Bolivia's dependency.

Theoretically, the drug war issue functioned as a vertically penetrated political system that was inherently vulnerable to the external manipulation of the United States. Rosenau's theory of foreign policy further suggests that the United States exerted a hegemonic influence within Bolivia's society and national system, regularly "outvoting" the government's domestic constituencies in the formulation of the country's coca policies. Although a nonmember of Bolivian national society, the United States directly participated in "the allocation of values" that determined Bolivia's domestic and foreign policies in the drug war (Rosenau 1966: 65). This extensive external penetration by the United States of national politics and society infringed on Bolivian sovereignty and both "bilateralized" and "narcotized" Bolivia's foreign policy.

FOREIGN POLICY FOR THE TWENTY-FIRST CENTURY

In terms of organization, professionalism, and global vision, Bolivian foreign policy has matured under democracy. In 1993, a new law governing Bolivia's foreign service defined its mission to preserve and protect Bolivian sovereignty and national interests. This core mission has been a major challenge for presidents and diplomats alike, given Bolivia's lack of geopolitical and power assets, and the hegemonic dominance of the United States in its internal affairs.

According to the Bolivian constitution (Article 96), the conduct of foreign relations is the prerogative of the president. The principal foreign policy institutions include the ministry of external relations and its Permanent Consultative Council of national leaders, ex-ministers, and diplomats. The president appoints the foreign minister, from the political, economic, and academic elite of the country, to serve as an officer of the executive branch. And as an important member of the cabinet, the minister of foreign relations and culture reports directly to the chief executive. Ambassadors are also appointed by the president but ratified by the National Senate. Among the important duties of the foreign ministry specified in the 1993 statute, is to give priority to all efforts and actions "that may be necessary to achieve Bolivia's inalienable right to its maritime reintegration" (Ministerio de Relaciones Exteriores y Culto de Bolivia 1993). The statute also lists other important foreign policy objectives, including regional integration, economic cooperation, internationalist activism, and promotion of the country's image abroad.

An important aspiration of Bolivia's foreign policymakers was to see their nation restored to its rightful place among the world's established democracies and prosperous economies (Messmer Trigo 1999). In this effort, both regional and international arenas served as indispensable sources of power enhancement and opportunity. In these forums, Bolivia's traditional national interests of maritime recovery, autonomy, democracy, economic development, and state security were recast and pursued within the wider context of hemispheric solidarity and global interdependence (Eguizabal 2000). Thus, for Bolivia as well as all the nations of the region, collective diplomacy emerged as a means of achieving and defending common interests, especially in the difficult areas of crime, corruption, money laundering, and drug trafficking. Collective and multilateral diplomacy helped Bolivia to promote its foreign policy and to offset its weakness and dependence on the United States. Multilateral arenas provided valuable vehicles to advance hemispheric coordination and to rally regional and international support for Bolivia's core foreign policy objectives.

For over a century, Bolivian foreign policymakers have struggled to overcome the limitations of geopolitics and the structural constraints that great power dominance and a landlocked status imposed on the country. Especially since the return to democracy, statesmen have sought to turn a geopolitical liability into a future potential. In every manner possible, Bolivian foreign policy has endeavored to capitalize on the country's geopolitical legacy "as the heart of South America" and become the natural nexus for regional cooperation and integration. Bolivia's location and participation in the major trading groups of the region favored such a pivotal role (Ministerio de Relaciones

Exteriores y Culto de Bolivia 2001b, 2001d; Messmer Trigo 1999). Therefore, these efforts form part of the wider strategy to mitigate Bolivia's international marginalization and peripheral status as a "taker" nation.

Close relations with Brazil, the dominant power in the region, became another integral component of Bolivia's strategy to break out of its geographic encirclement. Thus, when the presidents of the two countries met in 2001, they agreed to pursue bilateral efforts toward integration of the region's infrastructure, trade, development, and energy needs, as well as the resolution of Bolivia's maritime problem (Ministerio de Relaciones Exteriores y Culto de Bolivia 2001c). Both governments have lobbied for the unification of the continent's major trading associations, Southern Cone Common Market (MERCOSUR) and the Andean Community, into one formidable trading group (Hansen-Kuhn 1998; Ministerio de Relaciones Exteriores y Culto de Bolivia 2001c; Rohter 2000).

Bolivia's integrationist aspirations have inspired strong presidential rhetoric and the belief that "in unity there is power," and "united we can accomplish everything; divided, nothing" (Ministerio de Relaciones Exteriores y Culto de Bolivia 2001b, 2001d). Integration has also provided Bolivia's leadership with a new mission for Bolivian foreign policy—to place Bolivia in the center of continental unification. By aligning with the powerful forces of regionalism and globalization, Bolivia's leaders hope to develop the necessary diplomatic leverage to maintain cooperative bilateral relations with the United States and at the same time chart a more effective, activist and independent foreign policy.

Bolivia's successes and failures indicate that a stable democratic government, social development, and a strong economy are essential if the country is to progress beyond a reactive "small-state" diplomacy to a more proactive and autonomous one. Nevertheless, external and geopolitical factors have more consistently explained and limited Bolivian foreign policy in the past, and will most likely continue to do so in the century ahead. At the same time, a more integrated hemisphere and world will provide new opportunities for Bolivian governments to advance the country's foreign policy agenda and ultimately resolve its landlocked status.

DISCUSSION QUESTIONS

1. How has geopolitics impinged on Bolivian foreign policy?
2. In Bolivia's case, do you agree with Rosenau's hypothesis that small and weaker countries are more dependent on the international system?
3. What does it mean to say that Bolivian foreign policy operates like a "penetrated political system"?
4. Why did the foreign policy of certain Bolivian presidents oppose efforts of the international community to criminalize all coca production?

13

Chile
The Invisible Hand and Contemporary Foreign Policy

José A. Morandé

The structure of the international system as well as general trends in global politics have had important repercussions in Chilean foreign policy throughout the last fifty years. During this period, Chile's image on the international stage has been shaped primarily by the political-strategic context of the Cold War and, more recently, the globalization of the world economy. Despite the impact of international structural factors, successive Chilean governments have oriented foreign policy toward a search for increased national autonomy, based mainly on strategies of economic and sociopolitical development. In some instances, the personal protagonism of certain political leaders has been decisive in creating the direction for Chilean foreign policy. Nevertheless, it will be argued that the changing contours of the international system, as well as the complex interaction between systemic and domestic variables, provide the best framework within which to understand contemporary Chilean foreign policy.

Internationally, after World War II and until the end of the 1980s, the Chilean political landscape was marked by the global ideological confrontation of the Cold War and by the hemispheric security objectives of the United States. The Soviet Union's attempt to expand its influence in the Western Hemisphere was perceived by the United States as a serious threat to American leadership and dominance in the region. This would, in turn, have major repercussions for Chilean foreign policy. Nevertheless, by the

1990s, Chilean international conduct underwent a radical shift away from its traditional subordination to American interests.

With the end of the Cold War and the rearticulation of regional and world politics centered around the spread of democracy and the expansion of liberal economic competition, Chile's foreign policy has been characterized by a more international strategy. This strategy's logic and dynamic nature emphasize diversification and a broadening of political and economic options rather than the domination of traditional security concerns.

From a domestic perspective, Chile's foreign policy has been subject to the broad political and economic changes that have taken place in Chilean society. While it is true that national politics have been shaped by international political trends—namely, the ideological conflict of the Cold War and more recently the liberal globalization of global society—various Chilean governments have managed to develop (with different emphases, styles, and varying degrees of success) political projects oriented toward boosting national autonomy and diversifying Chile's participation in foreign affairs. In fact, this aspect of Chile's foreign policy is part of a long tradition anchored by the country's democratic institutions. Historically, Chile's international image has been accompanied by the predominance of a domestic political culture that has valued international participation in the Western world with specific regard for the West's political values and economic and social development.

Consequently, within the domestic context of the historical continuity of Chile's foreign policy, it is possible to identify structural changes as well as shifts in the political environment that have had a strong impact on Chile's international participation and image. The most visible and decisive changes occurred with the end of the democratic political government in 1973 and the installation of an authoritarian military regime, which ruled until March 1990 when representative democracy was recovered. During the seventeen years of military rule, Chilean foreign policy was marked by the international community's rejection of the Pinochet regime, which resulted in Chile's political isolation and its exclusion from many international arenas.

Chilean diplomacy, for its part, has provided support for the traditional goals of increasing national autonomy and amplifying Chile's international image, in particular through maintaining an active presence in regional and hemispheric political arenas. Even during the most difficult stages of international pressure on the military regime, the government managed to assert an international presence—which historically had characterized Chile's foreign policy—through an "economic diplomacy" anchored by the neoliberal globalization model.

At the individual level, the country's political leaders, particularly its presidents and—at times—their foreign ministers, have occasionally played important roles in actively promoting specific policies or general orientations. These goals were to either strengthen national autonomy or to pursue policies based on individual or group values or ideological motives. Individual leadership has played an important role in shaping Chilean foreign policy, and has indeed been a decisive factor with regard to certain specific policies. Nevertheless, it will be argued that, while this level of analysis helps us to understand some of the particular strands of Chilean foreign policy, it is the international and domestic political contexts—the latter being heavily influenced by the former—that have determined the direction of foreign policy in Chile.

Thus, by defining the various principles and values involved, as well as the interaction of domestic and external actors, we can identify stages of Chile's history that have been the product of an alignment between national and international factors: the "Freedom Revolution" of the 1960s; the "Democratic Path to Socialism" of the early 1970s; the market-based economic model of developing countries during the 1980s; and, most recently, the politics of economic globalization and the strengthening of democracy that began in the 1990s.

To summarize, in attempting to understand the dynamics that shape and give meaning to Chile's foreign policy, this chapter—following the questions regarding levels of analysis raised in earlier sections of this book—will focus on factors both in the international system as well as on the domestic level. Furthermore, we shall incorporate elements of the idiosyncratic level of analysis in explaining certain leadership factors that have contributed to shifts in the focus of Chilean foreign policy in recent decades. On this same level, we will consider the presidential nature of the Chilean political system that places foreign policy decision making in the executive branch—principally the president of the republic, who is advised by the Ministry of Foreign Relations based on the 1925 and 1980 constitutions.

With regard to methodology, this chapter will incorporate data related to Chile's position in the international economy, as well as recent empirical studies of the perceptions of domestic elites and interest groups in Chile. For the most part, the empirical aspect of this work will consider quantitative elements of Chilean foreign policy derived from official economic statistics, as well as field studies that I have carried out based on questionnaires and surveys about different domestic actors' perceptions related to political and commercial aspects of Chile's foreign policy.[1] In this way, it will be possible to illustrate and verify the central argument of this chapter and, at the same time, evaluate different opinions with respect to Chile's international image.

EVOLUTION OF CONTEMPORARY CHILEAN FOREIGN POLICY

The Cold War and the Structural Relationship with the United States: Some International Reasons for a Strategic Alignment

During most of the Cold War and because of the perceived threat from the Soviet Union and its allies, Chilean foreign policy was based on a political and strategic alignment with the United States—the latter in its role as superpower and leader of the Western bloc of nations. At the onset of this period, beginning in the 1940s, Chile entered into a relationship with the United States based on regional and hemispheric security. During this time, the Chilean government signed the Inter-American Mutual Assistance Treaty, a regional collective security agreement that entailed a Military Aid Pact between the United States and Chile.

In other words, the bipolarism that had defined the international system during the Cold War combined with the nascent institutions of the inter-American system, which were themselves based on the logic of anticommunist containment, created a subordinate role for Chile and the rest of Latin America with respect to the United States. Thus, U.S.-Chilean relations came to be centered on the economic and security interests of the United States, which had an increasing impact on the political and social systems in Chile.

From that moment on, the main concern and orientation of Chile's foreign policy has been toward creating and maintaining ties with the American superpower. Nevertheless, this structural relationship has also spurred Chile to broaden and diversify its links with other countries, globally as well as regionally. In this regard, the concern for strengthening political and economic ties with neighboring Latin American countries represents, for historical, geographic, and cultural reasons, a permanent priority for Chile's external image and international conduct.

The triumph of Fidel Castro's Marxist revolution in Cuba in 1959 triggered profound changes in U.S. policy toward Latin America that would also have a significant impact on Chile. The American government viewed the newly installed Castro regime as a grave threat to regional stability and moved quickly to isolate the Cuban government. Chile, however, expressed misgivings about U.S. efforts to cut off contact with Cuba, abstaining from Organization of American States (OAS) votes in 1962 and 1964 to break diplomatic relations with Cuba and to expel it from inter-American institutions.

Despite the increasingly independent position staked out by Chilean foreign policy at the start of the 1960s, the overall tendency toward alignment with the United States continued, albeit with dynamics that went beyond the previously narrow focus of security issues. The evolving nature of the communist challenge in the region generated a new set of strategies from Washington that put an emphasis on the need for structural reforms that would facilitate the development and modernization of Latin American societies. This new focus was articulated in the Alliance for Progress launched at the beginning of the new Kennedy administration.

Within this new Alliance for Progress framework, Chile—with its long history of democratic institutions and traditions—represented an ideal model in which to implement the new strategy of social and economic development favored by the new government in Washington. For example, the Alessandri government in Chile received $447.7 million in U.S. aid as opposed to the $69.1 million in aid doled out to the previous Chilean administration. Similarly, credits from the Export-Import Bank (EXIMBANK) to Chile rose from $50.7 million in the period 1952–1958 to $150.7 million between 1958 and 1964 (Muñoz and Portales 1987: 61–62).

During the Alessandri administration (1958–1964), Chilean foreign policy began a multilateral economic initiative within the region that formed the first steps toward trade integration in Latin America. This alignment, with proposals aimed at regional economic integration and cooperation, was part of a broader Chilean strategy that sought to diversify and deepen economic development as a means to increase national autonomy relative to the worldwide centers of economic and political power.

Domestic Reforms: Toward a More Active Foreign Policy in the Sixties

The administration of President Eduardo Frei Montalva (1964–1970) witnessed major transformations in the social structures of Chile that were intertwined with the dynamics of change taking place throughout Latin America. Nevertheless, the reformist tendency of the Frei Montalva government did not imply a breaking with the long-standing alignment of Chile's foreign policy with Western traditions; rather, it represented an attempt to diversify and broaden the available policy options with respect to the image of Chile's interests in the regional and international arenas.

It is against the backdrop of the changing nature of the relationship between the two world superpowers combined with increased levels of regional cooperation that Chile emerged as a showcase for the possibility of Third World countries to achieve social and economic development based on a democratic political model. With reforms under way to transform Chilean society, under the slogan "Revolution in Liberty," the Frei Montalva administration sought to match the traditional principles and instruments of Chilean foreign policy with the goals of increasing international support for Chile's reform project. The reformist vision of Frei Montalva—shared by his minister of foreign relations, Gabriel Valdés—was consistent with overall aims of the Kennedy administration's Alliance for Progress. The resulting juxtaposition of interests contributed to an increased awareness of and support for, the Chilean government—within domestic political circles, regionally, and also within the countries of Europe that had a shared ideological affinity with the Christian Democratic administration in Chile.

In spite of the commonality of interest between Chile and the United States regarding shared political values and the goals of economic and social development—particularly inasmuch as the Chilean experience offered a much preferable alternative (from the U.S. perspective) to the Cuban revolutionary model—the two countries entered a phase of increasing diplomatic confrontation toward the end of the 1960s as a result of the growing U.S. intervention in Latin America under the pretext of "anticommunist containment." The Chilean government, for its part, had opted for a strategy of increased political cooperation within the region.

This strategy sought to create more room for the maneuver of Chilean foreign policy in an external environment dominated by the rigid bipolarity of the Cold War. Related to this were a strengthening of economic and diplomatic ties with Western Europe and Japan, the reestablishment of diplomatic relations (broken since the 1940s) with the Soviet Union, and the creation of commercial and cultural links with Cuba and the socialist countries of Eastern Europe.

As was the case with the previous government of President Alessandri, Chile's foreign policy in the second half of the 1960s rested in large measure on the image of Chile as a country with a long-standing democratic institutional tradition. For various reasons, this strategy achieved a larger measure of success, both regionally and internationally, during the Frei Montalva government. This was due to the overlap of domestic and external factors centered on the reforms initiated in Chile with the existence of a feedback between national and international levels. The external actors that saw Chile as a possible model for development in the region created expectations, which in turn added legitimacy and impetus to reform initiatives at the domestic political level. At the same time, the international legitimacy accorded the Frei development project was leveraged as part of Chile's foreign policy strategy.

The Chilean Socialist Experience: Domestic Revolution and a Cautious Foreign Policy

The project of Socialist transformation in Chile under the presidency of Salvador Allende (1970–1973) that was aborted by the military coup of General Augusto Pinochet in September 1973 developed a foreign policy that in general followed the objectives of previous administrations in seeking to increase and consolidate national autonomy with respect to Chile's insertion in the international system. The diplomacy of the Allende government also stuck to the traditional parameters and styles of Chilean foreign policy.

Notwithstanding the strongly negative perceptions of the new government by many domestic sectors as well as serious reservations on the part of some Western governments regarding the "Chilean road to socialism," Chilean foreign policy at the time was in fact quite cautious. Nevertheless, the existence of a Marxist-oriented government in South America and the threat this represented to perceived American interests led the Nixon administration to use all available means to thwart the realization of socialist reforms in Chile. The covert U.S. intervention in Chile's economy and political arena in an effort to destabilize the Allende government was later revealed in the findings of a post-Watergate U.S. Senate investigation into the American role in the events leading up to the collapse of democracy in Chile (U.S. Senate 1975).

As for the Allende government, despite its anticapitalist discourse and talk of resisting the U.S. hegemonic role in the region—rhetoric designed mainly for domestic consumption—the administration in reality pursued a moderate international policy and sought to avoid confrontation with the Western powers, especially the United States. The overall objective was to maintain the international legitimacy that Chile had enjoyed and to counteract attempts to isolate the country diplomatically, which would have jeopardized the proposed structural reforms of Chilean society.

In a regional context, the Allende government favored a policy that looked for areas of increased cooperation and shared responsibilities between Chile and its neighbors. One result was the reaching of a settlement, through international arbitration, with Argentina regarding a long-standing border dispute in the southern section of the two countries.

A distinctive aspect of foreign policy under President Allende was the effort by Chile to reach out to the third world. The Third Assembly of the United Nations Conference on Trade and Development (UNCTAD) in Santiago in 1971 ratified the policy of creating a wider international forum in which developing countries would be able to formulate alternatives to the hegemonic vision of the United States. The Allende government also joined other developing nations (with the support of the majority of the UNCTAD participants) in calling for a "New Economic Order." The final result of the new administration's political orientation was that Chile was incorporated into the international "nonalignment" movement.

Despite its efforts to develop a moderate and nonconflictive foreign policy that would carry on the long-standing diplomatic traditions in Chile, the Allende government and its socialist experiment marked the end of a historical continuity in Chilean foreign policy.

Military Authoritarianism: A Foreign Policy Paradox

The authoritarian regime of General Augusto Pinochet, which took over in September 1973 and remained in power until March 1990, represented a profound break not only with Chile's democratic history but also with the tradition of Chilean foreign policy. In addition to representing a radical departure from the policies of the previous government, the military takeover also resulted in the international isolation of Chile due to the suppression of democratic institutions and the brutal internal repression based on an ideological mission to combat communism both on the domestic and international fronts.

The isolation of the military regime in Chile by the international community was heightened by changes in the structure of the international system. A thawing in East–West relations and the politics of détente took away potential support for an international policy based primarily on a militant anticommunist stance, as represented by the Chilean military regime. In other words, the authoritarian government in Chile increasingly became an international anachronism and its military project, and virulent anticommunist orientation became increasingly less compatible with the direction in which the international system was moving.

With respect to Latin America, Chile's withdrawal from the Andean Group in 1976, due to the incompatibility of the group's protectionist economic policies with the neoliberal economic strategy adopted by the Chilean military government, further heightened Chile's political isolation and the limits of its image within the region.

U.S.–Chile relations during the military regime evolved through different stages beginning with initial support from Washington for the policies of economic liberalization pursued under the Pinochet government. During the period of 1974–1976, Chile received $183.6 million in economic aid, as compared to the $19.8 million in U.S. assistance given to Chile during the Allende administration (Muñoz and Portales 1987: 91). This substantial financial support for the military regime showed a clear preference on the part of the Nixon administration for the new authoritarian government compared to the overthrown elected socialist government.

The changing political climate in the United States and the election of President Jimmy Carter in 1976 significantly altered the nature of U.S.–Chile relations. Increasingly, the issue of human rights and the restoration of democracy dominated the diplomatic agenda between the two countries. The Carter administration's concern over these issues were heightened by the 1976 assassination of Orlando Letelier, former foreign relations minister in the Allende government, in broad daylight in Washington, D.C., which also resulted in the death of Ronni Moffit, an American colleague of Letelier.

President Carter saw Chile as a "test case" for his foreign policy's human rights emphasis. Furthermore, the rejection by Chile's Supreme Court in 1979 for the extradition of the Chilean agents involved in the Letelier assassination resulted in a series of economic and diplomatic sanctions against Chile's military regime that would last until the transition to democracy in 1990.

When President Ronald Reagan took office in 1981, Washington adopted a softer line than the previous administration toward the military regime in Chile. His administration opted for what they called a "silent diplomacy" whose logic was that a policy of engagement with countries like Chile offered a better possibility to promote U.S. human rights goals than the confrontational approach taken by President Carter.

Despite the Reagan administration's initial support for the Pinochet government, the systematic, long-term violation of human rights in Chile (made worse by the catastrophic economic recession of 1982–1985) contributed to the formulation of a new U.S. policy toward Chile. The Reagan administration came to the determination that Pinochet was unwilling to relinquish power and allow a return to democracy, and that the repressive means necessary to stay in power against a rising democratic opposition movement had the possibility of resulting in the polarization of Chilean society and the destabilization of the country. As a result, the United States came to see the growing democratic movement as the best option to avoid the outbreak of civil conflict in Chile. Thus, by 1986, the United States made the restoration of democracy a primary objective in its foreign policy toward Chile, even though it gave continued support for the neoliberal economic model instituted by the Pinochet regime.

The widespread and long-term diplomatic isolation of Chile during the military government meant that the Pinochet regime had to seek nontraditional means to pursue its international objectives. Due to the structural changes in Chile initiated in the mid-1970s and the orientation toward a liberal market economy, Chile's foreign policy increasingly adopted a new model of international participation that, in the short term, sought to reverse the effects that the state-centered, socialist policies of the Allende government had had on Chile's participation in the world economy. In other words, the military regime's neoliberal experiment and the opening of its markets to foreign investment and trade allowed Chile to become integrated into the global economy as well as becoming a role model for economic development—regionally and internationally.

This "economic diplomacy" aspect of the military regime's foreign policy enabled the Chilean government—despite some setbacks—to create the conditions for sustained economic growth, a restructuring of its foreign debt, increased access to international capital, and the diversification of export production to avoid the extreme dependency on the export of a single product—copper—that characterized the Chilean economy in the twentieth century. As a result, the Chilean economy experienced a period of dramatic growth beginning in the mid-1970s. Despite the severe economic recession at the beginning of the 1980s, the Chilean economy grew steadily throughout the second half of the decade, reaching a record high of 10.6 percent growth in the gross domestic product (GDP) in 1989.

Similarly, in the period between the mid-1970s and the end of the 1980s, the country's foreign debt rose from $4.267 billion to $13.279 billion. At the same time, Chile's exports went from $2 billion to $8 billion, while imports rose from $2 billion to $6.5 billion. Overall, Chile maintained a positive trade balance during this period, with surpluses ranging between $135 million and $1.57 billion (see table 13.1). As a result, the Pinochet military government was able to reinitiate and strengthen international economic and commercial ties as part of Chile's traditional external image.

In summary, from 1973 to 1990 under Pinochet's leadership, the traditional diplomacy based on international prestige for Chile's democratic history was abandoned and replaced by a diplomacy founded on a reactionary ideology that, confronted with international efforts to isolate Chile, sought to establish order and stability for its authoritarian national project. Despite Chile's political isolation during this time, the successful economic model constructed by the Pinochet government made it possible for the country to restore its credibility in the eyes of the international financial community.

The Return of Democracy: Consolidation of Chile's New International Image

The complete reintegration of Chile into the international community of nations was achieved with the restoration of democracy in 1990. From that time until the present, the successive governments of Patricio Aylwin (1990–1994), Eduardo Frei Ruiz-Tagle (1994–2000), and the current president, Ricardo Lagos, in addition to continuing the economic opening predicated on the neoliberal model as an important part of Chile's foreign policy, have also consolidated and strengthened external links based on democratic principles and institutions. With the transformation from a military regime to a democratically elected government, Chile has been able to restore the political legitimacy of its international image, deepening even further Chile's economic and commercial ties with an increasingly globalized international community.

Since the transition to democracy, Chile has vigorously sought to penetrate international markets within the context of a strategy of "open regionalism"—in other words, a unilateral and dynamic opening of the Chilean economy to trade with the various regions or trading blocs that make up the global economy.

The result has been a decade of remarkable economic development and growth, notable for the balanced diversity of Chilean trade with different economic regions. For example, in a period of only ten years (1990–1999), Chile doubled its overall foreign trade (from $15 billion to $30 billion), with 90 percent of total trade being almost evenly divided between the United States, Latin America, the European Union, and the Asian member-states of APEC (see table 13.2).

Since 1990, the three democratic governments—representing the political alliance named the Concertación de Partidos por la Demócracia (Concertation of Parties for Democracy)—not only have reiterated the traditional

Table 13.1. Chilean Main Economic Indicators (1960–1999)

	1960	*1965*	*1970*	*1975*	*1980*	*1985*	*1989*	*1990*	*1995*	*1999*
GDP (%)	4.8	0.8	2.1	−12.9	7.8	2.4	10.6	3.7	10.6	−1.1
Consumer Price Index (%)	5.5	25.8	34.9	340.7	31.2	26.4	21.4	27.3	8.2	2.3
Foreign debt* (U.S.$ million)	622.0	1,469.0	2,767.0	4,267.0	9,413.0	17,650.0	13,279.0	14,043.0	21,736.0	33,887.0
Public	400.0	970.0	2,218.0	3,597.0	4,720.0	12,515.0	10,350.0	9,808.0	7,501.0	5,820.0
Private	222.0	499.0	549.0	670.0	4,693.0	5,135.0	2,929.0	4,235.0	14,235.0	28,067.0
Payment balance (U.S.$ million)	−28.4	46.7	114.0	−285.0	776.0	−99.0	437.0	2,368.0	1,060.8	−683.3
Trade balance (U.S.$ million)	−85.7	68.0	156.0	135.0	−1,055.0	884.0	1,578.0	1,273.0	1,542.0	1,758.0
Exports	469.7	684.0	1,112.0	2,151.0	4,722.0	3,804.0	8,080.0	8,310.0	16,445.0	15,914.0
Imports	−555.4	−616.0	−956.0	−2,016.0	−5,777.0	−2,920.0	−6,502.0	−7,037.0	−14,903.0	−14,156.0

*Preliminary data.
Source: Central Bank of Chile.

Table 13.2. Chilean Commercial Exchange 1990–1999 (U.S.$ million)

	1990	*Percentage*	*1995*	*Percentage*	*1999*	*Percentage*
Exports						
United States	1,469.2	18	2,375.0	14	3,088.8	19
Latin America	1,014.3	12	3,049.3	19	3,330.6	21
European Union	3,203.1	39	4,448.0	27	4,123.9	26
Asia*	2,245.9	27	5,421.9	33	4,321.4	27
Total	8,309.9		16,446.5		15,914.0	
Imports						
United States	1,373.4	20	3,792.9	25	3,022.6	21
Latin America	1,741.0	25	4,036.2	27	4,467.5	32
European Union	1,518.4	22	3,155.4	21	2,848.5	20
Asia*	932.0	13	2,513.9	17	2,197.7	16
Total	7,037.0		14,903.1		14,156.0	

*Asian countries at APEC.
Source: Central Bank of Chile.

principles of Chilean foreign policy with a strong respect for democratic development and human rights but have also emphasized Chile's economic image in the context of the globalization of the current international system.

The Aylwin government, representing the first democratic administration in Chile after seventeen years of military rule, was successful in enhancing Chile's international image based on significant domestic and international transformations. The changing orientation of Chile's international image coincided with changes in world politics. With the end of the Cold War, the renewed emphasis on democratic values and free market economic institutions were also important elements of Chile's new foreign policy.

Within this context, the Aylwin administration reestablished political and economic ties with countries with which ties had been severed during the military government (the former Soviet Union, Mexico, and Cuba, among others) and also reestablished Chile's participation in the political context of regional, democratic cooperation (such as the Grupo de Río). These were the first steps taken by the new democratic government in Chile to end the previous period of political isolation. Similarly, the return of democracy to Chile enabled the Aylwin government to mend relations with the United States. The full normalization of relations between the United States and Chile was reached in 1992 when those accused of responsibility for the Letelier–Moffit assassination were brought to justice in Chile, thereby removing the most important obstacle for full cooperation between the two countries. Two years before in 1990, President George H. W. Bush reestablished the Overseas Protection Insurance Corporation (OPIC) backing for American investment in Chile—according them most favored nation status within the

General Agreement on Tariffs and Trade (GATT) framework—and gave White House certification to Chile in order to lift the restrictions of military sales included in the Kennedy Amendment. All of these restrictions had their origin during the military government in Chile and were a response to the systematic violations of human rights that occurred under the Pinochet regime.[2]

Thus, the restoration of democracy in Chile brought about a dramatic transformation in relations with the United States, offering a chance for the United States to support the process of political and social transformation under way in the South American nation. The U.S. government, whose traditional strategic objectives were linked with the universal promotion of democracy and a market economy, found in Chile a resurrected symbol of the model for democratic, market-oriented development. This vision was confirmed by the proclamation of the Initiative for the Americas, formulated by President Bush in 1990. Since then, various U.S. officials have spoken of the possibility for a free trade agreement with Chile (an area that has included talks between the two governments that continue to the present day). American interest in a trade agreement with Chile was made official at the Summit of the Americas in Miami in 1994 when the presidents of the United States, Canada, and Mexico officially invited Chile to become a member of the North American Free Trade Association (NAFTA).

In the regional context, one of the most important goals of the Aylwin administration was the definitive resolution of border disagreements with Argentina and the initiation of close economic and political ties. In a global context, the new Chilean administration sought to widen and diversify its international presence through bilateral or multilateral agreements that include treaties for commercial exchange and economic cooperation with most of Latin America and Canada, as well as Chile's membership in APEC. Furthermore, Chile increased commercial links to the European Union (EU) and began an initiative that resulted in the signing of a landmark trade agreement between Chile and the EU in May 2002.

During the Frei Ruiz-Tagle administration, Chilean foreign policy sought to consolidate the previous phase of the Aylwin government's new international image through the increased internationalization of the Chilean economy, the development of stable relations, and the promotion of an environment favorable to democratic stability—particularly in a Latin American context. In a similar fashion, the Frei Ruiz-Tagle government took an active role in promoting democracy and human rights, participating in international peace initiatives, and supporting processes associated with international development and equality. In this respect, Frei Ruiz-Tagle looked to link Chile's economic development with increased social equality, which was also emphasized in the government's foreign agenda through proposals for social development made at international forums.

During the Frei administration, Chile became an associate member of the

Southern Cone Common Market (MERCOSUR), a political and economic decision that has meant a more Latin American emphasis compared with previous administrations. In summary, Chilean foreign policy under the Frei Ruiz-Tagle government was marked by, with varying degrees of emphasis, a strong commitment to expanding Chile's international economic image and a reaffirmation of the link between development and democratic stability.

The presidency of Ricardo Lagos (2000–2006) marks the current phase of the posttransition democratic government's foreign policy—representing the same Concertación center-left coalition. With his own personal leadership style, President Lagos, in addition to ratifying the permanent principles of Chilean foreign policy based on a legalistic and institutional legacy and a *latinoamericanista* emphasis inherited from the previous administration, has undertaken an activist foreign policy stance with regard to Chile's international economic image. The direction of this economic focus has been balanced between the different commercial and regional areas with which Chile has relations, with the overall aim of reducing Chile's economic vulnerability especially regarding its export economy.

As a result, in recent years Chile has been negotiating a trade agreement with the European Union at the same time that it has been discussing a deepening of economic integration with the MERCOSUR. Similarly, the Chilean government has continued to increase ties with APEC (Pacific Asia) and has placed a high priority negotiating a bilateral free trade agreement with the United States as well as the goal of a Free Trade Area of the Americas (FTAA). This policy is consistent with the international economic strategy pursued by the Concertación governments of the last decade in the framework of economic diplomacy.

To summarize, the foreign policy of President Lagos has placed an emphasis on the social and economic aspects of Chile's international image, deepening the country's political ties abroad through high-profile presidential visits and participation in regional and hemispheric summits. Thus, the Lagos government has stuck to a policy of strengthening democratic institutions, promoting human rights, and supporting the processes of regional cooperation and integration.

AN ANALYTIC FRAMEWORK FOR CHILEAN FOREIGN POLICY

Systemic Level of Analysis

Due to many different factors—historical, geopolitical, economic, and cultural among others—the international system has played a determining role in the orientation and conduct of Chile's foreign policy. From the mid–

twentieth century until the present, both the political-strategic context of the Cold War and, more recently, the globalization of the international scenario have constituted essential points of reference for understanding the external priorities and the different modalities of Chile's international image. For most of the Cold War, Chile aligned itself with the United States against the perceived threat of communist expansion. This strategic alignment with the United States in turn shaped and constrained options available to foreign policy decision makers in Chile.

The constraining effects of Chile's subordination to U.S. interests in the context of the Cold War can be seen in the Chilean government's response to U.S. efforts aimed at isolating and punishing the communist government in Cuba. Consistent with long-held principles of nonintervention and the primacy of sovereignty, the Alessandri and Frei Montalva administrations in 1963 and 1964 argued against the marginalization of the Castro government and Cuba's expulsion from the inter-American system. In the end, though, Chile decided against opposing the United States on an issue of strong importance to the latter. The result was that Chile abstained in the OAS vote to oust Cuba and to implement sanctions against the island nation, an outcome that, while not completely conforming with the U.S. position, represented a compromise of Chile's traditional defense of sovereignty and nonintervention principles. Thus, with respect to issues of hemispheric security, the margins of autonomy for Chilean foreign policy were much smaller compared with other international issue areas.

On a Latin American subsystemic level, particularly with respect to neighboring countries, Chilean foreign policy has also been marked by historical controversies deriving from border problems that date back to the nineteenth century. Even though border controversies have been a recurring foreign policy issue, it was essentially under the Pinochet military regime that Chile faced the most critical stages in its relations with its neighbors. In addition to Bolivia's historic claim on Chilean territory (demanding lost access to the Pacific Ocean), there were also military tensions with Peru in 1974 and later with Argentina in 1978.

However, it is worth pointing out that in the post–Cold War era, this systemic factor in Chilean foreign policy has changed dramatically. As a result, since the transition to democracy in 1990, Chile has been able to settle bilateral issues that had been a source of past conflict with Peru and Argentina while at the same time contributing to the implementation of strategic measures designed to foster mutual trust between Chile and its neighbors.

Notwithstanding the continuity and dynamics of regional and hemispheric factors that have had a structural impact on Chile's international image, the transformation of the international system since the end of the Cold War has been a determining factor that has permitted a greater degree of autonomy and diversity for Chile's foreign policy. Thus, with the reduced importance of strategic concerns, Chile has had the possibility to design and implement a broader and economically more diverse policy of international image. As a result, during the past decade the Chilean economy expanded its commercial exchange to different regions of the world (see table 13.2).

In a similar fashion, growing global interdependence has provided momentum for the increasing development of multilateralism, which has in turn fortified recent efforts at regional integration such as the EU, APEC, and MERCOSUR. From the perspective of regional political coordination, the Grupo de Río has played an important leadership and issue articulation role that has been largely absent in the hemisphere, without discounting the renewed protagonism of the OAS in the post–Cold War era. In this sense, the changes in the international system have been functional to recent attempts by Chile's foreign policy to broaden, diversify, and deepen the spaces available for its international relations.

State Level of Analysis

One constant of Chilean foreign policy has been the emphasis on a democratic tradition. This effort to leverage the traditional democratic nature of its governmental institutions to achieve a greater degree of international prestige and legitimacy has generated an increased relative capacity for maneuver in the international arena. For obvious reasons, this foreign policy strategy was not an option under the military dictatorship. After the loss of international prestige with the overthrow of the democratic regime in 1973, Chile had to wait until the restoration of democracy in 1990 to regain its international status and legitimacy.

Similarly, in different areas of economic strategy, the Chilean state has sought, in addition to domestic development, to broaden and diversify the levels of national autonomy in the international sphere. Despite the disparity of economic models adopted by various administrations, the constant factor has been the effort at boosting national development and increasing the welfare of the domestic society as part of a requisite for state sovereignty.

In the present context, we can find ideological correspondence between domestic and external factors of Chilean economic policy. Essentially, until the change of political regime in 1973, the foundations and principles of economic strategy were based on a high level of state participation in the national economy and the need for government intervention in international markets. With the onset of the military regime in Chile and its market reforms in the domestic economy, the economic strategy has been to promote free trade and direct foreign investment. In this regard, the foreign economic policy of recent Chilean governments has been consistent with the neoliberal economic model with respect to a reduced government role in the domestic economy and an enhanced role in fostering international trade.

With regard to economic foreign policy, it is interesting to observe the strong level of support for international trade agreements among different sectors of the Chilean elite. Among government officials, for example, a recent survey shows that a majority believe that such trade initiatives are "very important," although the importance given to different regions or trading blocs varies significantly. Thus, 94 percent stress the importance of a trade agreement with members of APEC, 88 percent strongly support a trade agreement with the EU, and 76.5 percent consider the U.S.-sponsored FTAA to be "very important." In contrast, a relatively smaller number of government officials stress the importance of trade agreements with NAFTA and MERCOSUR (53 percent and 41 percent, respectively) (see table 13.3).

Overall, these priorities are shared by the Chilean business class as well as

Table 13.3. International Economic Agreements: Priorities of Chilean Elites (%)

	Low Priority	*Neither Low nor High*	*High Priority*	*Doesn't Know*	*Doesn't Answer*
MERCOSUR					
Businessmen	9.8	43.9	41.5	2.4	2.4
Government	0	47.1	41.2	0	11.8
Political parties	8.3	36.1	47.2	2.8	5.6
Total survey	8.3	45.5	39.3	1.4	5.5
NAFTA					
Businessmen	7.3	39.0	46.3	4.9	2.4
Government	0	47.1	52.9	0	0
Political parties	0	25.0	72.2	0	2.8
Total survey	6.2	32.4	57.2	2.1	2.1
FTAA					
Businessmen	7.3	34.1	48.8	7.3	2.4
Government	0	23.5	76.5	0	0
Political parties	5.6	19.4	66.7	0	8.3
Total survey	5.5	27.6	60.0	3.4	3.4
European Union					
Businessmen	4.9	19.5	68.3	4.9	2.4
Government	0	11.8	88.2	0	0
Political parties	2.8	16.7	72.2	5.6	2.8
Total survey	2.1	17.2	73.8	4.1	2.8
APEC					
Businessmen	2.4	24.4	65.9	4.9	2.4
Government	0	5.9	94.1	0	0
Political parties	2.8	13.9	83.3	0	0
Total survey	1.4	23.4	72.4	2.8	0

by political party leaders (both the EU and APEC are considered the top priorities, followed by NAFTA, the FTAA, and finally MERCOSUR, with slight variance among the groups surveyed). One consistent result of the survey is the relatively low priority given to a trade agreement with the MERCOSUR, compared to agreements with other trading groups outside the region. Additionally, it is interesting to note that there is significantly stronger support for international trade agreements in general, independent of the region, among government officials than among business leaders (see table 13.3).

Furthermore, when the nation's elite were asked to indicate the country that they considered to be Chile's most important trading partner (considering individual countries and not trade blocs or associations), 54 percent of the total of those surveyed named the United States, with the next closest country in terms of economic importance for Chile being Japan (named by only 18.5 percent of respondents) (see table 13.4).

Interestingly, but perhaps not surprisingly, the majority of the Chilean elite share a positive view of the globalization of the world economy. Survey results show that more than 70 percent either fully or partially agree with the idea that it is necessary to adapt to the present trend of globalization (see table 13.5). In a similar fashion, a strong majority (73 percent) of the Chilean elite believes that the globalization process boosts national competitivity and prosperity, although more than half those surveyed feel that wealthy countries receive greater benefits from globalization than do poorer nations (see tables 13.6 and 13.7).

Another current in the state level of analysis in the Chilean case, is made up of two tendencies—the legalistic tradition and a preference for maintaining a regional status quo (both of which have roots dating back to the nine-

Table 13.4. Most Important Chilean Trade Partner (%)

	Businessmen	*Government*	*Politicians*	*Total Survey*
Germany	2.1	5.3	0	2.9
Argentina	4.2	5.3	0	9.8
Brazil	0	5.3	8.3	5.9
China	4.2	0	8.3	2.9
Spain	0	0	0	2.4
United States	66.7	68.4	50.0	54.1
France	0	0	0	0
Holland	0	0	0	0
England	0	0	0	0.5
Italy	0	0	0	0
Japan	18.8	15.8	25.0	18.5
No answer	4.2	0	8.3	2.9

Table 13.5. Levels of Agreement Regarding Economic Globalization (%)

	Completely Disagree	*Partly Disagree*	*Partly Agree*	*Completely Agree*	*Doesn't Know*
Businessmen	26.8	0	12.2	58.5	2.4
Government	17.6	0	35.3	41.2	0
Political parties	11.1	0	22.2	63.9	2.8
Total survey	22.8	1.4	24.1	49	1.4

Table 13.6. World Economic Competitiveness with Globalization (%)

	Completely Disagree	*Partly Disagree*	*Partly Agree*	*Completely Agree*	*Doesn't Know*	*Doesn't Answer*
Businessmen	22.0	2.4	29.3	43.9	2.4	0
Government	5.9	5.9	58.8	17.6	0	11.8
Political parties	5.6	11.1	41.7	38.9	2.8	0
Total survey	14.5	9.0	38.6	34.5	1.4	2.1

Table 13.6. Economic Globalization and Rich Countries' Advantages (%)

	Completely Disagree	*Partly Disagree*	*Partly Agree*	*Completely Agree*	*Doesn't Know*	*Doesn't Answer*
Businessmen	29.3	22.0	43.9	2.4	2.4	0
Government	11.8	35.3	35.3	5.9	0	11.8
Political parties	13.9	30.6	47.2	5.6	2.8	0
Total survey	15.2	28.3	46.9	5.5	1.4	2.8

teenth century)—has contributed to the orientation and the shape of Chilean foreign policy. The legalistic tradition consists largely of a strict respect for international treaties and the defense of the principles of nonintervention and self-determination.

Finally, due to the current economic and commercial aspects of Chile's international relations, there are not only greater demands for specialization and increased professional development for foreign service officials but also new challenges that have arisen for other sectors of the foreign policy bureaucracy, particularly the departments of economy, agriculture, and finance. Consequently, agenda proposals as decisional conflict of a political-bureaucratic nature increasingly can be found on this level, especially with respect to the processes of commercial negotiation (van Klaveren 1998: 147–49).

The Individual Level of Analysis

In general, the individual/idiosyncratic level of analysis plays a subordinate role to state- and systemic-level factors in the orientation and formulation of Chilean foreign policy. Even though it is possible to observe some permanent idiosyncratic elements that permeate the formulation of foreign policy in Chile, these become especially relevant in specific situations that involve change in the direction of foreign policy or when certain leaders or presidents have used these elements to legitimize Chile's international image. In the period under study in this chapter, personal leadership by the president or minister of foreign relations has been a determining factor in moments of major transformation in the domestic structure or in the case of legitimizing these internal transformations to the international political community.

A greater emphasis of personal leadership can be found in situations where the aforementioned diplomacy of prestige is used to achieve an increased regional or international presence. An example is the use of the traditional democratic nation by President Frei Montalva to gain support for his developmental reforms and plans aimed at increasing cooperation and integration within Latin America in the 1960s. In a different domestic and international context, President Salvador Allende, in attempting to justify his socialist experiment in Chile, attempted to leverage the country's "international prestige-based diplomacy" to gain leadership among third world countries and political respectability with Western democracies.

Allende's successor, General Pinochet, whose military dictatorship resulted in a loss of international political prestige for Chile, utilized neoliberal economic reforms launched under his government in an attempt to rescue the country's tarnished image. Downplaying the loss of democracy, Pinochet touted his administration's economic plan as a way of showing the world that Chile was serious about getting its house in order. And, of course, once stability was restored and the success of the economic model based on "liberal" free market values was assured, democracy would eventually be reintroduced. Similarly, since the return of democracy in 1990, it is worthwhile to note the reiterated emphasis that Presidents Frei Ruiz-Tagle and Lagos have put on the widely touted Chilean economic success, using it as a calling card for increased international participation.

CONCLUSION

Chilean foreign policy in recent decades reflects elements of change and continuity as a consequence of the dynamic between domestic and international factors. Chile enjoyed a consistency in its external policies until the change in political regime in 1973. Within this continuity, while taking into account efforts to increase national autonomy through different strategies of socioeconomic development, there was a congruence between the international system and the policies of Chile's external image. This was the case in Chile from the onset of the Cold War to the fall of democracy in 1973. Thus the first shift or transformation of Chile's international conduct took place during the Cold War and was the result of a dramatic and unprecedented transformation of the domestic political regime from a longstanding democracy to the authoritarian military government under General Pinochet's rule.

Despite the pervasive influence that the international system has on Chile's external conduct, the development of domestic political and economic strategies that tend toward a lessening of national vulnerability is a constant of Chilean foreign policy. This permanent search for national autonomy as a political expression of the Chilean state is complemented by its being a country with a long democratic tradition, which has contributed to a positive regional and international image.

The weakening of these factors and the loss of international legitimacy during the first decade of the Pinochet government contributed to its isolation in the international arena. This loss of prestige and tradition, however, forced the military regime to find other means of improving its international image while the domestic political system remained authoritarian and until democracy was returned to Chile. This search was made easier by the neoliberal restructuring of the domestic socioeconomic system in the 1980s, by which Chile found the means for strengthening its international image through its links with the international economic and commercial system. This can be seen as the second transformation generated by the military regime during the Cold War.

As a result, recent Chilean foreign policy, in addition to a tendency toward a diplomacy based on economic and commercial issues, has initiated the recuperation of its political tradition and international legitimacy with the end of the military regime and the restoration of democracy in Chile. Consequently, and in coincidence with the end of the Cold War, Chile began the 1990s with a foreign policy that was both new and traditional. The legacy of its democratic international image merged with the increasing internationalization of its economy. A decade after these dramatic changes, it is possible to observe the permanent characteristics of stability and congruency between the domestic and international forces that shape and give meaning to Chilean foreign policy.

DISCUSSION QUESTIONS

1. In what way did the Cold War influence the pursuit and development of national autonomy in Chile's foreign policy?

2. What impact did the change of regimes have on the policy orientations of Chilean foreign policy during and after the Cold War?
3. What is the role of the neoliberal strategy of development on Chilean foreign policy, and what is the degree of change and continuity in Chile's foreign relations?

NOTES

The author would like to thank Jason R. Weidner for his assistance in preparing this chapter.

1. The field study refers in a very partial manner to a section of the survey that I carried out at the beginning of 1998 and that was addressed to elites and different Chilean interest groups in order to know their perceptions on Brazil. This survey was part of the Chilean chapter (under my responsibility) of the research "Percepciones de Brasil en el Cono Sur" proposed and requested by ECLA-Brasilia. The findings of the study applied to this chapter are used in the form of tables in the final section of this research paper.

2. According to official documents, 2,279 people were victims of human rights violations during the Military Regime in Chile. See *Informe de la Comisión Nacional de Verdad y Reconciliación* (Santiago: February 1991).

III

BRAZIL AND THE SOUTHERN CONE

14

Brazil

From Dependency to Globalization

José Augusto Guilhon Albuquerque

This chapter deals essentially with Cold War and post–Cold War features of Brazilian foreign policy. As an introduction, we shall discuss briefly the major principles of Brazilian foreign policy as delineated by diplomatic bureaucracy. Also, to understand the nature of Cold War politics in Brazilian domestic and external relations, the period of "special alliance" with the United States shall be analyzed. We shall examine the politics of *desenvolvimentismo* ("developmentalism" in Portuguese) and its impact on foreign policy in the 1950s, as well as the *política externa independente* (independent foreign policy) adopted in 1960 by President Jânio Quadros and confirmed by his successor João Goulart. Then we shall turn to the authoritarian period, particularly to the so-called responsible pragmatism. The next period to be examined is the *neodesenvolvimentismo* introduced by the first postauthoritarian government of José Sarney in the late 1980s. The consequences of the end of the Cold War shall be addressed in the two remaining sections; the first deals with regional and interregional policies and the second one with trade, especially multilateral and trade agreements.

GENERAL FEATURES OF BRAZILIAN FOREIGN POLICY IN THE TWENTIETH CENTURY

In the Brazilian officialdom's rhetoric, the country's foreign policy is based on general, permanent, abstract principles that have long gathered respect and credibility among international partners. The five basic principles of Brazilian foreign policy include (1) peaceful conflicts settlement, (2) self-determination of nations, (3) nonintervention in the domestic affairs of third countries, (4) abiding to norms and principles of international law, and (5) multilateralism.

These principles are not different from those of the United Nations' charter, and indeed they are most of the time celebrated in the great majority of the rhetoric statements of international politics. Brazilian diplomacy is very faithful to this set of principles, which can be found in every official statement made before the UN General Assembly since its first meeting (Ministério das Relações Exteriores 1995). Like every nation-state, Brazil has often not followed all these principles.

Therefore, to understand Brazilian diplomatic motives and practices, it is perhaps more useful to look to its stated and nonstated goals rather than to its expressed principles. My hypothesis in this chapter is that, for the entire Cold War and post–Cold War period, Brazilian foreign policy goals have been essentially three:

1. to secure an international environment favorable to Brazilian economic development;
2. to avoid any semblance of submissive compliance to the United States and, more generally, to any of the U.S. major allies; and
3. to avoid or, at least, to delay any further integration into the U.S. economy.

The first of these goals entails three specific targets, the most important of which is to grant special support for the country's economic development. As a matter of fact, Brazilian diplomacy has consistently championed the adoption of multilateral programs of investments aimed at the industrialization and economic growth of underdeveloped countries. In this context, Brazil was one of the most conspicuous sponsors of the so-called New International Economic Order that inspired the creation of the United Nations Conference on Trade and Development (UNCTAD).

Another specific objective is to grant exception to the country's international commitments, especially concerning free trade and external debt. Consistent with this goal has been the Brazilian agenda in the General Agreement on Tariffs and Trade (GATT) rounds of trade negotiations at least since the Tokyo Round. In both the Tokyo and Uruguay rounds of trade talks, Brazil led a coalition of underdeveloped and developing countries demanding the adoption of a special status with a specific array of exceptions to GATT rules to be afforded to them.

Finally, Brazilian foreign policy has consistently tried to avoid any limitations to its freedom to fully exploit its domestic resources. Indeed, besides leading the collective resistance to the introduction of investment, subsidies, and property rights in the trade talks of the GATT, Brazil has also unilaterally resisted the recent trend of interventionism linked to the new transnational themes such as environmental protection, human rights, and labor standards.

The second major goal can be understood as a reaction of Brazilian bureaucracy and political leadership to the shift in post–World War II U.S. global orientations. Brazilian expectations of a special alliance with the United States were frustrated when the Cold War commitments directed U.S. vital interests far away from Latin America. Brazilian elite, so hesitantly engaged on the U.S. side in World War II, strongly resented the lack of peace dividends generously provided to its enemies in Europe and Asia.

But the anticipated U.S support to Brazilian industrial development and military modernization was never fulfilled. Technological cooperation was submitted to the rules of the Cold War. And investment and debt negotiations did not guarantee special conditions similar to wartime or even similar to those afforded to Germany and Japan. As a consequence, the Brazilian military and political elite regarded alignment with global U.S. goals as concessionary.

The third major Brazilian goal in foreign policy is a corollary of the two previous objectives. This became increasingly important to Brazilian domestic and external politics as a consequence of the growth in hemispheric interdependency, principally in the 1990s. It may be defined as the objective to avoid or at least delay any further integration with the U.S. economy. The reasons are twofold: First, Brazilian bureaucracy and business communities strongly fear an increased competition from U.S. industry in the context of an increased opening of the country's economy. Second, the Brazilian elite still resents the shift in U.S. priorities during the Cold War and persistently perceives U.S. long-term interests as incompatible with Brazilian growth and modernization.

Another singular feature of Brazilian foreign policy is the central role of the country's diplomatic bureaucracy (Itamaraty[1]) decision making. In every single constitution since the beginning of the republic (1889), the president has been entrusted with the entirety of foreign relations. The senate exerts very limited functions, such as the confirmation of appointed ambassadors, and the congress as a whole ratifies formal international treaties. With the growing impact of globalization on domestic policies and regulations, though, the congress tends to exert negative pressure in delaying the approval of legislation that reflects external commitments of the executive.

Other federal agencies, such as the Ministries of Treasury, Commerce, Labor, and Health, are increasingly involved in foreign policymaking. Among the bureaucracy, the military is the most capable in affecting the formulation and implementation of foreign policy, but as a disciplined corps it tends to abide by Itamaraty's leadership in this particular field. Party politics is generally far away from foreign policy, and the official agenda of major parties either ignore or simply mirror Itamaraty's views (Almeida 2000). The same applies to union leaders, the mass media, and the public opinion at large. Academic research is very incipient, and most authors are limited to commenting approvingly on Itamaraty's foreign policy choices.

All this is due to the extraordinary ability of the Brazilian diplomatic corps to earn credibility as a unique champion and efficient guardian of Brazilian external vital interests.

From 1822 to the advent of the republic in 1889, foreign policy was centered on obtaining international official recognition. The country had one single major counterpart besides the former Portuguese metropolis: the British (Ricupero 1995, 1996). In the early twentieth century, until the international and domestic crisis of 1930, Brazil's major goal was to preserve its territorial integrity, a very sensitive issue for a country with ten different nations bordering its frontiers. This period was marked by diffuse international counterparts and by an unwritten alliance with the United States, both countries sharing similar views about South American political instability and a similar mistrust concerning the European powers (Ricupero 1995, 1996).

In the aftermath of the international economic crisis of 1929 and the domestic revolution of 1930, Brazilian external politics focused on its major domestic objectives of modernization and economic development, which have been its main international goals. That had been the rationale for the political and military alliance with the United States during World War II. When in the 1960s Brazil adopted the so-called *política externa independente* (PEI; independent foreign policy), in an attempt to find alternatives to economic and political dependency on the United States, Brazil's focus was also on economic modernization and growth. And the same orientation applied again when Brazil championed a New International Economic Order at the Cancún meeting of UNCTAD. The current alignment with the so-called Washington consensus through the neoliberal adjustments, initiated in 1989, may also be attributed to the need to foster economic development.

Throughout the twentieth century, systemic change was the most important dimension in the shaping of Brazilian foreign policy. Unable to affect the international system as a whole, different Brazilian governments had to adjust the country's international goals and priorities to respond to policies adopted by the major international players. Keeping Brazilian options compatible with the interests of major European powers before World War II and with those of the United States in the postwar period was a central concern for all Brazilian governments.

Regime changes—from monarchy to republic in 1889, from liberal democracy to modernizing authoritarianism in 1930, to liberal democracy again in 1946, to military rule in 1964, and again to liberal democracy in 1985—always resulted in short-range impacts. Soon those changes had to be adjusted to cope with the demands of the country's major international counterparts.

Domestic political forces and social movements have had little impact on foreign policy. Quite the opposite, the bureaucracies along with the political leadership have played a major role. The military in the World War II period and the diplomats during the Cold War were responsible for translating the demands of the international system into policy choices. In association with the bureaucracies, either backing or further specifying their options, Getúlio Vargas (1930–1945, 1951–1954), Ernesto Geisel (1974–1979), and Fernando Henrique Cardoso (1995–2003) had a significant impact in major policy decisions.

SHIFTS IN THE BRAZILIAN FOREIGN POLICY FROM POST-WORLD WAR I TO THE COLD WAR

Until 1930, Brazilian foreign policy was essentially defensive. Its unwritten alliance with the United States permitted Brazil to shield itself against both European interventionism and South American instability on its frontiers. The internal and external effects of the 1929 crash reshaped Brazilian foreign policy. Its main goals were converted into negotiating the external debt and securing minimum prices for its major commodities, mainly coffee and sugar. Modernization of the economy and society provided the general framework for bilateral relations. Both internally and externally, this was a period of oscillating friendships from Berlin to London, to Rome, to Paris, always in search of economic and technological support for the modernization of the economy and armed forces (Seitenfus 1985; Seitenfus 1996).

With the war escalating, U.S. pressures finally prevailed, leading to a rupture of diplomatic relations with the Axis, later to a declaration of war, and finally to a direct participation in the conflict (Moura 1996). The wartime alliance with the United States was in clear opposition to the prevalent ideological preferences of the military and the political elite. In fact, the dominant mood was one of an overt ideological sympathy for the German and Italian dictatorships, most of all the corporative features of fascism that had already inspired the ongoing reforms of the Brazilian state.[2] Realpolitik prevailed over ideology, though, and the military played an important role in making clear that the Brazilian economy and military forces were not in a position to choose autonomously between the sides or even to embrace neutrality.

As a result, Brazil contributed extensively to the U.S. war effort. Most important of all was the concession of military bases in the far northeast, providing closer communication with the North African war theater. Moreover, the Brazil–U.S. accords secured industrial and military procurements, including strategic materials, which were vital to the U.S. war effort. Finally, Brazil sent troops and equipment (about twenty thousand men) to participate with U.S. troops in Italy. Brazilian participation in the conflict and its support for U.S. policies were to have a significant impact in favor of U.S. political priorities in Latin America, such as the strengthening of the Inter-American Security System.

In exchange for its contribution to the war effort, Brazil received significant support from the United States, in terms of military equipment, training, and, most of all, industrial investment. The first big industrial complex in Brazil, until today a symbol of the country's modern industrialization, the Volta Redonda steel complex, was built as a result of the wartime Vargas–Roosevelt deals (Wirth 1970).

In the aftermath of World War II, Brazil's expectations were accordingly very high. The United States was expected to fulfill its commitments to support the modernization of the economy and of the military and provide science and technology transfers necessary for sustained growth. From a political point of view, in exchange for its strong support for U.S. priorities in inter-American forums, Brazil played a more than proportionate role in the negotiations of the new international institutions. Brazil was the U.S. candidate for a permanent seat at the UN Security Council together with the USSR, China, the United Kingdom, and the United States itself, but it was vetoed by the USSR and replaced by France (*Fontes Vivas* 2000).

With the advent of the Cold War, U.S. regional priorities were superseded by its global commitments to the containment of Soviet expansion. Europe and especially Germany became the cornerstone of American diplomacy. Different from other peripheral areas, such as the Far East and the Middle East, Latin America lost much of its strategic significance. So, the Brazilian military and diplomatic bureaucracy resented that, despite having faithfully fulfilled its promises, the country's core problems still persisted. The rupture of diplomatic and commercial relations with the Soviet countries, trade and exchange liberalization, and military and political cooperation with the United States in the hemisphere did not help in tackling the country's debt, trade deficit, and stalled industrial growth.

The brief wartime and postwar honeymoon was followed by a long period of ambivalent policies, concerning both Brazil–U.S. relations and Brazilian general foreign policy orientations. The whole period from World War II to 1961, when President Jânio Quadros adopted the PEI, is generally regarded in the literature as one of automatic alignment with the U.S. foreign policy priorities. Nevertheless, a malaise was in place since 1949. Brazil–U.S. bilateral relations were the object of a lasting stalemate over the issues of the financial debt, renegotiation, and new investments; support to industrial development and military modernization; transfers of science and technology; and nonproliferation (*Fontes Vivas* 2000).

Systemic changes, including the advent of the United States as a global power, the downfall of the European balance of power, and the prelude to a new polarized international order, were to induce major shifts in Brazilian foreign policy. Despite its domestic leadership's political inclinations, Brazil was not free to challenge the U.S. regional leadership and join the Axis powers.

The military, during Vargas's dictatorship, and Itamaraty, during the subsequent democratic regime, were crucial in seeking to shape a special alliance with the United States. When the global commitments of the United States to the Cold War resulted in a sharp decline of its commitments to the hemisphere, the task of adjusting the Brazilian alignment with the West to its domestic needs of economic development and political modernization became ever more difficult. The role of diplomatic rhetoric became central in making foreign policy compatible with domestic politics.

During this period, despite the changing domestic forces, which were powerful enough to result in regime change, the need to adjust to the changing role of the United States in the international system prevailed over domestic considerations. The nature of the central conflict also varied. The ideological and political divide of the Cold War followed the military clash of World War II. Similarly, the diplomats replaced the military in decision making.

DEVELOPMENTALISM AND INDEPENDENT FOREIGN POLICY

We can define *desenvolvimentismo* in Brazilian foreign relations as a policy aimed at supporting a cooperative international environment favoring the government's industrial and trade policies. It implies obtaining external support for, or at least tolerance of, Brazilian import substitution policies, state-led industrial policies, protectionism, and control of exchange and foreign investment. It also implies obtaining official technical and financial assistance to Brazil's development.

In such terms, desenvolvimentismo is a good definition of Brazilian foreign policy goals in the twentieth century. As a matter of fact, exceptions to that definition are only to be found on rare occasions. It was the case of the defensive policies of the post-Depression period, in the period of the post–World War II alliance with the United States until 1949, in the brief period of ideological frontiers after the military coup in 1964, and again during the Collor administration, between 1990 and 1992.

The entire period, however, was one of conflicting orientations. Brazil aligned with the Western powers and diverged from them for the same reasons: They were supposed to command the political power and economic resources that would either facilitate or impede Brazilian development. It combined political and military alignment with a policy of frictions in the areas of trade, nonproliferation, disarmament, and official aid to developing countries. Different periods combined alignment and estrangement in different amounts. Eventually it evolved toward a growing generalized opposition.

Postwar developmentalism began with the Cold War and remained until President Juscelino Kubitschek's Pan-American Initiative (Operação Pan-Americana) in 1958. It involved two different movements: disillusionment (with President Eurico Gaspar Dutra, 1946–1951) and activism (with Presidents Getúlio Vargas, 1951–1954, and Juscelino Kubitschek, 1956–1961). Until 1950, Dutra's foreign policy expressed a malaise toward the meager dividends provided by the economic liberalization and anti-Soviet moves. Kubitschek started his government in 1956 rolling back from the strong activism of Vargas's final years. He tried again to draw official aid and debt relief. He searched for an alternative to American support among European and Japanese governments (Vizentini 1995, 1996).

After 1958, with a growing indebtedness, stagnation of exports, and high internal inflation, Brazilian domestic politics shifted to a more nationalistic orientation. Kubitschek skillfully played with a nationalist rhetoric and a liberal economic diplomacy. The Kubitschek administration was very active in attracting international investments and in searching for new markets, including socialist countries (Vizentini 1995, 1996; *Fontes Vivas* 2000).

Kubitschek's Pan-American Initiative aimed at the adoption of a program of economic development for Latin America, involving debt relief, special trade regimes with protection against flotation of commodities prices, industrial investments, and technical and scientific cooperation (Ministério das Relações Exteriores 1995). This program was to be funded by developed countries. It started with a letter from Kubitschek to Eisenhower following the frustrated visit of then–vice president Richard Nixon to Latin America (Correa 1995).

With the Pan-American Initiative, political and military alignment and opposition in trade and investments attained their highest limit of balance. Rhetoric and action were largely convergent. With Jânio Quadros, Kubitschek's successor (January–August 1961), rhetoric and action were dissociated and symbolic. Opportunistic actions were disconnected from permanent commitments. Quadros adopted incompatible policies and orientations in almost all domestic issues. His sole apparent criterion was the impact of his actions on the public in order to accomplish some momentary image building. His motives in foreign policy were also directed to influence public opinion (Araújo 1996; Schneider 1991).

Examples of symbolic, opportunistic actions were the appointment of a black Brazilian journalist as ambassador to Ghana—who was dismissed by the local elite. On another occasion, Quadros dispatched a special envoy to the German Democratic Republic while negotiating an important program of investments and technological cooperation with the Federal Republic of Germany (FRG). And a fatal example was the award of the highest Brazilian decoration to Che Guevara in an almost-clandestine ceremony, amid the strongest American pressures to exclude Cuba from the inter-American system.

Quadros's rhetoric achieved enormous (though undue) credibility domestically and externally. A number of his actions, irrespective of his motivations, finally acquired consistency and inspired a highly respected foreign policy. Although ambivalent, Quadros's independent foreign policy (IFP) was more consistent than Kubitschek's policies (Fonseca 1996).

The Sixteenth Session of the UN General Assembly in 1961 was the perfect stage for a statement on IFP. Foreign Minister Affonso Arinos clearly defined Brazil's vision of international relations during the Cold War:

> The leading problem is that of peace consolidation. The unpredictable consequences of nuclear war made it a devastating threat to all and every one and, for that very reason, improbable. But the Cold War threatens the accomplishment of every man, not only because of the expenses with the armaments race, but also because of the universal insecurity, which abolishes both trust in the present and hope for the future. . . . We either shall build peace based on free acquiescence of the self-determination of peoples, or shall make nationalism a pretext for war, leading only to the expansion of economic or ideological oppression. (Ministério das Relações Exteriores 1995)

In the UN General Assembly's 1962 session, Foreign Minister Arinos, now under the Goulart administration, added, "The international ideal consists in securing peace and prosperity to all nations. Peace is based on disarmament, and prosperity depends on technical and financial assistance to underdeveloped countries. Neither disarmament nor development can be really achieved on the basis of cold war and competition between ideologically hostile blocs" (Ministério das Relações Exteriores 1995).

The IFP continued during the João Goulart administration (1961–1964) and was only interrupted by the military coup of 1964. But the new automatic alignment with the so-called ideological frontiers of the Western bloc did not outlive the first military administration. The second military president, General Costa e Silva (1967–1969), reintroduced populist orientations and a new demand for international investments and official aid that prompted again disappointment and resentment against the Western developed countries, especially the United States.

During this period, Brazilian foreign policy had to tackle conflicting trends. It had to adjust to the waning importance of the region for the global order. It had also to respond to the growing need for external support, as a condition to secure Brazilian economic growth, which was deemed necessary to guarantee domestic political stability. The increasing domestic pressures for economic growth and political participation accounted for the mounting weight of political leadership in foreign policymaking, especially in the definition of external goals. Disappointment with the lack of reciprocity in Brazil–U.S. relations eventually changed the perception of political leaders, such as Kubitschek and Quadros, and diplomats, regarding the mere feasibility of an enduring special relationship between the two countries.

Reflecting the changing perception of U.S. priorities, the Brazilian diplomatic rhetoric changed as well. Starting with skepticism on whether all U.S. external goals were compatible with Brazilian economic development and political modernization, the perception that major U.S. goals conflicted with Brazilian interests later reflected bilateral relations. Finally, with Goulart (1961–1964), the dominant mood in Brazilian domestic politics was that U.S. interests were ultimately opposed to the growth of the Brazilian economy, to the country's modernization, and even to the stability of its democracy. For the first time, Brazilian foreign policy underwent a significant change in rhetoric, if not in policies, echoing domestic pressures rather than external constraints. The critical factor here is the changing perceptions of both the political leadership and the bureaucracy about the friendliness of the international environment with respect to Brazilian vital interests.

FROM "IDEOLOGICAL FRONTIERS" TO "RESPONSIBLE PRAGMATISM"

One of the major reasons why the military intervened in Brazilian domestic politics, initiating twenty-one years of authoritarian rule, was a deep belief that internal and external political conflicts as well as internal and external foes were the same, or at least strongly linked.

Because the freedom of Western democracies was at stake in the containment of Soviet expansion, all the options in foreign policy as well as all domestic policies were regarded as subsumed to the vital interests of the West. At stake was not so much an automatic alignment of the country's foreign policy to U.S. goals and priorities, as the alignment of the country's foreign policy goals to its domestic priorities.

In that sense, Brazil's contribution to world peace and prosperity—and to its own domestic stability and economic development—should have been consistent with the politics of the Cold War, despite the fact that Western powers gave priority to mutual containment rather than to growth and equality among nations. Therefore, the cost of sacrificing the country's particular domestic goals to Western security priorities—or to U.S. goals, for that matter—was the price to be paid for securing the country's own freedom and prosperity.

As a consequence, the solutions for the vital domestic problem of underdevelopment and political instability should have been a natural consequence of the identity of domestic and external threats. The much-anticipated peace dividends, once denied by the need to assist an unstable postwar Europe, were now to be granted by the need to assist the self-styled last stronghold of democracy and Christianity—Brazil.

This was a time for a fast dénouement for U.S. political and military ventures in Latin America as far as its potentially stronger opponent—Brazil—was less inclined to dissent. From the exclusion of Cuba from the inter-American system, to the political and military support for U.S. interventions in Central America, U.S. Cold War priorities in Latin America were accomplished more smoothly. Accordingly, this was a time of rising costs for the Brazilian leadership in South America. Brazilian support for the destabilization of Allende's government in Chile by the United States was resented by both Chileans and Argentines as a regional threat (Bernal-Meza 1989).

Again, the peace dividends did not come to Brazil. The Marshall Plan was not reshuffled for the sake of the underdeveloped Latin American targets of Soviet expansion as it had been adopted for the sake of its Western European and Asian targets.

As a result, the previous ambivalent orientations toward the United States resumed once more. Again, Western support for austerity measures attempted by the military government was limited to political declarations but it was not followed by the expected debt relief, fresh investments, and favored International Monetary Fund (IMF) assistance. There were no special preferences for Brazilian exports, no price stabilization for Brazilian commodities, and no transfer of advanced industrial and military technology.

Between 1969 and 1974, during the administration of General Emílio Garrastazu Medici, the overall ambivalent relationship persisted but was kept subdued for two reasons. First, the internal front was in a critical situation. Urban and rural guerrilla wars were being waged by a clandestine opposition, increasing the need for a stronger cooperation between the two governments in terms of police and security policies. Second, a period of global economic expansion supported a program of huge investments in infrastructure that prompted significant increases in earnings for the upper working class and financial gains for the middle class (Schneider 1991; Skidmore 1988).

The so-called Brazilian economic miracle provided a background of self-confidence to the military and its civilian supporters that permitted it to play down the conflicting views with Western powers on industrial and trade policies in addition to monetary and exchange measures. In the United States, for its part, by and large, the domestic opposition to military ventures and political interventions abroad increased, prompting at first a decrease in U.S. foreign activism.

Soon after Medici's term, a new U.S. activism began with the administration of President Jimmy Carter. The dirty wars carried out by the Latin American military and security agencies to preserve Western values and freedom were now perceived as a sin, requiring repentance and chastisement (*Fontes Vivas* 2000). During the same period, the first oil crisis and the corresponding world recession provoked a slowed Brazilian industrial growth.

To go beyond the easy imports substitution period, the Brazilian industrial sector had to achieve a huge program of investments in infrastructure and capital goods. It did not have the export income, the foreign direct investment, or the domestic savings to support such a program. This was the domestic and external context in which General Ernesto Geisel (1974–1979) took over the presidency.

The first time he addressed his cabinet, Geisel applied the expression of "responsible pragmatism" to define his foreign policy orientations. By that he meant that Brazilian foreign policy would primarily serve "national interests in terms of foreign trade, vital industrial and consumer supplies, and access to state-of-the-art technology." This was scarcely news, but to be able to attain those goals, his government would "make the necessary options and realignments" (Souto Maior 1996).

These changes entailed, first, a regional policy. During the period of "ideological frontiers," Brazilian foreign policy was much more Atlantic oriented than Latin America and Africa oriented. For the first time in decades, Brazilian support for decolonization and self-determination did not exclude the Portuguese colonies. Also, an important objective was the search for a more diversified oil supply and new alternative sources of energy. Brazil looked to the Middle East and to Latin America to guarantee oil supplies and started an ambitious program of nuclear power plants. When the Carter administration enacted new restrictions on American suppliers of nuclear equipment and supplies, Geisel turned to the FRG for cooperative ventures (Souto Maior 1996; Batista 2000; *Fontes Vivas* 2000).

Differently from Quadros's IFP, Geisel's responsible pragmatism was more tactical than ideological (Roett and Perry 1977). In many statements, Brazil's foreign minister Azeredo da Silveira reiterated that both bilateral relations with the United States and multilateral orientations would target practical goals instead of speculating about convergence or dissension. Brazilian foreign policy orientations would be subject to shifts and limited in time and scope as every pragmatic orientation is. The Carter administration did not share the same perspective. And its interventionism in the areas of human rights, indigenous rights, and nonproliferation prompted the highest degree of bilateral friction ever between the two countries (Souto Maior 1996; *Fontes Vivas* 2000).

Besides the nuclear power plants program, two other initiatives may be considered as emblematic of the responsible pragmatism. The first is the accreditation of an ambassador to Angola, before its formal independence from Portugal. At that moment, the two major political factions, the Marxist Popular Movement for the Liberation of Angola (MPLA) and the National Union for the Total Independence of Angola (UNITA), supported by South Africa and the United States, were still struggling for the military and political control of the country. Portugal and the MPLA, which controlled Luanda, the capital of Angola, had already agreed on a transition period before formal independence (Melo 2000).

The appointment of an ambassador to Luanda at that precise point was the equivalent of an official recognition of a political-military faction as an independent state. It provoked a faster outcome to a long-lasting internecine conflict and placed before the U.S. government an unwelcome fait accompli.

Another important initiative was the construction of the Itaipu hydroelectric complex, a binational venture in partnership with Paraguay on the border of the two countries. Itaipu fed a long conflict between Brazil and Argentina, a country that borders both Brazil and Paraguay. It initiated a dispute over the issue of the international utilization of rivers that lasted many years. The dispute with Argentina was only settled in the military presidency of General João Baptista Figueiredo (1979–1985), in 1979. A trilateral treaty was signed that set the way for a more cooperative relationship between Brazil and Argentina (Bernal-Meza 2000).

A series of agreements and other initiatives, both economic and military, were adopted that prepared the elite of both countries for the political and economic integration of the 1980s (Amorim 1991; Flores 1991; Guilhon Albuquerque 1992, 1997). Nevertheless, the Itaipu complex marked both Geisel's search for strengthening Brazilian regional interdependency and the difficulties of its novel Latin America–oriented foreign policy.

Changes in this period reflected both external and domestic pressures. The critical factor is an alteration of the perception by domestic pressure groups of the relationship between the domestic and the international arenas. Until then, the task of foreign policy decision making was to close the gap then perceived as existing between the two arenas. That task consisted in adjusting the weakest arena (domestic) to the dominant one (international).

The "ideological frontiers" doctrine supposed quite the opposite: that such a gap did not exist and that the interests and goals in both arenas were a perfect match. While in the early stages of the military rule, the coup was a forceful consequence of Brazilian commitment to the West and a new convergence with U.S.–Latin American policies, a corollary of the domestic anticommunist stance, which later provoked a fresh estrangement between the two countries.

As soon as the expectations concerning massive U.S. support were disappointed and the Brazilian economy started facing the consequences of the external crises, the perception of Brazilian external goals changed dramatically. Brazilian contribution to international stability was to be measured by its own sustained development, which was to be sought not so much in the alignment with the United States as in alternative ventures with other Western powers or even with nonaligned countries.

In the early military rule, the military bureaucracy exerted a major role in drawing the foreign policy consequences of the ideological frontier doctrine. The bureaucracy as a whole, rather than its political leadership, was entrusted with this mission. The responsible pragmatism, while initially formulated by Geisel, general and president, was mostly a diplomatic endeavor. The president used the diplomatic rhetoric to legitimize his choices before his fellow officers, and Itamaraty used Geisel's assertiveness to advance its own vision of Brazilian degrees of freedom in the international arena.

FROM *NEODESENVOLVIMENTISMO* TO NEOLIBERALISM

In the late 1980s, the first civilian democratically elected presidents of Argentina and Brazil in several years were facing similar challenges. Argentina's Raul Alfonsín was challenged by high inflation rates and lasting conflicting relations with the military. Brazil's José Sarney, as a vice president–elect of a president who died before the inauguration, besides illegitimacy, faced a waning majority, growing inflation rates, an increase in unemployment, and ever-higher pressures from the left-of-center political forces. Both had to deal with inflated popular expectations for economic growth and monetary stability.

It is a very widespread understanding that these reasons prompted both presidents to envisage a shift in bilateral relations that aimed at putting an end to old rivalries and establishing a pact addressing the mutual defense of their fragile democratic institutions against the threat of a military revival. It is well established that the two countries adopted two sets of cooperative initiatives, one among the military bureaucracies of both countries and the other aimed at the integration of the two economies. Both presidents ever since have stated clearly that their motivation was primarily political, with the defense of democracy its primary goal (Alfonsín 1994).

The rationale for the rapprochement was that both governments assumed that the increase in bilateral interdependency would enhance their need for cooperation, which would reinforce their mutual protection against political instability. A program of cooperation and economic integration was adopted with a view to integrating sectoral policies, such as transportation, science and technology, development policies, and macroeconomic harmonization. Finally, the decision to create a free trade area between the two countries surfaced as the first stepping stone toward the creation of the Southern Cone Common Market (MERCOSUR) (Flores 1991; Amorim 1991, Amorim and Pimentel 1996). However, the growing monetary instability and the huge external debt frustrated the political decision to foster economic integration.

During the entire Sarney administration (1985–1990), Brazil was the target of continuous transnational pressures emanating from a number of relevant actors: governments, financial institutions, the investment and financial communities, and nongovernmental organizations. Brazilian foreign relations were the target of three simultaneous crises, the first and more important of which was the debt crisis. That was the main reason for the stoppage of capital flows to the country, which only resumed in 1993. The dispute with creditors, the international financial authorities, and governments, particularly with the United States, would become critical after the Sarney administration declared a unilateral default, exacerbating the loss of the country's credibility.

The second critical issue was the hyperinflation—a stability crisis. More than growing inflation rates, it was the volatility of macroeconomic policies that constituted the critical factor for the assessment of the country's international image. Succeeding finance ministers and Central Bank presidents in the same administration tried to adopt their own adjustment programs, either heterodox or orthodox, contributing to increasing unpredictability.

The third crisis affected the development model. Brazil is probably the most successful case of import substitution industrialization. The very success of industrial growth and modernization made it even more difficult to adopt new policies. Because the abandonment of successful policies is deemed to be risky, it increased significantly the cost of neoliberal reforms following the so-called Washington consensus model. As a consequence, Brazil was one of the last countries of Latin America to enact the neoliberal reforms.

The neoliberal period in Brazilian foreign policy started with Fernando Henrique Cardoso's term as Itamar Franco's finance minister (1993–1994) and was consolidated during Cardoso's two presidential terms (1995–2003).

It is best understood as a consequence of changes in its regional and multilateral policies, as described in the two remaining sections.

REGIONAL AND INTERREGIONAL PRIORITIES

Since Brazil's political independence in 1822, the country's regional goals in South America and in the hemisphere were mutually entangled (Ricupero 1995, 1996). With minor changes, until the Cold War, Brazil's goals included a tacit alliance with the United States to guarantee stability in its frontiers, meaning especially South America.

In the Cold War era, Brazilian interest in Latin America was conditioned by U.S. priorities in the hemisphere (Ricupero 1995, 1996). In the post–Cold War, Brazilian priorities are twofold: Check the U.S. unilateralism in the region, and avoid isolation in South America. In this sense, one could argue that the restraint to conflict with the United States is the risk of becoming isolated in a South American context of growing interdependency with the U.S. economy. And the limit to increasing integration with the subregion is the Latin American countries' apparent willingness to increase their interdependence with the United States, leading to unchecked U.S. unilateralism in the region.

This leads to a diversity of subregional policies: As for the northern countries of South America, the Andean-Amazonian subregion, Brazilian prospects for an assertive policy are low. These countries are generally more oriented to the Northern Hemisphere and the Caribbean than to South America for what concerns trade and investments. They tend to be of critical relevance for the U.S. security for reasons of oil supply (Venezuela, Ecuador) or drug trafficking (Peru, Colombia). As a whole, they tend to be less attracted by the Brazilian market and political leadership.

One can hardly distinguish any discerning Brazilian policy toward Central America and the Caribbean, with the exception of Cuba. During the entire period of peace negotiations in Central America, Brazil was conspicuously absent. It was not before the eleventh hour that Brazil joined the Support Group to the Contadora Peace Initiative, later becoming, with the Contadora Group, the Rio Group of Latin American countries.

The reason for the exceptionality of Cuba in Brazilian foreign policy is that Cuba is an almost perfect case of U.S. unilateral interventionism in the hemisphere. Whatever the United States does and whatever Cuba's reaction, and vice versa, Brazil has a good case to check the U.S. moves and assert its own independence.

Brazil did not adopt specific regional priorities concerning North America. Until very recently, both Canada and Mexico were perceived as an extension of the United States In the late 1990s, Brazilian diplomats blocked the conclusion of trade agreements between MERCOSUR and those two countries, allegedly because they were part of the North American Free Trade Agreement (NAFTA) and had special trade relations with the United States.

As for the Southern Cone and its closer neighbors, Bolivia and Chile, MERCOSUR is the most conspicuous example of that twofold priority. Indeed, MERCOSUR is an alternative to unilateral initiatives of the United States such as George H. W. Bush's Enterprise for the Americas and Bill Clinton's Free Trade Area of the Americas. MERCOSUR avoids, or at least postpones, the enthusiastic integration of Brazilian fellow MERCOSUR countries in the U.S. economy. That was the rationale for the "Rose Garden Agreement," a framework agreement signed in 1991 between the United States and the four member states of MERCOSUR (Argentina, Brazil, Paraguay, and Uruguay), as a part of the Enterprise for the Americas Initiative (Amorim and Pimentel 1996). MERCOSUR should be singled out from Brazilian hemispheric policies and shall be addressed at the end of this section.

As for the European countries, since the Cold War, Brazil has tried to expand and deepen relations with the region, as a consequence of its disappointment with U.S. Cold War priorities. In the late 1940s, Brazilian officials tried secretly to procure alternative nuclear technology from German scientists, in an attempt to bypass the U.S. embargo (*Fontes Vivas* 2000). In the 1950s, President Kubitschek, after being disappointed with the lack of U.S. support for his project of automotive industry, turned to European governments. He finally succeeded in obtaining two major investments from France (the state-owned Renault) and West Germany (Volkswagen, where the government is a major stakeholder). In the late 1970s, as already mentioned, Brazil tried again a European partnership to accomplish an ambitious plan of alternative nuclear technology aimed at developing a huge program of power plants.

Generally speaking, the Brazilian elite looked to Europe searching for political support, an ideological model, and financial and technological aid. Brazil's most significant relations in Europe have been with the European Union (EU) countries, especially with France and Germany. But the intent to further integrate the economies of both regions, as an alternative to integration in the U.S. economy have not yet made relevant progress.

In the case of Africa, Brazilian policies have been cyclical. It suddenly attains high levels of activism and then slows down very rapidly. Such has been the cases of Nigeria, Senegal, Angola, Mozambique, and the oil countries of northern Africa. During the period of IFP, Africa had highly symbolic significance. With the responsible pragmatism goals, it acquired a more practical profile, involving oil supply and the export of engineering projects and military equipment.

MERCOSUR is the most important Brazilian endeavor in regional politics. It is the final result of a shift in Brazil–Argentina relations that started in the late 1970s. As described in the previous section, both countries then started a rapprochement, trying to put an end to a decade of severe competition between the two countries for the leadership in the region. This shift occurred when Brazil finally agreed in conceding to the conditions that would be acceptable to both Paraguay and Argentina in terms of common utilization of water power, settling the disputes over the Itaipu hydroelectric complex in 1979 (Flores 1991).

The second period of rapprochement is that of the political integration of Alfonsín-Sarney initiatives. It is clear from its goals that the initiative was oriented to a regional industrial policy aimed at import substitution. The framework for the free trade area then envisaged was that of lowering bilateral tariffs and keeping high external barriers. At any rate, the opening of both economies to external trade and investments only began in Argentina in the succeeding government of Carlos Menem and, in Brazil, in the second to last year of Sarney's administration, 1989.

MERCOSUR proper—that is, the Menem–Collor agreements, involving further Uruguay and Paraguay—is a totally new endeavor. It is a process of both intra- and extraregional economic openness. Its most important feature was not a series of sectoral industrial programs but an automatic and lineal process of tariff reduction. And its rationale was not the protection of infant industries against international competition but an exercise of regional competition to achieve global competitiveness (Guilhon Albuquerque 1997).

Struggling with diverging macroeconomic goals and performances in the two leading countries, MERCOSUR achieved its consolidation after Brazil's successful economic stabilization with President Fernando Henrique Cardoso (1995–2003). The weight of converging macroeconomic policies and mutual confidence between Cardoso and Menem set the stage for a durable cooperation, which resisted the ensuing debacle of the Argentine economy in 2001.

MULTILATERAL OBJECTIVES AND PRIORITIES

Brazil was an early GATT member, having participated since the very beginning in the talks aimed at the creation of the International Trade Organization that originated instead of the General Agreement on Tariffs and Trade. Until the Tokyo Round of GATT negotiations, Brazil's participation was marginal, targeting the defense of specific products, such as sugar and coffee. During the Tokyo Round, Brazil premiered the role of leader of underdeveloped and developing economies, claiming exceptions and special rules for that group of countries.

In the Uruguay Round, together with India, Brazil led a veto group, opposing the whole agenda of the Organization for Economic Cooperation and Development (OECD) countries, led by the United States. The Brazil–India group wished to restrict the negotiations to the traditional GATT agenda on tariffs of industrial goods and on the removal of nontariff barriers and fair trade rules adopted by the developed countries. It opposed any inclusion of trade-related matters such as services, intellectual property rights, and subsidies. It finally evolved from veto to a conflicting participation, accepting the new issues with exemption clauses for the developing economies.

After the creation of the WTO, Brazil resumed, in the beginning of Cardoso's term, very defensive tactics, opposing any inclusion of new issues, such as labor and environment norms, information technology agreements, and investment rules. Later it evolved to a coalition with the EU aimed at the launching of a new round of talks, to be called at the WTO ministerial meeting in Seattle. The Brazilian agenda in Seattle was limited to agriculture. It wanted the substantial lowering of tariff and technical barriers and the total elimination of subsidies to agriculture. The EU's main objective, quite the opposite, was to avoid any substantial concession in agriculture. But both expected to advance their common political agenda, which is to bypass the U.S. leadership at the WTO. Indeed, the failed Seattle Ministerial was expected, for the first time, to call a round of trade talks without an agenda led by the United States.

In any case, the margin of agreement between the United States and the EU is much greater than any margin of agreement between Brazil and the EU. This is true both in terms of trade-related issues (opposed by Brazil) and in terms of elimination of tariff and technical barriers and subsidies to agriculture (proposed by Brazil).

Besides MERCOSUR, Brazil is engaged in another huge multilateral negotiation, that of the Free Trade Area of the Americas (FTAA). Both Bush's Enterprise for the Americas, involving a free trade area "from Yukon to Patagonia," and Clinton's call for a Summit of the Americas later involving the FTAA, were initially opposed by Brazil. The rationale for this defensive stance was that Brazil had already opened "too much, too fast, and without reciprocity." This should have been a time for digesting the neoliberal adjustment. Brazil was also engaged in complex talks in the WTO, especially inside MERCOSUR, and was also involved in even more complex talks with the EU aimed at adopting an interregional comprehensive arrangement.

From the first Summit of the Americas in Miami to the second one in Santiago, Brazil's stance was limited to procrastination. In Santiago, accepting finally the beginning of formal negotiations, Brazil managed to format an agenda leaving market access—that is, the issue of freer trade—to the end. But the secondary agenda of the FTAA, involving the business community and the union leadership, followed its own path. While the Brazilian union leaders, initially favorable to hemispheric integration, changed their minds after socializing with their fellow U.S. union leaders, the opposite occurred in the business community. Brazilian industrial and agribusiness communities, initially opposed to any further integration with the U.S. economy, began to consider things in terms of gains and losses and pressed the diplomatic bureaucracy to review its agenda. Cardoso's foreign policy team was finally sensitive to such pressures.

Initially, the official rhetoric was "FTAA is totally detrimental to Brazil. As we cannot have any gains, let's retard the losses. Anything is better then starting an FTAA, so let's delay its entry in business as much as possible." The message from Itamaraty to the business community and the opinion leaders was "We are not prepared to compete in the U.S. economy. With the FTAA our industrial plants shall be dismantled. So, let's avoid any FTAA."

In the Third Summit of the Americas in Quebec, Cardoso set the stage for the final consolidation of the so-called neoliberal foreign policy. The new message is now "We are not prepared to compete in the U.S. economy. With the FTAA we will have to further compete in the U.S. economy. So, let's be prepared to increase competitiveness."

CONCLUSION

It is not an easy endeavor to summarize fifty years of a complex and diverse period of international relations and its impact on a modern regional power like Brazil. Many changes have occurred in the twentieth century that could have affected Brazilian international relations. System changes as well as regime changes were frequent. Leaders succeeded each other regularly, with the exception of the Vargas dictatorship, which lasted for fifteen years, from 1930 to 1945. Many had a strong personality and left indelible marks on Brazilian politics, like Vargas himself, Quadros, and Geisel. A new bureaucracy was created under the Vargas regime in the late 1930s and early 1940s, with a distinctively modern professional training. Bureaucratic modernization included a brand new school of diplomacy providing professional training and well-established standards for the *carrière*.

Every change in the international system affected deeply and clearly Brazilian international objectives and priorities. Goals and methods and alliances changed again, after the 1929 crash, in the prewar period. The special alliance with the United States prevailed only during World War II and the immediate postwar period. Then, bilateral relations between the United States and Brazil were deeply affected by the Cold War.

Regime changes did not have a comparable effect in foreign policymaking. The Brazilian pro-West stance during World War II prevailed until 1949 although a new democratic regime replaced the old Vargas era in 1946. Many elements of continuity can be found between the independent foreign policy of Quadros and Goulart and the succeeding military administrations. Again, the basic traits of the so-called responsible pragmatism of General Geisel have been maintained since 1985 by the democratically elected governments.

Some strong leaders did affect Brazilian foreign policy goals and methods; others did not. Quadros's policies largely survived his very short term in government. The same might be said about Geisel, whose term lasted five years. But the most prominent among Brazilian leaders in this century, Getúlio Vargas, while managing to make dramatic decisions, kept a low profile in external affairs, and his very pragmatic approach to diplomacy did not provide long-lasting doctrines and policies.

After its reform in the late 1940s, Brazilian diplomatic bureaucracy has been the single most conspicuous source of foreign policymaking. Itamaraty's peculiarity is its resiliency. Goals, methods, and tactics are supposed, in Itamaraty's traditional approach, to be the permanent traits of Brazilian foreign policy. Intergenerational changes in the diplomatic corps have occurred, though, and change in their intellectual training, too, for that matter. Until now, however, such changes did not seem to affect the policymaking.

My hypothesis is that the most important factors in Brazilian foreign policy changes originate from changes in the international system, affecting the Brazilian role in that system. Itamaraty's role in policymaking consists of interpreting that change in terms of so-called permanent principles, methods, and goals. Until now, Itamaraty has been exceedingly successful in its endeavor.

DISCUSSION QUESTIONS

1. Assess the importance of economic growth and development in the shaping of Brazilian foreign policy in the immediate postwar and post–Cold War periods.
2. What accounts for the shifts toward an independent foreign policy and responsible pragmatism in Brazil's foreign relations?
3. How consistent is Brazil's more open approach to external economic relations today with previous foreign economic policies?

NOTES

1. Named after the Palace of Itamaraty, its longtime house in the former national capital, Rio de Janeiro, both the Brazilian Ministry of Foreign Relations and its diplomatic corps are generally known as "the Itamaraty."

2. In 1937, a coup d'état staged by then-president Getúlio Vargas initiated the so-called Estado Novo (New State), which dictated a new authoritarian constitution and adopted a full range of industrial and social legislation inspired by the fascist corporatism.

15

Argentina

Between Confrontation and Alignment

Aldo C. Vacs

For most of the twentieth century, Argentina's foreign policies were characterized by an unwieldy mix of nationalism and internationalism, assertiveness and subordination, hegemonic aspirations and pragmatism, and neutralism and alignment that resulted in periodic shifts between challenging the prevailing international distribution of power and attempting to insert the country into the existing world order. However, since the mid-1980s, Argentina's democratization has been associated with the emergence of a pro-Western foreign policy approach that has shown an unprecedented degree of coherence and continuity throughout the presidential administrations of Raúl Alfonsín (1983–1989), Carlos Menem (1989–1999), Fernando de la Rúa (1999–2001), and Eduardo Duhalde (2002–2003).

This chapter examines the contemporary evolution of Argentina's foreign policies, devoting particular attention to the last twenty-five years that comprise, at the international level, the final stages of the Cold War and the post–Cold War period, and, at the domestic level, the rise and collapse of the last authoritarian regime (1976–1983) and the emergence and relative consolidation of liberal democracy since then. In terms of the relevance of Rosenau's (1971) levels of analysis—idiosyncratic, domestic, and systemic—in conditioning foreign policy behavior, the Argentine case seems to indicate that their relative importance has varied throughout time depending on changing historical economic and political circumstances, both national and international. From the late nineteenth century until the mid–twentieth century, as Argentina's economic prosperity and political stability rose and declined, the role of domestic variables—governmental and socioeconomic—in determining the country's Eurocentric and relatively independent foreign policy fluctuated. As economic and political problems accumulated, the relative significance of the systemic and idiosyncratic variables in determining foreign policy actions increased, although at times they contradicted each other. For example, in the 1940s and early 1950s, while systemic circumstances encouraged Argentina's Western alignment and the establishment of closer relations with the United States, idiosyncratic variables related to the political rise of Juan D. Perón led to the formulation of populist nationalistic and nonaligned foreign policies. As a result of these contradictory influences and the changing relative importance of the different variables shaping its international approach, Argentina's foreign policies became more inconsistent and erratic as they included conflicting components and fluctuated between contradictory poles. Authoritarian military regimes only contributed to sharpen these contradictions as domestic economic and political crises as well as systemic transformations made Argentine foreign policies oscillate between accepting U.S. leadership and adopting Western alignment, and welcoming idiosyncratic attempts by authoritarian military leaders to regain control by embracing nationalistic foreign policies.

However, since the late 1980s, the contradictions affecting Argentine foreign policies gradually ebbed as the three sets of variables influencing Argentina's foreign policies converged in the direction of favoring a Western oriented strategy of reinsertion into the world order: (1) systemic international economic and strategic trends—such as growing economic interdependence and transnationalization, the rise of global markets, and the drive toward privatization, as well as the collapse of the Soviet bloc and the end of the Cold War; (2) domestic Argentine developments—including the exhaustion of the import substitution model of industrialization, the debt crisis and renewed financial dependence, the changes in the social structure associated with the economic transformations, and the decline of populist and authoritarian experiences; and (3) the idiosyncratic role played by emerging political leaders that favored liberal democracy, free markets, alignment with the West, and close relations with the United States.

FROM PROSPERITY TO DECLINE: CONTINUITY AND FLUCTUATIONS IN ARGENTINA'S FOREIGN POLICY

Between the late nineteenth century and 1930, Argentina's rapid economic growth was associated with the formulation of foreign policies aimed to deepen its insertion into the world economy as an agricultural exporter while trying to secure for the country an influential role in hemispheric and global affairs. Argentina's foreign policy strategy called for the establishment of close relations with European importers of grains and beef and suppliers of manufactures—particularly Great Britain—while pursuing a preeminent role in Latin America, thus clashing with the Monroe Doctrine promoted by the United States. This approach led to displays of foreign policy independence including the rejection of U.S.–Pan American initiatives and Caribbean interventions, the proclamation of nonintervention doctrines, and the maintenance of neutrality during World War I.

During the Great Depression, Argentina's agricultural export–based model of growth was gradually replaced by a process of import substitution industrialization. However, some features of its foreign policy such as the close relationship with Great Britain, the confrontations with the United States, and the attempts to attain a position of regional leadership remained unchanged (Rapoport 1980). Thus, during most of World War II, Argentina remained neutral even when the U.S. pressure intensified after 1941. Argentina's declaration of war on the Axis came only in early 1945 and was aimed at securing the country's participation in the United Nations.

Throughout the first Peronist government (1946–1955), Argentina's foreign policies included both elements of confrontation and rapprochement with the West (Lanús 1984: 17–92). Perón's "Third Position Doctrine" championed nonaligned foreign policies and opposed the U.S. hegemonic stance over Latin America. Initially, Perón's government tried to reduce the U.S. influence by maintaining close economic ties with Great Britain, opening relations with the USSR, and creating a regional sphere of influence in South America. However, as Argentina's economic situation deteriorated and U.S. power increased, the Peronist regime sought closer bilateral ties to solve the country's growing balance of payments crisis. Thus, in the early 1950s, Perón refused to recognize the People's Republic of China (PRC), ratified the Rio Treaty, and granted U.S. oil companies important concessions to attract them to the country.

In 1955, after Perón's fall, the military government promoted even closer economic relations with the United States, joining the International Monetary Fund (IMF), the World Bank, and the General Agreement on Tariffs and Trade (GATT). Afterward, successive civilian and military administrations continued to seek U.S. and European loans and direct investment but often followed a moderate nationalistic approach imposing restrictions on foreign investment, nationalizing some activities, and rejecting controls on nuclear technology and supplies. Ultimately, these actions generated a climate of uncertainty among investors and lenders that resulted in a relatively sparse inflow of foreign capital.

Argentina's diplomacy was also affected by contradictions resulting from a combination of a pragmatic awareness of the country's weakening economic and political position with the idiosyncratic nationalistic refusal to abandon regional power aspirations. When the "pragmatic" mood of accepting the unfavorable systemic and domestic circumstances prevailed, Argentine policymakers accepted U.S. leadership in the Cold War and sought a dependent association with the United States and other developed capitalist countries. When the "nationalistic" disposition was on the rise, they challenged U.S. hegemony and envisioned the creation of an autonomous industrial power. These confrontational policies obstructed some U.S. hemispheric initiatives and generated bilateral antagonism. In turn, the United States greeted the successive Argentine attempts at rapprochement with distrust as the cyclical character of these initiatives did not guarantee long term cooperation.

This fluctuating nature of Argentina's foreign policies was clearly shown during the 1966–1973 period of military rule. General Onganía's administration (1966–1971) emphasized Argentina's "Western and Christian" ascription, and its doctrine of "ideological frontiers" called for closer relations with the United States and rejected friendly ties with socialist and nonaligned countries. However, when this approach was not rewarded with the expected U.S. military and economic aid, it was abandoned, and General Lanusse's administration (1971–1973) pursued an approach including warmer relations with the socialist Chilean and revolutionary Peruvian governments, closer ties with Western Europe, the opening of diplomatic relations with the PRC, and trade agreements with the USSR.

In the strategic realm, although supporting the anticommunist stance heralded by the United States, the Argentine governments of the postwar period were reluctant to align themselves unconditionally behind the United States (Lanús 1984: 70–275). U.S. rebuffs of Argentina's requests for military aid and Argentine nationalistic proclivities led to the development of its own armament industry and the purchase and licensing to produce Western European military equipment. Meanwhile, different Argentine governments refused to join U.S.-sponsored multilateral initiatives, declining to send troops to Korea and to participate in the Inter-American Peace Force created after the U.S. invasion of the Dominican Republic. Moreover, Argentina developed its own nuclear program and refused to ratify the Non-Proliferation and Tlatelolco Treaties, procuring its nuclear supplies from Canada, West Germany, Switzerland, and the USSR. The return of Peronism to power in 1973 reinforced this trend: Argentina joined the Non-Aligned Movement; established relations with Cuba, North Korea, and Vietnam; forced U.S. subsidiaries to ignore the trade embargo against Cuba; implemented an economic and diplomatic "opening to the East"; and urged the reform of the Rio Treaty system (Moneta 1988; Camargo and Vásquez Ocampo 1988: 197–237).

However, the Argentine policymakers' awareness of the negative consequences of confronting the United States occasionally resulted in more cooperative attitudes including the acceptance of a U.S. permanent military mission and a military assistance accord, the ratification of the Rio Treaty and joining the Interamerican Defense Board, the training of military personnel in the United States and the Canal Zone, the participation in joint military exercises with U.S. forces, and the quarantine of Cuba during the missile crisis. After Perón's death in 1974, the administration of his widow, Isabel Perón, also tried to overcome a growing domestic economic and political crisis by establishing closer relations with the United States and other Western powers. Nevertheless, these initiatives were implemented expecting tangible returns in the form of U.S. economic and military assistance; when the anticipated gains did not materialize, Argentina's approach reverted to its usual state of distrust toward the United States.

AUTHORITARIANISM AND FOREIGN POLICY CONTRADICTIONS

The authoritarian regime (1976–1983) that replaced Isabel Perón's government represented the culmination of the inconsistency characteristic of Argentina's traditional foreign policies (Russell 1988; Camargo and Vásquez Ocampo 1988: 238–356). The military rulers pledged to preserve the country's "international position in the Western and Christian world, maintaining its capacity for self-determination and ensuring the strengthening of Argentina's presence in the international community" while implementing an economic program that called for free market and trade policies and the lifting of foreign exchange and capital regulations that led to a sudden increase in private financial inflows and imports and an explosive growth of the Argentine foreign debt and trade deficits.

However, while these ideological and economic elements favored close alignment with the West, the regime also contained strong nationalistic features that led to confrontation with the West (Escudé 1984, 1987). In the territorial disputes with neighboring Chile over the Beagle Channel and with Great Britain over the Falklands/Malvinas Islands, the authoritarian regime adopted an aggressive attitude and refused to make concessions. As the international demands to stop the violations of human rights multiplied, the military government also played the nationalistic card, denouncing these pressures as an inadmissible interference in domestic affairs that was offset by having easy access to private commercial bank lending and alternative weapons suppliers, establishing closer ties with governments confronting similar situations (El Salvador, Guatemala, Paraguay, South Africa) as well as with the USSR and Eastern European countries that overlooked the military's human rights abuses.

In the economic realm, however, Argentina remained highly dependent on its exports of grains and beef to improve its trade balance and pay its financial obligations. Faced with competition from other agricultural producers and with the protectionist policies implemented by the European Community (EC) and Japan, the Argentine government turned its attention toward the USSR, which became the main importer of Argentine agricultural products. In 1980, when the Carter administration imposed the grain embargo on the USSR following the invasion of Afghanistan, Argentina refused to join the embargo and contributed, through massive sales of grains, to facilitate the ultimate failure of the U.S. sanctions.

In the early 1980s, as a domestic financial debacle was compounded by the emerging debt crisis, Argentina made a short-lived attempt to realign itself behind the anticommunist strategy of the Reagan administration in the expectation of receiving economic and political support. The Argentine military agreed to coordinate its activities with the United States in Central America, obtaining covert funds to supply military training and equipment to the anti-Sandinista groups located in Honduras and to assist the Salvadoran military (Armony 1997). In exchange, the Reagan administration asked Congress to lift the sanctions against Argentina—although opposition to this proposal prevailed—and ordered its representatives before the multilateral credit institutions to support its loan applications.

However, this was not enough to overcome the acute socioeconomic crisis that threatened the stability of the authoritarian regime. Faced with this situation, the military rulers searched for an initiative that could divert attention and unify the Argentine people behind the government. In this regard, the recovery of the Falklands/Malvinas Islands, controlled since 1833 by Great Britain, represented a lasting nationalistic aspiration shared by the majority of the population. The occupation of the islands, implemented in April 1982, seemed to fulfill the military expectations as it was met with a surge of nationalistic pride that stifled most domestic opposition or dissent (Cardoso et al. 1992).

In planning the invasion, the military had expected that Great Britain and its allies would react with diplomatic protests but ultimately accept the occupation of the islands as a fait accompli. However, it rapidly became apparent that this was a complete miscalculation. Great Britain reacted forcefully and organized a military expedition to recover the islands. After a brief mediation attempt, the United States condemned the invasion, announced sanctions against Argentina, and granted the British logistic and diplomatic support. The Western European countries backed Great Britain and also imposed sanctions on Argentina. Most Latin American and Third World countries rhetorically supported Argentina but refused to become involved in the dispute. The Argentine government reacted to this fiasco with a drastic foreign policy turn, denouncing the Western powers' policies as colonialist, withdrawing its forces from Central America, suspending foreign debt payments, and canceling its participation in joint military maneuvers with the United States. Meanwhile, it established close relations with the Non-Aligned Movement and acknowledged the support offered by Nicaragua, Cuba, the USSR, and Libya throughout the crisis.

After the surrender of the Argentine forces, the military were forced to call elections in October 1983. Faced with a government in decomposition and retreat, neither the banks nor the multilateral institutions were interested in trying to reach permanent agreements that could be subsequently rejected by the elected administration. The Western governments came to a similar conclusion about the futility of trying to establish closer relations with the military regime and decided to wait until the civilian government's inauguration before taking any steps toward rapprochement.

DEMOCRATIZATION AND THE LIMITS OF FOREIGN POLICY HETERODOXY

In his inaugural speech, the newly elected president, Raúl Alfonsín, criticized the military regime's foreign policies and stated that his approach would be "based on the recognition of ideological pluralism and the strong condemnation of all forms of imperialism, colonialism and neocolonialism" and result in an "independent foreign policy that will grant priority to the insertion into Latin America and be projected into the nonaligned movement" (*Clarín*, December 11, 1983). Friendly relations with the Latin American countries and regional integration, particularly with Brazil and other neighboring nations, were considered the best means to overcome Argentina's international isolation and economic vulnerability. The territorial disputes with Chile and Great Britain would be solved peacefully through negotiations. Active participation in the Non-Aligned Movement would follow the principles of "respect for democracy and human rights" and "the original postulates of nonalignment that favored detente as the true guarantee of world peace." Concerning the relations with the United States, Alfonsín defined them as "asymmetric and difficult" and stated that improvement in the bilateral relations could take place if the Reagan administration revised its "discriminatory commercial practices" and modified "its behavior in Central America." Alfonsín announced that Argentina would follow a flexible foreign debt negotiation strategy but that it "would not accept measures resulting in more economic recession or . . . in poverty or misery for the population."

Alfonsín's minister of foreign relations, Dante Caputo, was successful in reestablishing with presidential backing the supremacy of the foreign relations ministry in shaping Argentina's international relations, with the exception of the debt negotiations, which became the responsibility of the

Ministry of Economics. In this context, Argentina's foreign policy became the combination of initiatives promoted by a popular president working in close collaboration with a foreign minister who tried to pursue a relatively pragmatic course, and an economics minister determined to follow a tough course in negotiations with the foreign lenders, developed countries' governments, and multilateral organizations.

Soon after Alfonsín's inauguration, the government fulfilled his promise to resolve peacefully the Beagle Channel dispute with Chile. A peace declaration proposed by the Vatican was signed and bilateral negotiations progressed rapidly until a final agreement was reached on the basis of a proposal presented by the pope's representative. The Treaty of Peace and Friendship granted sovereignty on the island in dispute to Chile but established a territorial demarcation in the maritime area that satisfied the Argentine demands for sovereignty on the Atlantic waters. The government overcame any domestic opposition by organizing a referendum in which 81 percent of the voters supported the agreement. After this result, the treaty was ratified by a slim majority in the senate, against Peronist opposition.

In contrast, the Falklands/Malvinas problem was not as tractable as the Beagle dispute (Cardoso et al. 1992: 349–75). The initial Argentine probes did not yield results, as the Argentine side insisted on the sovereignty issue, while the British demanded a formal cessation of hostilities and the reestablishment of diplomatic and commercial relations as preconditions for negotiations. In 1984, after a meeting between Argentine and British representatives in Switzerland broke down as a result of the intransigent positions held by both sides, Argentina was able to gather support in the General Assembly of the UN for a resolution calling for both sides to resume talks, but the British response to this call was negative.

In the economic sphere, the attempts made by the minister of economics, Bernardo Grinspun, to address the foreign debt issue from a position that rejected the imposition of stringent stabilization and adjustment programs were unsuccessful. In January 1984, the government announced a temporary suspension of payments until mid-June and took a hard line in the negotiations, with creditors expecting that the threat of default would compel them to offer better terms of repayment (Bouzas and Keifman 1990). The viability of this "debt brinkmanship" depended, however, on the government's capacity to make its threat to the lenders credible by establishing a united front of Latin American debtors, gaining support from some developed countries' governments, and securing a trade surplus. In Latin America, Argentina tried to strengthen ties with other debtor countries promoting meetings such as the ones in Cartagena (June 1984) and Mar del Plata (September 1984) to demand lower interest rates, easing of IMF conditionality terms, and more favorable treatment for their exports. However, the largest debtors—Mexico, Brazil, and Venezuela—rejected the calls for joint action in the expectation that they would obtain better terms negotiating bilaterally. The European governments refused to support Argentina and made an agreement with the IMF and the banks a prerequisite for economic aid. In commercial terms, the Soviet Union remained the most important customer of Argentine grains (40 percent of the total) but refused to increase its purchases, preventing the trade surplus from growing.

This failure of the international debt strategy, combined with growing domestic difficulties, finally forced the administration to follow a more pragmatic course, attempting to reconcile the quest for economic and political stability and the recognition of the external constraints imposed on the country by establishing cooperative relations with the international financial community and the developed countries to obtain the necessary financial and investment flows. In early 1985, Juan V. Sourrouille was appointed minister of economics and announced the implementation of an economic stabilization and adjustment program, the "Austral Plan," that attended some of the demands of the foreign actors, including cuts in public expenditures, raises in indirect taxes and public services tariffs, and constraints on the growth of the money supply. A new debt negotiation approach was adopted that continued to reject demands for a sudden liberalization and opening of the economy but accepted reductions in export and import taxes and privatization of state-owned enterprises. The plan was welcomed by the United States, the IMF, and the World Bank, but financial support was conditioned to the introduction of deeper structural reforms including the elimination of import barriers, exchange controls, and subsidies, and deregulation of economic activities (Russell 1987: 24–26).

Meanwhile, acknowledging that this austerity program would generate some negative domestic reactions, the Alfonsín administration could not afford to give the opposition other rallying points by completely ignoring nationalistic demands. Continuous participation in the Non-Aligned Movement was seen as a means to appease the domestic opposition that opposed the rapprochement with the United States. Similarly, though it created tensions in the relations with the Western powers, the administration could not renounce its claim of sovereignty over the Falklands/Malvinas or support the U.S. intervention in Central America without being accused of acquiescing to external pressures in matters of sovereignty and non intervention. Thus, Argentina participated in the creation of the support group for Contadora (with Brazil, Peru, and Uruguay) and called for a peaceful resolution of the Central American crisis while supporting the Arias Peace Plan. In 1986, a joint meeting of the Contadora and Support groups in Rio de Janeiro led to the creation of the "Permanent Mechanism of Consultation and Political Concertation" (called the Rio Group) that organized annual presidential summits aimed to strengthen democratic institutions in the region and adopt common policies on trade and financial relations with the developed countries, environmental issues, drug traffic, economic integration, and security crises (Yopo 1991). Regarding Cuba, Argentina refused to support the U.S. motions at the UN Human Rights Commission demanding the investigation and condemnation of human rights abuses in Cuba, stating that its strong condemnatory language prejudged the case. In relation to Panama, Argentina denounced the coup orchestrated by Panamanian strongman, Manuel Noriega, but opposed military intervention and offered to mediate in the U.S.-Panamanian dispute.

Simultaneously, the Alfonsín administration strongly favored the development of closer economic and political relations with Brazil (Hirst 1989, 1990). Between 1985 and 1989, Alfonsín and the Brazilian president, José Sarney, moved toward the elimination of old rivalries and cooperation in areas such as economic integration, nuclear technology, and diplomatic initiatives. Successive summits established the basis for joint nuclear and biotechnological research; cooperation in sectors such as capital goods, the automobile industry, and food production; creation of binational enterprises and investment funds; and inclusion of Uruguay and Paraguay as new partners in the integration process. In the nuclear and military fields, agreements were signed calling for the mutual supply of enriched uranium, reaffirming both countries' rights to develop nuclear programs for peaceful purposes, and planning the joint production of military aircraft.

Argentina's policy toward Western Europe did not deviate from its original purposes of obtaining economic and political support and was helped in attaining these goals by the initial success of the Austral Plan and the agreement with the banks and IMF in stabilizing the economy. In particular, cooperation agreements were signed with Spain and Italy in which these two countries offered Argentina development credits and included an unprecedented clause that made cooperation conditional on the maintenance of Argentina's democratic regime.

The Falklands/Malvinas dispute, however, remained unresolved (Cardoso et al. 1992: 377–90). Argentina's demand that negotiations on all issues, including sovereignty, should start simultaneously were rejected by the British, who insisted on a formal cessation of hostilities and the reestablishment of diplomatic ties as preconditions for any talks. In 1987, in retaliation for Argentina's concession of fishing rights to the Soviets in the waters surrounding the islands, Great Britain established a 150-mile exclusion zone. The Alfonsín administration was only able to obtain some symbolic victories in the UN General Assembly, where calls for bilateral negotiations on all aspects of the controversy were approved by large majorities.

In the Non-Aligned Movement, Argentina established closer relations with India and Yugoslavia, trying to promote a return to the original principles of the movement, gather support in its confrontation with Great Britain, and create conditions for international peace. Concerning nuclear disarmament, Argentina played an active role in the creation of the Group of Six for Peace and Disarmament (with India, Mexico, Tanzania, Greece, and Sweden) that called for a global process of reduction in nuclear weapons proliferation.

Argentine relations with the USSR remained focused on economic issues. Ratification of a five-year grain supply agreement, signing of fishing agreements, the concession of Soviet credits for purchases and public work projects, and the discussion of possibilities of expanding and diversifying bilateral trade were complemented with exchanges of notes and visits in which broader diplomatic issues were discussed. Bilateral discussions were centered on the need to promote new types of cooperation—joint enterprises and mixed companies—and to increase bilateral trade, allowing for the reduction of the Soviet trade deficit and the diversification of Argentine exports.

It was in the economic sphere that this foreign policy strategy of promoting economic growth and political stability by combining a closer association with the United States and Western Europe with a moderately nonaligned diplomatic course, closer ties with the Latin American countries, and adequate relations with the USSR began to unravel. The initial success of the Austral Plan was followed by growing difficulties as the expected stability and growth did not materialize. While inflation, recession, and unemployment increased, successive economic packages aimed to open and deregulate the economy, privatize public enterprises, reduce the size of the state, and cut public expenditures failed to solve the problems. In 1988, the Bush administration's announcement of the Brady Plan calling for reductions in the value and interests of the debt and more flexible IMF lending policies raised some hopes, but it rapidly became clear that Argentina would not be one of the countries initially favored by the plan and that any economic relief would not come before the 1989 presidential election. Finally, in early 1989, a frantic run on the dollar depleted the Central Bank reserves and led to a hyperinflationary explosion, shortages and riots that facilitated the victory of the Peronist candidate, Carlos S. Menem, in the May presidential elections and forced a premature transfer of power in July 1989.

ECONOMIC LIBERALIZATION, POLITICAL PRAGMATISM, AND THE CULMINATION OF WESTERN ALIGNMENT

Faced with a dramatic economic crisis, Menem decided to discard the nationalistic, nonaligned, and autarchic elements of the Peronist "third position" and follow a course aimed at promoting Argentina's reinsertion into the world capitalist system through liberal economic policies and close alignment with the West. Accordingly, Menem's foreign policy goals were to promote closer links with the United States, reestablish normal relations with

Great Britain, remove any remaining problems in the relations with the EC, maintain the policy of integration with Brazil and other South American countries, and modify any other policies—nuclear, military, or commercial—that could hinder the development of closer economic and political relations with the advanced nations and neighboring countries (Centro de Estudios en Relaciones Internacionales de Rosario [CERIR] 1994; Escudé 1997).

The appointment of Domingo Cavallo—a Harvard-trained economist, former president of the Central Bank during the military regime, and Peronist representative since 1987—as minister of foreign relations reasserted these goals. Cavallo (1982) believed that Argentina's economic problems were the result of the existence of a "socialism without plan and capitalism without market," and he advocated an outwardly oriented liberal strategy of growth instead of the traditional Peronist approach based on the expansion of the domestic market.

The continuous feud with Great Britain over the Falklands/Malvinas was seen as one the main impediments for this project as it hindered the establishment of closer relations with the United States and the European countries. To remove this obstacle, the ban on British imports was lifted in 1989 before Argentine and British representatives met in Madrid to start bilateral negotiations. The Madrid talks led to a number of agreements, including the reestablishment of consular relations, the lifting of remaining economic sanctions, and the opening of air and maritime communications. The issue of sovereignty was circumvented by stating that these agreements would not affect the sovereign rights asserted by both sides. In exchange for Argentina's formal declaration of an end to the hostilities, Great Britain offered to withdraw its objections against closer relations between Argentina and the European Economic Community (EEC). The negotiations culminated in February 1990 with the reestablishment of bilateral diplomatic relations and the elimination of the British exclusion zone around the Falklands/Malvinas Islands.

At the same time, the establishment of friendlier relations with the United States became a key priority for the Menem administration as the president expected that these ties would help to overcome the economic crisis. Menem's populist rhetoric during the presidential campaign had generated misgivings in the United States, and once in power, he tried to dispel them by openly championing a policy of close alignment. In his first visit to the United States, Menem met with President George H. W. Bush and declared his support for the U.S. war against drugs, promised to honor Argentina's debt obligations, and supported the restoration of democracy in Panama. Back in Argentina, Menem refused to condemn the U.S. invasion of Panama and announced his intention to accept nonproliferation safeguards on the Argentine nuclear program, discontinue the Condor II missile project, and lower its profile in the Non-Aligned Movement (Russell 1990). During the Persian Gulf crisis, Argentina voted in the UN in favor of the U.S.-sponsored war, supporting the sanctions imposed against Iraq and becoming the only Latin American country that sent ships and troops to join the coalition (García 1992). This presidential decision was severely criticized by domestic opponents who saw it as a violation of Argentina's traditional neutrality but it helped to cement good relations with the United States. Support for Menem was clearly shown in December 1990 when President Bush, arriving in Buenos Aires a few hours after the end of a military uprising, congratulated Menem for his victory over the rebels and promised to support Argentina in its foreign debt negotiations.

In 1991, amid growing economic difficulties, Menem decided to heighten the application of free market policies and deepen the country's Western alignment. Cavallo was appointed minister of economics, and the Argentine ambassador to the United States, Guido Di Tella, became the new foreign relations minister. Di Tella strongly advocated the enhancing of the existing foreign policies having stated that Argentina "wants to belong to the Western club. I want to have a cordial relation with the United States and not a platonic love. We want carnal relations [*sic*] with the United States [because] it will be beneficial for us" (Bologna 1991: 58).

Cavallo's economic program—the "Convertibility Plan"—satisfied the demands of the United States, banks, and multilateral institutions by completing the trend toward economic liberalization through the introduction of a new currency freely convertible in dollars at a fixed parity rate of one for one, further privatization of public enterprises, acceptance of the Brady Plan as the means to reduce foreign debt, taxation reform, deregulation, and further opening of the economy. These economic policies succeeded in accomplishing some impressive results: Inflation was contained, the economy grew at a significant rate, privatization moved forward, the rate of exchange remained unchanged, and capital inflows increased. At the same time, however, the program reinforced the trends toward regressive income distribution and concentration of wealth, facilitated imports and generated growing trade deficits, and promoted deindustrialization and unemployment.

Economic liberalization and a deeper insertion into the Western capitalist world were presented by the Menem administration as the only viable strategy to promote Argentina's development considering not only the failure of previous economic policies but also the contemporary disintegration of the communist bloc, the collapse of the USSR, the turn toward market reforms in the PRC, and the crumbling of socialist and populist experiences in other parts of the world. This trend was seen as connected to the surge of transnationalization and interdependence that prompted the emergence of a global capitalist political economy in which the role of the states was severely limited by their growing incapacity to control or modify the nature and the outcomes of free market interactions that affect economic, social, and political developments within and across national boundaries. In Latin America, this pressure for the application of neoliberal programs was intensified by the existence of the so-called Washington Consensus that advocated fiscal discipline, elimination of subsidies, broad and moderate taxation, market-determined interest and exchange rates, trade and foreign investment liberalization, privatization of state enterprises, deregulation, and respect for private property rights. From the strategic perspective, the collapse of the USSR and the emergence of the United States as the only remaining superpower created a situation that denied to Argentina the chance of using relations with the Soviet bloc to counterbalance U.S. dominance and follow a nonaligned course. These transformations were perceived by the Argentine government as crucial and interpreted by Di Tella as generating circumstances in which "the total defeat of the communist system" and the "spectacular preeminence of the United States" left for "a country [such as Argentina] that could only aspire at a second or third rank" position in Latin America only one option: to try to develop a "preferential relationship" with the United States (República Argentina 1991).

From this perspective, the main objective of Argentina's foreign policy became the elimination of any remaining tensions with the United States, including those related to missile production, nuclear proliferation, U.S. drug patents, obstacles affecting the activities of foreign companies, and the participation in the war against drugs. In all these respects, the Menem administration policies complied with U.S. demands. The development of the Condor II missile had already been stalled but had not been discarded in the expectation of obtaining U.S. consent for its production and utilization for peaceful purposes (Barcelona and Villalonga 1992). When the United States refused to accept this alternative, Cavallo and then Di Tella advocated the cancellation of the project against the opposition of the military. Finally, Menem ordered the total dismantling of the program and the destruction of the missile components. Concerning nuclear proliferation, the Argentine government negotiated with Brazil the establishment of a joint accounting and control system to be applied to all nuclear activities to prevent the use of materials for nuclear weapons or explosions, then together with Brazil accepted International Atomic Energy Agency (IAEA) safeguards and supervision, and finally ratified the Tlatelolco Treaty. The acceptance of U.S. medicine patents was more difficult to attain as the Argentine pharmaceutical laboratories opposed it and lobbied Congress to reject a bill sent by the administration. Concerning drug traffic, several officials linked to the president's family who had been accused of involvement in the laundering of drug receipts were removed from office as the Menem administration announced its intention to cooperate with the U.S. drug enforcement agencies.

The U.S. response to these Argentine deferential policies included rhetorical compliments as well as some limited tangible support. Among the latter, in December 1992, the backing given by the U.S. administration facilitated the signing of a final agreement with the banks to reschedule the foreign debt. Finally, in 1993, Argentina entered the Brady foreign debt reduction plan, accepting an agreement that resulted in a reduction of the size of the debt and its partial rescheduling for a thirty-year term.

The inauguration of Bill Clinton as president in 1993 did not modify the nature of the bilateral relationship. During a visit to the United States in June 1993, Menem defined the relations as "excellent," while Clinton praised Argentina's positive role in the international arena and stated his support for agricultural trade liberalization, promising to consider the impact of U.S. agricultural export subsidies on the Argentine economy (*Clarín*, June 30; July 1, 1993). Menem's presidential reelection in 1995 contributed to reinforce the close ties with the United States. In the following years, the bilateral ties remained extremely cordial, with only occasional disagreements focused mostly on issues such as U.S. trade barriers affecting some Argentine exports and the existence of Argentine governmental corruption affecting American companies. The trend toward close cooperation culminated in visits by Clinton to Argentina and Menem to the United States in 1997 and 1998, respectively, which resulted in a series of announcements ranging from the naming of Argentina as a major non-NATO ally of the United States to the elimination of visa requirements for Argentine citizens and the reopening of the U.S. market to Argentine beef exports.

In the Western Hemisphere, Argentina did not challenge U.S. policies, following Di Tella's dictum of avoiding rhetorical involvements in issues that did not affect the national interests. However, the traditional Argentine reluctance to criticize other Latin American governments' domestic policies was replaced in some cases by a determination to support U.S. policies. In the Cuban case, Argentina broke ranks with the Rio Group and supported condemning human rights violations and demanding on site inspections by the UN Committee on Human Rights, while Menem criticized the authoritarianism of Castro's regime. In the case of Haiti, Argentina strongly condemned the military coup that overthrew President Jean Bertrand Aristide and supported the application of sanctions in an effort to reestablish democracy. After the appointment of the former foreign relations minister, Caputo, as the UN secretary's special envoy to Haiti, Argentina backed his attempts to reach a negotiated solution and, when this failed, joined the embargo decreed by the Security Council and supported joint military actions to remove the military from power.

Concerning the relations with Brazil and the process of economic integration in the Southern Cone, the Argentine government intensified its efforts to establish new institutional mechanisms for the creation of a regional common market. Menem and the Brazilian president, Collor de Mello, invited Paraguay and Uruguay to join the Southern Cone Common Market (MERCOSUR). In March 1991, a final agreement was reached between the four countries on the nature and mechanisms of the integration process to be completed in 1994 with the establishment of a regional free trade area. The cooperative character of the relations with Brazil was reaffirmed with the establishment of the joint accounting and control system of nuclear materials and the creation of the bilateral agency in charge of its application as well as by the joint acceptance by both countries of the IAEA safeguards and supervision (Carasales 1992). The impeachment and removal of Collor de Mello did not affect the cordial nature of the relationship, which continued under the new Brazilian president, Itamar Franco, and his elected successor, Fernando Henrique Cardoso. However, Brazil's political economic fluctuations affected the bilateral economic relations as successive Brazilian devaluations favored its exports vis-à-vis Argentina and contributed to generate trade imbalances, slowing down the integration process and hindering the possibility of incorporating new members to MERCOSUR, such as Chile and Bolivia.

Argentina's policy toward Western Europe was focused on establishing normal ties with the United Kingdom and trying to gain European economic support. New agreements were signed with Great Britain that reduced the military presence in the area and promoted economic cooperation. Argentine authorities referred for the first time to the likelihood of arbitration as a way to resolve the dispute and stated the need to consider the "wishes" and not only the "interests" of the Falkland islanders in order to reach an acceptable solution. In relation to the rest of the European Community, Argentine interest was focused in obtaining the participation of private and public enterprises in the process of privatization and reactivation of the economy while trying to modify the protectionist and subsidy policies that affected its exports. In this regard, the Menem administration was relatively successful in attracting European participation in the privatization of some public enterprises but less so in removing European trade barriers and agricultural subsidies.

Regarding the developing world, Menem argued that in the new world order, there was no room for the Third World, and Di Tella called for Argentina's withdrawal from the Non-Aligned Movement. Although there was some domestic resistance to this proposal, in September 1991, Argentina announced its exit from the movement, denouncing the fact that its proposals supporting freedom of the press, respect for human rights, and democratization had been rejected in the Ghana meeting (*Clarín*, September 19, 1991). The Argentine government argued that in the post–Cold War era, the Non-Aligned Movement had become superfluous as the UN and the Security Council were the most appropriate forums for international cooperation.

Concerning the relations with Russia and other Soviet successor states, the Menem administration recognized the Commonwealth of Independent States, established diplomatic relations with several newly independent republics, and declared its interest in maintaining cooperative ties with the Yeltsin administration in Russia (Zubelzú de Bacigalupo 1999). However, the bilateral economic relations declined abruptly as the new states experienced foreign currency shortages and cut down their imports of foodstuffs and consumer goods. These circumstances convinced the Argentine policymakers of the impossibility of establishing profitable ties, at least in the short term, and reinforced the trend toward closer relations with the United States, Western developed countries, and South American nations.

In the late 1990s, in part as a reflection of the Mexican and Asian financial crises, Argentina experienced a severe capital flight that led to a steep recession and a dramatic rise in unemployment. In this context, the Menem administration's inability to promote recovery, reduce unemployment, and eliminate corruption affected the Peronist electoral chances. Meanwhile, an Alliance composed of the Radical Party and the center-left Front for a Country in Solidarity (FREPASO) gained popular support promising to preserve democracy and promote economic growth while fighting corruption. Fernando de la Rúa, a Radical center-right politician, became the candidate of the Alliance and won the 1999 presidential elections by a respectable margin.

However, after his inauguration, de la Rúa implemented a foreign policy that did not differ in any substantial aspect from the one implemented by Menem. The new administration stated its intention to maintain close ties with the United States, particularly advocating the establishment of a hemispheric free trade area and supporting the U.S. positions in relation to Cuba, while emphasizing the country's trustworthiness as a permanent ally of the Western powers. Throughout his two years as president, de la Rúa's foreign policies became ever more closely aligned with the U.S. positions in the expectation of gaining economic support to overcome the crisis and political backing to remain in power. As the economic debacle continued, de la Rúa attempted to solve the crisis by deepening the application of free market adjustment policies, including sharp budget cuts, labor market flexibility, and further deregulation and tariff reductions. A political consequence of these measures was the collapse of the ruling Alliance as the FREPASO members resigned from the cabinet and refused to support the administration in the congress. In a last desperate attempt to control the situation, de la Rúa appointed Cavallo as minister of economics, but his attempt to avoid a devaluation, balance the budget through salary and pension cuts, and stop a run on the banks by restricting the public's access to checking and savings accounts utterly failed. These measures led to an explosion of popular discontent but did not result in any favorable reaction by the IMF and the

United States, which demanded more radical structural reforms before offering any relief.

Finally, amid growing turmoil, de la Rúa resigned in December 2001, and, after a series of frustrated attempts to stabilize the situation, Eduardo Duhalde, a former Peronist vice president, governor, and defeated presidential candidate in 1999, was appointed to complete the presidential term. The Duhalde administration tried to solve the economic crisis reaching an agreement with the IMF but found it extremely difficult to impose the measures demanded by the IMF with the support of the United States and other developed countries without generating further domestic upheaval. However, it emphasized that there was no intention of modifying the course of Argentina's foreign policy, neither by abandoning the neoliberal economic approach nor by moving back to some kind of nonaligned position that could result in confrontations with the United States.

THE TRANSFORMATION OF ARGENTINA'S FOREIGN POLICY: BALANCE AND PROSPECTS

Since the 1950s, the decline in Argentina of the import substitution industrialization model and the collapse of the populist experience marked the beginning of a series of political economic experiments aimed to reestablish conditions for economic growth, social peace, political stability, and reinsertion into the world in the new circumstances created by the Cold War and consolidation of the U.S. hegemony. Different attempts made by democratic and authoritarian governments to attain these goals failed due to adverse international trends and the effective opposition mounted by domestic actors.

The 1976–1983 authoritarian regime attempted to accomplish them by combining the use of domestic repression with the implementation of neoliberal programs aimed at disarticulating this opposition while generating the conditions for the establishment of a liberal export-oriented economy and a stable conservative political regime. In the foreign policy realm, this approach called for a closer alignment with the West in order to obtain the political and economic support necessary to complete this transformation. However, as it became apparent that the authoritarian regime's entreaties were not enough to stop the growing pressure concerning human rights or to obtain the capital flows required to stimulate economic growth, the military rulers began to pursue a contradictory foreign policy course that included nationalistic rejections of Western pressures and an economic and diplomatic rapprochement to the USSR and other communist countries. These foreign policy contradictions culminated in the early 1980s, after the coming of the debt crisis and the emergence of internal turmoil, in the ill-fated attempt to gain popular support by occupying the Falklands/Malvinas and engaging in a confrontation with Great Britain, the United States, and the rest of the Western developed world. This adventure ended in complete defeat and forced the military to transfer power to a civilian elected government leaving behind a legacy of domestic crisis and international isolation.

After some vacillations, the emerging elected administration turned to policies that, without eliminating the democratic features of the regime, represented an effort to overcome these problems through the application of increasingly liberal economic policies and the restoration and consolidation of closer relations with the Western developed countries. The Alfonsín administration concluded that most domestic problems, including stagnation, inflation, debt crisis, social tensions, and relative weakness of the fledgling democratic system, could not be solved without relying on a considerable degree of external support. In turn, the international conditions, characterized by a global trend toward free markets and free trade and the privatization of financial flows combined with the decline of the Soviet bloc and the end of the Cold War, seemed to require a deeper insertion into the world capitalist economy. To a large extent these circumstances indicated that the influence of the international systemic factors had become overwhelming vis-à-vis the diminishing capacity of the Argentine domestic economic, political, and social structures and actors to promote the implementation of nationalistic, unorthodox, and nonaligned foreign policies and the ability of individual decision makers to formulate and pursue idiosyncratic initiatives.

From this perspective, the Alfonsín administration represented a transitional stage in which the clash between the remnants of the old national and idiosyncratic drives and the ever–more powerful systemic pressures was still intense, although the capacity of the former to persist ebbed as time went on. The growing domestic crisis and the narrowing range of international options led to the application of increasingly liberal economic plans and the acceptance of orthodox stabilization and adjustment programs demanded by the multilateral credit organizations, private banks, and Western developed governments. A similar course was followed in foreign policy, passing from the initial attempts to implement a heterodox and somewhat independent approach to the foreign debt, Central American crisis, nonalignment, nuclear development, and the redefinition of the relations with Latin America, the United States, and the third world to the adoption of a lower international profile and a growing alignment with the United States and the Western countries.

However, the hesitant course followed by the Alfonsín administration fell short of completing the neoliberal restructuring and international reinsertion of Argentina. It was the Menem administration that implemented a more radical program of liberal economic restructuring and foreign policy realignment in an attempt to overcome the acute economic and social crisis of the late 1980s. At the idiosyncratic level, Menem adopted a pragmatic, Western-oriented approach that discarded any proclivity to pursue the nationalistic and nonaligned policies practiced in the past. At this same level, the ministerial appointments of Cavallo and Di Tella—both strong supporters of the neoliberal economic strategy and of Argentina's close alignment with the United States—cemented the policy shift. The statements and decisions made by Menem and his ministers repeatedly showed their determination to follow this course and to prevent any tensions in the relations with the United States. Many of their foreign policy initiatives were severely criticized by the opposition and even Peronist politicians, who denounced them as violations of Argentina's traditional principles of sovereignty, nonintervention, and neutrality, but the administration ignored all these negative reactions.

The systemic transformations simultaneously occurring in the rest of the world reinforced this trend as most countries moved in the same direction as Argentina, adopting neoliberal economic programs and pursuing closer relations with the Western developed countries. Friendlier relations with Brazil and economic integration with neighboring countries into MERCOSUR remained part of Argentina's foreign policy strategy due to the expected economic and political benefits that these ties generated, but they were linked—and to some extent, subordinated—to the maintenance of the neoliberal economic program and the close alignment with the West, particularly with the United States.

The end of the Menem administration, the rise and fall of the de la Rúa administration, the crisis of late 2001, and the coming to power of Duhalde did not alter Argentina's foreign policy approach. The completion of the country's process of neoliberal economic restructuring and the existence of international economic and strategic conditions favorable to capitalist globalization and U.S. hegemony have narrowed the range of foreign policy options that could be explored by Argentine policymakers. These international systemic transformations have converged with neoliberal structural domestic changes and the emergence of a group of supportive policymakers, increasing the likelihood that Argentina's international policies will remain unaltered in the future, unless some radical domestic and international transformations create the opportunity for a substantial shift in its Western-aligned foreign policy course.

DISCUSSION QUESTIONS

1. In your view, what factors contribute to explaining the contradictory features of Argentina's foreign policies during most of the twentieth cen-

tury? What relative importance do you assign to idiosyncratic variables, domestic factors, and systemic influences in generating the fluctuations of Argentine foreign policies. Why?

2. In your view, what are the main reasons why Argentina's foreign policy has followed in recent years a more stable and coherent pattern? What has been the importance of political leaders' personalities and preferences? What has been the impact of domestic developments such as democratization and economic decline? What has been the influence of changes in the international system, such as the end of the Cold War and the rise of economic globalization, on Argentina's international policies?
3. In your opinion, is the current Argentine foreign policy of Western alignment, neoliberal economic policies, and close strategic relations with the United States a trend that will not be modified in the near future as long as the international systemic circumstances remain unaltered? Or do you believe this is a temporary approach that will soon be abandoned if Argentina's domestic crisis continues and new leaders come to power?

16

Paraguay

The Legacy of Authoritarianism

Frank O. Mora

As scholars have often noted, democratization is very much a path-dependent process. This chapter suggests that the structure and nature of the democratization process shape foreign policy decision making and priorities. The path of Paraguay's transition *from above and within*—provoked by a crisis of internal decomposition in the sultanistic regime of President Alfredo Stroessner—allowed many institutional and structural vestiges of the regime to survive and shape the foreign policy of Paraguay's incomplete and precarious democracy. Moreover, Paraguay's strong *caudillo* (strongman) heritage, exaggerated personalism, and weak institutionalization have led to the dominance of the executive in all areas of public policy (Lezcano Claude 1989). Therefore, presidentialism or the overwhelming influences and autonomy of the executive is an important legacy and determinant of Paraguay foreign policy during the authoritarian and democratic periods.

Despite democratization, Paraguay's institutions and bureaucracy are still permeated by patrimonial and clientelist networks. Personal networks and membership in the ruling Colorado party remain the sine qua non of public sector employment. The Ministry of Foreign Affairs, like many other organs of the state bureaucracy, lacks the professionalism, modernization, and rationalization needed to become an efficient actor in foreign policy formulation and decision making. It remains stranded in the improvisation and institutional deficiency of the previous authoritarian regime, highly dependent on the whims and initiatives of the Palacio de Lopez. In other words, the incompetence of the foreign ministry resulted in a more executive-dominated foreign policy decision-making process. As reflected in the analysis of personalism in Latin America small state foreign policy, "weak countries with limited foreign policy bureaucracies provide ample opportunities for individual leaders to leave their mark" (Hey 1998: 112). This is certainly the case of Paraguay with the important caveat that after 1993, when the executives were weak and increasingly illegitimate, foreign policy was left in disarray because of the vacuum at the top. Therefore, because of the structural continuity and immobilism of Paraguay's "protected democracy" and its continuing status as a small, underdeveloped, and dependent state, the determinants that conditioned and shaped Paraguay's foreign policy during the Stroessner era have not changed dramatically in the post–Cold War, postauthoritarian period.

This excessive presidentialism and weak institutionalization and participation of society and the state bureaucracy in foreign policy does not serve the national interests of democratic regimes, particularly if the executive branch is itself weak and discredited. This was the case under the administrations of President Raul Cubas Grau (1998–1999) and President Luis Gonzalez Macchi (1999–present), who were not able, because of political crises and weak leadership skills, to fill the large vacuum of presidential leadership needed to formulate and implement public policies. As a result, Paraguayan foreign policy was left ill defined and in disarray as neither state organs nor society had the capacity, interests, or practice of engaging in matters related to international relations and Paraguay's foreign policy interests. Therefore, Paraguay's foreign policy has suffered from, at best, improvisation or, at worst, inaction.

Finally, in addition to these idiosyncratic and national characteristics of Paraguayan foreign policy, important systemic or external determinants are also of tremendous value in explaining Paraguayan foreign policy. The literature on small state foreign policy has emphasized that because of their weak political and economic power base, small states are vulnerable and constrained in their behavior by the structure of the international system (Elman 1995). The international environment is not only an important determinant of Paraguayan foreign policy but is, as with many small states, a critical factor in the consolidation of a regime type. Whether it is the Argentina–Brazil subregional rivalry, the Cold War and U.S. policy, or the globalization of democracy and markets, Paraguay's external behavior (and regime type) is strongly influenced and dependent on power relations and paradigmatic changes in the international system.

This chapter will examine Paraguay's foreign policy during the Cold War (authoritarian period) and post–Cold War (democratic transition) periods, focusing on patterns of change and continuity between both eras of the international system and regimes. The analytical section of the chapter will use James Rosenau's (1966) set of explanatory variables of foreign policy (i.e., levels of analysis) to answer the question "What explains foreign policy behavior and change in Paraguay?"

COLD WAR FOREIGN POLICY TRENDS IN PARAGUAY

Since the end of the Triple Alliance War (1870), when Paraguay's economy was decimated and sovereignty compromised, Asunción has been extremely vulnerable and dependent on external forces and actors that often penetrated and shaped the country's political and economic system. As a result, Paraguay suffered from marginalization, economic underdevelopment, and foreign intervention. Between 1870 and 1954, Paraguay was characterized by staggering levels of underdevelopment and economic dependence and high levels of political instability, specifically military coups and dictatorships, civil wars, and conflict with Bolivia. Political instability (constant presidential changes and social turmoil) and economic dependence impeded Paraguay from developing a coherent foreign policy that served the interests of the nation rather than that of a very small and narrow elite and/or external hegemon (i.e., Argentina) (Mora 1993).

The personalist-patrimonial regime of President Alfredo Stroessner (1954–1989) put an end to the instability that had plagued Paraguay for decades. An important factor that helped to strengthen and consolidate the Stroessner regime was the international environment (i.e., Cold War). The regime lacked any ideology other than xenophobic nationalism and a virulent anticommunism. Stroessner identified with the West in the Cold War and wasted no time in declaring the regime's full support for the Truman Doctrine. As a result of Stroessner's strong support for U.S. containment policy, Asunción received political support/legitimacy and invaluable material support in the form of military aid and economic and financial assistance that helped prop up his regime (Mora 1997). International factors have historically impacted Paraguayan politics and, in the case of Stroessner external actors such as Brazil and the United States, contributed to the regime's longevity, at least until the mid-1980s.

Fernando Masi (1991b: 3) characterized Alfredo Stroessner's foreign policy during much of the regime as "benign isolation." This approach consisted of discriminating and diversifying economic and commercial relations with select states, necessary in overcoming Paraguay's geopolitical prisonality (and in strengthening his domestic position), while maintaining a "low profile" in order to minimize criticism and pass unnoticed under the façade of "representative democracy." In other words, the Stroessner regime did not seek an active role in world affairs for fear that it would attract attention, resulting in pressures against his regime, but made sure to solidify bilateral ties with states that could directly help to sustain his regime. Conveniently, political instability and dictatorship in many of Paraguay's neighbors and U.S. preoccupation with communism in the region diverted attention from Stroessner's repressive but stable regime. President Alfredo Stroessner, the dominant foreign policymaking actor, was skillful in taking advantage of an ideological and polarized international system (i.e., the Cold War) that proved propitious for the type of "ideological and praetorian-caudillist" foreign policy that helped him to strengthen and consolidate his patrimonial regime.[1]

At this point, it is also important that we briefly discuss Stroessner's principal foreign policy objectives. First, as mentioned earlier, Stroessner wanted to maintain a low-profile foreign policy to avoid undue attention to the repressive nature of the regime while seeking political and economic support and legitimacy from key allies: Argentina, Brazil, and the United States. Second, he strove to enhance and balance political, economic, and commercial ties with the United States and the two powerful neighbors. In addition to attracting much-needed capital and aid for development and modernization, this pendulum policy would diminish Paraguay's vulnerabilities. Third, Stroessner sought to expand trade and contact with regional organizations and ideologically sympathetic or neutral regimes, especially South Korea, Taiwan, South Africa, and Japan. This not only diversified Paraguay's external relations but provided alternative sources of economic and financial support for development. Fourth, his administration wanted to maintain a strong anticommunist stance in regional and global organizations consistent and supportive of the internal objectives of the national security doctrine regime. Finally, his foreign policy tried to support national and regional integration and cooperation through multinational communication and transportation projects.[2] In sum, if there was one overriding goal of Paraguay's foreign policy that encapsulates these objectives, it is that Stroessner sought (with considerable success) to obtain the support of anticommunist external actors needed to sustain the stability of the regime.

A significant external-determining factor of Paraguayan foreign policy was the Cold War and Stroessner's relationship with the United States.[3] Stroessner seized and internalized the opportunity offered by the Cold War to align his regime and foreign policy closely with the United States. Once again, foreign policy and security is not defined by a set of national interests or priorities but by the prerogatives and interests of Stroessner and his regime. Stroessner and his close advisers, particularly Foreign Minister Raul Sapena Pastor (1956–1976), understood that Washington's economic and diplomatic support could be counted on if Paraguay became a fearless defender of U.S. containment policy. Upon assuming power, Stroessner's regime immediately identified with the West. It adopted the U.S. National Security Doctrine that emphasized the use of security and armed forces to counter all internal and external "communist threats"—the lever used by many Latin American dictators to suppress all opposition, while ensuring U.S. political and economic support, critical to extending the life of the regime (Yore 1992). Stroessner became a vociferous anticommunist, following the U.S. position on all matters in return for aid and legitimacy (Fernández Estigarribia and Simon 1987: 20; Abente 1988: 82–87). In addition to voting consistently with the United States in the United Nations and the Organization of American States (OAS), Stroessner offered, as he said during a meeting with President Eisenhower in 1956, "Paraguayans and land" (Miranda 1987: 45). In 1965, Asunción supported and offered troops to the U.S. intervention in the Dominican Republic, and in 1968, he offered to provide the United States with troops to fight in Vietnam (Hoyer 1975: 296). In terms of "land," in 1955, Defense Minister Herminio Morinigo told State Department officials that the Stroessner government would sign an agreement permitting the United States to build an air force base in Paraguay for the continent's defense (Miranda 1987: 72).

In return for this almost-unconditional support, the United States provided exactly what Stroessner had hoped for to strengthen and consolidate his repressive regime: aid and legitimacy (Mora 1998). In addition to public and diplomatic pronouncements of support, which translated into legitimacy, Stroessner wanted the United States to express its appreciation by offering material rewards in the form of economic aid, technical assistance, loans, grants, foreign investments, military security assistance, and trade concessions. Economic and financial assistance was needed by Stroessner to prop up his regime; he used this aid to finance infrastructure projects that were used as instruments by which the government procured a degree of legitimacy for itself.

In the critical years of the regime's consolidation (1954–1961), the total U.S. aid package plus loans via U.S.-controlled international banking institutions reached $53.2 million, an average of more than $6 million a year. This is a considerable amount when one considers that the total Paraguayan state budget for 1959 was $21 million (Abente 1988: 83). Aid increased even further during the Alliance for Progress, partly as a product of, but also in response to, the activity of small guerrilla groups in the late 1950s and 1960s. The Stroessner regime exaggerated the influence of communists and Fidel Castro in the financing and organizing of these guerrilla groups in order to raise fears in, and, consequently, funds from the United States. As Andrew Nickson (1993: 607) concludes, "relations between the Stroessner regime and successive U.S. administrations became extremely close and contributed much to the consolidation of the regime"—the key objective of Stroessner's foreign policy.

Another critical determining element of Paraguay's foreign policy between 1954 and 1983 was Asunción's ties with its two powerful neighbors, which had exercised influence over the nation's politics and economic development since before Stroessner's rise to power. Paraguay remained vulnerable to the geopolitical rivalry between Argentina and Brazil (Kelly and Whigham 1990). Since the end of the Triple Alliance War, Argentina and Brazil competed for influence in Paraguay, often supporting one party or politician (or general) in elections, civil conflicts or factional infighting. Politics in Paraguay became almost the responsibility of Argentina and Brazil, which believed that every domestic issue had strategic importance to their respective interests. However, between 1904 and the 1960s, Argentina was the dominant actor, largely because of Asunción's overwhelming economic dependence on Buenos Aires. In the 1950s, 90 percent of Paraguayan exports were shipped through Buenos Aires, and nearly 40 percent of Paraguay's trade was with Argentina. Moreover, Argentine investors had controlling interests in Paraguay's key industries, specifically livestock and agriculture (Baer and Birch 1987).

By the time Stroessner assumed power in 1954, some of his predecessors had already initiated a pendular foreign policy where Asunción played one regional hegemon against the other in order to enhance Paraguay's autonomy while obtaining economic and political support from Buenos Aires and Rio de Janeiro (see Birch 1988; Birch 1992; Lezcano 1990). However, Stroessner moved the pendulum clearly toward Brazil. More than just reducing Argentina's economic stranglehold, Stroessner was concerned with protecting his regime from Argentine political meddling, which he believed was the greatest external threat to his plans for complete control of the Paraguayan political system (Seiferheld and De Tone 1988: 65). Broader ties with Brazil would translate into economic advantages for the nation and political support for Stroessner. Brazil was more than willing to take advantage of Stroessner's preferences for closer military and economic ties and nonintervention in domestic affairs. Brazil and Paraguay shared concerns about the communist threat, particularly after the 1964 coup that brought to power in Brazil a national security doctrine regime. Military and security cooperation rapidly became the cornerstone of Brazil–Paraguay relations. Stroessner maintained friendly and cordial relations with Argentina, but Brazil's massive economic expansion and Argentina's political and economic crises of the 1960s made the choice clear; Brazil offered a stable partnership with tremendous economic and political benefits (Abente 1988: 79).

Economically, Brazil provided massive amounts of aid in addition to signing accords that offered trade concessions and financing to build roads, bridges, and port facilities—all mostly completed by the late 1960s. More importantly, duty-free port facilities were granted to Paraguay in Paranagua and Concepción and, after years of negotiation and study, construction on the $12 billion Itaipu dam began, which became a great source of wealth to the Paraguayan economy. Finally, changes in trade patterns were also significant.

Paraguay's exports to Brazil increased from less than 1 percent in 1965 to 25 percent by 1981. Imports experienced a similar trend (Rodriguez Silvero 1987; Franco 1988). Therefore, as Alfredo da Mota Menezes describes, Brazil, principally for geopolitical reasons (though there were some economic gains to be made), was more than happy to provide Paraguay with another "economic lung" that would free it from its historical dependency on Argentina.

POST–COLD WAR FOREIGN POLICY TRENDS

In terms of foreign policy, there has been no significant change and only shifts in emphases. The transition and the new international context of the post–Cold War period dramatically altered the regional and global context of Paraguay's international relations. However, its foreign policy has not been successful in adapting itself to the new context, largely because of the institutional and administrative deficiencies of the new democratic regime. As a result, Paraguay lacks a cohesive, well-defined, and well-articulated foreign policy. Therefore, immobilism and improvisation have characterized Paraguayan foreign policy (Simon 1990c). Two Paraguayan scholars of international relations describe the country's foreign policy as "presidential"—because of the dominance of the executive—and "dragged," with respect to how Paraguay is pulled and pressured into regional political organizations and economic integration arrangements by its neighbors (Argentina, Brazil, and Uruguay) (Masi and Simon 1993; Masi 1991a). The absence of a professional diplomatic service coupled with the level of bureaucratic politicization institutionalized by Paraguayan sectarianism allowed foreign policy to be manipulated by ambitious politicians, as in the case of former foreign minister Luis Maria Argaña. The incompetence and passivity of the foreign ministry coupled with the tradition of caudillism are the principal reasons why foreign policy was entrusted or delegated to the Palace of Lopez and regional capitals.

From the time General Andres Rodriguez staged his successful coup on February 3, 1989, and was elected president three months later, the most notable feature of his government's foreign policy was the active and personal diplomacy of the executive, characterized by the frequency and intensity of his international contacts (Yopo 1989). The Ministry of Foreign Affairs, under the leadership of Luis Maria Argaña (1989–1990), a longtime Colorado Party boss with no experience in international relations, was plagued by the legacy and weight of the previous regime's bureaucratic perversions. Argaña showed little interest in foreign policy matters and spent most of his time engaged in domestic politics, using the ministry as a staging point for his political ambitions.[4] The ministry was incapable of redefining a modern and coherent national foreign policy, mostly because the ministry itself lacked a modern and professional structure and personnel sufficiently independent of partisan politics.

The foreign ministry continued to operate under the same ideological, anticommunist paradigm of the previous regime until 1991, and it only changed course, not because of a process of modernization but by simply being "dragged" along by changes in the international system (i.e., the collapse of communism in the USSR and regional political and economic cooperation). Argaña's replacement, Alexis Frutos Vaesken, made an effort at reforming and modernizing the foreign ministry, but it was largely superficial and insufficient to turn the ministry from a passive observer to an active participant of the nation's international relations.

As a result of these limitations, the responsibility of reintegrating Paraguay into the international system, particularly the Rio Group and the regional economic integration process, fell to Paraguay's neighbors (Argentina, Brazil, and Uruguay), which pushed President Rodriguez to take the lead in accelerating Asunción's participation in light of the deficiencies of the foreign ministry (Masi 1991a: 12). For example, Uruguayan president Julio Sanguinetti directly pleaded and convinced President Rodriguez to attend the 1989 inauguration of Bolivian president Jaime Paz Zamora in order to end a long-standing bitter relationship and begin the process of regional infrastructure integration. Moreover, on the insistence of Argentina and Uruguay, Paraguay was invited to join the Rio Group. In 1990, it was President Sanguinetti who initiated the process by which Paraguay was invited to participate in the regional economic integration process that ultimately led to the signing of the Treaty of Asunción (1991) and the creation of the Southern Cone Common Market (MERCOSUR) (Masi 1993). Despite these cases of successful "pull," many opportunities were squandered because of the absence of a coherent and functional foreign policy bureaucracy. For example, Paraguay's role in the negotiations leading to the Treaty of Asunción was minimal at best. The lack of experts on economic integration and negotiations in the foreign ministry resulted in Uruguay taking on the role of Paraguay's negotiator (Masi 1990). As can be expected, Uruguay and Paraguay's interests did not always coincide. Therefore, the failure to respond to new opportunities with regard to neighboring countries revealed the limitations of the Rodriguez policy of presidential diplomacy, the absence of expert advisers on foreign policy formulation, and the weakness of the Ministry of Foreign Affairs when faced with new challenges and opportunities (Simon 1995a).

The Rodriguez administration (1989–1993) pursued three key foreign policy objectives: (1) end Paraguay's international isolation from which it suffered during the latter years of the Stroessner era; (2) reactivate a ravaged economy by joining regional economic integration systems and attracting foreign investments and credits; and (3), perhaps the most important objective, overcome his reputation of a corrupt Stronista and seek international support for his government. President Rodriguez considered such support and the reintegration of Paraguay into the community of democratic nations to be vital to the regime's legitimacy (see Simon 1989; Salum Flecha 1989; Labra 1990). His government hoped that by demonstrating a commitment to democracy and economic reform, Paraguay would gain access to foreign investments, trade concessions, and credit that were needed to reactivate the economy and sustain the process of democratization. In other words, Rodriguez considered international support of his regime and the transition process a critical requirement for domestic legitimacy. Interestingly, the external factor, which had played a secondary role in the demise of the Stroessner regime, acquired new potency and relevance to the strength and legitimacy of the Rodriguez government. The weakness of Paraguay's democracy has made external actors particularly influential in mediating conflict and safeguarding democracy (Mora 2000).

Since the president's image and legitimacy were so intricately linked to Paraguay's reintegration into an international system—one that insisted on democratic rule for participation—Rodriguez expressed in international forums a strong commitment to the strengthening of democracy in the country. For example, he constantly assured the international community that he would not seek reelection or extend his rule beyond 1993. President Rodriguez immediately ratified the Pact of San José (American Convention on Human Rights) and signed other agreements that demonstrated his commitment to democracy and human rights. The president dropped the virulent ideological-praetorian content of the previous regime's foreign policy, and he replaced Stroessner's pendulum policy with a more balanced approach in its relations with Argentina and Brazil. President Rodriguez made a concerted effort to mend relations with Argentina. He had four private visits with Argentine president Carlos Menem and signed a series of agreements on trade, communication, customs, and transportation, and he moved toward resolving pending problems concerning the Yacyreta hydroelectric plant and the Río Pilcomayo ecological dispute (Simon 1991). In terms of Brazil, relations maintained their steady course with respect to trade and investments, while diplomatic contacts and negotiations on Itaipu and foreign debt were emphasized. In the end, as Paraguayan analyst Fernando Masi (1997) asserts, "the Rodriguez government sought to avoid conflict with neighboring countries for fear that it might hinder its overriding diplomatic objective of securing a new democratic image for the country" (180).

The Rodriguez government also considered improving relations with the United States a key priority of its foreign policy. Again, Asunción understood that U.S. approval of Rodriguez and his government was an essential condition for Paraguay's reinsertion into the international system, which would translate into certain economic benefits needed to reactivate the economy and consolidate democratic rule. The fact that the United States stood as the only superpower in the post–Cold War period and as leader of the "free and democratic world" had tremendous symbolic meaning for Paraguayan elites and a regime that desperately sought to translate international support into domestic legitimacy (Mora 1997: 71). United States support not only helped in promoting a new democratic image in the international arena but also strengthened Rodriguez's position against the opposition and sectors of the Colorado Party opposed the transition. In the end, Paraguayan policy toward the United States during the transition did not change much from that of the previous authoritarian regime. Asunción still looked to the United States for support, much as Stroessner had done during the Cold War. The United States continued to play a pivotal role in regime stability and consolidation.

The Bush administration not only conferred recognition and full support for the Rodriguez government but also restored General System of Preferences (GSP) trade concessions and military assistance and cooperation agreements. Between 1989 and 1992, there were five visits by U.S. political and diplomatic officials, including Vice President Dan Quayle. During the same period, five visits by high military officials, mostly from the U.S. Southern Command, visited Asunción to restore and enhance military and antinarcotics cooperation and to observe several joint operation exercises. Rodriguez effectively translated the presence and expression of support from U.S. officials into domestic legitimacy by holding up the U.S. stamp of approval as a necessary requirement for legitimacy (*abc color* 1991).

Since 1993 Paraguay's democracy has been under tremendous stress and pressure from authoritarian enclaves (particularly within the Colorado Party and armed forces), socioeconomic deterioration, labor protests, and weak and ineffective institutions, all of which eroded the credibility of the government and regime. As a result, governments and society looked inward concerned with threats to the democratic system while completely disregarding critical foreign policy issues. The government and society, particularly political parties, were too engrossed in domestic political crises to engage in an open and effective debate on foreign policy. The bureaucratic-administrative structures remained highly politicized and corrupt, incapable of meeting the political, economic, and international challenges of Paraguay.

The fragility of Paraguay's democracy and political impotence of President Juan Carlos Wasmosy (1993–1998), who was beholden to civil-military interests that had brought him to power, increased the degree to which Paraguay relinquished responsibility for not only its international relations, but the stability of the transition, to regional neighbors and other external actors, such as the OAS, MERCOSUR, and the United States. The predominant role played by these external actors in safeguarding democracy from an internal threat in April 1996 confirms the extent to which external actors impact and shape the domestic.[5] In other words, a weak president (owing his presidency to an alliance of civilian and military nationalists opposed to an active foreign policy agenda for Paraguay) grappling with insurmountable domestic challenges, specifically the indefatigable threat from General Lino Oviedo, further crippled public policymaking. As a result, a number of important foreign policy matters remained unresolved, such as the Río Pilcomayo dispute with Argentina, fluctuating relations with the United States (drug trafficking and intellectual property), Itaipu renegotiations, MERCOSUR, and a deteriorating international image. In each of these cases, the Wasmosy administration did not fashion a response, nor did it formulate a national policy to effectively deal with these issues in favor of Paraguayan interests (Simon 2001). In other words, the need to focus inward diverted attention and interest away from framing a foreign policy that a complex and challenging international system required.

Although the Rodriguez administration suffered from excessive presidentialism and "drag" in its foreign policy, it was able to design a policy consistent with the stated interest and objectives of the president (i.e., improve his stained reputation and consolidate the democratic regime). However, the weakness and increasing illegitimacy of President Wasmosy created a vacuum that contributed to a foreign policy that can only be characterized as suffering from drift and near total neglect. Initially, President Wasmosy tried to personalize Paraguay's international relations by taking an inordinate amount of foreign trips attempting to establish a direct and personal relationship with other presidents. However, Paraguay's incomplete and precarious democracy, exacerbated by a distraught president and a public disinterested in international matters, contributed to disarray and neglect of foreign policy (Rehren 1994). As a result, Paraguay's international image and interests suffered (Simon 1995b: 10).

This situation of foreign policy inaction worsened as Paraguay sunk deeper into political crises after President Wasmosy left office in August 1998. The embattled administrations of President Raul Cubas (1998–1999) and President Luis Gonzalez Macchi (1999–present) continued to lack the strength, legitimacy, and focus to address critical foreign policy issues, such as challenges emanating from disputes within MERCOSUR. Between January 1998 and August 2001, Paraguay had three presidents and eight foreign ministers. Moreover, during this period, there were several impeachment proceedings held against each president, the assassination of Vice President Luis Maria Argaña, two failed coup attempts, over a dozen labor and peasant strikes and protests (including road blocks), and a quickly deteriorating socioeconomic crisis. The lack of leadership in the executive and the relative disinterest of the legislature and society (deeply preoccupied with the deteriorating domestic situation) in regional and global matters of importance to

Paraguay's national interest contributed to what can best be characterized as a nation without a foreign policy.

PARAGUAYAN FOREIGN POLICY: LEVELS OF ANALYSIS

Any analyst comparing Paraguayan foreign policy before and after the end of the Cold War and the inception of democratization in 1989 would be surprised to discover the degree of consistency in the potency of several of the key variables or levels of analysis used to explain foreign policy. That is, using some of James Rosenau's (1966) sets of explanatory variables of foreign policy—particularly, idiosyncratic (individual), governmental (domestic), and systemic—we find no significant difference in the weight of the variables used to explain the foreign policies of Paraguay's authoritarian and democratic regimes. This is not unique to Paraguay. In fact, it is typical of small (in terms of perception) vulnerable states, such as Paraguay, that have a long tradition of isolation, underdevelopment, dependency, and patrimonial-authoritarian rule. Paraguay's long tradition of personalism and autocratic rule, since before the patrimonial-authoritarian regime of President Alfredo Stroessner, emphasizes the role of leadership or the executive over the legislature and society in foreign policy decision making. The important difference, however, between authoritarian and democratic regimes is that under the former, foreign policy was designed solely by and for the interests of the authoritarian ruler, while in the latter, if there is an absence of a decisive and respected executive (in a society accustomed to the centralization of authority and decision making) foreign policy falls into disarray.

The importance of political culture in foreign policy has been studied (Ebel et al. 1991). Latin American foreign policy, more so than domestic policy, has traditionally been the preserve of the executive and a narrow elite. In stable monistic regimes, such as that in Paraguay, where there is a high concentration of power and authority in the caudillo, the chief executive enjoys sweeping autonomy in foreign policy (Ferguson 1987: 149). One basic and enduring factor of Paraguayan foreign policy is its geographic and cultural isolation (Gonzalez 1990). Paraguay's vulnerable geographic position as a landlocked buffer state between two powerful and menacing neighbors was an overwhelming determinant of Stroessner's foreign policy. In other words, feelings of insecurity and vulnerability caused by geopolitics and defeat in the Triple Alliance War contributed to certain hermetic and nationalist attitudes that shaped its politics (patrimonial-authoritarianism) and foreign policy (chauvinism and low profile) well into the Stroessner period.

Few observers would consider Stroessner's personalist-patrimonial regime to be an aberration of Paraguayan political history. In fact, the regime was the result and culmination of a long history of authoritarianism, caudillism, corruption, foreign machination, and political party factionalism that have plagued Paraguay since independence.[6] The only difference is that the Stronato was a more sophisticated, modern, and institutionalized form of autocratic rule consistent with the "neosultanistic" type of regime, in which the "binding norms and relations of bureaucratic administration are constantly subverted by personal fiat of the ruler."[7] Paraguay's geopolitical and cultural isolation and the concomitant ideological tradition of national chauvinism enhanced the position and power of *el actor único* in the decision-making process of foreign policy. As a result of the monopolization and personalization of power, the foreign policy of Paraguay was categorically designed and executed by el actor único.[8] Stroessner made all the important and minor foreign policy decisions.

As described earlier, the importance of *el actor único* in foreign policy decision making continued during the transition. Foreign policy remained very much within the purview of the executive and his close aides. In fact, President Rodriguez, in relation to Stroessner, who in the last few years of the regime seemed to devolve foreign policy authority to others in the executive branch, enhanced the degree to which the Palacio de Lopez reasserted full control over foreign policy. Distrust between the president and a highly political foreign minister and Rodriguez's desire to clean his reputation and enhance his democratic credentials led to strong presidentialism in Paraguay's foreign policy.

It stands to reason that Paraguay's political culture and deep-seated tradition of executive dominance over public policy issues will contribute to confusion and disarray when presidents in a democratic system are weak, illegitimate, and discredited (Abente 1996). This was the case with President Wasmosy, who was beholden to authoritarian civil-military interests that brought him to power in less than free and fair party and general elections (Nickson 1997). The political impotence of the president and threats to his government and the democratic regime did not allow for the formulation and implementation of a coherent foreign policy. Important regional and global matters surfaced that required Asunción's attention, but the political crises coupled with weakness and disorientation in the executive left issues such as MERCOSUR, Itaipu, and drug trafficking unattended, at a tremendous cost to the country. Needless to say, a strategic vision of Paraguayan foreign policy was never formulated in light of the vacuum and disarray at the top. This condition was exacerbated under Presidents Cubas and Gonzalez Macchi, who showed no interest or knowledge of foreign policy, and, as a result, Paraguay was unable to confront the challenges and opportunities that regional and global developments had to offer. In short, the absence of a strong and respected executive in a system that required decisive leadership at the top, coupled with the deterioration of Paraguay's democratic institutions, has contributed to uncertainty, paralysis, and negligible public policy outcomes.

At the governmental or domestic level, we find no real role, influence, or interest in foreign policy matters. The autocratic and patrimonial structure of the Stroessner regime secured a pliant and weak bureaucracy and society that were penetrated and absorbed by the dictatorship. By 1959, Stroessner had skillfully penetrated and seized the state bureaucracy and society, specifically the armed forces and the Colorado Party. He used the party effectively to mobilize support and repress opposition. In the end, all government and societal organizations were stripped of their professionalism and independence by a dictatorship that restricted any discussion of public policy matters not sanctioned by the ruler.

Through an adroit mixture of democratic trappings, repression, and cooptation, Stroessner was able to demobilize and deactivate society successfully, reducing all possibility for political mobilization and public policy discussion independent of the state (Simon 1990a). Paraguay's authoritarian tradition and the strong intolerance and exclusion for things *different*, particularly those coming from society, did not allow for much space or patience for societal participation in public policy matters. The social sciences at universities during the Stronato were viewed as subversive and ideological, and thus only a few programs and courses were offered. Not until the 1980s were any courses offered on international relations. Social science research remained very much within the closed and isolated walls of a few nongovernmental organizations such as the Centro Paraguayo de Estudios Sociologicos (CPES) (Simon 2000). The lack of knowledge, a result of the regime's repression and neglect of social science research and education, kept society ignorant and out of the loop of public policy decision making.

If there is one distinctive feature of Paraguayan foreign policy during transition, it is improvisation and immobilism. One of the limitations of a *transition from above and within* is that there is little change in the structure and elites from the previous authoritarian regime. The structural legacies of the Stroessner regime coexist with democratization and political and civil rights. The transition relied on the support of many of the political, economic, and military interests associated with the previous regime. Democratization provided the means to an end for an authoritarian elite seeking to manipulate and "control the pace and scope of the transition" in order to retain a "high degree of political and economic power" (Nickson 1989; Galeano 1989). Therefore, change in this "protected democracy" is occurring in the context of structural continuity and immobility. The antidemocratic political culture and the legacy of patronage, prebendarism, and corruption impede consolidation and the modernization and professionalism of the state bureaucracy.

The foreign ministry, like much of the state bureaucracy, continued to suffer from the same institutional deficiencies and politicization. The foreign ministry under President Rodriguez was largely absent with respect to foreign policy decision making as the executive, realizing the high degree of politicization and incompetence in the ministry, assumed complete control over public policy. The Wasmosy administration's three foreign ministers (Diogenes Martinez, Luis Maria Ramírez Boettner, and Ruben Melgarejo Lanzoni) were deficient in their knowledge of international relations and had little interest in modernizing and pushing the ministry into the center of Paraguayan foreign policy decision making. Ramírez Boettner was an experienced diplomat, but perhaps more than any of his predecessors (and successors), he reacted negatively to suggestions that the ministry needed restructuring.[9]

In the first six months of the administration, Foreign Minister Martinez assembled a group of journalists, scholars, and other experts of international relations to present a plan that would help the ministry design a foreign policy for the Wasmosy administration (*Ultima Hora* 1993; *abc color* 1993).[10] Several programmatic and strategic plans were presented but were immediately shelved and ignored once Martinez resigned and the government's attention focused on domestic political crises.[11] The absence of any significant role by the foreign ministry actually worsened under the embattled administrations of Cubas and Gonzalez Macchi. Between 1998 and 2001, foreign ministers lasted an average of five months in office, each one removed, not because of incompetence, but for reasons of political expediency.

Finally, there was no attempt by either the Rodriguez or Wasmosy administrations to include other key government agencies or the legislature in the process of foreign policy decision making. For example, Martin Sannemann (1995), the former president of the Commission on Foreign Relations of the Chamber of Deputies and a member of the opposition, noted with some consternation the absence of the legislature and society in formulating a national foreign policy. For the most part, the absence of the legislature was supported by the institution's lack of interest and expertise on issues related to Paraguay's foreign policy interests. If either chamber focused on an issue, such as MERCOSUR, foreign debt, or the Pilcomayo River/border dispute with Argentina, it was largely to gain political advantage over a weak executive, especially during the administrations of Presidents Cubas and Gonzalez Macchi.

It is important to note, however, that since the mid-1990s, several Paraguayan nongovernmental organizations, particularly universities and think tanks, have developed programs in international relations and foreign policy. In the early 1990s, CPES inaugurated a program on international relations, headed by José Luis Simon, that published several important studies on international relations and Paraguayan foreign policy.[12] CPES also published a biannual journal of international relations titled *Perspectiva Internacional*

Paraguaya. Due to a lack of resources and interest, CPES closed the section and finished editing the journal after only three years and eight issues.

The two largest universities, National University of Asunción and the Catholic University of Asunción, expanded their graduate and postgraduate programs in international relations and diplomacy. Student enrollment in these programs is growing, but the lack of resources and qualified faculty has placed severe constraints on the curriculum and professionalism of these academic programs (Simon 2000). Recently, the first nongovernmental organization strictly devoted to the study and discussion of international relations was created in 1997. The stated goal of the Centro Paraguayo de Estudios Internacionales (CEPEI) is to "help Paraguay integrate itself more effectively into the international system with the goal of strengthening its democratic institutions and development."[13] CEPEI is working closely with the foreign ministry offering technical, administrative, and policy advice. It has also published two documents: the first, an analysis of the participation of civil society actors in international relations and foreign policy decision making (CEPEI 2000) and the second, a report for the Ministry of Foreign Affairs outlining the basic elements in the formulation of Paraguayan foreign policy (CEPEI 2001). Despite these important first steps, there is still much to be desired from a disinterested society that lacks the knowledge and experience to be an effective actor in Paraguay's foreign policy process.

The foreign policy objectives of the Stroessner regime were centered on using the systemic, the structure of the international system, to sustain the domestic authoritarian project. During the Cold War, Asunción understood the domestic political and economic value of closely aligning its foreign policy with that of Washington. In the 1980s, however, the internal dynamic of the regime and the systemic forces that had sustained the political order for nearly thirty years began to change in ways that ultimately brought its collapse in February 1989. The decomposition of Stroessner and his regime, coupled with significant international changes, such as regional democratization and a shift in U.S. foreign policy priorities, undermined the regime's ability to continue using foreign policy to support domestic legitimacy and stability. Increasingly, as Stroessner's grip weakened and Paraguay found itself isolated in a community of democracies, the regime's unwillingness to liberalize and adapt its foreign policy to the new international context led to an obstinate and highly bunkered approach to its international relations that only accelerated its isolation and downfall (Simon 1988).

The systemic weighed heavily on the foreign policy of President Andres Rodriguez, largely because the consolidation of democracy and the rehabilitation of Rodriguez's negative image and reputation abroad could only be achieved by adopting a foreign policy that accepted emerging international norms, such as democratization and integration. As a result, as described earlier, Paraguayan foreign policy was often shaped or "pulled" by Asunción's neighbors as Rodriguez was willing to hand over the nation's foreign policy interests to Argentina, Brazil, or Uruguay if it helped Paraguay and the president end their isolation and dubious international image. The result, as in the case of MERCOSUR when Uruguay assumed the role of Paraguay's chief negotiator, was that Paraguay's national interests were neglected and sacrificed at the altar of Rodriguez's crusade to be a respected leader.

The abdication of Paraguay's foreign policy continued under President Wasmosy despite early attempts by the president to formulate and assert an independent and coherent policy. The difference with the previous administration was that Paraguay's neighbors were less willing to assume a role in Paraguay's foreign policy as they focused on other more pressing domestic and international concerns. The disinterest of Paraguay's neighbors, coupled with the inability of an embattled administration to design a coherent foreign policy, contributed to disarray, confusion, and the muddling through of Paraguay's foreign policy (Simon 2001). This process worsened under the very unstable and illegitimate administrations of Presidents Cubas and Gonzalez Macchi. In the meantime, the pace of regional changes and globalization and the inability of Asunción to design a coherent foreign policy contributed to the africanization of Paraguay in the international system. In other words, Paraguay finds itself increasingly isolated and abandoned, unable to formulate and implement a coherent, national foreign policy that could help Paraguay to confront and benefit from the tremendous challenges and opportunities offered by globalization.

CONCLUSION

This study of foreign policy during Stroessner's patrimonial or neosultanistic regime and that of the democratic transition governments demonstrates the potency of three explanatory variables of Paraguayan foreign policy. The state-executive level of analysis of foreign policy is particularly significant because of the weight of Paraguay's personalist and authoritarian heritage on politics and foreign policy decision making. Stroessner was the culmination of this tradition, except that he created a political system that enhanced the degree to which power was vested in the executive. The personalization of foreign policy by el actor único allowed Stroessner to design a foreign policy whose objective was to help strengthen and consolidate his regime. In other words, it was Stroessner's foreign policy, not Paraguay's.

The role of the president remained critical in the foreign policy of the democratic transition, particularly under Andres Rodriguez. The absence of a functional and professional Ministry of Foreign Affairs forced the president to assume full responsibility for the country's international relations at a critical time when the regime needed international support to strengthen democratic rule. When the executive neglected or was ineffective in pursuing a "presidential" foreign policy, Paraguayan foreign policy drifted, and Paraguay's international image suffered as a result.

In the domestic level of analysis, Paraguay's democracy has not been able to overcome the penetration and personalization of the state bureaucracy and the engulfing and atomization of society by the Stroessner regime. There has been no attempt at reforming and professionalizing the bureaucracy, while the legislature, submerged in political crises, has developed little interest or knowledge of international relations and Paraguayan foreign policy, thus delegating complete authority and responsibility to a weak and disoriented executive. Since the transition began, society has also expressed little interest in foreign policy matters. Universities, nongovernmental organizations and think tanks, and the media have been more preoccupied with the problems of governance and socioeconomic decline than with international relations, which is believed to be unimportant and elitist. For the most part, domestic actors in society and the military remained largely oblivious to international developments of importance to Paraguay.

The other important explanatory variable of Paraguayan foreign policy was systemic. As noted earlier, because of Paraguay's weak political and economic power base and its landlocked position between two regional powers, its foreign policy is vulnerable to external actors and strategic realities. Paraguayan foreign policy under the Stronato and democracy is conditioned by the regional or international context of the Cold War and the United States, Argentina–Brazil rivalry, or democracy and globalization. In fact, domestic stability, in large part, hinged on the ability of the authoritarian and democratic regimes to use foreign policy for purposes of obtaining much-needed political and economic support and legitimacy. Small states such as Paraguay, with a long tradition of authoritarianism, economic dependency, and a vulnerable geopolitical position, are bound to have a "presidential and/or dragged" foreign policy regardless of regime type.

DISCUSSION QUESTIONS

1. What are the elements of change and continuity in Paraguayan foreign policy between the authoritarian period (Stroessner era) and democratic transition?
2. How does the systemic or external explain the consolidation and longevity of Stronato?
3. How is Paraguayan foreign policy (post-1989) characterized by "immobilism and improvisation"?

NOTES

1. Research on Paraguayan foreign policy during the Stroessner era include Hoyer (1975); Fernández Estigarribia and Simon (1987); Mora (1988); Simon (1990a); Yopo (1991); Mora (1993).

2. For a discussion of Stroessner's foreign policy objectives, see Yopo (1991: 31–36); Mora (1988; 1993: 89–90); Simon (1993: 47–67).

3. For studies on U.S.–Paraguay relations, see Mora (1997, 1998).

4. For a scathing criticism of Argaña's poor performance as foreign minister, see a series of six articles authored by José Luis Simon in *abc color* (July 1989).

5. For an analysis of the role of external factors in Paraguay's democratization, see Valenzuela (1999) and Mora (2000).

6. For an excellent study of the historical and cultural roots of the Stroessner dictatorship, see Lewis (1980).

7. A description of a sultanistic regime is offered by Linz (1975). For the application of sultanism to the Stroessner case, see Riquelme (1994).

8. For an analysis of the extraordinary formal and informal powers of Stroessner, see Lewis (1980: 105–23). The legal basis of Stroessner's control of foreign policy was stipulated in the constitution of 1967 in article 180, section 6, which grants the executive branch complete authority over Paraguay's international relations.

9. For an analysis of Paraguayan foreign policy during the Wasmosy administration as explained by the foreign minister, see Ramírez Boettner (1995).

10. The specialists assembled by Foreign Minister Martinez included Jeronimo Irala Burgos, Carlos Plate, Ramon Silva Alonso, José Luis Simon, Ramon Casco Carreras, Fernando Masi, Hugo Marinoni Rodriguez, Juan Andres Cardozo, and Mauricio Schwartzmann.

11. One very elaborate and detailed study presented to the foreign ministry is Masi and Simon (1993).

12. The most important book-length study published by CPES was Simon (1990b).

13. See the CEPEI website at www.cepei.org.py.

17

Uruguay
A Small Country Faces Global Challenges

Lincoln Bizzozero

This chapter examines the modifications carried out in the foreign policy of Uruguay as a consequence of the post-1973 regime changes when the democratic regime was replaced by an authoritarian government. It also considers the period after 1985, when the return to a constitutional regime took place that coincided with the end of the Cold War and the organization of the Southern Cone Common Market (MERCOSUR) in the early 1990s. In so doing, this chapter reflects on the changes accomplished by a small country in response to mutations in internal and external variables affecting the definition of public policies.

To achieve these goals, this chapter starts with an overview of the principal characteristics of Uruguay and the evolution of its foreign policy. Subsequently, it discusses the change in Uruguayan foreign policy focusing on three main dimensions: transitions in the political regime in the 1970s and 1980s, the impact of the end of the Cold War, and the integration of Uruguay in MERCOSUR. In explaining changes and continuity in the foreign policy of Uruguay, this chapter emphasizes the nation-state as the level of analysis that holds greater explanatory power. However, interactions with the international system and the regional subsystem are carefully considered as crucial sources of explanation for the changes especially in the period following the end of the Cold War. The last section discusses the new priorities and perspectives brought about by the new presidential administration in 2000.

To introduce conceptual precision to the central subject of this chapter, it should be noted that foreign policy is not conceived as a whole, but different dimensions are analytically identified in order to understand it. Consequently, it considers the following aspects: the basic principles of the foreign policy as defined by the country's place in the structure of the *world* system; the external agenda set up by the presidential administrations after 1973; the continuity or variations in the choice of issues; the regional priorities selected by governments; and, finally, the change in the relationship between civil society actors in the decision-making process. Additionally, with respect to the dynamics change-continuity, this chapter includes, between these two conceptual axes, other possibilities to make the foreign policy process visible in addition to adding breadth to its analysis. All in all, what is relevant is the degree of the variations and not the classification into one of these categories.

According to this line of thought, it is possible to identify different degrees of variation in Uruguayan foreign policy. They may be conceptualized either as accommodation and adjustment or as innovation in response to specific international or internal conjunctures. Therefore, "accommodation" corresponds to a minor level of variation, while "innovation" actually represents a change, although both concepts may be understood as degrees in a continuum of mutations in foreign policy. Moreover, change in foreign policy requires a new definition of external projection expressed in terms of goals and policies, and visible in the priorities accorded to the issues included in the agenda. The theory created by James Rosenau for the interpretation of the change/continuity dynamics in the so-called postinternational politics contributes useful concepts for the analysis of the Uruguayan case. His theory is particularly helpful for understanding the instability in interdependence relations, the trends toward decentralization, and the emergence of nongovernmental actors and their participation in decision-making processes (Rosenau 1990b: 100, 253–60, 308–12, 454–59).

This analytic approach makes it possible to advance that, although there were no changes in the position of Uruguay in the international system, some long-lasting variations occurred from the 1970s on and especially during the post–Cold War era, as a consequence of changes in the political regime and the decision to join MERCOSUR. In the 1970s, the most important changes were effected in the economic development model and in the agreements with Latin American countries (border, commercial, energy, and transport agreements). In the 1980s, the main modifications that were put into effect were the support for a series of regional cooperation agreements, the reincorporation of the country into the international system, and the adoption of democracy as the basis for the regional integration policy. Finally, in the 1990s, the most relevant change was the decision to join the effort for the organization of MERCOSUR.

EVOLUTION AND CHARACTERISTICS OF URUGUAYAN FOREIGN POLICY

Uruguay is a small country with an area of 176,215 square kilometers and a population of 3.3 million. Asymmetries in territory and population in comparison with Argentina and Brazil, concentration of population and economic resources along the southern coast, as well as the condition of the capital city as the main oceanic port during the colonial era marked, from the beginning of the history of Uruguay, some decisive features of its foreign policy. Uruguay distinguished itself by its support for free navigation, by being a country open to the sea not having serious conflicts with the naval power of the time (Great Britain), by the defense of the principles of free determination and noninterference in internal affairs of other countries, and by the practice of a "pendulum" diplomacy toward its two powerful neighbors (Herrera 1988, 1991).

From the colonial period, the area surrounding Uruguay was the object of disputes first between Spain and Portugal and then between Argentina and Brazil, after independence. During the first decades of the nineteenth century, there were projects for its annexation to either its western- or its northern-bordering country before its emergence as a sovereign nation at the end of the 1820s. Uruguay was created as a consequence of mediation by Great Britain in order to put an end to conflicts in the area and to secure free navigation by means of the organization of an independent state controlling the northern bank of the River Plate and the Atlantic Ocean, the waterway that communicated the whole Basin of the Plate and the hinterland of South America to the rest of the world. Therefore, the beginning of independent Uruguay was marked by this instance of mediation and regional involvement, and this circumstance gave rise to debates about the viability of the nation and its capacity for having a foreign policy of its own. The emergence of Uruguay and the first decades of its republican history were characterized by the internationalization of its national politics. British and French interventions; British diplomacy in the area of the Plate; the Convention of 1828 that secured Uruguayan independence; links among Argentine, Brazilian, and Uruguayan political parties across borderlines; conflicts in the Plate Basin such as the question of navigation of the internal rivers; the struggle between "*federales*" and "*unitarios*"; the overthrow of Rosas as the result of a multilateral war; the Great War of 1839–1851; the Treaty of the Triple Alliance; the intervention of Brazil and the war against Paraguay—are all the main events that caused the internationalization of Uruguayan internal political debate. In this context, Uruguayan foreign policy had to be internationalist and moderately interventionist (Romero-Bizzozero 1987).

Between 1828 and 1870—when the internationalization of national politics culminated—the government defined Uruguayan foreign policy. In other words, it is not yet possible to identify a state policy because the political party in power designed foreign policy. This situation was partly due to the fact that it was not until 1870 that the foundations of the modern state were established and political parties were the only structures articulating the Uruguayan polity. After 1870, this role was taken up by the state. The internationalization of Uruguayan foreign policy during the first decades of independent life was caused by the regionalization of domestic conflicts as a result of links among Argentine, Brazilian, and Uruguayan political parties. This feature singularizes the foreign policy of Uruguay up to the war of the Triple Alliance. After 1870, Uruguayan political parties began to conceive policy formulation separately from the regional context. Politics became national, and the state asserted its presence laying the bases for the pendular equilibrium between Uruguay and its two neighbors.

The emergence of the national state was complete by the end of the nineteenth century and coincided with the separation of Uruguay from the regional context and the beginning of an era of prosperity marked by European immigration, almost nonexistent Native influence, and differentiation from the rest of Latin America. For these reasons, the attributes associated to Uruguayan national identity were development, national peace, and democracy. Uruguayan differentiation from Latin America in relation to the process of state formation as well as economic development and national identity, was contemporary with the previously mentioned retreat of the nation from the regional political context. Nonintervention and political self-determination became the bases on which that differentiation was built. At the same time, these principles represented the protecting shield of Uruguayan foreign policy (Trías 1972; Turcatti 1981).

It was not until the Spanish civil war and World War II that Uruguay, led again by its political parties, participated in the international debate, integrating the international conflict in the national perspective. World War II, its characteristics, and the participation of Uruguay in it were the objects of a controversy that divided Uruguayan society and political parties. Those who argued that the war was creating a new international scenario and advocated Uruguayan participation in it opposed the position maintaining that the war was not a problem affecting Latin American interests. This view prevailed, and consequently Uruguay took an active role in the beginning of the organization of the United Nations and other institutions created in the postwar period, although the declaration of war against the Axis was made when the war was about to end (Oddone 1985).

Another controversy raised during the war originated in the U.S. proposal for the construction of military bases aimed at controlling the Southern Cone: The critical question was Argentina's reaction to this idea. Public opinion and political parties actively participated in this debate. While the

Colorado Party, in office since the beginning of the century, was favorable to the American proposal, the opposition represented by the National Party led by Luis Alberto de Herrera defeated the project after a memorable debate in the senate (Haedo 1974; Alzaga 1985). The intensity of this controversy, which went on beyond the limits of the state bodies and involved a variety of nongovernmental actors, shows the early emergence in Uruguay of well-informed individuals who are interested in the events of world politics, a feature that Rosenau (1990: 335–37) has identified as a characteristic of the period following 1959.

The political system internationalized the debate and again the options and means depended on the proposals of each political party. However, this internationalization did not transform the bases of the bipartisan consensus that had shaped the formulation of Uruguayan foreign policy. Once the war was over, Uruguay participated in the organization of the new international order while persisting in its retreat from the regional scene (Real de Azúa 1987). Nevertheless, the drama that originated in the emergence of a new North–South axis, changes in the international order following the end of World War II and the Korean War, the recommendations expressed by the Economic Commission for Latin America (ECLA), and analysts concerned with the inequality prevailing in international commerce and its consequences for Latin American economic growth and technological development brought about a new trend toward the reincorporation of Uruguay into the Latin American region. The conclusion of the Treaty of Montevideo in 1960 creating the Latin American Association of Free Trade perfected the new relationship between Uruguay and its sister nations.

In the last forty years, two changes of regime (from democracy to authoritarian rule in 1973, and from dictatorship to democracy in 1985), various changes of government by elections (1959, 1963, 1967, 1972, 1985, 1990, and 2000), and four changes of political parties at the presidency (in 1959 the victory of the National Party; in 1967, the return of the Colorado Party to power; in 1990, the comeback of the National Party, and in 1995, the victory of the Colorado Party) have occurred. These events have influenced a series of transformations in Uruguayan foreign policy and present a sharp contrast with the political stability that had characterized the first decades of the twentieth century. As noted earlier, our analysis will focus on the changes caused by the transition from the authoritarian regime to democracy. Subsequently, it will concentrate on the impact of the changes of political parties at the government. Finally, the conclusion will examine some trends of the administration inaugurated in March 2000, whose accession to power implied a significant shift in power within the Colorado Party.[1]

THE AUTHORITARIAN REGIME AND ITS CONSEQUENCES FOR URUGUAYAN FOREIGN POLICY

It is possible to identify three different phases in the foreign policy carried out by the authoritarian regime organized after the coup of June 1973. They correspond to variations at the top level of Uruguayan government and changes in the international context. During the first phase, from 1973 to 1976, the government obtained international approval for implementing an economic policy dismantling protectionism and seeking the opening of the Uruguayan economy. This international backing may be explained by the characteristics of the coup: Even though the parliament was dissolved, there was continuity in the presidency, then held by Juan Maria Bordaberry who had been elected in 1971. The violent coup in Chile attracted the attention of the world, while in the United States, the government and public opinion were mainly concerned with the war in Vietnam. In 1976, a new phase in the relationship between Uruguayan dictatorship and the international system started: a conflict arising out of denunciations for violations of human rights was followed by reiterated resolutions issued by international institutions condemning the Uruguayan regime. Furthermore, a year later the Carter administration adopted a position of defense of human rights and isolated the Southern Cone countries from the rest of the Western world. Finally, the refusal of the citizenry to back a project of constitutional reform submitted to a plebiscite marked a historic defeat of the authoritarian regime and the beginning of a transition toward democracy. It is in the first two phases that the main changes in Uruguayan foreign policy took place (Caetano and Rilla 1987).

The foreign policy of the authoritarian regime adopted the bipolar logics of the time, moving away from any alignment with the third world, socialist policies, and proposals for the revision of the established model of economic development. It was consistent with a new orientation in the model of development characterized by the abandonment of the imports substitution policy. Numerous measures adopted from 1974 on were intended to open the economy, encourage foreign investment, and promote comparative advantages. These measures implemented a model of development similar to that adopted throughout the Southern Cone, in opposition to practices of economic regulation. A series of decisions showed a determination against any regulation of markets and any protection over raw materials, in a way that affected the relationship with many third world countries. For this reason, the position adopted on the occasion of the energy crisis reveals to what extent the ideological definition of Uruguayan foreign policy reduced the range of options open to negotiation by means of trade agreements, excluding alternatives that would have been better suited for the interests of the country.

During the 1970s, the Uruguayan government made known its position against the Organization of Petroleum Exporting Countries (OPEC) and joined an alliance to confront the "cartel." It refused to conclude agreements for regional integration on the lines adopted by the Andean countries. Some facts demonstrated a clear absence of orientation toward the periphery in the external economic activities of the military regime. For instance, during the conjuncture created by the rise in oil prices, not only did Uruguay confirm its opposition to the cartel, but also no efforts were made to seek a rapprochement with Latin American oil-exporting countries. Therefore, opportunities for either the better condition of payment or credit facilities in the supply of oil were not explored. This line of conduct was due to the fact that the governments of Latin American oil-exporting countries had backed Southern Cone opposition movements.

Neither was the Uruguayan government in favor of encouraging integration agreements. The basic idea underlying this attitude was that it would not be possible to benefit from comparative advantages, as integration would necessarily imply the adoption of protectionist rules. The response of the military regime to the Andean Pact code of investments, which admitted that the member states could share the profits of multinational companies, was the law on foreign capital.[2] The creation of the Latin American Economics System (SELA), which pursued goals such as promotion of cooperation among the countries of the area and the defense of their products in the international market, did not arouse much enthusiasm. Besides the changes introduced by the military regime in the development model, certain steps taken in relation to the subregion and the maritime space established precedents that had consequences later, especially on the relationship between Uruguay and its neighbors. Particularly, it is important to note the following measures: the support accorded to the Treaty of the Plate Basin, the adoption of a geopolitical approach in the discussion over the Waterway ("Hidrovía"), border agreements respecting the definition of the boundary with Argentina in the River Plate, the conclusion of trade and cooperation agreements with Argentina and Brazil, and the claim on the maritime area along the lines adopted by various coastal countries.

The approval of the Plate Basin Treaty made the region visible as a whole as to resources and opportunities. The support accorded by the Uruguayan government to this instrument was due to the fact that it emphasized almost exclusively geopolitical aspects and questions of infrastructure. Furthermore, it was an alternative to the challenge posed by the integration of the Andean region. The participation of Chile as an observer after its separation from the Andean Pact—which was due to its rejection of the code of foreign investment—revealed a division of the continent into two different integration projects. The problem of transport, particularly the connection of internal rivers and the sea, was an important theme of the Plate Basin Treaty, according to the priorities of the agenda in the 1970s. The series of agreements that followed the Plate Basin Treaty confirm the role of Uruguay as a supplier of energy, a path of transit between centers of development, and a place for tourism. The treaty left open the debate over the potential usage of the waterway, the deep waters port, and the energy resources of the region. However, the process that started with the conclusion of the Treaty of the Plate Basin was interrupted by the controversy between Argentina and Brazil over the hydroelectric dam at Itaipu, the war of the Falklands, and the transition to democracy in the Southern Cone countries.

The conventions of trade concluded by Uruguay and its neighboring countries with the purpose of balancing the commercial movement among them inaugurated a new type of agreement, more flexible than those conceived within the framework of Asociación Latinoamericana de Libre Comercio (ALALC, or the Latin American Free Trade Association), and paved the way for the new Treaty of Montevideo, signed in 1980, which organized the Latin American Association of Integration (ALADI). Moreover, two trade agreements, the Argentine-Uruguayan Convention for Economic Cooperation (CAUCE) and the Protocol of Commercial Expansion (PEC) with Brazil, confirmed and expanded after the return of democratic rule, increased the ties between Uruguay and its neighbors (Magariños 1994).

Another orientation that left lasting results was the importance of border agreements. In a short period of time, a series of treaties dealing with definitions of Uruguayan territorial and maritime space were signed. Uruguay joined the claim to two hundred maritime miles supported by several coastal countries. This defense of the maritime space coincided with the promotion of fisheries, a nontraditional business in Uruguay.

A difficult problem still pending was the legacy left by the participation of Uruguay in the regional networks of repression. Forced disappearance of persons, violations of human rights, and Plan Condor activities have been a lasting outrage in Uruguayan life. This theme is still on the political agenda of the Southern Cone countries and has conditioned the orientations and practices of their foreign policies, as was evident in the case of the trial of General Augusto Pinochet. In Uruguay, the constitution of a Peace Commission attempts to bring the matter of forced disappearances to an equitable issue.

CHANGES DURING THE TRANSITION TO DEMOCRACY: REINSERTION OF URUGUAY IN THE INTERNATIONAL SYSTEM

The foreign policy of the first Sanguinetti administration (1985–1989) was shaped by the transition from authoritarian regime to democracy and by decisions on economic questions related to the international system (foreign debt, international trade). Although the modifications associated with the restoration of democratic rule may be characterized, in general terms, as a mere return to the situation existing before the authoritarian coup, in the case of Uruguay they were significant and oriented foreign policy by setting the conditions under which the country would assume the political transition. This was visible in the new aspect of themes that had been overlooked in the 1960s but appeared under a new light after the mid-1980s. Therefore, democracy acquired a new value as the main basis of international relations, particularly for the advancement of new forms of cooperation and integration within the Latin American region. Furthermore, the orientation of Uruguayan foreign policy came back to political mechanisms, to representative institutions, and involved new actors and groups of Uruguayan society. The diplomatic style abandoned the ideological rhetoric that had characterized the authoritarian period and took on a pragmatic and rational approach more consistent with the vision of an interdependent world (Bizzozero and Luján 1992).

For these reasons, although there were no relevant changes in the model of development, which stuck to the fundamentals of the policy for the opening of the economy, and a conflicting issue such as the payment of interest on foreign debt was transferred to the productive sector and the salaried workers, it is possible to identify long-standing changes in political relations, in the definition of criteria, and in the decision-making process. The most enduring changes in foreign policy were that Uruguay kept itself aloof from the East–West conflict; it adopted a pragmatic approach for its inclusion in the West; it promoted democracy as the main basis for its foreign relations, especially in the negotiation of agreements with countries of the Western hemisphere; political as well as economic cooperation received the highest priority; the People's Republic of China was recognized; a modernizing reform in the procedures and orientations of the Ministry of Foreign Relations was brought into effect; and a variety of actors got increasingly involved in the decision-making process.

New Criteria in Policy Formulation

Former president Sanguinetti announced Uruguayan aloofness from the East–West conflict at the moment of his inauguration on March 1, 1985. At the same time, he confirmed his government's adhesion to the international doctrine of human rights with its signature of the Convention of San José de Costa Rica. The doctrine of national security was abandoned, and the political principles that had shaped the early history of the republic were reinstated. Distance from ideological conflicts did not mean renouncing belonginh to the West. In his inaugural speech, President Sanguinetti made this distinction clear: "Likewise, we say that we are Westerners; not because of the assumption of any automatic alignment with any great power, but that we are Westerners because the spirit of the West is the creed of freedom that was born with the dawn of our civilization."[3]

This confirmation of occidental identity in terms of tradition, culture, and ways of living and thinking was expressed in a scale of priorities that replaced the old conception of ideological frontiers. According to this, the highest priority was accorded to the neighboring countries; Latin America came immediately after, followed by the West (Europe, the United States, Israel, and Japan). The role of the United States as a "security key" of the West was not questioned, but the possibility of low-level controversies about Latin American issues, among them those related to the South Atlantic and Central America, was also accepted. The change of regime made it possible to make a visible shift in the criteria ruling Uruguayan foreign policy (respect for human rights and obedience to international law were now the core values) and in the relationship with the international community. Moreover, it allowed Uruguay to play a new role in the inter-American system, and this fact produced successful diplomatic results such as the General Agreement on Tariffs and Trade (GATT), Uruguay Round. The international clout of Foreign Relations Minister Enrique Iglesias was adequate for leading the transition in Uruguayan foreign policy. The diplomatic style of the former general secretary of CEPAL proved to be helpful for an effective reincorporation of Uruguay into the international system.

In his inaugural speech, the minister explained the new orientation of the Ministry of Foreign Relations:

> We will pursue a policy loyal to the fundamental principles ruling the practice of the Ministry throughout the history of the nation: the defense of law, multilateral institutions of negotiation and national sovereignty at every level; and, in response to our own vocations, such as pacifism and, very especially, Latin American integration . . . we must adopt a policy based on principles of dignity . . . that is, everything that is related with the idea of republic, defending peace, multilateralism, international law and dialog.[4]

Changes in the Decision-Making Process

The decision-making process in foreign policy was affected by the change of regime, which had a clear impact on the conception of the international role of the country. Along with the transition from authoritarian rule to democracy, there was another transition from the perception of Uruguay as a rational and unitary actor interacting under the rules of a zero-sum game, to a conception that recognized various actors participating in that process. Consequently, foreign policy was considered the result of interactions among several organizations and individuals taking part in a complex political game at the national level, and in new forms of cooperation within a more interdependent world, at the international level.

The recognition of the People's Republic of China's government is an example of the changes effected in the relationship between the executive and legislative powers as well as in the decision-making process. It was a consequence of the new intervention of the national political system and civil society actors. This decision put an end to a long-standing controversy that had involved political actors and several interest groups that promoted contradicting interests. The discussion over this recognition and the subsequent rupture of relations with Taiwan, which meant immediate costs in terms of investment and importation of soy, involved different factions of political parties. On the one hand, influential members of the political system invoked the principle of free determination to defend continuity in the relations with Taiwan, an important partner for Uruguayan prospects of trade, investment, and cooperation and a market for Uruguayan exportations. A minority inside this group maintained that Taiwan also represented the values of democracy while China was a totalitarian regime. On the other hand, the majority of political actors were in favor of recognition on the grounds that this was the prevailing trend in the international system and the position of the United Nations. One actor that played a significant role in the final decision was the wool-exporting sector since the recognition of China was the condition for the exportation of considerable amounts of that material (Bizzozero 1988).

This decision demonstrated that the change of regime made it possible for the national political system not only to debate but also to participate along the lines set up by the constitution. In Uruguay, foreign affairs are a sphere of almost-exclusive action of the executive power. This means that decisions are made at the presidency, the Ministry of Foreign Relations (particularly, at the office of the minister), meetings of the president with his ministers, and the Council of Ministers.[5] Nevertheless, it should be noted that other constitutional articles limit the action of the executive (article 6, relative to the use of pacific means and the collective defense of Latin American production) and stipulate the intervention of the legislative power (article 85 establishes the obligation to consult the General Assembly for declaring war, concluding peace, and approving treaties, conventions, and contracts with foreign powers; the General Assembly is the only state body that can permit or forbid the transit of foreign troops across the national territory and the sending abroad of national armed forces).

The international context was functional to Uruguayan change of regime and made it possible that the separation from the East–West conflict be accompanied by a positive reincorporation of Uruguay within the regional and hemispheric contexts by means of various agreements of political and economic cooperation. For this reason, the first years of the transition period were crucial for setting up the possibilities and perspectives of Uruguayan foreign policy. An example of the change in the orientations of foreign policy was the Uruguayan initiative to form a group of support to the peace process in Central America, on the grounds that Latin America ought to be excluded from the bipolar conflict. This was the Grupo de Apoyo a Contadora, which later was transformed into the Río Group, the mission of which was to promote democracy, peace, and cooperation. Furthermore, Uruguay played an important role in the Consensus of Cartagena, holding its Pro-Tempore Secretariat, and obtained the nomination of Carlos Pérez del Castillo as general secretary of SELA. Finally, these regional initiatives and the ability of Minister Iglesias made it possible for Uruguay to be the first developing country where a GATT meeting took place.

Initiatives for agreements of cooperation during this period had a special impact on the relationship with Argentina and Brazil. Uruguay accompanied the Argentine-Brazilian process of integration from its beginnings, although this policy was almost exclusively limited to the political level. As to the economic relationship, Uruguay was able to renew the commercial agreements with Argentina and Brazil on favorable terms.

URUGUAYAN FOREIGN POLICY AFTER THE COLD WAR: THE ROLE OF REGIONALISM

The change of government in March 1990 when President Luis Alberto Lacalle, leader of the National Party took office, was the occasion for the culmination of systemic modifications. First, the 1990s anticipated the end of the century because strategic bipolarity and ideological differentiation in the international system came to a close. Second, in the American continents, regional groups with the purpose of creating new links with the international order emerged. Third, the change of government in Uruguay meant a change in the political party in power. This fact had special meaning due to the National Party's orientation in relation to foreign policy.

These changes influenced the development of Uruguayan foreign policy, shaping a scenario that differed from that of previous decades. The most important event of the beginning of the 1990s was the decision to join an initiative of subregional integration that culminated in the emergence of MERCOSUR. This process began with diplomatic protests addressed to the governments of Brazil and Argentina since the conclusion of the Treaty of Buenos Aires in June 1990 (for the creation of a binational common market) had excluded the participation of other ALADI countries (Bizzozero 1997a).

The decision to enter MERCOSUR was unanimously ratified by the senate and by the majority of the Chamber of Representatives, showing that this initiative received a strong support from the political system.[6] What is more, civil society actors backed the idea. Chambers of foreign trade and associations of businessmen expressed their approval, and the central association of trade unions did not adopt a clear position in the beginning, although some leaders later expressed their concern about the possible outcomes, especially the increase of unemployment.

Uruguayan participation in MERCOSUR influenced foreign policy in the 1990s and caused new changes as a consequence of the emergence of new goals and the development of new forms of cooperation among the countries of the subregion. As to the policy goals, the adoption at the beginning of the 1990s of the program for the liberalization of trade gave new legitimacy to the economic policy established during the authoritarian period. The definition of a common external tariff conditioned the national commercial policy and led to joint negotiations for new instruments of commercial policy in the relationship between MERCOSUR and other countries. The aims to create a common market and coordinate macroeconomic policies led to definitions of criteria and indicators.

In addition to these changes in economic and commercial policies, the organization of MERCOSUR affected Uruguayan foreign policy in other respects. This was because the integration process brought about a complex institutional network that included several sectors—education, health, environment, industry, and quality certification—especially after the end of the transition phase in 1994. The ratification of the Protocol of Ouro Preto and the beginning of a new phase of consolidation of MERCOSUR caused the emergence of new issues—namely, the organization of a common market, proposals of a global MERCOSUR, and cooperation at various levels.

Other aspects of Uruguayan foreign policy were affected by participation in MERCOSUR. First, not only were foreign relations modified by the obligation stipulated by the Treaty of Asunción to negotiate en bloc every commercial agreement with other countries or groups of countries, but the Protocol of Ouro Preto ratified in November 1995 accorded a new juridical status to MERCOSUR. Second, and partly as a result of this new status, MERCOSUR began to act en bloc in every multilateral institution, and this fact originated a process of negotiations inside the bloc. This is the reason why MERCOSUR concluded en bloc the Agreement with the European Union for the creation of a common economic space, and has decided to negotiate in the same way to join the Agreement of Free Trade of the Americas.[7] Finally, the structure of foreign policy decision making was revised. This is due to the fact that the Council of the Common Market, the political institution of MERCOSUR, is formed by the Ministers of Economy and Foreign Relations of the four countries, and the Group Common Market, the executive body, is formed by representatives of those ministries and the presidents of the Central Banks of the state members. Therefore, the Ministries of Economy and Foreign Relations, as well as the presidents of the Central Banks, acquire a relevant position when it comes to formulating proposals or making decisions. The Ministry of Foreign Relations has played a relevant role as negotiator in matters related to timing and rhythm of the opening of the economy and the internationalization of the country. For this reason, from the 1990s on, a closer relationship has been seen between the said ministry and a variety of actors of the civil society, particularly those connected with industrial and commercial activities. Nevertheless, this new role of nongovernmental actors coexists with the direction of the integration process by the state bodies.

The process of regionalization involves not only the Ministries of Foreign Relations and Economy. MERCOSUR's goals and the institutional development have expanded the action of other state bodies. This is the case in several sectors such as health, education, judicial cooperation, policy, and security, among others. The integration of the country into a common space has led to the inclusion in the governmental agenda of new themes, such as the role of small countries, the case of borderlands, regional security, and the use of fluvial resources for transport—particularly the waterway, ports, and the need for a territorial policy.[8] The government adopted a geopolitical approach and established a set of priorities taking into account the position of Uruguay as a small country. Foreign policy was associated to a strategy based on the idea of concentric circles on a sliding scale of priorities, as follows: Argentina and Brazil, the Southern Cone, the region, the American continents, Ibero-America, Europe, and the rest of the world (Abreu 2000).

Another change brought about by the end of the Cold War affected the armed forces. On the one hand, as a result of the emergence of a common regional space, issues of security began to be thought of as regional and continental problems. Therefore, Uruguayan armed forces participated in many joint activities with their counterparts of other countries. On the other hand, after 1990 and in response to international requirements, Uruguay increased the participation of its armed forces in United Nations missions. This new trend is illustrated by the agreements between Argentina and Brazil (and of both countries with Paraguay) for the security of the Triple Frontier and the meeting of Presidents Carlos Saúl Menem and Fernando Henrique Cardoso in Buenos Aires in April 1996.

PERSPECTIVES OF FOREIGN POLICY AT THE BEGINNING OF THE TWENTY-FIRST CENTURY

The changes that have occurred in Uruguayan foreign policy in the last decades have been the consequence of modifications in the political regime and in the international system. Recent changes in the post–Cold War era have obeyed this logic: The emerging new international order led to different interpretations of the national political system and civil society, and this fact influenced the orientations and priorities of Uruguayan foreign policy, depending on the political party in power. For this reason, various elements of domestic politics are relevant for the orientation of foreign policy—namely, the election returns, the composition of the government, the political weight of the winning party, the personality of the minister of foreign relations, the political party he represents, and the representation of political parties in the parliament.

Changes in foreign policy after the 1960s led to enduring results, putting a definitive end to the vision of Uruguay as a country isolated from the region and the world. From the economic standpoint, the development model was abruptly modified during the 1970s with the decision to open the economy. The transition to democracy in the mid-1980s sought to mitigate the effects produced by the implementation of the economic policy of the military government, while maintaining the core ideas of said policy. The incorporation of Uruguay into MERCOSUR legitimized the adoption of the Program for Commercial Liberalization. Moreover, participation in the regional agreement has caused other consequences in economic regulations (law of defense of competition, antidumping measures), in negotiations en bloc and in the relationship with civil society.

Concerning the national territory, border agreements were concluded with neighboring countries, infrastructure undertakings brought about new energy resources and promoted tourism, and policies for the development of fisheries and the defense of the territory were designed. In the 1990s, the integration of Uruguay in the subregional group led to a new approach of the problem of territory. Recent debates related to the projected Colonia–Buenos Aires Bridge, the regional electric connection, the use of the waterway, the deep-waters port, and the use of sea resources are some examples of the difficulties arising out of the new regionalism and its impact on the national territory. Other changes are the result of the new relation with the world. Democracy has been considered as the basis of foreign policy since the transition to democratic government in the mid-1980s and has made possible an increasing cooperation within the region.

Finally, in the 1990s, MERCOSUR was the major change marking the beginning of a new period. Foreign policy was no longer the business only of the Ministries of Foreign Relations and Economy but acquired a global dimension involving governmental and nongovernmental actors such as entrepreneurs, trade unions, and cultural organizations, in the discussion of specific policies such as health, education, labor, and social security policies.

Uruguay has regionalized and internationalized itself and the current debates on the orientation of foreign policy concentrate on the priorities that

MERCOSUR should adopt and the options open to the country inside the bloc. In the near future, Uruguay should define its strategy as a small partner in MERCOSUR as the interests and perspectives of the various actors participating in the process of regional integration and internationalization are significant variables.

The current administration of President Jorge Batlle, who came to power in March 2000, has proposed a foreign policy with continental scope, emphasizing cooperation with other small partners within the continent and with the United States, liberal reforms, and opportunities for trade (Fernández Luzuriaga 2000). These new issues have had an effect on global, continental, and regional negotiations as well as on the strategy for MERCOSUR and the mechanisms of decision making (Bizzozero 2000).

DISCUSSION QUESTIONS

1. Which were the most important changes in Uruguayan foreign policy post-1973?
2. What impact did joining MERCOSUR have on Uruguayan foreign policy?
3. What permanent effects did the transition to democracy have on Uruguayan foreign policy?

NOTES

This chapter was written with the cooperation of Wilson Fernández Luzuriaga, who works in the Area of Comparative Studies on Foreign Policies, and Isabel Clemente, a professor at the Area of Studies on Uruguayan Foreign Policy, at the Program of International Politics and International Relations, School of Social Sciences.

1. The Colorado Party has two main groups: the Foro Batllista, led by ex-president Julio Maria Sanguinetti, and the 15, headed by President Jorge Batlle. The differences between them arise out of the role of the state, its relationship with actors of the civil society, and the timing and conditions of the insertion of Uruguay into the international order.

2. This was Law 14.179, strongly criticized by many analysts and jurists. See Astori et al. (1975).

3. President Sanguinetti's inaugural speech was published by several mass media at the time. See *El País*, March 2, 1985.

4. See *Busqueda,* March 7, 1985.

5. Meetings with ministers (*acuerdos*) and Councils of Ministers are two constitutional mechanisms for the expression of the will of the executive power (article 168, constitution of 1967).

6. At the senate, the unanimity was supported by the thirty-one members of this

state body, while at the chamber, only three members out of a total of ninety-nine voted against it.

7. See Protocol of Ouro Preto and Acuerdo Marco MERCOSUR–European Union, as well as other MERCOSUR documents on the website of the Administrative Secretaryship of MERCOSUR: www.mercosur.org.uy.

8. With respect to this subject, see the analysis by Wilson Fernández Luzuriaga (1998) on the foreign policy of the second Sanguinetti administration (1995–1999). The coalition government had a representative of the National Party, Alvaro Ramos, in the position of minister of foreign relations. The importance accorded to territory, borderlands, and transport illustrates the permanence of local and regional interests and its influence on policy formulation.

Glossary

Ad libitum alternare utrumque principium: A term used to express the idea of a hybrid principle in which Colombian foreign policy has alternated between *respice polum* and *respice similia* doctrines at will, depending on the issue area, historical moment, and administration in question.

Agreement to disagree: An understanding between Mexico and the United States whereby the Mexican government can disagree with U.S. policies on issues which are of fundamental importance to Mexico but not to the United States. The Mexican government agrees with the United States on issues that are of fundamental importance to the United States but are not to Mexico.

Alternative development: Forms of legitimate economic development in agriculture and light industry that can provide a livelihood to coca farmers displaced by coca eradication and disruption of the illegal drug economy.

Andean Group: A customs union founded in 1969 (composed of Bolivia, Colombia, Chile, Ecuador, and Peru) to promote economic integration, industrial planning, and establishing a set of common rules for foreign investment. Venezuela joined in 1974, and Chile withdrew in 1976.

Anti-Haitianism: A prejudice against Haitians who often occupy the lowest rungs of the socioeconomic ladder in the Dominican Republic. During the era of Trujillo (1930–1961) when nation-state building was still nascent, anti-Haitianism was used as one means of unifying the Dominican nation. It has since been used consistently by former president Joaquin Balaguer and other politicians.

Apertura: This term refers to the opening of a political system, economy, or diplomatic relations. Beginning in 1990, Colombia embarked on a process of opening and internationalizing of the economy, designed to promote economic growth, reduce inflation, and reform the country's commercial structure. Two of the primary motors of this process included export-oriented growth and economic integration.

Arias Peace Plan: The 1987 plan proposed by Costa Rica president Oscar Arias and agreed to by the other four Central American presidents, committing them to mutual nonaggression and political opening. The plan led to the end of the war in

Nicaragua; the electoral defeat of Sandinista president, Daniel Ortega; and eventually cease-fires and political openings in El Salvador and Guatemala Arias successfully promoted the plan over the opposition of the Reagan administration.

Autogolpe: Literally "self-coup," used to refer to Alberto Fujimori's dismissal of the legislature and courts in Peru to become an "elected dictator."

Benign isolation: Foreign policy consisting of discriminating and diversifying economic and commercial relations with select states, necessary in overcoming Paraguay's geopolitical isolation, while maintaining a low profile in order to minimize criticism.

Betancourt Doctrine: Policy in support of defending democracy in Latin America. Venezuelan president Romulo Betancourt, the author and main proponent, argued that democratic states in the hemisphere should sever diplomatic ties with governments that came to power by overthrowing democracies.

Bolivarianism: Admiration, adherence, and, on occasion, cult following to a set of very complex ideas expressed by Latin American independence leader Simón Bolívar during the course of his life. In terms of foreign policy, Bolivarianism emphasizes independence, Latin American unity and solidarity, and the search for security for Venezuela and Latin America.

Brain drain: A phenomenon with migration whereby people who are relocating (e.g., from the Caribbean to the United States) tend to be the brightest and most ambitious. Such migration can be very detrimental to the developmental prospects of the society losing its citizens.

Castro, Fidel: The Marxist-Leninist revolutionary leader of Cuba since 1959 and leader of the Non-Aligned Movement.

Centro Multilateral Antidrogas (CMA): An effort by Panama and the U.S. government to retain a U.S. military presence after 1999, by establishing a multilateral antidrug center with a small, but permanent, U.S. military contingent. After serious negotiations, Panamanian president Pérez Balladeres rejected the accord (in 1998), resulting in the departure of all U.S. troops from Panama at the end of 1999.

Charter States' Economic Rights and Duties: Document drafted in the 1970s and presented at the United Nations General Assembly that included the provisions for a New International Economic Order (NIEO), and the role of states in it, that would benefit less developed countries. The NIEO sought a more just and equal international order.

Chilean road to socialism: Slogan of the administration of President Salvador Allende to emphasize the need for a democratic path toward socialism in Chile. This political and economic experiment negatively affected Chile's relations with the West; however, it deepened its relations with the socialist camp, facilitating Chile's participation in third world international forums.

Communidad Andina (CAN): Spanish acronym for the Andean Community, a cooperative economic agreement among Venezuela, Colombia, Ecuador, Peru, and Bolivia. Previous names for the organization include the Andean Group and the Andean Pact.

Contadora: The name given to the group of four governments—Mexico, Venezuela, Colombia, and Panama—which intended to reach a negotiated and peaceful solution to the Central American conflict between 1983 and 1986. Negotiations emphasized the local causes of conflict as opposed to an East–West confrontational approach, security and dimensions, and the need for democratic governments in the region.

Contras: Armed forces seeking to overturn the Sandinista government in Nicaragua who were active from 1981 to 1989. The term *contras*, from the Spanish word for "counterrevolutionaries," became the popular name of the forces. Backed by the United States, they formed an umbrella organization called the Nicaraguan Democratic Force.

Core: Refers to the center, as opposed to the periphery, which refers to less developed countries that are on the margin or away from the core. It is a term borrowed from dependency theory, which characterizes countries as being in the center or the periphery.

Cotonou Agreement: Drafted in 2000; provides a framework for the European Union to extend trade preferences and developmental aid programs to a large group of developing nations (including CARICOM's members). It is, say many observers, less generous than the Lomé Accords, which it replaced.

Democratic transition from above and within: A process of democratic regime change led by discontented actors and institutions of the previous authoritarian regime. Many of the authoritarian regime's structural-institutional rigidities continue within new democratic rules, thus impeding democratic consolidation.

Dependency: Refers to dependency theory as developed by Brazilian sociologist Fernando Henrique Cardoso, later twice elected Brazilian president (1995–2003), and the Chilean sociologist Enzo Faletto, among others. Dependency theory establishes that the underdevelopment of backward economies is essentially due to their economic links with industrialized countries, especially former colonial or semicolonial rulers. According to dependency theory, economic growth and modernization of dependent countries tend to perpetuate their economic, social, and political backwardness. The focus is on the unequal, exploitative, and dependent relationship between developed and dependent/underdeveloped economies.

Diaspora: A conglomeration, often unplanned, of people from the same country of origin living within a host country while maintaining their cultural, linguistic, ethnic, religious, and national ties to their country of origin.

Dilemma of Mexican foreign policy: The need to maintain an anti-interventionist position and not to oppose the United States too much (Ojeda 1976: 80).

Diversification of dependence: A way of establishing relations with other countries to get away from the core. It is a search for a greater autonomy in foreign policy by a country that moves away from the core.

Economic diplomacy: Chile's new global approach directed toward sustaining the principles and policies of economic neoliberalism. It emphasizes official support for trade expansion and diversification.

Economic liberalization: The elimination of government intervention in the economy by deregulating, downsizing, privatizing, and introducing market mechanisms to align the economy based on market mechanisms.

Effective sovereignty: A situation in which a government and a society have the power to make and implement decisions affecting their own country's destiny. A nation with a high degree of effective sovereignty would register rather low on the Rosenau penetration scale.

Entregismo: An open policy of surrendering national patrimony or sovereignty to foreign interests.

Falklands/Malvinas Islands: An archipelago located in the South Atlantic occupied since 1833 by Great Britain. The territorial dispute between Argentina and the United Kingdom over these islands culminated in 1982 in an Argentine invasion and a short war that ended with the defeat of the Argentine forces.

Figueres Ferrer, José: The leader of the Army of National Liberation that overthrew President Picado in 1948. Figueres was the principal founder of the Costa Rican democratic regime. Figueres founded the Party of National Liberation and was elected president twice (1953–1958, 1970–1974).

Foreign policy paradox: A policy orientation of the Chilean authoritarian regime of General Augusto Pinochet whereby political and diplomatic isolation was pursued simultaneously with economic opening and expansion of Chile's role in the global economy.

Free trade: Trade under which goods and services are determined by market forces without state interference or barriers.

Furezas Armadas Revolucionarias de Colombian (FARC): The largest insurgency group in Colombia, established in the 1960s.

Geopolitics: Political geography or the combined environmental, geographical, and physical (or topographical) aspects of national power, which includes factors such as a state's size, population, and natural resources.

Group of 77: A collection of developing countries originally formed by seventy-seven countries not aligned to the centers of power.

Hay–Bunau–Varilla Treaty: A 1903 treaty signed by the United States and Panama that allowed the U.S. government to build the Panama Canal and establish the ten-mile, U.S.-controlled Canal Zone. The treaty was a key source of conflict between the United States and Panama since the Panamanians felt they accepted the treaty under duress and the accord gave the U.S. government the power to intervene in the isthmus perpetually.

Ideological pluralism: An attempt by Venezuelan president Rafael Caldera to expand and diversify diplomatic relations with a broad array of nations regardless of any political-ideological consideration.

Import substitution: A deliberate policy tool used to promote industrialization through the protective use of tariffs, subsidies, and foreign exchange controls.

Independent foreign policy: Adopted by Brazilian president Jânio Quadros (January–August 1961) with a view toward opening and diversifying Brazil's international economic and political relations, in contrast with the previous economic and political alignment with U.S. foreign policy goals. President João Goulart (1961–1964), who succeeded Quadros in the presidency, adopted the same approach, before being ousted by the military in March 1964.

Intermestic conflicts: *Intermestic* is a term that is used to explain the increasingly common phenomenon of fusion between international and domestic affairs. The Cold War, and the new security agenda that this has implied, led to conflicts being understood without the traditional distinction between domestic and international politics.

Itamaraty Peace Declaration: A 1996 agreement signed by Peru and Ecuador to end their conflict over the disputed border zone.

Junta: A Spanish word meaning "assembly" or "council."

Landlocked status: The geographic condition whereby a country lacks direct access to the sea or a major external body of water. This condition contributes to isolation and underdevelopment, as in the case of Bolivia and Paraguay.

Martí, José: A nineteenth-century Cuban independence leader and well known as a poet, writer, and journalist throughout Latin America.

MERCOSUR (Southern Cone Common Market): An agreement involving Argentina, Brazil, Paraguay, and Uruguay aimed at creating a free trade area as well as promoting further economic integration.

Militarization of the drug war: The use of a country's military and security forces and other militarized enforcement measures as a form of counternarcotics control.

Military internationalism: Also known as "proletarian internationalism," this term refers to the role of the Cuban military in the 1970s when it was used by the Castro regime to serve in military missions protecting friendly governments in the developing world.

Money laundering: A problem related to the international narcotics trade involving the utilization by drug cartels of banks and other financial institutions in third countries (e.g., in the Caribbean) to transform their illegal profits into legitimate assets. The (third-country) laws that allow such activities to occur have generated tensions between the U.S. government and some Caribbean governments.

NAFTA parity: Refers to arrangements that would give a country many of the benefits of the North American Free Trade Agreement (NAFTA) without becoming a formal participant in NAFTA. The U.S.-Caribbean Trade Partnership Act of 2000 is illustrative of efforts to achieve/provide elements of NAFTA parity.

Narcotization of foreign policy: Viewing a country's international relations primarily in terms of the drug war, or reducing relations with a country to its drug enforcement activities.

New regionalism: A country's political and strategic insertion into international regimes via economic integration.

Non-Aligned Movement: A group of nations that chose not to be militarily associated with either the West or former communists. The group continued to meet after the end of the Cold War.

National autonomy: The permanent approach of Chilean foreign policy to seek greater independence and economic and political flexibility vis–à-vis great powers.

Neoliberalism: A political-economic doctrine advocating free market and trade policies, balanced budgets, deregulation, privatization, and respect for private property. In foreign policy terms, it resulted in programs favoring economic opening in financial, commercial, and investment terms and closer relations with the United States, other developed countries, and organizations such as the International Monetary Fund, the World Bank, and the International Trade Organization.

Pact of Punto Fijo: An agreement signed in Caracas, Venezuela, by the principal political parties (Acción Democratica, COPEI, and Union Republicana Democratica) in October 1958 to ensure the stability and consolidation of a new, fragile democracy. The accord was established on the basis of elite consensus, shared responsibility, and no public antagonism on critical issues.

Panama Canal Treaties: Signed in 1977; two treaties that fundamentally changed the

U.S.–Panama relationship in that they ended the Canal Zone in 1979, gave to Panama control of the Panama Canal, and ended the long-standing U.S. military presence on the isthmus at the end of 1999. The accords, however, still allow the U.S. government to intervene in Panama for the purpose of defending the canal.

Panamanian Defense Forces (PDF): In 1983, General Manuel Noriega renamed Panama's National Guard the Panamanian Defense Forces, in an effort to give the military greater prestige and control. The PDF supported Noriega throughout the 1980s, becoming extensively involved in vote fraud during the 1989 national elections. The PDF was eliminated by Panama's president Guillermo Endara in 1990, just after the 1989 U.S. invasion.

Patrimonal rule: Traditional type of rule characterized by clientelism and personalism.

Pendulum foreign policy: Foreign policy strategy utilized by small, weak states to mitigate vulnerability vis-à-vis regional powers. In the case of Paraguay, Asunción played one regional hegemony against the other in order to enhance its autonomy while obtaining economic and political support from Argentina and Brazil.

Penetrated political system: James Rosenau's term for a system wherein the boundaries between the national and international have been eroded, and nonmembers of a national society are able to participate directly and authoritatively in the weaker state's policymaking process.

Petrostate: A state that has control over the economically dominant and dependent petroleum industry and its rents. The fragility of state institutions and social organizations combined with economic vulnerability and volatility are key components of a petrostate.

Political culture: The values, beliefs, and orientations that influence and shape a political system and its foreign policy. Political culture by revealing patterns of orientations to political actions helps us to understand the cultural idiosyncratic sources of foreign policy.

Praetorian: Caudillist foreign policy; foreign policy dominated by an authoritarian ruler and influenced by a strong anticommunism (national security doctrine) and nationalist ideology. There is a high concentration of power and authority in the caudillo or authoritarian despot.

Presidentialist foreign policy: Decision making and implementation of foreign policy dominated by the executive branch. This type of foreign policy is typical of societies with a long tradition of authoritarian rule and weak institutionalism.

Privatization: Refers to selling off of state assets to domestic and foreign investors. Privatization is an essential component of a neoliberal economic strategy.

Process of integration: A plan intended for the construction of a common market. States involved in this process share policies, territorial areas, and institutional structures that articulate national and regional interests.

Protected democracy: Weak democracies safeguarded against authoritarian threats by external actors (states and intergovernmental organizations).

Regional cooperation: Adaptation of directions and priorities among various states to seek goals of common interest.

Regional integration: An economic coalition among countries within a subregion promoting increased trade cooperation.

Respice polum: This term, which implied that Colombia should align its foreign policy with that of the United States, was coined by Colombian president Marco Fidel Suárez (1918–1922) and historically led the country to adopt a rationalized position of subordination toward the United States.

Respice similia: A term coined by Colombian president Alfonso López Michelsen (1974–1978) in order to suggest that Colombian foreign policy should revolve around relations with similar countries, especially in Latin America, to gain greater leeway vis-à-vis the United States.

Responsible pragmatism: Describes the goals and actions of Brazilian foreign policy from the early 1970s to the early 1980s, particularly during General Ernesto Geisel's term (1974–1979). Inspired by previous notions of independent foreign policy, responsible pragmatism involved a higher degree of conflict with U.S. foreign goals and policies.

Revolution in liberty: Slogan of the administration of Chilean president Frei Montalva during the 1960s to justify a peaceful and democratic process of reform of Chilean society. This was viewed as an alternative to violent, radical change espoused by many in Latin America following the Cuban model.

Rio Protocol: A 1942 agreement that temporarily ended conflict between Peru and Ecuador over the disputed Amazonian territory and finalized all but a tiny portion of the current border. It was a "guarantee" by international agents Argentina, Brazil, Chile, and the United States. That small portion saw numerous violent eruptions between troops from both sides in the 1990s.

Sandinistas: Given name of the Sandinist Front for National Liberation (FSLN), the revolutionary movement that overthrew Anastasio Somoza in 1979 and ruled until 1990. It transformed itself from a guerilla organization into a ruling party and then a major opposition party.

Special relationship: A perception held by some analysts and policymakers especially during World War II and immediately after of the unique nature of U.S.-Mexican relations largely as a result of geographic proximity. Relations were supposed to be close and understandings easily achieved given the special status of Mexico to the United States and vice versa.

State autonomy: The capability of a state to act with a relative degree of independence in its domestic and foreign policy decision making.

Statist: When government plays a leading role in the management of the economy.

Structural adjustment: Drastic economic measures taken by a country to establish economic balance. Often conditional measures are taken on loans from the International Monetary Fund and the World Bank, which request the removal of state controls and the liberalization of economic affairs.

Tercermundismo: "Third worldism"; refers to a "third path" of nonalignment in a bipolar world of two superpowers.

Third position: Nonaligned foreign policy approach adopted in Argentina by Juan Perón, his followers, and other nationalistic groups. This notion rejected any permanent alliance with the capitalist and socialist blocs led by the United States and the USSR during the Cold War and called for an autonomous foreign policy opposed to any hegemonic attempt.

Third world: Refers to the less developed countries of Asia, Africa, and Latin

America. They are characterized by low levels of economic development relative to industrialized nations.

Tico: Costa Rican.

Torrijos, General Omar: Panama's military dictator who took power soon after a military coup ousted the democratically elected president, Arnilfo Arias, in 1968. Torrijos, a populist leader, was known for his anticommunism as well as his social and political reforms. He negotiated the 1977 Panama Canal Treaties with U.S. president Jimmy Carter and ruled until 1981, when he died in an airplane crash.

Western alignment: Foreign policy approach supported by recent Argentine administrations that called for close cooperative ties with the United States in the expectation of establishing a beneficial preferential relationship in economic, diplomatic, and strategic terms.

Suggested Readings

Argentina

Cisneros, Andrés, and Carlos Escudé, eds. 1998–2000. *Historia general de las relaciones exteriores de la República Argentina*. Vols. 1–14. Buenos Aires: Nuevohacer, Grupo Editor Latinoamericano.

Escudé, Carlos. 1997. *Foreign Policy Theory in Menem's Argentina*. Gainesville: University Press of Florida.

Lanús, Juan A. 1984. *De Chapultepec al Beagle: Política exterior argentina (1945–1980)*. Buenos Aires: Emecé.

Norden, Deborah, and Roberto Russell. 2002. *The United States and Argentina: Changing Relations in a Changing World*. New York: Routledge.

Perina, Rubén M., and Roberto Russell, eds. 1988. *Argentina en el mundo (1973–1987)*. Buenos Aires: Latinoamericano.

Russell, Roberto, ed. 1993. *La Política exterior argentina en el nuevo orden mundial*. Buenos Aires: FLACS/ Latinoamericano.

Tulchin, Joseph S. 1996. "Continuity and Change in Argentine Foreign Policy." Pp. 165–96 in *Latin American Nations in World Politics*, ed. Heraldo Muñoz and Joseph S. Tulchin. Boulder, Colo.: Westview.

Bolivia

Farthing Linda, and George Ann Potter. 2001. "Bolivia: Eradicating Democracy." Foreign Policy in Focus, Interhemispheric Resource Center and the Institute for Policy Studies 5, no. 38 (March): 1–3.

Gamarra, Eduardo A. 1997. "Fighting Drugs in Bolivia: United States and Bolivian Perceptions at Odds." Pp. 243–53 in *Coca, Cocaine, and the Bolivian Reality*, ed. Madeline Barbara Léons and Harry Sanabria. Albany: State University of New York Press.

Lehman, Kenneth D. 1999. *Bolivia and the United States: A Limited Partnership*. Athens: University of Georgia Press.

Menzel, Sewall H. 1996. *Fire in the Andes: U.S. Foreign Policy and Cocaine Politics in Bolivia and Peru*. Lanham, Md.: University Press of America.
Morales, Waltraud Queiser. 1984. "Bolivian Foreign Policy: The Struggle for Sovereignty." Pp. 171–84 in *The Dynamics of Latin American Foreign Policies*, ed. Jennie K. Lincoln and Elizabeth G. Ferris. Boulder, Colo.: Westview.
———. 1992. *Bolivia: Land of Struggle*. Boulder, Colo.: Westview.
Shumavon, Douglas H. 1981. "Bolivia: Salida al mar." Pp. 179–90 in *Latin American Foreign Policies: Global and Regional Dimensions*, ed. Elizabeth G. Ferris and Jennie K. Lincoln. Boulder, Colo.: Westview.
St. John, Ronald Bruce. 1977. "Hacia el Mar: Bolivia's Quest for a Pacific Port." *Inter-American Economic Affairs* 31: 41–73.
———. 2001. "Same Space, Different Dreams: Bolivia's Quest for a Pacific Port." *Bolivian Research Review* 1, no. 1 (July 9). Available on-line: www.bolivianstudies.org.

Brazil

Albuquerque, J. A. Guilhon, ed. 2000. *Prioridades, atores e políticas: Sessenta anos de política externa brasileira*. São Paulo: University of São Paulo Center for International Relations.
Guedes da Costa, Thomaz. 2001. "Strategies for Global Insertion: Brazil and Its Regional Partners." Pp. 91–116 in *Latin America in the International System*, ed. Joseph S. Tulchin and Ralph H. Espach. Boulder, Colo.: Westview.
Hirst, Monica. 1996. "The Foreign Policy of Brazil: From the Democratic Transition to Its Consolidation." Pp. 197–224 in *Latin American Nations in World Politics*, ed. Heraldo Muñoz and Joseph S. Tulchin. Boulder, Colo.: Westview.
Hurrell, Andrew. 2002. "The Foreign Policy of Modern Brazil." Pp. 146–69 in *Comparative Foreign Policy: Adaptation and Strategies of the Great and Emerging Powers*, ed. Steven W. Hook. Upper Saddle River, N.J.: Prentice Hall.
Lafer, Celso. 2000. "Brazilian International Identity and Foreign Policy: Past, Present and Future." *Daedalus* 129 (Spring): 207–38.
Tollefson, Scott. 2002. "Brazil: The Emergence of a Regional Power." Pp. 283–301 in *Foreign Policy in Comparative Perspective: Domestic and International Influences and State Behavior*, ed. Ryan K. Beasley, Juliet Kaarbo, Jeffrey S. Lantis, and Michael T. Snarr. Washington, D.C.: CQ Press.
Vizentini, Paulo. 1995. *Relações internacionais e desenvolvimento, o nacionalismo e a política externa independente (1951–1964)*. Petropolis: Vozes.

Caribbean

Braveboy-Wagner, Jacqueline. 1989. *The Caribbean in World Affairs: The Foreign Policies of the English-Speaking States*. Boulder, Colo.: Westview.
Bryan, Anthony T., ed. 1995. *The Caribbean: New Dynamics in Trade and Political Economy*. New Brunswick, N.J.: Transaction.
Klak, Thomas, ed. 1998. *Globalization and Neoliberalism: The Caribbean Context*. Boulder, Colo.: Rowman & Littlefield.

Mullerleile, Christoph. 1996. *CARICOM Integration Progress and Hurdles: A European View*. Kingston, Jamaica: Kingston.
Rodriguez Beruff, Jorge, and Humerto García Muniz, eds. 1996. *Security Problems and Policies in the Post–Cold War Caribbean*. New York: St. Martin's.
Tulchin, Joseph, and Ralph H. Espach, eds. 2000. *Security in the Caribbean Basin: The Challenge of Regional Cooperation*. Boulder, Colo.: Rienner.

Chile

Fagen, Richard R. 1975. "The United States and Chile: Roots and Branches." *Foreign Affairs* 53, no. 2: 297–313.
Leiva, Patricio. 1996. "Las Relaciones de Chile y la Unión Europea." Pp. 113–56 in *América Latina y la Unión Europea: Construyendo el siglo XXI*, ed. Patricio Leiva. Santiago: Celare.
Morande, José A. 1990. "Chile y los Estados Unidos: Distanciamientos y aproximaciones." *Estudios Internacionales* 97: 3–22.
———. 1995. "Relaciones internacionales entre Chile y los Estados Unidos." *Estudios Internacionales* 111: 323–37.
Muñoz, Heraldo. 1984. "The International Policy of the Socialist Party and Foreign Relations of Chile." Pp. 150–67 in *Latin American Nations in World Politics*, ed. Heraldo Muñoz and Joseph S. Tulchin. Boulder, Colo.: Westview.
———. 1986. *Las Relaciones exteriores del Gobierno Militar Chileno*. Santiago: Ediciones del Ornitorrinco.
Wilhelmy, Manfred. 1996. "Politics, Bureaucracy and Foreign Policy in Chile." Pp. 61–80 in *Latin American Nations in World Politics*, 2d ed., ed. Heraldo Muñoz and Joseph S. Tulchin. Boulder, Colo.: Westview.

Colombia

Ardila, Martha, Diego Cardona, and Arlene B. Tickner, eds. 2002. *Prioridades y desafíos de la política exterior colombiana*. Bogotá: Fescol-Hanns Seidel Stiftung.
Bagley, Bruce, and Juan Gabriel Tokatlián. 1985. "Colombian Foreign Policy in the 1980s." *Journal of Interamerican Studies and World Affairs* 27, no. 3 (Fall): 27–62.
Drekonja, Gerhard. 1983. *Retos de la política exterior colombiana*. Bogotá: CEREC-CEI.
Matthiesen, Tatiana. 2000. *El Arte político de conciliar: El Tema de las drogas en las relaciones entre Colombia y Estados Unidos, 1986–1994*. Bogotá: FESCOL-CEREC-Fedesarrollo.
Pardo, Rodrigo, and Juan Gabriel Tokatlián. 1989. *Política exterior colombiana: De la subordinación a la autonomía?* Bogotá: Tercer Mundo–Uniandes.
Randall, Stephen J. 1992. *Aliados y distantes*. Bogotá: Tercer Mundo–Uniandes–CEI.
Restrepo, Luis Alberto, and Socorro Ramírez, eds. 1997. *Colombia entre la inserción y el aislamiento: La Política exterior colombiana en los años noventa*. Bogotá: Siglo del Hombre–IEPRI–Universidad Nacional de Colombia.
Tokatlián, Juan Gabriel. 1988. "National Security and Drugs: Their Impact on

Colombian-U.S. Relations." *Journal of Interamerican Studies and World Affairs* 30, no. 1 (Spring): 133–60.

Costa Rica

Arcaya Incera, Manuel. 1990. *Las Bases historicas de la política exterior costarricense: Algunas consideraciones*. Heredia: Escuela de Relaciones Internacionales, Universidad Nacional.

Hurwitz, Jon, Mark Peffley, and Mitchell Seligson. 1993. "Foreign Policy Belief Systems in Comparative Perspective: The United States and Costa Rica." *International Studies Quarterly* 37: 245–70.

Longley, Kyle. 1997. *The Sparrow and the Hawk: Costa Rica and the United States during the Rise of José Figueres*. Tuscaloosa: University of Alabama Press.

Rojas Aravena, Francisco, ed. 1990a. *Costa Rica y el sistema internacional*. Caracas: Nueva Sociedad.

———.1990b. *Política exterior de la administración Arias Sánchez, 1986/1990*. San José: FLACSO.

Schifter, Jacobo. 1986. *Las Alianzas conflictivas: Las Relaciones de Estados Unidos y Costa Rica desde la segunda guerra mundial a la guerra fria*. San José: Libro Libre.

Sojo, Carlos. 1991. *Costa Rica: Política exterior y Sandinismo*. San José: FLACSO.

Cuba

Dominguez, Jorge I. 1989. *To Make the World Safe for Revolution: Cuba's Foreign Policy*. Cambridge, Mass.: Harvard University Press.

———. 2001. "Cuban Foreign Policy and the International System." Pp. 183–206 in *Latin America in the International System*, ed. Joseph S. Tulchin and Ralph H. Espach. Boulder, Colo.: Rienner.

Erisman, H. Michael. 2000. *Cuba's Foreign Relations in a Post-Soviet World*. Gainesville: University Press of Florida.

Erisman, H. Michael, and John M. Kirk, eds. 1991. *Cuban Foreign Policy Confronts a New International Order*. Boulder, Colo.: Rienner.

Fernández, Damián. 1992. "Opening the Blackest of Black Boxes: Decisionmaking in Cuban Foreign Policy." *Cuban Studies* 22: 24–36.

Glejeises, Piero. 2002. *Conflicting Missions: Havana, Washington and Africa*. Chapel Hill: University of North Carolina Press.

Luxenberg, Alan. 1989. "Did Eisenhower Push Castro into the Arms of the Soviets?" Pp. 13–38 in *Cuban Communism*, 7th ed., ed. Irving Louis Horowitz. New Brunswick, N.J.: Transaction.

Pavlov, Yuri. 1994. *Soviet-Cuban Alliance: 1959–1991*. New Brunswick, N.J.: Transaction.

Dominican Republic

Atkins, G. Pope, and Larman C. Wilson. 2001. *The Dominican Republic and the United States: From Imperialism to Transnationalism*. Athens: University of Georgia Press.

Espinal, Flavio. 2000. "La nueva Visión de la OEA: Implicaciones para la política exterior de la republica Dominicana." Pp. 120–41 in *La Republica Dominicana el umbral del siglo XXI: Cultura, política y cambio social*, ed. Ramonina Brea, Rosario Espinal, and Fernando Valerio-Holguín. Santo Domingo: Pontifícia Universidad Católica de Madre y Maestra.

Graham, Pamela, and Jonathan Hartlyn. 1996. "The United States and the Dominican Republic: Toward the Year 2000: Marginality, Unilateralism or Cooperation?" Pp. 45–60 in *The Dominican Republic Today: Realities and Perspectives, Essays in English and Spanish*, ed. Emilio Betances and Hobart A. Spalding Jr. New York: Bildner Center for Western Hemisphere Studies.

Latorre, Eduardo. 1995. *De Política dominicana e internacional y desarrollo humano*. Santo Domingo: INTEC.

Wiarda, Howard, and Michael J. Kryzanek. 1988. *The Politics of External Influence in the Dominican Republic*. Stanford, Calif.: Praeger.

Ecuador

Corkill, David, and David Cubitt. 1988. *Ecuador: Fragile Democracy*. London: Latin America Bureau.

Herz, Monica, and João Pontes Nogueira. 2002. *Ecuador vs. Peru: Peacemaking amid Rivalry*. International Peace Academy Occasional Paper Series. Boulder, Colo.: Rienner.

Hey, Jeanne A. K. 1995. *Theories of Dependent Foreign Policy and the Case of Ecuador in the 1980s*. Athens: Ohio University Press.

———. 1996. "Political Manipulation of Foreign Policy in the Duran Ballen Presidency." *Canadian Journal of Latin American and Caribbean Studies* 21, no. 42: 293–310.

Palmer, David Scott. 1997. "Peru–Ecuador Border Conflict: Missed Opportunities, Misplaced Nationalism, and Multilateral Peacekeeping." *Journal of Interamerican Studies and World Affairs* 39, no. 3 (Fall): 109–48.

Mexico

Centro de Estudios Internacionales–Instituto Matias Romero de Estudios Diplomaticos. 1997. *Política exterior de Mexico: Un Analisis*. Mexico City: CEIIMAR.

Chabat, Jorge. 1996. "Mexican Foreign Policy in the 1990s: Learning to Live with Interdependence." Pp. 149–64 in *Latin American Nations in World Politics*, ed. Heraldo Muñoz and Joseph S. Tulchin. Boulder, Colo.: Westview.

Domínguez, Jorge I., and Rafael Fernández de Castro. 2001. *The United States and Mexico: Between Partnership and Conflict*. New York: Routledge.

Fernandez de Castro, Rafael, ed. 2002. *Cambio y continuidad en la política exterior de Mexico*. Mexico City: Ariel-ITAM.

Ferris, Elizabeth G. 1984. "Mexico's Foreign Policy: A Study in Contradictions." Pp. 213–27 in *The Dynamics of Latin American Foreign Policies*, ed. Elizabeth G. Ferris and Jennie K. Lincoln. Boulder, Colo.: Westview.

Garza, Elizondo, Humberto. 1984. "Desequilibrios y contradicciones en la política exterior de Mexico." *Foro Internacional* 24, no. 4 (96) (April–June): 443–57.
Garza Elizondo, Humberto, and Susana Chacon, eds. 2002. *Entre la Globalización y la dependencia: La Política exterior de Mexico, 1994–2000*. Mexico City: Colegio de Mexico-ITESM.
Mexico, Secretaria de Relaciones Exteriores. 1985. *Política exterior de Mexico: 175 anos de historia.* Mexico City: Author.
Sepulveda, Bernardo. 1984. "Reflexiones sobre la política exterior de Mexico." *Foro Internacional* 24, no. 4 (96) (April–June): 407–14.
Snarr, Michael T. 2002. "Mexico: Balancing Sovereignty and Interdependence." Pp. 302–20 in *Foreign Policy in Comparative Perspective: Domestic and International Influences and State Behavior*, ed. Ryan K. Beasley, Juliet Kaarbo, Jeffrey S. Lantis, and Michael T. Snarr. Washington, D.C.: CQ Press.

Nicaragua

Aviel, JoAnn Fagot. 1988. "Nicaragua and the United Nations." *Review of Latin American Studies* 1, no. 2.
Close, David. 1999. *Nicaragua: The Chamorro Years.* Boulder, Colo.: Rienner.
Merrill, Tim L. 1994. *Nicaragua: A Country Study.* Washington, D.C.: U.S. Government Printing Office.
Morley, Morris H. 1994. *Washington, Somoza, and the Sandinistas: State and Regime in U.S. Policy toward Nicaragua, 1969–1981.* Cambridge: Cambridge University Press.
Vanden, Harry E. 1991. "Foreign Policy." In *Revolution and Counterrevolution in Nicaragua*, ed. Thomas W. Walker. Boulder, Colo.: Westview.
Vanderlaan, Mary B. 1986. *Revolution and Foreign Policy in Nicaragua.* Boulder, Colo.: Westview.
Walker, Thomas W., ed. 1997. *Nicaragua without Illusions: Regime Transition and Structural Adjustment in the 1990s.* Wilmington, Del.: Scholarly Resources.
Walker, Thomas W., and Ariel C. Armony. 2000. *Repression, Resistance, and Democratic Transition in Central America.* Wilmington, Del.: Scholarly Resources.

Panama

Anguizola, Gustave. 1977. *The Panama Canal: Isthmian Political Instability from 1821 to 1977*. Washington, D.C.: University Press of America.
Araúz, Celestino Andrés. 1994. *Panamá y sus relaciones internacionales: Estudio introductorio.* 2 vols. Panama City: Editorial Universitaria.
Conniff, Michael L. 1992. *Panama and the United States: The Forced Alliance*. Athens: University of Georgia Press.
Ealy, Lawrence O. 1951. *The Republic of Panama in World Affairs, 1903–1950*. Westport, Conn.: Greenwood.
LaFeber, Walter. 1989. *The Panama Canal: The Crisis in Historical Perspective*. New York: Oxford University Press.

Ropp, Steve C. 1982. *Panamanian Politics: From Guarded Nation to National Guard.* New York: Praeger.

Paraguay

Estigarriba, José Felix, and José Luis Simon. 1987. *La Sociedad internacional y el estado autoritario del Paraguay.* Asunción: Aravera.

Hoyer, Hans. 1975. "Paraguay." Pp. 294–305 in *Latin American Foreign Policies: An Analysis*, ed. Harold E. Davis and Larman C. Wilson. Baltimore, Md.: Johns Hopkins University Press.

Mora, Frank. 1993. *Política exterior del Paraguay, 1811–1989.* Asunción: Centro Paraguayo de Estudios Sociologicos.

———. 1997. "From Dictatorship to Democracy: The U.S. and Regime Change in Paraguay, 1954–1994." *Bulletin of Latin American Research* 17, no. 1 (January): 59–79.

Simon, José Luis, ed. 1990. *Política exterior y las relaciones internacionales del Paraguay contemporáneo.* Asunción: Centro Paraguayo de Estudios Sociologicos.

———, ed. 1995. *Política exterior y democracia en el Paraguay y sus vecinos.* Asunción: Fundación Hans Seidel/Universidad Nacional de Asunción.

Yopo, Mladen. 1991. *Paraguay-Stroessner: La Política exterior del régimen autoritario.* Santiago: PROSPEL.

Peru

Bakula, Juan Miguel. 2002. *Peru: Ante la Realidad y la utopia.* Lima: Fondo de Cultura Economica.

Herz, Monica, and João Pontes Nogueira, 2002. *Peru vs. Ecuador: Peacekeeping amid Rivalry.* Boulder, Colo.: Rienner.

Masterson, Daniel M. 1991. *Militarism and Politics in Latin America: Peru from Sanchez Cerro to Sendero Luminoso.* New York: Greenwood.

McClintock, Cynthia, and Fabian Vallas. 2003. *The United States and Peru: Cooperation at a Cost.* New York: Routledge.

Tulchin, Joseph S., and Gary Bland, eds. 1994. *Peru in Crisis: Dictatorship or Democracy?* Boulder, Colo.: Rienner.

Wise, Carol. 2003. *Reinventing the State: Economic Strategy and Institutional Change in Peru.* Ann Arbor: University of Michigan Press.

Uruguay

Atkins, G. Pope. 1975. "Uruguay." Pp. 273–93 in *Latin American Foreign Policies: An Analysis*, ed. Harold E. Davis and Larman C. Wilson. Baltimore, Md.: Johns Hopkins University Press.

Bizzozero, Lincoln. 1989. "Definición de política exterior, toma de decisión y oportunidad de resolución." PROSPEL working paper no. 14. Santiago: Universidad Academia de Humanismo cristiano.

———. 1991. "La Política exterior del Uruguay en una perspectiva histórica." *Síntesis* 13 (January–April): 347–58.

Bizzozero, Lincoln, and Carlos Luján. 1992. *La Política exterior del gobierno de transición democrático en Uruguay (1985–1989)*. Montevideo: Facultad de Ciencias Sociales, Universidad de la República.

Castillo, María Eliana. 1987. "Uruguay: Profundización del camino trazado en la política exterior democrática." Pp. 345–60 in *Las Políticas exteriors de América Latina y el Caribe: Continuidad en la crisis*, ed. Heraldo Muñoz. Buenos Aires: PROSPEL.

Lujan, Carlos. 1990. "Política internacional del Uruguay: Tendencias presentes y escenarios posibles." *América Latina/Internacional* 7, no. 24: 4–15.

———. 1993. *Cambio de régimen y política internacional: El Caso uruguayo*. Montevideo: Intendencia Municipal de Montevideo.

Venezuela

Cardozo Da Silva, Elsa. 2000. "El mundo no es ajeno: El Juego de poder visto desde aquí." Pp. 431–58 in *Venezuela siglo XX: Visiones y testimonios*, vol. 1, ed. Asdrúbal Baptista. Caracas: Fundación Polar.

Consalvi, Simón Alberto. 2003. "Historia de las relaciones exteriores de Venezuela: 1810–2000." In *Enciclopedia multimedia de Venezuela*. Caracas: Planeta.

Hillman, Richard S. 1994. *Democracy for the Privileged: Crisis and Transition in Venezuela*. Boulder, Colo.: Rienner.

Josko de Guerón, Eva. 1984. "La Política exterior: Continuidad y cambio, contradicción y coherencia." Pp. 350–75 in *El caso Venezuela: Una ilusión de armonía*, ed. Moisés Naím and Ramón Piñango. Caracas: IESA.

Kelly, Janet, and Carlos Romero. 2002. *The United States and Venezuela: Rethinking a Relationship*. London: Routledge.

Nweihed, Kaldone G., ed. 1999. *Venezuela y los países hemisféricos, ibéricos e hispanohablantes*. Caracas: IAEAL, USB.

Polanco Alcántara, Tomás, Simón Alberto Consalvi, and Edgardo Mondolfi Gudat. 2000. *Venezuela y Estados Unidos a través de 2 siglos*. Caracas: Cámara Venezolano–Americana de Comercio e Industria.

Romero, María Teresa. 2002. *Política exterior venezolana: Proyecto democrático*, 1959–1999. Caracas: Libros El Nacional.

Bibliography

Abarca Vásquez, Carlos. 1995. *Rodrigo Carazo y la utopía de la dignidad, 1970–1983.* San José: Editorial de la Universidad Nacional.

abc color. 1991. "Estados Unidos: Vínculos entre legitimidad internacional y doméstica." February 4, 3.

———. 1993. "Entredicho entre Wasmosy y el embajador." *Asunción*, November 11, 8.

Abente, Diego. 1988. "Constraints and Opportunities: Prospects for Democratization in Paraguay." *Journal of Interamerican Studies and World Affairs* 30, no. 1 (Spring): 82–87.

———. 1996. "Paraguay: Transition from *Caudillo* Rule." Pp. 118–32 in *Constructing Democratic Governance: South America in the 1990s*, ed. Jorge I. Dominguez and Abraham Lowenthal. Baltimore, Md.: Johns Hopkins University Press.

Abreu, Sergio. 2000. "Uruguay: Socio pequeño del MERCOSUR." Pp. 41–81 in *Los países pequeños: Su rol en los procesos de integración*, ed. Lincoln Bizzozero, Sergio Abreu, and Fernando Masteo. Buenos Aires: Banco Interamericano de Desarrollo, Departamento de Integración y Programas Regionales del INTAL.

Aguilar Bulgarelli, Oscar. 1980. *Costa Rica y sus hechos políticos de 1948.* San José: Editorial Universitaria Centroamericana.

Alemán, Arnoldo. 2000. *Tercer informe de gobierno 1999.* Managua: Presidencia de la República.

Alfonsín, Raúl. 1994. "La Cumbre de las Américas y las alternativas de América Latina." Proceedings of the II Foro MERCOSUR-NAFTA, São Paulo. *Cuadernos del Parlatino* 6 (October): 19–23.

Almeida, Paulo R. 2000. "A Política da política externa: Os Partidos políticos na política externa do Brasil, 1930–1990." Pp. 381–448 in *Sessenta Anos de politica externa brasileira*, ed. J. A. Guilhon Albuquerque, *Vol. 4: Prioridades, atores e políticas,* ed. Ana Blume. São Paulo: University of São Paulo Center for International Relations.

Alzaga, Álvaro. 1985. "El 'NO' de Herrera a las bases aeronavales: 1940–1944." *Hoy es Historia* 2, no. 12 (October–November).

Ameringer, Charles D. 2000. *The Cuban Democratic Experience: The Auténtico Years, 1944–1952*. Gainesville: University Press of Florida.

Amnesty International. 2001. "Bolivia, Torture and Ill-Treatment: Amnesty International's Concerns." AMR 18/0008/2001, June 15. Available on-line: http://web.-amnesty.org/ai.nsf/print/AMR180008200l/OpenDocument (accessed July 10, 2001).

Amorim, Celso L. N. 1991. "O Mercado Comum do sul e o contexto hemisférico." *Série Política Internacional* 4. São Paulo: University of São Paulo Center for International Relations.

Amorim, Celso L. N., and Renata Pimentel. 1996. "Iniciativa para las Américas: O Acordo do Jardim das Rosas." Pp. 103–34 in *Sessenta Anos de politica externa brasileira: Vol. 2. Diplomacia para o desenvolvimento*, ed. J. A. Guilhon Albuquerque. São Paulo: University of São Paulo Center for International Relations and Cultura Editora.

Angell, Alan. 1993. *Chile de Alessandri a Pinochet: En Busca de la utopía*. Santiago: Bello.

Anguiano, Eugenio. 1977. "México y el tercer mundo: Racionalización de una posición." *Foro Internacional* 18, no. 1 (July–September): 177–205.

Araníbar Quiroga, Antonio. 1987. "Bolivianizar la lucha contra el narcotráfico: Elementos de una doctrina nacional." *Movimiento Bolivia Libre* (September).

———. 1999. *Bolivia, Chile y Perú: Hacia un futuro compartido*. La Paz: Centro de Información para el Desarrollo.

Araújo, Braz J. 1996. "A Política externa no governo de Jânio Quadros." Pp. 253–81 in *Sessenta Anos de política externa brasileira: Vol. 1. Crescimento, modernização e política externa*, ed. J. A. Guilhon Albuquerque. São Paulo: University of São Paulo Center for International Relations and Cultura Editora.

Araya Incera, Manuel. 1990. *Las Bases históricas de la política exterior costarricense: Algunas consideraciones*. Heredia, Costra Rica: Escuela de Relaciones Internacionales, Universidad Nacional.

Ardila, Marta. 1991. *Cambio de Norte? Momentos críticos de la política exterior colombiana*. Bogotá: Tercer Mundo.

Armony, Ariel C. 1997. *Argentina, the United States, and the Anti-Communist Crusade in Central America, 1977–1984*. Monographs in International Studies, Latin America Series, no. 26. Athens: Ohio University Center for International Studies.

Armstrong, Adrienne. 1981. "The Political Consequences of Economic Dependence." *Journal of Conflict Resolution* 25: 401–28.

Arriola, Carlos. 1974. "El Acercamiento mexicano-chileno." *Foro Internacional* 14, no. 4 (April–June): 507–47.

Associated Press. 2001. "Bolivian, Powell Discuss Drugs." Media Awareness Project. April 24. Available on-line: www.mapinc.org/drugnews/v01/n727/a11.html (accessed July 11, 2001).

Astiz, Carlos, and José Z. García. 1972. "The Peruvian Military: Achievement, Orientation, Training and Political Tendencies." *Western Political Quarterly* 25 (December 4): 667–85.

Astori, D. R. Zerbino, J. Rodríguez Lopez, and A. Tisnés. 1975. *Inversión extranjera y desarrollo económico*. Montevideo: Fundación de Cultura Universitaria.

Aviel, JoAnn Fagot. 1988. "Nicaragua and the United Nations." *Review of Latin American Studies* 1, no. 3: 81–90.

———. 1990. "'The Enemy of My Enemy': The Arab-Israeli Conflict in Nicaragua." Pp. 13–41 in *Central America and the Middle East*, ed. Damián J. Fernández. Miami: Florida International University.

———. 1992. "El Papel de España en el proceso de pacificación de Centroamérica." Pp. 295–312 in *La Reconstrucción de Centroamérica: El Papel de la comunidad europea*, ed. Joaquín Roy. Miami: University of Miami Press.

Axline, W. Andrew. 1979. *Caribbean Integration: The Politics of Regionalism*. New York: Nichols.

———. 1996. "External Forces, State Strategies, and Regionalism in the Americas." Pp. 199–218 in *Foreign Policy and Regionalism in the Americas*, ed. Gordon Mace and Jean-Philippe Thérien. Boulder, Colo.: Rienner.

Baer, Werner, and Melissa Birch. 1987. "The International Economic Relations of a Small Country: The Case of Paraguay." *Economic Development and Cultural Change* 35 (April): 601–27.

Bagley, Bruce M. 1981. "Mexico in the 1980's: A New Regional Power?" *Current History* 80, no. 469 (November): 353–55, 386–94.

———. 1982. "Mexican Foreign Policy and Central America: The Limits of Regional Power." Washington, D.C.: School of Advanced International Studies.

———. 1983. "Mexican Foreign Policy: The Decline of a Regional Power?" *Current History* 82, no. 488 (December): 406–9, 437.

———. 1989. "La interdependencia y la politica de Estados Unidos hacia Mexico: La decada de los ochenta." Pp. 45–67 in *Mexico-Estados Unidos, 1987*, ed. Gerardo M. Bueno and Lorenzo Meyer. Mexico City: El Colegio de Mexico.

Bagley, Bruce M., and Juan Gabriel Tokatlián. 1987. "La Política exterior de Colombia durante la década de los ochenta: Los Límites de un poder regional." Pp. 151–76 in *Continuidad y cambio en las relaciones América Latina–Estados Unidos*, ed. Monica Hirst. Buenos Aires: Latinoamericano.

Balaguer, Joaquín. 1985. *La Isla al revés: Haití y el destino dominicano*. Santo Domingo: Libreria Dominicana.

Banco de la República. 2001. *Indicadores Económicos: Primer Trimestre de 2001*. Bogotá: Author.

Barcelona, Eduardo, and Julio Villalonga. 1992. *Relaciones carnales: La Verdadera historia de la construcción y destrucción del misil Cóndor II*. Buenos Aires: Planeta–Espejo de la Argentina.

Barrios Morón, Raúl. 1989. *Bolivia y Estados Unidos: Democracia, derechos humanos y narcotráfico (1980–1982)*. La Paz: HISBOL-FLACSO.

Batista, Paulo N. 2000. "O Acordo Nuclear Brasil–República Federal da Alemanha." Pp. 19–54 in *Sessenta Anos de política externa brasileira*, ed. J. A. Guilhon Albuquerque, *Vol. 4: Prioridades, atores e políticas*, ed. Ana Blume. São Paulo: University of São Paulo Center for International Relations.

Bell, John Patrick. 1971. *Crisis in Costa Rica: The Revolution of 1948*. Austin: University of Texas Press.

Bendana, Alejandro. 1982. "The Foreign Policy of the Revolution." Pp. 319–27 in *Nicaragua in Revolution*, ed. Thomas W. Walker. New York: Praeger.

Bernal-Meza, Raul. 1989. "Teorias, ideas politicas y Percepciones en la formulacion de la politica exterior chilena: 1970–1989." Pp. 22–49 in *Politica, Integracion y*

Comercio Internacional en el Cono Sur Latinoamericano, ed. Raul Bernal-Meza, Oscar Mendoza, Mario M. Pouget, and Pedro Ruiz. Mendoza: Universidad Nacional de Cuyo.

———. 2000. *Sistema Mundial y Mercosur*. Buenos Aires: Grupo Editor Latinoamericano.

Berríos, Rubén. 1980. "La Regulación de la tecnología y la inversión extranjera." *Comercio Exterior* 30, no. 5 (May): 490–94.

———. 1986. "The Search for Independence." *NACLA Report on the Americas* 20, no. 3 (June): 27–32.

Berríos, Rubén, and Cole Blasier. 1991. "Peru and the Soviet Union: Distant Partners." *Journal of Latin American Studies* 23, no. 2 (May): 123–40.

Betancourt, Rómulo. 1969. *Hacia América Latina democrática e integrada*. 3d ed. Madrid: Taurus.

Biddle, W., and J. Stephens. 1989. "Dependent Development and Foreign Policy: The Case of Jamaica." *International Studies Quarterly* 33 (December): 411–34.

Biesanz, Mavis Hiltunen, Richard Biesanz, and Karen Zubris de Biesanz. 1979. *Los Costarricenses*. San José: Editorial Universidad Estatal a Distancia.

Birch, Melissa. 1988. "La Política pendular: Política desarrollo del Paraguay en la posguerra." *Revista Paraguaya dé Sociología* 25, no. 73: 73–103.

———. 1992. "Pendulum Politics: Paraguay's National Borders, 1940–1975." Pp. 203–228 in *Changing Boundaries in the Americas*, ed. Lawrence Herzog. San Diego: University of California Regents.

Bizzozero, Lincoln. 1988. "Toma de decisiones en política exterior uruguaya: El Caso de las dos Chinas." Cuadernos del CLAEH [Centro Latinoamericano de Economía Humana] 48. Montevideo: Centro Latinoamericano de Economía Humana.

———. 1989a. "Definición de política exterior, toma de decisión y oportunidad de resolución." PROSPEL, working paper 14. Santiago: Universidad Academia de Humanismo Cristiano.

———. 1989b. "Las Relaciones de Uruguay con la Unión Soviética durante el actual régimen representativo." Cuadernos del CLAEH [Centro Latinoamericano de Economía Humana] 51. Montevideo: Centro Latinoamericano de Economía Humana.

———. 1990. "Las Relaciones de Uruguay con la Unión Soviética." Pp. 22–41 in *Nuevos Rumbos en la relación Unión Soviética/América Latina*, ed. Roberto Russell. Buenos Aires: Facultad Latinoamericano de Ciencias Sociales/Argentina–Latinoamericano.

———. 1991. "La Política exterior del Uruguay en una perspectiva histórica." *Síntesis* 13 (Spain): 345–59.

———. 1997a. "Uruguay en el proceso de integración del Mercosur: ¿Hacia un rol de articulador regional?" *Lateinamerika: Analysen-Daten Dokumentation* (Hamburg): 273–95.

———. 1997b. "La Política internacional de Uruguay a principios del siglo XXI: ¿Un socio pequeño de carácter regional, continental, occidental o mundial?" Pp. 43–55 in *Cuadernos del Claeh: Vol. 21. Uruguay en la Región y el mundo: Retrospectivas/ Prospectivas*. Montevideo: N.p.

———. 1998. "La Política exterior de los nuevos regionalismos: El Uruguay de los noventa." Serie Documentos de Trabajo 36. Montevideo: Unidad Multidisciplinaria, Facultad de Ciencias Sociales.

———. 1999. "La Política exterior de Uruguay en el MERCOSUR." *Carta Internacional* 79 (San Pablo, Brazil): 6–7.

———. 2000. "Los Resultados electorales en Uruguay: Su Impacto en la política exterior y las relaciones regionales." *Carta Internacional* 83 (São Paulo): 1–4.

Bizzozero, Lincoln, and Carlos Luján. 1992. *La Política exterior del gobierno de transición democrático en Uruguay (1985–1989)*. Montevideo: Facultad de Ciencias Sociales, Universidad de la República.

Bizzozero, Lincoln, and Marcel Vaillant. 2000. *Inserción internacional de socios pequeños: Los Casos de Chile y Uruguay*. Cuaderno de Integración. Montevideo: Facultad de Ciencias Sociales, Universidad de la República.

Blasier, Cole. 1978. "The Cuban-U.S.-Soviet Triangle: Changing Angles." *Estudios Cubanos–Cuban Studies* (January): 1–9.

Boersner, Demetrio. 1978. *Venezuela en el Caribe: Presencia cambiante*. Caracas: Monte Ávila.

———. 1987. "Cambios de énfasis en la política exterior venezolana, 1958–1978." *Política Internacional* 8 (October–December): 8–15.

Bologna, Alfredo. 1991. *Dos modelos de inserción de Argentina en el mundo: Las presidencias de Alfonsín y Menem*. Rosario: Cuadernos de Politica Exterior Argentina.

Bond, Robert D. 1977. "Venezuela's Role in International Affairs." Pp. 227–62 in *Contemporary Venezuela and Its Role in International Affairs*, ed. Robert D. Bond. New York: New York University Press.

Booth, John A. 2000. "Costa Rica: Buffeted Democracy." Pp. 89–110 in *Repression, Resistance, and Democratic Transition in Central America*, ed. Thomas W. Walker and Ariel C. Armony. Wilmington, Del.: Scholarly Resources.

Bouzas, Roberto, and Saul Keifman. 1990. *Deuda externa y negociaciones financieras en la década de los ochenta: Una Evaluación de la experiencia argentina*. Documentos e Informes de Investigación 98. Buenos Aires: Facultad Latinoamericano de Ciencias Sociales.

Boye, Otto. 1974. "La Política exterior de Chile entre 1964–1970." *Estudios Sociales* 3 (April): 48–66.

Braveboy-Wagner, Jacqueline. 1989. *The Caribbean in World Affairs: The Foreign Policies of the English-Speaking States*. Boulder, Colo.: Westview.

———. 1995. *Caribbean Diplomacy: Focus on Washington, Cuba, and the Post–Cold War Era*. New York: Caribbean Diaspora Press at the Caribbean Research Center of the City University of New York.

Brea, Ramonina, Isis Duarte, Ramón Tejada Holgún, and Clara Báez. 1995. *Estado de la situación de la democracia dominicana (1978–1992)*. Santo Domingo: Pontifícia Universidad Católica de Madre y Maestra.

Breitenecker, Rudiger. 1992. "The Caribbean Basin Initiative—An Effective U.S. Trade Policy Facilitating Economic Liberalization in the Region: The Costa Rican Example." *Law and Policy in International Business* 23, no. 4 (Summer): 913–49.

British Broadcasting Corporation (BBC). 1995. "Amazon Region Countries Sign Lima Declaration on Sustainable Development." BBC Summary of World Broadcasts.

———. 1998. "Ecuadoran Congress Authorizes Signing of Peace Agreement with Peru." BBC Summary of World Broadcasts, October 19.

———. 1999. "Chile Reportedly Pushing for Full Diplomatic Ties with Bolivia by March 2000." Lexis-Nexis Academic Universe, excerpted from *La Tercera de la*

Hora (Santiago), December 27. Available on-line: http://web.lexis-nexis.com (accessed April 12, 2001).

———. 2000. "Colombian Rebels Warn Ecuador to Remain Neutral in Colombian Conflict." BBC Summary of World Broadcasts, July 20.

———. 2001. "Bolivia Pledges Coca-Eradication by 2002." Media Awareness Project, April 24. Available on-line: www.mapinc.org/drugnews/v01/n727/a13.html (accessed July 11, 2001).

Burke, Melvin. 1991. "Bolivia: The Politics of Cocaine." *Current History* 90, no. 553 (February): 65–68, 90.

Bustamante, Fernando. 1991. "La Política exterior chilena y los partidos políticos." *Cono Sur* 10, no. 1 (January–February): 33–36.

Caetano, Gerardo, and Pedro Rilla. 1987. *Breve Historia de la dictadura.* Montevideo: Centro Latinoamericano de Economía Humana.

Camacho Omiste, Edgar. 1986. "Bolivia en 1986: La Política exterior del neoliberalismo." Pp. 183–204 in *Las Políticas exteriores de América Latina y el Caribe: Continuidad en la crisis*, ed. Heraldo Muñoz. Buenos Aires: Programa de Seguimiento de las Políticas Exteriores Latinoamericanas/Latinoamericano.

———. 1989. "Política exterior independiente." Unpublished manuscript, La Paz.

———. 1996. "Democracy and Regional Multilateralism in Chile." Pp. 181–98 in *Foreign Policy and Regionalism in the Americas*, ed. Gordon Mace and Jean-Philippe Thérien. Boulder, Colo.: Rienner.

———. 2000. "Nuevas Perspectivas de la cuestión marítima." Pp. 345–70 in *Bolivia: Temas de la agenda internacional*, ed. Alberto Zelada Castedo. La Paz: Unidad de Análisis de Política Exterior (UDAPEX), Ministerio de Relaciones Exteriores y Culto.

Camargo, Sonia de, and José M. Vásquez Ocampo. 1988. *Autoritarismo e democracia na Argentina e Brasil (um a decada de politica exterior, 1973–1984).* São Paulo: Convivio.

Canak, W. 1989. "Debt, Austerity, and Latin America in the New International Division of Labor." Pp. 9–27 in *Lost Promises: Debt, Austerity, and Development in Latin America*, ed. W. Canak. Boulder, Colo.: Westview.

Carasales, Julio. 1992. "Argentina and Brazil: Nuclear Non-Acquisition and Confidence-Building." *Disarmament* 15, no. 3: 91–101.

Carazo, Rodrigo. 1989. *Carazo: Tiempo y marcha.* San José: Editorial Universidad Estatal a Distancia.

Cardona, Diego. 1990. "Evaluación de la política exterior de la administración Barco." Documentos Ocasionales 16. Centro de Estudios Internacionales, Universidad de los Andes (July–August).

———. 1997. "Colombia: Una Política exterior hacia el futuro." Pp. 340–69 in *Colombia: Entre la Inserción y el aislamiento*, ed. Socorro Ramírez and Luis Alberto Restrepo. Bogotá: Siglo del Hombre.

Cardona, Diego, Carlo Nasi, Liliana Obregón, Arlene B. Tickner, and Juan Gabriel Tokatlián. 1992. *Colombia–Venezuela: Crisis o negociación?* Bogotá: Centro de Estudios Internacionales.

Cardona, Diego, and Juan Gabriel Tokatlián. 1991. "Los Desafíos de la política internacional colombiana en los noventa." *Colombia Internacional* 14 (April–June): 3–10.

Cardoso, Oscar, Ricardo Kirschbaum, and Eduardo van der Kooy. 1992. *Malvinas: La Trama secreta.* Buenos Aires: Sudamericana-Planeta.

Cardozo Da Silva, Elsa. 1992. *Continuidad y consistencia en quince años de política exterior venezolana: 1969–1984.* Caracas: Universidad Central de Venezuela.

———. 1997. "Política exterior para la gobernabilidad democrática." Pp. 71–121 in *De una a otra gobernabilidad: El Desbordamiento de la democracia venezolana*, ed. Richard S. Hillman and Elsa Cardozo Da Silva. Caracas: Universidad Central de Venezuela.

———. 2000. "El Mundo no es ajeno: El Juego de poder visto desde aquí." Pp. 431–58 in *Venezuela siglo XX: Visiones y testimonios*, vol. 1, ed. Asdrúbal Baptista. Caracas: Fundación Polar.

Carey, James. 1964. *Peru and the United States: 1900–1962.* Notre Dame, Ind.: University of Notre Dame Press.

Carreras, Rodrigo X. 1990. "Costa Rica y Panamá: Asimetría bajo penetración." Pp. 117–136 in *Costa Rica y el sistema internacional*, ed. Francisco Rojas Aravena. Caracas: Nueva Sociedad.

Carrillo, Justo. 1985. "Vision and Revision: U.S.-Cuban Relations." Pp. 163–74 in *Cuba: Continuity and Change*, ed. Jaime Suchlicki, Antonio Jorge, and Damián Fernández. Coral Gables, Fla.: University of Miami Press.

Castañeda, Jorge G. 1987. "¿Qué hacemos en Centroamérica?" Pp. 55–73 in *México: El Futuro en juego.* Mexico City: Joaquín Mortiz–Planeta.

Castillo, María Eliana. 1986. "La Reinserción internacional del Uruguay democrático." Pp. 469–86 in *América Latina y el Caribe: Políticas exteriores para sobrevivir*, ed. Heraldo Muñoz. Santiago: N.p.

———. 1987. "Uruguay: Profundización del camino trazado en la política exterior democrática." Pp. 457–78 in *Las Políticas exteriores de América Latina y el Caribe: Continuidad en la crisis*, ed. Heraldo Muñoz. Buenos Aires: Programa de Seguimiento de las Políticas Exteriores Latinoamericanas.

———. 1988. "Uruguay 1987: Manteniendo la continuidad externa." Pp. 458–78 in *Las Políticas exteriores de América Latina y el Caribe: Un Balance de esperanzas*, ed. Heraldo Muñoz. Buenos Aires: Programa de Seguimiento de las Políticas Exteriores Latinoamericanas–rupo Editorial Latinoamericano.

———. 1989. "Política exterior de Uruguay en 1988." Pp. 462–81 in *Las Políticas exteriores latinoamericanas: A la Espera de una nueva etapa*, ed. Heraldo Muñoz. Caracas: Nueva Sociedad.

Cavallo, Domingo. 1982. *Volver a crecer*. Buenos Aires: Sudamericana/Planeta.

Centro de Apoyo a Programas y Proyectos (CAPRI). 1992. *Directorio ONG de Nicaragua, 1991–1992.* Managua: El Amanecer.

Centro de Documentación e Información (CEDOIN). 1990. "Campaña de soberanía nacional: Militarización no, desarrollo sí!" *Informe R* 10, no. 194 (May 1). La Paz: Author.

Centro de Estudios en Relaciones Internacionales de Rosario (CERIR). 1994. *La Política exterior del gobierno de Menem.* Rosario, Argentina: Author.

Centro Paraguayo de Estudios Internacionales. 2000. *Bases para la agenda internacional del Paraguay: Una Visión desde la sociedad civil.* Asunción: Author.

Centro Paraguayo de Estudios Sociologicos. 2001. *Lineamientos básicos para la formulacón de la política exterior paraguaya.* Asunción: Author.

Cepeda Ulloa, Fernando. 1985. "El Proceso de paz en Colombia y la política internacional." Pp. 11–22 in *Contadora: Desafío a la diplomacia tradicional*, ed. Fernando

Cepeda Ulloa and Rodrigo Pardo García-Peña. Bogotá: Centro de Estudios Internacionales–Oveja Negra.
Cepeda Ulloa, Fernando, and Rodrigo Pardo García-Peña. 1989. "La Política exterior colombiana (1930–1946)"; "La Política exterior colombiana (1946–1974)"; La Política exterior colombiana (1974–1986)." Pp. 9–90 in *Nueva Historia de Colombia,* Vol. III, comp. Alvaro Tirado Mejía. Bogotá: Planeta.
Cerdas Cruz, Rodolfo. 1992. "Costa Rica." Pp. 280–99 in *Latin America between the Second World War and the Cold War, 1944–1948*, ed. Leslie Bethell and Ian Roxborough. Cambridge, Mass.: Harvard University Press.
Chabat, Jorge. 1992. "La Política exterior de Miguel de la Madrid: Las Paradojas de la modernización en un mundo interdependiente." Pp. 91–104 in *México: Auge, crisis y ajuste*, ed. Carlos Bazdresch, Nisso Bucay, Soledad Loaeza, and Nora Lustig. Mexico City: Fondo de Cultura Económica.
Child, Jack. 1992. *The Central American Peace Process, 1983–1991.* Boulder, Colo.: Rienner.
Cisternas, Carlos. 1996. "'El Loco' Wins Ecuador's Presidential Election." Associated Press, July 8.
Clark, Mary. 1997. "Transnational Alliances and Development Policy in Latin America: Nontraditional Export Promotion in Costa Rica." *Latin American Research Review* 32, no. 2: 71–98.
Clayton, Lawrence A. 1999. *Peru and the United States: The Condor and the Eagle.* Athens: University of Georgia Press.
Close, David. 1999. *Nicaragua: The Chamorro Years.* Boulder, Colo.: Rienner.
Cockcroft, James D. 1996. *Latin America: History, Politics, and U.S. Policy.* Chicago: Nelson-Hall.
Coleman, Kenneth M., and Luis Quiros-Varela. 1981. "Determinants of Latin American Foreign Policies: Bureaucratic Organizations and Development Strategies." Pp. 39–59 in *Latin American Foreign Policy: Global and Regional Dimensions*, ed. E. Ferris and J. Lincoln. Boulder, Colo.: Westview.
Conaghan, Catherine. 1988. *Restructuring Domination: Industrialists and the State in Ecuador*. Pittsburgh, Pa.: University of Pittsburgh Press.
Conaghan, Catherine, and James M. Malloy. 1994. *Unsettling Statecraft: Democracy and Neoliberalism in the Central Andes.* Pittsburgh, Pa.: University of Pittsburgh Press.
Connolly, Willam E. 1991. *Identity/Difference: Democratic Negotiations of Political Paradox.* Ithaca, N.Y.: Cornell University Press.
Consalvi, Simón Alberto. 1997. "Los Mitos de la política exterior." Pp. 141–50 in *El Perfil y la sombra*, ed. Simón Alberto Consalvi. Caracas: Tierra de Gracia.
———. 2000. "La Relación de Venezuela–Estados Unidos durante la primera mitad del siglo XX." Pp. 137–319 in *Venezuela y Estados Unidos a través de 2 siglos*, ed. Tomás Polanco Alcántara, Simón Alberto Consalvi, and Edgardo Mondolfi Gudat. Caracas: Cámara Venezolano–Americana de Comercio e Industria.
Cope, Orville G. 1975. "Chile." Pp. 309–37 in *Latin American Foreign Policies: An Analysis*, ed. Harold E. Davis and Larman C. Wilson. Baltimore, Md.: Johns Hopkins University Press.
Corkill, David, and David Cubitt. 1988. *Ecuador: Fragile Democracy*. London: Latin America Bureau.
Corlazzoli, Pablo. 1987. *Los Regímenes militares en América Latina: Estructuración e ideología en los casos de Brasil, Chile y Uruguay*. Montevideo: Nuevo Mundo.

Correa, Luis Felipe S. 1995. "Introduction." Pp. 2–17 in *A Palavra Do Brasil nas Nacioes Unidas, 1946–1995*, ed. Ministry of Foreign Relations. Brasília: Fundacao Alexandre Gusmao.

Cotonou Agreement. 2000. Available on-line: www.apcsec.org/gb/cotonou/accord1.htm.

Covarrubias, Ana. 1999. "El Problema de los derechos humanos y los cambios en la política exterior." *Foro Internacional* 39, no. 4 (October–December): 429–52.

Crabtree, John. 1992. *Peru under García: An Opportunity Lost*. Pittsburgh, Pa.: Pittsburgh University Press.

Crawley, Eduardo. 1979. *Dictators Never Die: A Portrait of Nicaragua and the Somoza Dynasty*. New York: St. Martin's.

De la Mora, Luz María. 1995. "Comercio internacional y medio ambiente: El Caso del embargo atunero en las relaciones entre México y Estados Unidos." Pp. 205–39 in *México–Estados Unidos–Canadá, 1993–1994*, comp. Gustavo Vega Cánovas. Mexico City: Colegio de México.

Del Castillo, Gustavo, and Gustavo Vega. 1995. "The North American Free Trade Agreement in Context: A Mexican Perspective." Pp. 83–151 in *The Politics of Free Trade in North America*, ed. Gustavo del Castillo and Gustavo Vega. Ottawa: Center for Trade Policy and Law.

Del Pilar Gumucio, Maria. 1995. "U.S. and Bolivia at a Crossroads: Between Cooperation and Collision." Master's thesis, Florida International University. Miami.

Demas, William. 1986. *Consolidating Our Independence: The Major Challenge for the West Indies*. Distinguished Lecture Series. St. Augustine: Institute of International Relations, University of the West Indies, Republic of Trinidad and Tobago.

Dempsey, Mary. 2001. "In Spite of Everything." *Latin Trade* (February): 21–23.

d'Escoto, Miguel. 1992. Interview with author, Managua; July.

Diaz Espino, Ovidio. 2001. *How Wall Street Created a Nation: J.P. Morgan, Teddy Roosevelt, and the Panama Canal*. New York: Four Walls Eight Windows.

Domínguez, Jorge I. 1978a. *Cuba: Order and Revolution*. Cambridge, Mass.: Belknap Press of Harvard University Press.

———. 1978b. "Cuban Foreign Policy." *Foreign Affairs* (Fall): 97.

———. 1980. "The Success of Cuban Foreign Policy." Center for Latin American and the Caribbean Studies Occasional Papers 27. New York: New York University.

———. 1998. "Ampliando horizontes: Aproximaciones teóricas para el estudio de las relaciones México–Estados Unidos." Pp. 25–56 in *Nueva Agenda bilateral en la relación México–Estados Unidos*, coordinated by Mónica Verea Campos, Rafael Fernández de Castro, and Sidney Weintraub. Mexico City: Instituto Tecnológico Autónomo de México, Universidad Nacional Autónoma de México–Centro de Investigaciones sobre América del Norte, Fondo de Cultura Económica.

Domínguez, Jorge I., and Rafael Fernández de Castro. 2001. *The United States and Mexico: Between Partnership and Conflict*. New York: Routledge.

Drekonja, Gerhard. 1983. *Retos de la política exterior colombiana*. Bogotá: Centro de Estudios Internacionales.

Dunkerley, James. 1984. *Rebellion in the Veins: Political Struggle in Bolivia, 1952–1982*. London: Verso.

Durán, Roberto. 1996. "Democracy and Regional Multilateralism in Chile." Pp. 181–98 in *Foreign Policy and Regionalism in the Americas*, ed. Gordon Mace and Jean-Philippe Thérien. Boulder, Colo.: Rienner.

Durch, William J. 1978. "The Cuban Military in Africa and the Middle East: From Algeria to Angola." *Studies in Comparative Communism* 11 (Spring–Summer): 34–74.
Ebel, Roland, Raymond Taras, and James D. Cochrane. 1991. *Political Culture and Foreign Policy in Latin America: Case Studies from the Circum-Caribbean.* Albany: State University of New York Press.
Ecocentral. 1996–1998. Albuquerque, N.M.: Latin American Data Base. Available on-line: http://ladb.unm.edu.
The Economist. 1996. U.S. Edition, Special; November 30, 19.
———. 1999. "Awaiting Rescue." August 7, 14.
———. 2000. "Ecuador's Post-Coup Reckoning." January 20, 21.
Economist Intelligence Unit (EIU). 2001. "Economic Data." May 4.
Edelman, Marc. 1983. "Costa Rica: Seesaw Diplomacy." *NACLA Report on the Americas* (November–December): 40–43.
Eguizabal, Cristina. 2000. "Latin American Foreign Policies and Human Rights." Pp. 54–69 in *Human Rights and Comparative Foreign Policy: Foundations of Peace*, ed. David P. Forsythe. New York: United Nations Press.
Einaudi, Luigi. 1999. "El Proceso de paz peruano-ecuatoriano." *Análisis Internacional* 16 (January–June): 3–9.
Elman, Miriam Fendius. 1995. "The Foreign Policies of Small States: Challenging Neorealism in Its Own Backyard." *British Journal of Political Science* 25: 171–217.
Erisman, H. Michael. 1985. *Cuba's International Relations: The Anatomy of a Nationalistic Foreign Policy.* Boulder, Colo.: Westview.
Escobar, Gabriel. 1996. "Free Market Is No Sacred Cow in Ecuadorean Election." *Washington Post*, March 31, A23.
Escudé, Carlos. 1984. *La Argentina: ¿Paria internacional?* Buenos Aires: Belgrano.
———. 1987. *Patología del nacionalismo: El Caso argentino.* Buenos Aires: Tesis.
———. 1997. *Foreign Policy Theory in Menem's Argentina.* Gainesville: University Press of Florida.
Espinal, Flavio. 2000. "La nueva Visión de la OEA: Implicaciones para la política exterior de república dominicana." Pp. 137–57 in *La República dominicana el umbral del siglo XXI: Cultura, política y cambio social*, ed. Ramonina Brea, Rosario Espinal, and Fernando Valerio-Holguín. Santo Domingo: Pontifícia Universidad Católica de Madre y Maestra.
Espinal, Rosario. 1994. "The 1994 Elections in the Dominican Republic." *Report to the Inter-American Dialogue* (November).
———. 1998. "Electoral Observation and Democratization in the Dominican Republic." Pp. 359–81 in *Electoral Observation and Democratic Transitions in Latin America*, ed. Kevin Middlebrook. La Jolla, Calif.: Center for U.S.-Mexican Studies.
Eurodad. 1998. "Nicaragua: IMF and Aleman Government Sign the ESAF Programme for 1998–2000, Civil Society Platform Looks for Improvement and Alternatives." Eurodad briefing period, March. Available on-line: www.eurodad.org.
Evanson, Robert K. 1985. "Soviet Political Uses of Trade with Latin America." *Journal of Interamerican Studies and World Affairs* 17, no. 2 (Summer): 99–127.
Facio, Gonzalo. 1979. "Política exterior." Pp. 159–88 in *Costa Rica Contemporánea*, vol. 1, ed. Chester Zelaya. San José: Editorial Costa Rica.
Fagen, Richard R. 1975. "The United States and Chile: Roots and Branches." *Foreign Affairs* 53, no. 2 (January): 297–313.

Faiola, Anthony. 1998. "Peru–Ecuador Peace Treaty May Be Near." *Washington Post*, February 8, A31.
———. 2001. "In Bolivia's Drug War, Success Has Price." *Washington Post*, March 4. Available on-line: www.mapinc.org/drugnews/v01/n383/a08.html (accessed July 11, 2001).
Falcoff, Mark. 1986. "Chile: The Dilemma of U.S. Foreign Policy." *Foreign Affairs* 64, no. 4 (Spring): 833–44.
Farrell, Cathleen. 1998. "Setting the Next Agenda." *Time*, July 6, 26–27.
Farthing, Linda, and George Ann Potter. 2001. "Bolivia: Eradicating Democracy." Foreign Policy in Focus, Interhemispheric Resource Center and the Institute for Policy Studies 5, no. 38 (March): 1–3. Available on-line: www.fpif.org.
Ferguson, James. 1994. "Presidential Elections: Loser Takes All." *NACLA Report on the Americas* 28, no. 3: 5–11.
Ferguson, Yale H. 1987. "Analyzing Latin American Foreign Policies." *Latin American Research Review* 22, no. 3: 142–56.
Fermandois, Joaquin. 1991. "De una Inserción a otra: Política exterior de Chile 1966–1991." *Estudios Internacionales* 24, no. 96 (October–December): 433–55.
Fernández, Damián J. 1987. "The Duty of a Revolutionary: Cuba's Foreign Policy as a Third World Model." *Harvard International Review* 11, no. 2 (January): 29–32.
———. 1988. *Cuba's Foreign Policy in the Middle East*. Westview Special Studies on Latin America and the Caribbean. Boulder, Colo.: Westview.
Fernandez de Cordoba, Marcelo. 1998. *Itamaraty: Seiscientos veintisiete días por la paz*. Quito: V&G.
Fernández Estigarribia, José Felix, and José Luis Simon. 1987. *La Sociedad internacional y el estado autoritario del Paraguay*. Asunción: Aravera.
Fernández, Janina. 1988. *Inestabilidad económica con estabilidad política*. San José: Editorial de la Universidad de Costa Rica.
Fernández, Leonel. 1996. *Leonel: Temas de campaña, Octubre de 1993–Marzo de 1996*. Santo Domingo: Alfa y Omega.
Fernández Luzuriaga, Wilson. 1998. *Los Nicios de la política exterior en la actual administración*. Serie Documentos de Trabajo 37. Montevideo: Unidad Multidisciplinaria, Facultad de Ciencias Sociales.
———. 2000. *El Presidente electo en la transición: Variables afectadas de la política exterior*. Working paper 53. Montevideo: Unidad Multidisciplinaria.
Ferré, Alberto Methol. 1973. *El Uruguay como problema*. 2d ed. Montevideo: Banda Oriental.
Ferrero Costa, Eduardo. 1987. "Peruvian Foreign Policy: Current Trends, Constraints and Opportunities." *Journal of Interamerican Studies and World Affairs* 29, no. 2 (Summer): 55–78.
———, ed. 1995. *Hacia una agenda nacional de políitica exterior*. Lima: Centro Paraguayo de Estudios Internacionales.
Ferrigni Yoston, Carlos Guerón, and Eva Josko de Guerón. 1973. "Hipótesis para el estudio de una política exterior." *Estudio de Caracas*, Gobierno y Política, VIII-2. Caracas: Universidad Central de Venezuela.
Ferris, Elizabeth G. 1979. "Foreign Investment as an Influence on Foreign Policy Behavior: The Andean Pact." *Inter-American Economic Affairs* 3, no. 2: 45–70.
Ferris, Elizabeth G., and Jennie K. Lincoln, eds. 1981. *Latin American Foreign Policies: Global and Regional Dimensions*. Boulder, Colo.: Westview.

———, eds. 1984. *The Dynamics of Latin American Foreign Policies: Challenges for the 1980s*. Boulder, Colo.: Westview.

Fishlow, Albert. 1998. "Estrategia económica colombiana: La Dimensión internacional." Pp. 325–36 in *Colombia y Estados Unido: Problemas y perspectivas*, ed. Juan Gabriel Tokatlián. Bogotá: Tercer Mundo–Colciencias.

Flores Neto, Francisco. 1991. "Integração e Cooperação Brasil-Argentina." Série Política Internacional 3. São Paulo: University of São Paulo Center for International Relations.

Fonseca, Gelson. 1996. "Mundos diversos, argumentos afins: Notas sobre aspectos doutrinários da política externa independente e do pragmatismo responsável." Pp. 299–336 in *Sessenta Anos de política externa brasileira: Vol. 1. Crescimento, modernização e política externa*, ed. J. A. Guilhon Albuquerque. São Paulo: University of São Paulo Center for International Relations and Cultura Editora.

Franco, Andrés. 1998. "La Cooperación fragmentada como una nueva forma de diplomacia: Las Relaciones entre Colombia y Estados Unidos en los noventa." Pp. 37–83 in *Estados Unidos y los países andinos, 1993–1997: Poder y desintegración*, ed. Andrés Franco. Bogotá: Centro de Estududios Judiciales.

Franco, José. 1988. *Intercambio comercial paraguayo-brasileno: Análisis de su incidencia en la economía Paraguaya*. Asunción: Centro Paraguayo de Estudios Sociologicos.

Fundación Arias. 1997. *Diagnóstico sobre la incidencia en Centroamérica: Proyecto la formación de una cultura democrática en Centroamérica: El Papel socializador de las ONG*. San José: Arias.

Fundación Polar. 1988. *Diccionario de historia de Venezuela*. Caracas: Ex Libris.

Furlong, William. 1987. "Costa Rica: Caught between Two Worlds." *Journal of Interamerican Studies and World Affairs* 29, no. 2 (Summer): 119–54.

Furtak, Robert K. 1983. "Cuba: Análisis." Pp. 461–88 in *Teoría y práctica de la política exterior latinoamericana*, ed. Gerard K. Drekonya and Juan G. Tokatlián. Bogotá: Universidad de los Andes.

Galeano, Luis. 1989. *De la Apertura otorgada a la transición pactada*. Working paper. Asunción: Centro Paraguayo de Estudios Sociologicos.

Gamarra, Eduardo A. 1997. "Fighting Drugs in Bolivia: United States and Bolivian Perceptions at Odds." Pp. 243–52 in *Coca, Cocaine, and the Bolivian Reality*, ed. Madeline Barbara Léons and Harry Sanabria. Albany: State University of New York Press.

Gambone, Michael D. 1997. *Eisenhower, Somoza, and the Cold War in Nicaragua 1953–1961*. Westport, Conn.: Praeger.

Gamus Gallegos, Raquel. 1994. "La Política exterior de Pérez Jiménez hacia Estados Unidos: Entre la autonomía y la dependencia." In *Anuario 1994: Instituto de Estudios Hispanoamericanos*, vol. 6. Caracas: Universidad Central de Venezuela.

García, Miguel V. 1992. *Argentina en el Golfo*. Buenos Aires: Pleamar.

García Bedoya, Carlos. 1981. *Políitica exterior peruana: Teoríia y práactica*. Lima: Mosca Azul.

García y Griego, Manuel, and Mónica Verea Campos. 1998. "Colaboración sin concordancia: La Migración en la nueva agenda bilateral México–Estados Unidos." Pp. 107–34 in *Nueva Agenda bilateral en la relación México–Estados Unidos*, coordinated by Mónica Verea Campos, Rafael Fernández de Castro, and Sydney Weintraub. Mexico City: Instituto Tecnológico Autónomo de México, Universidad Nacional Autónoma de México–Centro de Investigaciones sobre América del Norte, Fondo de Cultura Económica.

Gil Villegas, Francisco. 1992. "La nueva 'Relación especial' de México y Estados Unidos durante 1990: Cordialidad en medio de situaciones conflictivas." Pp. 21–53 in *México–Estados Unidos 1990*, ed. Gustavo Vega. Mexico City: Colegio de México.

Gonzales de Olarte, Efraín, ed. 1996. *The Peruvian Economy and Structural Adjustment*. Miami: North-South Center Press, 1996.

González, Anthony P. 1989. "Recent Trends in International Economic Relations of the CARICOM States." *Journal of Interamerican Studies and World Affairs* 31, no. 3 (Fall): 63–95.

González, Bayardo. 2000. *Nicaragua Monitor* (January–February).

Gonzalez, Edward. 1977. "Complexities of Cuban Foreign Policy." *Problems of Communism* 26, no. 6 (November–December): 1–15.

Gonzalez, Luis. 1990. *Paraguay: prisonero ge-politico.* Asunción: Instituto De Estudios Geopoliticos e Internacionales.

———. 1993. *Paraguay: Prisonero geo-político*. Asunción: Instituto de Estudios Geopolíticos e Internacionales.

González y González, Guadalupe. 1983. "Incertidumbres de una potencia media regional: Las nuevas Dimensiones de la política exterior mexicana." Pp. 15–81 in *La politica exterior de México: Desafíos en los ochenta*, ed. Olga Pellicer. Mexico City: Centro de Investigación y Docencia Economicas.

———. 1986. "La Política exterior de México (1983–1985): ¿Cambio de rumbo o repliegue temporal?" Pp. 241–71 in *Fundamentos y prioridades de la política exterior de México*, ed. Humberto Garza Elizondo. Mexico City: Colegio de México.

———. 2001. "Foreign Policy Strategies in a Globalized World: The Case of Mexico." Pp. 141–82 in *Latin America in the New International System*, ed. Joseph S. Tulchin and Ralph H. Espach. Boulder, Colo.: Rienner.

Goodsell, Charles T. 1974. *American Corporations and Peruvian Politics*. Cambridge, Mass.: Harvard University Press.

Gorman, Stephen M., and Ronald Bruce St. John. 1982. "Challenges to Peruvian Foreign Policy." Pp. 179–96 in *Post-Revolutionary Peru: The Politics of Transformation*, ed. Stephen M. Gorman. Boulder, Colo.: Westview.

Goss, Jasper, and Douglas Pacheco. 1999. "Comparative Globalization and the State in Costa Rica and Thailand." *Journal of Contemporary Asia* 29, no. 4: 516.

Graham, Pamela, and Jonathan Hartlyn. 1996. "The United States and the Dominican Republic: Toward the Year 2000: Marginality, Unilateralism or Cooperation?" Pp. 97–125 in *The Dominican Republic Today: Realities and Perspectives, Essays in English and Spanish*, ed. Emilio Betances and Hobart A. Spalding Jr. New York: Bildner Center for Western Hemisphere Studies.

Green, Duncan. 1995. *Silent Revolution: The Rise of Market Economics in Latin America*. London: Cassell.

Green, Rosario. 1977a. "Deuda externa y política exterior: La Vuelta a la bilateralidad en las relaciones internacionales de México." *Foro Internacional* 18, no. 1 (July–September): 54–80.

———. 1977b. "México: La Política exterior del nuevo régimen." *Foro Internacional* 18, no. 1 (July–September): 1–9.

———. 1986. "México: Deuda externa y política exterior." Pp. 221–39 in *Fundamentos y prioridades de la política exterior de México*, ed. Humberto Garza Elizondo. Mexico City: Colegio de México.

Gudmundson, Lowell. 1996. "Costa Rica: New Issues and Alignments." Pp. 78–91 in *Constructing Democratic Governance: Latin America and the Caribbean in the 1990s*, ed. Jorge Domínguez and Abraham Lowenthal. Baltimore, Md.: Johns Hopkins University Press.

Guerón, Carlos. 1991. "La Política de estado y el estado de la política para un debate sobre política exterior." *Política Internacional* 23 (July–September): 4–10.

———. 1993. "Introduction." Pp. 1–18 in *Venezuela in the Wake of Radical Reform*, ed. Joseph S. Tulchin and Gary Bland. Boulder, Colo.: Rienner.

Guevara Mann, Carlos. 1994. *Ilegitimidad y hegemonía: Una Interpretación histórica del militarismo panameño*. Panama City: Litho Editorial Chen.

Guilhon Albuquerque, J. A. 1977. "O Mercosul: Balanço Atual e Perspectivas de Consolidação." Pp. 3–17 in *Debates* no. 14. São Paulo: Fundação Konrad Adenauer.

———. 1991. "MERCOSUR: South America's Economic Regional Integration after the Cold War." Pp. 167–83 in *Regional Economic Integration: Proceedings of the International Colloquium, São Paulo, December*. N.p.

———. 2000a. *Fontes vivas da política externa brasileira*. São Paulo: University of São Paulo Center for International Relations.

———. 2000b. "La nueva Geometría del poder mundial en las visiones de Brasil y de la Argentina." Pp. 79–113 in *El Futuro del MERCOSUR: Entre la retórica y el realismo*, ed. Felipe de la Balze. Buenos Aires: Consejo Argentino de Relaciones Internacionales y Asociación de Bancos de la Argentina.

———. 2000c. *Percepções das Elites e da Sociedade sobre as Relações Internacionais do Brasil*. São Paulo: University of São Paulo Center for International Relations.

Gumucio, Jorge A. 1987. "Toward a Sociology of International Relations: The Case of Bolivian Quest for an Outlet to the Sea." Ph.D. diss., University of Pittsburgh.

———. 1993. *El Enclaustramiento marítimo de Bolivia en los foros del Mundo*. La Paz: Academia Boliviana de la Historia.

Gutiérrez, Carlos José. 1956. "Neutralidad e intervención: Dirección y problemas de la política internacional costarricense durante el primer tercio del siglo XX." *Revista de la Universidad de Costa Rica* 14 (November): 2–61.

Gutiérrez González, Carlos. 1987. "México en el Congreso estadounidense: El debate sobre política interna." Pp. 211–47 in *México–Estados Unidos 1986*, ed. Gerardo M. Bueno. Mexico City: Colegio de México.

Haedo, Eduardo Víctor. 1974. *El Uruguay y la política internacional del Río de la Plata*. Buenos Aires: Editorial Universidad.

Hansen-Kuhn, Karen. 1998. "Free Trade Area of the Americas." *Foreign Policy in Focus* 3, no. 6 (April): 1–4. Available on-line: www.foreignpolicy-infocus.org/.

Hargreaves, Clare. 1992. *Snowfields: The War on Cocaine in the Andes*. New York: Holmes & Meier.

Hartlyn, Jonathan. 1988. *The Politics of Coalition Rule in Colombia*. New York: Cambridge University Press.

Hausmann, Ricardo. 2001. "Prisoners of Geography." *Foreign Policy* (January/February): 45–53.

Healy, Kevin. 1988. "Coca, the State, and the Peasantry in Bolivia, 1982–1988." *Journal of Interamerican Studies and World Affairs* 30, nos. 2 and 3 (Summer/Fall): 105–26.

———. 1997. "The Coca-Cocaine Issue in Bolivia: A Political Resource for All Seasons." Pp. 227–41 in *Coca, Cocaine, and the Bolivian Reality*, ed. Madeline Barbara Léons and Harry Sanabria. Albany: State University of New York Press.

Heller, Claude. 1984. "El Grupo Contadora en la crisis centroamericana." Pp. 27–40 in *México–Estados Unidos, 1983*. Mexico City: Colegio de México Centro de Estudios Internacionales.

Hermann, Charles F. 1990. "International Crisis as a Situational Variable." Pp. 185–93 in *Classics of International Relations*, 2d ed., ed. John A. Vasquez. Englewood Cliffs, N.J.: Prentice Hall.

Herrera, Luis Alberto de. 1961. *La Formación histórica rioplatense.* Buenos Aires: Coyoacán.

———. 1981. *El Uruguay internacional.* Serie Teorización Política 1. Montevideo: Cámara de Representantes. (1st ed., 1911.)

———. 1988. *El Uruguay internacional.* Montevideo: Camara de Representantes de la Republica Oriental del Uruguay.

———. 1990. *La Clausura de los ríos.* 2d ed. Serie revisión historiográfica. Montevideo: Cámara de Representantes.

———. 1991. *La doctrina Drago y el interes del Uruguay.* Montevideo: Camara de Representantes de la Republica Oriental del Uruguay.

Herrera Zúniga, René, and Manuel Chavarría. 1984. "México en Contadora: Una Búsqueda de límites a su compromiso en Centroamérica." *Foro Internacional* 24, no. 4 (April–June): 458–83.

Herrera Zúniga, René, and Mario Ojeda. 1983. *La Política de México hacia Centroamérica, 1979–1982.* Mexico City: Colegio de México.

Hey, Jeanne A. K. 1995. *Theories of Dependent Foreign Policy and the Case of Ecuador in the 1980s.* Athens: Ohio University Press.

———. 1996. "Political Manipulation of Foreign Policy in the Duran Ballen Presidency." *Canadian Journal of Latin American and Caribbean Studies* 21, no. 42: 293–310.

———. 1997. "Three Building Blocks of a Theory of Latin American Foreign Policy." *Third World Quarterly* 18: 631–57.

———. 1998. "Is There a Latin American Foreign Policy?" *Mershon International Studies Review* 42 (May): 106–16.

———. 2000. "Ecuador and the Organization of American States: A Marriage of Convenience?" Pp. 182–93 in *Beyond the Ideal: Pan Americanism in Inter-American Affairs*, ed. David Sheinin. Westport, Conn.: Greenwood.

Hey, Jeanne A. K., and Thomas Klak. 1999. "From Protectionism towards Neoliberalism: Ecuador across Four Administrations (1981–1996)." *Studies in Comparative International Development* 34, no. 3: 66–97.

Hey, Jeanne A. K., and Lynn Kuzma. 1993. "Anti-U.S. Foreign Policy of Dependent States: Mexican and Costa Rican Participation in Central American Peace Plans." *Comparative Political Studies* 26, no. 1 (April): 30–62.

Hillman, Richard S. 1994. *Democracy for the Privileged: Crisis and Transition in Venezuela.* Boulder, Colo.: Rienner.

Hillman, Richard S., and Elsa Cardozo Da Silva, eds. 1997. *De una a otra Gobernabilidad: El Desbordamiento de la democracia venezolana*. Caracas: Universidad Central de Venezuela.

Hirst, Mónica, ed. 1989. *Argentina-Brasil: El largo Camino de la integración*. Buenos Aires: Legasa.

———. 1990. *Argentina-Brasil: Perspectivas comparativas y ejes de integración*. Buenos Aires: Facultad Latinoamericano de Ciencias Sociales/Tesis.

Honey, Martha. 1994. *Hostile Acts: U.S. Policy in Costa Rica*. Gainesville: University Press of Florida.

Hoyer, Hans. 1975. "Paraguay." Pp. 294–305 in *Latin American Foreign Policy: An Analysis*, ed. Harold E. Davis and Larman C. Wilson. Baltimore, Md.: Johns Hopkins University Press.

Hudson, Rex A., and Dennis M. Hanratty, eds. 1991. *Bolivia: A Country Study*. 3d ed. Washington, D.C.: Federal Research Division, Library of Congress, U.S. Government Printing Office.

Huerta, John E. 1977. "Peruvian Nationalization and the Peruvian-American Compensation Agreements." *New York University Journal of International Law and Politics* 10, no. 1 (Spring).

Hunt, Shane. 1975. "Direct Foreign Investment in Peru: New Rules for an Old Game." Pp. 302–49 in *The Peruvian Experiment: Continuity and Change under Military Rule*, ed. Abraham Lowenthal. Princeton, N.J.: Princeton University Press.

Hurwitz, Jon, Mark Peffley, and Mitchell Seligson. 1993. "Foreign Policy Belief Systems in Comparative Perspective: The United States and Costa Rica." *International Studies Quarterly* 37: 245–70.

"Indian Farmers' Protests Turn Deadly in Bolivia." *Dallas Morning News*, April 10, 2000. Available on-line: www.mapinc.org/drugnews/v00/n474/a08.html (accessed July 11, 2001).

Ingram, George M. 1974. *Expropriation of U.S. Property in South America: Nationalizations of Oil and Copper Companies in Peru, Bolivia and Chile*. New York: Praeger.

Instituto de Investigación, Capacitación, y Asesoría Económica (INICAE). 1991. *Entre la Agresión y la cooperación, la economía nicaraguense y la cooperación externa en el periódo 1979–1989.* Managua: Author.

Insulza, José Miguel. 1993. "Chile y Estados Unidos: Entre Bush y Clinton." *Cono Sur* 12, no. 1 (January–February): 15–19.

International Monetary Fund (IMF). 1986. *Direction of Trade*. Washington, D.C.: Author.

———. 1999. *Dominican Republic: Selected Issues*. International Monetary Fund Staff Country Report No. 99/117. Washington, D.C.: Author.

International Press Service (IPS). 2000. "Economy: Caribbean Looks Inward to Solve Regional Problems." January 6. Available on-line: www.cnn.com/WORLD.

Iturralde Andrade, Monica. 1995. "Colombian Traffickers Use Ecuadorans to Smuggle Narcotics." Inter Press Service, May 16, 4.

Jácome, Francine. 1999. "Venezuela: Old Successes, New Constraints in Learning." Pp. 99–125 in *Political Learning and Redemocratization in Latin America: Do Poli-*

ticians Learn from Political Crises? ed. Jennifer L. McCoy. Miami: North–South Center/Rienner.

Janson Pérez, Brittmarie. 1997. *Golpes y tratados: Piezas para el rompecabezas de nuestra historia*. Panama City: Instituto de Estudios Políticos e Internacionales.

Jaworski, Helen C. 1984. "Peru: The Military Government's Foreign Policy in its Two Phases (1968–1980)." Pp. 200–15 in *Latin American Nations in World Politics*, ed. Heraldo Muñoz and Joseph S. Tulchin. Boulder, Colo.: Westview.

Jervis, Robert. 1976. *Perception and Misperception in International Politics*. Princeton: Princeton University Press.

Jimenez Polanco, Jacqueline. 1999. "El nuevo liderazgo politico en la Republica Dominicana: del liderazgo carismatico al liderazgo contingente." Revista Ciencias Sociales 7 (June): 153–194.

Jorden, William J. 1984. *Panama Odyssey*. Austin: University of Texas Press.

Josko de Guerón, Eva. 1978. "El Congreso y la política exterior en Venezuela." *Politeia* 7: 329–441. Caracas: Universidad Central de Venezuela.

———. 1984. "La Política exterior: Continuidad y cambio, contradicción y coherencia." Pp. 350–75 in *El Caso Venezuela: Una Ilusión de armonía*, ed. Moisés Naím and Ramón Piñango. Caracas: Instituto de Estudios Sociales.

———. 1992. "Cambio y continuidad en la política exterior de Venezuela: Una Revisión." Pp. 41–75 in *Reforma y política exterior en Venezuela*, ed. Carlos Romero. Caracas: Nueva Sociedad.

Juárez Anaya, Carlos. 1993. "Economía política y apertura económica: Desarrollo económico y comercio exterior en Colombia, 1967–1991." Monografías 36. Bogotá: Facultad de Administración, Universidad de los Andes.

Kaplan, Mario. 1989. *Integración regional: Un Camino posible*. Montevideo: FESUR.

Kegley, Charles, and Steven Hook. 1991. "U.S. Foreign Aid and UN Voting: Did Reagan's Linkage Strategy Buy Deference or Defiance?" *International Studies Quarterly* 35 (September): 295–312.

Kelly, Janet, and Carlos Romero. 2002. *The United States and Venezuela: Rethinking a Relationship*. New York: Routledge.

Kelly, Philip, and Thomas Whigham. 1990. "Geopolítica del Paraguay: Vulnerabilidades regionales y propuestas nacionales." *Perspectiva Internacional Paraguaya* 2, no.1 (January–June): 41–77.

Kisic, Drago. 1987. *De la Correspondencia a la moratoria: El Caso de la deuda externa peruana 1970–1986*. Lima: Centro Paraguayo de Estudios Internacionales–Fundación Friedrich Ebert.

Kohl, Ben, and Linda Farthing. 2001. "The Price of Success: Bolivia's War against Drugs and the Poor." *NACLA Report on the Americas* 35, no. 1 (July/August): 35–41.

Krauss, Clifford. 2000. "Bolivia Wiping Out Coca at a Price." *New York Times*, October 23. Available on-line: www.mapinc.org/drugnews/v00/n1595/a02.html (accessed July 11, 2001).

Labra, Fernando. 1990. "Paraguay: Nuevo perfil internacional." *Perspectiva Internacional Paraguaya* 2, no. 4: 7–33.

Lacalle, Carlos. 1947. *El Partido Nacional y la política exterior del Uruguay*. Montevideo: Directorio del Partido Nacional.

Lama, Abraham. 1995. "Peru-Drugs: War with Ecuador Led to Rise in Drug Trafficking." Inter Press Service, March 14, 3–4.

Lanús, Juan A. 1984. *De Chapultepec al Beagle: Política exterior argentina (1945–1980)*. Buenos Aires: Emecé.

Latin American Bureau. 1980. *Paraguay Power Game*. London: Russell.

Latinamerica Press (LP). 1995. "Getting a Boost from War." March 30, 6.

Latin Finance. 1997. "Ecuador: Convertibility and Reform on Their Way." (January/February): 104.

———. 1998. "Banking Profiles: Ecuador." August 20.

Latorre, Eduardo. 1995. *De Política dominicana e internacional y desarrollo humano*. Santo Domingo: Instituto Nacional de Economia y Comercio.

Lehman, Kenneth D. 1999. *Bolivia and the United States: A Limited Partnership*. Athens: University of Georgia Press.

Léons, Madeline Barbara, and Harry Sanabria, eds. 1997. *Coca, Cocaine, and the Bolivian Reality*. Albany: State University of New York Press.

Lewis, Paul. 1980. *Paraguay under Stroessner*. Chapel Hill: University of North Carolina Press.

Lezcano, Carlos Maria. 1990. "Relaciones exteriores del Paraguay y percepciones de amenaza: La Política pendular del régimen de Stroessner y las perspectivas de cambio después del golpe de febrero de 1989." Pp. 369–92 in *Política exterior y relaciones internacionales del Paraguay contemporaneo*, ed. José Luis Simon. Asunción: Centro Paraguayo de Estudios Sociologicos.

Lezcano Claude, Luis. 1989. *El Poder ejecutivo en el Paraguay*. Asunción: Intercontinental.

Lincoln, Jennie K. 1984. "Peruvian Foreign Policy since the Return to Democratic Rule." Pp. 137–50 in *The Dynamics of Latin American Foreign Policies: Challenges for the 1980s*, ed. Jennie K. Lincoln and Elizabeth G. Ferris. Boulder, Colo.: Westview.

Linz, Juan. 1975. "Authoritarian and Totalitarian Regimes." Pp. 259–69 in *Handbook of Political Science*, ed. Fred Greenstein and Nelson Polsby. Reading, Mass.: Addison-Wesley.

Longley, Kyle. 1997. *The Sparrow and the Hawk: Costa Rica and the United States during the Rise of José Figueres*. Tuscaloosa: University of Alabama Press.

López Michelsen, Alfonso. 1989. "La Cuestión del canal desde la secesión de Panamá hasta el Tratado de Montería." Pp. 145–86 in *Nueva Historia de Colombia*, Vol. I, ed. Alvaro Tirado Mejía. Bogotá: Planeta.

Lozano, Olga Lucia, and Sandra Zuluaga. 2001. "Del Acuerdo de Cartagena al establecimiento de la Comunidad Andina." In *Las Américas sin barreras: Negociaciones comerciales de acceso a mercados en los años noventa*. Washington, D.C.: Banco Interamericano de Desarrollo.

Lujan, Carlos. 1990. "Política internacional del Uruguay: Tendencias presentes y escenarios posibles." *América Latina/Internacional* 7, no. 24: 347–51. Buenos Aires: Facultad Latinoamericano de Ciencias Sociales/Argentina.

———. 1991. "Redemocratización y política exterior en el Uruguay." *Síntesis* 13 (Spain): 359–77.

———. 1993. *Cambio de régimen y política internacional: El Caso uruguayo*. Montevideo: Intendencia Municipal de Montevideo.

Mace, G., and J. P. Therien. 1996. *Foreign Policy and Regionalism in the Americas*. Boulder, Colo.: Rienner.

Mace, Gordon, and Louis Bélanger. 1999. *The Americas in Transition: The Contours of Regionalism*. Boulder, Colo.: Rienner.

Madalengoitia, Laura. 1987. "Las Relaciones Perú–Estados Unidos: Una Visión desde Perú." Pp. 293–322 in *Continuidad y cambio en las relaciones América Latina/Estados Unidos*, ed. Monica Hirst. Buenos Aires: Latinoamericano.

Magariños, Gustavo. 1994. *Comercio e Integración: Mundo, continente, región*. Montevideo: Federación Comercial del Uruguay.

Major, John. 1993. *Prize Possession: The United States and the Panama Canal, 1903–1979*. Cambridge, Mass.: Cambridge University Press.

Marín Ibáñez, Rolando. 2000. "Bolivia y la integración de América del Sur." Pp. 239–64 in *Bolivia: Temas de la agenda internacional*, ed. Alberto Zelada Castedo. La Paz: Unidad de Análisis de Política Exterior (UDAPEX), Ministerio de Relaciones Exteriores y Culto.

Martz, John D. 1987. *Politics and Petroleum in Ecuador*. New Brunswick, N.J.: Transaction.

———. 1995. *U.S. Policy in Latin America: A Decade of Crisis and Challenge*. Lincoln: University of Nebraska Press.

Masi, Fernando. 1990. *Paraguay en el proceso de integración del Cono Sur: Discusión y análisis*. Asunción: Instituto de Integración de America Latino.

———. 1991a. "Paraguay: ¿Hasta cuando la diplomacia presidencialista?" *Perspectiva Internacional Paraguaya* 3, no. 5 (January–June): 7–21.

———. 1991b. *Relaciones internacionales del Paraguay con Stroessner y sin Stroessner*. Working Paper 3. Asunción: Instituto Paraguayo para la Integración de América Latina.

———. 1993. "El Contexto internacional en la transición a la democracia." Pp. 131–46 in *Paraguay en transición*, ed. Diego Abente. Caracas: Nueva Sociedad.

———. 1997. "Foreign Policy." P. 176 in *The Transition to Democracy in Paraguay*, ed. Peter Lambert and Andrew Nickson. New York: St. Martin's.

Masi, Fernando, and José Luis Simon. 1993. "Lineamientos estratégicos y programáticos para la política exterior del Paraguay de la consolidación democrática." Document prepared at the request of Foreign Minister Diogenes Martinez, December, Asunción.

Masterson, Daniel M. 1991. *Militarism and Politics in Latin America: Peru from Sanchez Cerro to Sendero Luminoso*. New York: Greenwood.

Matthiesen, Tatiana. 2000. *El Arte político de conciliar: El Tema de las drogas en las relaciones entre Colombia y Estados Unidos, 1986–1994*. Bogotá: Centro de Estudios de Realidad Colombiana–Fedesarrollo.

Mazza, Jacqueline. 2001. *Don't Disturb the Neighbors: The United States and Democracy in Mexico, 1980–1995*. New York: Routledge.

McClintock, Cynthia. 2001. "Peru: El viejo Cuento de la estabilidad, tolerancia de Washington frente a Fujimori." *Foreign Affairs en Español* 1, no. 1: 19–25.

McConnell, Shelley A. 2001. "Ecuador's Centrifugal Politics." *Current History* 100, no. 643: 73–79.

McShane, John. 1979. "Cuban Foreign Policy: Global Orientations." *Latinamericanist* 14 (March 31): 1–4.

Melo, Ovídio de A. 2000. "O Reconhecimento de Angola pelo Brasil em 1975." Pp. 345–92 in *Sessenta Anos de politica externa brasileira: Vol. 3. O Desafio geoestratégico*, ed. J. A. Guilhon Albuquerque. São Paulo: University of São Paolo Center for International Relations and Anablume.

Menkhaus, Kenneth J., and Charles W. Kegley. 1988. "The Compliant Foreign Policy of the Dependent State Revisited: Empirical Linkages and Lessons from the Case of Somalia." *Comparative Political Studies* 21: 315–46.

Menzel, Sewall H. 1996. *Fire in the Andes: U.S. Foreign Policy and Cocaine Politics in Bolivia and Peru*. Lanham, Md.: University Press of America.

Merrill, Tim. 1994. *Nicaragua: A Country Study*. Washington, D.C.: U.S. Government Printing Office.

Mesa-Lago, Carmelo, and June S. Belkin, eds. 1982. *Cuba in Africa*. Pittsburgh, Pa.: University of Pittsburgh Press.

Messmer Trigo, Fernando. 1999. "Bolivia: Continuidad democrática, estabilidad económica e inserción internacional." Unpublished document, Discursos-Autoridades del Ministerio, Madrid, Ministerio de Relaciones Exteriores y Culto de Bolivia, September 13. Available on-line: www.rree.gov.bo/DOCUMENTOS/Madrid.htm (accessed August 2, 2001).

Meyer, Lorenzo. 1972. "Cambio político y dependencia: México en el siglo XX." *Foro Internacional* 13, no. 2 (October–December): 101–38.

———. 1985. "México–Estados Unidos: Lo especial de una relación." Pp. 15–30 in *México–Estados Unidos, 1984*, ed. Manuel García Griego and Gustavo Vega. Mexico City: Colegio de México.

———. 1991. "Mexico: The Exception and the Rule." Pp. 83–110 in *Exporting Democracy: The United States and Latin America*, ed. Abraham Lowenthal. Baltimore, Md.: Johns Hopkins University Press.

———. 1992. "Las Relaciones con los Estados Unidos: Convergencia y conflicto." Pp. 105–26 in *México: Auge, crisis y ajuste*, ed. Carlos Bazdresch, Nisso Bucay, Soledad Loaeza, and Nora Lustig. Mexico City: Fondo de Cultura Económica.

Milenski, Edward S. 1975. "Peru's Diplomatic Offensive: Solidarity for Latin American Independence." Pp. 93–114 in *Latin America: The Search for a New International Role*, ed. Ronald G. Hellman and H. Jon Rosenbaum. New York: Sage.

Ministerio de Cooperación Externa. 1992. *Cooperación externa 1991 y perspectivas 1992*. Managua: Author.

Ministerio de Relaciones Exteriores y Culto de Bolivia. 1993. "Ley No. 1444." El Ministerio, Ley de 15 de Febrero de 1993, Ley del Servicio de Relaciones Exteriores. www.rree.gov.bo/JURIDICA/ley1444.htm (accessed August 2, 2001).

———. 1999. "Tema Marítimo Boliviano. Declaración del Excmo. Señor Presidente de Bolivia, Gral. Hugo Banzer Suárez, IX Cumbre Iberoamericana, La Habana, 16 de noviembre de 1999." Discursos, Señor Presidente de la República. *www.rree.gov.bo/ACUALIDADES/cuba1.htm* (accessed August 14, 2001).

———. 2001a. "Declaración Presidencial de Tarija, 27 de junio de 2001." Actualidades, Nota de Prensa, June 6. Available on-line: www.rree.gov.bo/ACTUALIDADES/2001/junio/notaprensa06_06_2001.htm.

———. 2001b. "Mensaje de S.E., Ing. Jorge Quiroga Ramírez, Presidente de la República, en el Día de su Asunción al Mando de la Nación." Discursos, Señor Presidente de la Republica, August 7.

———. 2001c. "Palabras del Excmo: Presidente de la República en Ejercicio, D. Jorge Quiroga Ramírez, en el Acto Inaugural de la I Reunión de Ministros de Relaciones Exteriores: Diálogo Político Comunidad Andina–MERCOSUR y Chile." Discursos, Señor Presidente de la República, July 17.

———. 2001d. "Palabras de S.E., el Señor Presidente de la República, Gral. Hugo Banzer Suárez, en ocasión del almuerzo ofrecido en honor del Excmo. Sr. Presidente de la República Federativa del Brasil, D. Fernando Henrique Cardoso, en el marco de su visita de Estado a Bolivia, La Paz 26 de junio de 2001." Actualidades, Nota de Prensa, June 6. Available on-line: www.rree.gov.bo/ACTUALIDADES/2001/junio/notaprensa04_06_2001.htm.

Ministerio de Relaciones Exteriores de Nicaragua. 2001. Available on-line: www.cancilleria.gob.ni.

Ministerio de Relaciones Exteriores del Peru. 1986. "FMI declara al Peru inelegible para sus préstamos." *Boletín Informativo* 262 (August 20).

Ministério das Relações Exteriores. 1995. *A Palavra do Brasil nas Nações Unidas 1946–1995*. Brasília: Fundação Alexandre Gusmão.

Miranda, Anibal. 1987. *EEUU y el régimen militar paraguayo, 1954–1958*. Asunción: Lector.

Mondolfi Gudat, Edgardo. 2000. "La Relación Venezuela–Estados Unidos durante el último medio siglo." Pp. 245–70 in *Venezuela y Estados Unidos a través de 2 siglos*, ed. Tomás Polanco Alcántara, Simón Alberto Consalvi, and Edgardo Mondolfi Gudat. Caracas: Camara Venezolano–Americano de Comercio e Industria.

Moneta, Carlos. 1988. "La Política exterior del peronismo, 1973–1976." Pp. 49–97 in *Argentina en el mundo*, ed. Rubén M. Perina and Roberto Russell. Buenos Aires: Latinoamericano.

Moon, Bruce. 1983. "The Foreign Policy of the Dependent State." *International Studies Quarterly* 27: 315–40.

———. 1985. "Consensus or Compliance? Foreign Policy Change and External Dependence." *International Organization* 39 (Spring): 297–329.

Mora, Frank O. 1988. "Política exterior del Paraguay: A la Búsqueda de la independencia y el desarrollo." *Revista Paraguaya de Sociología* 25, no. 73 (September–December): 253–73.

———. 1990. "Relaciones EEUU–Paraguay: Conflicto y cooperación." *Perspectiva Internacional Paraguaya* 2, no. 3: 79–94.

———. 1993. *Política exterior del Paraguay, 1811–1989*. Asunción: Centro Paraguayo de Estudios Sociologicos.

———. 1997. "From Dictatorship to Democracy: The U.S. and Regime Change in Paraguay, 1954–1994." *Bulletin of Latin American Research* 17, no. 1 (January): 59–79.

———. 1998. "The Forgotten Relationship: United States–Paraguay, 1937–1989." *Journal of Contemporary History* 33, no. 3 (July): 451–73.

———. 2000. "Paraguay y el sistema interamericano: De Autoritarismo y parálisis a democracia y la aplicación de Resolución 1080." Pp. 235–60 in *Sistema interameri-*

cano y cemocracia: Antecedentes y perspectivas futuras, ed. Arlene Tickner. Bogotá: Universidad de los Andes.

Morales, Waltraud Queiser. 1984a. "Bolivian Foreign Policy: The Struggle for Sovereignty." Pp. 171–91 in *The Dynamics of Latin American Foreign Policies*, ed. Jennie K. Lincoln and Elizabeth G. Ferris. Boulder, Colo.: Westview.

———. 1984b. "La Geopolítica de la política exterior de Bolivia." *Documentos de Trabajo PROSPEL* 2: 1–31 (monograph). Santiago: Centro de Estudios de la Realidad Contemporánea.

———. 1988. "Bolivia." Pp. B23–B47 in *Latin America and Caribbean Contemporary Record: Vol. 5. 1985–1986*, ed. Abraham F. Lowenthal. New York: Holmes & Meier.

———. 1992a. *Bolivia: Land of Struggle*. Boulder, Colo.: Westview.

———. 1992b. "Militarising the Drug War in Bolivia." *Third World Quarterly* 12, no. 2: 353–70.

Morandé, José A., and Roberto Durán. 1993. "Percepciones en la política exterior chilena: Un Estudio sobre líderes de opinión pública." *Estudios Internacionales* 26, no. 104 (October–December): 595–609.

Moreno, Darío. 1994. *The Struggle for Peace in Central America*. Gainesville: University Press of Florida.

Morgan, Lynn. 1990. "International Politics and Primary Health Care in Costa Rica." *Social Science and Medicine* 30, no. 2: 211–19.

Morley, Morris H. 1994. *Washington, Somoza, and the Sandinistas, State and Regime in U.S. Policy toward Nicaragua, 1969–1981*. New York: Cambridge University Press.

Mota Menezes, Alfredo. 1990. *La Herencia de Stroessner*. Asunción: Schaumann.

Moura, Gerson. 1996. "O Brasil na Segunda Guerra Mundial." Pp. 87–114 in *Sessenta Anos de politica externa brasileira: Vol. 1. Crescimento modernização e política externa*, ed. J. A. Guilhon Albuquerque. São Paulo: University of São Paulo Center for International Relations and Cultura Editoria.

Muñoz, Heraldo. 1986. *Las Relaciones exteriores del gobierno militar chileno*. Santiago, Chile: Ediciones del Ornitorrinco.

———. 1996. "Dominant Themes in Latin American Foreign Relations: An Introduction." Pp. 1–16 in *Latin American Nations in World Politics*, ed. Heraldo Muñoz and Joseph S. Tulchin. Boulder, Colo.: Westview.

———, ed. 1987. *Las Políticas exteriores de America Latina y el Caribe: Continuidad en la Crisis*. Buenos Aires: Programa de Seguimiento de las Políticas Exteriores/ Latinoamericano.

Muñoz, Heraldo, and Carlos Portales. 1987. *Una Amistad esquiva: Las Relaciones de Estados Unidos y Chile*. Santiago: Pehuén.

Muñoz, Heraldo, and Joseph S. Tulchin. 1984. *Latin American Nations in World Politics*. Boulder, Colo.: Westview.

Muñoz, Heraldo, and Joseph S. Tulchin. 1996. *Latin American Nations in World Politics*, 2d ed. Boulder, Colo.: Westview.

Mytelka, Lynn Krieger. 1979. *Regional Development in a Global Economy: The Multinational Corporation, Technology and Andean Integration*. New Haven, Conn.: Yale University Press.

National Democratic Institute. 1994. "Interim Report: The May 16, 1994, Elections in the Dominican Republic." *National Democratic Institute.* Available on-line: www.ndi.org/ndi/worldwide/latinamerica/dominicanrep/1994_dominica_elections/1994_dominica_elections.htm (August 15).

———. 1996. "Preliminary Statement of the NDI International Observer Delegation to the May 1996 Presidential Elections in the Dominican Republic." *National Democratic Institute*. Available on-line: www.ndi.org/ndi/worldwide/latinamerica/dominicanrep1996/prelimstatement05196 (May 18).

NICCA Bulletin. April–June 1992. Nicaragua Center for Community Action.

Nickson, Andrew. 1989. "The Overthrow of the Stroessner Regime: Re-establishing the Status Quo?" *Bulletin of Latin American Research* 8, no. 2: 185–209.

———. 1993. *Historical Dictionary of Paraguay*. Metuchen, N.J.: Scarecrow.

———. 1997. "The Wasmosy Government." Pp. 185–99 in *The Transition to Democracy in Paraguay*, ed. Peter Lambert and Andrew Nickson. New York: St. Martin's.

NotiCen. 1999–2001. Albuquerque, N.M.: Latin American Data Base. Available on-line: http://ladb.unm.edu.

Oconitrillo García, Eduardo. 1991. *Los Tinoco (1917–1919)*. San José: Editorial Costa Rica.

Oddone, Juan. 1985. "Uruguay frente a la Segunda Guerra Mundial: La Política internacional del compromiso." *Hoy es Historia* (Montevideo) 12: 3–18.

Office of the President of the Republic. 1999. "Plan Colombia: Plan for Peace, Prosperity and the Strengthening of the State." Bogotá: Author.

Ojeda, Mario. 1976. *Alcances y límites de la política exterior de México*. Mexico City: Colegio de México.

———. 1980. "El Poder negociador del petróleo: El Caso de México." *Foro Internacional* 21, no. 1 (July–September): 44–64.

———. 1983. "La Política de México hacia Centroamérica en el contexto de las relaciones México–Estados Unidos." Pp. 73–96 in *Centroamérica: Futuro y opciones*, ed. Olga Pellicer and Richard Fagen. Mexico City: Fondo de Cultura Económica.

———. 1984. "El Lugar de México en el mundo contemporáneo." *Foro Internacional* 24, no. 4 (April–June): 415–26.

———. 1986. *México: El Surgimiento de una política exterior activa*. Mexico City: Secretaría de Educación Pública.

Olson, Richard S. 1975. "Economic Coercion in International Disputes: The United States and Peru in the Expropriation Dispute of 1968–1971." *Journal of Developing Areas* 9, no. 3 (April): 395–413.

Orias Arredondo, Ramiro. 2000a. "Bolivia: La Diplomacia del mar en la OEA." Pp. 387–413 in *Bolivia: Temas de la agenda internacional*, ed. Alberto Zelada Castedo. La Paz: Unidad de Análisis de Política Exterior (UDAPEX), Ministerio de Relaciones Exteriores y Culto.

———2000b. "El Derecho internacional y las negociaciones marítimas con Chile." Pp. 371–85 in *Bolivia: Temas de la agenda internacional*, ed. Alberto Zelada Castedo. La Paz: Unidad de Análisis de Política Exterior (UDAPEX), Ministerio de Relaciones Exteriores y Culto.

Oxfam International. 1998. "Debt Relief for Nicaragua: Breaking Out of the Poverty Trap." Position paper. Available on-line: www.oxfam.org.

Painter, James. 1994. *Bolivia and Coca: A Study in Dependency*. Boulder, Colo.: Westview.

Palacios, Marco. 1983. "El Interés nacional y el ingreso a los No Alineados." Pp. 61–72 in *Colombia No Alineada*, ed. Marco Palacios. Bogotá: Biblioteca Banco Popular.

Palmer, David Scott. 1992. "United States–Peru Relations in the 1990s: Asymmetry and Its Consequences." Pp. 3–23 In *Latin America and Caribbean Contemporary Record: Vol. 9. 1989–1990*, ed. Eduardo Gamarra and James Malloy. New York: Homes & Meier.

———. 1997. "Peru–Ecuador Border Conflict: Missed Opportunities, Misplaced Nationalism, and Multilateral Peacekeeping." *Journal of Interamerican Studies and World Affairs* 39, no. 3 (Fall): 109–48.

———. 1998. "Relaciones entre Estados Unidos y el Peru durante el decenio de 1990: Dinámicas, antecedentes y proyecciones." *Politica Internacional* 53 (July/September): 9–25.

Pardo, Diana, and Arlene B. Tickner. 1998. "La Política exterior en el proceso electoral colombiano." Pp. 17–34 in *Elecciones y democracia en Colombia 1997–1998*, ed. Ana María Bejarano and Andrés Dávila. Bogotá: Fundación Social, Departamento de Ciencia Política, Universidad de los Andes, Veeduría Ciudadana a la Elección Presidencial.

Pardo, Rodrigo, and Juan Gabriel Tokatlián. 1989. *Política exterior colombiana: ¿De la subordinación a la autonomía?* Bogotá: Tercer Mundo–Uniandes.

Pastor, Robert A. 1992. *Whirlpool: U.S. Foreign Policy toward Latin America and the Caribbean*. Princeton, N.J.: Princeton University Press.

Peeler, John. 1998. *Building Democracy in Latin America*. Boulder, Colo.: Rienner.

Pellicer, Olga. 1965–1966. "México en la OEA." *Foro Internacional* 6, no. 2 (October–December): 288–302.

———. 1972a. "Cambios recientes en la política exterior mexicana." *Foro Internacional* 13, no. 2 (October–December): 139–54.

———. 1972b. *México y la revolución cubana.* Mexico City: Colegio de México.

———. 1980. "Veinte años de política exterior mexicana: 1960–1980." *Foro Internacional* 21, no. 2 (October–December): 149–60.

———. 1983. "México en Centroamérica: El difícil Ejercicio del poder regional." Pp. 97–110 in *Centroamérica: Futuro y opciones*, ed. Olga Pellicer and Richard Fagen. Mexico City: Fondo de Cultura Económica.

Pérez, Orlando J., ed. 2000. *Post-Invasion Panama: The Challenges of Democratization in the New World Order*. Lanham, Md.: Lexington.

Perez-Stable, Marifeli. 1993. *The Cuban Revolution*. New York: Oxford University Press.

Perina, Rubén M., and Roberto Russell, eds. 1988. *Argentina en el mundo (1973–1987)*. Buenos Aires: Latinoamericano.

Petrásh, Vilma. 1999. "Dos Siglos de relaciones con los Estados Unidos." Pp. 615–67 in *Venezuela y . . . los países hemisféricos, ibéricos e hispanohablantes*, ed. Kaldone G. Nweihed. Caracas: Universidad Simón Bolívar.

Pike, Frederick. 1963. *Chile and the United States: 1880–1962*. Notre Dame, Ind.: University of Notre Dame Press.

Pinelo, Adalberto J. 1973. *The Multinational Corporation as a Force in Latin American Politics: A Case of the International Petroleum Company in Peru*. New York: Praeger.
Pino, Ricardo. 1992. "¿Cómo marcha el plan económico?" *El País*, May.
Polanco Alcántara, Tomás, Simón Alberto Consalvi, and Edgardo Mondolfi Gudat. 2000. *Venezuela y Estados Unidos a través de 2 siglos*. Caracas: Cámara Venezolano–Americana de Comercio e Industria.
Presidencia de la República. 1990. *Estratégia nacional de desarollo alternativo*. La Paz: Author.
Purcell, Susan K. 1981–1982. "Mexico–U.S.: Big Initiatives Can Cause Big Problems." *Foreign Affairs* 60, no. 2 (Winter): 379–92.
———. 1985. "Demystifying Contadora." *Foreign Affairs* 60, no. 1 (Autumn): 74–95.
Quagliotti De Bellis, Bernardo 1976. *Uruguay en el Cono Sur: Destino geopolítico*. Montevideo: Biblioteca del Palacio Legislativo.
Quest Economics Database. 1998. "Country Profile: Ecuador." March.
Ramírez Boettner, Luis Maria. 1995. "La Política exterior de la administración Wasmosy." Pp. 89–98 in *Política exterior y democracia en el Paraguay y sus vecinos*, ed. José Luis Simon. Asunción: Universidad Nacional de Asunción/Fundación Hanns Seidel.
Ramírez, Socorro. 2000. *Los No Alineados: ¿Voceros del Sur?* Bogotá: Colciencias–Tercer Mundo.
Randall, Stephen J. 1992. *Aliados y distantes*. Bogotá: Tercer Mundo–Uniandes–Centro de Estudios Internacionales.
Rapoport, Mario. 1980. *Gran Bretaña, Estados Unidos y las clases dirigentes argentinas*. Buenos Aires: de Belgrano.
Real de Azúa, Carlos. 1987. "Política internacional e ideología en Uruguay." Pp. 233–66 in *Escritos*, ed. Carlos Real de Azúa. Montevideo: Arca.
Rehren, Alfredo. 1994. "Wasmosy frente al Estado prebendario-clientelista: Desafíos del liderazgo presidencial democrático." Pp. 93–127 in *La Democracia en Paraguay: Cinco años despues*, ed. José Luis Simon. Asunción: Fundación Hanns Seidel/ Universidad Católica.
República Argentina. Ministerio de Relaciones Exteriores. 1991. *Conferencia del señor canciller Guido Di Tella en el Círculo de Empresarios Católicos* [April 5]. Buenos Aires: Author.
Rey, Juan Carlos. 1983. "El Sistema político venezolano y los problemas de su política exterior." Pp. 57–79 in *La Agenda de la política exterior de Venezuela*, ed. Instituto de Estudios Políticos. Caracas: Universidad Central de Venezuela.
———. 1989. *El Futuro de la democracia en Venezuela*. Caracas: IDEA.
Rey, Juan Carlos, and Charles W. Kegley. 1989. "Trade Dependence and Foreign Policy Compliance: A Longitudinal Analysis." *International Studies Quarterly* 24 (March): 191–222.
Richardson, Neil R. 1978. *Foreign Policy and Economic Dependence*. Austin: University of Texas Press.
Richardson, Neil, and Charles W. Kegley. 1980. "Trade Dependence and Foreign Policy Compliance: A Longitudinal Analysis." *International Studies Quarterly* 24, no. 2 (June): 191–222.

Rico F., Carlos. 1986. "El Proceso de Contadora en 1985: ¿Hasta dónde es posible incorporar las preocupaciones de Estados Unidos?" Pp. 105–16 in *México–Estados Unidos, 1985*, ed. Gabriel Székely. Mexico City: Colegio de México.

———. 2000. *Hacia la globalización: México y el mundo. Historia de sus Relaciones Exteriores*. Vol. VIII. Mexico City: Senado de la República.

Ricupero, Rubens. 1995. *Pensando o Brasil*. São Paulo: Paz e Terra.

———. 1996. "O Brasil, a América Latina e os EUA desde 1930: 60 Anos de uma Relação Triangular." Pp. 37–60 in *Sessenta anos de politica externa brasileir: Vol. 1. Crescimento, modernização e política externa*, ed. J. A. Guilhon Albuquerque. São Paulo: University of São Paulo Center for International Relations and Cultura Editora.

Riquelme, Marcial Antonio. 1994. "Toward a Weberian Characterization of the Stroessner Regime, 1954–1989." *European Review of Latin America and Caribbean Studies* 57 (October): 35–62.

Rivera Urrutia, Eugenio. 1982. *El Fondo Monetario Internacional y Costa Rica, 1978–1982*. San José: Departamento Ecuménico de Investigación.

Roberts, Kenneth, and Mark Peceny. 1997. "Human Rights and United States Policy Toward Peru." Pp. 192–222 in *The Peruvian Labyrinth: Politics, Society, Economy*, ed. Maxwell A. Cameron and Philip Maureci. University Park: Pennsylvania State University Press.

Rodriguez Silvero, Ricardo. 1987. *La Integración económica del Paraguay en el Brasil*. Asunción: Historica Fundación Friedrich Nauman.

Roett, Riordan, and William Perry. 1977. "Recent Trends in Brazilian Foreign Policy." *The World Today* (August).

Rohter, Larry. 1997. "Backlash from NAFTA Batters Economies of Caribbean." *New York Times*, January 30.

———. 2000. "Latin Leaders Rebuff Call by Clinton on Colombia." *New York Times*, September 2. Available on-line: www.wola.org/summit_nytimes_2sep00.htm.

Rojas Aravena, Francisco, ed. 1990a. *Costa Rica y el sistema internacional*. Caracas: Nueva Sociedad.

———. 1990b. *Política exterior de la administración Arias Sánchez, 1986/1990*. San José: Facultad Latinoamericano de Ciencias Sociales.

Rojas Aravena, Francisco, and Luis Guillermo Solís. 1988. *¿Súbditos or aliados? La Política exterior de Estados Unidos y Centroamérica*. San José: Facultad Latinoamericano de Ciencias Sociales.

Rojas Bolaños, Manuel. 1992. *Los Años ochenta y el futuro incierto*. San José: Editorial Universidad Estatal a Distancia.

Romero, Aníbal. 1986 *La Miseria del populismo*. Caracas: Centauro.

Romero, Carlos. 1992. "La Complejidad organizacional en el sector externo de Venezuela." Pp. 209–38 in *Reforma y política exterior en Venezuela*, ed. Carlos Romero. Caracas: Nueva Sociedad.

———. 1998. "Las Relaciones entre Venezuela y Estados Unidos durante la presidencia de Clinton: Coincidencias, estratégicas y diferencias tácticas." Pp. 141–72 in *Estados Unidos y los países Andinos 1993–1997: Poder y desintegración*, ed. Andrés Franco. Santa Fe de Bogotá: Universidad Javeriana.

Romero, María Teresa. 2002. *Política exterior venezolana: Proyecto democrático, 1959–1999*. Caracas: Libros El Nacional.

Romero, Pérez Antón. 1983. "Hacia una impostergable política exterior." *Cuadernos del CLAEH* 25. Montevideo: Centro Latinoamericano de Economía Humana.

Romero, Pérez Antón, and Lincoln Bizzozero. 1987. "A Política internacional do Uruguai na democratizaçao." *Contexto Internacional* 4/5. Río de Janeiro: Instituto de Relaçoes Internacionais, Pontificia Universidade Católica.

Ropp, Steve C. 1992. "Explaining the Long-Term Maintenance of a Military Regime: Panama before the U.S. Invasion." *World Politics* 44 (January): 210–34.

Rosenau, James. 1966. "Pre-Theories and Theories of Foreign Policy." Pp. 17–93, 95–149 in *Approaches to Comparative and International Politics*, ed. R. Barry Farrell. Evanston, Ill.: Northwestern University Press.

———. 1971. *The Scientific Study of Foreign Policy*. New York: Free Press.

———. 1990a. "Pre-theories and Theories of Foreign Policy." Pp. 164–75 in *Classics of International Relations*, ed. John A. Vásquez. Englewood Cliffs, N.J.: Prentice Hall.

———. 1990b. *Turbulence in World Politics: A Theory of Change and Continuity*. Princeton, N.J.: Princeton University Press.

———. 1996. "Pre-theories and Theories of Foreign Policy." Pp. 179–90 in *Classics of International Relations*, ed. John A. Vásquez. Upper Saddle River, N.J.: Prentice Hall.

Rosenzweig, Gabriel. 1983. "La Cooperación económica de México con Centroamérica a partir de 1979: Perspectivas para los próximos años." Pp. 235–72 in *La Política exterior de México: Desafíos en los ochenta*, ed. Olga Pellicer. Mexico City: Centro de Investigación y Docencia Economicas.

Rovira Mas, Jorge. 1988. *Costa Rica en los años 80*. San José: Porvenir.

Rudolph, James D. 1992. *Peru: The Evolution of a Crisis*. Westport, Conn.: Praeger.

Russell, Roberto. 1987. "Las Relaciones Argentina–Estados Unidos: Del 'Alineamiento heterodoxo' a la 'recomposición madura.'" Pp. 12–31 in *Continuidad y cambio en las relaciones America Latina/Estados Unidos*, ed. Monica Hirst. Buenos Aires: Latinoamericano.

———. 1988. "La Política exterior del régimen autoritario (1976–1983)." Pp. 99–128 in *Argentina en el mundo (1973–1987)*, ed. Rubén M. Perina and Roberto Russell. Buenos Aires: Latinoamericano.

———. 1990. "Argentina: ¿Una nueva Política exterior?" Pp. 15–30 in *El Desafío de los '90*, ed. Heraldo Muñoz. Anuario de Políticas Exteriores Latinoamericanas series. Caracas: Programa de Seguimiento de las Políticas Exteriores Latinoamericanas–Nueva Sociedad.

———, ed. 1993. *La Política exterior argentina en el nuevo orden mundial*. Buenos Aires: Facultad Latinoamericano de Ciencias Sociales–Grupo Latinoamericano.

Sáenz Carbonell, Jorge Francisco. 1996. *Historia diplomática de Costa Rica (1821–1910)*. San José: Juricentro.

Salazar Paredes, Fernando, Jorge Gumucio Granier, Franz Orozco Padilla, and Lorena Salazar Machicado. 2001. *Charaña: Una Negociación boliviana, 1975–1978*. La Paz: Centro de Estudios de Relaciones Internacionales.

Salisbury, Richard. 1974. "Domestic Politics and Foreign Policy: Costa Rica's Stand on Recognition, 1923–1934." *Hispanic American Historical Review* 54, no. 3 (August): 453–78.

Salum Flecha, Antonio. 1989. "Nueva Proyección de la política internacional del Paraguay." *Perspectiva Internacional Paraguaya* 1, nos. 1–2: 157–61.

Sanabria, Harry. 1997. "The Discourse and Practice of Repression and Resistance in the Chapare." Pp. 169–93 in *Coca, Cocaine, and the Bolivian Reality*, ed. Madeline Barbara Léons and Harry Sanabria. Albany: State University of New York Press.

Sanchez, Peter M. 2003. "Panama's 'Hegemonized' Foreign Policy: The Struggle over a U.S. Military Presence on the Isthmus." Pp. 53–74 in *Explaining Small State Foreign Policy*, ed. Jeanne A. Hey. Boulder, Colo.: Rienner.

Sánchez, Rebeca. 1999. "La Organización de Países Exportadores de Petróleo (OPEP)." Pp. 1013–38 in *Venezuela y . . . los países hemisféricos, ibéricos e hispanohablantes*, ed. Kaldone G. Nweihed. Caracas: Universidad Simón Bolívar.

Sannemann, Martin. 1995. "Reflexiones sobre los desafios internacionales que enfrenta el Paraguay." Pp. 109–14 in *Política exterior y democracia en el Paraguay y sus vecinos*, ed. José Luis Simon. Asunción: Universidad Nacional de Asunción/ Fundación Hanns Seidel.

Sanz de Santamaría, Mauricio. 1993. "Ministerio de Comercio Exterior: Una nueva Forma de gobernar." Pp. 37–49 in *La Internacionalización de la economía colombiana*, ed. Ministerio de Comercio Exterior. Bogotá: Imprenta Nacional de Colombia.

Schemo, Diana Jean. 1997. "New Horizons in Ecuador, but Paralysis Sets in Early." *New York Times*, April 3, A8.

———. 1998. "3 Years after War, Ecuador and Peru Agree to Peace Talks." *New York Times*, January 20, A4.

Schifter, Jacobo. 1982. *Costa Rica 1948: Análisis de documentos confidenciales del Departamento de Estado*. San José: Editorial Universitaria Centroamericana.

———. 1986. *Las Alianzas conflictivas: Las Relaciones de Estados Unidos y Costa Rica desde la Segunda Guerra Mundial a la Guerra Fría*. San José: Libro Libre.

Schneider, Ronald M. 1991. *Order and Progress: A Political History of Brazil*. Boulder, Colo.: Westview.

Schwalb Lopez-Aldana, Fernando. 1979. *El Convenio Greene–De la Flor y el pago a la IPC*. Lima: Populista.

Scranton, Margaret E. 1991. *The Noriega Years: U.S.–Panama Relations, 1981–1990*. Boulder, Colo.: Rienner.

Seiferheld, Antonio, and José Luis De Tone. 1998. *El Asilo a Perón y la caida de Epifanio Mendez*. Asunción: Histórica.

Seitenfus, Ricardo A. S. 1985. *O Brasil de Getúlio Vargas e a Formação dos Blocos: 1930–1942*. São Paulo: Nacional.

———. 1996. "Quatro Teses sobre a política externa brasileira nos anos 1930." Pp. 115–60 in *Sessenta anos de politica externa brasileira: Vol. 1. Crescimento, modernização e política externa*, ed. J. A. Guilhon Albuquerque. São Paulo: University of São Paulo Center for International Relations and Cultura Editora.

Semple, Kirk. 1999. "Colombia's Drug Problems, Internal Conflicts Worry Neighbors." *Boston Globe*, September 19, A19.

Seoane Flores, Alfredo. 2000a. "Ampliación y profundización de la relación especial con el MERCOSUR." Pp. 265–90 in *Bolivia: Temas de la agenda internacional*, ed. Alberto Zelada Castedo. La Paz: Unidad de Análisis de Política Exterior (UDAPEX), Ministerio de Relaciones Exteriores y Culto.

———. 2000b. "Estado actual y proyecciones de la Comunidad Andina de Naciones." Pp. 291–312 in *Bolivia: Temas de la agenda internacional*, ed. Alberto Zelada Castedo. La Paz: Unidad de Análisis de Política Exterior (UDAPEX), Ministerio de Relaciones Exteriores y Culto.

Seoane, Alfredo, Humberto Zambrana, Fernando Jiménez, and Rafael González. 1997. *Bolivia y Chile: Complementación económica y asimetrías*. La Paz: Unidad de Análisis de Políticas Económicas (UDAPE), and Unidad de Análisis de Política Exterior (UDAPEX), Ministerio de Relaciones Exteriores y Culto.

Serbin, Andrés. 1994. "Towards an Association of Caribbean States: Raising Some Awkward Questions." *Journal of Interamerican Studies and World Affairs* 36, no. 4 (Winter): 61–90.

SEREX. "Principal Achievements of the Ministry." Available on-line: http://196.3.85.11/english/serex/serex_foreign_acheivements_1.htm.

Shapira, Yoram. 1978. "Mexican Foreign Policy under Echeverría." London: Sage.

Sharp, Daniel A. 1972. U.S. *Foreign Policy and Peru*. Austin: University of Texas Press.

Sheetz, Thomas. 1986. *Peru and the International Monetary Fund*. Pittsburgh, Pa.: Pittsburgh University Press.

Shumavon, Douglas H. 1981. "Bolivia: Sálida al mar." Pp. 179–90 in *Latin American Foreign Policies: Global and Regional Dimensions*, ed. Elizabeth G. Ferris and Jennie K. Lincoln. Boulder, Colo.: Westview.

Sigmund, Paul E. 1977. *The Overthrow of Allende and the Politics of Chile, 1964–1976*. Pittsburgh, Pa.: University of Pittsburgh Press.

———. 1980. *Multinations in Latin America: The Politics of Nationalization*. Madison: University of Wisconsin Press.

Simon, José Luis. 1988. "Aislamiento político internacional y desconcertación: El Paraguay de Stroessner de espaldas a America Latina." *Revista Paraguaya de Sociología* 25, no. 73 (September–December): 185–236.

———. 1989. "Del Aislamiento a la reinserción internacional: El Paraguay de la inmediata transición post-stronista." *Perspectiva Internacional Paraguaya* 1, no. 1: 163–200.

———. 1990a. "Una Política exterior de automarginamiento: El Paraguay en la crisis terminal del autoritarismo de Stroessner y America Latina en la década de los ochenta." Pp. 323–68 in *Política exterior y relaciones internacionales del Paraguay contemporáneo*, ed. José Luis Simon. Asunción: Centro Paraguayo de Estudios Sociologicos.

———, ed. 1990b. *Política exterior y la relaciones internacionales del Paraguay contemporáneo*. Asunción: Centro Paraguayo de Estudios Sociologicos.

———. 1990c. "Transición política pero inmovilismo e improvisación en relaciones exteriores." Pp. 7–12 in *Estado, partidos políticos y sociedad: Análisis de la transición política*, ed. Domingo Rivarola. Asunción: Centro Paraguayo de Estudios Sociologicos.

———. 1991. *Modernización insuficiente, carencia de una vision global y condicionamientos de un estado prebendario en crisis*. Asunción: Mimeo.

———. 1995a. "Los Deficit de la actual política exterior paraguaya frente a los avances de las democracias vecinas." Pp. 201–16 in *Politica exterior y democracia en el Paraguay y sus vecinos*, ed. José Luis Simon. Asunción: Fundación Hans Seidel/Universidad Nacional de Asunción.

———. 1995b. "Las Pesadillas de Wasmosy y del canciller." *Hoy*, February 18, 10.

———. 2000. "Universidad, instituciones académicas y relaciones internacionales en el Paraguay." Pp. 107–31 in *Bases para la agenda internacional del Paraguay: Una visión desde la sociedad civil*, ed. Centro Paraguayo de Estudios Internacionales. Asunción: Centro Paraguayo de Estudios Internacionales.

———. 2001. "Una Propuesta para discutir las prioridades de la política exterior paraguaya en la perspectiva de la construcción del estado de derecho democrático." Report presented to the Paraguayan Foreign Ministry on behalf of the United Nations Development Program.

Singer, J. D. 1961. "The Level-of-Analysis Problem in International Relations." *World Politics* 14: 77–92.

Skidmore, Thomas. 1988. *The Politics of Military Rule in Brazil*. New York: Oxford University Press.

Smith, Clint E. 2000. *Inevitable Partnership: Understanding Mexico–U.S. Relations*. Boulder, Colo.: Rienner.

Smith, Wayne S., ed. 1991. *Toward Resolution? The Falklands/Malvinas Dispute*. Boulder, Colo.: Rienner.

Snarr, Michael T. 1995. *Latin American Foreign Policy towards the United States from 1948–1978: Exploring the Salience of Development Strategies*. Columbus: Ohio State University Press.

Sojo, Carlos. 1991. *Costa Rica: Política exterior y Sandinismo*. San José: Facultad Latinoamericano de Ciencias Sociales.

Souto Maior, Luis A. P. 1996. "O 'Pragmatismo responsável.'" Pp. 267–96 in *Sessenta Anos de politica externa brasileira: Vol. 1. Crescimento, modernização e política externa*, ed. J. A. Guilhon Albuquerque. São Paulo: University of São Paulo Center for International Relations and Cultura Editora.

Spanakos, Anthony Peter. 2000. "The Dominican Republic: A New Way." Pp. 527–41 in *Latin American Politics and Development*, 5th ed., ed. Howard J. Wiarda and Harvey F. Kline. Boulder, Colo.: Westview.

Spencer, Bill, with Gina Amatangelo. 2001. "Drug Certification." *Foreign Policy in Focus* 6, no. 5 (March): 1–4. Available on-line: www.foreignpolicy-infocus.org.

St. John, Ronald Bruce. 1977. "Hacia el mar: Bolivia's Quest for a Pacific Port." *Inter-American Economic Affairs* 31: 41–73.

———. 1992. *The Foreign Policy of Peru*. Boulder, Colo.: Rienner.

———. 2001. "Same Space, Different Dreams: Bolivia's Quest for a Pacific Port." *Bolivian Research Review* 1, no. 1 (July 9). Available on-line: www.bolivianstudies.org.

Suchlicki, Jaime. 1984. "Is Castro Ready to Accommodate?" *Strategic Review* (Spring 1984): 22–29.

Swansbrough, Robert H. 1975. "Peru's Diplomatic Offensive: Solidarity for Latin American Independence." Pp. 115–30 in *Latin America: The Search for a New International Role*, ed. Ronald G. Hellman and H. Jon Rosembaun. New York: Sage.

Tarre, Maruja. 1999. "Relaciones petroleras entre Estados Unidos y Venezuela." Pp. 668–89 in *Venezuela y . . . los países hemisféricos, ibéricos e hispanohablantes*, ed. Kaldone G. Nweihed. Caracas: Universidad Simón Bolívar.

Tickner, Arlene B. 2002. "U.S. Foreign Policy in Colombia: Bizarre Side-Effects of the 'War on Drugs.'" In *Democracy, Human Rights and Peace in Colombia*, ed. Gustavo Gallón and Christopher Welna. Notre Dame, Ind.: University of Notre Dame Press.

Tokatlián, Juan Gabriel. 2000a. "La Mirada de la política exterior de Colombia ante un nuevo milenio: Ceguera, miopía o estrabismo?" *Colombia Internacional* 48 (January–April): 35–43.

———. 2000b. "La Polémica sobre la legalización de las drogas en Colombia: El Presidente Samper y los Estados Unidos." *Latin American Research Review* 35, no. 1: 37–83.

Tokatlián, Juan Gabriel, and Diego Cardona. 1991. "El Futuro de la política exterior colombiana." *Revista Cancillería de San Carlos* 7: 90–94.

Tokatlián, Juan Gabriel, and Arlene B. Tickner. 1996. "Colombia's Assertive Regionalism in Latin America." Pp. 103–20 in *Foreign Policy and Regionalism in the Americas*, ed. Gordon Mace and Jean-Philippe Thérien. Boulder, Colo.: Rienner.

Toranzo Roca, Carlos F. 1997. "Informal and Illicit Economies and the Role of Narcotrafficking." Pp. 195–209 in *Coca, Cocaine, and the Bolivian Reality*, ed. Madeline Barbara Léons and Harry Sanabria. Albany: State University of New York Press.

Toro Hardy, Alfredo. 1986. *Venezuela, democracia y política exterior*. Caracas: Proimagen.

———. 1992. *La Maldición de Sísifo: Quince años de política externa venezolana*. Caracas: Panapo.

Toro, María Celia. 1983. "El Comercio México–Estados Unidos: La Realidad desigual y los límites a la colaboración norteamericana." Pp. 187–234 in *La Política exterior de México: Desafíos en los ochenta*, ed. Olga Pellicer. Mexico City: Centro de Investigación y Docencia Economicas.

———. 1995. *Mexico's "War" on Drugs: Causes and Consequences*. Boulder, Colo.: Rienner.

———. 1998. "La Política mexicana contra el narcotráfico: Un Instrumento de política exterior." Pp. 135–57 in *Nueva Agenda bilateral en la relación México–Estados Unidos*, ed. Mónica Verea Campos, Rafael Fernández de Castro, and Sidney Weintraub. Mexico City: Instituto Tecnológico Autónomo de México, Universidad Nacional Autónoma de México–Centro de Investigaciones sobre América del Norte, Fondo de Cultura Económica.

Torres-Saillant, Silvio. 1998. "Visions of Dominicanness in the United States." Pp. 139–52 in *Borderless Borders: U.S., Latinos, Latin Americans and the Paradox of Interdependence*, ed. Frank Bonilla, Edwin Melendez, Rebecca Morales, and María de los Angeles Torres. Philadelphia: Temple University Press.

Trías, Vivián. 1972. *El Uruguay y sus claves geopolíticas*. Montevideo: Banda Oriental.

Tugwell, Franklin. 1977. "The United States and Venezuela: Prospects for Accommodation." Pp. 199–226 in *Contemporary Venezuela and Its Role in International Affairs*, ed. Robert D. Bond. New York: New York University Press.

Tulchin, Joseph, and Ronald H. Espach, eds. 2001. *Latin America in the New International System*. Boulder, Colo.: Lynne Rienner.

Turcatti, Daniel. 1981. *El Equilibrio difícil: La Política internacional del batllismo*. Montevideo: Centro Latinoamericano de Economia Humanista.

Ultima Hora. 1993. "Cancilleria diseñara nueva política exterior paraguaya." September 2, 12.

United Nations. 1991. *Index to Proceedings of the General Assembly, 45th session 1990/91*. New York: Author.

United Nations Development Program (UNDP). 2002. *Human Development Report 2000*. New York: Oxford University Press.

United Press International (UPI). 1995. "Latin American Leaders Gather in Ecuador." September 2.

Urbaneja, Diego Bautista. 1992. *Pueblo y petróleo en la política venezolana del siglo XX*. Caracas: Centro de Formación y Adiestramiento de Petroleos de Venezuela y Sus Filiales.

Uriarte, Manuel. 1986. *Transnational Banks and the Dynamics of the Peruvian Foreign Debt and Inflation*. New York: Praeger.

U.S. Department of State. 1999. "Voting Practices in the United Nations 1998: Report to Congress." March 31.

———. 2000. "Background Notes: Nicaragua." September.

———. 2001a. "Country Program: Bolivia." Fact Sheet, Bureau for International Narcotics and Law Enforcement Affairs, April 16. Available on-line: www.state.gov/g/inl/rls/fs/2001/may/index.cfm?docid=2201 (accessed September 13, 2001).

———. 2001b. "South America." Available on-line: www. State.gov/g/inl/rls/nrcrpt/2000/index.cfm?docid+883 (accessed April 3, 2001).

———. 2001c. "USAID Bolivia." Fact Sheet, U.S. Agency for International Development, March 16. Available on-line: www.state.gov/g/inl/rls/fs/2001/may/index-.cfm?docid=3186 (accessed September 13).

U.S. Senate. 1975. *Covert Action in Chile: 1963–1973*. Washington, D.C. : U.S. Government Printing Office.

Vacs, Aldo C. 1984. *Discreet Partners: Argentina and the USSR since 1917*. Pittsburgh, Pa.: University of Pittsburgh Press.

———. 1989. "A Delicate Balance: Confrontation and Cooperation between Argentina and the United States in the 1980s." *Journal of Interamerican Studies and World Affairs* 31, no. 4 (Winter): 23–59.

———. 1991. "Abandoning the 'Third Position.'" *Hemisphere* 4, no. 1 (Fall): 28–29.

Valenzuela, Arturo. 1999. *The Collective Defense of Democracy: Lessons from the Paraguayan Crisis of 1996*. A Report of the Carnegie Commission on Preventing Deadly Conflict. New York: Carnegie Corporation of New York.

Van Cleeve, John V. 1976. "The Latin American Policy of President Kennedy: A Reexamination Case: Peru." *Inter-American Economic Affairs* 30, no. 1 (Summer).

Vanden, Harry E. 1991. "Foreign Policy." Pp. 295–320 in *Revolution and Counterrevolution in Nicaragua*, ed. Thomas W. Walker. Boulder, Colo.: Westview.

Vanderlaan, Mary B. 1986. *Revolution and Foreign Policy in Nicaragua*. Boulder, Colo.: Westview.

van Klaveren, A. 1994. "Chile: La Política exterior de la transición." *América Latina Internacional* 1, no. 2 (Fall–Winter): 47–64.

———. 1996. "Understanding Latin American Foreign Policies." Pp. 35–60 in *Latin American Nations in World Politics*, ed. Heraldo Muñoz and Joseph S. Tulchin. Boulder, Colo.: Westview.

———. 1998. "Insercion Internacional de Chile." Pp. 147–149 in *Chile en los noventa*, ed. Cristian Toloza and Eugenio Lahera. Santiago: Dolmen Ediciones.

Vázquez, Josefina Zoraida, and Lorenzo Meyer. 1982. *México frente a Estados Unidos: Un ensayo histórico 1776–1980*. Mexico City: Colegio de México.

Vega, Bernardo. 1996. *La Agenda pendiente: Reformas, geopolítica y frustración; artículos y conferencias 1990–1995*. Santo Domingo: Fundación Cultural Dominicana.

Vega, Mylena. 1990. "Dinámica Política y procesos de toma de decisión en Costa Rica: El segundo Préstamo para el ajuste estructural y el Parlamento Centroamericano." Pp. 281–302 in *Costa Rica y el sistema internacional*, ed. Francisco Rojas Aravena. Caracas: Nueva Sociedad.

Velázquez, Carlos. 1968. *La Política internacional en el pensamiento de Luis Alberto de Herrera*. Shrewsbury, U.K.: Wilding.

Vigevani, Tullo. 1996. "Os Militares e a Política Externa Brasileira: Interesses e Ideología." Pp. 61–86 in *Sessenta Anos de Politica Externa Brasileira: Vol. 1. Crescimento, modernização e política externa*, ed. J. A. Guilhon Albuquerque. São Paulo: University of São Paulo Center for International Relations and Cultura Editora.

Villanueva, Victor. 1974. *Ejército peruano: Del Caudillaje anárquico al militarismo reformista*. Lima: Mejia Baca.

Vivas G., Freddy. 1999. *Venezuela: Política exterior y proyecto nacional: El pretorianismo perezjimenista (1952–1958)*. Caracas: Universidad Central de Venezuela.

Vizentini, Paulo. 1995. *Relações Internacionais e desenvolvimento: O Nacionalismo e a política externa independente (1951–1964)*. Petrópolis: Vozes.

———. 1996. "A Política externa do governo JK (1956–1961)." Pp. 231–52 in *Sessenta Anos de politica externa brasileira: Vol. 1. Crescimento, modernização e política externa*, ed. J. A. Guilhon Albuquerque. São Paulo: University of São Paulo Center for International Relations and Cultura Editora.

Walker, Thomas W., ed. 1997. *Nicaragua without Illusions, Regime Transition and Structural Adjustment in the 1990s*. Wilmington, Del.: Scholarly Resources.

Walker, Thomas W., and Ariel C. Armony. 2000. *Repression, Resistance, and Democratic Transition in Central America*. Wilmington, Del.: Scholarly Resources.

Warner, Matt. 2001. "Investing in Ecuador: Pipe Dreams." *Financial Times*, May 25, 46.

White House Office of the Press Secretary. 2000. "The Trade and Development Act of 2000: Strengthening Our Economic Partnership with Sub-Saharan Africa and the Caribbean Basin." May 18.

Wiarda, Howard J. 1996. "The 1996 Elections in the Dominican Republic." Washington, D.C.: Center for Strategic and International Studies.

Wiarda, Howard J., and Michael J. Kryzanek. 1988. *The Politics of External Influence in the Dominican Republic*. Stanford, Calif.: Praeger.

Wilhelmy, Manfred. 1984. "Politics, Bureaucracy and Foreign Policy in Chile." Pp. 61–80 in *Latin American Nations in World Politics*, ed. Heraldo Muñoz and Joseph S. Tulchin. Boulder, Colo.: Westview.

———. 1995. "De Aylwin a Frei: Continuidad política e internacional." Pp. 165–78 in *Política exterior y democracia en el Paraguay y sus vecinos*, ed. José Luis Simon. Asunción: Fundación Hans Siedel, Universidad Nacional de Asunción.

Williamson, J. 1990. *Latin American Adjustment: How Much Has Happened?* Washington, D.C.: Institute for International Economics.

Wilson, Bruce. 1994. "Why Social Democrats Choose Neoliberal Economic Policies: The Case of Costa Rica." *Comparative Politics* 26, no. 2: 149–69.

———. 1998. *Costa Rica: Politics, Economics, and Democracy*. Boulder, Colo.: Rienner.

Wirth, John D. 1970. *The Politics of Brazilian Development, 1930–1954*. Stanford, Calif.: Stanford University Press.

Wittkopf, Eugene R. 1973. "Foreign Aid and United Nations Votes." *American Political Science Review* 67 (September): 868–888.

World Bank. 2001. *World Development Report 2000/2001*. New York: Oxford University Press.

World Politics and Current Affairs (WPCA). 1996. "The Ogre Beams." July 13, 42.

Wucker, Michelle. 1999. *Why the Cocks Fight: Dominicans, Haitians, and the Struggle for Hispaniola*. New York: Hill & Wang.

Yashar, Deborah. 1997. *Demanding Democracy: Reform and Reaction in Costa Rica and Guatemala, 1870s–1950s*. Stanford, Calif.: Stanford University Press.

Yopo, Boris. 1991. "The Rio Group: Decline or Consolidation of the Latin American *Concertación* Policy?" *Journal of Interamerican Studies and World Affairs* 33, no. 4 (Winter): 27–44.

Yopo, Mladen. 1986a. "Política exterior boliviana: Continuidad y cambio en la crisis." Pp. 203–24 in *América Latina y el Caribe: Políticas exteriores para sobrevivir*, ed. Heraldo Muñoz. Buenos Aires: Programa de Seguimiento de las Políticas Exteriores Latinoamericanas–Latinoamericano.

———. 1986b. "La Política exterior del Paraguay: Continuidad y cambio en el aislamiento." Pp. 447–67 in *America Latina y el Caribe: Políticas exteriores para sobrevivir*, ed. Heraldo Muñoz. Santiago: Programa de Seguimiento de las Políticas Exteriores Latinoamericanas–Latinoamericano.

———. 1988. "Bolivia 1987: Una Política exterior de sobrevivencia." Pp. 147–68 in *Las políticas exteriores de América Latina y el Caribe: Un balance de esperanzas*, ed. Heraldo Muñoz. Buenos Aires: Programa de Seguimiento de las Políticas Exteriores Latinoamericanas–Latinoamericano.

———. 1989. "Política exterior del Paraguay: Continuidad, reacómodo y transición." Pp. 266–86 in *Anuario Política Exterior Latinoamericana*, ed. Heraldo Muñoz. Caracas: Nueva Sociedad.

———. 1991. *Paraguay-Stroessner: La Política exterior del régimen autoritario*. Santiago: Programa de Seguimiento de las Políticas Exteriores Latinoamericanas.

Yore, Fatima Myriam. 1992. *La Dominación stronista: Orígenes y consolidación*. Asunción: BASE–Investigaciones Sociales.

Youngers, Coletta A. 2000. *Deconstructing Democracy: Peru under President Alberto Fujimori*. Washington, D.C.: Washington Office on Latin America.

Zubelzú de Bacigalupo, Graciela. 1999. *La Argentina y las repúblicas post-soviéticas*. Rosario, Argentina: Centro de Estudios en Relaciones Internacionales de Rosario.

Index

Numbers in italics refer to figures and tables.

About the Editors and Contributors

Editors

Jeanne A. K. Hey is an associate professor of political science and international studies at Miami University. Professor Hey is also the director of international studies at Miami University. She is coeditor of *Foreign Policy Analysis: Continuity and Change in its Second Generation* (1995) and author of *Theories of Dependent Foreign Policy and the Case of Ecuador in the 1980s* (1995). She has published numerous scholarly articles on foreign policy in small states, especially Latin America, in journals including *Comparative Political Studies*, the *Mershon International Studies Review, Third World Quarterly*, and *World Development.* Between 1998 and 2000, she was in residence at Miami University's European Center in Luxembourg, where she pursued research projects on Luxembourgish foreign policy.

Frank O. Mora is an associate professor of international studies at Rhodes College in Memphis, Tennessee. Professor Mora also holds the Senior Latin American Research Fellowship at Rhodes. He is the author of numerous articles and chapters on Paraguay foreign policy, U.S.–Latin American relations, and democratization published in the United States, Europe, and Latin America, including *Politica exterior del Paraguay, 1811–1989* (1993). He is also the coeditor, with Michael LaRosa, of *Neighborly Adversaries: U.S.–Readings in Latin American Relations* (Rowan & Littlefield, 1999).

Authors

JoAnn Fagot Aviel is a professor of international relations at San Francisco State University. She served as a Fulbright professor in 1999 at the University of Costa Rica and in 1984 at the Diplomatic Academy of Peru. She recently coedited, with James P. Muldoon Jr. and others, *Multilateral Diplomacy and the United Nations Today* (1999). She has published encyclopedia articles on Nicaragua and journal articles and book chapters on Nicaraguan foreign policy as well as on other topics in comparative foreign policy and international relations.

Rubén Berríos has worked for nearly two decades on development issues as researcher, teacher, and practitioner. Much of his research has concentrated on Peru, Central America, and Cuba. He is the author of *Contracting for Development* (2000) and of many book chapters and articles for specialized journals. He is currently an assistant professor of economics at Clarion University of Pennsylvania.

Lincoln Bizzozero is the coordinator of the Program on International Politics and Relations of the Social Sciences Faculty of the Universidad de la Republica, Uruguay. Professor Bizzozero has taught in several universities in Europe, North America, and Latin America, including the Free University of Brussels, University of Montreal, Universidad Catolica Argentina, and Universidad de Jaen y Granada. He is the author of several published articles and monographs on regional integration, foreign policy, and civil society in the international system.

Elsa Cardozo Da Silva has a graduate degree in international studies and a doctorate in political science (1989), both from the Universidad Central de Venezuela (UCV). She is a full professor at the UCV and was a Fulbright Scholar in residence at Macalester College in Minnesota, a researcher as part of the Faculty Research Program sponsored by the Canadian government, and a visiting professor at St. John Fisher College as part of the Affiliation Program that created the Institute for Democracy and Human Rights. She is the author of several works, including *Continuidad y consistencia en quince años de política exterior venezolana: 1969–1984* (1992).

Ana Covarrubias has been a faculty member of the Center for International Studies of El Colegio de México since 1995, and she became its academic coordinator in August of the same year. She is also a member of the Sistema Nacional de Investigadores in Mexico. Her research focuses on Mexican and Latin American foreign policies and the inter-American system.

H. Michael Erisman is a professor of political science at Indiana State University in Terre Haute. His main fields of interest are U.S. policies toward Latin America, transnationalism/political economy in the Caribbean Basin, and Cuban foreign affairs. He is the author of *Cuba's International Relations: The Anatomy of a Nationalistic Foreign Policy* (1985), *Pursuing Postde-*

pendency Politics: South–South Relations in the Caribbean (1992), and *Cuba's Foreign Relations in a Post-Soviet World* (2000). He has also edited *The Caribbean Challenge: U.S Policy in a Volatile Region* (1984), and has also coedited, with John Martz, *Colossus Challenged: The Struggle for Caribbean Influence* (1982).

Damián Fernández is an associate professor of International Relations at the Florida International University. He has published widely on Cuban politics and foreign policy. His most recent books are *Cuba and the Politics of Passion* (2000) and *Cuba, the Elusive Nation: Interpretations of National Identity*, coedited with Madeline Camara (2000).

José Augusto Guilhon Albuquerque is a professor of international relations in the Department of Economics, University of São Paolo, Brazil. He is a former Jacques Leclerq Chair Visiting Professor at Louvain, Belgium, and most recently (2002) Rio Branco Chair Professor and Visiting Fellow at the Royal Institute of International Affairs, Chatham House, London. His research centers on regional economic integration and Brazilian foreign policy.

Richard S. Hillman is a professor of political science and the director of the Institute for the Study of Democracy and Human Rights at St. John Fisher College in Rochester, New York, and the Central University of Venezuela, Caracas. He is the author or editor of several books on Venezuela, including *Democracy for the Privileged: Crisis and Transition in Venezuela; De una a otra gobernabilidad: El desbordamiento de la democracia venezolana* (with Elsa Cardozo Da Silva, 1994); and *Democracy and Human Rights in Latin America* (coeditor with John Peeler and Elsa Cardozo Da Silva, 2002). Professor Hillman was a Fulbright Scholar in Venezuela in 1987, 1992, and 1996.

Waltraud Quesier Morales is a professor of political science at the University of Central Florida. Her teaching and research areas include international relations and comparative politics with an emphasis on third world development, Latin America, and the Andean region. She is the author of *Bolivia: Land of Struggle* (1992). She was awarded a Fulbright teaching and research grant to Bolivia in 1990 and a research sabbatical leave in 2001.

José A. Morandé received his Ph.D. in international studies in 1983 from the University of Denver, Colorado. He is presently an associate professor and researcher at the Institute of International Studies at the University of Chile, where he also serves as its assistant director. He has served as a visiting professor at the Institute of Political Science at the University of Chile; the School of Journalism at Gabriela Mistral University in Santiago, Chile; as well as in the Department of Political Science of the University of Texas, Austin. Dr. Morandé presently serves as the vice president of the Chilean Political Science Association.

John Peeler is a professor of political science at Bucknell University, where he has taught since 1967. He holds his Ph.D. from the University of North Carolina at Chapel Hill. He is the author of two books: *Latin American Democracies: Colombia, Costa Rica, Venezuela* (1985), and *Building Democracy in Latin America* (1998), as well as numerous articles and chapters. He has taught at the University of Costa Rica on two occasions, once as a Fulbright lecturer. His current research interests include democracy in Latin America, indigenous politics in Latin America, and democratic theory.

Peter M. Sanchez is an associate professor of political science at Loyola University in Chicago. He has held teaching positions at Soka University, Virginia Tech (1993), and the U.S. Air Force Academy (1989–1992). Professor Sanchez has published research and commentary in a number of journals, including *Peace Review, Alternativa, Global Development Studies, International Journal on World Peace*, the *Harvard Journal of Hispanic Policy*, *Journal of Developing Areas*, *Journal of the Third World Spectrum*, *Conflict Quarterly*, and *Air Force Law*.

Anthony P. Spanakos is a visiting assistant professor at Manhattanville College and a guest scholar at Princeton University's Program in Latin American Studies. He has published articles on the Dominican Republic, the concept of race and citizenship in the Dominican Republic and Brazil, citizenship and social movements in Brazil, and citizenship in Latin America more generally. Professor Spanakos is currently a Fulbright Scholar in Brazil.

Arlene B. Tickner is the director and an associate professor at the Centro de Estudios Internacionales (CEI), Universidad de los Andes, Bogotá, Colombia, an institution where she has worked since 1991. Professor Tickner has been an assistant professor of international relations at the Universidad Nacional de Colombia since 1999. Her most recent publications include "La Política exterior y el Proceso Electoral Colombiano," in *Elecciones y democracia en Colombia 1997–1998*, edited by Ana Mariá Bejarano and Andrés Dávila (Bogotá, 1998); and "Colombia's Assertive Regionalism in Latin America," in *Foreign Policy and Regionalism in the Americas*, edited by Gordon Mace and Jean-Phillipe Thérien (1996).

Aldo C. Vacs is a professor of political science at Skidmore College. He teaches courses on international political economy, Latin American politics, and Latin American relations with the United States. Dr. Vacs completed his Ph.D. in political science at the University of Pittsburgh (1986). His publications include studies on Russia–Latin America relations, the process of Latin American democratization, and relations among political democratization, economic liberation, and structural reform.

Howard J. Wiarda is a professor of political science and the Leonard J. Horwitz Professor of Iberian and Latin American Studies at the University of Massachusetts, Amherst. He is also Senior Associate of the Center for Strategic and International Studies (CSIS) and Senior Fellow at the Woodrow Wilson International Center for Scholars. Professor Wiarda is the author/editor of more than forty books, including *American Foreign Policy: Actors and Processes* (1996); *The Politics of External Influence in the Dominican Republic* (with Michael J. Kryzanek, 1988); *Dictatorship and Development: The Methods of Control in Trujillo's Dominican Republic* (1968); *Latin American Politics and Development*, 5th ed. (2000); and *The Soul of Latin America: The Cultural and Political Tradition* (2001).